THE MERC
The Emergence of a Global Financial Powerhouse

Bob Tamarkin

HarperBusiness
A Division of HarperCollins*Publishers*

HarperCollins books may be purchased for educational, business, or sales promotional use. For information please write: Special Markets Department, HarperCollins Publishers, Inc., 10 East 53rd Street, New York, NY 10022.

FIRST EDITION

Library of Congress Cataloging-in-Publication Data

Tamarkin, Bob.
    The Merc : the emergence of a global financial powerhouse
  / by Bob Tamarkin.
      p. cm.
    Includes index.
    ISBN 0-88730-516-4
    1. Chicago Mercantile Exchange—History. 2. Commodity exchanges—
Illinois—Chicago—History. I. Title
HG6049.T35   1993   91-31500
332.64'4'0977311—dc20   CIP

93 94 95 96 97 PS/HC 10 9 8 7 6 5 4 3 2 1

Books by Bob Tamarkin

The Merc

The Leader Within

Rumor Has It: A Curio of Lies, Rumors, and Hoaxes

The New Gatsbys

The Young Executive Today

Hefner's Gonna Kill Me When He Reads This (ghost author)

Ideal

Egg and butter,
shank and udder,
and the gamesmanship
of free gentlemen:

build us a house of prosperity
from the brick
of sweat and temerity
and ye shall know

the transcendence
of dull eternity.

J. J. Tindall

Contents

Photographs follow pages 146 and 290.

Foreword

The people and the politicians of the beleaguered countries of Eastern Europe and the former Soviet Union have been learning an important lesson the hard way. It's not enough merely to wish for a market economy. Somebody has to take care of the details.

Taking care of the details is particularly crucial for those special market institutions known as *exchanges*. Exchanges are more than just crowded rooms in which noisy people in wildly colored jackets wave their hands and throw paper on the floor. They are business organizations whose product is transaction, clearing, and settlement services. Running such a service enterprise and keeping it stable in the face of stiff competitive challenges is a task as daunting as any facing managers and entrepreneurs in manufacturing or retailing.

The Chicago Mercantile Exchange has been blessed through its long and often stormy history by having savvy and energetic leaders come loping onto the scene just in time to rescue the exchange from threatened stagnation and propel it to renewed growth and vigor. The challenges were daunting in the 1960s when Leo Melamed and his colleagues rescued the Exchange and, in the process, revolutionized the world of finance. Melamed retired with a noble legacy, but the challenges are no less daunting for Jack Sandner, who has chaired the Merc through eight terms and now leads a preeminent global financial institution in a rapidly changing field of competition at home and overseas. During my own years as a Public Governor of the Exchange, I have admired the wisdom and good judgement of these veterans and their colleagues. Reading about their past travails and triumphs in this history has for me been something like looking at the faded pictures in a family album. Bill Muno, was that really you? And Phil Glass? And Jerry Hirsch, John Geldermann, and Larry Rosenberg?

That the vision of these architects may not have been implemented but for a skilled professional staff, from the legendary Everett B. Harris through Clayton Yeutter to current CME President Bill Brodsky. That staff has great strength across the board. But, as an academic economist, I cannot resist singling out for special mention the CME's outstanding economic research division, headed currently by Todd Petzel and before him by Rick Kilcollin, now the Chief Operating Officer (and both University of Chicago Ph.D.'s I am proud to say).

The modern history of the Chicago Mercantile Exchange is the story of a fundamental shift in the world financial markets. In my view, financial futures represent the most important and far-reaching financial innovation of the last 20 years. They have changed forever, and for the better, in the way business firms here and throughout the world manage and control the exchange-rate risks, interest-rate risks, and portfolio risks they face. The times were indeed ready for just such an innovation as foreign currency futures in the early 1970s. That an exchange originating in the butter and egg trade should have triggered such a financial revolution remains a great irony of our time.

The story of how this came to be deserves to be as widely known as the corresponding stories of Edison, Ford, Bell, and Firestone. The chapters of this book are a good place to begin catching up on this important piece of American, and indeed world, economic history.

Merton H. Miller

Introduction

Once enclosed in a glass box at the Chicago Historical Society was an odd relic of pre-Chicago: the bones of fur trader Jean Lalime, the "little Frenchman" killed in a fight with John Kinzie, a founding father of the city. The slaying had climaxed a gnawing antagonism between independent fur traders and those who were employed by the government. Lalime's 180-year-old bones were a macabre reminder of what may have been the earliest local triumph of private enterprise. The legacy endures, shaped by the ebb and flow of economic cycles that have since transformed Chicago from the smokestack capital of the Midwest to a mogul of world-class finance.

Nobel economist Milton Friedman, the free-market spirit, left the Windy City more than a decade ago to take up residence in San Francisco. Yet there's still something that grabs him and won't let go when you mention Chicago's players in the evolution of risk management: "Chicago is a much more brash, raw, uncivilized, but also innovative and entrepreneurial city than any other place. It's possible to be a maverick in Chicago and still be in the main stream."

Back in 1971 Friedman put his reputation where his mouth was by publicly encouraging the Chicago Mercantile Exchange to launch currency futures trading in the wake of monetary anarchy among the industrialized nations. President Nixon had closed the gold window, bringing an end to Bretton Woods and fixed exchange rates pegged to an anemic gold standard. The action set off shock waves in financial ministries around the world. For the first time in history, every nation had an irredeemable paper standard. From then on, the world's monetary system entered uncharted waters: Foreign exchange traders could now transfer their risk to the willing speculators floating on a sea of volatility.

As foreign exchange rates were allowed to move freely in the marketplace, the Merc's International Monetary Market began trading foreign currencies in 1972. A year later the Chicago Board of Trade spun off the Chicago Board Options Exchange to create the first market for fungible options. And Chicago had staked its claim as the mogul of financial futures and options, obscuring Carl Sandburg's turn-of-the-century vision of Chicago as the world's hog butcher, toolmaker, wheat stacker, and freight handler. Now resting on the big shoulders are the exchanges, banks, brokers, and speculators that today make up the vortex of the world's major derivative markets, where some 70 percent of all the futures and options traded globally swirl through Chicago's trading pits. In 1992 the Merc and CBOT bet their share would grow even more through a global computerized marketplace called GLOBEX®, a 24-hour electronic trading system for futures and options, which is Big Business at its biggest. The underlying value of all contracts traded on the Merc annually totals more than $50 trillion—in contrast to the value of all equities traded on the New York Stock Exchange, about $1.3 trillion.

The Merc has come a long way from a faltering butter-and-egg exchange on the brink of extinction in the 1950s. Through self-assertiveness and a fiercely competitive drive that constantly overcame the conventional wisdom of the day, it has forged itself into one of the world's major financial institutions in the 1990s, where the trading pits are a whirl of flailing hands, emotional jags, and screaming orders—a bastion of raw capitalism, say traders. From the beginning it traveled a hard road, pitted by war, depression, scandal, and stock market crashes. At times, the road appeared to be a dead end. In 1958, for example, in the wake of a speculative binge, the Merc was brought to its knees by the congressional ban on onion trading, the first such congressional edict on a commodity. But the Merc refused to resign itself passively to fate. The Merc's is a long day's journey of travails and survival that now continues into the night with round-the-clock trading.

Sometimes the importance of a journey is not the destination, but what you learn along the way. The idea to do a history of the Chicago Mercantile Exchange came to me in 1985, in the course of doing another book about futures traders. In my research I was astounded to find out that no book had ever been written on the Exchange. There had been several histories of the Chicago Board of Trade, although no current ones. But nothing on the Merc other than a slim 1954 volume entitled *Evolution of Futures Trading*, written by Harold S. Irwin, a former U.S. Agriculture Department economist. But Irwin's study of the early days of egg trading—published when the Merc was deep in the shadows of the CBOT—did not show up in any library computer search. There was no record of the Merc in any card catalog anywhere. In fact, any reference to commodity trading or futures generally referred to the CBOT histories. How, I wondered, could such a dominant institution be the best-kept secret around? To be sure, there were hundreds of newspaper and magazine articles, but no chronicle of the Exchange, which had revolutionized futures trading not only in the United States, but worldwide. The Chicago Mercantile Exchange was a major business story waiting to be told.

That's when I began my journey. It initially brought me to a dank warehouse on Chicago's West Jackson Street, where I discovered musty ledgers of the Butter and Egg Board—the predecessor to the Merc—dating back to 1895. Poring over the thousands of pages of scribbled notations, egg and butter prices, inventories, memoranda, and comments gave me a glimpse of an early exchange trying to plant roots at a time when farmers were hauling their produce to selling houses on South Water Street. Unfortunately, there were significant gaps in the story I was trying to piece together. For example, when in 1972 the Merc relocated from Franklin Street to Jackson Street, boxes of documents, letters, Merc memorabilia, even minutes of board meetings going back to 1919—much of it with historic relevance—were either arbitrarily discarded or simply lost in the move. Fortunately, some of the historic void was filled by the institutional memories of such individuals as E. B. Harris, Bill Katz, Kenneth Mackay, and Saul Stone, and Michael Weinberg, Jr., who spent untold hours providing me with details and recollections derived from their personal histories. Thanks also to Princeton Professor and former Merc member Stanley N. Katz (Bill's son) who encouraged me early on.

There are others to thank as well. My deepest thanks go to Irene Macauley, Alysann Posner, and Sue Finucane, who at one time or another were my links to the Merc and patiently helped me track down sources and materials whenever I got stuck, which was often. There is also gratitude to Mort Edelstein for his talks on momentum; to Sherlene Branscomb for her tireless work in transcribing oral interviews and to Maryanne Martinez, who guided me through the new-fangled systems of word processing (which still cause me nostalgic pangs for my old Underwood). I am also appreciative of the efforts of Lee Froehlich, Anthony Barnett, Betty Hanning, Karen McCoy, Larry Norals, Raymond Wild, and Bruce Frost, manager of the Merc's library and resource center. My thanks, too, to John Geldermann, Bill Muno, Girard Miller, Jack Sandner, and in particular Larry Rosenberg, who all took time to advise me on the manuscript in progress. I am indebted to Bill Brodsky for his encouragement and critical comments and to Leo Melamed for all that he shared. A special thank-you must go to Elisa Tamarkin, who helped organize the bibliography, to Theresa Wilkerson, who went well beyond the call of duty as a first-rate copyeditor; to Sheryl Lilke, who showed great patience in coordinating production; to Mark Greenberg and Martha Jewett, both of whom believed in the relevance of this book; to Virginia Smith, for taking over a difficult project; and to Joan Daley, the Merc's diligent archivist who was extremely helpful in digging up facts, sharing some of the oral histories in her files, and doing the photo research for this history while painstakingly assembling the Merc's archives for use by future researchers and historians. And, finally, to my wife, Civia, my deepest appreciation for enduring.

The Merc's is a story that grew out of the ashes of Chicago's great fire of 1871 as a new city rose, full of steam and commercial vitality, at a time when farmers were hauling their grain and eggs in buckboard wagons. The Merc reflected America's melting pot, and the anecdotes used to render its story serve as pearls strung together with an overarching theory: The Merc learned to survive because its leaders were themselves survivors. Some were European immigrants, others came from the backwaters of rural America, and still others from the mean streets of the cities. They were highbrow, middlebrow, and lowbrow; they were entrepreneurs who faced off like gladiators in miniature coliseums called trading pits. In order to survive, the Merc continually had to reinvent itself; that is, it had to create new products to keep itself in the forefront of innovation. From onions, it was pork bellies, then currencies and stock indexes, Eurodollars, and options on futures. It was the first exchange to open offices in Washington, London, and Japan. It was the first to establish a historic bridge to the markets of the Pacific Rim with its mutual offset trading link to the Singapore Monetary Exchange in 1984. Finally, there is GLOBEX, a kind of United Nations of futures exchanges. The Merc's story is thus one of ideas and ideals—a story about Chicago's "second exchange" and its struggle for respectability, about innovation and commerce intersecting to create progress. And it is a story about a capitalistic institution—which sees itself among the last strongholds of free enterprise—trying to control its destiny.

For the uninitiated, the futures market is a strange creature shaped by time and rhythm. The beats are nanoseconds. And the pits have their own metabolism—fueled by the chemistry of physical energy and greed. ("An exchange is a place that harnesses greed," former Merc president E. B. Harris likes to say.) To those individuals who waited impatiently for this particular history, I can only say that history needs a period of gestation after seminal events. The perspective on events such as the 1987 stock market crash and the 1989 Justice Department investigation of the trading pits is far different from what it was when they first exploded in eye-grabbing headlines. The meltdown of the market and the Merc's image have since rebounded.

Every industry has its thieves, knaves, and weasels that draw the fire of reformers. Over the years the futures markets had their share of detractors, and certainly the Merc had its dark side, just as Wall Street did with its insider-trading scandals. As I've tried to show in this history, maligning the futures markets is not something new. The Merc has certainly had its share of wrongdoers, problems, and other failings. Futures markets are easy targets because they are very visible, noisy, and colorful and because huge sums of money swirl about them daily. There has never been any shortage of mindless attacks from politicians and journalists, many of whom to this day refuse to see commercial value in futures contracts. For them, the futures exchanges will always be gaming establishments. Yet the growth of these exchanges over the past two decades has been nothing short of phenomenal, attesting to both the speculative and commercial use of the markets. Consider the fate of Sir Freddie Laker, the founder of Laker Airways. Long-term "overvaluation" of the dollar caught Laker Airways by surprise in 1982. The company had left its dollar borrowings unhedged, and the rising dollar had pushed its sterling interest costs sky-high, thus contributing to Laker Airway's bankruptcy. An airline went under, and with it went jobs. Over the years, American multinational companies learned the hard way, too. For example, Eastman Kodak Company's pre-tax earnings were depressed by $3.5 billion between 1980 and 1985 because of the rising dollar. The dollar's subsequent fall, however, revived its fortunes by adding 60 cents a share in 1986. But its overseas market share—in 1991 some 46 percent of Kodak's $19 billion in annual sales come from foreign countries—took time to recover. Today, Kodak uses mainly options to make sure it at least breaks even on currency swings, and as with all multinationals, exchanges-rate risks have become crucial to Kodak in foreign plant location, finding new suppliers, or choosing markets. The lesson is clear: Exchange rates go through swings that do not relate to economic reality as perceived by importers and exporters. The futures markets can hedge such exposure and, in turn, save jobs in the long run.

Not surprisingly, then, the Merc and the Chicago Board of Trade, in particular, have been emulated by virtually every financial center the world over, with new exchanges developed in London, Paris, Hong Kong, Sydney, Toronto, Singapore, Rio de Janeiro, Osaka, Zurich, Frankfurt, and Tokyo. Moreover, the exchanges never argued against the fact that futures trading is a risky venture for the small investor. But today it is mainly the commercial entities—not the small investor—who use the futures markets to reduce risk and lower the costs of doing business. Stock index futures, for instance, offer greater liquidity than individual stocks, are far less vulnerable to manipulation than individual stocks, and provide greater leverage than stocks.

History teaches us the most basic lesson of life: To see where we might be going, we must understand where we've been. We go forward by looking back. The purpose of this book is neither to glorify the Merc nor to present a gossipy insider view, but to chronicle its development as a significant American business story that had been largely ignored. The Merc is in good part responsible for the birth of the Global Exchange, and like "a citizen of the world" it is heading into the twenty-first century by turning itself into the "exchange of the world," a boundaryless entity guided by speed and innovation.

Part I

The Age of Enterprise
(1850 to 1958)

1

The Gathering

On the sultry Chicago evening of 4 June 1982, some 1,400 commodity traders, spouses, brokers, bankers, politicians, and academicians gathered at the Hyatt Regency Hotel to clink glasses of champagne in honor of the tenth anniversary of the Chicago Mercantile Exchange's International Monetary Market (IMM).

It was a lavish black-tie affair, part celebration, part rally, part "I told you so"—and all Chicago Mercantile Exchange (CME) bravado. The high-spirited crowd feasted on rare tenderloin, smoked salmon, raspberries, and chocolate sweets. As waiters poured coffee, a hush fell in deference to the man at the podium who was about to introduce the evening's guest of honor, Nobel Laureate economist Milton Friedman, a friend and consultant to the Exchange over the years who had been dubbed by some "mentor" of the IMM.

But first, Leo Melamed, four-time chairman of the CME and IMM, briefly reminisced, raising and lowering his voice with the theatricality of the actor he was as a youth on the Yiddish stage:

> It seems like only yesterday when the first IMM board of directors took its very first European trip to tell the world about our great idea. And no one came to listen.... Who were we? We were traders to whom it didn't matter whether it was eggs or gold, bellies or the British pound, turkeys or T-bills. We were babes in the woods—innocents—in a world we didn't understand. Too dumb to be scared. We were audacious, brazen, raucous pioneers. Too innocent to realize we couldn't win; that the odds against us were too high; that the banks would never trust us; that the government wouldn't let us; that Chicago was the wrong place ....

Melamed's 10 minutes of verbal shorthand sketched the history of the Mercantile Exchange from its rough beginnings as a butter-and-egg exchange in 1918. Melamed had, however, conveyed more than just a string of broken images. He had traced the Merc's long journey from obscurity with its detours of despair along the way. Through a blend of scrappiness, hustle, street smarts and a damn-the-torpedoes attitude, the Merc had bolted through the 1970s and into the 1980s as a pioneer and innovator. It seemed to be making up for lost time, but never lost opportunity.

Then CME chairman Jack Sandner summed it up at the semiannual members' meeting shortly after the IMM gala: "We are determined people; we are aggressive people. We are doers; we are originators. We are a mixture of formally educated and practically experienced people. We are planners. We are challengers. We are interested in the past only as a prelude to the future. We are opinionated, sometimes stubborn. We think pragmatically, and we are very profit oriented."

The kind of hard-scrabbling people Sandner described weren't all that different from what historian Henry Adams found the average Chicagoan to be a century earlier—"a pushing, energetic, ingenious person, always awake and trying to get ahead of his neighbors."

Trying to get ahead of its neighbor may indeed have been a factor in the Merc's growth. A few blocks away stood the venerable Chicago Board of Trade, the granddaddy of futures trading, with more than a 70-year head start— a lifetime—over the Mercantile Exchange. Did it make the Merc try harder? That's a matter of opinion. However, among the nation's futures exchanges, the Merc certainly proved itself shrewder, quicker, and more flexible when it came to diversifying than did the others.

Over the years, such Merc leaders as Leo Melamed, Laurence Rosenberg, Jack Sandner, and Brian Monieson had the charisma to inspire Exchange members with "win one for the Gipper" homilies. From time to time, members had to be fired up like players for the big game. Ideas became markets; the IMM was proof of that. But without the trading impetus—the liquidity that comes with people buying and selling—markets simply died. A market either worked, or it didn't; and once it did, it took on a life of its own, filtering information and responding like a human brain. As for the economic justification of a futures contract, "only the marketplace knows," Melamed emphatically stated.

There was more than slick rhetoric and economic gospel to fall back on. There was an impressive record of rapid growth, especially in the wake of the IMM. When trading on the IMM began in 1972 with seven foreign currencies, it was the first major effort by a U.S. exchange to open a financial market in currencies to the general public. Merc officials never looked back.

Membership expanded from 500 to 1,150 in 1972 and to 2,600 in 1982. During this period, the number of contracts traded more than quadrupled to 33.5 million. (In 1985, a record 56.6 million contracts changed hands.) The Merc had also scored another first among futures exchanges when, in 1977, it opened an office in Washington, D.C., to give it a more formidable presence. All along, new contracts were being added to the list of interest rate and financial futures. The Merc had spawned the financial futures revolution and paved the way for the markets of the 1980s; nearly every other exchange followed. In 1983 the world's second-largest futures exchange moved into the world's largest and most advanced trading complex and within months was considering expansion.

The idea of a mercantile exchange was rooted in the nineteenth century, a time when farmers were hauling their grain, butter, and eggs to the big city in buckboard wagons. Since its beginning, the Exchange has traveled a hard road, often shaken by war, depression, recession, scandal, and government price supports. At times, the road appeared to be a dead end. For example, in 1958, in the wake of a speculative binge, the Exchange was brought to its knees by a congressional ban on onion trading, the Merc's principal commodity at the time. But as always, the resolute Merc managed to assess, regroup, and then move ahead like a well-disciplined trader who learns from his mistakes. In doing so, the Merc was as far-seeing as it was unconventional.

Among the guests at the IMM anniversary were children and grandchildren of the members of the Merc when it was the teetering Butter and Egg Board in 1918, nervously wondering whether it could survive by trading futures in butter and eggs. History had answered that question, just as it had for the IMM. As it turned out, the IMM was not an evolution, but a revolution with a profound effect on the history of the futures markets in particular and financial markets in general.

An overwhelming sense of victory filled the massive Hyatt ballroom as the architects of the Exchange's modern era were now gathered to toast both the past and the future. There was Melamed, the charismatic driving force behind the Exchange since the 1960s, whose idea it was to give business and financial managers the same price risk–transfer opportunities that their agribusiness counterparts had been using for more than a century. Also in attendance were the philosophic statesman Everette B. Harris, who had served as the Exchange's president for 25 years until his retirement in 1978, and the man who replaced him, the loquacious and quotable Clayton Yeutter, destined to become the U.S. Secretary of Agriculture. There was the numbers man, Dr. Mark Powers, the Merc's chief economist—and the first economist on any futures exchange anywhere—who drew up the specifications and delivery mechanism of the first foreign currency contracts. As previously mentioned, also in attendance was the renowned Dr. Milton Friedman, who had authored a study for the Merc in December 1971 that became the intellectual foundation for the birth of currency futures, giving Melamed's idea, as he himself put it, "credibility." Jack Sandner, the tireless chairman in 1982, who carried the leadership mantle into the 1990s, was present. And there were the dignitaries too: Mayor Jane Byrne, a friend of Chicago's exchanges; and the Lord Mayor of London, Sir Christopher Lever, who came to thank the first American exchange to open a London office. Scores of others who had either been Exchange governors or had served on the various committees that helped launch the IMM attended, as well as the hundreds of traders who made it go. The success of the IMM had made visionaries of them all.

The IMM had thrust the Mercantile Exchange into a new dimension that was neither time nor twilight zone, but perhaps a bit of both. The Merc had entered the international arena of high finance, the shadowy and very exclusive world of the large banks, which traded currencies among themselves in a "forward market" in such world money centers as New York, London, Paris, Zurich, and Tokyo. The Exchange had made itself vulnerable to the ridicule of skeptics in the United States and abroad. On 16 May 1972, the very day trading opened in the currencies, *The Wall Street Journal* quoted a New York foreign exchange dealer in a bitter outburst: "I'm amazed that a bunch of crapshooters in pork bellies have the temerity to think that they can beat some of the world's most sophisticated traders at their own game."

Unfortunately, the dealer had missed the point. The Mercantile Exchange, its officials were quick to point out, had no intention of beating anyone. The new IMM had been designed as an adjunct and alternative to the world's interbank market. Simply put, foreign exchange traders could transfer their risk to the willing speculative world. That world had changed dramatically in 1971.

There was no historical precedent for the monetary standard after 1971, the year in which President Nixon closed the gold window to bring an end to the Bretton Woods agreement, which fixed exchange rates pegged to an anemic gold standard. Before 1971, the value of money had been linked in the mind of the beholder to a commodity of some kind or another—from feathers in Brazil to hubcap-sized stones on the island of Yap. The Japanese had used iron as a monetary standard during the nineteenth century. The Western world, too, had metals mania, as summed up by Karl Marx: "Money is, by nature, gold and silver." Until the administration of Lyndon Johnson, the American dollar bill carried the legend, "Payable in silver to the bearer on demand."

Britain adopted the gold standard in 1816, but it carried no weight along the coast of Guinea in Africa, where all the gold bullion in the world couldn't buy a spear. However, a string of cowrie shells could. Some tribes of Native Americans used wampum, small beads made of shells (a black or dark purple bead was worth twice as much as a white one), and the early settlers in Virginia used tobacco to stoke their pipe dreams of wealth.

There were, of course, blips in the panorama of monetary history when governments cranked out irredeemable paper money with nothing more than a prayer behind it, if that. During the Revolutionary War, for example, the Continental Congress switched from coin, or "specie," to paper money, and the new currency dropped in value faster than the temperature at Valley Forge. It depreciated so quickly, in fact, that "not worth a Continental" became a phrase in the American lexicon synonymous with worthlessness. In the second year of the Civil War, to avoid bankruptcy, the North printed large quantities of "greenbacks," paper money that was green on the back, and declared them legal tender for debts. Six months later, they weren't worth a Continental, and the Lincoln administration was forced to levy new taxes on manufactured goods and income taxes on railroad and steamboat companies. In 1911 American economist Irving Fisher dourly proclaimed, "Irredeemable paper money has almost invariably proved a curse to the country employing it."

That's what made 1971 so special in a monetary sense. It was the first time in history that every nation had an irredeemable paper standard. Moreover, it was not a temporary situation. From that point on, the world's monetary system, as Friedman sees it today, remains "uncharted territory." The International Monetary Market is a means to help individuals and institutions navigate the rocky shoals of world financial markets. "It's a very important service," Friedman said of the IMM at a press conference on the morning of 4 June. "It isn't going to change the world fundamentally, but it is going to enable the world to operate more smoothly and effectively."

The IMM, like the Chicago Mercantile Exchange itself, wasn't an overnight success. It took time, as well as coddling, courting, and cajoling the brokerage community and banking establishments before the IMM's currency contracts were accepted. For Merc officials, however, that was par for the course. They had long learned how to endure and be persistent. It was part of their century-old legacy that Everette B. Harris had once stated as the Merc's unwritten motto: "We didn't know it couldn't be done."

The Exchange was obviously more than just a glass-and-granite shell for a bunch of boisterous risk takers. It was a place that brought buyer and seller together—a mechanism, said Harris, that epitomized the free-enterprise system in the United States, a thriving example of how people build institutions for the sake of profit in a free market for free individuals.

2

A Crossroads

Under milky clouds, an icy wind ripped through the streets of Chicago, which was still on the mend from the Great Fire that two years earlier had burned a swath through its heart, destroying a third of its wealth. The winter of 1873 was particularly bitter—for some, catastrophic.

All year long, banks and businesses across the nation fell like dominoes, pushed over the brink by financial panic that froze commerce in most American towns. The panic of 1873 claimed legions of investors, budding entrepreneurs, and economic titans. Big railroads and eastern financial firms went belly-up, closing the New York Stock Exchange for 10 days. The entire banking system imploded like a black hole, sucking down 22,000 businesses and millions of depositors. Eventually 500,000 Americans became unemployed with no safety net as global depression swept across the oceans.

The streets of Chicago were a reminder of the scope and severity of the problem that brutal winter. Some people froze. Some died of hunger. Others without jobs and homes huddled under rags in the corridors of public buildings, including the first floor of City Hall. Still others took to the streets, waving protest signs declaring "Bread or blood!" through the frigid air. Remarkably, no shots were fired in the incident known as the "Bread Riot." Though economic depression would pass, the stage was set for social unrest in the future.

Throughout those lean and harsh months of 1873, Chicago withstood the general collapse of confidence better than other big cities on either side of the Mississippi River. The city's merchants even managed to stage the Inter-State Industrial Exposition, which included the construction of a Crystal Palace modeled on the iron and glass convention hall in Victorian London. The exposition drew some 60,000 visitors, who gazed upon an array of the latest machines and tools produced across Illinois. Such seeming resiliency did not occur because Chicago had shrewder businessmen or because its methods of doing business were superior; it was instead the agricultural garland the city wore that buffered the hard times—access to the immense granaries of the West, upon which, more than anything else, the nation depended for relief. The golden fields of grain had contributed far more to the country's economic progress than had the gold fields of California. Geography was destiny, and Chicago was square in destiny's path.

Decades before the railroads crisscrossed the Midwest, when people, goods, and ideas traveled slowly, the "Caravans of Faith," as the wagon trains were called, rolled across Illinois filled with men and women in search of their futures. Trundling against the backdrop of the opalescent waters of Lake Michigan, about 200 wagons rattled into Chicago weekly during the 1830s.

"Like the finger of destiny," wrote Edward Dies in *The Wheat Pit*, "the historic pilgrimage of pioneers pointed ever westward, straggling onward in unending lines." Destiny's finger also pushed the Native Americans into pockets of despair, scattering tribes like chaff in the wind. Between 1840 and 1860, Illinois, Ohio, Indiana, Michigan, and Wisconsin doubled their populations and tripled the production of their fields.

Immigrants poured into Chicago with Old World perseverance, a willingness to sweat, and a certain naïveté that came with their unfettered optimism. They began replacing American labor in railroad and canal construction work. There were more immigrants in Chicago in 1850 than natives, and at the turn of the century, immigrants made up more than 70 percent of the city's population.

It was the opening of the Erie Canal in 1825 that spurred the migration, helping to transform Chicago from a sleepy, mud-drenched prairie hamlet into a rapidly growing town. Eventually, Chicago became the junction of America's two great inland waterways. The water route for commerce stretched westward from the Erie Canal through the Great Lakes to the Chicago River, then through the Illinois and Michigan Canal and down the Mississippi, to the thriving ports of St. Louis and New Orleans.

The first shipment of grain to the East was more by chance than by plan. In 1838, Walker & Company shipped $15,000 worth of hides on its steamer, the *Great Western,* bound for Buffalo. Along with the hides were added 39 bags of wheat (about 78 bushels) as a trial of sorts. The next year, Newberry & Dole Company shipped 1,678 bushels of wheat aboard the brig *Osceola,* and the grain trade began in earnest.

The volume of grain coursing through the city in 1851 turned Chicago into the nation's primary corn market. By 1854, it was the largest center for wheat; six years later, the greatest lumber market; and, during the Civil War, the foremost meat-packing point.

With the emerging grain trade came a modern American tool of commerce: the futures contract. During those early years, the long distances from which grain came to Chicago led to the use of "to arrive" sales and forward contracts, in which buyer and seller agreed upon payment for delivery of a specified quantity of goods at a specified future date. The early commodity markets existed primarily for spot or cash transactions with immediate delivery on foodstuffs, textiles, hides, metal, and lumber. However, spot trading and forward contracting could not handle the problems created by the dramatic shifts in supply, demand, and price that played havoc with the emotions and pocketbooks of farmers who brought their grain and livestock to markets for a given period each year.

There was no area in Chicago that reflected this chaos better than South Water Street, nestled along the South Branch of the Chicago River. During the early 1800s, pistol-toting hunters on horseback ambled down South Water, selling their game to the meat commission houses, where the fly-covered carcasses of deer and black bears hung on the walls. For two dollars a dozen, one could choose from a variety of fowl that included teal, partridge, jacksnipe, quail, prairie chicken, and grouse. In the corners and on the shelves of the stores, bags of corn and wheat piled up, often serving as a buffet for famished rats. At other times, however, the walls were barren and shelves empty. For both man and beast, it was a feast or famine situation. Little changed when South Water became the haven of Chicago's wily butter-and-egg men, who peddled their merchandise from one-horse wagons that clippity-clopped across the city from dawn to dusk.

The grain trade, though it was the mainspring of Chicago's commercialism, had numerous problems. There was a shortage of storage and transportation facilities, and weather often proved hellish. Most of the year, rain and snow made the dirt roads from country farmlands to the city impassable. Thus, there was either a river of grain or extreme shortage; these fluctuations were exacerbated by crop failures. Even when yield was abundant, supplies of grain and livestock were quickly exhausted, causing prices to soar and people to go hungry. There were also periods, following good harvests, when short-term demand could not absorb the glut of meat and grain at any price, however low, and grain was actually thrown into the streets or dumped into Lake Michigan for lack of buyers. By spring, grain supplies were tight and prices soared.

In 1841 wheat trading was hailed as the harbinger of better times. Six years later, under the pressure of severe shortages, buyers were cursing it as the scourge of the prairie. In 1847 prices rose from 70 cents a bushel in late March to $1.30 in early June. Such speculative flurries turned the grain trade into a cutthroat business. When buyers weren't forming minicartels to fix prices, they were sending runners speeding to the rim of the prairie to meet incoming wagons and bargain for the contents. Terminals awash with grain one moment, then dry as a water hole in the Sahara the next, had a ripple effect on an economy tied to agriculture. Without crops to sell, the farmer lacked income to buy plows, hammers, overalls, and other manufactured goods, thus forcing businessmen to face bankruptcy.

Out of this chaotic frenzy, the necessity for a central market where buyers and sellers could meet became clear. Forward contracting was a step in that direction. Grain traders had used forward contracts in Chicago shortly after the city was incorporated in 1833. (Even before the Chicago Board of Trade was founded in 1848, price quotations of forward contracts appeared in Chicago newspapers.)

But there was no physical exchange, no marketplace where parties could haggle over price face-to-face.

As early as the 1700s, Japanese merchants saw the value of exchanges. Unlike those in the United States and Europe, commodity exchanges predated stock exchanges in Japan, where forward contracting on the Osaka Rice Exchange began in 1730, along with markets for edible oils, cotton, and precious metals. An exchange in New York began trading domestic produce in 1752, but transactions were made in cash and deliveries were immediate. It took nearly one hundred years for the notion of an exchange to evolve in Chicago, spurred by farmers, and merchants, shippers, and grain dealers seeking greater profits and predictability for their markets in a nation that was fast becoming market driven. From the late 1840s through the 1880s, the system that balanced the gaps between supply and demand grew more sophisticated. It included not only futures trading, but also standardization of grades, the expansion of warehouses and elevators, and the use of warehouse receipts as negotiable instruments. The need for a central meeting place where merchants and businessmen could air their common concerns and resolve mutual issues led to the founding of boards of trade. The Buffalo Board of Trade began in 1844, followed by the Detroit Board of Trade in 1847; then it was Chicago's turn.

On a February afternoon in 1848, Thomas Richmond, a Chicago grain elevator operator, and William L. Whitney, a grain broker, met to discuss the prospects of an exchange. It was more a meeting of the minds than a debate. Two months later, the two men invited eighty others with interests in the grain trade to help form the Chicago Board of Trade. In the following months, a president was elected, a constitution and by-laws adopted, and rooms rented for $110 a year with meetings held daily and annual dues of three dollars.

Initially, the Board was more a trade association than a marketplace for the rationalization of the grain trade. Among its 25 directors were a druggist, a bookseller, a tanner, a grocer, a coal dealer, a hardware merchant, and a banker. From the start it was vocal on and off the trading floor. For instance, in 1850 the Board vigorously protested the removal of the toll collector's office to another location on the Illinois and Michigan Canal. The change, argued the Board, would harm the prosperity of Chicago. It wasn't civic pride that moved the Board's members to rally for such a seemingly mundane cause; it was self-interest. Grain meant possible profits to speculators, warehouses, processors, and those who financed its movement. Any obstacle—no matter how trivial—that might alter the course of grain flowing into Chicago terminals was bad for business.

For the next six years, the Exchange struggled for survival. In the beginning, few were inclined to use the Board, and the reluctance showed in its flagging support. With only 53 members in 1852, there were many days when no one showed up, not even the president of the Board. Weeks could go by without a single transaction taking place. The malaise in those early years prompted this wry observation from local historian Everett Chamberlin: "To be sure, there was a Board of Trade, frequently in session, discussing public measures, applauding eloquent harangues, ridiculing strange ideas and interchanging all the blunt, frank and hearty offices of western good fellowship. But this body of men could not overcome the habit of feeling that the time spent on 'Change' was in derogation of the stern exactions of real business."

And so it went. To drum up support, the Board tried luring members with a daily free lunch of cheese, crackers, and ale. For a time, it drew the trading crowd, along with every freeloader who sauntered by the corner of South Water and LaSalle Streets. The Board countered by posting a bouncer at its doors to deal with the crashers. Such perquisites, however, weren't enough to stimulate trading. Short of perhaps doling out free room and board, it is doubtful anything could have done so.

Businessmen, it seemed, were simply too slow and too cautious to recognize the value of time contracts. "The conservative men who controlled affairs at the time, however, seemed to think there was too much of the element of chance in this method of trade," remarked Board of Trade historian Charles Taylor. A bit of jealousy may also have had something to do with it. The strongly financed and influential firms on the Board tended to snub speculators with limited capital who were active in trading time contracts. Finally, the Board retrenched at its annual meeting on 7 April 1856 at the Tremont House.

Forty-five additional members were elected, and the newly installed officers pledged to set a new course that involved establishing grades and standards for greater surety in the quality of grains. Shortly thereafter, the Board ordered daily telegraph reports of the markets in New York, Montreal, Buffalo, and Oswego. Not even the panic of 1857, which depressed grain and cotton prices severely, curbed the Board's growth. Membership ranks swelled within two years to 520, and business on the Exchange was restricted to members only. In 1859 a committee of arbitration and appeals was formed whereby inspectors were appointed whose certificates would be binding upon members. The Board was fast becoming an economic, political, and social force in Chicago. Its shaky start behind, there was no doubt that this institution of commerce was here to stay.

Meanwhile, the momentum of the grain trade was ensuring a rosy future for the Board. Grain arrived in Chicago faster than it could be sold, which created a need for expanded storage capacity. Elevator operators began issuing receipts indicating the grade and amount of grain that was stored. These receipts, in effect, were ownership titles, enabling the grain dealer to sell his wheat and transfer it to the buyer by mere delivery of the elevator receipt.

The receipts allowed speculation by those outside the grain business who anticipated a drop in prices even though they didn't own the grain. Now a speculator could sell and borrow elevator receipts for an amount of grain equivalent to the amount sold. At first, the elevator receipts represented specific lots of grain. Later, they reflected grain of a given grade without regard to one specific lot.

The Civil War gave impetus to the use of contracts of this sort. Board members no longer needed free lunches to draw them to the trading floor, as long as they could savor risk and taste profits instead. Wheat for the stomachs of the Union Army and oats for its horses meant a booming business for grain traders. The war that split a nation—costing 620,000 lives—acted as a catalyst to push the grain trade out of its Middle Ages. The stock exchange also began to flourish, boosted by factories and railroads in the North that had built the Union war machine, as well as the emergence of the "modern" corporation and its need for an amount of capital no individual could muster alone. In 1863 the New York Stock and Exchange Board changed its name to the New York Stock Exchange, and two years later it moved into its permanent home on Broad Street, just south of Wall Street. America stood on the brink of prospering and Americans, at least those who were inured to risk, loved the appeal of common stocks, which in the decades after the Civil War helped Cornelius Vanderbilt unify his railroads, J.P. Morgan fund his mergers, and Jay Gould play the market for fun and profit. From across the nation, millions of dollars flowed into New York, strengthening its position, observed social historians Thomas Cochran and William Miller, "as the real capital of the nation."

One month after Lee surrendered to Grant at Appomattox to end the Civil War, the Board of Trade adopted its first rule, which dealt specifically with time contracts. It provided for the deposit of margins on time contracts not to exceed 10 percent of the value of the commodity specified in the contracts. A rule similar to this would be adopted 45 years later also as the first by the Chicago Butter and Egg Board, nearly a decade before the start of organized trading in butter-and-egg futures on the Chicago Mercantile Exchange. It wasn't until 1868 that the Board of Trade passed its first rules regulating grain futures contracts in an effort to curb manipulation of the markets through the widespread abuse known as a *corner* or a *squeeze*. A corner was the attempt to acquire a sufficient quantity of a commodity or security in order to gain control over its price and supply. (Wall Street had its share of corners in the late 1800s and early 1900s, when the securities markets were virtually unregulated.) Corners in the wheat market not only hurt traders caught short, but even worse, they affected the price one paid for a loaf of bread. Every corner artist had the same source of inspiration: greed. With a harshly worded resolution, CBOT directors fired the first volley in their war against corners:

> The practice of corners, of making contracts for the purchase of a commodity, and then taking measures to render it impossible for the seller to fill his contract, for the purpose of extorting money from him, has been too long tolerated by this and other commercial bodies to the injury and discredit of legitimate commerce;... these transactions are essentially improper and fraudulent, and should any member of this Board hereafter engage in any such transactions, the directors should take measures for his expulsion.

Unfortunately, the board had fired a volley of blanks, for the resolution was ineffectual, according to Jonathan Lurie in his study titled *The Chicago Board of Trade, 1859–1905.* The old-boy network endemic to both the nation's stock and futures exchanges, which were run like private clubs, had little use for reform. The sense that an exchange was a quasi-public organization had not taken hold with the nineteenth-century speculators, for whom "corner" was a shibboleth. The CBOT made little effort to enforce the resolution, observed Lurie, "choosing again not to interfere with members' market activity."

Even the anti-corner law passed by the Illinois legislature in 1874 couldn't stop the shenanigans of William Sturges, a former CBOT director. Known among his pals as "King Jack," Sturges tried to squeeze the corn market in the summer of 1874 at precisely the time the new anti-corner law went into effect. Corners and squeezes died hard in the futures markets, as witnessed by the machinations of Nelson Bunker Hunt and his brother William Herbert Hunt, the one-time Texas billionaires, who set out to be the King Jacks of their day when they began gathering up soybean contracts like two children hoarding baseball cards. In 1977 the Hunts bought some 24 million soybean contracts on the CBOT— eight times the position limit allowed—before the CFTC forced them to sell off their holdings. They were fined a half million dollars and could not dabble in the soybean market again for at least two years. The brothers were at it again in 1979, when they tried to corner the silver market on the CBOT, where eventually they controlled 70 percent of the supply for delivery and 50 percent of the supply on the Commodity Exchange of New York (COMEX). Again they were caught, and again they were forced to liquidate into a declining market; this time, it cost them their billions. As recently as 1989 the corner appeared still to be in vogue when the giant Italian grain merchant, Ferruzi Financiaria S.P.A., amassed soybean contracts exceeding hedging limits.

By the turn of the century, the complexion of commodity exchanges had been transformed from that of essentially cash markets to financial markets in which the ability to buy and sell the actual commodity became secondary to protection against the financial risk of price volatility. Oddly, though, the use of futures contracts as a hedging tool developed slowly even among the giants of the grain trade like James Pillsbury, the tycoon flour miller. Over brandy one evening, F. H. Peavey, head of the biggest grain elevator company at the time, gave Pillsbury a tip. "Fill up your elevators with wheat," he advised. Then he instructed Pillsbury to sell "May" as a hedge. There would be a profit of several cents a bushel, he assured.

Pillsbury mulled over the prospect for a moment, showing concern and grave skepticism. A deal like that was impossible, he was convinced, for no business was assured a profit without effort. More convincing was his belief that neither farmer nor miller had much influence over prices in the Chicago Board of Trade wheat pits. He, in fact, went one step further, insisting that if there were no futures markets there would be no need for speculation. The need to hedge, he thought, was created by speculators, who had destabilized the markets over the years. No, thank you, he told Peavey and passed up the tip.

All along, the key to a thriving commodity trade—whether it was grain, cattle, or eggs—was transportation. Fortunately, Illinois legislators realized that early. Congress had authorized construction of the Illinois and Michigan Canal in 1836 (it wasn't completed until 1848), just three years after Chicago was incorporated. That year, Illinois built its first railway, the Galena and Chicago Union Railroad, when there was barely a thousand miles of track in all of America. The rail link connected Chicago with the Mississippi barge trade and the grain fields in the northwestern part of Illinois. As the railroads pushed west, the bankers stalked like bloodhounds. In 1854, Chicago boasted 25 investment bankers, compared to the 18 in New York and 10 in Boston. The reason: Railroads were the growth industry of the nineteenth century and represented one-fourth of the total active capital in the country. Between 1850 and 1857, about twenty-three hundred miles of railroad tracks, which included the Rock Island and the Illinois Central, were built annually, at a cost of $60 million. However, the transcontinental system turned Chicago into the husky, brawling "city of big shoulders" that poet Carl Sandburg celebrated nearly fifty years after the coasts of a half-wild continent were linked. In 1869, the year the Board of Trade began regulating trading in futures contracts, the tracks of the Central Pacific and Union Pacific railroads were joined at Promontory Point, Utah, linking America and accelerating its commerce. From the West Coast alone, some 53 million pounds of commodities began pouring into Chicago yearly, including everything from borax to butter, and wood to wine.

Chicago's stockyards bulged with 800,000 head of cattle shipped out of Dodge and Abilene for points in the East. The month-long trip from San Francisco to Chicago by the combination of railroad and rickety stagecoach was now cut to a week by train, which shuttled big-city ideas to small towns via hungry salesmen with order blanks for every product imaginable.

By 1871 Chicago, now the lumber capital of the continent, had pushed St. Louis aside to become the major emporium for farmers of the West to buy their goods. Much of the lumber went into shaping Chicago's skyline, dominated by giant wooden monoliths along the lakeshore and river banks; these structures were the massive grain elevators that swallowed wheat like a hungry dog devouring a mouthful of meat, as one observer who marveled at the sight described it. Before the rail union between East and West, there were few cities between Chicago and San Francisco at all, and none whose population numbered more than 35,000 persons. Suddenly towns sprouted over the prairie where only gophers and jack rabbits had lived. Railroad euphoria spread across the nation, bolstered by President James A. Garfield, who heralded the train as "the greatest centralizing force of modern times."

It wasn't the only force at work. As railroads prodded Americans on a faster and farther track, a bumper crop of gizmos and gadgets were introduced to expand man's output. In the 1840s some 5,942 new patents were issued. In the 1850s the number quadrupled to include wheat thrashers, mechanical drills, water wheels, steam engines, and pumps. Cyrus McCormick's Chicago factory sold 1,558 reapers and sowers in 1854 and was planning for 3,000 machines in 1855. Before the Civil War, it took 61 hours of labor to produce one acre of hand-grown wheat. By the late 1800s, machinery yielded the same amount of wheat in under three-and-a-half hours.

As Chicago was going out to the world, the world was coming to Chicago. Immigrants were arriving almost as fast as the grain. In a single week in 1854, some 12,000 immigrants arrived on trains in Chicago, many of them Irish and Germans who had fled famine and depression in Europe. There were Jews, Italians, Poles, Lithuanians, and Greeks, too, crowding and squeezing into the wooden shanties of the south and west sides of the city, and all eager to earn a living that would provide something extra to send for their relatives.

From the burgs and shtetls of Europe, the peasantry perceived America as the land of the wealthy. With visions of greenbacks dancing in their heads as they huddled on steerage decks, the immigrants wasted little time rolling up their sleeves and hustling once they reached the Atlantic shore. Turn-of-the-century *Chicago Daily News* columnist Finley Peter Dunne summarized the drive that made the New World go 'round in the droll wit of his classic creation, Mr. Dooley, the saloon keeper with the tart Irish brogue: "The crownin' wurruk iv our civilization is th' cash raygister."

Among the wave of immigrants was a hearty and enterprising youngster named Max Weinberg, who became a charter member of the Chicago Mercantile Exchange when it was created in 1919. Weinberg had left Kassel, Germany, in 1879 and boarded a tramp steamer for America. In one respect, it was a remarkable journey because Max was alone and only 12 years old at the time. He was on a single-minded mission: to make enough money to bring the rest of the family to America. An older cousin was to have gone instead, but when he was conscripted by the German army, the burden fell on Max. If he had any qualms about taking on the assignment, Max never let anybody know.

Along with other "greenhorns," Max arrived at Castle Garden (Ellis Island wasn't opened until 1892) at the Battery on the southern tip of Manhattan. While being processed through the stockadelike depot, he was lonely, bewildered, fearful, and unable to speak a word of English. There were no friends or relatives waiting to greet him, only uniformed officials barking orders in English, which was unintelligible to Max's ears, and performing fearful eye examinations. His senses were bombarded with the lower East Side; he was terrified and at the same time excited. Never had he seen such buildings or such masses of people scurrying around, or heard such noises, or smelled such odors wafting from the pushcarts crammed along streetcurbs and sidewalks. The screaming hawkers, screeching streetcars, eerie lights, and gloomy shadows cast from the forlorn rows of tenements added to his confusion. Homesick, he wanted to cry *"Oy gevalt!"* and go back home. But he wouldn't. He held back his tears and went about the mission, no matter how long it would take. For the next several months, Max worked as a busboy, picking up tips and English phrases. With a few dollars in his pocket, he headed for Chicago, the heart of the nation's meat-packing industry and one of its most congested cities, having passed Philadelphia as the runner-up to New York in size.

Max arrived in Chicago at a time when wages were rising commensurate with who you were. Department store magnate Marshall Field, for instance, was making $500 an hour in 1880, while most of his nonexecutive employees were making around $12 for a 59-hour week. Max landed a job with a meat processor, a business he had learned a little about in Kassel, where he had worked in his father's butcher shop. For the next six years he saved. By 1885 Max was able to pay passage from Germany to Chicago for his parents, two brothers, and three sisters, and there was enough left over to start a business.

At 18 Max Weinberg was in business for himself. His sister made sausages, and he sold them door-to-door. The brothers eventually joined the company, and by 1891 Weinberg Brothers & Co. had added groceries, tallow, hides, furs, and game to its meat, poultry, and egg business. Subsequently, Weinberg Brothers & Co. became America's oldest commodity firm owned by a single family, having become a major processor and wholesaler of poultry, eggs, butter, and related products. Besides wholesaling, Max concentrated customer business in butter-and-egg futures too.

Max learned early not to take anything for granted. The lesson occurred when he was haggling with a meat processor and the language barrier began to go up. As communication faltered, Max started flashing his fingers to indicate price. The other man responded and quickly raised all the fingers on his right hand. Max nodded "yes," sealing the deal. Later, when the processor returned to collect, he wanted more than Max had agreed to pay. Tempers flared briefly, but Max ended up paying the higher price. There on the man's right hand was the freakish proof of the transaction: six fingers.

It was a story Max would repeat to his son, Michael, and grandson, Michael Jr., over the years. To this day, Michael Weinberg, Jr., admits that he doesn't know whether the story is apocryphal. Regardless, there is a lesson in it—one should never assume anything when it comes to a business deal, however basic, even if it means counting the fingers on someone else's hand.

In an age of enterprise, people like Max Weinberg were pioneers. They were egg packers, meat merchants, and produce peddlers, anxious to feed their own families, but also helping to feed a city and nation on the move. They were small businessmen, fiercely independent, who had carved their commercial niches among the Philip Armours, Gustavus Swifts, Marshall Fields, Cyrus McCormicks, Potter Palmers, William Wrigleys, and George Pullmans—the giants of Chicago commerce.

These early butter-and-egg men, emerging from a crude Chicago commerce, had a certain audacity, the kind the Mercantile Exchange leaders would talk about a century later in reference to their own accomplishments. They were the first movers and shakers behind the Chicago Mercantile Exchange. In fact, it was Max Weinberg, his brothers, friends, and rivals on South Water and Fulton Streets who banded together to form the Chicago Butter and Egg Board in 1898, when egg packers were paying a paltry five cents per dozen. In many ways, they reflected Chicago itself, a city of vigor and resiliency that had amazed a nation by the speed at which it rebuilt itself after the Great Fire.

What better place to launch enterprise than in a city that by its nature stood at the right place at the right time? Chicago was a city of commerce loaded with characters of every ilk and fashion, and a political city where subterfuge was the normal way for doing business in the city council, dominated by the likes of such slippery First Ward politicians as Hinky Dink and Bathhouse John, a pair of Picassos in the art of boodle. That was Chicago at the turn of the century: the melting pot of humanity, the smudge pot of industry, and the honey pot of corruption. The butter-and-egg men had come to make their fortunes and build their futures in Chicago, which had derived its name from *checagou,* an Algonquian word that meant *wild onion*—a fitting omen of things to come at the Chicago Mercantile Exchange.

3

From Steerage to Storage

Of all the arguments, philosophic and otherwise, that ensued on the Chicago Mercantile Exchange over the years, one was indisputable: The egg came before the chicken. Indeed, trading in egg futures preceded chicken futures by more than four decades.

While the Midwest was becoming the nation's breadbasket in the nineteenth Century, it was turning into its hen house as well. As long as they had shells, eggs were eggs—a highly seasonal commodity with oversupply in the spring and a scarcity in the winter. During the Civil War, Illinois exported eggs to New York, and by 1880, the farms scattered across Illinois, Iowa, Nebraska, and Minnesota had collectively become the nation's largest producers of poultry and eggs, according to the first census to include such data.

During the long peace that followed the Civil War, American wealth grew rapidly. America's exclusive club of just three millionaires in 1860 had swelled to 3,800 millionaires by 1900, when one-tenth of the population owned nine-tenths of the wealth. The reign of agrarianism was replaced by a kingdom of tough-minded businessmen, trusts, corporations, and Washington railroad lobbyists—all calculating to accumulate capital. In the scramble, hardly anyone minded that seven out of ten industrial workers were earning no more than 10 cents an hour or that children under 15 were sweating in coal mines, steel mills, and tobacco fields for as little as 25 cents per day.

Even those of the upper middle class didn't mind working ten hours a day, six days a week. "The husbands are content to slave in business in order that their wives and families may live in ease and affluence," observed two visiting Englishmen in their *Reminiscences of America,* published in the early 1870s when the Victorians with their garish tastes and tasteless palates had taken over the parlors of America, filling them with wicker rockers, lamps, pianos, and countless knickknacks.

Technology had moved hand-in-hand with wealth. In 1870, there was no such thing as a telephone, but by 1900 there were 19,000 telephone operators and 200 American cities with 30,000 electric trolley cars. The population rose from 39 million to 76 million, along with an increase in per capita income from $779 to $1,164.

Meanwhile, as large sections of the big cities were becoming ethnically rich but pocket-poor, more and more farmers were becoming urban dwellers, pushed off land by mechanized farm implements that enabled one man to do the work of six. Despite the farm exodus, in 1890 the nation's eight million farm workers still outnumbered jobholders in all other industries. Few farmers were turning profits, however.

Practically every Midwest farm had a mongrel flock of chickens, and farm wives used eggs to barter for food at the general store, which accommodated customers in order to retain their business. But during the flush season, when farmers were happy to get five cents per dozen, the money wouldn't go very far to buy a pound of flour or bolt of yarn. In Chicago, a nickel could buy a mug of beer along with a lunch of rye bread, cheese, and bologna at the Tremont, or a stack of flapjacks and coffee at Pittsburgh Joe's restaurant on Van Buren Street, not far from the butter-and-egg district that supplied this city and those in the East.

Egg marketing in the 1890s was hardly a well-oiled machine. It was, in fact, quite crude, with little concern for the quality of the eggs. As the railroads pushed deeper into the Midwest, egg shippers and packers began to establish themselves as a link with the big cities. By 1895, the abundance of shippers prompted the publication of the first trade journal—*The Egg Reporter* in Waterloo, Iowa—to cover the Iowa Wholesale Butter and Egg Association, one of a number of state groups organized in Iowa, Illinois, Missouri, Indiana, and Ohio that met monthly to deal with problems of freight classifications, freight rates, and grading practices.

Egg prices were perhaps the biggest concern. Traders didn't set prices outright, but rather massaged them with a flurry of verbal speculation. What would be the price of eggs prior to the opening of a new season? At season's end? For refrigerated eggs? Were prices too high? Too low? What seemed fair? Every egg dealer walked away from a meeting with a sense of fair price. These associations bolstered fair trade practices at a time when the Populist revolt, led by the farmers, focused on the Interstate Commerce Act of 1887, which placed controls over railroads, and the Sherman Antitrust Act of 1890, which tried to harness monopolies. Moreover, labor disorders—the Haymarket riot and Pullman strike among them—had ricocheted across Chicago, shaking the foundations of business. By this time, American sectionalism had been replaced by a new spirit of nationalism, created by a blend of transportation and communication: completion of the transcontinental railroad, the telegraph and telephone system, news services like the Associated Press, and national markets for magazines and books. The boundaries shrank even further as manufacturers churned out standard factory products.

In essence, the egg men, through their trade groups, were banding together with a single-minded purpose: to survive in an era when monopoly was the mother of expansion. Practically every small entrepreneur faced the recurrent pattern of nineteenth century business; first the machine, then the monopoly. Even the mundane egg business, drastically altered with the advent of mechanical refrigeration, was no exception. Steel, oil, railroads, utilities, and meat packing were among the industries dominated by impatient, tyrannical individuals (coronary-prone type-A executives in today's corporate world) who pushed themselves and their competitors to the limits of endurance. They squeezed smaller competitors into submission.

Why not? After all, in the animal kingdom, fate was governed by survival of the fittest. Why not in man's domain too? The notion of social Darwinism had crept into the psychology of an expansion-minded America playing out its "Manifest Destiny" with an unbridled zeal for ships, colonies, and power. There were no new prairies to cross with railroads, no inland markets to turn into factories, and no native tribes to vanquish. It seemed that the only new worlds to conquer were those beyond American shores, if for no other reason than to break the monotony of dollar chasing. By 1898, Theodore Roosevelt wanted a war to give the United States "something to think about which isn't material gain." He got his war. With help from those newspaper barons of banality—Hearst and Pulitzer—yellow headlines whipped the public into a frenzy and America was at war with Spain.

The Spanish-American War raised American spirits quite well, along with profit levels. It took plenty of protein to charge up San Juan Hill, and, just as in the Civil War, the merchants of grain, meat, and eggs found the military a lucrative market. Now, thanks to Libby McNeil & Libby's canning methods, the nation's meat packers were feeding the U.S. troops compressed beef, otherwise known among the Rough Riders as "Red Horse." (Later the meat was called "embalmed beef" during public inquiries.)

Though the refrigerated rail car was hardly more than a crude icebox on wheels when it was developed in 1896, it transformed Chicago from a regional meat packer into a national purveyor of animal parts. Over the next two decades, there was a shift from the marketing of live cattle and hogs to their conversion into processed meat. Chicago's packers, with satellite plants in Nebraska, Iowa, and Missouri, had also tapped into the markets across the Atlantic, shipping dressed beef to England, France, and Germany. By 1886, the shippers of dressed beef were using some 1,500 refrigerated cars per year.

Indeed, Chicago had turned into hog butcher of the world: the Union Stock Yard had grown from a single slaughterhouse operated in 1827 by Archibald Clybourne, who had a government contract to supply Fort Dearborn with meat, to 475 acres of abatoir, handling annually 75,000 cattle, 50,000 sheep, 300,000 hogs, and 5,000 horses. Some 100 packing firms employed more than 30,000 men, most of whom belonged to the Amalgamated Meat Cutters and Butchers Workers of North America, which steadily grew in size and influence.

The nation's ravenous appetite for steaks and chops was matched by the packers' voracity for profits. They diversified into everything short of potatoes. Not only was there money in meat, but in bone and fat as well. Swift & Company was the first to eliminate waste by turning out a virtual sundries market of profitable by-products that included hairbrushes, buttons, chessmen, knife handles, fertilizer, soap, perfume, glue, leather goods, surgical sutures, violin strings, photographic film, gelatin, and oils.

Armour & Company, on the other hand, found a cash cow in wheat. At the turn of the century, the grain commission house established by Philip Armour's brother before the Civil War had grown into an immense operation with more storage elevators than any company in the world. When refrigeration replaced the icehouse in the late 1890s, both Swift and Armour scrambled to become egg merchants. They even influenced the price Chicagoans paid for so basic a necessity as ice. The large quantities of ice used by the packers (along with the breweries that chilled their beer during the long fermentation process) kept the demand and prices frozen at levels the poor could not afford. The two packers had huge icehouses, each with a capacity of 175,000 tons. Subsequently, the packers also dominated the egg business, owning most of the cold-stored eggs in Chicago through World War I. The balance was held by egg wholesalers and interior shippers. Naturally, Chicago, the butcher of hogs and stacker of wheat, became keeper of eggs.

The city was favored by its position between the surplus-producers of the Midwest and consumers of the East, joined by a rail system whose fingers reached above and below the Mason-Dixon line, reaching the heart of the South and Eastern seaboard. The rise of interior egg shippers eventually led to improved merchandising methods. They began to grade eggs and place them in uniform packs. Typical of these dealers was Jacques Havens & Company, based in rural Iowa in a low-slung wooden planked building. Inside, Jacques was dominated by a pot-bellied Franklin stove and a husky Irish immigrant named John Fitzpatrick, who cut hard-bargaining deals for poultry and butter. In dribs and drabs, country eggs moved through the pipeline to big city buyers. From Dubuque, Fort Dodge, Waterloo, and Sioux City, farmers would sell one or two cases of eggs to their local merchant on consignment. The storekeepers, in turn, delivered the eggs to packers like Jacques, or other *concentrators*, who became collection depots. The eggs would then be shipped to the egg men in Chicago, a terminal market. During the 1880s, the railroads gave interior egg shippers a competitive break by charging them less than carlot rates. In 1895, the Chicago dealers were jubilant when the rate advantage the interior enjoyed was abolished by the railroads.

Before refrigeration, egg marketing was strictly a seasonal affair, an odious situation by most standards. During the winter months, there were few eggs. Then the spring thaw brought a flood of them. Springtime production was heavy as egg sellers raced to push supply into the egg baskets of housekeepers, kitchens of restaurateurs, and mixing bowls of bakers. The pipeline dried up with the summer sun that sent the odor of rotten eggs wafting from boxcars whose destinations were too far to sustain freshness. By late fall, the farmers played a waiting game. They held back eggs with hopes for higher prices. Unfortunately, those with poor timing ended up knee-deep in spoiled eggs. And the cycle repeated.

There were, however, attempts to preserve eggs for winter use. For each trial there was an error, but never a solution. Some eggs were pickled, some packed in salt, and some in lime. Pickled and limed eggs seemed to have a longer life with one distinct drawback: They tasted strongly of the preservatives and could only be sold at substantial discounts under fresh eggs. Even when the first icehouses were used in the 1870s, the egg men continued to blunder by placing eggs next to fruit. For example, eggs stored near lemons acquired a lemon flavor. They still fetched a higher price than pickled eggs, and, fortunately, the lemons, apples, and oranges never tasted like eggs. Fresh Chicago eggs in the mid-winter of 1878, for example, sold at 20 cents a dozen compared with 14 to 18 cents for icehouse eggs and 5 to 12 cents for pickled eggs.

With mechanical refrigeration came stockpiling. As eggs were chilled, their prices cooled, too. But consumption of eggs rose. The market grew more complicated, since eggs were available to consumers year round. Dealers were faced with such marketing decisions as how many eggs to store and what prices to charge for refrigerated eggs. The terminal dealers were in a better position to make those judgments because they were in constant communication with egg marketers in other parts of the country.

As a result, the efficiency of the entire industry improved. Bigger storehouses were built, such as the Western Cold Storage Company of Chicago, which in 1895 began to solicit the business of smaller midwestern egg dealers by actually sending out promotional circulars. (The circulars, of course, neglected to mention the fact that Western Cold Storage favored the big Chicago dealers by charging the smaller ones five cents a case more for less than carlot quantities.) There was even a sharpened business acumen among the egg peddlers who moved about by wagon, compared with those who walked.

The butter market evolved in a similar fashion. The butter that could not be sold immediately was carried forward, first by the farmers in their spring houses and then by country stores. The surplus butter was salted heavily and held until it could be sold. Eventually, refrigeration moved butter from the cellars of commission merchants to cold-storage warehouses. The stage was set for time contracts in butter and eggs.

For the Chicago dealers, there was allure in the volatile world of butter and eggs because there were profits to be made. Chicago had become an aggressive forwarding market, and dealers sought to maintain that position from early on. They did so by organizing, as did their counterparts in other thriving areas of Chicago commerce. The grain traders had their Board of Trade, operating since 1848. The Pork Packers Association was formed in 1864 to consolidate the smaller stockyards around the city's periphery, and the Illinois and Wisconsin Dairymen's Association was founded in 1867. Now the butter-and-egg men took their turn.

On 20 May 1874, some 20 years before the Iowa Wholesale Butter and Egg Association got its start Chicago's produce dealers, along with a few margarine makers, established the Chicago Produce Exchange. At the northeast corner of Clark and Lake Streets, a hall was opened on 2 June with little fanfare but high hopes of building a market to attract eastern and southern buyers for butter, cheese, eggs, and poultry. Soon the ranks grew to 300 members, but there was hardly any activity other than the compilation of trade statistics.

The members of the Produce Exchange had no desire to emulate the Board of Trade. Certainly no one had applied the notion of futures trading in wheat, corn, and oats contracts to eggs, butter, and chickens, perhaps with good reason. The Board of Trade could hardly serve as a role model in 1874, the year public opinion prodded the Illinois legislature to pass an anti-corner bill to curb unscrupulous speculation, pegged by miffed farmers as "urban chicanery." Even the regulations designed by the Board of Trade to prevent price manipulation and to promote adjustments on defaulted contracts couldn't stop the misdeeds of the daring. Two years later, seven traders on the Board of Trade were jailed after the Illinois legislature had passed a short-lived law that declared futures trading to be illegal gambling.

By the late 1880s, approximately 200 such bills had been introduced into Congress to kill all futures trading or trading in one or more commodities. Every one was defeated, and the fiery rhetoric that stirred them up dissipated in an atmosphere of confusion. The reason was simple: No one had come up with a better plan to replace futures trading. For that matter, the government did not intend to fix prices on each commodity by edict. Congress therefore backed off each time it reared its regulatory head, retreating with conviction that a free market for free men was in the spirit of raw-boned capitalism. In addition, a new wave of speculators predictably rushed in chasing corners and squeezes each time, in the same way a wine connoisseur would pursue a good vintage.

In 1891, the Board of Trade heralded the glories of speculation as the American way. To be a risk-taker, the Board asserted, was patriotic, Darwinian, and quite in character with the notion of Manifest Destiny. Speculation was the noblest of endeavors, the way the Board viewed it in its thirty-fourth annual report:

> Speculation stimulates enterprise; it creates and maintains proper values; it gives impulse and ambition to all forms of industry—commercial, literary, artistic; it arouses individual capacities; it is aggressive, intelligent, and belongs to the strongest and ablest of the race; it grapples undismayed with possibilities; it founded Chicago, and developed the great West, which is the Nation's prosperity and the impelling commercial power of the continent.

They believed they weren't mere traders of futures contracts, but businessmen using new techniques, dealing more in the rights to property than in physical property itself.

During the 1870s and 1890s the shift was apparent. Merchants, financiers, manufacturers, and developers began using checks cancelled through central clearinghouses, rather than cumbersome commercial paper, and commodity transactions were increasingly being conducted through negotiable contracts rather than in raw products themselves. Commodity exchanges were bringing buyers and sellers together to create immediate contact. In essence, the exchanges were time-savers, a way to cut through the unnecessary legal paraphernalia of tedious and competitive contract making, bypassing the jargon, endless details, the interminable oaths and affidavits. There was little need to travel to musty dockside warehouses or country elevators to feel, smell, and taste a particular commodity in order to test quality. The varying qualities of cotton, wheat, corn, oats, rye, and such were classified by the exchanges and samples of each displayed on tables along the perimeter of the trading floors. This attempt to standardize quality and codify trade practices was an effective means of speeding up transactions and turning the flow of commodities into smoothly running tributaries of an enormous river.

There were still plenty of scams, frauds, and bucket-shop operators to contend with. Poor produce was sometimes passed off as the best, just as unauthorized stock was sold as gilt-edged securities. There would always be plungers, insiders, and schemers, luring, then fleecing the public—and each other.

4

The Street

The spirit of the fledgling Chicago Produce Exchange was broken early. By 1878, just four years after it was founded, the Exchange became inactive, a victim of member apathy. However, the produce markets proved too active to keep the doors closed for long. Activity was revived in 1882, and within three years, the Exchange was back on its feet, although in modest quarters at the corner of Clark and South Water Streets, the fulcrum of the early produce markets.

South Water had undergone obvious changes from its rough-and-tumble beginnings. The narrow wooden-planked street was now replaced by a wider cobblestone one. Instead of saddle-sore hunters on horseback ambling along, there were scores of archetypical peddlers hunched over the reins of their mares pulling open wagons. But its soul hadn't changed; the streets still ran on sweat, hustle, and capitalistic enterprise. For those who worked along the teeming commercial artery, South Water was simply known as "the Street," a kind of haggler's bazaar spiked by the pungent odors of ripened fruits, vegetables, poultry, and meats that clung to the area like a fine morning mist. The eastern end was anchored by the fruit and vegetable dealers, while the merchants of meat, poultry, and dairy products worked the western district. The south side of the Street was the "busy side" because it had the advantage of being shady during the summer. The various businesses stood like row houses, the ground floors used for storage and sales. The general offices were usually on the second floor, and the basements were often rented out to dealers of bananas, butter, and eggs.

Across the Chicago River, just north of the Street, were the auction rooms and cold storage warehouses on Kinzie Street. On nearby Lake Street, where the butter-and-egg men eventually relocated their exchange, stood the National Produce Bank, offices of trade organizations and trade papers, shippers' representatives, inspectors, and other related businesses.

Chicago's coffers also bulged a bit more from the swirl of South Water's commerce. On a good day, anywhere from three hundred to four hundred wagons rolled through the area, paying city collectors 10 cents per day for a single team and 15 cents for a double. Market hours varied, depending on the season: from

10:00 A.M. to 2:00 P.M. in the winter, and from 4:00 A.M. to 10:00 A.M. in the summer.

For nearly a decade, the Chicago Produce Exchange served the butter-and-egg dealers well. But, as cold storage heated up markets, the need for more accurate pricing became apparent. Disenchantment among dealers began to spread over the crude way wholesale prices were determined by the Exchange secretary, who each day informally polled selective commission merchants and came up with a consensus price. Thus, the power of pricing lay in the hands of the secretary alone, who decided which merchants to query. The disgruntled dealers sought to give pricing a more democratic scope. They formed a 15-member committee to fan out among many more merchants, but petty squabbling among the committee members detracted from the efficiency of that plan. Finally, on 26 May 1894, the committee invited all of Chicago's wholesale butter-and-egg dealers to join in its daily sessions. The new system apparently worked to everyone's satisfaction.

There was strong need among the butter-and-egg dealers to reorganize. Just a year before, the nation had sunk into yet another depression, plunging commodity prices to new lows and forcing many farmers in Kansas, Nebraska, Minnesota, and the Dakotas to mortgage their spreads in order to stay afloat. Despite the enormous concentration of robber-baron wealth, America had now become a country of small- and medium-sized businesses with 11 out of 12 families earning an annual income of $380. With the Depression behind them, the butter-and-egg merchants were determined to insulate their industry from future economic shocks. On 9 November 1895, they organized the Produce Exchange Butter and Egg Board as a group within the Chicago Produce Exchange. There was no grand strategy, other than to establish equitable price quotations for butter and eggs. From among the 20 members, they chose a board comprising a chairman, secretary, treasurer, and sergeant at arms. Board meetings were held once a week, and the annual dues were five dollars. The first expenditure by the new board was $10 for a "suitable" blackboard to display sales and daily prices. There were few rules and little regard for conflict of interest. For instance, the butter inspector appointed by the board was "allowed to in any way use his office for advertising his own business . . . ." It wasn't long before the volatility of egg prices attracted a hoard of speculators from the street. The industry's leading trade journal *The Egg Reporter* made the following wry observations in 1895:

> At present, the indications are that there will be active speculation in eggs this season. There are men of moderate means outside the produce business who make a practice of investing in a car of so every year. Nearly all these outside investors have friends among the produce houses who act as their agents. Not a great deal of money is required to carry a car of eggs. At 12 cents, it will take 3 cents a dozen, or one-fourth the original cost to be put up by the speculator. The other 9 cents will be advanced by the cold storage companies for the purpose of securing the carrying charges. The latter very often lose money by making a three-quarter advance and the amount of money loaned on eggs varies in different markets.

There is no way of telling just how many outside speculators dabbled in butter and eggs, but the board wasn't taking any chances that the situation would get out of hand. By early December 1895, it moved rather quickly to close the Exchange doors to outsiders by passing a motion to admit "only members to the floor" who were bona fide butter-and-egg dealers. The gathering of traders became a clearinghouse of information, gossip, and opinion as to the movement of stored goods. Oddly enough, in those early years, the butter-and-egg men faced the same painful problems as had their counterparts in both the grain and cotton markets, yet there is no indication they learned from those who had passed through a similar stage a half-century earlier. Regardless, the growth of the egg market in size and complexity set the stage for trading time contracts in eggs.

Time contracts in eggs were traded in 1882 on the Chicago Produce Exchange. There were two types: the first called for the delivery of refrigerated eggs in fall and early winter, and the second was used to obtain eggs for refrigeration with delivery in April. These contracts were informal, based largely on the reputations of dealers and brokers in the trade. After jousting over prices, quality, and packaging, a handshake and a simple memorandum closed the deals, many of which were made in state association meetings like the annual Iowa Dairymen's Convention, or the national Dairy Union in Springfield, Illinois, or even the lobby of the posh Palmer House Hotel.

There were numerous time contracts traded in the 1890s when demand for refrigerated eggs was on the rise. Brokers representing smaller dealers had to find new egg shippers, since the established ones preferred to deal in large units with the eastern egg dealers. What better place to match up buyer and seller than on the floor of an exchange? Though the volume of these contracts was fairly substantial, it was small compared to the cash transactions in eggs; that eventually changed. As the markets expanded, the dealers grew more sensitive to price—so much so, that if any colleague stepped out of line, the others would pounce. For example, on 8 January 1896, a complaint was filed with the board by J.H. Palmer & Company against Earl Brothers Incorporated "on a low-priced circular letter issued." The next day, Mr. Earl appeared before the board "regretting the circular . . . as having gone out without his knowledge or approval." The apology was accepted and the matter closed. Underselling fellow members of the Chicago Produce Exchange was against the grain of the typical nineteenth century trade association, formed to enforce limits on production and price, and in some cases, to combat the labor unions.

Early on, the Exchange bucked heads with the local press in an era long before media relations. Reaction was hostile on both sides. In January 1896, the board appointed egg dealer John Low to draft a resolution repudiating the charges "published in a scathing article in the *Chicago Tribune* and reflecting on the integrity of the produce trade of this city." Precisely what the draft denounced is unknown because no record appeared in the board's minutes. Apparently, the board was sensitive to the need for public relations. The very next month, it approved the establishment of a Bureau of Information to handle public inquiries and to deal with press matters. Unfortunately, harmony was short-lived. Just two years later, the Chicago Produce Exchange was churning with dissent in its own civil war. On one side stood the butter people and on the other, the oleo faction. The clash was inevitable. The Produce Exchange had never been pure, but rather an alloy of butter and margarine. That blend became unstable after a third element was added—politics.

The butter dealers wanted to use the Exchange to win Illinois legislation that would control, and thus limit the sale of margarine statewide. The oleo makers successfully fought off the effort, but the result led to a mutiny. On 8 February 1898, the butter-and-egg dealers walked out of the Chicago Produce Exchange and formed the Chicago Butter and Egg Board with the following objective:

> The purposes for which this corporation is formed are to establish for the benefit of its members daily market quotations on butter, eggs, and other products and to furnish general information to its members regarding the market for such commodities, and to facilitate the speedy adjustment of business disputes among its members, and to secure to its members the benefits of cooperation in the furtherance of their legitimate pursuits.

Though no one knew it then, the spin-off exchange was to become the immediate predecessor to the Chicago Mercantile Exchange. The new Butter and Egg Board had 48 members; among them were packers Swift & Company and Armour & Company, along with the major storage outfits, Union Cold Storage Company, Western Cold Storage Company, and North America Cold Storage Company. In addition to a slate of four officers, the board was expanded to nine so-called "trustees" who served either a one- or two-year term. The board was composed of three committees: membership, arbitration, and trade and statistics. With its emotional rift behind it, the Butter and Egg Board was eager to gain distance from its past. The first order of business was to find new quarters and reasonable rents.

By May, the Exchange had moved into the Marine Building at 136 West Lake Street, paying $27 a month for rooms 27 and 28. The two-year lease included some sprucing up with painting, papering, tearing out partitions, and carpeting throughout. The trading floor was to be hardwood, and there were incidental expenses such as $20 for a new rug in the directors' room and $3 for lettering windows with the exchange name. Total moving expenses ran about $150. (Eighty-five years later, when the Chicago Mercantile Exchange moved over a Thanksgiving Day weekend from Jackson Boulevard to its current Wacker Drive location, it took an army of movers and a logistical team to complete. The moving cost: $37,946.) Once in place, the Butter and Egg Board began to concentrate on the well-being of its members. In a startling move, the board sought to abandon official price quotations. The reason became clear for such drastic action in the impassioned minutes penned by exchange secretary Thomas Gallagher following the board meeting of 24 August 1898:

The greatest evil in the trade today lies in the prevailing contract practice which is rapidly dealing a death blow to the Commission Business from the fact that it is continually drawing away from the large receiving centers the smaller jobbing trades which have heretofore looked to the Butter houses of these Centers for their stock . . . . Therefore we recommend as a remedy for this evil to discontinue the practice of establishing any fixed market quotations, as has been the custom at your daily Butter and Egg Board meetings; that the daily market reports be written more as a review of the daily transactions in Butter without taking upon itself to name a fixed price for any one grade; the board also recommends that each house furnish the Secretary before Board meetings daily lists of their sales to be posted, believing that while such sales would not furnish a sufficiently substantial foundation upon which to base a contract, they would still indicate the pulse of the market as a guidance for the members.

Exchange membership grew to 63 by July 1899. "The tendency to buy and sell futures in eggs is increasing alarmingly," noted *The Egg Reporter* that year. "A few years ago it was done to some extent by a few speculators, but this year we find many old established firms doing it." Typical of the kind of member drawn to the Exchange was William S. Moore, a second-generation butter-and-egg wholesaler, who played a dominant role in organizing the Chicago Mercantile Exchange in 1919. Earlier he had served as a butter inspector for the Chicago Produce Exchange before he resigned in 1895. Moore's father had moved the family to Chicago in 1885 to buy butter for a Memphis wholesale grocer.

Much of the butter traded in Chicago at that time was farm butter that came directly from the 60 cooperative creameries and 54 private ones that dotted the Midwest. Shipped in kegs and tubs, butter was a highly seasonal commodity. Yields were heavy in the late spring and early summer when pastures were flush, but small during the winter months. The butter was usually traded at the country stores; the three grades were called *extras*, *firsts*, and *seconds*. Some stores sold to local buyers; others shipped to commission merchants like Moore's father, who started his own brokerage operation on South Water shortly after arriving in Chicago. As a youth, William Moore helped his father after school hours and on weekends, learning how to grade and buy butter and eggs in the process. There was no doubt he would become a wholesaler like his father. Moore became a full-time butter-and-egg man in 1889 and remained one until his death in 1953.

South Water was filled with a host of fabled characters in an area of business where there was considerable competition for such distinction. Many butter-and-egg men were immigrants who picked up in Chicago where they had left off in Europe. By that time, some 280,000 of the city's more than one million residents were foreign-born. A number of South Water Street outfits were "mom-and-pop" operations, informally run and physically demanding in labor requirements. Often youngsters worked beside their Popeye-armed fathers who tossed crates around as if they were over-stuffed cushions. Hours were long and profits small, but to be in one's own business was worth it. Besides, a stake in the Street was relatively modest at the turn of the century, as the following sales contract dated 2 August 1900 discloses:

> For the sum of Two Hundred Dollars, $200.00, we hereby sell to Doe & Co., of Market Street, Chicago as follows: One black mare, one single top wagon, one set single harness, one large ice box, one floor scale, one spring scale, one hundred empty egg cases, together with the good will and trade of all our customers. We further agree in consideration of the above purchase from us, to sell one hundred cases of fancy April storage eggs, at current prices at time of purchase on customary terms allowed by cold storage companies, and to carry same in storage without deposit from said Doe & Co., during regular storage season, not later that Jan. 1st, 1901. We further agree to use our influence with our former customers to secure their continued patronage for said Doe & Co.

As the Butter and Egg Board thrived, its fight against the margarine makers continued to rage. One resolution called for congressional action that would take margarine out of competition with butter through an increase in the national tax from two cents to ten cents per pound. The law was never passed because the oleo faction also had a strong and active lobby at both the state and federal levels.

By 1900, the Exchange once again welcomed outsiders, although sparingly. Each member was issued a "visitor's ticket" good for one guest on one day in any one month. Of course, visitors weren't allowed to trade on the floor, or in any other rooms and offices of the Exchange. The next year, the Exchange showed its patriotic side; not only did it close its doors for the day when President William McKinley died, but it dispatched a committee of three to Canton, Ohio, to attended the slain President's funeral.

Another concern that was always on the minds of the trustees was press relations. A press committee was appointed in 1901, to which the city's newspapers could go directly to obtain information on prices, market conditions, stocks, and so forth, "so that articles as published by said papers may be authenticated." In another instance, the board went as far as to ask the City Press Association to assign a full-time reporter to cover South Water and Randolph Streets "so more current quotations will be sent out by the daily papers and produce trade." The Exchange had come up with a short-hand way of characterizing the daily market action: "tone steady," "market same," "tone firm," and "unchanged."

The Butter and Egg Board was hardly a well-oiled machine, but it worked. Members met each morning at 9 A.M. in the daily session known as *the call*. Wholesalers offered butter and eggs, and jobbers and buying brokers bid based on the prospect of the market. There were days on which perceived values were too far apart and no sales would take place. Each day, the quotations committee would list a set of prices. In 1915, much to the consternation and chest-pounding of the board, the practice was abandoned when the federal government sued the Exchange under the Sherman Antitrust Act, the very law that was intended to shield the small entrepreneurs of the nation.

Monopolies over the necessities of life had been under attack since the 1870s when a grass-roots revolt grew out of the agrarian Midwest called the "Granger movement," named after *granges* or farms. In 1871 there were eight Granges in Illinois; two years later there were more than five hundred. By mid-1873 local farmer clubs had joined the Grange to form the Illinois State Farmers' Association, with more than 1,000 local branches. Seeking to eliminate the profits of the middleman, Grangers founded cooperatives for buying and selling, for milling and storing grain, and even for banking and manufacturing. The movement left its imprint on politics and laws adopted in the early 1870s by midwestern states to regulate grain elevators and railroads. Eight Granger cases came before the U.S. Supreme Court in 1877, and in *Munn vs. Illinois*—the most significant of them—the court upheld the "police power" of state regulation. The state laws, however, were never very effective in regulating the railroads or the trusts, the industrial giants formed after John D. Rockefeller's Standard Oil Company pointed the way. The problem of regulation was left up to the federal government.

By 1890 when the Sherman Antitrust Act became law, the Granger movement was played out. However, the Grangers had helped stir the congressional debate over the concern for the consumer and small businessman. It brought to the surface the folklore of the old capitalism, which harbored the trusts and robber barons, and the apprehension of the new. At first, clever lawyers found plenty of loopholes in the act. But as time went on, the muckraking press added monopolies to the lengthy list of public evils, and the politicians tightened the laws. That's not to say that the exchanges had no support in high places. On the contrary, the very man who coined the word *muckraker,* in his pledge to bust the trusts, spoke out in favor of the exchanges. "The great bulk of the business transacted on the exchanges is not only legitimate," President Theodore Roosevelt said, "but is necessary to the working of our modern industrial system, and extreme care would have to be taken not to interfere with this business in doing away with the bucket-shop type of operations."

By 1901 the CBOT had won its long-fought battle with the bucket shops,[1] which were gambling dens where wagers could be made on current prices of stocks or commodities without any intention to purchase or deliver. If a person bet the price would go up, the operator would take the opposite position and vice versa. The loser would pay the difference as reflected in the CBOT price quotations.

When the CBOT cut off the market quotations to the bucket shops, the shops sued. Two of the cases went before the U.S. Supreme Court in 1905, and the Board won. In citing the majority opinion, Chief Justice Oliver Wendell Holmes observed the Board was "a great market, where through its eighteen hundred members, is transacted a large part of the grain and provision business of the world" and that speculation was "the self-adjustment of society to the probable." Success of the strong, Holmes concluded, "induces imitation by the weak." As for the bucket shops' contention that the CBOT was also a gambler's paradise, Holmes responded, "Set off has all the effects of delivery." The sales—contracts made between members—Holmes emphasized, were not pretended, but were meant to be binding. Thus the CBOT was postured as a place that facilitated an orderly and competitive market for the economic advantage of all concerned. Even the *Chicago Tribune,* a harsh critic of the CBOT, conceded that without the trading pits, "the smaller men in the business would be hopelessly crowded out of the race by the big ones who would control the situation as against them if the market ceased to be an open one."

Two years later the knees of the American economy buckled. Roosevelt was being blamed for the financial panic that struck in the autumn of 1907. Production had expanded beyond the nation's capacity to consume, but that lull could have been withstood if the banking and monetary systems had been stronger, and if speculation had not been excessive. Panic set in after depositors discovered that several New York trust companies failed in an attempt to corner the copper market. Runs began on banks in New York and some failed. In Chicago, the banks faced a currency famine as people hoarded cash out of fear that the banks wouldn't honor checks. Roosevelt condemned the "speculation, corruption, and fraud" that fueled the panic, and he sought financial reforms that would strengthen the nation's banking system. It took six years before the monetary system was taken out of the grip of the J. P. Morgans and put in the hands of the federal government with the passage of the Federal Reserve Act of 1913. Setting up the Federal Reserve Board and the regional Reserve Banks was considered the most important statute of Woodrow Wilson's administration. He gave the nation its first efficient banking system since Andrew Jackson's term, and more reform followed a year later in a bill drafted by Louis Brandise to create the Federal Trade Commission which was established to prevent the unlawful suppression of competition.

The winds of reform blowing over the nation were being felt in Chicago. The CBOT's victories over the bucket shops, as well as the Holmes opinion, hardly stopped criticism of the exchange. Between 1905 and 1921 a number of congressional committees investigated the CBOT and its effect on grain prices. "On each occasion," Lurie points out, "a spokesman for the Board of Trade appeared before them clutching a copy of Holmes's decision as if it were a talisman that could neutralize all criticism leveled against the exchanges."

For the Butter and Egg Board, which under the Sherman Act had been found guilty of controlling distribution of market information, the dynamics of a true marketplace had not yet taken shape. (That would change within four years.) Meanwhile, the government's antitrust action was a stark reminder that the protective armor of laissez-faire had been dented. Thus, the forefathers of the Chicago Mercantile Exchange had learned a painful, but important, lesson about the mercurial futures business from which they made their livelihood: Every silver lining came with a cloud.

5

The Rise of the Butter-and-Egg Men

With its rise in stature, the Butter and Egg Board found itself wearing two different hats, neither of which fit quite right. One hat was a marketing tool whose potential had barely been tapped. The other was a trade association, policing credit abuses among its members, lobbying for legislation, and establishing an *entente cordiale* between the consumer and the despised cold-storage egg.

Ages before the cholesterol scare would turn the lowly egg into a dietary hazard, the Exchange set out to make it the object of everyone's affections. To bolster the consumer's taste for eggs, the board launched an "educational" campaign, starting with an advertisement in the *Chicago Tribune* on 21 October 1914.

> Eggs and Ham can't be beaten as a real man's breakfast by all the new fangled 'breakfast' foods on earth. Crisp, relishing, sizzling eggs and ham will enable you to start out with pep and snap on the cold days of winter. Eggs are sheer nutrient well divided between muscle-building protein and the energy-saving carbohydrates. And eggs have withstood the general rise in the price of food stuffs. The very best cold-storage eggs—which means a superior class of eggs—are now being sold to grocers at 24 cents to 26 cents a dozen. Remember that a cold-storage egg is simply one that has been scientifically cared for.... YOU NEED NOT FEAR TO EAT PLENTY OF EGGS IF YOU INSIST ON GETTING THE BEST CANDLED SELECTED COLD-STORAGE EGGS.
>
> – CHICAGO BUTTER AND EGG BOARD

The following January, the Chicago Butter and Egg Board took yet another try at luring the consumer to partake in cold-storage eggs. The caption in the ad, this time in the pages of *The Chicago Examiner*, boldly stated: "The Hen, the Egg, and the Unvarnished Truth."[1]

No one, least of all the Butter and Egg Board, knew whether such ads produced more egg eaters. It did make consumers aware of at least one thing:

34

Somewhere in Chicago there was an institution called the Butter and Egg Board. It so happens, that more eggs were in fact being consumed, according to annual receipts of carlots shipped through Chicago on their way to New York and other markets. In 1914, Chicago brokers handled 4,565,000 cases of eggs, compared with 3,114,000 in 1904 and 2,096,000 in 1899. The growth in population, of course, also ensured an expanding egg market for years to come. American production totaled 5.4 billion eggs a year in 1879, well before the science of breeding turned each hen into a miniature egg factory. By 1986, in spite of cholesterol bantering, hens laid a staggering 69 billion eggs a year, enough to feed every man, woman, and child on Earth an egg a day for weeks. Trying to get *real* men to eat eggs was one thing. Trying to get them to trade egg futures was another.

In eggs, the cash markets didn't give way easily to the futures market as it had in the grain trade. "The practice [of futures trading] was attacked both from within and from without the Board, as being of too speculative a character," remarked economist Edwin Griswold Nourse in his account of *The Chicago Produce Market,* published shortly before the end of World War I.

Only a minority of dealers used egg futures contracts in the early and mid-1900s; they were an influential group nonetheless. Time contracts, they insisted, were a convenience for shipments on the way, which dealers wished to sell in advance of arrival. They also helped as a sort of market guide when it came to buying operations, although the Exchange did not recognize contracts between its members and non-member egg packers. There was no doubt that the idea of futures trading had soured in the minds of the trustees of the Butter and Egg Board. Exactly why this happened is difficult to determine. Dealers would often blame the volatility of prices on the way time contracts were traded. Standard forms had been worked out to replace the crude memoranda of early days, and by 1911, rules provided margins of as much as one dollar on time contracts.

During periods of big price swings, the transfer of contracts became more like a game of hot potato. At times, traders would actually form rings on the trading floor, with contracts changing hands a dozen times or more. It wasn't the frequency at which the contracts were traded, but rather the aura surrounding them that stuck the nettles in the souls of purists. No longer were contracts personal affairs between honorable gentlemen with expectations that each contract would be fulfilled by delivery; in many instances, cash settlement replaced delivery and acceptance as the number of unfilled contracts increased during sharp price changes. In short, time contracts had changed the character of the market, and indeed some of the dealers themselves. The altered trading environment led to a war of wills in which emotions could not be cooled. There were those who saw time contracts as the wave of the trading future. Others, however, — the majority of dealers — saw them as a nuisance, a new way of playing five-card stud. Time contracts were clearly controversial.

The stage was set for definitive action on the part of the board. The butter-and-egg men's tenacity surfaced on 19 March 1915 when the board voted to quit trading futures contracts for the next two months. The decision, based on emotion more than anything else, was demoralizing for those who believed in the virtues of time contracts. To soothe tempers, the board simply called the ban "an experiment." Compromise healed the temporary rift; instead of eight weeks, trading resumed after five weeks, with one exception: futures contracts were limited to a 10-day period. Finally, 16 months later, in July 1916, the full status of time contracts was restored. The board voted unanimously to allow members to buy and sell for delivery at any time in the future. There was also some tightening of the rules. For instance, all contracts for more than 10 days in the future had to be in writing and signed by both parties. The margin for eggs was set at 30 cents per case and at 60 cents for a tub of butter. The margin was to be deposited with the treasurer of the Butter and Egg Board. (Two percent of the margin was retained by the Exchange to cover clerical costs involved in handling the transaction.) Like grain futures, contracts were to be made by future months. A *seller's option* allowed delivery of the goods on any day of the month named in the contract. However, one day's notice had to be given if delivery was to be made any day before the last day of the month. Similarly, the *buyer's option* demanded delivery at any given time during the specified month, provided three days' notice was given.

The visionaries had won out. In less than a decade, egg futures became the primary Exchange business, accounting for nearly 98 percent of the activity and only 2 percent of the spot merchandise. The road to dominance had been paved with egg shells. As soon as trading in egg time contracts resumed in 1916, it was brought to its knees again less than a year later by the advent of World War I.

Congress had granted President Woodrow Wilson broad wartime mobilization powers, which authorized him to set the prices of many commodities and to reg-ulate factories, meat-packing houses, food processing plants, and transportation facilities. The American War Industries Board controlled American manufac-turing, as the Food Administration, under the direction of Herbert Hoover, was responsible for civilian and military supply.

Shortly after America entered the war in the spring of 1917, both wages and commodity prices, including prices of butter and eggs, began rising sharply. The number of time contracts traded also soared. For instance, on 25 April—19 days after the United States declared war—a contract for 50 cars of eggs at 33.5 cents per dozen was bought, then sold the following day at 36 cents per dozen, for a net profit of nearly $15,000. Losses were equally heavy. In a number of contracts, delivery simply wasn't made—or, when it was, the eggs were of inferior quality. Many disputes arose, followed by a barrage of lawsuits as a means of attempting to force settlements.

Meanwhile, public opinion was also mobilized. Anything that smelled of speculative manipulation when it came to war prices was strongly condemned.

Thus, in May 1917, the Food Administration suspended trading in time contracts in butter and eggs. The public pressure was so great that other exchanges took voluntary action with a self-imposed ban. Some, like the Kansas City Butter, Egg and Poultry Board, even went further in their patriotic fervor. The Kansas City Board disbanded altogether in order to make doubly sure that it wouldn't become the target of public criticism.

The prohibition lasted until 1919. Oddly, despite the hiatus, trading seemed to have picked up where it left off. The problem of non-fulfilled contracts continued to linger like a persistent hangover, owing largely to rising commodity prices. It was evident that a new set of trading rules was needed that could somehow enforce the spirit of the contracts. The Chicago Butter and Egg Board had tried earlier to get a handle on time contracts, but it ended up with only a few minor changes in the rules. Concern for serious change was now mounting among veteran egg dealers.

There were more immediate problems to tackle that were caused by the controlled war economy. The government had halted antitrust suits during the war, but price competition was narrowed as well. Nevertheless both labor and the farmers shared extensively in wartime prosperity. The total wheat crop rose from 634 million bushels in 1916 to 952 million in 1919.

The orgy of production sent prices up rapidly, but wages climbed at a faster rate. Demand for commodities from apples to zinc was strong, and prices continued to rise after the armistice was signed on 11 November 1918, pushing American unions to resort to strikes. In 1919 alone there were more that 3,600 strikes across the nation.

On the world front, an idealistic President Wilson was trying to forge a plan for future peace through the League of Nations. At home, his administration continued to impose wartime controls in an effort to keep a lid on prices; this endeavor proved to be a source of antagonism for commodity exchanges, including the Butter and Egg Board.

The Chicago dairy merchants made a concerted effort to follow the rules, though it meant a squeeze on profits. Nevertheless, it was better than chancing the wrath of an angry public, who would accuse the butter-and-egg men of profiteering. It was better to seem cooperative, the Board reckoned, than competitive; perhaps it was in deference to those egg dealers who had returned to Chicago as World War I veterans. In any case, a passive mood prevailed, and for a while the Board became a watchdog of its own industry. During the first week of January 1919, for example, the Board posted a hastily composed memo notifying members, "The Food Administration reports that certain dealers are shipping eggs out of the city at a greater profit than that allowed by their regulations." The Board warned members that such practice had to cease, "or the parties doing it will be caused trouble." Apparently the culprits took heed, because no one was "caused trouble," according to records.

The following week, an official of the Food Administration appeared before the Butter and Egg Board members with good news and bad. All restrictions on fresh butter were removed, and it could be sold in the same way as it had been before the war, according to the official. Restrictions on stored butter and eggs were to continue until the new crop was marketed.

The announcement was a blow to the dealers, whose inventories were swelling by the day, because a mild winter had resulted in heavier than normal egg production. Egg prices were dropping faster than the temperature. Feeling compelled to do something to ease the situation, the Butter and Egg Board fired off a telegram in February to Charles M. Woolley, then chairman of the War Trade Board in Washington, pleading that the government permit Chicago dealers to export eggs to Canada, where demand would ensure a sharp reduction in stocks. The Board apparently was optimistic about its chances of obtaining the government's permission, for at the same time the telegram was sent, a committee was appointed to obtain export licenses. The Board had played its hunch correctly—within weeks, approval was granted.

As Chicago eggs were heading north, the traders were busy moving in another direction; they sought to crack the defensive armor of the Exchange by removing the debilitating trading rules that kept it from operating as a proper free-market enterprise. In a petition to the board of directors, 10 influential butter and egg dealers asked for rule changes on trading that had been in effect since 1917. Adopted in the spirit of the war effort, these rules, they believed, now threatened the spirit of the Exchange itself. One rule in particular forbade traders who bought goods on the call to offer them for resale during the same session. Another limited sales on the call to spot transactions. Such rules collectively placed a stranglehold on trading vitality and, in turn, caused a ground swell of resentment. The Chicago traders wanted a less restrictive system, one that would allow them more dealing than wheeling.

Compared with other butter-and-egg exchanges of the period, Chicago's Board was sluggish when it came to change. By 1900 the New York Mercantile Exchange already had in place a standard butter-and-egg contract that required the signatures of both parties, carried a margin equal to 10 percent of the contract price, and showed quantity, grade, price, and terms of delivery. (The Chicago Board of Trade had adopted a 10 percent margin requirement on grain contracts in May 1865, which suggests that, historically, difficulties with fulfillment of time contracts were common among members of the various exchanges.) Early in April 1919 the Board wavered. To avert a mutiny, a compromise on one of the thorniest rules was reached: Although a member could be both a buyer and seller during the same trading session, he still couldn't sell butter or eggs on the call. The Board also restored the 10-day trading rule, which meant that contracts to be fulfilled less than 10 days in the future required neither written agreement nor margin. Next, the Butter and Egg Board took on the state legislature. On 29 April 1919 the Board dispatched one of its members to Springfield in order to lobby against House Bill 299, which gave Chicago and other Illinois cities broad taxing and regulatory power over a number of industries, including the butter-and-egg business. The Board had the following opinion on the proposed law: "[It is] uncalled for as a Police Measure and [it] opens the door to pernicious interference with and restraint upon trade and commerce." The Board's victory in opposing the bill gave the butter-and-egg men a sense of confidence and purpose. The Board itself appeared to have developed a more forceful and willful character. Although the end of World War I brought with it the collapse of the farmer's purchasing power, the pursuit of new outlets for commodities remained strong, and those eager to preserve the old ways were about to face a new era.

Nerves began to fray as the Butter and Egg Board, perhaps out of frustration, grew somewhat defensive. Five months after the war ended, the Board sent a resolution to both Congress and the State Legislature with a belt-tightening plan of its own. It harshly criticized the market reports of the Bureau of Markets, an arm of the Agriculture Department, as a waste of taxpayer dollars.

"In butter and eggs, the sales on the street and on the Exchange establish a necessary trading basis early in the day," the Board argued. "This is reported by private agencies and immediately distributed by wires wherever needed, and the work of the Bureau of Markets which does not usually reach the trade until the next day is superfluous and unnecessary." Next, the Board turned its ire toward the U.S. Post Office and a relatively new service for which it was trying to drum up business, called *parcel post*. The Post Office had begun to encourage egg shippers to use parcel post. The Board saw this as "encroachment" on a system that was already working with enough competitive pressures.

There were certainly problems with the parcel post system. For example, parcel post offered neither the shipper nor the receiver satisfactory reimbursement for eggs broken in shipping. Moreover, there was no assurance that parcel post would mean lower egg prices for consumers. During the slow season, when egg supply was meager, the Post Office would have to operate its trucks at a loss. The litany of woes led the Board to emphatically conclude, "the advice of experienced and trained men in the business should be sought and heeded to the end that there shall be no disturbance of the normal course of trade and no further waste of the tax payer's money."

Obviously, the butter-and-egg men didn't like hearing the footsteps of the government tramping on their ground. They had grown protective of their business over the years. They had fought the railroads for reduced carlot rates and better shipping schedules, and they were still locked in the ongoing struggle with the margarine producers. The Board members, however, were smart enough to know when to back off from their squabbles with the government. If they were going to stand up to Washington, which tried to clamp down on runaway food prices by reestablishing wartime controls, they decided that they would pick and choose the issues.

Instead of blowing up over the matter, the Board shrewdly and calmly hoisted the red, white, and blue: A telegram was sent directly to President Wilson offering support in the name of patriotic duty. The wire, a goodwill (and public relations) gesture, reminded the President that the butter-and-egg men had placed patriotism before profit during the war. The Butter and Egg Board pledged, in part, its "hearty cooperation in the establishment of some form of temporary regulation of our industry, similar to that which prevailed during the late war period, especially along the lines of limitations of profits and co-ordination of purchases . . . . We express to the government our willingness to offer our services in the formulation and enforcement of such regulations." The Board and its members were beginning to shake their torpor at a time when the economy was about to spin giddily upward and the postwar world was at odds with itself. The Lost Generation was trying to find solace and a conscience on the Left Bank of Paris, while Germany, Austria, Russia, and Hungary, among other countries that had forsaken the gold standard during the war, were cursed with hyperinflation and huge debts. In the United States—where Prohibition would become the law of the land within a year—conservative political leaders were showing little enthusiasm for regulating business or disciplining monopolies. By appointing gaggles of pro-business bureaucrats to various agencies, including the Federal Trade Commission, Wilson had shown businessmen how to avoid government interference without a legislative assault on one popular reform— trust-busting.

With the transition from a wartime to a peacetime society underway, there was reason for optimism among most businessmen, including those who earned their livelihoods selling butter and eggs. Yet, there was a profound undercurrent of uneasiness among the nation's farmers, who had planted acres of crops as if the war's demand would never end. Now they were faced with an end to government-guaranteed prices, bracing themselves for a bin-bursting oversupply that would mean drastic cuts in farm prices across the board. The law of supply and demand had caught up with the farmer—and with the commodity exchanges, too.

6

The Birth of the Merc

It was by accident that the notion of a new exchange came about. One afternoon in the late spring of 1919, a score of dealers had gathered after trading hours in an exchange room to await the results of a candlers' strike. Among them was a young egg wholesaler named Oscar Olson, a low-key, earnest man, and other South Water Street merchants, including C. J. Eldredge, the first chairman of the Butter and Egg Board, Charles McNeil (then its current president), J. C. Borden, and Joseph Milnarik, each of whom would serve a term as Merc chairman during the 1920s.

As they waited, the dealers found themselves engaged in a discussion over the hottest issue then facing the Exchange—how to handle trading in time contracts. No one had a complete answer. Some wanted to trade these contracts, others were content with the cash markets. The impromptu brain-storming session ended in a consensus: No one, it seemed, really understood the value of trading futures contracts.

Shortly thereafter, the group sought the counsel of William S. Moore, the butter-and-egg guru of the era. Behind a mischievous smile, Moore was spontaneous, unhesitant, sure of himself, a merchant who knew the butter-and-egg business like the palm of his weathered hand. He, too, professed ignorance of futures trading, yet he agreed to look into the matter. That was enough for the dealers on the Street, who were anxious to form a new association for trading butter and eggs. They moved swiftly into action under the leadership of Moore, who appointed a committee to gather information on organized trading in grain, cotton, and other commodities. Hours were spent talking to traders, speculators and officials at both the Chicago Board of Trade and New York Cotton Exchange. (Time contracts in corn, pork, and cotton were reported in Chicago, Indiana, Ohio, and New York as early as 1851, nearly 20 years before the New York Cotton Exchange was organized.) Their findings, in turn, were reported to a central committee that was busy drafting rules and regulations for a new exchange.

All along, Moore was careful to avoid ending up with two exchanges of butter-and-egg men. He diplomatically solved the anticipated problem by con-

41

vincing the Butter and Egg Board to add the rules for organized futures trading to its rules book. In effect, Moore and his colleagues were allowed to operate as a unit within the Butter and Egg Board.

The new organization called itself the Chicago Mercantile Exchange with the foresight, Moore later explained, that some day commodity futures other than butter and eggs would be traded. Everyone agreed the new name was perfect, distinctive enough from the Chicago Board of Trade, with a tone that reflected a new direction.

On 5 October 1919 the Chicago Butter and Egg Board went out of existence. The next day, the Chicago Mercantile Exchange began operations, although organized trading in butter-and-egg futures did not begin until 1 December 1919. In its amended charter, filed with the Secretary of State of Illinois on 26 September 1919, the Mercantile Exchange set down its reasons for existence:

> The purposes for which this Exchange is formed are: To furnish a convenient meeting place where its members may buy and sell Butter, Eggs, and other commodities; to promote uniformity in the customs and usages of the trade; to gather and impart to our members general information useful to them; to facilitate the speedy adjustment of any business disputes that may rise amongst its members; and to secure the full benefit of co-operation in the furtherance of their legitimate pursuits.

Some 142 memberships of the Chicago Butter and Egg Board were transferred to the Mercantile Exchange, and the officers of the old Board continued their posts in the new organization until the following January. With little fanfare and amazing speed and efficiency, the transition had taken place. For Moore, Olson, and the others, it was far more than one organization melding into another. As they saw it, evolution was at work in the dawn of organized trading. They had fallen behind other commodity exchanges in this respect. They were, however, a determined bunch with every intention of catching up, and that meant even more change.

The newly reorganized exchange may not have aroused the public's awareness, but it caught the media's fancy. Under the title "Ode To Chicago's New Mercantile Exchange,"[1] *The Chicago Daily News* published an anonymous poem:

> Hail, noble shell of busy trade
> In butter, also eggs fresh laid,
> Or else, in pristine freshness stored
> In some chill, superarctic hoard,—
> Or else those eggs expected when
> It suits the mood of Mrs. Hen—
> Not egocentric in your art,
> For barnyard creatures play their part
> On your facade. We see the cow,
> Contentment sculptured on her brow;

The faithful hen here gets a show
Despite her lord and master's crow.
Like statesman, bard and soldier strong
The clucking bird in frozen song
Is here exalted. (If you please,
No wheeze on eggs upon the frieze.)
Hail, produce temple, multi-tiered,
Your white and sunny side upreared;
Well built to bear your workday yoke
You've cap'talized a Nation's joke
And though consumers feast or fast
Your butter'n'egg men laugh the last!

The Chicago Mercantile Exchange was more than just a new play with the same cast of characters. Membership still cost $100 plus $12.50 in annual dues, and the doors of the clubby place still were open only to white, American males, at least 21 years old, with "good" character and endorsements by two members. Changes in the constitution and bylaws began to prod the Exchange into the twentieth century as a viable marketplace. As expected, not everyone welcomed the transition with open arms; some resisted it with the opinion that the butter-and-egg market was too volatile in the wake of wartime price controls. With a new decade about to begin, and the war to end all wars over and done with, the idea of a fresh start was appealing to most. Besides, there was a certain logic to reconstructing the Exchange, just as there was in 1917 when the federal government had proclaimed, "Food will win the war." The postwar politicians promised that prosperity was around the corner, and the butter-and-egg crowd wanted to be ready. The consumer, economists kept insisting, would be the savior of private enterprise in America, even though the bushel of corn that could buy five gallons of gasoline in 1919 only bought half a gallon in 1920.

During the autumn of 1919, it became apparent to traders that the Exchange had indeed undergone more than just a facelift, although the Merc continued the basic activities of the Butter and Egg Board. The five committees expanded to a dozen, covering every aspect of Exchange business. The most dramatic change, however, was the manner in which butter-and-egg futures contracts were handled. For the first time, the Exchange had a clearinghouse, which was a means of offsetting not only money accounts, but contracts as well. In short, the clearinghouse matched and processed trades of buyers and sellers by transferring funds and guaranteeing the performance of all obligations. It was the first stage in putting the Merc on par with other commodity exchanges that had affected their respective industries. Throughout the previous summer, Board president Charles McNeil, a stickler for details, carefully laid the groundwork for a clearinghouse. He worked closely with Mancha Bruggemeyer, an attorney who had counseled the Exchange over the years. Bruggemeyer spent countless hours poring over and analyzing the Butter and Egg Board's constitution and bylaws in light of the then-current federal laws and state statutes. The existing framework, he concluded, was "sufficient to authorize the creation of the Clearing House as a convenient place." He reminded McNeill in a letter of the legal ground upon which the proposed new exchange was about to tread:

> Permit me to again impress upon you, in the face of the decree of the United States Court, and the Criminal Code of Illinois, and the provisions of the Sales Act, the law of 1915, that all of these transactions of future trades must be strictly bona fide. And I urge upon you, if the Exchange is established, not to suffer the practice to grow out of two parties to a contract directing the Secretary to make distribution of the deposit moneys in a manner that raises an inference of a settlement, instead of a consummated business transaction.

McNeill and the others hardly pondered the jargon-choked legal opinions of Bruggemeyer. They didn't have to. They knew that the purpose of an exchange was to facilitate business, and that was precisely what a clearinghouse did. It sped up the adjustment of contract obligations, among other things, to keep the Exchange machinery chugging ahead.

It was hardly a new idea. The clearing system dates back to the Middle Ages; commodity markets had their roots in medieval fairs. During the twelfth century, for example, so-called settlement days followed each of the four fairs of Lyons, France. Bankers promptly showed up with balance sheets in-hand, first to accept bills by those upon whom they were drawn, then to compare accounts, and finally to settle the accounts in cash. For centuries, clearinghouses had been used to offset debits and credits among banks.

Before they used a clearinghouse, the butter-and-egg traders were burdened with direct settlement. If matching sales against purchases was not possible before delivery, all accounts would remain open. The business of receiving deliveries and paying for them, of making deliveries, and of billing and collecting all would come afterward.

The clearinghouse also reduced the number of contracts on which margins were maintained. In effect, it meant a saving in clerical work, a saving in the use of credit, and a simplification of contract relations. The courts of the day saw economic sense in the clearing system. For instance, in a case involving two New York cotton traders in 1920, an appeals judge concluded, "It would be as idle to insist upon an actual delivery between the members of an Exchange as it would be to compel the banks to carry to each other's banking houses the actual money called for by the checks severally received by each upon the other."

Despite the apparent advantages in using a clearinghouse, members were ambivalent about the new trading tool. Some summarily resisted change. Others weren't interested in organized futures trading at all. Still others thought the risk was too great, reasoning that if the Clearing House guaranteed all futures contracts, no one would know what would happen if the losses exceeded the reserve fund; perhaps the members of the Clearing House would have to cough up the difference.

Any member of the Mercantile Exchange was eligible for membership in the Chicago Mercantile Exchange Clearing House as long as he could come up with a $500 deposit as a reserve against possible losses. To reduce financial exposure (and to allay fears among the skeptics), margins had to be deposited with the Clearing House by both parties to each contract cleared. The margin would then be adjusted each day to the market price. Another provision required a Clearing House member who was trading for customers to collect a margin from each one. There were stiff penalties for defaulters of contracts; the margin for a carload of eggs (12,000 dozen) was $300, of which $210 was deposited with the Clearing House until the transaction was completed. The $90 balance was kept by the Clearing House broker to use as a settlement margin. For butter, the margin was $400, of which $288 went to the Clearing House and $112 to the broker's margin account.

For all the objection they raised at first, the Exchange members acquiesced to the new policy easily enough. There was little opportunity to resist, since all futures contracts were required to be cleared through members of the Clearing House. Among the initial 46 Clearing House members were Beatrice Creamery Co., Bowman & Co., Harry H. Field & Co., The Peter Fox Sons Co., H. & J. Lepman, Inc., J.V. McCarthy & Co., J.T. Milnarik, H.H. Redfearn & Co., Schreiber & Falker, and Weinberg Bros. & Co.

To win the confidence of the trading public and to rally trader support, the Mercantile Exchange packaged its gospel in a 15-page booklet entitled *How to Buy and Sell Butter and Eggs*. Authored by the manager of the Clearing House, S. Edward Davis, the question-and-answer guide was written in a jargonless, breezy style and included a list of the Clearing House members and their addresses. The following passage is typical of the proselytizing pamphlet:

> You cannot afford to follow blindly just everyone's advice. Remember that it is your money that is seeking a profit and that you are entitled to up-to-the-moment information which will enable you to make up your mind and use your good judgment as to the trading to be done. The trailer is seldom a successful operator.

Such efforts did little to soothe the irate brokers who had made their living off of speculators. They were now competing with Clearing House members who charged reduced commissions of a quarter of a cent per pound of butter or per dozen eggs, compared with the two cents or more charged by brokers. A few traders, too, were annoyed with the fact that the days of casual contract making were over. Even some of the butter-and-egg wholesalers were losing out to the clearinghouse system. An egg jobber, for example, might accept delivery of a car of eggs instead of buying it from a given wholesaler. To win support for users of contracts, the Exchange established a new and more definite set of grades for both butter and eggs (there were no federal grades at the time) and provided a fully staffed inspection department.

In 1919 the Merc was ready for better times. Around the corner was another era with different fads, changing morals, and a new wave of materialism. The 1920s was a time of prosperity, normalcy, Warren G. Harding, Calvin Coolidge, and Herbert Hoover, who tried to give the nation a businesslike government with little idealistic promise. Hoover had emerged from wartime service with a grand scheme he pushed, first as Secretary of Commerce, and then as President: an alliance between the federal government, the trade associations, and the giant corporations. The result boosted the number of trade associations from a dozen in 1920 to more than 2,000 when Hoover left the White House in 1932. Hoover's call to rugged individualism had been pushed aside somewhere in his pragmatic engineer's mind. Federal activity in economic affairs under Republican administration had coiled back in the 1920s, allowing big corporations to grow, on the average, three times as fast as smaller ones. Concerns such as Kroger Company, for example, grew through vertical integration, buying up bakeries, packing houses, and coffee-roasting plants. The big meat packers bought ranches to raise their own cattle and farms for chickens and eggs. As for the nation's commodity exchanges, they were left to themselves for a time with little supervision from the government or anyone else.

Meanwhile, American farmers and industrialists grew fearful of being inundated with cheap produce and products from depressed European labor. A Republican Congress became protection-minded and rushed to passage in the spring of 1921 an "emergency" tariff bill, which outgoing President Wilson vetoed, arguing, "If there ever was a time when America had anything to fear from foreign competition that time has passed."

The following year, Congress passed the Fordney-McCumber Act, a tariff law that set the highest rates in U.S. history up to that time, and protectionism was in full bloom. The act authorized the president to raise or lower duties by as much as 50 percent if recommended by the Tariff Commission (Warren Harding and his successor Calvin Coolidge used the provision 37 times, 21 of which increased tariffs on such commodities as pig iron, chemicals, butter, and cheese, which the Merc began trading in 1929). The predictable result: a tariff war that cut deeply into the U.S. foreign trade. It was the tariffs of the 1920s, in fact, that a number of today's economists say sparked the Great Depression. Maybe so—but prosperity during the Roaring Twenties bulled ahead in spite of the tariffs rather than because of them, and few could argue against prosperity.

On the surface everything *looked* healthy; national income was high and unemployment low during the decade. But there was a flaw in the economic timber: Most of the wealth was in the hands of a few. For every 100 people in American cities in 1920, there were only thirteen bathtubs and six telephones, and one house in every ten city homes was wired for electricity. Only one in

10,000 persons had a radio. Nearly one-third of the country's breadwinners earned less than $2,000 a year, and one-fifth less than $1,000.

Saul Stone wasn't making much more than that in 1921 when he took a job as a 60-cent-an-hour egg candler for Becker Brothers on Fulton Street, which had replaced South Water that year as Chicago's dairy and produce hub. South Water had been torn down to make room for the double-decked Wacker Drive. A vestige of the Street remained, called New South Water Market, but the historic lane of commerce, which had been the link with the old Chicago, had vanished. Fortunately, the spirit of the butter-and-egg men remained intact, and the business continued to attract immigrants like Saul Stone, who had left Europe for better opportunity in America.

In 1986 the then-87-year-old Stone was a spry little man with fine white hair, sharp eyes, and a droll wit. He had been a member of the Merc for nearly a half-century, and during that period he built Saul Stone & Company into a major clearing firm and brokerage operation. Traces of his Russian-Yiddish accent still lingered from the first 22 years he spent in Romanow, a village in Russia, where in the wake of the 1917 Revolution, his father's flour mill was confiscated by the Bolsheviks. "Life was so tough after the Revolution," he recalled, "I came looking for freedom. I couldn't take the abuse there." As an egg candler, Stone literally learned the business of eggs from the outside in and from the inside out. Candling is the art of examining the size, color, and quality of eggs by passing them over the flame of a candle (eventually replaced by the electric light bulb) in a darkened room. Stone, however, didn't become a full-fledged member of the Merc until 1938, when he joined "for the purpose of being able to hedge my own eggs."

No one hedged eggs or butter in the Merc's early days. The main concern of those who backed futures trading was to ensure the fulfillment of contracts; the hedging interest simply wasn't there. Instead, dealers merely looked for speculative profits in accumulating butter and eggs, hoping that the profitable years would more than offset the losing ones.

A 1919 editorial in *Dairy Produce,* a leading trade paper of the time, noted that the Merc officials hoped the Clearing House would serve as an improved means of exchange. Likewise, in early 1920, the Clearing House itself did some public boasting in advertisements that pointed to the number of contracts that had cleared satisfactorily and emphasized that in the April future no disputes requiring arbitration had arisen. By 1921, however, many dissenting voices raised objections to the clearinghouse and the increased volume. The next year, in fact, there was a concerted effort to actually abolish the Merc's clearing operations, or at the very least to restrict them. Arguments broke out among various factions as if they were squabbling fiefdoms—and indeed they were.

Merc membership at this time could be divided into seven groups, based, oddly enough, on the territory from which they came: the North Side, Fulton Street, Haymarket, New South Water Market, the Stock Yards on the South

Side, the downtown Loop, and the out-of-towners, which then comprised 20 percent of the Merc's total membership.

"There is rivalry and even jealousy between the several groups of jobbers," observed William Moore in the 1920s. Exchange officials once more turned to "Billy" Moore for guidance in a crisis that threatened to split the Merc down the middle. Moore, who worked from both the mind and the gut, sized up the issue as a clear-cut one in which there were no subtleties or gray areas that could be compromised.

On one side stood those who hoped to turn the calendar back 20 years to the days when only the physical goods mattered and a man's word was his bond. On the other side were those who simply valued organized trading. Both sides sputtered with discontent until December 1922 when a frustrated Moore, along with Exchange officials, threatened to withdraw from the Merc and start a new trading organization. Faced with such a bleak prospect, the opposition backed off. Moore and his cronies had won a victory in the battle for organized futures trading.

The dissidence underscored the weaknesses in the Merc's organization. The Mercantile Exchange was like a strong stew prepared without regard for the tastes of its members. Although the Exchange itself lacked an impulsive nature, its officials appeared to be unreflective and without a sense of leadership style. As a group, they managed by whisper rather than by roar and evinced a certain skittishness when it came to confrontation. Among the egg men, though, there was reason to use soft-boiled diplomacy rather than hard-boiled tactics. In a nutshell (or an eggshell, as the case may be), Moore stated, "What we want is not a fight, but an earnest endeavor to get along." After all, every one of them was cast from the same occupational mold. The Board was elected from the ranks of the traders, as was president Charles McNeill and business manager S. Edward Davis. There were at this point no outsiders or professional managers; exchange management had a much different relationship with its members than business had with labor.

Though there were distinct cliques among the traders, in the end, the majority ruled over Exchange matters. The political nature of the Exchange had to be democratic because the members owned the Exchange. Business, on the other hand, was built around the tradition of leadership, with the archetypical strong-willed, decisive entrepreneur who demanded strict obedience as if he were a general or admiral in the military.

Around the time the Merc was getting its organizational house in order, there was a sharp drop in commodity prices. During the last six months of 1920, the average price of crops fell by 57 percent, and by May 1921, prices were a third of what they had been the preceding June. The plight of the farmer was relieved through a series of national laws designed to ease the agricultural crisis. In the process, the futures industry got what it had been trying to avoid for decades: federal regulation. For years, the prospect of government intervention lumbered toward the industry like some weighty glacier through a pristine alpine pass. Its impact was felt in 1921 with the first grain futures act, the basis of all federal commodities regulation since its passage. Upheld by the U.S. Supreme Court in 1923, the law forbade futures trading "unless the seller is at the time of the making of such contract the owner of the actual physical property covered thereby, or is the grower thereof," or "where such contract is made by or through a member of a board of trade which has been designated by the secretary of agriculture as a 'contract market.'"

Since then, the commodities exchanges have been under a combination of federal supervision and self-regulation. The government stops short of the daily monitoring of the trading pits and exchange membership, which is controlled by the exchanges themselves. Indeed, over the years the Merc, along with the nation's other major exchanges, has had its difficulties with the federal regulators as the market system evolved and the exchanges matured.

Even in 1923 the Merc was acutely aware of the importance of image. Promotion was coming into its own during this period. Cadillac was advertising its "runabouts," Camel its cigarettes, Atlantic its gasoline, and National its biscuits. Consumers were showered with premiums, prizes, and gifts for their patronage, along with reduced down payments, generous credit terms, and trade-in allowances.

The public relations man emerged in corporate America as a Mr. Fix-It for whom no detail was too trivial when it came to influencing the public favorably or unfavorably. Even Calvin Coolidge acknowledged advertising's power, calling the rising phenomenon "the most potent influence in adopting and changing the habits and modes of life—affecting what we eat, what we wear, and the work and play of a whole nation."

As part of a campaign to explain itself, the Merc published a series of booklets in 1923 that were aimed to give the reader "a comprehensive survey of the purposes, functions and operations of this important business." The subjects covered included "Chicago—The Central Market," "The Chicago Mercantile Exchange," "Hedging Butter and Eggs," "Getting Butter and Eggs to Market," "Cold Storage," and "Merchandising Butter and Eggs," the treatise that, in part, suggested that grocery store retailers promote butter and eggs as a "loss leader" instead of sugar. (Also noted were the peculiarities of egg merchandising, in that New Yorkers preferred white eggs, while Bostonians favored brown-shelled eggs, and each city was willing to pay a premium for the desired color.) Such promotional efforts were a sort of legacy to the saucy ads of the late 1960s and 1970s, when the Merc proclaimed in one newspaper display: "The Father of Our Exchange"—the caption beneath the picture of an egg.

As perplexing to the public as the Exchange was, the traders were at times a paradox to themselves. In 1925 Moore reminded the Merc membership just how far the Exchange had come in six years; he sent a letter to each trader in an attempt to rally support for the construction of a new Mercantile Exchange Building. "You may not realize it—I am sure the public does not know it," he wrote, "but the Chicago Mercantile Exchange is one of the big business enterprises of Chicago. It ought to take its place among them by having a home comparable with the buildings occupied by other big business enterprises in the Loop."

It was December 1925—Prohibition had been in effect for five years—and the Merc had but sixteen months to find new quarters. Located at 136 West Lake Street on the northeast corner of Lake and LaSalle streets, the Exchange was in the path of the wrecker's ball that was widening LaSalle Street in an effort to fashion the heart of Chicago's financial district. Davis had mailed each Merc member a questionnaire, hoping for a consensus as to where the traders wanted to relocate. Of the many options, one in particular was intriguing: moving into the planned $17.5 million Chicago Board of Trade Building to be constructed at the foot of LaSalle Street. The prospect of cozying up to the Board of Trade was seriously considered by the Merc officials. In Chicago, the Board of Trade had a certain stature and prestige. On one hand, the Merc, still trying to establish its identity and credibility, viewed an alliance as alluring. On the other hand, the trade-offs were too great. The Merc had no intention of forgoing its independence, the very quality its members prided themselves upon, even if it meant missing the opportunity to rub elbows with the grandfather of commodity trading. Perhaps equally important was the matter of character. Each exchange had evolved with its own distinct personality, shaped by the different backgrounds, businesses, and trading styles of its respective members. The Board of Trade was run by the descendants of predominantly Irish Catholic and German farmers, many of whom were still landholders. The tone of the Exchange was perceived by outsiders as stubborn and autocratic. There was indeed a strong influence among the Board of Trade elders to control membership as if the Exchange were an exclusive club for which acceptance was based on the proper pedigree, which made for a certain arrogance and snobbishness on the part of the Board and its members.

Over at the Mercantile Exchange, most of the butter-and-egg men had gotten their starts with pushcarts instead of plows, hawking their goods from door to door. A large number were Jews who came from Eastern Europe. There, too, was a more humble air of being second-best among the Chicago exchanges. With this in mind, the Merc officials kindly refused the Board of Trade's offer to become tenants (for a hefty rental price). Assuring them that the offer had been fully investigated, the irascible Moore told his fellow traders, "It was certainly flattering to be invited to join and reassuring to know that the Board of Trade doesn't fear being put out of business either by the government, or cooperative marketing, but we have no relish to join them on terms that bar us from any of the returns from the building and simply permit us to pay $150,000 per year rent and incidentals—alluring but too rich for our blood."

The Merc brokers, who accounted for 90 percent of Exchange business, were anxious to get under one roof. "They have paid in their money for several years with the understanding that sooner or later they would have a new home on the Franklin Street site," Davis explained in a letter to Merc members, "and they are at a loss to understand how anyone can seriously consider depriving them of that right and pleasure now that the time has come for the realization of their dreams." Moore added a bit more pressure, appealing to the members' sense of fair play. "While the brokers have paid for the land and are willing to pay for the building," he stated, "the ownership of the property is and will be in the entire membership. We think it is pretty soft for the members at large, and feel that the least the brokers can ask in return is to say where the building is to be."

There was no need for arm-twisting. All the friendly persuasion and advice from the old hand Moore, from Davis, Olson (then secretary of the Exchange), and the other officials did its job, and their wishes prevailed. The various factions, including the out-of-towners, rallied around the newly proposed venture with a sense of purpose: the building was a symbol, signifying that the Chicago Mercantile Exchange did exist and intended to be around for a long time. When the last vote was counted, the membership, some 300 strong by then, had overwhelmingly decided to build its own exchange on a piece of land 100 feet by 180 feet at the corner of Franklin and Washington Streets.

The property had been purchased by the Merc in 1922 for more than $500,000 with the intention of building an exchange; the cost of the 16-story structure was estimated at $9 million, 65 percent to be financed through Prudential Insurance Company and the balance to come from surplus funds of the Exchange and from rents of brokers and other tenants who were expected to occupy 14 of the 16 floors. Moore figured the Merc would pay off the mortgage within twelve years. The developers went to work.

So did the traders.

7

The Stormy Years

Even with LaSalle Street falling down around them, the butter-and-egg traders conducted business as usual, buying and selling at a record pace in 1925— 70,000 cars of eggs and 28,000 cars of butter compared with 11,000 and 4,000 respectively in 1919, when the Mercantile Exchange began operations. With its new building in the works, and membership at nearly 300, the original seats, which had cost $200 were now worth close to $500. Commodities markets, in fact, were booming across the nation. There were, at this time, at least 15 different types of commodities traded in 34 futures markets, in which grains, eggs, butter, and other foodstuffs together accounted for 80 percent of all commodities traded in the United States.

The hustle and bustle inspired Oscar Olson's secretary, Florence Sherman,[1] to put aside her shorthand for a bit of short verse as she penned a poem entitled "How It Looks At The Door," which appeared in a 1926 issue of *Exchange News*, the Merc's monthly house organ:

> One by one, they trickle in,
> Some just quiet, some with din,
> Some with lightly tripping toe,
> Some with faces filled with woe.
>
> And now approaches eleven o'clock,
> The markets cease to roll and rock,
> Hundreds of cars are bought and sold,
> The record of which the world is told.
>
> The bell has rung, the close at last,
> The sound of conflict is ebbing fast,
> The settlement price is posted too,
> It cannot suit each one of you.
>
> Now one by one they trickle out,
> Some are sure, some are in doubt,
> Some will gain, and some will pay,
> Ah, well, tomorrow's another day.

At times, the LaSalle Street demolition outside of the Exchange was too much for the boisterous traders inside. When the ear-piercing noise from the crashing bricks and mortar rose above the bedlam on the Exchange floor, tempers flared and members demanded relief. A few even stomped out of the Exchange in frustration, vowing not to return until the sounds of trading were back to normal. It took a series of telephone calls from the Merc's business manager, Ed Davis, to City Hall as well as some pleading with Chicago's strapping Mayor William ("Big Bill") Thompson before frazzled nerves could be soothed. "Davis had to call Big Bill Thompson to actually stop the demolition in order to save trading," recalled Kenneth Mackay, who started a 50-year career at the Merc in May 1927 as a clerk on the trading floor, immediately upon graduating high school. The wrecking crews were instructed by Mayor Thompson to ease up around the Exchange until after trading hours. His response was typical of the way Chicago's politicians related to the exchanges over the years: cordial, but not cozy. Most of the time the mayors—like the rest of the public—were bemused and bewildered by the machinations of the exchanges.

Local politicians were smart enough to realize early that thriving futures and stock exchanges were big pluses for big cities. They were a source of taxes and employment—an important part of the economic infrastructure, adding a dimension to the overall financial stature. The exchanges kept large sums in operating funds and margin money in the major downtown banks, which often lent money to would-be traders who sought to purchase exchange memberships. If anything, the exchanges were a stark metaphor of capitalism alive and thriving in the nation's second-largest city. The flamboyant styles of some of Chicago's and New York's butter-and-egg dealers of the era even captured the attention of Broadway producers, who backed a short-lived musical called *The Butter and Egg Man* that played to an apathetic audience and a hostile bunch of critics.

Meanwhile, there was a sharp increase in open contracts relative to the stocks of butter and eggs in storage, beginning in 1925. It was apparent that nearly all the short positions represented sales by butter-and-egg dealers against actual or anticipated holdings. It wasn't until 1939 when the pattern of open contracts became one of hedging positions on the short side and speculative positions on the long side. There was little interest in hedging at the Merc during the 1920s, but the Great Depression changed that. Dealers suffered heavy losses in butter and eggs on quantities they accumulated in 1929 and 1930, largely as a result of the Depression. From 1931 on, the advantage of transferring price risks on accumulations became more evident to dealers, as well as their bankers.

Just as with real estate, insurance, and securities, commodities were a roller-coaster ride during the 1920s. The peaks, valleys, speed, and intensity of an untethered economy tied to a boom psychology ended in a nervous breakdown when the 1929 stock market took its stomach-churning plunge on Black Tuesday and sent a nation spinning into darkness. Men and women alike hunched over the inverted glass bowls watching spools of ticker tape stamped with cryptic numerals unwind along with their lives. Politically and economically everything went wrong. Nobody seemed to be calling the shots. Responsibility was diffused through a society grown self-righteous, stubborn, and greedy, a system bent on self-destruction.

Five years earlier, no one seemed to have an inkling that such folly would result in the Great Depression. In 1925, in fact, grain trading was so active that directors of the Chicago Board of Trade authorized daily price limits for the first time. Trading at the Mercantile Exchange didn't need that kind of tempering; there were other anxieties to deal with. All during 1926 Merc officials, under the presidency of Charles Eldredge, an even-tempered man sporting a Chaplinesque mustache, were busy trading their butter and eggs, as well as their ideas about the new Mercantile Exchange building. The property, secured at the northwest corner of Franklin and Washington just five years after the Exchange opened, was more than a vacant lot with a vague future. Now there were blueprints and architectural plans to be carefully scrutinized by Eldredge and the other Merc officers and directors. Some $2.6 million in mortgage bonds had been sold to partially finance the building; this was as much a reflection of the Merc's success as was the rising cost of memberships.

The officers were anything but passive. They offered suggestions and stamped approval on every feature from lighting fixtures to elevator shafts. For instance, in September, Merc officials were quick to veto architects' proposals that called for elevator shafts to be located in the central part of the trading floor. The floor was to be an uninterrupted plain with no room for pillars, just bodies. In November, the Exchange members were told that the new home would be 17, not 16, stories high, and that the first nine floors would be steel frame and the remaining eight floors concrete. One economy-minded group of traders demanded that concrete be used throughout the building, since it was cheaper than steel. This proposal was voted on by the entire membership and defeated. It would have been necessary to string heavy pillars across the trading floor in order to support the building's weight. Like the elevator shafts, the pillars would have taken up valuable space in which more traders might be accommodated. Even more important, a pillar could interfere with the clear vision traders needed to see the trading boards. Thus, the Exchange designed its trading floor around the notion of equal trading opportunity for all.

The trading floor, 75 feet by 125 feet with a 30-foot-high ceiling, occupied the second floor and was reached by a marble stairway and six elevators. The third floor even included a studio for radio because Exchange officials anticipated someday broadcasting market results, trends, and public affairs programs. On the perimeter of the trading floor were two rooms, one for Postal Telegraph and the other for Western Union, the two major telegraph operators at the time. There were no clerks or runners in those days; all communication was via telephone or telegraph operators filling the airwaves with the clickety-click of Morse code.

Incoming orders and confirmations were telegraphed and the Exchange phones were strictly for incoming calls.

At one point in the planning stage, there was talk about doing away with the blackboard system of trading and replacing it with a form of pit trading similar to that of the Chicago Board of Trade. From its opening day on 1 December 1919, when three contracts traded in a 45-minute period (and only eight for the entire first week), the Merc used the blackboard in preference to the pit or post system used in grain and stock exchanges. The boards along the south wall were divided into sections, separating butter from eggs. On one panel of a section was written each offering, on another each bid, and on a third the completed sales. Board markers scribbling in chalk would turn an ear to the traders grouped en masse before the boards. A big day was 500 trades. Thus, the members, in a relatively unhurried but sometimes noisy fashion, either bought against the offerings or sold against the bids. The completed transactions were transferred to a sales board.

The blackboard system was kept for the new building despite the fact that, as the Board noted in its minutes, "It is not entirely satisfactory, and it is difficult to install boards to harmonize with the high-toned character of the trading room."

"We knew the traders by their voices," reminisces Rudi Gaimari, who was employed as a $15-a-week board marker in 1938. "We had eyes behind our heads. We had keen hearing. There were times when Harry Redfearn would buy the whole board. He'd always be on the buy side."

To this day, a remnant of the blackboard system remains like a crudely fashioned tool from the Stone Age in the midst of a space-age communications network linked by computerized quote boards. In one corner of the Merc's football field–sized trading floor, just beyond the Standard & Poor's 500 Stock Index pit jammed with hundreds of traders, is a time capsule of yesterday's trading world: three 6-foot by 2-foot blackboards used in butter trading. Each board represents a different grade; AA for top-grade, A for medium, and B for consumer-grade butter. Every Friday at 10 A.M., six traders huddle around the blackboards to do business. Brian Shannon of Berkshire Foods is one of them. "There hasn't been an active market lately," he mused, just before the butter call on a Friday morning in 1986. Rudi Gaimari oversees the butter trading. The banter begins:

"Drop it to 137¾," bids one trader on the consumer grade.

"Make it 135.50," counters another.

"Make it 137 even."

"Make it 136.50."

"136.25."

"136 even."

"Buy it!"

"We got a sale," gleefully shouts Gaimari as if he had just won a million-dollar lottery. "First call. Second call. Third call. Closed." Butter trading for the day is over. The time elapsed from the 10:00 opening to the close: three minutes. Another market, another day, another era.

The blackboard system of trading was replaced by the trading pit shortly after the end of World War II in 1945. A few years later, the government provided its own butter-and-egg inspectors, replacing those who worked for the Merc.

"The Exchange always moved with the times and like a fine wine mellowed with age," says the 72-year-old Gaimari, who managed the Merc's Clearing House from 1961 to 1968. "I never dreamed the Exchange would be this big." Nor did anyone else, for that matter, back on Armistice Day in 1928, when the members moved into the new Mercantile Exchange Building at 110 North Franklin, with its ornate ceilings festooned with fancy chandeliers that bathed the trading floor and its blackboards in the radiance of capitalism.

A dedication banquet was held on 25 April and presided over by Eldredge. The keynote speaker was the nation's cracker-barrel philosopher of the day, humorist Will Rogers, who showed up in black-tie without his lariat. "You can buy eggs on this market the same way you can buy General Motors stock," wryly observed Rogers in his Oklahoma drawl before a chuckling crowd that included Mayor Thompson among the dignitaries. "So, get you some eggs and hold 'em. Somebody will eat 'em. If you can't pay your cold storage bill, hardboil 'em and sell 'em for picnics." Rogers' commentary was a hit with the members and received ample coverage by Chicago's newspapers.

Ironically, just as the Merc was settling into the new building and working out the kinks, the Board of Trade moved to temporary quarters on Clark Street, just south of Van Buren, while its new quarters were under construction in 1929. By then, the price of a Merc membership sold at a record $4,500, while at the Board of Trade a seat also sold at a record $62,500, a record that wouldn't be surpassed until April 1973, some 44 years later.

The economy seemed to be marching along and Chicago's exchanges were right in step. The nation's economic expansion reached a peak of activity in August 1929 and then, almost without notice, started to slow down. The lag intensified. It was the onset of the worst business collapse in American history. Joblessness spiraled while production levels shriveled. Unemployment at 3.2 percent of the labor force in 1929 rose to nearly 25 percent by 1933, when the slump hit bottom.

During the same period, gross national product fell by 33 percent and factory output by more than one-half. As for the stock market, it had been a speculative timebomb wired with high interest rates and prices that were too high relative to earnings. There were no big institutional investors around similar to those who dominate today's markets and who can be a stabilizing influence in the long run. Rather, there were tens of thousands of individuals buying shares with down payments equal to just 10 percent of the purchase price of their shares.

When the margin calls came, many were wiped out. The crisis on the land was even worse than the industrial depression. The farmers, one-quarter of the population, had been in trouble throughout the 1920s. A bushel of wheat that sold in Chicago for $2.94 in 1920 dropped to $1 by 1929 and 30 cents by 1932.

"That's when I saw eggs sell for 10 or 12 cents a dozen early in the Great Depression, and decided to devote full time to trading eggs on the Exchange. I was losing my shirt in the wholesale eggs," Alex Kittner told a newspaper reporter in 1974 on the eve of his retirement as a Merc trader after 48 years. He was 80 years old at the time. An Austrian immigrant who sold eggs door-to-door, Kittner bought a membership in August 1926 for $500, saw it rise to $4,500 in 1929, and then drop to $1,000 in 1930. But for better and for worse, he stuck with the Exchange, and when he left in 1974 "to soak up some sunshine for a while" near Miami, he cashed in his membership for $75,000.

Other Exchange members like William Katz managed to hang on as egg dealers and traders. The business was founded by his father, Samuel, who arrived in the United States at the turn of the century from the province of Kiev in Russia, where he had been a feed buyer for the Russian cavalry. It was enough for him to pull his roots and eventually plant them in his own butter-and-egg store in Chicago at Fourteenth and Carpenter Streets. The store was a block from Maxwell Street, where the railroad stations became a magnet to the 50,000 Jewish immigrants pouring into Chicago in the late nineteenth century.

The area turned into a sweltering slum of burgeoning tenements and sweatshops fronted by open air stalls reminiscent of the ancient markets of Baghdad and Jerusalem. By 1912 the Chicago City Council passed an ordinance recognizing the melting pot of commerce as the Maxwell Street Market. Its heyday was in the 1920s, when it attracted 70,000 people a day. In staccato barks, the immigrants haggled and finagled as they tried to eke a living from "the streets" with the oldest form of selling—the pitch—and the oldest marketing strategy of all: "Have I got a deal for you."

Bill Katz, a former chairman of the Merc, remembers those days:

> At times, trading horses was more important than selling eggs. We had 14 rigs, you know doubles, singles. The biggest horse deal in Pa's life was the time when he palmed off a blind horse on some friend of his. It wasn't quite that bad. The horse was blind in only one eye.
>
> By 1914, we had a big business and Pa was driving a Buick. For my twenty-first birthday present, he bought me a Merc membership for $2,975, just before things got bad. When I got into the business in 1930, everything collapsed. Eggs were eight cents a dozen and chickens eleven cents a pound. We used to auction the memberships off on the floor for as little as $100. We bought 'em. It was like a market unto itself. The atmosphere was club-like. There were only 250 or so locals and they didn't come to the Exchange all the time. I didn't either. I just came for the cash market. Then both my brother, Isadore, and I spent our time there running the plant from the telephone.

A feisty man with a biting sense of humor, Sam Katz died in 1931, leaving the egg business to his sons. In one way or another, the Katz family managed to make money on eggs by retailing them, wholesaling them, trading them—even breaking them. In fact, at one time Sam Katz was one of the biggest egg breakers in Chicago. The process went something like this: Whole eggs were broken and the yolks went into one barrel, the whites into another, and the shells into a third. Each product had its own destination. The whites were used by bakers and mayonnaise producers. The yolks were dried and turned into powdered eggs for institutions and the U.S. military. The shells were processed by animal feed makers. In 1972, the Katz brothers sold out of the egg-breaking business, which had gotten them through the knocks of the depression and the rationing and price controls of World War II, when the federal government was their biggest customer.

"Pa's argument was that people will always eat eggs. That was one of the reasons for being in the business," said the high-spirited 79-year-old Bill Katz one afternoon in 1987 following the close of the markets. A lawyer who had passed the Illinois Bar shortly after joining the Merc in 1930, Katz never practiced law. But he served on the Merc's first law committee and as chairman of the Exchange in 1959 and then again in 1962 and 1963. At 77, this aged Marlboro man had cut back from smoking three packs of cigarettes a day to just one. One thing he refused to give up was the commodities business.

Katz was still in the thick of things on the trading floor of the Mercantile Exchange every day as vice president and floor manager for the clearing firm of Balfour Maclaine. To this day, the elder statesman of the Exchange thinks he knows what motivated immigrants like his father, as well as those of future generations who helped build the Exchange. "They understood survival," he said, "and they weren't shackled by preconceived notions."

Samuel Katz became a member of the Merc in 1919, and over the years traded alongside Ludwig D. Schreiber, John V. McCarthy, Oscar Olson, Miles Friedman, and Harry H. Field, one of his early partners, who was chairman of the Merc from 1930 through 1932. When Harry Field was elected chairman in 1930, he was one of the leading egg dealers at the time. "He was quite an operator," said Kenneth Mackay. "His firm was number one." But Field's business, like so many others, fell on hard times.

In the fall of 1929, nearly four times as many employers reported increases in wages to the Bureau of Labor Statistics as wage reductions. A year later, when the situation was reversed, the Chicago Board of Trade moved into its new building, a 45-story limestone edifice at Jackson and LaSalle Streets with its two-story-high polished granite base and a trading hall that stretched 165 feet by 130 feet, almost double the size of the Merc's. Though they didn't know it then, both the Merc and Board of Trade were about to fall on hard times, too.

At the Merc, a key management change had taken place in 1929. Edward S. Davis, the Exchange's first business manager, retired after 40 years in the butter-

and-egg industry. With the federal government moving toward a more dominant role in the futures markets, Field and his colleagues looked to Washington for Davis's replacement. They wanted someone who had roamed the bureaucratic corridors of the then-powerful Department of Agriculture. They also wanted a person with contacts on Capitol Hill and who understood the commodities business from both the farmer's and the trader's perspectives.

The search had lasted nearly a year before the Merc found its new business manager—Lloyd Tenny, an economist at the Department of Agriculture who spent his early years as a fruit inspector. A tall, bespectacled man with an aura of laconic authority, Tenny had broader visions for the Merc. He reflected on them in a letter to the Board in April 1943:

> I recall very definitely in the early days of my service here emphasizing the fact that a futures market was primarily for the purpose of hedging and that the proper operations of a market such as ours required that the members of the trade use futures for the purpose of eliminating price risks in their own merchandising operations. The public, who are the proper risk bearers, were not greatly interested in butter and egg futures.

Under Edward Davis, the position of business manager had become a powerful post. At times he could be cordial, but he could also be quite aloof. But as business manager he walked a straight line, favoring neither buyer nor seller, egg man nor butter man.

The Exchange was governed by its board of directors. Each year, the Merc members elected from their ranks a president, two vice presidents, a secretary, a treasurer, and a sergeant at arms. The president, in turn, appointed members to the various committees. However, it was the business manager—an outsider, a nonmember employee of the Exchange—who played the most important role in Exchange affairs. He supervised the trading, made sure that the rules were rigidly observed, and handled the administrative work of the Exchange. He alone had the authority to inspect the books of the Clearing House members, to survey their trades, and to assess their financial standing. In this respect, the Merc operated differently from the Board of Trade and other exchanges, which required their key personnel to own Exchange memberships. Simply, the Merc fathers believed that the business manager, without a membership stake, would be above compromise and passion when it came to voting on key issues.

When Tenny took the job, he, the Mercantile Exchange, and the nation were about to plunge into the worst financial depression the country had ever known.

There were several hundred women sleeping nightly in Grant and Lincoln Parks, by the count of Chicago's police department in the hot, muggy summer of 1931. Homeless and unemployed, the female derelicts were an image of an urban nightmare that had never existed before, a stark reminder of just how bad things were getting and that the Depression showed no bias toward gender. Oranges were a dime for three dozen; lamb chops, twelve and a half cents a pound; eggs, eight cents a dozen—all good buys, *if* you could afford them. Fewer and fewer could. Ironically, the fount of Democratic capitalism had come to suggest not a wellspring of wealth and growth, but a cesspool of poverty and stagnation. All this happened amid farm surpluses and lack of any mechanism to maintain prices.

That very summer, a 17-year-old lad named Everette B. Harris had hitchhiked from a farm near Norris City, Illinois, to Detroit, where he landed a job working on the loading docks for Kroger & Company. The strapping, gregarious Harris could never imagine then that someday he'd end up at the helm of the Chicago Mercantile Exchange, helping to guide it for 25 years as its president. He was too busy scrambling to save enough of his $18-a-week salary to pay room, board, and tuition at the University of Illinois, which he planned to attend in the fall.

Harris, like so many others across rural America, was on the move in the early 1930s. The nation had slipped into a kind of dreamy trance, and the tableau of soup lines, Hoovervilles, and street-corner apple hawkers was ineffably sad. Even Nature turned against humankind as droughts and dust storms afflicted the farm belt, forcing tens of thousands of ruined farmers to pack up their families in old jalopies and flee to what they hoped was the "promised land" in California.

By 1932, American voters threw out President Hoover and replaced him with Franklin Roosevelt, who earlier had flown through dangerous headwinds to Chicago to accept his party's nomination. There, he pledged "a new deal for the American people" to cheers and the strains of "Happy Days Are Here Again." Thus, under a banner of acronyms, a string of agencies were created in Roosevelt's New Deal era—agencies such as the SEC (Securities and Exchange Commission), TVA (Tennessee Valley Authority), FDIC (Federal Deposit Insurance Corporation), CCC (Civilian Conservation Corps), CAB (Civil Aeronautics Board), REA (Rural Electrification Administration), and NLRB (National Labor Relations Board).

It was crisis management by proxy. Big business hated Roosevelt with ferocity. The reason was obvious: They feared that the New Dealers would trample the spirit of free enterprise so thoroughly that it would never recover, and the country would forever lapse "from New Deal to New Dole," as detractors put it. But Roosevelt wasn't out to remake or redefine a social and economic structure, only adjust it. In essence, his role was more like that of a receiver in bankruptcy.

The solution to the farm problem had been long advocated by Milburn L. Wilson, an obscure Montana State College professor who believed in the restriction of production. That strategy would require an unheard-of amount of government supervision, but Congress went along with it in May 1932, when it passed the Agricultural Adjustment Act (AAA), sending an army of some 22,000 people, mostly volunteers, prowling through the country to persuade suspicious farmers to plow under one quarter of their crops for cash payments of $6 to $20 per acre. Destroying crops was a violation of American tradition, the critics bemoaned. They became even more furious when the Agriculture Department decided to slaughter six million baby pigs to keep production of pork down. The outcries reached the Supreme Court, which declared the AAA unconstitutional in 1936. Two years later, Congress passed a second and less drastic AAA, one Roosevelt himself considered more workable. The Roosevelt Administration had embarked on a risky course of replacing an open market with government management of agriculture. There were almost no precedents for such tricky devices as official price fixing, subsidies, and production controls.

By the end of 1932, American business had failed to respond to low costs and low interest rates of the previous three years. The mechanics of the free market had failed to operate effectively in situations of limited competition and rigid price control. This caused the Depression to linger. The situation also reinforced the importance of a futures exchange in the minds of the traders, as long as the government kept its tampering in check. The Merc felt the Depression shocks from its executive offices to the trading floor. "Trading was moderately slow," said Kenneth Mackay, who was a board marker at the time. An ill-timed cheese contract launched in October 1929 was delisted several months later because of a lack of interest. "We tried Maine green mountain potatoes too," said Mackay, "but we lost that contract to the New York Mercantile Exchange." In January 1931, a contract in Idaho russet potatoes was started almost out of desperation to offset the limping butter-and-egg trade. Even the normally full visitors' gallery was empty on most days.

The slowdown in trading forced the Merc, in turn, to tighten its own belt. There were cuts in overhead. "They let one person from each department go," said Mackay. "That accounted for at least five or six people. Then everyone had to take a pay cut. Those of us who stayed were more than willing since jobs were at a premium in those years." While the Exchange did not curtail trading hours, every Merc employee, including the business manager, had to take one day off without salary, according to Mackay. The Exchange managed to pay its bills, but even some of its investments went sour. In 1932, for instance, the Merc lost $78,000 in the sale of utility bonds that it held in its investment portfolio. (It hung on to some of the worthless bonds until 1941, when it took another loss of some $30,000.)

As the Depression deepened, the Merc took its biggest blow in both finances and pride. The very building that Billy Moore had fought so hard for was sold back to the Prudential Insurance Company as Lloyd Tenny bargained for a reduction in the rent to the new landlord. By the time the Merc recouped its earlier losses, it was too late and too costly to regain possession of the building. The Mercantile Building changed hands again after World War II and this time the landlord was Chicago financier Henry Crown, who had become a millionaire during the Depression from a sand-and-gravel business he started in 1919, the very year the Merc came into existence.

The Merc wasn't the only exchange to try drumming up business with new contracts during this period. All of the exchanges introduced new contracts, hoping to regain the momentum of the 1920s. One of the largest increases in the number of futures markets occurred between 1928 and 1935, when an additional

23 sprung up. During World War II government price controls and rationing rendered some markets absolutely useless, and by 1946 there were only 17. The following year, the number more than doubled to 36.

Prior to 1929 there were few hedgers at the Merc. The notion of taking opposite positions in the cash market and the futures market at the same time simply hadn't caught on. But by 1931, when dealers began taking heavy losses in the butter and eggs they had stored, locking in a guaranteed futures price looked outright shrewd. Along with a growing number of hedgers came yet another problem for the Exchange: a lack of speculators. For hedging to work, speculators were needed to take the other side of a trade. The market needed liquidity and there weren't enough members trading actively to provide it. Without the speculative flow, markets dried up and vanished.

The Merc put the call out for speculators as if it were trying to arouse the collective conscience of the Minute Men during the Revolution. The battle for liquidity was on. The only place to find an army of new speculators was outside of the Exchange, through a combination of newspaper ads, educational pamphlets, and telephone calls across Chicago and the nation. For the first time, brokers who dealt in other commodities and even securities were asked to become members of the Chicago Mercantile Exchange and, of course, to solicit trades in butter-and-egg futures from their customers. It took time, but the blitzkrieg eventually worked. By the end of August 1939, nearly 20 percent of the long positions in butter futures and 30 percent in egg futures were held by speculators outside of the butter-and-egg business. Sixty percent were held by the insiders and 20 percent by those in related businesses such as meat packing, cheese handling, and cold storage.

Not all traders had been oblivious to the virtues of hedging in the early years. Ludwig D. Schreiber saw the advantages before the Depression. "He actually was the first guy to learn how to hedge eggs. He was very bright, very smart," said Gilbert Miller, president of G.H. Miller & Company, a clearing member of the Merc since 1946.

At 6 feet 4 inches, Schreiber was an imposing figure on and off the trading floor. Some simply called him "L.D.," others "Barney." His partner, Elmer Falker, was a head shorter and the two were promptly dubbed "Mutt and Jeff" by their fellow traders. But once Schreiber began trading, the laughing stopped. Every era seems to have its trading knight, a sort of heroic figure who is looked on with envy and awe by his competitors. Schreiber was certainly the Lancelot of his time. "He was a role model," said Saul Stone. "He taught me the art of hedging, but not directly. I observed him on the trading floor and what he was doing. When he was selling I figured he was hedging. And when he was spreading, I figured he planned on taking delivery of whatever product he was trading. Eventually I did the same thing. It worked then. Everyone would always ask, 'What's Schreiber doing today?' "

Schreiber was quick with his mind, quick with a smile, and quick with a handshake. He loved to press the flesh and played the game of politics with finesse equal to his trading ability. Not only was Schreiber chairman of the Exchange from 1933 until 1935, replacing Harry Field, but he had been elected city clerk on the 1932 Democratic ticket, running with Anton Cermak, who became mayor. (Schreiber served out the position under Mayor Edward J. Kelly, who replaced Cermak after he had been accidentally killed by an assassin's bullet meant for President Roosevelt. The two were sitting next to each other at a rally in Miami). The fact that Schreiber was a butter-and-egg trader at the Mercantile Exchange gave the Exchange some positive publicity when he went knocking on doors for votes. "He was highly prominent," said Mackay. "No doubt about it."

He could also be stubborn. Miller tells the story of Schreiber and John V. McCarthy bucking heads at a board of governors meeting once: "These guys hated each other and it was the only time I ever saw Barney get flustered. Something came up at the board meeting and McCarthy, a vitriolic guy, said, 'I'll resign if you resign.' And they did."

8

The Winds of Change

As the Depression wore on, the Mercantile Exchange had learned to cling to solvency by the tips of its financial fingers. It was a lesson that would serve the Merc well in the years ahead. By 1940, the old days of laissez-faire were gone, replaced by a new age of capitalism. Government had stepped in when private initiative faltered, to form a union, restricting on one hand, yet opening new frontiers of economic freedom on the other.

The farmer, however, still faced a dilemma. Unlike the automobile maker, he could not stop production to meet market conditions. All the federal planning and controls only shifted the burden of overproduction. Instead of the farmer drowning in a sea of surpluses, the government was now treading water to stay afloat. The demands of World War II saved the day.

Across the Atlantic, the Nazi menace had driven the British back to their island, and by the end of 1940, Hitler controlled most of western Europe, including France. Back in the United States, the rumblings of war were growing louder. In a way, even the Mercantile Exchange began heating up with a special committee that was to cooperate with the army on butter purchases.

George B. Shawhan had replaced Miles I. Friedman as president of the Merc in 1940, inheriting a balance sheet whose bottom line was graying. Earlier cost-cutting measures had kept the Exchange profitable, though barely. Shawhan knew that all the penny-pinching in the world couldn't make for a healthy exchange. Only trading in the pink could put the Exchange in the black.

A folksy person with a strong sense of organization and solid business judgment, Shawhan wasted no time in attempting to move the Merc into a stronger financial position to buffer what winds a war might bring. There were still enough old-timers around to remind Shawhan, Friedman, Field, and other Merc officials of just how tight things were under the price controls of the First World War.

At the suggestion of Lloyd Tenny, the board once again lowered employee salaries by 10 percent in September 1940, including his own and Shawhan's, which was $2,000 a year. Committee members continued to receive five dollars for attending a meeting half an hour long and ten dollars for an hour. Next, the board approved liquidation of the Merc's bond portfolio, amounting to some $50,000, which was promptly reinvested in U.S. savings bonds.

Shawhan then tried, but failed, to push through a motion that would have extended trading hours. Though a proud man, Shawhan invested energy in board matters rather than ego. He could accept defeat on one issue, then quickly go on to another without pausing to mend political fences; his mind was receptive to new ideas. For instance, in September 1941, with some coaxing from Shawhan, the board gave Tenny authority to try an "experiment" on the trading floor: For the first time, clearing members were permitted to use telephone clerks and runners. Several of the board members balked over the prospect of a brigade of gofers scurrying about the floor in and among the traders. Such distraction, they argued, would be too much and surely take its toll on their concentration. Within six months, the experiment proved itself successful. The traders had learned to live with their clerks and even come to depend on them. Not only did the runners help to keep the floor machinery chugging over the years, but their ranks have become a minor league of sorts for aspiring traders, providing a pool from which new Exchange members come into the business. Running was a means of getting one's feet wet before taking the plunge. From the 1950s on, clearing firms used the system as a training ground.

In 1941 the Exchange did all it could to hang on to its veteran members. To drum up business, it ran full-page ads in such trade journals as *Who's Who in the Egg and Poultry Industries*. Business was so slow that for the first time, trading was curtailed on Saturdays during the months of July and August. To keep spirits up, the Board that summer restored the 10 percent cut in salaries it had instituted the year before.

By the fall of 1941, the pace began to quicken as the U.S. military needed an increasing amount of foodstuffs, including butter, eggs, and potatoes, on its way to mobilizing 12 million men and women. Thus, the government would become the biggest and most voracious consumer of every commodity imaginable from apples to zinc. The surpluses vanished. The Monday following the attack on Pearl Harbor, the Merc board hastily gathered to plan wartime strategy. The market was closed that day. There was little bantering among the directors, who were meeting in the patriotic spirit of national emergency. While a sense of collective uncertainty dominated the board room, one thing was clear: Price controls would freeze the markets. (At the Board of Trade, the only commodity that could be traded during the war was rye.) The Merc directors decided to limit price fluctuations in the markets when they opened again on Tuesday, 9 December. Price movements in butter and egg contracts were limited to one cent above or below the settling price on Saturday, 6 December. A 50-point swing would be allowed on potato contracts.

On Tuesday, 10 December at 3 P.M., after the markets closed, the Exchange received a telegram from the Commodity Exchange Authority which stated in part, "Temporary ceilings on certain commodity futures Tuesday and Wednesday will not be continued tomorrow. Trading in December eggs on Mercantile Exchange for remainder of month will be for liquidation purposes only. Effective Thursday, all other commodities will have usual permissible fluctuation limits, up or down, from today's close. Please advise your markets."

Shawhan gave no hint that business was hampered by the war. Among the motions passed late in 1941 was one calling for the annual members' dinner. Another sanctioned Christmas bonuses of one week's salary to each employee. In a burst of last-minute business before the New Year, the Board approved the trading schedule for an Idaho russet potato contract to open in April of 1942. In September of 1942, it would add onions to its markets. From 1930 until the United States' entrance into the war, there had been an active and well-developed cash market for onions but no futures market. The Exchange continued to invest heavily in defense bonds, and to contribute money to a number of wartime organizations ranging from the American Red Cross to United China Relief, Inc. Annual dues were waived for the duration of the war for Merc members who were in the armed services. In return, these members lost their privilege to vote on Exchange business.

Despite the facade of well-being, there were definite signs that the Exchange and its members had fallen on hard times. There was only one membership applied for in 1941 and eight in 1942, when Sol Schneider and Sol Rich picked up seats at $510 each as a result of defaults. Going into 1942, the Mercantile Exchange was braced for another round of cost-cutting measures. Early in January, the Exchange appointed Alfred Kraemer as assistant to Tenny. Kraemer's job was to ease the pressures on the aging Tenny by handling Exchange personnel from runners to inspectors. Now Tenny could direct his attention to Exchange policies and internal affairs. Backed by Shawhan and the Board, he looked for a solution to a problem that had given the Exchange a black eye more than once over the years: market manipulation.

During the late 1930s, several squeezes had been engineered in eggs by a group of traders. To most traders, cornering and squeezing the market was venturing on shaky ground. There were still a few who defended the practice as a private matter between the manipulators and the shorts—those involved in the sale of contracts that must be borrowed to make delivery in anticipation of a price decline—who were being squeezed. (The short squeeze is a result of sharp price increases or difficulty in borrowing the contract the sellers are short. The rush to cover losses forces prices even higher, which in turn causes a greater squeeze.) The Exchange, they argued, had no business interfering. In fact, in some of the older exchanges they pointed to, there was no ban on the practice. It was a short-term, myopic view of trading life, and certainly a dinosaur of an idea.

The government had already cracked down on the old Wall Street with the SEC. Commodity markets would face the same scrutiny if things got out of hand, opined the Merc officials. It was better to do your own policing than have someone else doing it, Shawhan and his colleagues believed. For that matter, no one in 1942 could speculate on the extent of government controls once the war was over. Just thinking about it made for queasy stomachs. As far as its clearing members were concerned, the Merc had run a tight financial ship. There had been no clearinghouse defaults in its 21 years. Just one unchecked squeeze could easily have broken that record and, in turn, would have blackened the Merc's financial integrity.

Shawhan and the other officials weren't about to take any chances; they decided to bring in nonmember directors. At the 1942 annual meeting, the membership overwhelmingly voted its approval on a unique proposition: to expand the board from 12 to 15 members, adding outside directors from the butter-and-egg business. Thus, the Merc was the first futures exchange to use outside directors, hoping for a more objective eye in its affairs.

The crunch came in the summer of 1942, when the Board turned its attention to bottom-line details. A special committee consisting of George Shawhan, Harry Field, Joseph Godow, and Maurice Mandeville spent hours poring over the books in an effort to find ways to save money. Tenny, who came up with his own cost-cutting plan, figured $15,000 could be trimmed from the budget without any layoffs, but his proposal did not satisfy the Board. In a letter to the Board, the committee had made its recommendation, explaining that $35,000 "is the minimum amount the Committee feels that we can save and operate the Exchange during the period of the war with any safety." In order to save that much, the committee concluded, "It is necessary to curtail the staff considerably."

The message spread like a tropical fever as morale among the Merc staffers dropped dizzyingly. Although no one panicked, there was a sense of urgency. Within hours after the committee's report, Tenny put his own job on the block by offering to retire immediately. Though the gesture was not hollow, the committee bluntly refused the offer, noting, "We feel however this should not be done on account of the Washington contacts and because of rather major administrative problems that are likely to arise at any time."

But Tenny's offer planted a seed in Shawhan's mind as he began to juggle positions on the organizational chart. Oscar Olson, who was paid the modest sum of $4,000 a year as an assistant to Tenny, was retained and given additional duties of supervising the Merc's inspection department. John Carole, the chief butter inspector, and Herb Hentschel, the chief egg inspector, would now do all the grading of products themselves. The shift eliminated the head of the inspection department, Joseph Milnarik, the second-highest-paid Merc official and former president from 1924 to 1925. The savings: $12,000. Three board markers and the Exchange's doorman were also dismissed. In addition to the layoffs, the wish list of cuts included the following:

Employees dismissed	$22,270	
Employees salaries reduced		4,350
Bonus for employees	1,200	
Governor's and committee fees reduced by one-half	2,050	
Contributions to dairy produce		754
Payment to Chicago Price Current	1,302	
Board of Trade translux		978
Exchange ticker on the board of Trade (estimated savings on telegraph messages largely because of the ticker service)		2,200
		$35,419

In its letter to the board, Shawhan's committee summed up the situation: "It regrets very much that it has to recommend the elimination of any of these valued workers, but the Committee feels that for the period of the duration of the war the organization should be cut to a point where it can handle easily from one hundred to one hundred fifty cars of trading per day and we feel that the above recommendations will in no great measure at least, hamper the fulfillment of the functions of the Exchange."

Such cost-cutting measures only proved to be a bandage for a deeper financial wound that reached the very core of the Exchange. The Merc was under the strict pricing thumb of the all-powerful Office of Price Administration, which set the limits on the cost of everything from rents and gasoline to steaks and chewing gum. Butter and eggs were among those commodities whose price limits had been set both by government decree and rationing. It was the kind of situation that could bring an exchange to its knees and eventually force it to close its doors. The fates of the nation's futures exchanges hung on the duration of a war whose outcome was still uncertain in 1942. Ironically, it was uncertainty in the first place that gave exchanges their reason to exist.

An exchange was the nerve center of the marketplace, but it could not make the price of a commodity any more than a thermometer can make the weather. It merely provided the machinery whereby price evolved and was registered. To function as such a system, it needed a lifeline of contracts and willing speculators to fill the breach between buyer and seller. It was impossible to match supply and demand at any given time unless there was someone to offer the commodity or to bid for it. Thus, to a great degree, futures buying and selling refined speculation, reducing the spread between producer and consumer.

During the war, the pros and cons of a market mechanism had little bearing on reality. "Trading was dead," Bill Katz said. "Most of us were in the dried-egg business, and we had powdered eggs for the army. Then again, the 1940s weren't as bad as the 1930s, when there were only five people on the floor. You could still trade up to the support levels."

Shawhan, whose tough Irish streak kept the Merc in tow through the first two years of the war, turned over the presidency to then-62-year-old Maurice Mandeville, a veteran egg dealer, whose firm, Bickley, Mandeville & Wimple, was an original clearing member at the Merc. The bald and bespectacled Mandeville, who favored bow ties, was a dry man with a Midwesterner's abhorrence of government meddling in other people's business affairs. Yet, like most everyone else in the nation at the time, he put patriotism before capitalism. "No one had it in his mind to make a killing or to get rich trading eggs and potatoes," said Katz. And there wasn't a waiting line for memberships; on most days there was a soporific calm on the floor.

By 1943, when Mandeville stepped in, the Board was confident that it could keep the Merc going without sacrificing any more employees. Apparently, though, Tenny felt the pressure as he began to question his own usefulness to the Exchange. After weeks of soul-searching, in mid-March he decided to resign.

> This action on my part is not taken hastily [he assured the Board in his letter of resignation], or for any reason than that I feel very much as if the work possible in Washington is not worth all it is costing the Exchange, and further . . . I can get a full year of work done at my farm, some of which things will require several years to develop along the lines that I hope they will.
>
> I still have great confidence in the future of the Exchange and have no recommendation to make other than what has been made, that we continue with a limited staff, if possible keep contracts open, do a little trading day by day, minimize losses as much as possible, and be ready when the time comes to pick up and go forward in a substantial manner.

The 14 years of Tenny's stewardship were stormy ones, and the Exchange at times was bewildered. Yet Tenny symbolized stability in the minds of members. There were fat years and lean years and though his contacts in Washington did little to favor the Merc, the scope of the Exchange had expanded through his vision. The Merc, he reminded his colleagues, "has a broader outlook and a more national viewpoint than existed in 1929 when I came here."

More sophisticated perhaps, but still rough around the edges, the Merc had a long way to go to be on par with other exchanges. Tenny believed that it was only a matter of time before it caught up. In his pragmatic manner, Tenny had pursued an active public relations program, defining the Merc and its function to the public and working to resist the encroachment of government into the futures markets. In his words, "I recall very definitely in the early days of my service here [at the Merc] emphasizing the fact that a futures market was primarily for the purpose of hedging and that the proper operation of a market such as ours required that the members of the trade use futures for the purpose of eliminating price risks in their own merchandising operations."

Tenny's comments were hardly news to the Board. They were, in fact, a bit sophomoric. But they did reflect how Tenny related to the Exchange over the years. He saw himself as a teacher of the futures markets competing with the distant past and an ignorant public. "The public, who are the proper risk bearers, were not greatly interested in butter and egg futures," he conceded. "Through the development of the public interest we have, to a large degree, corrected this situation."

This statement was typical of Tenny's optimism. On and off over the years, he had tried to push the Exchange to reach out to Congress, farm leaders, and the public. "The surface of this work has scarcely been scratched," he stated emphatically, "and if the opportunity is presented at some future date whereby an intensive educational program to show the importance of futures trading in the merchandising of agricultural products, I would like to see the Chicago Mercantile Exchange take a very leading part in such a movement if and when it comes."

Despite the Merc's cloudy financial picture, Tenny was upbeat in his fiscal summary. No one could hide the fact that the Merc had taken a bath during the Depression, as Tenny reported: "In 1932 we took a loss of something like $78,000 in the sale of bonds, in spite of the fact that at that time we still carried over a substantial number of worthless bonds, or bonds of very poor investment which were not closed out until 1941 when we cleaned out our portfolio completely with another loss of something like $30,000."

Having said that, Tenny, with stubborn pride, was quick to point out that from 1930 to the end of 1942, the Exchange had an aggregate profit, though modest, of $62,582. "I doubt if any other Exchange in the country can show during these thirteen years any increase in their financial backlog," he boasted, "and therefore I am exceedingly proud of what the Board and the management have done during these years to leave the financial picture of the Exchange substantially better than it was at the beginning of the worldwide depression."

By now the Merc was trading butter, eggs, potatoes, and an onion contract it had launched in September 1942. It also dabbled in cheese and frozen eggs, and even tried a contract in hides as "an experiment," that, according to Tenny, was "one of the expensive items." Trading volume was merely a speck of what it is today, but it was enough to keep the Exchange prosperous until the end of the war.

Ironically, as World War II pulled the nation out of its financial calamity, it pushed the Merc into a deeper one. By 1942, it was a matter of hanging on and keeping the doors open in anticipation of postwar readjustment. The Merc accountants had projected losses of just under $50,000 per year through 1944. Crucial to those projections was a reduction in rent, and, like any trader worth his voice, the Board was ready to bargain.

The plan that had started out as a shout in 1928 turned into a whimper. To finance its building, the Merc had borrowed $2.6 million, of which $2.1 million was a first mortgage (issued as mortgage bonds through a separate building corporation whose directors were also on the Merc's board) and $500,000 a second one. Both mortgages were held by the Prudential Life Insurance Company, with Continental Illinois National Bank and Trust Company as trustee of the first mortgage bonds.

Indeed, the situation looked bleak as Merc secretary Joseph Sieger described it in 1943:

> The Building Corporation is and has been for many years in default under both the First and General [second] Mortgages. The amount of the default has grown so large that it would seem that the Building Corporation and consequently, the members of the Exchange, as beneficial owners of its outstanding stock, have lost all equity in the building, unless as the result of a chaotic inflation, the value of the building in dollars is tremendously increased. Notwithstanding the extent of the default, no foreclosure suit has been brought. . . .

Desperate to buy time, the Merc was hardly in a position to make demands on Prudential, although it did not hide from the fact that it had to have relief from the monthly cash crunch if its doors were to remain open for the duration of the war. Not that Prudential was an unwitting landlord—the insurance giant did not need arm-twisting to be convinced. After all, it was far better to have a tenant making partial payments than to be stuck with a half-empty building and a cavernous trading floor collecting dust.

Without hesitation, Prudential agreed to reduce the Merc's rent from $66,500 per year, or $5,541 per month, to $42,000, or $3,500 per month, plus $1 for each contract over a volume of $42,000 traded during any calendar year. The lower rent was to be paid through February 1948, when the Merc's 20-year lease terminated.

On the surface, the Merc had cut a favorable deal, but in doing so, it took a gamble by putting its major asset on the line: the Exchange Building itself. In return for the cut-rate rent, the Merc was forced to place the deed to its building in escrow, to be forfeited to Prudential in the event that it reneged on the rent or that it failed to pay all outstanding bonds, together with interest, at the termination of the lease. It took a vote of the entire membership to approve the plan, which passed overwhelmingly with 312 votes in favor and three against. Among the three lonely dissenters was William Moore, who 18 years earlier had successfully led the fight to convince the membership that a new building on Franklin Street was in its best interests. Now the elder statesman's pleas that such a plan made the Exchange too vulnerable fell on deaf ears. He called for other options, but offered none specifically.

A dejected Moore knew that the Exchange would never be able to catch up by 1948 no matter how well business rebounded; but there remained a strain of optimism among the usually cynical directors, who saw no other way out for the languishing Mercantile Exchange. Unfortunately, Moore was right. Even in the wake of postwar prosperity and the end of price controls, the Merc came up short on its mortgage obligations and lost its building to Prudential. Shortly thereafter, Prudential sold the building to Henry Crown, who became the Merc's new landlord and the man to reckon with on lease renewals and rents until 1972, when the Merc moved to new quarters on Jackson Boulevard.

Before striking its deal with Prudential, the Merc replaced Lloyd Tenny with Oscar Olson in March 1943 at an annual salary of $7,200. Olson, a butter-and-egg man to the core, was like a honey-tongued politician on the campaign trail. Always ready with a firm handshake, he enjoyed talking about issues and seldom lost his temper. But he never backed down from traders who tried bending the rules.

Olson was well-liked throughout the industry and over the years made good contacts that later paid off. At one point he had worked with an enterprising fellow named Wynn Smith, who would later team up with several associates to open a brokerage house in New York known as Merrill Lynch, Pierce, Fenner & Smith. Actually, recalls Everette Harris, it was the Smith connection that led Merrill Lynch to become the first wire house (a multioffice brokerage firm using electronic communications to transmit customer orders) to have brokerage and clearing operations on the Mercantile Exchange. Olson knew his hands would be full just trying to keep the spirits of the Merc members up at a time when everything around them seemed to be caving in. With a positive outlook that was contagious, he moved around the Exchange floor pressing the flesh of fellow traders and reminding them that the war couldn't go on forever.

America was now in the full swing—and spirit—of the war effort. Army posters were urging civilians to "Do with less so they'll have enough" in a plea to help the GIs fighting overseas. Two-thirds of all production in the United States was fodder for the ravenous war machine. For example, Kaiser Industries was churning out a warship every 12 days. The pace was furious, but no one complained—least of all the manufacturers, who were making handsome profits on a cost-plus basis.

No commodity was wasted. Nylon stockings became nylon parachutes and pennies were being made of zinc-coated steel because copper had gone to war. Women had emerged as a substitute as well, making up one-third of the work force to fill the jobs of the men who were in the military. For the first time, income tax was withheld by employers instead of being paid in one lump sum.

Eggs had slipped to 23 cents a dozen; the price of a Merc membership also fell. In 1942, a seat cost $510. On 20 May 1943 Isadore Mulmat, Isadore Katz, and Sol Schneider each bought a seat for $285 from three traders forced to put their memberships on the auction block because they were delinquent in paying their dues.

The membership prices of an exchange function as a sort of litmus test of trading vitality. When things are booming, seats are at a premium. The opposite, of course, is true when the markets languish as they did during the Depression and the war years. But it was also during market lulls when Exchange leaders had a chance to pause and reflect on the future of their institutions, to reinspect the mechanism, and to sometimes indulge in self-examination. The 1940s provided the Exchange that opportunity—there was little else to do. For Maurice Mandeville and his colleagues, there indeed was light at the end of the tunnel in 1944, but the tunnel was long and the light dim. The Chicago Mercantile Exchange had literally fallen victim to the age-old trade-off between guns and butter.

9

Oscar and the Old Guard

Oscar Olson was the right man for the right job at the right time in the winter of 1944. A man of short stature and Swedish descent who was as dependable as a brown-bagger showing up to work on time every day, Olson was low-key on the outside, but keyed-up inside. He was anxious to keep the Merc from cracking internally by making sure the members weren't at each other's throats whenever a dispute arose.

"He was a great mediator," said E. B. Harris, who replaced Olson as president of the Mercantile Exchange in 1953. "Oscar was even-tempered and always sure of his facts."

A graduate from Chicago's Kent Law School in the class of 1913, the year Harris was born, Olson never practiced law. However, noted Harris, "He had sharp analytical skills from his legal training." Thus, while Olson had the feisty spirit of a Fulton Street egg peddler, he had the agile mind of a LaSalle Street attorney. The blend proved just right when it came to dealing with the traders, who, at times, could be hair-pulling stubborn. Olson stood his ground no matter how menacing the arguments became, which is why the Board readily gave him far more discretion than Tenny had been given to decide which disputes were to be arbitrated.

Olson worked closely with Merc counselor J. Arthur Miller, a tough negotiator who, at the request of the Board, had rewritten the trading rules in 1944 to make arbitration compulsory for Exchange transactions. The rule change was the result of a dispute that arose during the summer of 1943 between traders Samuel Midlin and Harry Field. The Board kept the tiff a private matter, referring to Midlin's mistake as "a minor offense." Field asked for arbitration, but Midlin refused to air his dirty laundry before the Board. The tiff was over an unmatched trade known as an *out-trade,* or a price discrpancy between buyer and seller. The Board found Midlin guilty, and though the infraction may have been minor, the penalty wasn't: Midlin was suspended from the Exchange for one year. The Board had used the Midlin affair as a clear message that it wasn't going to tolerate any Merc members thumbing their noses at the rules, or at the Board for that matter.

When news that 176,000 assault troops stormed the Normandy beaches to free the French on 6 June 1944 reached the Merc floor, the members knew the worst was over. "In a sense, the Mercantile Exchange was free too," said E. B. Harris, "from the depressing thought that it might not weather the war."

That year, total industrial output in Chicago reached a wartime peak of nearly $12 billion. The economists had calculated that the city's industrial district, comprising some 2 million workers, produced one-twelfth of the "bits and pieces" needed to fight the war. In Illinois alone, some $12 billion in victory bonds were sold during the war, second only to New York. Wartime inflation had been counteracted by price controls and raw materials preserved by rationing.

A planned economy had virtually put the nation's futures exchanges on hold, in a sort of organizational limbo, waiting for the free-market forces to come back into play. "These exchanges attempt to establish a market where there shall be as perfect competition as possible," wrote economist John R. Commons. "Their rules are directed towards establishing liberty, equality and mutuality through publicity and precision. What they do is eliminate practices and customs that are deemed to obstruct free competition, or deemed to tend towards inequality or concealment."

The war, of course, had changed the rules and such economic adages mattered little to the Merc members. With a war winding down, their thoughts focused on less lofty sentiments. Their concern was how to adjust to a postwar era that would suddenly be without life-sustaining government largess. Tough, though somewhat tattered, the Exchange had survived. Now the traders longed for the old days when memberships sold at a premium and per capita consumption of butter and eggs hit new peaks each year.

There were still plenty of traders around from the First World War who remembered the sting of an economy that fell with a thud following demobilization. Back then, price controls chief, Bernard M. Baruch, simply resigned the day after the armistice. Economists bemoaned the fact that such cavalier planning had delayed orderly peacetime conversion by more than two years.

Early in 1945, Olson met with the Board to discuss postwar strategy. As the Merc's first educational director, he realized the importance of reaching out to the public. Olson wanted to spend more money on public relations and advertising. There was talk about new contracts, perhaps in poultry. However, the problem of rekindling the momentum lost during the war remained. There had been no trading in egg futures in 1942 and 1943 and only a minimum amount of activity in 1944 and 1945 because of the ceiling prices set thereon. Before the Exchange could settle on a specific course, tragedy befell the nation with the death of Franklin Roosevelt on 12 April 1945. For one day, the Merc closed its doors in memory of the man who had dared to tamper with the free markets during the Depression, but who had championed the cause of the world.

About a month later, victory in Europe came. On 14 August 1945 the Japanese surrendered, and the war was over. This time, the Merc closed its doors for two days as a half-million people jammed the streets of the Loop in celebration. A few hours after the Japanese surrender, people were pasting their rationing coupons in their memory books. Two days later, the army sent manufacturers some 60,000 form telegrams canceling contracts worth $7.3 billion, as the giant industrial machine that helped to reshape the world's geopolitical face began to dismantle.

The American economy had thrived from war: During the period from 1940 to 1945, the gross national product more than doubled to $215.2 billion, while the cost of living remained stable, owing to tight price controls and rationing. Weekly earnings were pumped up to nearly twice their 1944 level and Americans itched to spend money on homes, cars, refrigerators, steaks, bacon, butter, sugar, coffee, chocolate, chewing gum, nylons, shoes, gasoline—anything and everything that was scarce during the war. Savings were high, and demand went up. There was promise in an economy converting its guns back to butter. The wartime production boom was being replaced by an insatiable demand for merchandise. Consumers stormed a new beachhead—the department stores, where sales in Chicago reached a postwar peak of $4.2 billion in 1948, nearly triple what they had been in 1940.

At the same time, however, the scramble for income alternatives was pandemic. The industrial renaissance had left a crop of factories loaded with the latest tools and machinery ready to produce for a peacetime economy. In Chicago, there were 9,058 manufacturing firms when the war began and more than 12,000 when it ended. Tank builders now built cars instead; shell producers churned out trucks, and smaller outfits that turned out time fuses used in anti-aircraft shells went back to making watches. A flock of manufacturers began producing a newfangled item called *plastic*.

The big question that had the politicians and economists scratching their heads was how fast to decompress. In January 1946 President Truman asked Congress for another year of the Office of Price Administration and a 65-cent-an-hour minimum wage. He wanted to lift controls, commodity by commodity, based on supply and demand.

The Truman Administration still didn't know what to do with the American farmers, who were miffed by a set-aside order that required them to sell the government one-half of the wheat they grew. It was acceptable during wartime, but went against the grain of rural independence after August 1945.[1]

In 1946, the control system was near collapse, reeling from a producer backlash. Meat became a rare commodity as ranchers kept cattle off the market because of low prices. Then came the consumer aftershock. With lower supplies and higher demand, prices soared. In the summer of 1946, the cost of living rose by 33 percent, and then by 75 percent more in the fall. Angry housewives calling themselves the Militant Marketers picketed food stores for relief.

At one point, the lack of supply forced store closings around the country. In Chicago during one week of June in 1946, about 36,000 head of cattle arrived at the Chicago stockyards, and Wilson & Company couldn't buy a single head at legal compliance prices. Three months later, Armour's main Chicago plant slaughtered just 68 cattle rather than the average 9,000 a week. A *Time* magazine survey of 139 cities found only six without acute meat shortages, and cattleranchers estimated that 75 percent of the nation's beef was being sold on the black market by shady outfits that simply ignored price ceilings. Something had to give.

As the shortages became more severe, public pressure to remove the controls increased. The OPA, itself a bureaucratic monster served by 73,000 people, seemed to be losing its grip. It became clear that farmers, consumers, and politicians detested controls. Finally, in a national radio address on the evening of 14 October 1946, Truman announced the end of price controls.

Swept up in postwar optimism, the Merc forged ahead as if it were breaking through a cocoon of dreamy withdrawal. A committee had been formed in late 1944 to explore the possibilities of trading new contracts. Less than two months after the war ended, Merc traders were buying and selling a new contract in turkeys,[2] and under consideration were new potato and onion contracts in addition to those already being traded.

Internally, the Merc had hardly changed. The war had made the membership more cohesive, and the Board remained a tight group influenced strongly by the chairman and business manager. In January 1946 the Board closed ranks even more when it unanimously voted to eliminate outside directors, thus reducing the number of governors from 15 to 12. The Board had been expanded to 15 members as an "experiment" in February 1942 with the notion that the outsiders would represent the public and those producers of the commodities traded on the Merc. But, as Olson pointed out, "Experience has shown that it has been most difficult to persuade suitable persons to accept appointment upon the board of an exchange with respect to which they are in no way directly connected. . . . Those persons who have accepted appointment have, generally speaking, not been diligent in attending meetings of the board, and it is the consensus of the board that the experiment has not been a success and that the rules should again be amended."

It was time for a change in leadership as well. Mandeville was tired, a bit cranky, and eager to return to running his egg business full-time. The pressures of keeping the Exchange from faltering were more demanding mentally than physically, and Mandeville simply needed time away from the Exchange. He was replaced by Charles S. Borden in the 1946 Merc election.

Borden was head of S.S. Borden & Co., located at 133 South Water St., which was a charter member of the Merc. He had a wide range of business associates on and off the Exchange and among his friends was Adlai Stevenson, whom he backed as governor of Illinois and then in the two presidential elections against Eisenhower. The Borden family had long established itself in the dairy industry and during the 1950s and 1960s, promotional efforts had made Elsie the cow a household name synonymous with dairy products. The good-natured Borden was introspective, and "a great gentleman," said Kenneth Birks, typical of the military veterans who had returned from the war eager to get back into the commodities business.

The Board that year was loaded with old guard traders, including Mandeville, Isadore Katz, Saul Stone, Hy Henner, Harry Redfearn, Frank Collyer, and Barney Schreiber. One of the Board's fair-haired boys was Joseph F. Sieger, who had moved up from secretary to first vice chairman and would become chairman from 1952 until 1954.

Annual dues in 1946 were set at $50 and committee members were still being paid five dollars per meeting. Though finances were tight, the Board increased Olson's annual salary by a few thousand dollars to $12,000. The raise was a vote of confidence more than anything, and Olson took it as such.

Though shaken, the nation's commodity exchanges pulled through the war years with remarkable resiliency, if not implacable confidence. At the beginning of the war, the system of futures trading was an integral part in the distribution of commodities. There were active futures markets in grains, eggs, sugar, coffee, cotton, cocoa, butter, flaxseed, lard, hides, wool, rubber, copper, zinc, tin, lead, cottonseed oil and meal, silk, onions, potatoes, soybeans, and peppers. All of the exchanges were hoping to add more contracts.

What was the spark that made the Merc and other exchanges function so effectively? The answer, in part, was provided by J. A. Higgins, Jr., executive vice president of the National Association of Commodity Exchanges and Allied Trades Inc. (NACEAT). Before the House Committee on Agriculture in July 1947, Higgins explained:

> All normal men possess in varied degrees a desire to be self-supporting, to make progress and to be a success....All efforts, through whatever avenue should be undertaken for a common purpose, namely: the capture of a reward in proportion to services rendered. These rewards will vary by the degree of intensity of competition existing in the particular field of effort or by the degree of skill with which efforts are applied. Accordingly, it is the incentive for personal reward that keeps the mechanism of a commodity exchange functioning.

As head of NACEAT, Higgins was the postwar spokesman for the futures industry, the man who was to explain to both the government and the public what exactly commodity exchanges did to justify their existence. He was, in the words of NACEAT's declaration of principles, "a pleader for the Commodity Exchanges with the prestige of a champion of the public weal."

Formed in 1945, NACEAT, of which the Merc was a charter member, was the forerunner of such current organizations as the National Futures Association and the Futures Industry Association. Such organizations, intent to get the message to the public, multiplied after the war. Advertising was emerging and so was

America's mass awareness of Madison Avenue, thanks largely to a best-selling novel by Navy veteran Frederic Wakeman called *The Hucksters* (and the motion picture starring Clark Gable). Although public relations had its pallid beginnings in the 1920s, it did not gain wide acceptance until after the war, when a skeptical public recognized the big corporations as having the power to grow.

The promotional-minded Oscar Olson saw value in both public relations and advertising and convinced the Board to increase its spending in these areas. In 1949, Olson hired the Merc's first full-time public relations director, Colonel Samuel Austin, a World War II Air Force veteran and friend of Harry Redfearn, then chairman of the Merc Board. Redfearn's view of his colleagues was laced with cynicism. Recalled Kenneth Birks: "I can remember when Harry used to say 'We're nothing but a bunch of retired chicken farmers—just a lot of characters.' "

Olson set out to change, or at least soften, the image of the world's largest market for futures trading in eggs, butter, onions, and turkeys. The Merc hired Aubrey, Finlay, Marley & Hodgson, Inc. to prepare a series of advertisements for *The Wall Street Journal* and various trade periodicals.

Educational in tone, the headline of one ad stated, "WHAT CAN HAPPEN IN 5 MINUTES ON THE CHICAGO MERCANTILE EXCHANGE." The ad copy went on to explain, "Within less than 5 minutes after the Chicago Mercantile Exchange onion market opened at 9:30 A.M. one morning recently, 149 carloads of onions were traded. That's an average of almost 30 carloads a minute—a total of 4,470,000 pounds!" The two short paragraphs that followed answered the questions "Who were the buyers and who were the sellers?" and "Why were so many trades made?"

So many trades? Not even the long-range future gazers could imagine the kind of trading volume that would exist 40 years later. Annual volume on the Merc in 1947 totaled 120,000 contracts. In 1990, almost 106 million contracts changed hands.

One thing that didn't change was the nature of trading. As Higgins described it in 1947, he could very well have been looking down into the pits from the visitors' gallery today: "This split-second buying and selling, and highly perfected marketing machinery, is carried on amid noise and seeming confusion that amazes an Exchange visitor. It is difficult to believe that the slightest order or system could in any way come from the turmoil of the Exchange floor. . . . Every shout, every movement of the hand has a distinct and important place in the Exchange. No other marketplace actually functions smoother, or due to rigid self-policing, with more meticulous conformity to inflexible standards. Nowhere in the world is the determination of price supply and demand, in accord with economic law, given more attention that it is in the American commodity exchange."

Although the nature of trading may not have changed in those post–World War II years, neither did the nature of greed. During the war, market manipulators were dormant like ice-age mammoths frozen in time. But when the wartime price freeze began to thaw, the manipulators began to stir again. True, LaSalle

Street plungers no longer dominated the Chicago markets as in the days of crafty Benjamin Peters ("Old Hutch") Hutchinson, the Massachusetts drifter who dabbled in meat packing before perfecting the corner in the wheat market during the 1880s and whose son was president of the Chicago Board of Trade in 1888. And the indomitable Edward Partridge, a former dry goods salesman from New York, became the "bear"—the trader who profits from market declines—of the Chicago grain pits from 1890 to 1894. James A. Patten, the Illinois farm boy who learned big-city ways fast, maneuvered to become the only person ever to have run successful corners in wheat, corn, oats, and cotton. (His biggest corner was in the Chicago wheat market in May 1910.) Let us not forget the penny-pinching, puritanical teetotaler Arthur Cutten—the "Great Bull"—who owned more grain at one time than probably any other man in history and whose zest for corners inspired Congress to pass the Futures Trading Act of 1921, aimed at regulating futures trading in grains. The U.S. Supreme Court ruled the law unconstitutional in an opinion written by Chief Justice William H. Taft, which implied that the decision may have been different if the act had relied more on the commerce clause of the constitution instead of on the congressional taxing power. A year later, on 21 September 1922, Congress passed basically the same legislation as before, calling it the Grain Futures Act. (This time the Act, in part, asserted that "fluctuations in prices are an obstruction to and a burden upon interstate commerce." In a decision written by Taft, the Act was upheld by the Supreme Court.)

A year later the Grain Futures Act was tested in Chicago. In a case called *Chicago Board of Trade v. Olsen*, the constitutionality of the Act was upheld. In response to contentions that there was no relation between prices in the futures market and those in the cash market, the Court dismissed the notion as "hardly consistent with the affidavits the plaintiffs present from the leading economists. . . . It is very reasonable to suppose that one influences the other as the time of actual delivery of the futures approaches, when the prospect of heavy actual transactions at a certain fixed price must have a direct effect upon the cash prices in unfettered sales."

The new law, which included trading in wheat, corn, rye, oats, flax, and barley, was based on the Federal Trade Commission's *Report on the Grain Trade*, which questioned the financial responsibility of speculators who were required to ante up less than 10 percent for margin. But the Grain Futures Act had an obvious loophole: the culprit had to be caught in the illegal act at the time he was arrested. Thomas W. Howell, who rigged corn in 1931, had slipped through the loophole without a statutory scratch. In doing so he drew the ire of grain belt legislators who feared that, in the wake of the stock market crash, shady stock speculators would swarm over the futures markets at the farmer's expense. It was an echo of nineteenth century populism and its antifutures crusaders, who viewed the commodity speculator as nothing more than a parasite to the farmer—the city slickers versus the country boys—and with good reason. The total number of bushels of grain and cotton traded on the futures exchanges exceeded the annual production from 1872. In some of the years toward the end of the century, the number of bushels traded in contracts amounted to seven times the annual crop. The implication seemed clear: Most of the buyers and sellers of futures contracts had no connection to the commodities business.

That was hardly news, good or bad. Nearly all of the futures contracts were liquidated by purchases or by sales of offsetting contracts in equal long and short positions that canceled against each other. Thus, speculators and hedgers were never interested in making or taking delivery on their futures contracts. They wanted to profit or protect themselves, respectively, from the movement of prices. The lawmakers, however, who attacked the exchanges in the 1800s with antigambling legislation, had relied on the small volume of deliveries as an indication of the useless character of futures trading. But minute quantities of deliveries merely indicated that a proper relation existed between cash prices and futures trading, argued economists. In other words, there was no point in making delivery. Agriculture Department economist Harold S. Irwin, who in 1954 did one of the rare studies on the butter-and-egg market during the early days of the Merc, explained it this way: "The objection that too few deliveries are made on contracts is inconsistent with hedging which requires that most contracts shall be offset [by buying or selling] rather than by taking delivery. At the beginning of butter and egg futures it appears that the transfer of ownership by means of delivery was common but with the development of hedging the transfer of price risks without giving up possession of the commodity became predominant."

The tension between the ideals of encouraging and discouraging deliveries was illustrated by economist Holbrook Working in *The Wheat Studies*, a 20-volume survey published by Stanford University's Food Research Institute, beginning in 1924. "Unreasonable exercise of the legal privilege to take delivery of cash wheat," Working wrote, "may well be compared with unreasonable exercise of the legal privilege of depositors to demand payment of their total bank deposits in cash."

Over the years speculation on commodity futures had been justified for a number of reasons. First, forecasting by speculators promoted short-run stability of prices and an adjustment in the use of fixed supplies. Futures markets were used for hedging in order to shift market risks. By doing so, dealers were (and are) able to operate on smaller profit margins, resulting in savings to consumers and help in financing inventories. In addition, the exchange served as a center for continuous price registration and as a clearinghouse for information, making it possible to promptly respond to changes in the cash market. Thus, any attempt to monopolize a commodity became incompatible with futures trading in it.

The premise was simple enough, but that didn't prevent the titans of speculation from treating the exchanges like a metaphorical theater in which they were puppeteers. They were by-products of inefficient and unregulated eras, who could send the markets soaring or plunging on rumor, tips, and sheer buying power. They were connivers, robber barons of the pits, whose characters darkened and hardened as time went on. They dominated the trading pits with ease and arrogance. The nineteenth-century Populist Revolt, the Jeffersonian clichés, and the constitutional quibbling could not tame their fiercely competitive and inbred universe. Not only did they scheme against the smaller speculator with little regard for the man on the street, but they took on each other as well. Their exploits became the stuff of legends. In the classic novel *The Pit*, author Frank Norris fashioned his protagonist, the fictional Curtis Jadwin, after Joseph Leiter, the hapless real-life manipulator who in 1898 tried to corner the wheat market in Chicago by going long. Leiter ended up bucking heads with Philip D. Armour, the meat-packing patriarch, who shorted the market. Leiter went broke, losing $10 million—an especially enormous sum in that era. His fiasco was a vivid reminder of the pitfalls around which manipulators must dance. In the end, the wheat cornered Leiter.

Although some of those notorious corners involved control of the visible supply in the United States, there were corners in local markets, too. The term *squeeze* was used to characterize corners of lesser extent or to sometimes reflect the degree of price increase. The long position is able to supply offsetting contracts at successively higher prices. The prices, however, are not driven high enough to warrant the shorts' expense of acquiring the cash commodity outside the terminal market in which the exchange is located. That wasn't the case when Leiter and Armour went at it. Consider the lengths Armour had to go to ward off Leiter's long wheat squeeze: Just three weeks before the 1 January delivery date in Chicago, Armour's grain warehouses stood empty. That's when he swung his millions into action. He dispatched his emissaries into the Northwest and Canada to buy up all the available wheat and ship it to Duluth, Minnesota. He then hired a Great Lakes shipping fleet of some thirty vessels to carry the wheat, along with a fleet of tugs loaded with dynamite to crash through the ice-choked Duluth Harbor into Lake Superior. The boats slowly made their way from Lake Superior to Lake Michigan and on to Chicago, where trains were arriving daily with millions more bushels of wheat. Armour's elevators began filling up so fast that he had a new one built, engaging hundreds of carpenters and laborers to work three shifts around the clock. Within two weeks Armour had one of the world's largest grain warehouses. He began dumping the wheat on an astounded Leiter, who was forced to sell the cash wheat he had collected, breaking the price and ruining himself. Suddenly, for Leiter—whose millionaire father, Levi, was a former partner of Marshall Field in the department store business— the 90s weren't so gay. Papa Levi had to bail out his son in a corner that had collapsed, shattering Joe's spirit and fortune.

It was the kind of corner Armour despised, the kind in which the shorts are driven to deliver large stocks from the outside, depressing the market as the cornerer disposes of the stocks—the kind, he grumbled, that posed the problem of "burying the corpse," a phrase he had coined years earlier when he faced a similar situation in the pork market. When told that there was a large speculative short interest in December pork and asked why he did not corner that delivery, Armour replied, "To commit murder is very simple; the trouble is to bury the corpse."

Thomas Howell certainly dug himself into a hole when he tried to bury the corpse in 1931. He had squeezed the corn market on the CBOT from 1 April to 31 July, garnering a profit of $270,214. In his subsequent effort to rid himself of his cash holdings, he lost $1,250,000. No one had a Tag Day for Howell, who had millions and would continue to corner markets throughout the late 1930s.

It took a special character to master the art of cornering. Aside from risk appetites, all who tried seemed to share a characteristic that stood out like a dominant gene: a knack for deceit. Although deceit wasn't necessary to corner markets, sneakiness helped. At times, in fact, the game of corners looked more like a rousing game of hide-and-seek. Cornerers would go to great lengths to conceal their positions to keep the regulators and competitors off guard. In 1931, for example, Arthur Cutten and his pal Thomas Howell had 35 and 16 accounts, respectively, with eight different firms in their play to squeeze the corn market. Not surprisingly, administrative proceedings against the the pair didn't begin until they had finished their attempts. Another favorite trick of the manipulator was to reduce the supply of the commodity to be delivered on long contracts. In 1897 John Cudahy cornered the pork-rib market by cutting the ribs in such a way as to make them undeliverable, and then he sold them. In 1926 Armour Grain Company stored rye in a public warehouse, rendering the entire load undeliverable. In 1938 Howell tried to hide his goods by shipping corn out of the Chicago market to Canada. In 1948 General Foods Corporation tried a host of schemes to lessen the deliverable supply: It bought long lines of the same commodity in another exchange and stood for delivery there; it sought to have deliverable grain in boats at Chicago declared undeliverable if a duty was not paid; and it attempted to merchandise its cash holdings by offering them to the government or to processors, who would not let them get into the hands of speculators. No cost, it seemed, would be spared in trying to perfect the corner.

Unfortunately, no one had ever bothered to tally the cost of manipulation on the public's pocketbook. It was certainly a burden that rippled all the way to the grocery store. Artificial prices were quoted as a basis for prices in the cash market; hedging, which depended on a reasonable level between cash and futures prices, was discouraged; the normal flow of commodities was thus disturbed, and speculators who supplied the market liquidity necessary for hedging were subjected to risks unrelated to supply and demand forces in the cash market. Moreover, a corner that failed because stocks could not be disposed of was as harmful to the public as one that was successful, since the loss occurred in the manipulated price—not in the individual gains or losses.

Oddly enough, there have been unintentional corners, too. One such corner, for example, took place during World War I, when some allied governments took large long positions in wheat, driving prices sharply higher on some exchanges. When it became apparent that wheat was unobtainable, the governments--only interested in getting the wheat—backed off and released the shorts from their obligations.

In the late 1940s the danger of corners was minimized by more rapid communication and improved storage facilities, which helped detect any artificial scarcity of deliverable supplies. In addition to establishing more delivery points by the exchanges, there was increased vigilance enforced through the law—the Commodity Exchange Act—that had replaced the Grain Futures Act. In June 1936, two years after the Securities and Exchange Act was passed to set up the SEC for protection of the public, the Commodity Exchange Authority was created to regulate the contract markets. The new law required actual margins of 10 percent, and, along with grains, covered for the first time mill feeds, rice, potatoes, butter, and eggs. (Onions remained an unregulated commodity and cotton was still covered by the ineffective 1916 Cotton Futures Act, which applied to the grading of cotton, but not to the regulating of the cotton markets.) The Commodity Exchange Act was designed to close the kind of technical window that Howell had passed through in 1931. It didn't stop others, including Great Western Food Distributors, which squeezed the Merc's December 1947 egg futures contract.

Great Western had acquired control of both the cash and futures markets separately. The result: price abnormalities. To better understand the corner, it's worth reviewing how the government built its case against Great Western. In order to prove manipulation, prosecutors had to prove that Great Western caused the price of refrigerated eggs in Chicago on December futures to be higher than they would have been if driven by only the forces of supply and demand. The government used historical justification for its findings, noting that the December 1947 to January 1948 futures price spread was abnormally wide. Over the period from 1932 to 1948, the December future was generally at a premium of less than one and a half cents over the following January future in the later weeks of December trading. But during the last week of trading in the December 1947 futures, the average spread was nearly six cents—more than three times the comparable spreads in each of the previous 10 years—reaching more than eight cents on the last day of trading. Figures also showed that from 1932 to 1948 December closing prices averaged 103 percent of January's, and that in December 1947, the ratio was 112 percent. Moreover, the December futures and storage egg prices were high in relation to the price of fresh eggs.

In its defense, Great Western characterized its strategy in terms of "economic hedges." The government countered, calling the position a "speculative spread." Great Western argued that the shorts could have closed out their positions by delivering out-of-town storage eggs (just as Armour did in his wheat play against Leiter). Although a monopolized resource seldom lacked substitutes, under the Sherman Act, "alternatives will not excuse monopolization." Besides, it was common knowledge that futures traders did not want to handle the cash commodity—in spite of the rules facilitating delivery—and would hang on until it was too late. Earlier, before government hearings, Commodity Exchange Authority economist William Blair Stewart explained the pathology of short sellers: "It is true that if the shorts would take the proper steps to secure the grain early enough in the delivery month, they could make delivery under existing circumstances, but anyone who has studied the market knows that shorts live in hopes, even though they may die in despair, and they continue to hold short positions up to times when it becomes practically impossible for them to deliver, and the result is the extreme congestion we find in the squeeze position."

Great Western's long position had exceeded the total stock of storage eggs in Chicago from 2 to 22 December. That put it in a position at the end of December trading that brought the shorts to its doorstep to offset their contracts. Its sales in the cash market early in the month had reduced the supplies available to the shorts later in the month because once refrigerated eggs were out of storage they were rendered undeliverable by the rules of the Merc.

It wasn't the first attempt by Great Western Distributors to corner a Merc market, nor would it be the last. Indeed, it was operators like Great Western that gave the Merc its casino image during the 1940s, 1950s, and 1960s. In 1941 Great Western had been suspended from trading for 10 days in a futile effort to corner the March 1940 butter future. The company struck again in 1949—this time it was the October egg futures. On 14 October there was more than a seven-cent increase in the spread between the October contract and the following November future, a gap big enough to rattle the Merc board into taking drastic action based on its so-called Emergency Rule 943. All trading was stopped in the October future contract on the 14th of the month, with all remaining contracts either fulfilled by delivery or settled at a specified price.

The action drew barbs from both sides of the market. The longs felt that the settlement price was too low and that the Exchange should not have taken any action, leaving instead the conflicting interests to work it out. The shorts, on the other hand, claimed the settlement price was too high, but were convinced that the situation had necessitated emergency action. Subsequently, criminal proceedings under both the Commodity Exchange Act and Sherman Act were brought against Great Western for the alleged corner in the October eggs. Not only did the Merc board have to listen to its disgruntled members, but it got an earful from the grand jury as well. During the grand jury hearings on the case, the Merc was criticized for its failure to have taken disciplinary action—in accordance with its own rules—against Great Western and other traders who were responsible for manipulating prices in the October future.

Another anticorner measure the regulators pushed was for tighter position and daily trading limits. Such limits, they believed, prevented speculators from building up commanding positions—the first step on the way to a cornering expedition. Limits were imposed before World War II. In 1938 they were placed on wheat, corn, oats, barely, and flaxseed; in 1940 on cotton (and amended in 1947); in 1945 on rye; in 1951 on soybeans and eggs; and in 1953 on soybean oil, cottonseed oil, and lard. Yet the problem of corners wouldn't go away. In 1953, for instance, the Commodity Exchange Authority charged 13 companies and individuals of acting in concert to manipulate December 1952 egg futures by means of a corner. It was obvious by now that the Commodity Exchange Act could not handle attempts to corner the futures markets in the commodities under its jurisdiction. When it came to those commodities outside of its domain, namely onions, it was open season. A bill introduced in both houses in 1949 called for 11 additional commodities, including onions, to be covered in the Commodity Exchange Act. Bogged down in politics, the bill never reached the floor. Four years later, however, wild price gyrations in the Merc's March 1953 onion contract grabbed the politicians' attention. In an abortive attempt to corner the contract, the shorts, the longs, the dealers, the growers, and the public all claimed to have been adversely affected. The result: the word *onion* was added to the definition of a commodity in the Commodity Exchange Act.

By 1949, the Merc was scrambling again. Volume was back to levels of two years earlier, primarily due to a sharp drop in the per capita consumption of eggs. In 1945 Americans were frying, boiling, and poaching a record 402 eggs per person, but the number dropped to 370 in 1948, and from all indications the demand would continue downward.

Once again, the Merc chiefs reached deep into their grocery bag of ideas to pull out another contract that could be traded. This time it was America's favorite fruit, the dependable apple. Just as Redfearn took over the chairmanship in January 1949, the Merc started trading apples. Five months later, a contract in dressed poultry was added and then in December a contract in frozen eggs. Under Redfearn, whom Harris described "as a progressive thinker," the Merc was growing again. When the new decade began, volume was just shy of 200,000 contracts a year.

Monthly trading volume early in 1950 had surpassed that for all of 1920. To the public, however, the futures industry held all the mystic aura of how Winston Churchill once described Russia—"A riddle wrapped in a mystery inside an enigma." Few knew much about the nation's 17 futures exchanges, including the financial press of the day. Yet what happened at an exchange like the Merc determined, for the most part, the prices of onions in Texas, eggs in Iowa, potatoes in Idaho, turkeys in California, and butter in Wisconsin. The Merc ironically was even being largely ignored in its own backyard. The *Chicago Tribune*, which published the daily grain prices at the Board of Trade in its financial pages along with the stock market tables, omitted the Mercantile Exchange's prices.

Sam Austin, who headed the Merc's public relations effort in the early 1950s, wrote and published several booklets, which were distributed to the media and made available free to the public in coupons accompanying various Merc newspaper ads. Two of the more popular ones were entitled *Is There a Future in Your Future?* and *How Commodities are Bought and Sold on the Chicago Mercantile Exchange.*

In June 1950 North Korean troops invaded South Korea and the United States and the United Nations rallied to South Korea's defense. War was bullish for commodity markets. Americans were already suffering a case of the jitters from the end of World War II when the Soviet Union gobbled down half of Europe with an arsenal that had three times as many airplanes and four times as many troops as the United States did.

Changes were taking place at the Merc too. Oscar Olson, now into his sixties, let it be known he was thinking of retiring. He began to cast for a successor.

It was the first telephone call of the morning for Everette Bagby Harris, executive secretary of the Chicago Board of Trade. On the other end of the line was his part-time friend, part-time antagonist, George Livingston, regional director of the Commodity Exchange Authority, which was the federal watchdog of the nation's futures exchange. Harris was somewhat surprised by the early call that was unofficial, curt, and cryptic.

"Do you know Oscar Olson?" Livingston asked.

"Why sure," Harris replied. "I sponsored his membership in the Union League Club some time ago."

"He wants to lunch with you Tuesday at the Club. Can you make it?"

"Yes."

"Make it noon. It'll just be the two of you."

Before Harris could flick the ash from his Pall Mall, Livingston had hung up. He sat back for a moment, inhaled deeply, and released twin plumes of smoke from his nose as he asked himself, "Why does Olson want to meet?" Harris couldn't come up with an answer.

The meeting was cordial and Olson quickly came to the point. Olson, then 64 years old, had been a part of the Merc for nearly 35 years, first as a trader, then an official. He talked freely about those years and what they had meant to him personally, while the normally loquacious Harris listened intently, barely uttering a word.

Then Olson asked: "E.B., would you be interested in taking my place? I'm planning to retire to spend more time with my wife. It's time."

Harris, slightly taken aback by the question, paused briefly before he answered Olson. "Oscar, I'm happy at the Board of Trade," he said, "but I'd be interested in possibly merging the two exchanges." Now Olson was a bit startled, but intrigued by the idea of a merger. The two parted, agreeing to ask their respective exchange board members.

A week later, they both met again, this time with the same answer—no. It was clear that neither exchange wanted to merge and that each was quite satisfied with its respective position.[3] Both exchanges had similarly defined public relations policies that essentially stressed maintenance of free markets and, of course, championed speculators as vital to a liquid market. But each exchange traded a different set of commodities, and, more important, each had its own culture and traditions. The Board of Trade had already celebrated its 100th birthday by 1953. The Merc was about to turn 34. However, the price of membership at both exchanges that year was $4,000. (In 1942 a Merc seat cost $225, moving to $2,350 by November 1945.)

Harris had done more than poll his board during the week. He did a little personal soul-searching as well. On one hand, the Merc had a reputation on LaSalle Street as a wild trading arena filled with cutthroat competitors who turned the egg and onion markets into speculative merry-go-rounds. On the other hand, the Merc had spunk and razzle-dazzle that caught Harris's fancy and provoked his imagination. There was plenty of room for growth and new ideas, and a dire need for public relations. Moreover, the Merc wasn't hamstrung by immutable tradition or by a congealed residue of stagnation; the atmosphere was charged with unpredictability. Despite the fact that it was the world's biggest exchange in the commodities it traded, it was nervous about its future.

"The entire futures industry had an inferiority complex at that time," observed Harris. "Many of its leaders feared further government intrusion, viewing it as creeping socialism."

The industry had to cope with a rural backlash as well. From his farm in Henderson, North Carolina, where he lived in retirement, Lloyd Tenny summed up the mood in September 1953: "Futures trading in agricultural commodities is a major factor in the marketing of these products and yet it is the least understood and often the most condemned part of the entire marketing system. Many farmers and farm leaders have felt that this speculation in their products was not in the interest of agriculture because they erroneously regarded it as a form of gambling; legislators have often maligned the subject of exchanges in their topics of discussion at farm meetings."

From practically the first days exchanges opened their doors, controversy transfixed skeptics and believers alike. Now the Merc and the other exchanges were on the defensive. "I wanted to go on the offensive," said Harris.

Olson suggested that Harris meet with other board members and arranged a dinner at the Standard Club. Those attending included Hy Henner, Bill Katz, Bill Rankin, and chairman Joseph Sieger, who had been elected in 1951 to replace Frank Collyer. They were eager to learn about Harris, grilling him as if he were seeking membership in some kind of exclusive club. In a way, he was.

Harris understood their motives and he sensed their reticence. Replacing Olson with an outsider (a "hired gun," as some mockers would later refer to Harris) was a big organizational step that hadn't been taken since the hiring of Lloyd Tenny in 1930. But Harris was used to dealing with an esprit de corps mentality. He did so for four and a half years at the Board of Trade, where the aloofness of some members began to gnaw at his psyche, giving him the feeling, he said, that "I was the employee and they were the employers."

In a number of ways, Harris was the opposite of Olson, who was a short, stout, bald individual, icy and grim with the anesthetized face of a Buster Keaton who spoke in measured tones. By contrast, the animated Harris, extroverted and bulky, stood at six feet two inches with slightly receding blond hair combed back and a pencil-thin mustache. Behind horn-rimmed glasses, his rapid-fire speech was peppered with bucolic anecdotes, off-color jokes, and a string of meandering homilies that could convert the crustiest foes in commerce and ply politicians of every persuasion. Seemingly always pumped with bonhomie, the good-old-boy back-slapping side of Harris combined an instant quip and a sturdy handshake. Some thought him too pushy in his eagerness to charm, but a Chicago newspaper article once characterized him as being "among the last *gentle* men in a cut-throat age."

Harris was pure Illinoisan, a fourth-generation farm lad whose grandfather received a land grant signed by John Quincy Adams in 1827 for a plot of land just outside of Norris City. He never denied his rural background. In fact, with a sort of backwoods charm he played off his roots when he dealt with farmers and ranchers with whom he could establish immediate rapport. What better spokesman for an agricultural exchange than one who could talk the language of farmers from first-hand experience?

Born 18 April 1913 on an 80-acre farm in Gallatin County, Illinois, near the converging borders of Indiana and Kentucky, Harris lived with his parents and two sisters. His father was George Harris, whose father, Robert Harris, had obtained the land. (To this day, Everette Harris possesses the sheepskin land grant signed by President John Quincy Adams, which vested title of the land on Robert Harris.)

When Harris was five, his father sold the property and bought 56 acres not far away, near Norris City, so the children could go to high school when the time came. His father died soon after buying the farm, leaving the family in the grip of the Depression at a time when, as Harris later related, "we were being starved off the farm." A small herd of dairy cows produced milk and butter for sales, with additional revenue from chickens and eggs. The family's food needs were supplied from the land, and the $1,000 per year cash income was generated from the sale of produce, which Harris helped haul to town.

Harris was 12 when the business world first beckoned. One day he and his mother paused before a store window of a merchandiser, Arthur Marlin. There in the window were a new pair of shoes and a wagon, one of which were to be given to the boy or girl who could make the most names out of "Buster Brown," the title of a comic strip from an earlier era and also the name of a line of shoes. Harris won, took the shoes instead of the wagon, and became fast friends with Marlin, who took an interest in Harris and gave the youngster a Saturday job selling dry goods.

By 18, Harris was attending the University of Illinois on a four-year academic scholarship. With a bachelor of arts degree in 1935, his first job was in the advertising department of Southern Indiana Gas and Electric Company. A few months later, and for higher pay, he joined the soil conservation service of the Department of Agriculture. After three years, he transferred to the Bureau of Labor Statistics, performing wage analysis with the war labor board. While still with the government, Harris added another educational stripe in 1945, earning a master's degree in business administration from the University of Chicago while taking courses at night in the first class of U of C's now-famous 190 MBA program.

Harris went private in 1946, landing a job with the help of a friend at Mandel Brothers, a Chicago department store chain with some 4,000 employees and $36 million in sales. The fit was wrong. Harris liked labor relations, but not the retail business. He stuck it out for three years and in 1949 was hired as secretary (the equivalent of business manager at the CME) at the Board of Trade. Though he never traded a contract, he was required to buy a Board of Trade membership during his tenure there.

A farm child of the Depression who had married a university classmate and was now a family man with two young sons, Harris naturally was interested in security. The years had fashioned him into a scrambler of sorts, a man who had dreams of his own but seemed more comfortable working with the visions of others. Now as he sat dining among the CME directors at the tony Standard Club on Plymouth Court, he assured them that he could be tough if had to be, as long as the Board backed him. Olson was certainly no patsy when it came to dealing with traders who bent the rules. Kenneth Birks remembered:

"Oscar Olson was a good administrator. He was also fair and firm. You'd walk in his office with your hat in your hand and he'd say, 'You know what you did. You're fined $500. Goodbye.' And you paid it and walked out. There was no arguing."

The Board, of which Birks was a member at the time, saw Harris as an ideal front man, an aggressive mover who could go outside the exchange and comfortably shake hands with the public.

Harris saw the Board as a group of hardnosed egg traders who knew their business and little else. It was a clash of stereotypes that ended in beautiful chemistry and subsequently a 25-year reign for Harris. He had accepted the job offer, agreeing to a three-year contract at a starting salary of $20,000 a year[4] and a new title, that of president.

Olson's tag had been executive vice president. The title of president had always been carried by the individual who headed the board; he would be chairman. Al Kraemer, Olson's long-time assistant who stayed on to team with Harris, became the executive vice president. All the title shuffling had been in line with modern organizational charts to give the Merc an updated look. Thus, officially Harris was the first named president of the Chicago Mercantile Exchange—and a nonmember to boot.

At Olson's retirement dinner on 8 July 1954, Harris good-naturedly played off the presidential title in brief remarks honoring his predecessor before hundreds of Merc members and friends:

> He [Olson] was our first unpaid President and our first paid President; his personality, his good judgment, his persistence and perseverance, his consistent application and other good attributes of character are woven throughout the fabric of this fraternity. And personally, I must say I appreciate most among his accomplishments that after thirty-five years he helped change the office of the President from an unpaid to a paid position! My wife and children appreciate it too!

The speech reflected Harris's breezy style and his knack for captivating an audience with wit, which he would use over the years to shield himself from some of his associates at the Merc. Harris had honed his talents the hard way, scrambling like the Merc itself to survive, and growing in the process. Years later he would look upon the Exchange through Emersonian eyes and declare: "The Mercantile Exchange is the lengthening shadow of many men."

Chicago's industrial landscape was changing rapidly when Harris settled in at the Merc on 1 June 1953. Some of the very industries that had made Chicago into a commercial powerhouse were dying. The biggest victim: the once venerable meat-packing industry. In the end, it wasn't all the journalistic muckraking and federal reforms that determined the meat packers' fate, but something far more basic — competition. The regional stockyards in places like Omaha and Kansas City were vying for the title of major meat market by the end of the decade. In 1954, the Chicago stockyards celebrated the sale of their one billionth animal, boasting a total of $31 billion in livestock sales since the yards opened.

Five years later, the *Chicago Tribune* sadly observed: "Chicago, which Carl Sandburg celebrated as hog butcher to the world, isn't killing enough hogs these days to feed its own citizens." Most of the steaks, chops, and bacon were coming to Chicago from the packing towns west of the Mississippi. The Chicago packers were dropping like cattle on a slaughtering line. In June 1953 — the very month in which Harris joined the Merc — Swift ceased its meat-packing operations, which had been going on since 1875. Two years later, Wilson was out of business, and in July 1959, Armour phased out. Modern communications and transportation had caught up with the meat packers, who had dominated as long as Chicago was the nation's preeminent rail terminus. But by the 1950s, farmers could catch the daily livestock quotes on their radios and within hours were hauling their animals by truck to the local slaughterhouse. The egg market had followed a similar course. No longer was there a need for a central city like Chicago.

Though Chicago withdrew from the actual receipt of livestock, it still played a vital role in the marketing and pricing of cattle, hogs, and the edible parts thereof. The interest would resurface a few years later, when the Chicago Mercantile Exchange began trading futures contracts on these items. It began first in 1961 with pork-belly (uncured slabs of bacon) contracts. Then in 1965, it pioneered trading in live cattle, followed by live hogs a year later. "The textbooks said you couldn't trade such a thing because the livestock wasn't storable like grain," Harris recalled. "But we argued that cattle in a feedlot of uniform quality were just as much in storage as graded cotton in a mill or wheat in an elevator. There was an inventory risk that indeed had to be protected."

Harris didn't waste any time getting down to the business of drumming up business. The Exchange was trading some 250,000 contracts per year when he replaced Olson, and the prospects were dim.

After the war, the Dairy Products Marketing Association, a major cooperative owned by the big creameries, supported the price of butter at 25 cents a pound. "It killed our futures market at the Merc and there was no butter trading after that," said Kenneth Mackay, who became head of clearing operations in 1954, replacing Carl Hilburn.

Essentially, that left eggs and onions as the Merc's major markets. But, as Harris saw it, it was more than enough to build on. Part of his strategy was to put the Chicago Mercantile Exchange on the map—at least on a Chicago map. That meant recognition in the local media. Harris's first stop was at the financial desk of the *Chicago Tribune*. Over a lunch meeting at the Sheraton Hotel, Everette Harris and Sam Austin met with *Tribune* financial editor Phillip Hampson. The object was to convince Hampson to publish the daily price movements of onions and eggs in the *Tribune's* financial pages.

"We're a Chicago institution," Harris argued, "And you should be running our prices instead of filler on linseed and cottonseed oils and things of that kind."

Hampson agreed, and within weeks, the *Tribune* was running the daily prices for onions and eggs. Under Harris, Austin was given more responsibility and encouragement to cultivate the financial press. That was no small task, given the attitude of business journalists during the 1950s. They paid little or no attention to the commodity exchanges, dismissing them as esoteric marts for professional speculators who wanted more volatile action than stocks offered.[5]

In fact, until 1965 only two studies had been done that revealed any information on traders and their trading styles, according to economist Seymour Smidt, a professor in the graduate school of business and public administration at Cornell University.[6] Smidt had run across the studies in his own research on amateur commodity speculators published in 1965.

Next, Harris and Austin turned their attention to the contingent of Merc members on the East Coast. The Merc hosted a party at the St. Moritz Hotel for its members in New York City, most of whom were big egg traders and also members of the New York Mercantile Exchange, where Maine potatoes were traded. It was an effort to strengthen membership ties for the Merc, which needed all the cheerleading that it could muster when Harris took over.

Harris's most aggressive step to this point was taken in October 1953, when he set out on a crusade in which he tried to persuade the securities industry of the virtues of speculating in commodities. For the first time, someone from the futures industry had taken the initiative to pitch to the stock men of Wall Street on the profit potential of customer trading in commodity futures.

The timing seemed right. The stock market had turned bearish and brokerage revenues were sharply down. Again Harris headed for Manhattan, where he played professor in two afternoon sessions attended by 150 registered representatives of New York Stock Exchange member firms, which also held memberships on the Mercantile Exchange (at least 30 of the dual-membership firms were headquartered in New York).

Harris offered the stockbrokers an "out" from the wave of red ink that engulfed their business. Deftly skirting the issue of futures volatility, Harris rattled off statistics. At the time, there were 17 commodity exchanges licensed as contract markets under the Commodity Exchange Act, trading 19 commodities. The dollar value of these commodities amounted to $45.5 billion, compared with $17.5 billion worth of stocks and bonds traded on 16 registered securities exchanges.

Harris, with bouncy grace, did not mince words. The public, he said, had begun to realize that the stock market "is a frozen market at most, first of all because a tremendous percentage of stocks is in the hands of women who are not by nature speculators."

Harris fielded questions and reviewed the history of the Merc and the commodities traded there, which included eggs, butter, onions, dressed poultry, cheese, frozen eggs, turkeys, and Washington apples. He talked about the growth[7] and the potential of new markets, and he passed out Merc literature as if he were a missionary somewhere in the heart of the jungle handing out Bibles. Harris was indeed seeking converts.

The Merc had prepared a new series of how-to booklets authored by experts. For instance, "Bank Financing of Commodity Hedge Loans" was written by Arthur G. Osgood, a vice president at Harris Trust & Savings Bank. Professor Lawrence Darrah of Cornell University contributed a brochure on "An Explanation of Hedging on the Chicago Mercantile Exchange." They were hardly best-sellers, but they were ideal calling cards and served the purpose of getting the name of the Mercantile Exchange in circulation. The media began to take notice. The New York sessions were covered by the trade periodicals as well as *The Chicago Daily News, The New York Times*, and *The Wall Street Journal*. The aggressive search for new business prompted Harris to reflect at the time:

> For years during the New Deal our public relations efforts were largely directed to explaining to legislators, the public and even school children why we should be allowed to continue to exist. Now, with the new Administration, we are in an era where we can take it for granted that we will be in business to stay. Instead of constantly having to prove the value of a free market place, we can now devote our efforts to increasing the effectiveness of our exchanges by increasing their trade.

In November, Harris was back in Chicago, talking to the American Statistical Society. This time, however, his pitch was to the amateurs, as *The Wall*

Street Journal reported: "The Chicago Mercantile Exchange, one of the largest commodity markets in the U.S., is setting out to convince the public of two propositions: That 'trading' in the sense of buying and selling on exchanges for speculative profit is not an evil word. That trading on commodity exchanges is more advantageous than trading on stock exchanges." Although the untrained eye looked upon an egg as merely an egg, Harris called eggs "the best speculative medium ever invented." He gave his explanation in a speech entitled "The Economic Functions of the Chicago Mercantile Exchange" at a $3 per plate luncheon hosted by the Economic Club of Chicago on 1 March 1954.

That was long before the go-go years of the mutual funds—during the 1950s, the strategies of the pension funds and institutions were tied to long-term investment rather than to quick speculative gain. The result was a drag on the volatility of the securities market. For those enticed by more action, Harris asserted, commodity futures were "by necessity an in-and-out trade with fast turnover." Then there was the 50 percent margin rule for stock buyers, he continued, which also required more capital than did margins for dealing in futures. As for commissions, Harris asserted, those on futures trading were so low "that on a pure chance basis, the odds are only 49 to 51 against your making money, against much longer basic odds on stock speculation because of higher commissions there."

It would be another 20 years before the public rode the crest of a commodity tidal wave set off by the United States' sale of huge amounts of wheat and other grains to the Soviet Union, before the world's monetary markets turned topsy-turvy when the wobbly Bretton Woods Agreement tore apart at the seams, and before the Merc traded futures in currencies, short-term interest rates, and equities—even before it shelved its storage mentality for the likes of live cattle and hogs (and shortly before a scandal that nearly put Harris, the traders, and the Merc itself out of business).

10

The Onion Fiasco

As McCarthyism was in high gear exploiting the nation's fears, Harris was busy traveling the chicken-a-la-king circuit, drumming up interest in the Merc and preaching the virtues of lunch-bucket capitalism with a zealot's fervor.

Harris had put on a few extra pounds from all those lunches along the way, but it was the other growth numbers that were most satisfying: Trading volume climbed to 550,000 contracts by 1955, a 65 percent increase over the volume of 1954, and more than twice the 1953 trading volume. The cost of a membership in 1955 reached a then-all-time high of $7,000, a far cry from the paltry $300 memberships of a decade earlier.

There were meetings and training courses in Chicago, Detroit, New York, and Kansas City; talks to the Economic Club, Executive Program Club, and Lions Club; and sessions with university groups and business editors that resulted in scores of newspaper and magazine articles being written about the Exchange. Did it all make a difference? Looking back on all the activity in 1959, Harris speculated on the significance in a letter to a Board member: "Whether or not there was any correlation between these efforts and the total volume of business on this Exchange since the start of 1953, exceeding the total business from the inception of the Exchange in 1919, can be debated. For whatever reason, the fact is obvious that speculation by the public and professionals was greatly stimulated during this period."

In some ways, the Exchange was like an emerging nation, inventing and reinventing itself with each new contract and change in economic climate. Harris added to the definition by describing his duties, as he saw them, in a memo to the Board.

> My conception of my function and responsibilities includes overall administration of the day-to-day operations of the Exchange, expense and income control, planning for future growth, promotion of new products, projection of an effective image for the Exchange through various public relations activities, contracts with federal and state officials, other commodity and securities exchanges, speaking at industrial conventions and other functions and all the miscellaneous duties necessary to maintain and expand the operation.

95

All of the above must be accomplished within broad and specific policies established by the Board of Governors and in closest cooperation with the chairman of the Board who is the general executive officer of the Board and the executive vice president, who is, in effect, my deputy.

The duties of president, of course, changed with the growth of the Exchange; they became narrower as new layers of management were added. But during the 1950s and 1960s, Harris wore a coat of many colors as the Mercantile Exchange vacillated from feelings of self-doubt to questions of character.

At the time Harris joined the Merc, the Board was under the autocratic hand of a second-generation Dutchman named Joseph Sieger, the head floor broker for Merrill Lynch. Tall, with a mop of brown hair that was graying at the temples, thick eyebrows, and a full face softened by a shy smile, Sieger also possessed a mercurial temper.

"He was known as a tough chairman," said Leo Melamed, who was a runner for Sieger while attending law school, and destined to become chairman himself. "It was a different era. Joe didn't have to listen to his critics, but he was smart. And very demanding. He wanted things done his way."

With his rich, deliberate baritone, Sieger sounded confident, yet not overbearing, and confidential, but not intrusive. "He could charm you out of your britches," said Harris. The two worked well together, trading suggestions like a pair of scalpers facing off in the pit. Sieger, whose mentor was an amicable and influential trader in Exchange politics named Charles Pratt, had replaced Frank P. Collyer, a Merrill Lynch broker who held the Merc chairmanship during 1950 and 1951. When Collyer died in 1951, Sieger hired Kenneth Birks to replace him as the other Merrill Lynch floor broker.

Two years later, Melamed was hired by Merrill Lynch to work for Sieger as a runner at $25 a week. For Melamed, it was an experience on a learning curve that moved straight up without a glitch. While grasping the fundamentals of how an exchange worked, Melamed was able to observe Sieger, though from a distance, and how he related to the membership as chairman. As a runner, Melamed was far-removed from Exchange politics and the pecking order of Exchange life. His mind was then on law, not on eggs and onions. His job was the means of helping him get through John Marshall Law School.

Young Leo Melamed had been bitten by the trading bug from the first day he set his eyes on the Merc trading floor. On an active day, there was the excitement of being part of a mechanism that seemed to have a mind of its own, a system that could stimulate the flow of adrenalin.

"Joe Sieger intimidated me immediately," said Melamed. "But I was so awed by the promises of 110 North Franklin that it didn't matter. I had a love affair with the Exchange that has never stopped."

Melamed wasn't the only one enthralled by the CME. "We all loved the old place," said Harry Hellman, who ran the back office operations for Saul Stone & Co. Though the Exchange stood like a forlorn dowager at the corner of Washington and Franklin, most of the members (and those associated with the clearinghouses) appreciated its character.

At the entrance of the trading floor stood a large bronze rooster, a mascot symbolic of the CME's roots, which was the gift of Frank Mudd, an early member of the Exchange. No one seems to know just how long the rooster had been perched at the doorway and there are no records of when—or why— Mudd gave the gift, but to many a superstitious trader, the rooster was a good omen. (Today the rooster stands in the Memorabilia Gallery outside the executive suite on the fourth floor.)

Each morning, it was common among the traders to pat the rooster's head for good luck as they entered the trading arena, made up of three sunken octagonal pits. Only two were in use; one for eggs, and the other for onions. The third pit, where butter once was traded, was empty because there was no longer a butter market. However, it was often used to launch new contracts, such as the short-lived contract in iron and steel scrap started September, 1954. (The contract was delisted in August 1955 because it was difficult to grade the scrap in an industry dominated by a few firms capable of controlling the price of scrap metal.)

Behind the pits were several rows of desks and telephones from which orders to buy and sell came to the floor. Prices posted on the CME's blackboards were flashed around the country as the Exchange's own ticker service reported every transaction almost instantaneously to hundreds of cities. Tom Peak, who in 1991 celebrated his 38th year as the Merc's longest-tenured employee, can still remember those blackboards like a vivid dream. They cost him many sleepless nights. Peak started at the Merc as a board marker in 1953, the same year E. B. Harris became president. "Every trade made was written on a blackboard and nothing cleared if it wasn't," Peak explained. "The trades would then be copied in a book and keypunched. It was the seller's duty to turn in a trading card. There were no out-trades with this system." The trading day was shorter then, from 9:00 A.M. to 1:00 P.M., but the nights were longer. Peak said he felt like a doctor on call. Many nights he'd work in the Clearing House, matching the clearing firm's records with the blackboard's totals, into the early morning hours, and then grab a few winks at the nearby Sherman House Hotel or Bismarck Hotel because it was too late to go home. And then there were those 24-hour days, when volume would reach 5,000 trades a day. "We'd get through just before trading opened and then go out on the floor and work all morning again," said Peak, who today is the Merc's director of trading floor operations. At times, the volume was so great that the Merc would run out of blackboards and be forced to photograph them with a Polaroid to keep track of prices before erasing the boards for use again.

The Merc of the 1950s, of course, was but a glimmer of the daz- zling 1990s version, with its high-tech tentacles of communication reach- ing into the far-flung financial markets of the world. Yet, throughout the decades, two elements remained constant that inextricably bound (and bind) the Exchange to its past, present, and future: the human voice bellowing in the open outcry system and the fact that the Exchange relied upon a mercurial essence for effectiveness. Face-to-face, eyeball-to-eyeball interaction of buyer and seller was, in fact, a capitalistic practice as old as traveling the ancient camel routes. There was—and still is—a timelessness in the Exchange halls, where commodities with the power to satisfy human wants and needs are traded, a reminder that low-tech can be a lot more sophisticated than people think it is.

In 1955, the price of a CME membership ranged from a low of $3,000 to a high of $7,000. There were some 65 clearing firms, each required to own at least two memberships. A clearinghouse had to put up a $50,000 reserve and a $10,000 bond to guarantee its financial ability to fulfill trades. Members, of course, paid only half of the commissions charged to the public—$16.50 for a contract of eggs (versus $33 for outsiders), from which the Exchange collected a small clearance fee used to pay its expenses. No longer was a trader referred to as a "butter-and-egg man," a term from an era when the markets were less regulated and some of the more flamboyant traders were the darlings of the flappers. Now there were potatoes, onions, and turkeys to trade, and the traders to trade them. By no means was the Exchange in short supply of characters during the postwar decade, nor could it ever be accused of practicing meritocracy. Credentials meant nothing in the trading pit and they still don't today.

"The pit is a total equalizer," Melamed said. "It doesn't care who you are or what you are." Chicago Mayor Michael Bilandic summed up the pit's lack of meritocratic culture in 1978 at the Board of Trade's 130th birthday party. Standing before a cake that was five feet high, weighed 300 pounds, and was shaped like the Board of Trade building, Bilandic sliced off a section of a yellow door trimmed in chocolate and marveled, "You have M.B.A.s from Harvard, and you have people who walked in off the streets. . . . "

The walk-ins included cops, taxicab drivers, high-school dropouts, former teachers, doctors, lawyers, anybody and everybody, young and old, male and female. Indeed, credentials meant nothing in the pit. It wasn't a matter of who you knew or what you knew that counted, but how you felt about the market at hand, because once in the pit, everybody was a trader. Even the dress code of the exchanges suggested a classless society, a culture without social distinctions, a melting of different sizes and shapes into the same uniform. All wear the unisex trading jacket, whose color may vary; by the 1970s, a tie for men would be mandatory and blue jeans would be out, but every man and woman wore the unisex trading jacket like a uniformed student in a parochial school.

The pit culture ignored not only credentials, but often civilized amenities as well. There were seldom any handshakes in the pits, or *thank-you*s, or *pardon-me*s, or *you-go-first*s. There wasn't time for anything but a quick nod to seal a buy or sell. Outside of the pits people could be friends; inside, they became adversaries who not only traded buys and sells and gibes, but sometime jabs, too. They could push, elbow, slap, punch, kick, bite, wrestle, step on toes, spray one another with saliva, and parry and thrust their pencils like sabers, accidentally jabbing a hand here, an arm there, and sometimes even a face—all in the name of communication. The pits legitimized conduct that in other times and places might have seemed irrational.

The pits were no place for shrinking violets. It took thick-skinned aggressiveness, self-confidence, discipline, and the instinct to survive to endure the pits and withstand those close encounters of the unkind. But in the end, any successful trader would say it was worth it as long as the cash flow was healthy. Money, after all, was the only means of keeping score in this game. That prospect was enough to keep a steady parade of traders heading for Chicago's trading pits, which were as rambunctious as any and were filled with characters of every background. The Merc certainly had more than its share over the years.

On any given day back in the 1950s, one could see strolling across the floor an elderly, cigar-chomping bachelor named Elmer Falker, still wearing spats and driving to and from the Exchange in his spiffy 1932 Franklin. He was a partner of L.D. Schreiber in the early 1920s and had made a great deal of money trading eggs. The two were a contrast of comic proportions, a Mutt-and-Jeff pair, with Schreiber at six-foot-two towering over the diminutive under-five-foot-tall Falker.

Falker was, in fact, a visionary. To anyone who would listen, he would relate an idea that was constantly rolling around in his mind: a Dow Jones futures contract. A disciple of this unlikely sage who had won and lost many fortunes was a young Merrill Lynch runner named Leo Melamed. One day in 1953, Falker sidled up to Melamed, grabbed his hand, and confided, "The ultimate futures contract is stock market futures."

Melamed stood mute. When Falker realized that Melamed didn't immediately understand, he whispered, "You know, like Dow Jones futures." Then, waving his cigar through the air, the Argus-eyed little man added, "But it will never happen 'cause you can't take delivery." Three decades later, cash settlement made Falker's "ultimate" contract a reality.

The CME could even boast a little royalty in its blood, thanks to Count Daniel Delattre, a French nobleman with a dry sense of humor blended with a connoisseur's taste for dry wines. Endowed with a lilting Parisian accent, he was the consummate raconteur as he doled out tales from a basketful of witty World War II stories he collected while serving as an advisor to General Eisenhower in North Africa. Harris remembered "the Count" as "a single-minded man of singular habits who was very French and not a bad egg trader." Naturally, to Harris and all the others, Delattre's wife—who inherited his membership upon his death—was known as "the Countess."

The Merc crowd still had some rough players in the 1950s. Among them were the nine Fox brothers of Fox Deluxe Foods Inc., a wholesaler of turkeys, butter, and eggs, with roots in South Water Street when the company was called Peter Fox & Sons. The Foxes were notorious for their alleged corners of the egg markets, according to John Geldermann, Merc chairman from 1974 to 1975 and again from 1989 to 1990. Geldermann's father-in-law was Bert Fox, who walked with two canes because of hip injuries sustained when he tried to stop a barrel of frozen turkeys from rolling off a freight car in South Dakota. Along his arms were knife scars from run-ins with the Teamsters who tried to organize the drivers on South Water in the 1930s. "He was the toughest man I had ever known," said Geldermann. Bert's nephew, Harold Fox, was among the biggest egg traders and a three-pack-a-day smoker. As he talked, a cigarette waggled up and down in his mouth, its ashes burning little spots on his ties. Bert's brother, Michael, was Merc chairman from 1936 to 1938. For a period the Foxes also ran their own brewery called Fox Deluxe Beer.

One of the early "true" scalpers was Al McKenzie, who would go long at the bid price or short at the offer price, grabbing five or ten points. Another quirky trader was Bob Kratoville, called by his colleagues "Scratch Him Over" because he would constantly buy and sell at the same price. And there was Miles Friedman, a tough, barrel-chested man who was chairman in 1939 and wore a flower in his lapel every day. One of Friedman's employees, Jimmy Boyle, had at one time six sons trading on the Merc floor. Friedman's son-in-law, Nathan Wertheimer, would become Merc chairman in 1966. Others of the era included George Hoffman, Roy Eldrige, Bill Rankin, Ruby Carl, Marlowe King, Bob O'Brien, Sidney Maduff, Gil Miller, Ken Birks, Sol Rich, Sam Becker, Bill Brodsky (no relation to the current Merc president), Saul Stone, Carl Sturm, Mike Weinberg, Marvin Prager, and Robert Ascher. Merc staffer Al Kramer made sure there were no duplicate trading badges as he doled out the symbols like vanity license plates.

There were family ties too: the Fox brothers, of course (of the nine, only Bert, Joseph, and Michael were listed as CME members) constituted a true Merc dynasty; also holding memberships were the brothers Schneider (Sol and Sam), Katz (Bill and Izzy), Siegel (Joe and Sam), and Mulmat (Izzy and Jack). Once on a slow trading day in the pork belly pit, William Muno, a Merc member since 1955, counted 16 sons of members (including his two) whose fathers were still traders. "Most people in the 1940s, 1950s, and 1960s came down to the Merc through a family connection," said Muno, who first came to the Merc in 1950 as a board marker. Behind the blackboards was the little room with the ping-pong table, the domain of Marvin Prager, who would spot nearly anyone 20 points in a 21-point game. In one marathon session, Prager and Bob Redfearn slammed away until 3:00 A.M. In a separate room, other people would play gin rummy. Sometimes they'd play gin at their trading desks on slow days. "It was a social club," recalled Muno. "There wasn't enough for them to do. A thousand carlots a day was a good day."

Indeed it was a club, small enough where everyone was on a first-name basis—informal enough not to have a dress code, and to allow a trader to chain-smoke his way from one pit to the next. In fact, most traders could be distinguished by their voices. The board markers, Muno said, wouldn't have to turn around to scribble the trades because they knew each one. That's why Joe Theisen would merely yell out his trades from his front-row desk.

For the most part, the Merc of the 1950s was upbeat and friendly, yet hard, even boorish—a world unto itself. It sustained life by offering traders a chance at making a living. It hosted death as well. In 1959 egg trader Joe Crilly died of a heart attack at 9:25 A.M., five minutes after the egg market opened.[1] Trading never stopped, even when the fire department paramedics carried his body off the floor. "We said prayers to ourselves," Muno said. "It was a good way to go." As always, a trader's scorecard was money. Back then a good day for any of these traders was a $400 profit. But there were always exceptions. In a feature story on the CME in September 1956, *Chicago Magazine* noted: "More adventurous traders have been known to go from rags to riches by their operations on the Exchange—and sometimes back to rags. An Exchange official cites an example of one man who made half a million dollars on onion futures within two years and lost it all again within the ensuing six months." Ironically, less than two years later, onions would cause the Merc itself to run with its proverbial tail between its legs and once again depend on the lowly egg for existence.

After 20 years of the New Deal and Fair Deal legislation, the conservative Republicans were anxious to undo the previous reforms. But for the most part, President Eisenhower continued to carry out basic New Deal policies. The farm population dropped by nearly 7 million during the 1950s, but farm output grew. Aided by postwar science, production continued to exceed demand.

The Administration, with a willingness to control and stimulate the economy through Federal management, decided to slow the accumulation of farm surpluses under the price support program. Secretary of Agriculture Ezra Taft Benson argued for lower price supports on a sliding scale. As a result, the farmers' share of national income dropped. To help the economy muscle its own way, Eisenhower dropped all price controls that had been instituted for the Korean War, and cut taxes for both individuals and corporations in 1954. That, coupled with reduced government spending, touched off a mild recession similar to the economic rattle of 1937 to 1938. At that time, defense spending and increased outlays for foreign aid and domestic programs spurred the economy, but partial cutbacks created a brief recession again in 1957 and 1958.

Through it all, the Merc held its ground on free markets. Harris carried the message. Appearing before the subcommittee on agricultural policy of the Congressional Joint Economic Committee, Harris argued that artificially high prices would solve neither the economic or social problems of American farmers—or the political problems of American congressmen.

"No system ever considered rations our agricultural commodities so efficiently," he told the subcommittee in 1957, "with such low middlemen's costs, higher returns to producers and lower costs to consumers, as our own free-to-change price system.

"Under a free price system, if there is overproduction one year the price falls, rations out the commodity and gives the producer a fresh and hopeful start the next year.

"If there is a short crop of some commodity some year under a free price system, the price would go high and ration out the commodity more sparingly, requiring some substitute product at a lower price at times, and spread the short supply over the entire following year until a new crop could be produced."

The last thing Harris wanted to do was to generate friction with needless remarks. Harris appeared before the congressmen, as he put it, "to fight the good fight." It wasn't apple pie or motherhood that Harris was defending, though the object of his defense was capable indeed of bringing tears to one's eyes. It was the onion, that lowly edible bulb of the lily family with its sharp smell and taste, whose demand among consumers was wholly inelastic. The onion had become an endangered commodity species. Congress had been ruminating about the fate of onion trading for some time: to ban or not to ban.

For months during 1956 and 1957, senators and representatives listened to the charges of the National Onion Growers Association and individual growers in Texas, Idaho, and Michigan, all of whom complained that there was too much opportunity for price speculation in onion trading. At first, proponents of the measure to ban trading did not win overwhelming support from the legislators. One of those who questioned the wisdom of such radical legislation was Illinois Senator Paul Douglas, a former economics professor at the University of Chicago. In debate, Douglas maintained that "trading in futures is a stabilizing device whereby possible futures suppliers are brought into relationship with the present market. Therefore futures trading is a necessary function and should not be outlawed."

Douglas's congressional colleagues were unmoved by his logic. Responding to the onion farmers in Michigan—the headquarters of the National Onion Association—a young Republican congressman named Gerald Ford wanted an end to the onion futures market. "He didn't make a lot of noise," recalled Harris, "but just enough to be heard." Not even Douglas's fellow Democrat, Senator Hubert Humphrey, agreed with him, despite Humphrey's torn loyalties to voters. With one ear, the Minnesota senator listened to the onion growers of his state. The other was bombarded with the arguments in support of the Merc from members of the Minneapolis Grain Exchange, which, like other futures exchanges, saw its fate tied in with the outcome. Humphrey, chairing one of the subcommittees that held hearings on the proposed ban, ended up in favor of it, according to Harris. The issue was so emotional that little attention was paid to a 1956 report adopted by the International Chamber of Commerce, which, in part, concluded, "Any factor which tends to restrict operations on a futures market prevents that market from effectively fulfilling its task."[2] In connection with that point, the Washington Congress of the International Chamber of Commerce had resolved 25 years earlier that, "The broader the market, the more efficient are the services rendered by it."

Congress had already slapped the hands of the onion traders and the Merc through the so-called King Bill, which gave the Commodity Exchange Authority control over futures trading in onions.[3] The Merc had not uttered a word in opposition to enactment of the Bill, which became law on 24 September 1955. Supervision of most other agricultural commodities (including eggs) and their derivatives were already under CEA regulations as part of an ongoing process that began in 1921.[4]

The final knell was sounded for onion trading after a furious burst of speculation in the March 1956 contract, called by some "March madness." Left in the wake were record low prices and boiling tempers among impassioned onion farmers, a small but vocal group led by the National Onion Growers Association. "Onion prices dropped to the point where the 50-pound bags that held the onions were worth more than the onions themselves," remarked E. B. Harris. "It was an extreme case of over-speculation coupled with oversupply that pushed onions below the cost of production." Charlie Keeshin, a Merc onion trader who owned a farm near Rockford, Illinois, took delivery on the 50-pound bags at 10 cents each and used the onions for fertilizer.

What happened on the March contract? It opened on 1 August 1955 at $2.40, went to $2.75, plunged to a low of 10 cents, and closed at 15 cents. On the last day, when prices broke to record low levels, three cars traded at 10 cents, none at 11 cents, none at 12 cents, five at 13 cents, two at 14 cents, and only three at 15 cents—a total of 13 cars at 15 cents or less.[5] The activity on that last day was so frantic that seven board markers had to handle the March contract. Were growers of onions that had been grown during the summer of 1955 still holding their perishable onions late in March of 1956?

"Of course not," Harris told a House Agriculture subcommittee in Washington on 18 May 1956, "They [the farmers] had sold or hedged their onions during the fall of 1955. Only the bravest speculator was holding long onion contracts in March 1956, and only the bravest speculator was holding any unhedged cash onions at that time."

Harris continued: "A man would not sell a car of onions in late March for less than production cost if there were not excessive supplies and danger of dumping. Dumping of onions or other perishables is quite common through the years when a new crop overtakes an excess of old crop. This merely clears the way for the next year and has no relation to futures trading."

"The futures market does not in any way set prices. We merely furnish the hall for trading and what we hope are fair and equitable rules. Supply and demand sets onion prices as it sets other prices which are not on government price support programs. The Exchange merely registers and disseminates these prices so that all may know them. We are like a thermometer which registers temperatures. You would not want to pass a law against thermometers just because we had a short spell of zero weather or break a barometer because the air pressure fell."

Political pressure from onion growers and onion dealers was well-organized, and there were reams of statistics to back up claims. The Commodity Exchange

Authority, for example, had prepared tabulations that classified all holders of onion futures contracts by occupation and the dates of their positions. The conclusion: These speculators were hardly competent judges of supply and demand conditions for onions. In other words, they weren't handlers of the commodity. They were, for the most part, speculators. In fact, the CEA pointed out, the nature of the onion speculation was "in-and-out-trading," which involved holding a position for two weeks or less. CEA Administrator Alex Caldwell—considered by Harris a friend of the Merc—told the congressional committees that such trading "necessitates guessing on . . . immediate and so-called technical conditions." He had begun his testimony by noting that recent price volatility in the onion contracts had been "both more rapid and of greater extent because of activity in the futures market." He added "This sort of price movement in [March] onion futures has occurred on many occasions prior to this most recent episode. . . . Price movements of this sort cannot be attributed to supply and demand, and force the conclusion that speculation, and in some instances manipulation, has been a dominant factor."

Caldwell then concluded, "Wide and rapid price swings attract speculation which at times further widens these swings, thus attracting more speculation. This speculative fever continues until the individual speculators have either lost their money or made enough to satisfy them for the time being." Caldwell believed that onions, more so than other commodities, were subject to speculative excesses due to rapid price changes. "The frequency of wide price movements," he said of onions, "attracts a type of speculator who is looking for quick action and who is likely to go into and out of the market in a short time."

The congressmen were told that the hedging of onions differed in character from the hedging of such commodities as wheat, corn, and cotton. "There is a tendency on the part of onion hedgers," Caldwell explained, "to hedge only partially and to place and remove their hedges sporadically, with changing appraisals of current market conditions."

Caldwell's testimony had dealt only with price tendencies in the presence of futures trading. "The investigating committees heard no evidence regarding the probable extent of unwarranted fluctuations in cash prices of onions in the absence of futures trading," economist Holbrook Working noted in 1960, three years after the hearings. And though the congressional committees had heard testimony that futures trading reduced the volatility of onion prices, the Senate Committee on Agriculture and Forestry concluded that speculative flurry in the futures markets "causes such severe and unwarranted fluctuations in the price of cash onions as to require complete prohibition of onion futures trading in order to assure the orderly flow of onions in interstate commerce." The House Committee on Agriculture essentially had reached the same conclusion.

The Mercantile Exchange had mounted a strong campaign to offset congressional sympathy for the onion growers. For the first time, the Merc hired an outside public relations firm, Chicago-based Selvage & Lee, Inc., to prepare special releases based on the testimony before the various congressional committees. The aging political war horse, L. D. Schreiber, through his Democratic network, lined up Hyman Raskin, a crack Washington lobbyist familiar on Capitol Hill and with close ties to Senator John F. Kennedy. Raskin, according to Harris, contacted Bobby Baker, a young staffer for Senator Lyndon Johnson, hoping to convince him to work on stalling the bill in-committee. To this day, Harris doesn't know whether Raskin's effort succeeded, but the bill was held up for several months. The Merc even extended an olive branch to the National Onion Association based in Benton Harbor, Michigan; on 6 April 1955 the entire Board of the Merc met with representatives of the onion association, including its strong-willed president, Veril Baldwin. The outcome was a series of recommendations designed to maintain tighter control on the onion contract.

But in the end, nothing mattered. After extensive congressional hearings, all the pros and cons of a free market system, and the promise of reform, Congress remained undaunted.

On 28 August 1958, the Merc was brought to its knees when trading in onion futures, the second-most heavily traded future contract on the Exchange, was outlawed by congressional edict. Congress had enacted Public Law 85-839—the Onion Futures Act—prohibiting futures trading in onions. It was a historical first—the first time that futures trading in any commodity was made illegal in the United States—and one that had the Merc and its members gasping for breath. Harris would later describe the drastic and unprecedented action as "the blow that was almost fatal to the Exchange." And to this day, he faults the Merc hierarchy for not going to the Supreme Court on the onion ban.

Part II

The Golden Age of Commodities (1959 to 1975)

11

Back to Eggs

Gloom spread across the floor of the Mercantile Exchange when word got around that the worst scenario had been played out. The unthinkable had happened: the government had closed a free market. "They stopped it as if they had shuttered a restaurant dishing out ptomaine," lamented 83-year-old Roy Simmons. In 1958 Simmons was one of the Merc's major onion traders. He was still actively trading on the Merc in 1988.

The entire futures industry did little to defend the Chicago Mercantile Exchange, other than to offer sympathy. "It was quite obvious that the Mercantile Exchange had paid the price for what was perceived as excessive speculation, and from that point all the other exchanges were gun shy," said Bill Katz, who became chairman in 1959, replacing Carl E. Sturm, who had served one term. The sinking feeling had become all too familiar to Katz and the others. They had been to the brink before, first during the Depression, then World War II. But somehow the Exchange always managed to stay afloat. This time, however, the mood was different. "There was pessimism all right," said Harris, "verging on panic."

For nearly three years, the axe of federal intrusion hung over the Merc's neck, and it finally fell in 1958. For all practical purposes, the Chicago Mercantile Exchange was now a one-commodity exchange. Earlier, government price supports ended futures trade in the butter market; now it was onions. Only eggs remained, and the obvious question was on everyone's mind: Could the Merc survive? No one was prepared to answer just yet. There were other questions, too. How could this have happened to the Exchange, which was heralded by *Chicago Magazine* just three years before as "easily the most important produce market in the world"? Did this mean an end to self-regulation—and, to a greater degree, self-determination?

"There were so many questions, we couldn't even begin to tackle them all," recalled Harris. "But the immediate question that needed to be answered dealt with strategy. Should we fight the congressional ban on constitutional grounds? If so, we had to prepare ourselves for going all the way to the United States Supreme Court."

Sixteen days before the official congressional ruling on the onion ban, the CME's public relations firm, Selvage & Lee, urged preparation of a counter-campaign that would hopefully keep the Exchange's image intact. Sam Bledsoe handled the CME account. He was a rough-hewn man with a passion for baseball and deep Southern roots that allowed him access to a number of Dixie senators. Harris chose him because of the political rapport and his smooth style. It was clear to Selvage & Lee that the ruling would go against the Exchange.

On 11 August 1958, Sam Bledsoe wrote Harris from Selvage & Lee's Washington office, expressing frustration over the situation and suggesting a defensive strategy:

> Dear E.B.
>
> I talked to Eastland but did no good. I talked to Anfuso and others also to no avail. Any day the House will approve the conference report. As I told you, I am upset by the entire matter and if it were to do over again—? Maybe, however, in a contest of this kind where there is a vocal, fairly numerous and determined group of producers pitted against an exchange, there could have been but one result.
>
> However, I would advise you to prepare a counter campaign immediately. It is apparent that the abolition of futures trading in onions will do nothing to improve the price situation. It will do the opposite for many growers will increase acreage, anticipating higher prices because there is no organized trading.
>
> The Exchange should keep in touch with the producers who opposed the abolition of trading and furnish them with material which can be used to show that conditions have not improved. Instances where prices paid growers are below market prices in Chicago should be stressed. The Exchange should keep in touch with members of the Chicago delegation and other Congressmen like Anfuso so that periodically, the attention of the Senate and House can be called to the failure of the abolition of futures trading to cure the ills in the onion industry. Material should be sent to the newspapers along the lines indicated and attempts made to inspire magazine stories which would say that no cure for the farm problem can be found in killing futures trading.
>
> The Exchange also should work systematically with the Farm Bureau, fruit and vegetable organizations to point out that, in the case of onions, the producers took the wrong approach. I am personally of the opinion that something can be done to encourage the consumption of onions through recipes, stories about the good qualities of the product, lack of calories, etc.
>
> All the Exchange should cooperate in the kind of program indicated, for if they do not other commodities will follow—potatoes, wool, etc.
>
> I know you are sick and tired of hearing about onions but the result most certainly is not your fault. You have tremendous drive, bulldog tenacity and the capacity for leadership. You did everything possible. I enjoyed working for you and no one could be fairer or more realistic. If ever there is anything I can do for you personally do not hesitate to call on me. . . . Don't let this thing discourage you too much. I predict that you will yet turn it into a victory.

The letter stirred the thorns in Harris's side. He felt a sense of outrage, but reminded himself to remain calm. He explains his thoughts at the time: "Here we were, a viable exchange that had been in existence for forty years, coping with the rules of chance and probability, and codes of conduct. And now we were fighting for our lives. The situation was nerve-wracking and frustrating. But I told myself that problems with outside groups and government regulations meant growing pains. And I'd rather have growing pains than be standing still."

Shortly after receiving the Selvage & Lee letter, Harris requested an emergency board meeting to discuss the Merc's next move. The Board, headed by Sturm, was willing to fight the ban. "We were nervous about survival," said Katz, a member of the Board at the time. "It felt as if we were sitting on a time bomb with the seconds ticking away." Time indeed was crucial.

One Board member, Harry Fortes, a University of Chicago–educated attorney turned futures speculator, offered the services of a friend—a bright constitutional lawyer and professor at Harvard Law School. Fortes was given the nod to make the contact without delay. "The Board didn't think twice," said Harris. "Everyone assumed we would challenge the constitutionality of the ban."

Following the meeting, Fortes called Boston, and his friend was on the next plane to Chicago. He would come, the friend assured him, because of his interest in the case and out of friendship for Fortes. There would be no fee for his opinion, only reimbursement for the air fare. "It was as if the Lone Ranger were coming into town to save the day," snickered Harris. "For a moment we breathed a sigh of relief with the thought of having the best legal mind on the case."

Fortes's legal eagle was a soft-spoken gentleman with dark bushy eyebrows who favored bow ties. His name was Archibald Cox, who 15 years later (in May 1973) would be hired by then–Attorney General Elliot Richardson as special prosecutor in a far more sensitive (and stickier) constitutional case known as Watergate.[1]

When Cox reached Chicago, everyone was ready to take on the federal government.

In his low-key manner Cox approached the question as if he were reviewing a case study with a class. "He asked very pointed questions, that seemed to skirt around the issue at hand," recalled Harris. "But he knew what he was after." Some of the questions dealt with the history of the Exchange, others with past regulatory problems.

The Merc had relatively few problems in the post–World War II years. Occasionally, the Commodity Exchange Authority's local office took after a Merc trader for trying to manipulate prices by cornering the market. A firm that found itself in violation of the Commodity Exchange Act bared itself to civil suits for damages by other traders who could allege financial injury as a result of the manipulation. In the extreme, a trader could be expelled from exchange membership, fined, and even sentenced to jail.

Such penalties had proved rather effective in preventing violations, but there were cases from time to time. In the decade through 1956, the CEA had only brought three charges against firms. In one, several of the officials of Great

Western Distributors, Inc., an egg dealer, were found to have attempted a corner in the market in December 1947. The firm was suspended from trading for a year, and under a criminal indictment filed by the Department of Justice, a fine of $32,000 was levied. But the biggest controversy to hit the Exchange involved onion futures.

Despite the longevity of futures exchanges in the United States, they were the least-understood of marketing mechanisms, Harris was convinced. Free markets, he emphatically told Cox and the Board, would be destroyed and replaced by a planned economy if the opponents of futures trading had their way, or they would be choked to death with excessive regulation. At one point, Harris sounded like a Minute Man during the American Revolution, trying to pump up his fellow colonists for the good fight. "The price of maintaining free markets is eternal vigilance," Harris told the Board members, pounding a fist on the long conference table.

The vigorous and continuous public relations campaign by the CME had accomplished little against the outcries and outrage of the National Onion Association, which represented only some 2,000 growers who blamed price volatility on the big city speculators. Nevertheless, the amount of onion trading had increased steadily from just 461 contracts in the first full year of 1943 to 20,000 in 1948 and well over 100,000 by 1955.

As if the outside pressures weren't enough, there was internal strife to cope with as well. Led by the grackle-voiced elder statesman, John V. McCarthy, a group of the traders attacked the politics of the Exchange at the time the congressional hearings were underway.

In a letter dated 6 March 1956, McCarthy, a wholesale distributor of butter, eggs, poultry, and potatoes by "carlots only" according to his firm's letterhead, complained to then-chairman Michael Weinberg Sr.:

> . . . During the years the structure of the Exchange has taken on the appearance of a ward organization and in the writer's opinion we are gradually but surely slipping into a very unstable position. . . . I suggest an immediate and drastic cut in the personnel of all committees, with the view of getting rid of the dreamers and hot air specialists. . . . An outstanding weakness of our Organization is the common desire to place self-interest above the interest of the Exchange and it is being said that we will eventually have to go outside of our own ranks for legislative talent if we expect to hold and maintain the respect of the trading public. What a pitiful plight to be in. For more than three years we have known the desperate need of changes in the conduct of our business and this can be said of both the onion and the egg business. . . .

The letter, emotional and hostile, reflected the indignation felt by McCarthy and some of his colleagues, but by no means did it represent a consensus. Yet, it caught the mood, a blend of fury and frustration that had left CME members such as McCarthy alienated and forlorn.

By the end of the year there was mutiny in the air. Merc governor Hyman Henner, an egg broker for Uhlmann & Company, sent a letter to the membership, which included Clarence Carlson, George Murlas, Earl Riley, E.E. Birks, Harry Fortes, and John Coleman. The slate was backed by McCarthy and L.D. Schreiber, the aging veterans who could still muster support based on their positions. The letter, mailed to the membership on 26 December 1956, accused the then-current board of dealing unwisely with the changing conditions in the egg and onion industries. Henner contended that the board, on which he had two more years to serve, had used "poor judgment" in dealing with the federal regulators and Merc members who were constantly trying to manipulate prices. "The unfavorable publicity the Exchange has received," Henner wrote, "cannot be glossed over by cold figures showing an increase in the volume of trading . . . the Exchange was created to serve the perishable commodity industries, so that these industries could buy price insurance . . . to attract speculators who are willing to assume the price risk . . . It is no longer a local butter and egg market but a national commodity Exchange. . . . "

Henner's comments fell like a slap on the face of at least one of his fellow board members, setting off a letter duel. On 3 January 1957, William Katz, a Merc governor who would become chairman three years later, fired his shot in response to Henner's views. In a letter to the Board, Katz charged Henner with violation of Rule 402 (c) — "conduct which has the manifest tendency to impair the dignity and good name of the Exchange." Henner's letter, maintained Katz, had accused the Board of incompetence without any attempt at proof. In doing so, it "lowers the prestige of the Board among the membership and abroad and brings a serious matter into public discussion in a most improper and condemnatory manner."

Perhaps the most intriguing aspect of the Katz letter was his reference to the Broker's Club, out of which the so-called Young Turks would emerge in the coming years to wrestle the Merc leadership away from the old guard led by Katz. It is the first time on record that confirms the club's existence, then characterized by Katz as "the young men who make up the organization within our organization." The entrenched Merc leadership at the time viewed the club as almost subversive, with the goal of shuffling the power structure. Being a member of the Broker's Club was one thing. Openly admitting it seemed quite another. "Recently Mr. Henner denied all connections with the so-called Brokers' Club [sic] and demanded an apology 'on my word of honor,'" wrote Katz. "This apology was not forthcoming. Now his letter, by strange coincidence, . . . endorses the exact same candidates for Governor as were endorsed by the Broker's Club. . . . " (Henner indeed says he had been a founder of the Broker's Club along with New York trader Hartley Harris. The club, Henner recalled, had some 25 members.)

Katz closed his letter by demanding a public apology from Henner in the form of a written retraction to the Board. Nothing in the record indicates that Henner changed his mind or that he was member of the Broker's Club. As for his proposed six-man slate, three were elected in January 1957—Clarence Carlson, E.E. Birks, and John Coleman—to the 12-man board whose chairman was Michael Weinberg, Sr., Max Weinberg's son. (Michael Weinberg, Sr., who served as chairman from 1955 to 1957, died in May 1991 at the age of 91. He was the youngest president of the Butter and Egg Board and had been a Merc member since 1921.) The dissidents could thus claim victory, planting the political seeds of the Broker's Club that wouldn't sprout again until four years later in a fight that brought a young man named Leo Melamed to the front lines of Merc politics.

Such squabbling among the Merc members had overshadowed the fact that time and circumstance had caught up with the Exchange. "The supply was dwindling anyway," Harris said. "With year-round production in eggs and onions, it was almost like trading in non-existent commodities."

Robert O'Brien, who a decade later became Merc chairman, summarily described those days: "The turmoil that preceded and followed the onion debacle left the Exchange administration weary and desperate; the membership was torn by internal strife. The image of the CME as a financial institution was at its lowest level. Public confidence was shattered."

Archibald Cox's assessment of the situation didn't do much to pull the CME out of its funk either. His opinion, in fact, threw ice water on those fired up to battle with Congress. The Merc, said Cox, would be ill-advised to pursue the fight into the highest courts. Why the timidity? It was simple logic. By risking a Supreme Court decision, Cox warned, the CME—and indeed the entire futures industry—could leave itself vulnerable. A precedent-setting decision against the Exchange would surely throw a dark cloud over the commodities markets for years to come, if not end them by threat of decree.

"Cox pulled no punches," said Harris. "After all, he could have collected sizeable fees defending us. But he calculated the legal odds and there was far too much at stake to test the waters of reason. At the time we really had little to fall back on. That is, the futures industry had no political clout. That was readily apparent by the onion growers' victory."

So the CME took its lumps. The Board voted against pushing the issue in the courts. Instead, Harris and company decided to take their case to the public. The Merc's fragile image had been cracked, but not shattered, believed Harris, who began making plans to meet with editors of newspapers and magazines around the country in an effort to counter criticism.

Perhaps there was no year-end president's letter—before or since—that fretted over the misfortune of the CME more than the one written to members on 23 December 1958. In it Harris tried to pump up spirits, but, given the conditions, "it would have been foolish to play Santa Claus," he said. "It was downhill after the introduction." The letter, in part, stated:

> To you, at this Holiday Season, may I send sincere greetings and my wish for a happy, prosperous 1959 for all members of the CME.
>
> This year 1958 was rather a critical period for your Exchange. Caught in a political tide in an election year we became the victims of legislation which would prohibit futures trading in onions. Many who voted against us did so with admitted misgivings. . . . The shadow of this legislation over our onion market restricted trade somewhat and onion volume for the year was down about 25 percent from 1957, totaling about 52,300 contracts. . . . It must be apparent to everyone in our business that the climate for commodity trading is not presently as pleasant as we would like. Government interference with free markets has taken many forms and trading has been restricted and markets prevented from fulfilling their full economic function in many cases.
>
> Never has it been more imperative that we all work together in the interest of commodity trading with complete cooperation. We must rededicate ourselves as men of good will to making our proper function better understood by producers, consumers, members of congress [sic], farm organizations, and the public generally. Suggestions toward this end are always welcome.
>
> Finally, it would be helpful if you would submit suggestions for new commodities which are being studied and more are needed [sic]. . . .

There was no way for Harris to know immediately whether his pep talk had boosted morale. But in the next two months, it became clear that the members were beginning to put pressure on Harris, chairman Katz, and the Board to rally business. Reflecting on those desperate days, Robert O'Brien remarked, "I now marvel at the courage of the Board members and administration of the time in being able carry on at all. But carry on they did. The Exchange was left with but one viable market—storage eggs and their counterpart, frozen eggs—their only hope for survival."

12

Inching Along

"We can't afford to sit around and wait to see what happens," Harris told Katz over breakfast at the Union League Club shortly after Cox headed back to Boston. "That's the Rip Van Winkle approach and we don't want any part of that strategy," added Harris.

Katz agreed with Harris and promised that he would push hard to move the CME into new areas. However, neither had any ideas for a substitute that would replace the onion contract. The consensus among members was to stick with the Merc's bread and butter: eggs. There was little choice. By April 1959 Harris had put together a strategy he thought viable, reaching back to the roots of the Exchange.

"The exchange was founded by butter-and-egg men and all attempts to branch into other fields—cheese, apples, scrap iron, onions, potatoes, turkeys, hides, and so forth—have been disappointing to date," Harris ruefully observed before a board meeting during which he outlined a plan of attack.

"In our egg contract we still have the best single commodity for public participation in a speculative market among the agricultural commodities traded today," he said. "We must constantly attempt to improve our contract, keep in step with changes in the trade so that as we increase the volume of trading we can keep the train on the track in the future."

In addition, Harris called for formation of a business conduct committee "if for no other reason than the necessity of giving a new look to our policing methods," promotional materials for member firms to promote volume, and an all-out effort to launch an advertising campaign supplemented with educational and training programs would be presented by Merc personnel in the field.

In closing, Harris noted, "We should continue to try new commodities but we should concentrate our efforts on eggs." And so they did. The alternative was of little comfort to such major onion traders as Roy Simmons and Joe Siegel. "I was disappointed," brooded Simmons one day in 1987 as he talked about those days.

Operating out of Oswego, New York, Simmons had converted an old steel foundry warehouse into a storage facility for some 200 carloads of onions in order to take delivery and to ship the onions along the Eastern Seaboard. "It was obvious the prices had become far too volatile," said Simmons, who spent at least three weeks out of every month trading in the onion pit of the CME. After the ban, he said, "I started to trade whatever moved, and that was usually the egg contract."

Another active trader was Joseph Siegel, who became a CME board member in 1960 when Cola A. Gray was elected chairman. In 1988, more than two decades later, from his luxurious Water Tower Place apartment on Chicago's Gold Coast, Siegel reminisced about the demise of onion trading. "Onions were a luxury, not a necessity," explained Siegel. "The growers used to play the long side of the market and they'd constantly accuse the shorts of maneuvering the market."[1]

A year before the onion ban, the Commodity Exchange Authority (CEA) completed a survey of the open interest on the CME. The number of speculators in the onion futures market was 405, or 89.6 percent of all traders. Those traders classified as hedgers numbered just 47, or 10.4 percent of the total. The results of the survey were similar to those in CME surveys taken in 1955 and 1956.

From the pattern, the CEA concluded that "relatively numerous speculative traders [hold] all but a very minor portion of the long side of the market, and a small number of hedgers [account] for the bulk of the short side." When the speculators' long positions were added to their short positions, the aggregate was 63.4 percent of the total positions in the market, compared with 36.6 percent classified as hedgers.

"This distribution of open contracts between speculators and hedgers in onions," noted the CEA report, "does not differ materially, however, with that observed in other commodities."[2]

Such surveys made no difference to traders like Siegel, whose sharp elbows went with the trading territory in the pits as well as the boardroom. Reared on Chicago's West Side, Siegel was the son of an Orthodox rabbi. Originally planning to follow in his father's footsteps, young Joseph had a last-minute change of heart. One month shy of becoming an ordained rabbi, he decided instead to pursue a career as a journalist and entered Northwestern University. After graduation, he worked in radio stations in Iowa and Indiana until 1950 when his brother, Sam, convinced him to return to Chicago and try his hand in the commodities business.

One year later, he opened Siegel Trading Company, a CME clearing member. While his brother handled the wholesale end of the produce business, Siegel developed into an aggressive trader. With the collapse of the onion market, he concentrated on trading eggs at the Chicago Merc and Maine potatoes at the New York Mercantile Exchange. "I was distressed because the onion ban was affecting my income as a clearinghouse," Siegel said.

To make matters worse, storage eggs were beset with many problems and, in the view of some traders, the usefulness of eggs as a futures vehicle was about to become as outmoded as the Model T. The futility of the situation was reflected in the loss of memberships. By 1960, noted Siegel, the Exchange supported the price of memberships at $3,000. Between 1960 and 1962, more than 30 memberships had been bought back. On top of the membership decline, self-esteem among the members was badly shaken. Suddenly, it seemed, the Exchange had all the appeal of poison ivy.

William Katz sadly summarized the situation: "From the late Fifties through the early Sixties, the storage egg contract was a constant attraction for would-be manipulators and attempted cornerers. Whatever remained of our public image as a place of investment was being replaced with the image that the CME was a place for highly trained professional speculators and immoral wolves of the money world."

It was a period during which the nation was disturbed by cold-war ultimatums and distracted by the Camelotish dazzle of the youngest president in American history. William Katz became CME chairman in 1959. He succeeded Carl E. Sturm, an out-of-towner from Manawa, Wisconsin, who had been a strong financial backer of Senator Joseph R. McCarthy.

"He was like a father to Joe McCarthy," Harris said. Sturm's one-term chairmanship reflected the impatience of a beleaguered membership, believed Harris. "He [Sturm] was a scapegoat," Harris said, "but the members were hoping for a different type of leadership, one hopefully that would restore a sense of unity."

Katz also served only one term. In 1960 the board elected Cola A. Gray, a former egg buyer for a Boston grocery chain, who had served under General Pershing in World War I. Gray, well into his sixties, was a dignified man with a rather droll style. He offered the members neither charisma nor quixotic solutions at a time when pressure for decisive action was building among the members, both young and old. The outcome of his tenure was predictable. Harris observed, "Few of the members would listen to him. And that made his job virtually impossible. He resigned because of the pressure."

In a special election, Katz was chosen to finish out Gray's term. By now the members were anxious to pick a strong chairman for what they saw as some tough years ahead of them. Perhaps no one expressed this attitude better than the elder statesman of the day, John V. McCarthy, whose lean, saturnine face and fiery rhetoric reflected honest, emotional indignation. A charter member of the Exchange and active in the business for more than fifty years, McCarthy served as a CME director during 1961.

In mid-December, shortly before the election of a new chairman, he summed up his feelings in a letter received by each of his Exchange colleagues:

> I proclaim to all our members that our legislative departments are sorely in need of a blood transfusion. Without new blood, our chance for progress is nil, and our chance for limited success is slim. . . . I cannot look into the future without becoming alarmed about our security. We are at a crossroads and no matter how hopeful we may be, I frankly say to you that never before have I seen so many hurdles in our path. Most of our troubles are of our own making and as long as we continue to perpetuate professional and pleasurable office seekers in our legislative departments, we can't go anywhere but downhill.

For most of the year, McCarthy had been urging his fellow board members to discuss the creation of a research department. His repeated requests, however, were ignored to the point where he told his colleagues, "My associates on the board have treated my recommendations as though research is something foreign to our line of business."

McCarthy was right, and Harris was the first to admit it. Research had become "foreign" to the Exchange. "We had become so preoccupied with the onion problem in trying to save what we had, that indeed we did lose our grip on researching new futures contracts," admitted Harris. "You see, in our hearts we really didn't believe Congress would ban onion trading."

McCarthy's plea was seen as more than just the ranting of an old warhorse about to head for the pastures of retirement. "His comments and observations made a lot of sense," said Bill Katz. For many institutions and corporations, the inability to shrug off the past eroded confidence, thereby preventing clear and decisive strategy. Instead, an organization became passive and it was only a matter of time before managerial atrophy set in. Though they hadn't stated the problem exactly in this manner, the CME officials (prodded by the McCarthyists of the day) were anxious to push the Exchange forward, breaking away from the past. This meant that the CME needed an infusion of both contracts and younger members.

"The most crippling thing in our line of business is physical and mental laziness," McCarthy stated. "We may be able to plug along under existing conditions, but to go forward to success is comparable to operating an insurance association with a membership limited to people over 70 years of age. . . . Unless we make a drastic change, both in our thinking and management, we will simply dry up and blow away. . . . All that is needed is foresight, energy, a willingness to work, and a crop of new engineers at the throttle."

Predictably, Bill Katz won the chairmanship in 1961. He was the logical choice, having been a director for a number of years and having served as chairman in 1959. Moreover, he was popular among the members. About four months later, the CME was set to begin trading frozen broilers on 1 April 1962.

In January of that year, however, Harris found himself back in Washington—this time testifying before the Agriculture Department in an effort to head off legislation that would limit the production of turkeys through the so-called Turkey Marketing Orders.

"It seems logical," Harris told the committee members, "that artificially high prices can reduce consumption and invite substitutions. We wouldn't want Polish ham or hot dogs to replace turkey for Thanksgiving."

Harris argued that strict government controls, if successful, could stabilize prices, but only at the expense of individual initiative and will. Through farm programs that were born in the 1890s, grew to giant proportions in the New Deal days of the 1930s, and kept growing in the 1940s and 1950s, the U.S. government underwrote the American farmer. And it was continuing to do so into the 1960s. Whenever the government in its infinite wisdom thought that the city folks might object to grocery store prices, it could, and sometimes did, manipulate commodity prices by dumping from the huge and expensive surpluses accumulated under the price support programs.

It was this point of view that Harris and other CME officials in subsequent years would continually present to congressional hearings whenever the threat of government price fixing reared its head. After all, Harris would remind congressmen, the commodity exchanges were auction markets where interested persons met and, through a formalized system, established the price of commodities according to their best judgment of the free-market forces of supply and demand.

"While one is willing to make sacrifices for the public good," Harris reasoned, "one rejects such sacrifices for a cause which would seem to further lead this country toward a regimented society."

By now it was becoming clear—even to former critics—that the ban on onion trading had been premature. In the 29 January 1960 edition of *The Produce News*, a popular trade publication, a headline in the lead story stated: "Futures' End Has Not Aided Onion Market."

Reporting on the weakness in onion prices, the article somberly noted,

> For a number of years there was trading in onion Futures, and a good many people, including some members of the trade such as dealers and growers, believed that all the onion business needed was to get rid of Futures. So they got rid of Futures and the market has gone from bad to worse. This is not to say the market would have been better if Future trading had been permitted to continue. However, it could not have been worse.
>
> It was a victory for those who like to pass restrictive laws, but it put no money in growers' pockets. Some evidence would indicate that it has taken money out. . . . Growers held back their onions in the belief that better prices were coming. They didn't come, and now growers would like to sell.
>
> This should prove once and for all that you have to do something besides abolish Future trading to make people eat onions. . . .

Such journalistic diatribes were too little too late. "The damage had been done," said Harris. "All the government analysis, miscalculations, and apologies from those who were quick to shoot from the hip meant little to an exchange that was forced into a defensive posture. Our momentum had come to a screeching halt."

The CME was no longer in overdrive, but inching along in second gear. The onion loss left many Merc members morose and distracted. Their characteristic ebullience did not reemerge until 1961 with the introduction of a strangely named commodity called *pork bellies*—and the rise of the Young Turks.

"At this point, the outlook for the Chicago Mercantile Exchange might have been judged hopeless," observed economist Holbrook Working of the period immediately following the onion futures ban. In a 1970 paper entitled "Economic Functions of Futures Markets," Working put the CME's plight in perspective, along with the historical relevance of an exchange teetering on the brink of extinction.

"There is drama in the story of the Chicago Mercantile Exchange," Working wrote, "and reason why the highlights of the story should be noted at the beginning of what may seem a prosaic set of inquiries into economic questions. The dramatic aspects of the story are directly related to major economic issues concerning the functions of commodit[ies], their usefulness in society, and the framing of public policy toward them."

By 1960 the CME had lost all merchandising trade, as had the nation's other exchanges. Its commodities had dwindled to less than a grocery bagful. Futures trading in butter had long since died. Egg futures were an endangered species faced with changes in seasonal output, which reduced the need to store eggs. The potato futures showed little prospect as well, since most traders preferred to use the larger and more liquid New York market. The CME's feeble potato future was the sole survivor from thirty years of trying to drum up new business. The outlook, by any stretch of the imagination, was rather dismal. Had the time come to throw in the towel? "Some, especially our competitive exchanges, might have said 'yes' at the time," said Harris. "It was a thought that never entered our minds." Working put it another way: "The Exchange refused to accept the verdict that it must be a victim of technological unemployment at the age of 40." Nearly a decade later, Harris could point to statistics that showed that in August 1969, the Chicago Mercantile Exchange had done more business than any other exchange in the United States, including the Chicago Board of Trade, which meant, in effect, more business than any other exchange in the world.[3]

A great deal took place over those years as the Exchange moved ahead, twisting and turning, careful to keep on track, yet bold enough to innovate. During the three prior decades, Working pointed out, the CME had made a long series of attempts to add new futures contracts to a short list of those that worked. All but two of the attempts failed, but between 1960 and 1966, three new contracts were launched. Each succeeded. Why the change in the CME's fortunes? Working thought he knew the answer and explained it this way: "Among the reasons for this remarkable change in the fortunes of the Exchange was the emergence and acceptance of a new idea to guide the choice of a commodity in which to introduce futures trading: the idea that a futures market could succeed only to the degree that it could attract business from handlers of a commodity."

Today that idea seems obvious. But it wasn't until 1953, when Working published "Futures Trading and Hedging" in the *American Economic Review*. In fact, some economists initially considered it rather a dubious theory. But Working had the statistics to support his views and, "Almost immediately," he said, "it received striking confirmation." Actually, primary credit for the idea, Working noted, was based on the research of J.W.T. Duvel, the first chief of the Grain Futures Administration in 1922. Trained in the natural sciences, Duvel—

a strong advocate of research based on quantitative information—produced the first evidence that something was wrong with the traditional concept of a futures market. Over the vigorous objections of the grain exchanges in the 1920s, he began to gather statistics on open futures contracts, compiling two sets—one for hedgers, another for speculators.

Duvel had learned about the futures markets directing grain standardization investigations for the Department of Agriculture. During World War I he served with the U.S. Grain Corporation and for a while after the war was a grain merchant. By the late 1920s, the statistics he had accumulated revealed a fact that shattered the conventional wisdom of the day: Futures trading was not solely dependent on speculators. To the contrary, the open contracts on each futures market showed a tendency to vary in relation to the number of hedging contracts outstanding. Duvel's findings were published in a 1941 Department of Agriculture bulletin. A year later, Harold S. Irwin, an economist brought to the Commodity Exchange Authority by Duvel, began his study of the Chicago Mercantile Exchange. It was the first statistical study of the butter and egg markets by an economist. His conclusion: Futures trading in both commodities developed from the need of the handlers to hedge. Irwin's conclusions didn't reach print until 1954, despite the fact that he had sent his report to Working in 1946.

It took more than hedgers, however, to keep the gears of futures markets turning. Liquidity was the lubricant. Speculators were needed—lots of them. "Without a liberal volume of speculation," Working observed, "no futures market could pay its way from commission charges as low as those on true futures markets. . . . And volume of transactions depends much more on speculative trade than on use of the futures contract by handlers of the commodity."

The Merc, for instance, had lapsed into a liquidity lull for three years after trading in onions had resumed, following World War II. But the situation changed in the 1949 to 1950 season, when a moderately sized crop brought prices to growers three times as high as they had been the previous year. Many of the dealers thought the price was too high and chose to hedge in the futures market, and that brought on a corresponding increase in speculative activity. From that time on, the market prospered until the ban.

There were, of course, other reasons for the CME's survival in the wake of the onion ban. Much of it had to do with unrest among the younger rank-and-file members who believed in the CME's future, but not in its internal politics. They saw the leadership as staid, nepotistic, and unable to let go of the past.

The Board of that era was, for the most part, made up of sons, in-laws, or associates of the founding fathers of the Exchange. Among the Merc leaders at the time were William Katz, Nate Wertheimer, Robert Asher, Michael Weinberg, and Lee Freeman, Sr., the Exchange's outside counsel. Harris called the coterie the "Highland Park Five," in reference to the affluent North Shore suburb along Lake Michigan where many of them lived. "Their tenure of office was always a foregone conclusion," said Robert O'Brien, who would go on to become chairman. "They held omnipotent power over the decisions of the Exchange and seemed financially satisfied with their share of things as they then stood."

The rumblings became louder among the so-called Young Turks, one of whom was Melamed, a member of the Broker's Club, which he described as a "half-clandestine group." The Broker's Club was certainly all cloak and no dagger, yet it was visible enough to have its own stationery with the letterhead stating in bold uppercase **THE BROKER'S CLUB.** Beneath that appeared "Room 1203" and the CME address, 110 North Franklin Street, Chicago 6, Illinois.

The Broker's Club was part social and part activist. Kenneth Birks and Robert O'Brien, John V. McCarthy's son-in-law, were founding members of the Club in 1951, but it remained dormant throughout most of the 1950s. Initially the Club was more of a social organization, but there was little need for a club within a club, explained Birks. "After all, the entire Exchange was like one big club in the early Fifties. I can remember Harry Redfearn saying we were nothing but a bunch of chicken farmers, just a lot of characters. There was less competition and more camaraderie. The place was small."

No one can recall the exact date on which the club was founded. O'Brien, 72 years old in 1991, can muster only vague recollections about the organization. Neither can anybody quite pinpoint the motivation of its members, but the primary purposes of the club stand clear in Birks's memory: "To somehow exert pressure on the governing body in order that it move forward with what we considered progressive and constructive policies and programs; and to work energetically for the election to the Board of new members."

Membership of the Broker's Club, as Melamed put it, "was a dramatic contradiction" to the make-up of the existing Board of Governors. "We were then all relatively young, aggressive and without a stake in the establishment. Moreover, we were, for the most part, financially insecure and had nothing to lose. We were very much dissatisfied with the status quo."

Melamed's faith had been shaped by his own history. Born in Bialystok,[4] Poland, in 1932, Leo was the only child of Faygl and Isaac Melamdovich. His mother had taught first grade in Bialystok and his father was a high school mathematics teacher (*Melamed* means *teacher* in Hebrew) who had published three math books in Yiddish. In 1938, Isaac was elected a councilman of Bialystok, 80 percent of whose population was Jewish.

The Germans invaded in September 1939, and after a harrowing escape involving a 14-day train ride across the frozen expanse of Siberia, and a journey that took one and a half years, the family reached Vladivostok. It was only the beginning of a white-knuckle Odyssey for the then-six-year-old Leo and his parents.

In December 1940, the family arrived at the Japanese port of Niigata, but Isaac made his way to nearby Kobe, a departure point for thousands of Eastern European Jewish immigrants on their way to Shanghai, where they settled. Eventually, he obtained a visa to the United States, based on "the luck of the draw," as Leo remembered it. The family reached Seattle, Washington, in April 1941. They then moved on to New York, as nearly all Jewish immigrants did.

Two months later, the family moved to the northwest side of Chicago, where both his father and mother became teachers at the local Jewish parochial school. By now, young Leo had attended schools in Poland, Lithuania, Russia, Japan, and the United States, and when he entered the Chicago grade school, his primary language was Yiddish. Those early years left him skeptical, wary, and somewhat superstitious. Looking back on the scramble for survival, Leo would one day recall it with levity as the Bialystok Syndrome: Disaster lurks around the next corner and you invite it when you begin bragging about your success. As for the notion of risk, he once told a *New York Times* reporter, "I come from a family of risk-takers. I wouldn't be alive today if my parents hadn't taken incredible risks."

Leo Melamed eventually went to the University of Illinois at Navy Pier and then graduated from John Marshall Law School. While at law school, he began his career at the Merc as a $25-a-week clerk in 1953, and borrowed $3,000 from his father two years later to buy his first seat (probably his father's entire life savings). He still jokes about naïvely mistaking Merrill Lynch Pierce Fenner and Smith for a law firm when he applied for the clerk position. Apocryphal or not, once he stepped on the Merc floor into the tumult, he knew that was where he wanted to be someday. Almost from the start he became part-time lawyer and part-time trader.

While practicing law with partner Maury Kravitz, the two founded a futures trading firm called Dellsher Investment Company, Inc. in 1964. (The name was derived from the combined first names of Melamed's daughter Idel and Kravitz's daughter Sheryl.) A year later Melamed gave in to the trading itch. Kravitz got the law firm and Melamed took Dellsher, along with their heavily mortgaged 33-foot cabin cruiser, which he had won on the toss of a coin. In 1965 he teamed up with a savvy trader, George Fawcett, and turned Dellsher into a clearing firm. (Six years later, Kravitz traded in his law shingle for a trading badge on the Merc and has been there ever since.) But well before Melamed had established himself on Merc turf, he had tangled with the Merc's inner circle, the sons and grandsons of the Exchange founders, who could control both the trading and politics. The trading cliques that dominated the Merc's traditional butter-and-egg futures was well entrenched. But Melamed, a charismatic and articulate young man who had acted in Chicago's Yiddish Theater, relished the Merc's rough-and-tumble political arena.[5]

By May 1961 the battle lines had been drawn. "A lot of people who weren't in the butter and egg crowd were clamoring to have a voice," the late Stephen Greenberg, who was named chairman in 1964 at the age of 34, told the *Chicago Tribune*.

Melamed characterized the period as the "beginning of a war which was to continue for the better part of the next five years." The rules of the Exchange at the time were "pretty arcane," as Birks put it. They had been neglected for years with little update. One rule in particular centered on the quorum needed to hold a membership meeting. Of the 500 CME members, 300—or about 60 percent—were needed to hold a meeting. The percentage was so high that it effectively prevented a meeting from being held. Consequently, the chairmanship was virtually controlled by a small group of traders, passed on like a baton in a relay race.

Melamed, the only attorney-member of the Broker's Club at the time, was thrust into the role of legal advisor. He persuaded the Club that no matter what the Board of Governors might say, the CME was an Illinois corporation and as such was subject to corporate state laws. He explained: "It was my contention that a duly-passed resolution of the members, lowering the quorum requirements at a duly qualified members meeting, would necessarily have to be accepted by the Board. I cautioned, however, that a court process might be necessary."

No one at the time wanted an intramural fight that would split the Exchange into two factions—the old guard and the new blood. But perhaps the feistiness of the younger traders was a reflection of the times. After all, youth was a part of the New Frontier, whose destiny was directed from the White House, the home of the youngest man ever elected to the office of president of the United States. There was a sense of immediacy, a push for equality in the administration of John F. Kennedy. That mood seemed to carry across the nation, filtering into all sorts of organizations and institutions. It had always been present among the futures exchanges.

From the early days, the intent of the CME and the others was simple enough: to promote an egalitarian environment. The exchanges were based on the notion that free markets for free men was the purest form of competition. Moreover, the traders did indeed own the Exchange. A membership gave an individual the right to trade on the floor of the Exchange and to vote for a board of governors that handled the business of the not-for-profit corporation, which in some ways bore resemblance to a trade association. The Exchange was "a complete Copernican system," as CBOT archivist Owen Gregory described it, "with the trader in the middle." As the exchanges grew more sophisticated, they became more like self-contained universes with everything—financial, legal, and logistical support packaged down to the lighting and heating—in orbit around the trader.

The Young Turks weren't caught up in any kind of grand scheme to create a sleeker institution with a youthful air. Their strategy was driven by a more practical sense—survival. "We were very conscious of the fact that we were about to be driven to oblivion because we were a one commodity exchange," Melamed said to explain the motivation some years later. Thus, the new guard found an ally in a chain-smoking, black-haired, wiry coiled spring of a man they called Leo, who was a novice attorney with a flair for rhetoric. They set out to rebuild the infrastructure of an exchange fallen on hard times. Many had blamed the entrenched Board for some hasty and poorly executed decisions, such as backing away from a Supreme Court verdict on the onion ban.

"It wasn't exactly a palace revolt," said Harris. "The younger members didn't set out with a sweeping series of management changes aimed at calming warring factions. They had legitimate gripes."

The strategy was to call for a special meeting of the Merc membership in order to revise the quorum requirements. The number set was 100, or 20 percent, as opposed to the 60 percent in the existing rule, otherwise known as Rule 109. But there was a catch-22: A quorum of 300 members was needed to call the special meeting.

It was difficult to be optimistic in those days, as there was a gray mood in the air to begin with. The traders were hoping for a tomorrow no worse than the bleak days that had overtaken the Exchange. They set about the business of obtaining sufficient proxies for the meeting, a task which was next to impossible and never before attempted. Among the Broker's Club members who solicited proxies were Bill Henner, Ken Birks, Marlowe King, Jerry March and Leo Melamed.

Methodically, the group launched a letter-writing campaign to solicit proxies from the out-of-town members, while rallying the Chicago-based members with the cry of reform. Smugly, the old guard and the Board were positive that the meeting would never take place. "The thought of trying to contact members and solicit proxies was considered too much trouble by the then-Exchange establishment," said Harris. But the rather small group of traders that constituted the core of the Broker's Club was determined. "We worked hard to make sure the letters went out to the members," said Birks. "We were pretty well organized."

They were indeed. On 14 June 1961 there were present in person or by proxy the required number of members for a legal quorum. Thus, the meeting was held on a warm, humid afternoon, as Harris recalled, "after the close of trading when everyone could concentrate on the matters at hand."

The proposition was presented and adopted by the membership as the Turks held their breaths. There was a complicated mix of emotions to deal with, based on a campaign that illuminated character and vision. The mechanics had kicked into place a sort of momentum, yet no one was certain what the autocratic Merc Board would actually do. In the minds of many of the board members, Katz conceded, nothing was accomplished until *they* voted to lower the quorum requirements.

Under the chairmanship of Bill Katz, the Board immersed itself in discussion of the matter the following day. Sometimes talk bordered on polite debate, but more often than not, it lapsed into heated argument. "Tempers were hot and there was plenty of cursing," recalled Katz, who "let the tempers fly so they could get it out of their systems." Within an hour, Katz had the meeting under control and the Board was voting on what already had been voted on—and approved—by the membership. Joe Sieger moved that the Board adopt the amendment to Rule 109, John Coleman seconded the motion, and there was unanimous approval.[6] Thus, the board gave its nod and the requirement was lowered to the realistic number of 100.

The matter was over, and from all appearances, there were no apparent hard feelings between the camps. Clearly it wasn't a case of generational chauvinism that pushed the Turks to seek change, nor was it the iconoclasm of the Sixties. There was genuine need for change from the old ways, if the Merc intended to keep up with the times, or indeed survive at all.

For the Board and the old guard, there was a lesson to be learned: compromise was inevitable and the old ways could no longer be kept merely for the sake of tradition. For the Broker's Club, it was a victory, but not the kind that it could savor and boast about with chest-pounding smugness. Rather, it was the kind to be grabbed for the moment, then quickly let go of in order to continue the business at hand. It was also a sign of the times and what the Merc elders could expect in the months ahead.

It represented the first major breakthrough for the members in imposing their will on the administration of the Exchange.

13

Slicing the Bacon

On the afternoon of 1 September 1960, the CME Board approved an additional $1,000 for the committee in search of new futures contracts. Six months later, Glenn Andersen, chairman of the committee, reported that progress had been made in the development of a potentially new contract that had most of the members scratching their heads in bewilderment.

"What the hell is a pork belly?" Katz asked Andersen.

"It's the part of the pig that bacon comes from," he answered, adding, "the uncured bacon slabs from which breakfast rashers are cut."

"Can't we call them another name?" wondered Katz.

"The government won't let us. That's what they're called and that's what we have to call them."

Thus, the unlikely name for a new futures contract began to take shape. There was some discussion that perhaps "unprocessed bacon" be used, and one radio announcer called them "pork tummies." But "pork bellies" stood. "As it turned out," notes Mark Powers, the CME's first economist, "the name 'pork bellies' was so unusual it worked to the advantage of the Exchange." Nevertheless, pork bellies were a rather obscure commodity, and for that reason, among others, they were slow getting off the trading ground.

Helping Andersen work on the belly contract was Henry F. Adlam, hired as a special consultant. At a special board meeting on 11 May 1961, the business of putting together a belly contract took on a serious note. "The Board recommended trading in bellies for the December 1961 contract and that the February and April 1962 contracts be opened simultaneously," recalled Kenneth Mackay, who a week earlier had been named assistant to Harris at $12,000 a year, replacing the retired A.M. Kraemer. "We also decided that the publicity committee would begin a campaign to advertise pork bellies," said Mackay.

It would be at least 18 months before the crest of a speculative wave in pork bellies washed over the pits of the CME, bringing with it record volume and bedlam to the rickety old quarters. There were several reasons why the pork belly market was slow to take off. First, the initial contract did not appeal to hedgers.

Without hedgers, speculators would not be drawn into the market. And without enough trading volume and open interest to ensure sufficient orders in the pit, the spreads between bids and offers ebbed to their competitive minimums.

A second reason was equally basic: a lack of marketing. Like any other financial service, futures contracts had to be marketed, packaged, advertised, promoted, financed, and distributed. After all, image was important. The extent to which the public could identify with a particular commodity provided the clue as to the ease or difficulty with which the contract could be marketed. One of the reasons futures trading in live cattle a few years later was such an immediate success, according to Mark Powers, "is that the public speculators knew what a steer looked like and knew that steers became steaks. Trading in live beef futures conjured up romantic images of old west cattle drives and cowboys. People who bought cattle futures felt just like the cattle barons."

Over-romanticism? Perhaps, and perhaps not. In any case, pork bellies were about as well known to the average trader as was the theory of particle physics. "They were not easily recognized, identified with, or understood by people at the start of trading," observed Powers in a doctoral dissertation he had done on the pork belly contract some years later, before joining the CME.

Prior to the opening of the contract, in fact, there was some lively debate among Merc members as to whether to list the new contract as pork bellies or simply as "unprocessed bacon." However, much more important to the readers than the name of the commodity were the amount, kind, quality, and frequency of information about the price-making forces affecting pork bellies. That's what spun the markets—information, the constant flow of it like a tributary leading to a vast river basin. Sometimes that flow moved at a snail's pace, and at other times it poured in with a rush that sent traders into a frenzy, firing off bids and offers at each other.

Exchanges did not set prices, but merely registered them, and because the prices paid on an exchange like the CME were monitored by merchants and shippers from Rotterdam to Singapore, the key to success was communications— from the very basic to the most sophisticated of an era. Information moved markets.

On 3 August 1961 the Board set the date for opening trading in pork bellies to be 18 September 1961. (Initial margins were set at $500 for speculative, $400 for hedging, and $200 for straddling.) Before the opening, word went out about the new contract. Members of the commodities committee met on the floor of the Exchange on 22 August at 3:15 P.M. with brokers and customers' representatives to answer any questions about the new contract, which was to trade between the hours of 9:30 A.M. and 12:55 P.M.. Each contract was for 30,000 pounds of uncured, frozen bacon slabs, which were two inches thick and weighed about twelve pounds each. So convinced that pork bellies would take off, the board appropriated $2,000 for the continued services of Henry Adlam as "Frozen Pork Bellies Consultant."

Had their enthusiasm merely masked a veneer of skepticism? Despite the fact that a new contract was about to be tested, there was still a deep-seated longing for the old days. A week before the belly contract was to open, the Board retained H.B. Raskin for $2,000 until the end of the year. His assignment: to survey the mood in Washington with a view to open a campaign to resume trading in onion futures. The politicians, he found out, weren't ready to reconsider. His advice: Forget it. And they did.

Nevertheless, the pork belly contract began trading in September 1961 as green-jacketed traders squeezed into the pit the size of a small pigpen to launch the new contract. That year, cash commodities had risen modestly.[1] But while a growing population clamored for more protein, heavy beef production, plentiful hogs, and a record number of turkeys and broilers exerted downward pressures on meat prices. The result for the pork belly contract was disastrous. In the first 16 months of trading, less than a thousand pork belly contracts were traded.

"The early contracts in pork bellies were poorly written and poorly marketed," said Harris, "and the timing was off due to sizable production in beef, hogs, and broilers. There was too much of everything and prices were soft."

Harris and the Board, however, hadn't stopped with pork bellies. A single-commodity exchange, they had painfully learned, was too vulnerable. Even if a new contract took off like a rocket, it was still subject to the cyclical nature of supply and demand. "The basics, we could never forget the basics," said Harris. So, in an attempt to hedge their strategy, they began casting for other possible contracts.

In 1962, for instance, Harris tried to convince the board that there was viability in a futures market in Florida orange juice concentrate that would benefit the orange growers. He had based his convictions on a study completed in June 1962 by a group of Harvard Business School faculty members on behalf of the Florida Citrus Mutual. The Harvard professors had strongly recommended a frozen orange juice concentrate futures market. The CME board voted against it. Harris even looked into pecans as a possibility for a futures contract.

The Board did settle on a contract to its liking. On 1 April 1962 the Merc opened trading in frozen broilers. The way for trading in broilers had been paved in August 1957, when President Eisenhower signed into law a long-debated mandatory inspection program for all poultry moving in interstate commerce. The bill standardized and improved the quality and grading of broilers, a prerequisite for any commodity to be efficiently traded on a futures exchange. Hedgers didn't use the contract, and a year later, in February 1963, it was delisted.

The Merc didn't stop there. In September 1963, Harris, addressing the National Poultry, Butter & Egg Association convention in Chicago, announced plans to initiate trading in frozen shrimp. Suddenly the Merc found itself in the pages of *Fishing Gazette*. The contract began trading on 11 November 1963, with initial delivery made only to Texas warehouses. First it was brown shrimp only, then white and pink shrimp in addition, with delivery expanded to warehouses in the twelve Gulf states.

The idea of a shrimp contract wasn't all that fishy. The U.S. per capita consumption of shrimp had grown 75 percent since the years just after World War II, to 1.56 pounds in 1964. (Total consumption had hit a record 299 million pounds in 1964, a 6 percent gain over the previous year, for a dollar value of roughly $270 million.) Moreover, the shrimp contract had the blessings of the shrimp industry and the federal government's Bureau of Commercial Fisheries.

Shrimp certainly offered traders plenty to speculate on. As admitted shrimp-lover Gilbert Miller, then a CME governor who headed the committee that recommended the shrimp contract, put it for the *Chicago Daily News*: "It's a perfect commodity. It's mysterious, glamorous. You can get figures on how many cattle, hogs, chickens there are, but I dare you to try and say how big the shrimp crop out in the sea will be." There were no takers.

Modestly successful at first, the shrimp contract never got going even after it was revised in April 1965 with delivery to take place at any exchange-approved warehouse, regardless of location. (Because imported shrimp accounted for more than 50 percent of the shrimp introduced into commercial channels each year since 1960, the new rules permitted shrimp to be caught anywhere in the Western hemisphere, not just in the Gulf of Mexico.) Six months later, the contract was delisted.

For a time, it appeared as if pork bellies might suffer the fate of shrimp. Trading had gotten off to such a slow start that Barry Lind, who became a CME member in 1962, remembered that "the men played gin rummy in the afternoons because there was nothing to do." He was 24 years old at the time, and he and his young colleagues would take long breakfasts to console one another.

The times, to say the least, were unsettling. The shock of the assassination of President Kennedy on 22 November 1963 had stunned the nation. President Lyndon Johnson pledged to continue the New Frontier, adding some humanitarian embellishment under a fresh slogan, the Great Society. He had set in motion the most ambitious program of social improvement in thirty years, including a landmark education bill, a major civil rights bill, and a series of anti-poverty projects. It was a time when the American economy was still bulling ahead through the postwar years. There were some 90,000 Americans who were millionaires, compared with just 27,000 in the early 1950s. The stock market had come full circle from the crash of 1929: More than 20 million Americans held stocks listed on the New York Stock Exchange worth $410 billion, nearly a ten-fold increase from the holdings since World War II. The migration of poor rural blacks and whites from the South to the North continued. American agriculture was also booming, producing 60 percent more food than it did in 1940 with far more efficiency. (The number of labor-hours needed to do the nation's farming dropped from 20 million in 1940 to 9 million in 1963.) The once-mighty farm bloc had lost its political clout as the number of Americans living in urban and suburban areas swelled to 75 percent of the total population by 1963.

Ironically, amid all the prosperity, the Chicago Mercantile Exchange found itself scrambling for an economic foothold. Anxiety and paranoia and a corrosiveness that wore down the spirits of even the CME veterans who had endured the Depression pervaded the atmosphere. The Exchange still hadn't found a contract to replace onions and eggs as 1963 trading volume in the first half was lagging some 25 percent behind that during the same 1962 period. To make matters worse, the CME had to cope with some bad publicity. The Exchange had conducted an investigation in the fall of 1962 of an alleged attempt to manipulate the shell egg market. In the following August, two dealers were expelled for violating rules in connection with trading in the tom-turkey contracts.

Self-doubt began to loom among the Exchange officials. The normally confident and insouciant Harris was feeling the heat from disgruntled members who were blaming their misfortunes on misguided leadership. "I felt the pressure from some," remarked Harris, who abruptly announced his resignation on 1 August 1963. In a letter to the board, Harris said he would resign on 1 November to take a job with Hayden Stone & Company, Inc. as a senior vice president in charge of its rapidly expanding commodity operations. He had served a decade and perhaps it was time to move on, he thought.

The announcement had caught some members off guard. "While the announcement about your plans was indeed a shock," wrote Michael Weinberg, Jr., in a letter to Harris five days later, "I can well imagine that heading the Exchange has been the height of frustration! Please accept my heartfelt wishes for happiness, success and peace of mind in your new work!"

On 24 September 1963 the Board appointed a search committee to find candidates to replace Harris. "We looked from coast to coast and interviewed dozens of prospects," said Bill Katz, who was chairman at the time. "But the committee kept coming up short. No one knew the Exchange like Harris or problems the industry faced. We needed someone to get us through a transition. That someone, we realized, was Harris."

Less than a week before he was to resign, the CME board made an eleventh-hour plea, asking Harris to remain as president. All along, Katz had urged him not to resign at such a crucial point, with new contracts under consideration and the Exchange in flux. "My heart was in the Exchange and I knew I had a lot more to offer," said Harris, who agreed to stay on as president, signing a five-year contract with a raise to boot. Though disappointed, Hayden released Harris from his commitment.

Even with Harris in place, most of the younger members like Barry Lind wondered, "Could the Exchange make it?" The average age of the traders, Lind estimates, was then about 50 and the feeling was that "they had no place to go." But there was one thing that the older traders could teach the younger ones: patience. "We had nothing to lose, just time," said Lind. Trading mainly eggs his first year, Lind earned $3,400. He then turned to pork bellies. By the end of 1963 he was up to $1,000 a month, and in 1964, $1,000 a week, as bellies rose from 40 cents a pound to 55 cents. By 1965, through customer business, he was pulling down $10,000 a month. Pork bellies had caught on. And so had the Barry Linds of the Exchange.

By 1965 the cacophony from the pork belly pit told the story. Supply and demand played a part in the resurgence of the contract that people once laughed at. The speculative wave was unleashed 18 months earlier by a dwindling pig crop. In August 1965 it was about 10 percent smaller than it had been a year earlier with warehouse holdings of frozen bellies—7.4 million pounds on 1 July—down from a 1965 peak of 121 million pounds on 1 May. Moreover, the public's craving for bacon and eggs had risen, despite higher retail prices.

More important, however, was the fact that there was liquidity in the market that began attracting speculators eager for profits and appetites for low margin requirements. Equally happy were the hedgers, pig farmers, feed lot managers and packing companies, all of whom sought insurance against price fluctuations between the farrowing period and a customer's visit to the supermarket.

Suddenly the Merc was fat and happy. A membership now sold for $8,500, up from $3,000 in 1964. And there was talk about modernizing and expanding its shabby trading facilities. An accounting firm had been hired to study the procedures, and some of the younger Exchange members wanted to install a computer and discard the venerable chalkboards. Thanks to the belly of the lowly hog, the Merc was about to turn a profit for the first time since 1961. In the interim, its deficits had totaled $500,000. In all of 1964, trading added up to 249,554 contracts worth about $2 billion, the lowest volume since 1952. But that was all in the past. Now there was a new future to consider. In the first half of 1965, volume soared to a record 343,838 contracts—a 224 percent increase over volume in the first half of 1964—valued at about $3 billion. Nearly 90 percent of the first-half volume was accounted for by pork bellies.

Business was so bullish, in fact, that Lind opened his own retail firm, borrowing $50,000. Four years later, B.J. Lind & Company would be employing 60 people with offices in southern Illinois, Ohio, and California, all pulling in more than $1 million per year in commissions. Lind's was typical of other success stories that were beginning to take shape at the once stodgy exchange, so long dominated by the ghosts of the butter-and-egg men.

Lind was in the vanguard of a youth movement that was sweeping the Exchange and symbolized by Stephen Greenberg, a vice president and national commodity sales manager for Walston & Co., who had become CME chairman in 1964. He was only 34. Half of the Merc Board had been removed from office, replaced by younger members such as Gerald Hirsch, who at 29 became the youngest CME member ever elected a director. He had been a member for several years, having bought a seat with a $6,000 loan from his father-in-law, Saul Stone, then already a 30-year veteran of the butter-and-egg business. But it was only the beginning. It would be another two years before the revolt that gave the Exchange members—both young and old—their full rights.

14

Futures on the Hoof

A renewed wave of optimism rolled across the trading floor of the Chicago Mercantile Exchange on 30 November 1964. At 9:05 A.M., the commodity tickers across the nation flashed:

> The first transaction in Live Beef cattle came in the April contract. The buyer was Larry Ryan of Francis I. Du Pont & Co. The seller was Marlowe King of King & King, Inc., commodity brokers in Chicago representing Stanley Waldner, the Ayionorous Cattle Co., Leavenworth, Kansas. The sale was made at 24.00 dollars cwt.

Thus, the CME stepped into a new dimension of futures trading. Here, for the first time, was a market for a product that was not only non-storable, but alive.

"As the seller for the first contract, I felt I had made a tangible demonstration of my faith and confidence in activity that in my opinion had much to offer the livestock industry," Stanley C. Waldner later wrote in a first-person article in *Feedlot*, a farm magazine for cattle and lamb feeders. "However," he continued, "I didn't regard the decision of the Chicago Mercantile Exchange to treat live beef as a tradeable commodity as the panacea for a collection of near-broke cattlemen."

It was a far cry from a blue Monday that morning when live cattle trading opened active, loud, and colorful. Just before the opening bell, CME employee Susan Kein guided a black Angus steer onto the trading floor, compliments of Colonel Herman E. Lacy[1] of Shamrock Farms in McHenry, Illinois. The steer was flanked by Glen Andersen, chairman of the Beef Cattle Committee, and Harris, in Texas-style garb complete with string tie and ten-gallon hat. In a flurry of noisy bidding, 32 cars of April contracts were traded within minutes of the opening call and 55 during the first half hour. Initial prices ranged from $23.50 to $24 per hundredweight (abbreviated *cwt.*, it is a British unit of measurement equal to 100 pounds) for April, and 16 cars of June were traded quickly at $24.35 to $24.60 per cwt. The first day's tally amounted to 191 contracts representing 4,775 head of choice cattle. The CME was on its

134

way to providing a unique hedging and marketing tool for the nation's then $10 billion per year livestock industry. "The opening of live cattle futures trading was by far the most aggressive of any commodity traded on our exchange up to that point," Harris said.

Although cattleman Waldner believed that the cattle contract had the potential of being an effective management tool for his industry, his feelings were hardly unanimous. "To my dismay," he mused, "I found few other cattlemen who seemed inclined to agree with this thinking."

Trading live cattle indeed was a revolutionary plan, a bold and unique experiment, a mixture of promise and problems that had been greeted with varying degrees of encouragement and suspicion by the livestock and meat industries. Harris envisioned the contract as "a valuable market stabilizer and price-insurance tool for the cattle feeder."

The meat-packing industry, on the other hand, through its American Meat Institute (AMI) spokesperson, stated flatly: "It won't work." At the outset, the AMI was fearful that futures trading in live cattle could become a vehicle for expanding government control over the livestock and meat industry. There were those, too, who envisioned a swarm of speculators engulfing the pit. Gerald Leighton, president of the Chicago Livestock Exchange, noted that "farmers were leery about futures because they don't know the ins and outs of the market. We have not found a great deal of interest among our customers. Maybe it's because of a lack of education in futures trading."

CME chairman Stephen Greenberg countered with a simple summation of intent, one that had been the rationale for virtually all exchanges. "The Exchange," he said, "with futures trading is not supplanting the packer, the cattle feeder or rancher. We are merely giving the buyer and the seller a place to meet and trade under a specific set of rules."

Somewhere in between the CME and its staunchest critics stood the producer organizations, which had adopted a hopeful wait-and-see attitude. "It was pointed out, for example, that during a period of rising prices the futures market might remove speculative profits to cattle feeders as well as speculative losses. Thus, the futures market would limit the cattlemen's profit to feeding efficiency and to the spread between the price of feeder cattle and cattle finished for the market," observed co-authors Jack Sampier and Jerry March in their *Cattle Futures Handbook*.

Regardless, argued the CME officials, the futures market offered something to offset such possible limitations: inexpensive price insurance that would provide stability to cattle production. A farmer with properly hedged feeder cattle could find himself with a much happier banker when the market price began to dip. Pat DuBois of Saulk Centre, Minnesota, vice president of the national Independent Bankers Association, agreed when he told the *Minneapolis Tribune* that very first day shortly after live cattle trading opened, "A farmer will certainly improve his credit standing if he has reduced his loan risks. This could be just one more thing for the farmer and his banker to hang their hats on when they're talking short-term credit."

The critics of the new contract also attacked it on the basis that official grades for live beef were less precise than for other commodities such as grain and frozen pork bellies. Problems would develop, they feared, where contract deliveries were actually made. But the Merc had carefully anticipated that possibility and had worked out satisfactory arrangements with the grading service of the USDA. The delivery plan was based on a series of correlation studies that compared on-the-hoof grading with the later grading of the dressed meat.

Anderson-Clifton Company, specialists in price forecasting and inventory control for packers, had surveyed all aspects of the livestock industry. Their unqualified conclusion: The futures market would be accepted by the livestock industry. "We were convinced that suitable deliveries could be made for both buyers and sellers," said Harris. "And we knew that the beef futures market would stand or fall on the service it provided the industry, just as the pork bellies did."

At first there seemed to be more doubters than believers in the new cattle contract. Waldner painted this bleak picture:

> Paradoxically, the most experienced and highly successful cattlemen in the business found little hope for the tenure of the contract. The decision makers in some of the country's largest commission firms doubted that the delivery conditions which are set forth in the contract could be equitably met to the satisfaction of both the seller and buyer.
>
> Packer order buyers were vocal in their disbelief that a government representative could provide the degree of discrimination required in the evaluation of a contract of steers delivered against the hypothetical "par delivery unit" [25,000 pounds of choice grade or better live steers]. Finally, many of the knowledgeable cattle bankers had mixed emotions as to the desirability of superimposing commodity loan practices on already overburdened cattle accounts. In general, this was the situation that prevailed throughout most of December, January, and February.

By March, the doomsayers were scratching their heads. Trading volume in live beef and the open interest in contracts were beginning to shape a viable market. Could the experts have been wrong? "It had surpassed the goals attained by pork bellies, the wonder commodity," reflected Waldner, "after the latter had been offered for trading by the exchange for an equal period." With some 150 contracts traded daily during March, the success of the beef contract seemed ensured. In the first eight months, more than 32,000 cattle contracts had been traded.

"Cattlemen, packers, and speculators were learning to use the contract," noted Waldner. "Some had begun to appreciate its worth and spoke strongly in favor of it in the face of the sphinx-like reservation which characterized the livestock industry as a whole."

Both the futures market and the spot market in cattle had closed in line with each other. Only one test remained. How well would delivery work? There were

20 contracts involved, of which the first two were to be delivered to Chicago on 26 April at the Union Stockyards through the commission house of Walters & Dunbar. The cattle had been consigned by Lloyd Ewald and Cliff Haden of Rochelle, Illinois and were shipped on 25 April.

Shortly after 10:00 A.M. on Monday, 26 April, two USDA inspectors—David Mangum and John McKenna—arrived at the pens. They spent about five minutes at each cattle pen, assessing the cattle in accordance with grading regulations. Twenty-one of the cattle were graded "choice" and four "good." The yield of the steers was estimated as within the specifications of the futures contract (61 percent), and although four of the head were considered to be potentially over-weight, none exceeded one inch of fat over the twelfth rib, reported the graders. And so it went. The first delivery was considered an unqualified success in the eyes of Waldner and his colleagues. Why shouldn't it have been? As Greenberg put it, "enormous amounts of time and effort went into the development" of what the Exchange believed to be "a fair and workable program."

Timing, too, had helped. The new contract was launched just as the nation's cattle feeders were reeling from nearly two years of depressed markets. More-over, Americans were beginning to eat more beef, a trend that would carry through the 1970s and beyond.

Of the historic live cattle contract, University of Wisconsin professor Henry H. Bakken in 1970 remarked, "Some futures contracts have been formulated prematurely and failed because those concerned were not ready for change. Similarly, some contracts have been offered belatedly with indifferent success. In forming the live cattle futures in 1964, it appears from subsequent events that the timing was propitious. The officials of the Chicago Mercantile Exchange are to be commended for their foresight, whether they were clairvoyant or just lucky."

By the end of 1964, it was evident that the CME's strategy was more than a cow-jumped-over-the-moon fantasy. "In retrospect," observed Sampier and March, "the year 1965 went into the record books as a phenomenal year for the Chicago Mercantile Exchange—the year that brought home the Beef and Bacon."

The live cattle contract had become the third most actively traded on the Merc in 1965, behind frozen pork bellies (638,031 contracts traded) and frozen eggs. In total, some 900,000 contracts traded that year, triple the 1964 volume and nearly double that of 1960, the previous record year. The activity was duly reflected in the price of memberships, which had climbed from $4,500 in November 1964, when cattle trading began, to $15,000 in December 1965.

The CME didn't stop there. Exactly a year to the day after the original cat-tle contract traded, a second cattle contract was inaugurated. This one was a live cattle futures contract for Western delivery at Artesia-Los Angeles. On 30 November 1965 the first contract was traded in a historical encore: Stanley Waldner sold the first contract. Waldner's Western contract for April 1966 was bought at $23.65 by the Elkhorn Valley Cattle Company of Norfolk, Nebraska. Only five contracts traded that day.

The West Coast contract was part of the Merc's long-range strategy for cattle futures. Harris explained that strategy in the *Cattle Futures Handbook*: "Our decision to open a live cattle contract for Los Angeles delivery in addition to existing contracts calling for Chicago and Omaha deliveries was no hasty decision. When we first drew up specifications for the live cattle contract in 1964, we delayed launching the West Coast delivery until we felt that the live cattle contract had gotten off to a good start."

This time, Greenberg emphasized, the Merc was responding to the industry demands. "[The] West Coast cattle industry and bankers had wanted a western delivery because of existing price differentials," he said. "They told us they wanted to take part in futures trading on the Chicago Mercantile Exchange. Now they have the chance."

Just how successful the CME's live cattle contract was became apparent five months later. On 15 April 1966 the Chicago Board of Trade's executive vice president Warren Lebeck announced plans to trade a live cattle contract. "If imitation is a form of flattery, then we were flattered," said Harris. "But we were also mad." So much so that shortly after Lebeck's announcement, the CME delivered a petition, signed by nearly every member, to the directors of the Board of Trade. Dated 10 May 1966, the petition stated:

> The recent proposal to open live cattle trading on the Chicago Board of Trade has serious implications for the orderly trading of commodities. We are vigorously opposed to such a course of action because we believe:
>
> 1. Trading in the same commodity at two exchanges will cause confusion and uncertainty in the minds of those using the markets.
> 2. Markets on both exchanges will be watered down and the effects of a thin market could be fatal to both contracts.
> 3. Establishment of competing contracts could lead to commission cutting, variance in trading hours and other complications.
>
> Most of all, the opening of a commodity contract on an exchange in the same city is without precedent and has been strongly opposed by industry groups including the National Livestock Feeders Association. The integrity of commodity markets is an important part of our free enterprise system. We believe that your sense of justice and fair play will prevail and you will reconsider your decision which could have a seriously detrimental effect on both the Chicago Board of Trade and the Chicago Mercantile Exchange.

The lobbying effort did not stop there. Along with the petition, Harris and new CME chairman Nathan Wertheimer, who had replaced Greenberg in 1966, sent a letter directly to the Board of Trade's chairman, Robert L. Martin. The letter, aimed at the conscience of Martin, a long-time friend of Harris, was fashioned as an appeal to reasonable business judgement. It stated, in part,

Please consider this a formal request to your Board of Directors to please refrain from opening a futures contract in live cattle. . . . Much of the speculative buying business which comes to both of our markets and provides liquidity for hedgers as well as commissions to the wire houses and floor brokerage for floor members flows through such commission firms as Merrill Lynch, Bache, Thompson & McKinnon, etc. If we trade in the same commodity in the same city there will be much confusion as where orders should go, contracts at both markets will be thin and watered down and the market on either Exchange may never be allowed to mature fully. . . . If competition starts in one commodity, it might well spread to others and the harmful effects [could] be very damaging at a time when we are all attempting to survive and get back to free markets for all commodities. . . . Please do not interpret any of this as critical of the Chicago Board of Trade, which obviously is the dominant Exchange for commodity trading in the entire country and doing from eighty to ninety percent of the total commodity business. . . . I do not believe that it would be the desire of your organization or to its long-run advantage to have a virtual monopoly on all commodity trading. . . . I am sure you know that we have spent many thousands of dollars and hundreds of hours of hard work researching, promoting and inaugurating this exciting new market in live beef cattle which so far has been successful and won favorable acceptance from all elements of the livestock industry. . . .

In a subsequent letter, Martin told the CME officials that the wheels had already been set in motion. A vote among the Board of Trade members to establish trading in live cattle was scheduled for late summer. On 29 August 1966 the CBOT members voted on the proposed contract. The result was predictable: 416 for and 267 against. Trading was to begin on 4 October 1966.

The CBOT was no stranger to beef trading. It had begun trading a steer carcass beef contract on 5 April 1965, and by the end of 1966, the contract was delisted because of a lack of open interest and liquidity. The counterpart to the steer carcass contract of the CBOT was the dressed beef contract offered by the CME. It had a shorter life than the CBOT's carcass contract. The first carlot of dressed beef carcasses traded 15 February 1965, and the last carlot nine months later, on 19 November 1965. The total number of trades during the life of the contract was a paltry 689 carlots.

With the dressed beef contracts, the two Chicago exchanges had met head-on for the first time. The result, reported *BusinessWeek* in August 1965, was that potential investors were so confused that neither contract caught on. (Significantly, the CBOT had no plans for trading either pork bellies or live hogs.) Nevertheless, the CBOT remained determined to challenge the CME head-to-head with a "fat-cattle" contract. The CBOT, it turned out, wasn't the only competitor. The Kansas City Board of Trade also ventured into live cattle with a "feeder cattle" contract that began trading on 20 June 1966, two months before the CBOT was to launch its live steer contract. Moreover, the CBOT was about to face an unwanted competitor of its own. The New York Produce Exchange was set to begin trading a soybean contract on 2 September 1966—one of the CBOT's major grains. (The Produce Exchange contract called for 2,500-bushel units, compared with 5,000-bushel units for the CBOT contract.)

Meanwhile, the CME found itself an ally in at least one wirehouse. A month before the CBOT was to commence trading in its live cattle contract, Werner Lehnberg, head of commodities trading in Goodbody & Company's New York office, sent a memo to the firm's partners, branch office managers, and retail brokers.

> It is unfortunate this second live cattle futures contract was permitted to come into existence in the same city. As you know, trading in an identical live cattle futures contract was inaugurated on the Chicago Mercantile Exchange on 30 November 1964. This contract has attracted the widespread interest of the livestock industry as well as speculators, and the success of this market is best illustrated by the fact that the current open commitments in live cattle futures on the Chicago Mercantile Exchange amount to over 13,000 contracts.
>
> In the interest of our customers we strongly recommend that you continue to use the cattle futures market on the Chicago Mercantile Exchange, because it is the primary market and enjoys a relatively high volume of trading which has recently exceeded 1,000 contracts a day. It goes without saying, an active futures market serves the trade and trader best as it offers greater fluidity.
>
> Another factor we must consider is the probability that trading in the same futures contracts on two different exchanges in the same city will create confusion and will lead to many errors. Hence, our recommendation is to confine trading in cattle futures contracts to the Chicago Mercantile Exchange. . . . Unless specified "Board of Trade" we will consider all live cattle futures orders pertaining to the Chicago Mercantile Exchange with the usual differentiation between "live cattle" (which refers to Midwest cattle) and "Western cattle". . . .

In spite of all the pressure from the Merc, the Board of Trade wouldn't back down. "It (the CBOT) saw us as the upstart exchange and was betting on its stature to push us aside," said Harris. The CBOT launched its live cattle contract on 4 October 1966. The contract lasted for some five years (it was delisted in 1971), but it never attracted the trading volume that the CME's cattle contract did. Volume, in fact, for the CBOT's cattle contract peaked in 1969, when it reached a total of only 67,000 contracts, whereas the CME still trades in live cattle futures today. The CBOT's entry into live cattle futures supported a lesson that most exchanges had to learn the hard way: Get to the market first with a unique contract.

A new contract, of course, still had to make economic sense among its users.[2] "Just because we were successful with one contract didn't ensure the success of a related contract," said Bill Katz. The CME officials realized that fact in May 1967 when they received a report from the Andersen-Clifton Company, which had been hired to do a feasibility study on trading cattle carcasses. The study revealed only a limited demand for the contract and that because carcass cattle were not owned by a firm or person long enough, there was no great importance in shifting price risk. In addition, the report stated, "The trade has already developed market channels for the marketing of carcass cattle. The suggested 'pit trading' of carcass cattle would tend to be a duplication of existing services. . . . " The CME therefore took a pass on the notion of carcass cattle and instead considered live hogs as the next area of expansion. There was no longer any question that a live product could be successfully traded on a futures market as well as serve the industry involved.

In his conclusion, however, G. Alvin Carpenter had drawn on two authorities who had studied the influence of futures trading on prices of commodities. One was Holbrook Working, former professor of prices and statistics at Stanford University, who had made a thorough study of hedging. Working said, "It is a form of arbitrage, undertaken most commonly in expectation of a favorable change in the relation between spot and futures prices. The fact that risks are less with hedging than without is often a secondary consideration. The prevalent tendency to regard curtailment of business risks as the main service of futures markets has diverted attention from their probably more important service of promoting economically desirable adjustment of commodity stocks, thereby reducing price fluctuations." In short, Working says hedging is a profitable operation for those who do it right; it makes stocks of commodities available at all times and helps to hold down violent price movements.

The second authority, Deane W. Malott, former president of Cornell University, reported his conclusions in a booklet titled *Does Futures Trading Influence Prices?* He stated,

> The consistent pattern of price trends month by month for products going to market through various types of marketing organizations seems to me to indicate that it must be the supply and demand features of the commodities which determine the price trends—and not the mechanisms which have been set up for serving the buyer and seller. . . . So far as we are able to ascertain, with no axes to grind, the organized futures exchanges do not cause any dislocation of prices, and prices for commodities in which there is futures trading do not vary from fluctuations common to other agricultural products.

15

The Palace Revolt

Frigid arctic blasts were slamming Minneapolis in November 1966 when E. B. Harris arrived at the Leamington Hotel to present a paper before the 15th National Agricultural Credit Conference American Bankers Association. Harris was part of a panel that included Iver M. Brook, a vice president of Bache & Co., and Arthur G. Osgood, a vice president of Harris Trust & Savings Bank in Chicago. Both were CME members and students of futures trading.

"I remember it was bitter cold outside," said Harris, "and there were a lot of icy glares inside too."

Harris and his two colleagues had found themselves in a room full of skeptical bankers who, for the most part, sniffed at the term "speculator" as something unwholesome. Harris began his speech with an historical spin.

"The Chicago Mercantile Exchange has been the old Butter and Egg Exchange and we were sort of running out of gas due to technological change, the modernization of American agriculture, integration, disappearance of small producers and the onslaught of agri-business after World War II." He went on to explain that butter had become an item that was no longer traded on a futures market because it had no price risk due to the government support program. In addition the Midwest was no longer the egg basket of the nation, and millions of cases of eggs no longer went into spring storage.

By the time Harris got around to talking about live cattle, he detected an uneasiness among the bankers, a few of whom were tapping their fingers on the white tablecloths out of boredom. Then Harris began talking about "the father" of the cattle market, and suddenly there was interest. "I could feel them starting to listen more carefully when I mentioned the late Arthur Longini of the Mellon Bank of Pittsburgh," said Harris.

Longini had been in charge of area development for the bank. He had been studying the live cattle market and wrote a paper on the subject, which he presented to Harris and the CME directors as early as 1961. Not long afterward, Harris received a call from James Sartwelle, a cattleman tied in with the Port City Stockyards in Houston, Texas. Sartwelle told Harris that rumor had

142

it that the CME was about to start trading in live cattle. A month later, Harris met Sartwelle in Houston for his ideas on developing a contract. "The rest was history," Harris told the group.

Finally, Harris gave proper credit to the CME's friends in the banking industry. He referred to Ellmore C. Patterson, vice chairman of Morgan Guaranty Trust Co. in New York, as "helpful in the success of the beef cattle market." Harris began quoting from a speech presented by Patterson before the American Meat Institute annual meeting a year earlier. The speech, a strong commentary on futures trading and speculation, added credence to what the CME and other exchanges were trying to do. After all, the words were coming from the mouth of a well-known Wall Street banker, who was strictly bonds and blue-chips. In part, Patterson stated,

> I am aware that this Institute came out originally against the idea of futures trading in live cattle, and I understand the reservations that many of you probably have about this kind of trading, which to be successful must attract speculative capital. I can appreciate that speculation has unpleasant connotations for many. Actually, speculative capital serves a useful economic purpose by assuming certain kinds of risk that other capital does not wish to bear.
>
> The existence of an effective futures market has proved indispensable in a number of processing industries. Sugar refining is a classic example. In the banking business, the ability to buy and sell currency futures is essential to trading foreign exchange. The history of futures markets shows that they take time to develop. Where the industry that utilizes or processes the commodity makes active use of the market, futures trading tends to contribute to price stability rather than detract from it. A market evolves in response to the needs it is supposed to fill and the uses that are made of it. The evolution in turn can enlarge the area of usefulness. . . . It may seem odd for a banker to be speaking favorably of futures transactions in any commodity, after the vegetable oil bath of nearly two years ago. But the trouble there was not futures, but fraud. From a banker's standpoint, I would say in general that a processing industry which is able to hedge its price risks gains added attractiveness both as a borrower and as an investment."[1]

This was the kind of support the CME needed and would continue to seek in the years ahead. Bankers made good allies, Harris believed. But they needed educating. "As Patterson pointed out even back in the Sixties, the banks were in the futures business trading their currencies," said Harris, who a decade later would team up with Melamed and others to try to convince the banks of the need for financial futures.

Back at the CME, another kind of storm was brewing. The cattle and pork belly markets were in place, but there was still a current of political unrest among the younger members. In spite of all the efforts of the Broker's Club, the membership still had little, if any, voice in the affairs and administration of the Exchange. Committees on which members served were totally powerless and their usefulness nonexistent. Complaints, opinions, criticisms, and suggestions usually fell on deaf ears.

The Board of Governors continued to rule the CME as it saw fit, often in total opposition to the consensus of the general membership. Predictably, a strain of distrust evolved, spreading among the members like a virus. The notion of egalitarianism had dissipated along the way. And now the CME's junior members, allied with a group of veterans, were pushing for a palace revolt of some kind. The Board had obviously lost touch with its members, who were the ultimate producers of business for the exchange. Without their support, the best of Board actions simply would go to waste. A we-versus-them attitude began to prevail between the rank and file and the board. It was time to revive the Broker's Club.

It had been five years since the members reared their collective heads and challenged the establishment. It was no longer an isolated sign of urest in the CME culture, but rather an indication of what was on the minds of individuals who were being suffocated by a tightly controlled bureaucracy. "You could virtually feel the change in mood with the times," said Ronald Frost, a former Merc vice president.

Indeed, both moods and times were changing. The Silent Generation of the fifties had slouched into the Beat Generation of the sixties, a time when go-go investing spurred the growth of the huge corporate funds as the ravenous institutional investors began to dominate the securities markets. The institutional thrust pushed prices higher, sending the Dow Jones Industrial Average above the 1000 mark for the first time on 18 January 1966, along with a blizzard of paper that jammed back office operations of many brokerage houses.

There was also inflation to contend with, the result of President Johnson's effort to build a Great Society with a package of domestic social changes while fighting a war in Vietnam. The guns-and-butter economy ended the bull market with a sudden jolt as European economies and their currencies tied to the dollar by Bretton Woods faltered.[2]

Even food had found its way into the channels of diplomacy. The Johnson Administration during the period from in 1965 to 1968 sought unsuccessfully to use food aid in persuading India to support its policies in Southeast Asia.[3]

While the Broker's Club was preparing a strategy for changing the CME by-laws, the Board was busy studying the results of a survey that it had commissioned. The public relations firm Beveridge, Penney & Bennett, Inc. was hired to assess attitudes of the nation's major wirehouses toward the CME.[4]

The results were rather humbling. One-third of the fifteen wirehouses surveyed did not hold the CME in very high regard. Among the reasons most often noted for this attitude were floor executions, time limits for openings and closings, physical appearance of the statistical sheet, the advertising campaign, an element of the membership and floor brokers, and the inability to put up bonds. On a positive note, the houses generally agreed that the CME was a progressive exchange and that business would probably continue to boom ahead.

"In all, the survey didn't do a lot to bolster the spirits of the board," said Harris. "But for the first time in years we had a reference point from which to launch a set of improvements and to do some much needed housecleaning."

Such views by the wirehouses, which were growing in importance and prestige to the exchanges, helped to stoke the coals of insurrection. The CME found itself strapped with an image problem perceived from the inside as well as the outside.

Meanwhile, the man who spoke only Yiddish when he arrived in the United States was fast becoming one of the Merc's foremost orators. Leo Melamed had rallied the Broker's Club with the help of people like Kenneth Birks and Robert O'Brien, pushing for a referendum rule to the by-laws. It was the only way to give the membership a meaningful voice and to make the board fully responsible to its members. After all, the referendum was one of the most basic principles in American law and justice. "I reasoned that such a rule would probably never be used, except under extreme circumstances," Melamed later recalled. But it would be an effective threat, one that Melamed would eventually have to deal with two decades later when his leadership was challenged.

Again, the key was the proxy. Unlike before, proxies were not needed to raise a quorum. This time they were needed to win a majority number of votes in order to propose and approve an amendment to the by-laws. Again they were advised that such a proposal would not be binding to the Board. The Young Turks were determined for a showdown with the establishment.

The battle lines had been drawn. On one side stood Melamed, Birks, Jesser, Henner, March, and the other Young Turks. On the other side was the Board led by chairman Nathan Wertheimer, president E.B. Harris, and CME attorney Lee Freeman. It was mid-December and snow packed the Chicago streets in record drifts. Shortly after the closing bell rang, the members gathered on the trading floor to listen to a debate. For weeks before, Birks had methodically mustered the necessary number of proxies. Now came the speeches blasting across the floor by microphone. First, by several of the Board members, and then one by attorney Freeman, arguing that a referendum as proposed had no legal justification in the context of CME by-laws. He threatened a court battle if such an amendment were adopted.

Then it was Melamed's turn. Suddenly he was thrust into the role of the floor's leader, attorney, and speaker on behalf of the membership. It was a move, he recalls, critical to his career at the Exchange. Tightly grasping the microphone, Melamed countered with an explanation of precisely why the referendum was legally binding to the Board. The words from both sides echoed across the trading floor as tempers flared. Some 45 minutes later, a motion was made, seconded, and voted on. Rule 206, as it was called, was overwhelmingly adopted.

A month later, in January 1968, Melamed was elected to the Board with the highest number of floor votes to his credit, and a new chairman was elected.

He was 48-year-old Robert J. O'Brien, an ally to Melamed and the Broker's Club members. At the same time, the Board elected Melamed as secretary, a position he used to communicate with the membership and to further his ideas. Melamed was no longer an outsider, nor was he a son, son-in-law, or grand-son of any Exchange member. O'Brien, the son-in-law of John V. McCarthy, represented the transition—the link between the old guard and the new wave of Exchange members. To be sure, there were still such veterans on the board as Michael Weinberg, Jr., John V. McCarthy, Jr., Samuel Becker, Gilbert Miller, Glenn Andersen, Carl Anderson, Harry Fortes, William Ferguson, and William Katz. The blend of old and new blood seemed to mix well. Old rivalries were forgotten.

O'Brien was receptive to new ideas. Although he was a generation removed from the Young Turks, they considered him to be of "new blood vintage" because of his willingness to broaden the horizons of the Exchange and to work closely with the younger members. O'Brien had taken the first major step in years toward decentralization of the administrative power. Committees were expanded and he began to use the executive committee—Board members who were CME officers—as a steering force.

"I wanted to enhance our image," recalled O'Brien. "The CBOT was viewed as a bunch of angels and the Merc a bunch of crooks. I wanted the new board to fashion a moral code and at the same time put the good old boy network behind us."

Rule 206 was a step in that direction. The new by-law was heralded as one of the most democratic of its kind among the nation's exchanges. It was one of the most basic—and dramatic—policy revisions since the CME's founding. In effect, it allowed the Board to share with the membership the power of creating and cancelling rules. A three-member rules committee, which included Melamed, Weinberg, and Miller, was selected to refine Rule 206 on six basic points:

1. Strengthening of the committee responsibility
2. Delaying of rule effect for five days (except in the case of emergency) to enable members to amend or rescind
3. Circulation to all members within 24 hours of passage
4. Permitting of petitions to institute a members' referendum to propose new rules or cancel old ones
5. Allowing the Board 15 days to enact the proposal before a referendum is issued
6. Limiting of an identical proposal by members to once in a six-month period[5]

In addition to the rule change, the Board doubled the number of annual meetings, set for the third Wednesday in January and the third Wednesday in

The Chicago Mercantile Exchange's 1921–1928 location at the corner of Lake and Wells is shown here. The building no longer stands. (CHICAGO HISTORICAL SOCIETY)

The first building constructed expressly for Chicago Mercantile Exchange trading
was built at the corner of Washington and Franklin. The CME occupied
the building from 1928 to 1972.

Skidmore, Owings, & Merrill designed the home of the CME from 1972 to 1983 at
444 West Jackson Boulevard to accommodate twenty-one futures and options contracts,
including the new International Monetary Market. The trading floor encompassed
23,000 square feet after the 1978 expansion.

The Chicago Mercantile Exchange Center is in the heart of Chicago's financial district at 30 S. Wacker Drive. The CME's home since 1983, the building includes two trading floors. (JESS SMITH/PHOTOSMITH)

The original charter of the Chicago Butter and Egg Board which was the predecessor to the CME was formally signed on February 5, 1898.

Peter Fox & Sons was one of the original member firms of the CME. Pictured is William J. Fox in 1904 at age twenty. (COURTESY OF KATHLEEN KENNEDY ISRAEL, FOX DELUXE)

S. Water Street, later Wacker Drive, was a bustling market area at the beginning of the century. This and other markets provided impetus for butter and egg futures trading. (CHICAGO HISTORICAL SOCIETY)

Listing price quotations on blackboards was well established by 1919 when the CME used this trading floor at Lake and LaSalle streets.

Will Rogers is shown as the guest speaker at the CME's 110 N. Franklin building dedication on April 25, 1928.

Members gather on the trading floor of the CME for the formal dedication on April 26, 1928.

The "Our Founder" bronze rooster statue continues to represent the CME's beginning as a butter and egg market.

CME Business Manager Oscar Olson (*right*) was responsible for recruiting then Chicago Board of Trade Secretary Everette B. Harris (*left*) to the newly created position of CME President in 1953.

From left to right (*above*), CME Clearinghouse Manager Rudy Gaimari, member Stephen Greenberg, and President Everette B. Harris mark the 1961 opening of the revised Tom Turkey contract.

The new Pork Belly futures contract, opened on September 18, 1961, would eventually bring trading volume to new highs.

CME President Everette B. Harris leads the ceremony to open Live Cattle futures trading on November 30, 1964. Behind President Harris is Chairman Stephen Greenberg.

Live Hog futures trading opens at the CME on February 28, 1966. A "sample" of the commodity is on display for the first session.

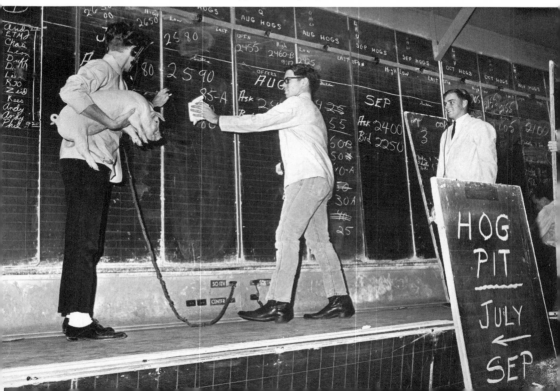

An overview of trading activity in December 1967 at 110 N. Franklin. A total of eleven commodities were traded at this time.

A meeting of the 1969 CME Board of Governors and Executive Staff, who were the architects of the International Monetary Market which brought currency futures contracts to the floor of the Exchange. From bottom left, clockwise: Samuel H. Becker, Ronald J. Frost, Carl E. Anderson, Robert J. O'Brien, Daniel R. Jesser, Gerald Hirsch, William S. Katz, Everette B. Harris, Leo Melamed, Michael Weinberg, Jr., Kenneth Mackay, John T. Geldermann, Glenn H. Andersen, Ray L. Elster, Jr., William C. Muno, and William Phelan.

The CME donates the Poultry and Egg Building in the Farm-in-the-Zoo at Chicago's Lincoln Park Zoo to mark the Exchange's fiftieth anniversary. From the right, Chicago Mayor Richard J. Daley, CME President E. B. Harris, and, to the left, CME Chairman Leo Melamed look on as Clifford M. Hardin, U.S. Secretary of Agriculture, unlocks the door to the new barn on October 16, 1969.

CME Cattle Committee Chairman Lloyd F. Arnold (*left*) and Floor Facilities Committee Chairman John T. Geldermann (*right*) examine the first electronic quotation board that went into service in late 1971.

The ceremonial cutting of a ribbon of currencies marks the opening of the International Monetary Market on May 16, 1972. From left to right, assisting are CME Chairman Michael Weinberg, Jr., Chicago City Controller David Stahl, IMM Chairman Leo Melamed, International Monetary Fund Executive Director William B. Dale, and CME President Everette B. Harris.

Economist Milton Friedman rings the opening bell for Treasury Bill futures in January 1976. This was the first interest rate futures contract traded on the CME.

The opening of the Stud Lumber contract on December 1, 1977, is celebrated by, from left to right, H. A. Roberts, Executive Vice President, Western Wood Products Association; CME President Everette B. Harris; and John Mulrooney, Executive Vice President, National American Wholesale Lumber Association.

CME President Clayton Yeutter and former President Everette B. Harris look on as Alan Greenspan speaks at the Financial Writers Seminar sponsored by the CME in March 1978.

From left to right, John Geldermann, Chairman of the CME Building Improvement and Real Estate Committee; Beverly Splane, CME Executive Vice President; and Larry Rosenberg, CME Chairman, undertake the symbolic demolition of a wall to expand the trading floor at 444 W. Jackson in mid-November 1978.

Pictured is floor activity on the newly expanded trading floor at 444 W. Jackson in 1979.

Republican presidential candidate Ronald Reagan is welcomed to the trading floor by CME Chairman Jack Sandner and CME Special Counsel Leo Melamed on March 17, 1980.

Past CME Chairmen gather at a reception in July 1980 honoring former President Everette B. Harris, who served from 1953 to 1978. From left to right, seated are Michael Weinberg, Jr. (Chairman 1972–1973); Nathan A. Wertheimer (Chairman 1966); Everette B. Harris; Michael Weinberg, Sr. (Chairman 1955–1957); and William S. Katz (Chairman 1959, 1961–1963). From left to right, standing are John T. Geldermann (Chairman 1974–1975); Laurence M. Rosenberg (Chairman 1977–1979); John F. Sandner (Chairman 1980–1982); Leo Melamed (Chairman CME 1969–1971, 1976; IMM 1972–1975); Stephen Greenberg (Chairman 1964–1965); and Robert J. O'Brien (Chairman 1967–1968).

CME Special Counsel Leo Melamed (*seated, left*), CME Chairman Jack Sandner (*seated, center*), and John T. Geldermann, Chairman, CME Building Improvement and Real Estate Committee (*seated, right*), sign the first three leases for office space in the new CME Center. From left to right, standing are Lawrence F. Levy, President, and Holly Youngholm, Vice President, The Levy Organization, consultants to the Exchange; Elayne Adams, CME Center Director of Leasing; and Bernard Weissbourd, Chairman, Metropolitan Structures, codevelopers.

CME Chairman Jack Sandner, President Clayton Yeutter, and Special Counsel Leo Melamed field questions at the press conference marking the official opening of Eurodollar trading on the Exchange on December 9, 1981.

Milton Friedman, 1976 Nobel Laureate–Economics (*center*), joins CME Special Counsel Leo
Melamed (*left*) and CME Chairman Jack Sandner (*right*) at a press conference
on the occasion of the CME's 10th Anniversary celebration of the
International Monetary Market on June 4, 1982.

Louis Rukeyser (*left*) hosts a "Wall Street Week" broadcast at the CME in
May 1983. His panelists were Monte Gordon (*center*), Director of Research for
Dreyfus & Company, and Martin Zweig (*right*), a market strategist.

July. To keep the out-of-town members apprised of what was going on, the CME published a list of the various committees[6] and the names of committee members with encouragement "to make their thoughts known to the appropriate committees."

Along with the political changes came some physical ones. The Merc was getting a new face to go with its new disposition. Expansion of the CME trading floor was under way, with some $22,000 in scaffolding and barricades installed at the south end of the trading floor in preparation for demolition. Completion of the 25 percent increase in space was scheduled for 16 February 1968.

The translux tickers were to be relocated in units at the end of the floor with a new set of catwalks and ticker booths. The former Board room became a temporary coffee room, and the coffee room a committee-office room. Between 5 September and 15 December new trading boards were built behind the old ones, which eventually were removed. There were five pits (two sharing the same base at either end), an additional nine double desks, and six 12-foot teletype enclosures at the south end of the floor. The remodeling had forced the Exchange's general offices to move to temporary quarters in an adjoining building.

The CME's members and their machines also did some adjusting. A new IBM data processing center was set up that included a 1401 processing unit. Dan Hackett manned the key punch; Walter Erikson did the card sorting; Rudi Gaimari and Thomas Peak collated; and Dave Derring supervised the recording of out-trades. The Merc had yet to become fully automated, but it was on its way.

The CME was still far from a smooth-running operation internally. It wasn't long after the transition that the new Board and Chairman O'Brien realized that the Young Turks had inherited a set of archaic, and often cryptic, by-laws that had been handed down through the generations like the legendary sagas of a tribe. "They were bits and pieces of rules, as if each had been added in a vacuum," said Melamed, lifting up the old CME rule book held together by yellowed Scotch tape, paste, paper clips, and the good intentions of the early boards, dating back to 1898. Some of the pages were typed and others written in an almost indecipherable scrawl. It was a hodge-podge, full of contradictions that made little sense when taken together. Particular amendments in the context of others often meant something different. The history of each change was neither understood nor explained.

Up to that point, it was all in the memory of one man, Kenneth Mackay, who was CME executive vice president, secretary, manager of the clearinghouse, and administrator of the Exchange. "He was everything," said Melamed. "Everything was in his mind."

16

Sir Francis Pork Belly

Gerald Hirsch had a problem.

What, he wondered, was the best way for the Merc to tell the public about its success? When Hirsch wasn't trading cattle or pork bellies, he was concerned about the CME's image, for it was his responsibility to think about such matters as chairman of the publicity committee. But his thoughts were fairly well-limited to the rather modest annual budget the Merc had come up with for both public relations and advertising: $25,000.

Until then, the Merc's advertising was rudimentary—usually a series of small strip ads with pictures of various commodities placed in the *Chicago Daily News* or the *Chicago Tribune*. Nevertheless, Hirsch began searching for a small advertising agency to replace the one the Merc was using. And quite by accident, he found a creative gold mine. Chatting with a friend in the advertising business during a morning train ride to work, Hirsch had casually asked him whether he would be interested in handling the Merc account. The friend politely turned down the business and suggested that Hirsch contact an up-and-comer who had just opened his own one-man ad agency.

The following day, Hirsch called Martin Cohen. Cohen had opened his agency, Martin A. Cohen Inc., a month earlier and was in need of a client. Like a well-timed trade, the Merc showed up. "The ad budget was small and the Exchange really didn't know what it wanted," said Cohen. The Merc, too, was fortunate, for in Cohen they had found not only a highly creative mind, but one that was familiar with the futures markets. Cohen was pure Chicagoan, born and bred in the city; and, as a high school student in the summers of 1948 and 1949, he was a runner at the Chicago Board of Trade, earning $15 a week. He knew traders at both the CBOT and the CME.

Hirsch and his committee hired Cohen, who immediately convinced the CME to raise its advertising budget from $25,000 to $100,000. The partnership between Cohen and the CME was to last for 17 years, resulting in award-winning advertising campaigns that were both highly creative and controversial.

Cohen had fancied himself a disciple of hot-shot Madison adman Bill Bernbach of Doyle Dane & Bernbach, who was the creator of a series of snappy Volkswagen ads during the 1960s and early 1970s. Martin A. Cohen Inc. was off and running with the blessings of Hirsch and his committee. The mandate was direct: to be creative.

After talking to various traders and roaming the floor himself to get a feel for the pit action, Cohen began to understand how active pork belly trading had become. He fashioned his first ad around the Merc's fastest growing futures contract. For an adman, the notion of conveying what went on in a futures exchange was indeed a challenge.

"It was a complex perception which had to be simplified," said Cohen. "We wanted to attract public speculators as well as professionals." The first Cohen ad, which appeared in The *Wall Street Journal* was simply the picture of a hefty pig with the caption "Capitalist Pig."

The CME officials and members did not know what to make of that first ad. "It was so radical for an exchange to take a sassy approach, some of us had difficulty adjusting to that style of creativity," said E.B. Harris, who wasn't a Cohen fan at the start.

"E.B. was one of my early detractors. He thought the ads initially were insane," said Cohen, "but he became an early convert." If not insane, some of the ads tilted toward the eccentric side, as far as exchange promotion went. Those early ads were aimed straight at the public's pocketbook. "If you have a little risk capital," stated one, "we've got the risk." Within 18 months, Cohen was producing award-winning ad campaigns for the CME.

"Why not be bold if you have a story to tell?" reasoned the Exchange officials. After all, as Harris would later say, "Business is show business." The CME eventually became one of the most aggressive marketers, with an ad campaign to match. A typical ad promoting pork belly trading showed a portrait of English philosopher Sir Francis Bacon with the caption "Sir Francis Pork Belly." Another Merc ad touting lumber futures even took a good-natured swipe at rival Chicago Board of Trade with a picture of a two-by-four and the caption "The Chicago Mercantile presents the board of trade."

At times, the ads were coated with a veneer of romanticism, such as one in which Cohen compared futures trading to the last frontier: "Starting with little more than ingenuity, guts and the courage of his convictions, the frontiersman achieved incredible success." It went on to assert that a commodity trader succeeded or failed on the basis of nothing more than his own abilities, and that "the Chicago Mercantile Exchange is dedicated to preserving the spirit of the frontier."

The Merc wasn't shooting from the hip with such an ad campaign. It knew precisely which prospects it was aiming at. An ad in *Playboy* magazine, for example, drew some 900 responses from readers who wanted to know about the futures markets. In an attempt to gain more insight into a potential universe of traders, the Merc did its own marketing research.

"The results were fascinating," said Ronald Frost, the CME's former vice president of public relations, of a profile study involving some 4,000 commodity traders. The typical trader was pegged as someone between the ages of 35 and 55 with at least a bachelor's degree and an income of close to $20,000 a year. There were some 5 million people in the United States who fit that description at the time, and according to projections, there would be 9 million such people by 1990. But only a fraction traded commodities.

The Merc study also showed that most of the commodity speculators lived in Illinois, California, New York, Texas, and Florida, and were relatively new to the market; 73 percent of them had been trading for fewer than four years. It also showed that 70 percent of them had securities accounts as well as commodities accounts.

The CME moved on a broad marketing front. To shore up its public relations efforts, Harris hired Ronald Frost in October 1968. Frost had handled the Merc over the previous three years as an associate of the public relations firm, Beveridge, Penney & Bennett, Inc., who continued to service the account. It was the first time the exchange had a full-time public relations specialist internally, as well as an outside firm. Frost, a graduate of Loyola University, had worked on the *National Provisioner* before joining the Beveridge group and was well-versed in agricultural commodities.

A year later, on the eve of the CME's 50th birthday, Leo Melamed was voted into office as the Exchange's 23rd chairman. He concentrated on three goals:

1. To organize and rewrite the Merc's foundation laws
2. To improve the image of the Merc by cracking down on those who tried to manipulate prices
3. To diversify the product line

Under O'Brien's guidance the CME had made steady progress and hit record volume. In the area of raising standards, the Exchange had increased the limits on fines for infractions, tightened rules on discretionary accounts, imposed guidelines with specific requirements for approved solicitors, and instituted new and higher financial requirements for clearing members.

"We consider the CME a quasi-public institution, not a private club in any sense," E.B. Harris told the members in his year-end report. The Commodity Exchange Authority had seemed pleased with the CME's progress in self-policing through its Department of Audits and Investigations under the direction of vice president William M. Phelan.

Harris viewed the CME as a conglomerate of sorts, a multimarket institution trading effectively in a number of qualified and diversified commodities. Financially, treasurer William C. Muno assured his fellow traders that the Exchange was on firm footing. Income had been voluntarily reduced by the use of Treasury bills as margin, which passed the interest income on to CME members and their customers. Moreover, clearing fees had been reduced by 50 percent, passing additional profits back to member firms. To round out its golden year, the CME, for the first time in its history, awarded honorary memberships to old-timers Miles Friedman, Jack Friedman, Frank Darby, and Sam Schneider.

The CME had come a long way from its butter-and-egg days. It periodically had been brought to its knees, but it always managed to rise again like a distraught marathon runner who suddenly got a second wind after a quick swig of Gatorade. Now, at the close of a decade, there was time to look back and think about the future. It was a time when business was unpopular, war was unpopular, and government was unpopular—a period of social upheaval. For all the progress the CME had made in its 50 years, there was still a long way to go.

Despite this progress, Melamed, the new chairman, had no intention of looking back and becoming complacent. At this juncture in the CME's history, there was no compromise, no middle ground, no coasting on past achievements. The tendency of the institutional animal, and indeed all corporate entities, was to mark time once a comfortable operating plateau had been reached. In this regard the Young Turks were cynical toward big institutions that became cash cows. It was the entrepreneurial firms that maintained close touch with their customers and markets. The Exchange membership was composed of entrepreneurs, each a profit and loss center unto himself, all competing in the same marketplace, yet all with the same objective.

"In business, to stand still is equivalent to retreating," Melamed said. "Rebirth is certainly more difficult than continuation," he stated in the annual chairman's message of 1968. Melamed's management style was fluid. With a fixation on the future, he was determined to remove the stigma of past sins that had besmirched the CME's name. He did not want to flout tradition, but merely tease it, along with the other Young Turks who kept rebellion marginal but firm. Some former CME leaders had wanted to maintain a hold with as little compromise as possible. Melamed's instincts dictated flexibility, yet he hoped to sidestep any confusion over the direction the Exchange had to take. In that first letter he was tough and blunt and even a bit philosophical:

> It should be abundantly clear to anyone who has studied our record that some time ago we endured a long period of complacency. Suddenly we realized that we had waited too long and the process of rebirth—new ideas, new commodities, new blood, new rules—began to formulate. But, because the hour was late, we found it agonizingly difficult to proceed. . . . Today we are witnessing the fruition of those painful years. Today we are once again a successful institution. . . . I submit that our choice must be to use our momentum for continued forward motion. The problem with forward motion, however, is that it has no magic formula, particularly when it relates to a large institution. What may be good for one business may be fatal to another. . . .

In essence, the old model of an exchange had to be scrapped for a progressive one whose leaders could look ahead to the next 50 years. To expect such prescience from traders who pegged their livelihoods on short-term goals was asking a lot. Yet the new board wanted to get the members to think long-term when it came to building the CME for the generations of future traders. At that point, however, there was no way to anticipate the rapid-fire growth that would take place over the next two decades.

The elections of 1968 and 1969 dramatically changed the entire makeup of the Board with new and younger members. The price of membership had risen to a new high ($32,000), and the bitter memories of strife and quarrel were on the wane. But from a management standpoint, the CME was far from a smoothly running machine. It desperately needed a tune-up, if not a complete overhaul.

"We were, it was true, the second largest commodity exchange in the nation," Melamed said, looking back at the period, "but what a bad second we were." At the time, the Merc was doing less than 20 percent of the nation's futures business. As bad as those statistics were, the Merc's lowly stature in the financial world was even worse. The agenda was simple enough: continued business expansion, internal reorganization, and programs aimed at changing the Merc's stature in the financial community.

The leadership set out to capitalize on the momentum of the Exchange, careful not to cut through the organization like a Samurai gone amok. The first order of business was to evaluate personnel. Melamed focused on E.B. Harris, who had already been president for 15 years. His tenure had been a controversial one and many were betting that he would be the first to go under the new regime. But Melamed reserved judgment.

"To me, Mr. Harris was an unknown quantity," said Melamed, who had served on the Board for two years, and had had little contact with Harris. Nevertheless, there was indeed a bias, concedes Melamed. He explains, "The fact that he had been president during the past years of the Exchange had substantially prejudiced me and others against him, but I vowed to reserve final judgment."

Harris, too, had his doubts about Melamed. What were the intentions of this young CME chairman, Harris wondered. Was he capable of running an exchange, given his inexperience in such matters? Was he diplomatic enough to bridge the generation gap that now existed?

Melamed wasn't about to move hastily, and perhaps unwisely. The easiest way to smooth ruffled feathers, he knew, was to find a replacement for Harris. But instead, he began to gather facts first-hand. By talking to former Merc governors and garnering opinions and observations among members, it didn't take him long to separate fact from fiction. Melamed concluded that Harris had been caught up in circumstances often beyond his control.

"He had always served as frontman for the decisions of previous chairmen and previous boards," concluded Melamed. "If a crucial decision were made, he would often find that after he took a stand the Board would vacillate and, often as not, back him up. It was difficult for him to develop a leadership role under such conditions."

Harris was kept in place as president. In doing so, the elder Harris shifted his operational mode, gearing it to the younger and more spirited new board. The partnership between Melamed and Harris bridged the generation gap at the time and served notice to the rest of the Merc members that the transition between the past and present would be virtually painless. Melamed also made it clear that no longer would one individual serve as a whipping boy for any future failures of the Exchange.

Melamed tried not to allow his ego to cloud business judgment. Hadn't he maintained his once arch-antagonist, Lee Freeman Sr., as the CME's counsel, despite their prior differences? Now they had were close allies. Melamed recognized the value of Freeman's tenacity and loyalty. If anything, the new board of governors understood the value of maintaining continuity in an organization in flux. It generally meant keeping key people in place, especially those with expertise and a sense of history to draw from. More importantly, replacements weren't easily found in the futures industry that was still emerging in the late 1960s and early 1970s. To most outsiders, regardless of their financial savvy, commodities trading was an enigma. (It would be a problem that the industry would have to cope with throughout the 1980s as well.)

The management-by-crisis syndrome that had so dominated the CME's strategy for decades suddenly took on a new look. "There seemed to be a more professional management air," recalled Kenneth Mackay. "You got the feeling a new era was about to begin." Indeed it was.

While the reorganization did not mean a new president, it did require a top-to-bottom reorganization—and redefinition—of each department. "It also meant that the lax attitude by many employees was no longer acceptable, and each person would have to carry his weight or leave," said Melamed.

A number of new committees were created whose members were able to make meaningful contributions. The committee chairmen, many of whom were governors, were to work closely with department managers and to report their work to the Board. The notion of a more participatory organization began to take hold. As change swept over the Merc, it became necessary to redefine committee functions and powers. This brought the Board the thorniest problem facing the Exchange: a set of archaic by-laws that desperately needed updating.

17

Happy Fiftieth

Melamed had set out to convince the CME members that the reinvigorated leadership was in touch with their needs. But it took more than a college try to fulfill those needs. It required anticipating future trends in domestic and world markets. The board had set in motion its plans to reconstruct its capital base while conveying to outsiders the growth and ambition of the Exchange. The reasoning was simple enough: If members knew that their exchange were successful, they would maintain a genuine interest.

The time was ripe for change. Investors were looking at futures a bit differently than they had in the early 1960s, and with good reason. The 16-year postwar bull market crested in January 1966, when, for the first time, the Dow industrials surpassed 1000. By October, however, it sank to 754 and did not rise again above the 1000 mark until 1972. Investors were fidgety over inflation. The rapidly growing expenditures for the Vietnam War coupled with the billions poured into Lyndon Johnson's war on poverty, sent the cost of living spiraling upward.

The CME scored a first among futures exchanges when in 1966[1] it allowed a young woman named Sandra J. Stephens, working for R.J. O'Brien & Associates, Inc., on the floor as a clerk. (Lois Berger Knight, however, claims that she was the first female to work on the Merc trading floor in 1959 as a phone clerk for John E. Coleman. "It was hear no evil, see no evil, speak no evil. There was a real chauvinist attitude," said Knight.) In the era of the Beatles and bell-bottoms, madras and miniskirts, the CME Board had no intention of letting the traders' minds wander. So as the barrier for women was lowered, so were their hemlines, which had to fall from two to three inches above the knee. (Bowing to the rising women's rights movement, the New York Stock Exchange admitted its first female member a year later. In 1968, the Chicago Board of Trade rewrote its membership rules to include women traders also.)

But it would take another six years—on 16 May 1972, the day the IMM opened—before the first female entered the inner sanctum of the pits as a trader. She was Carol (Mickey) Norton, who got her start by charting commodities for

Melamed's firm, Dellsher, on a once-a-week basis, and subsequently bought an IMM membership. The 5-foot-2-inch, 105 pound Norton made the first IMM trade—in deutsche marks—with Daniel Jesser. Her profit on the trade: $70.

Also in May 1972, the Merc admitted its first black member—Valerie Turner, who also owned an IMM seat. Sandra Stephens became an IMM member that year as well. Seven months later, Barbara Diamond began trading on the IMM. In 1973 Miriam Schmitt became a floor broker for L.D. Schreiber & Company in the cattle and pork belly pits.

By the end of 1967, stock prices had recovered to around 900 on the Dow, but corporate America was quaking in its boots as the "conglomerateurs" used their high-priced shares to gobble up acquisitions as if they were collector's items. While the go-go mutual funds were still on the go, some economists were skeptical over the use of convertible securities, so-called Chinese money, used to acquire the companies. (Two decades later junk bonds would be the corporate chips of acquisition.)

Over the next twelve months, both the stock and futures markets were whip-sawed in a year of turmoil, stirred by such events as the Tet Offensive in Vietnam, Lyndon Johnson's decision to drop out of the presidential race, and the assassinations of Robert Kennedy and Martin Luther King, Jr. By the time Richard Nixon was elected president, the era of fixed commissions in stocks had ended.

While Nixon's transition team was still working out the kinks, University of Chicago economist Milton Friedman was busy working on another agenda. Friedman and fellow economist Arthur Burns were part of a presidential task force concentrating on economic matters. "One of the first things I urged Mr. Nixon to do upon taking office was to close the gold window," recalled Friedman, who had prepared a confidential memorandum for president-elect Nixon on resolving the United States' balance of payments problem.

Presented to Nixon in December 1968, the memo began, "The first few weeks of the new administration that takes over in January 1969, will offer a unique opportunity to set the dollar free and thereby eliminate for years to come balance of payments restraints on U.S. economic policy." [2]

Friedman argued that if the administration waited too long, it would have to do it later under more difficult circumstances. "I talked to Nixon about it, but he didn't follow my advice because Arthur Burns didn't agree with me". Burns, in fact, strongly opposed the idea with a "maintain and retain" attitude, as Friedman put it. It was a cordial disagreement between two old friends whose relationship began in 1931, when Burns had been Friedman's economics professor at Rutgers University.

Burns, a pipe-smoking, implacable conservative was mostly an economic pragmatist, sometimes veering from being a crusty advocate of fiscal restraint to being a cautious fueler of the money supply. During the Eisenhower Administration, he headed the Council of Economic Advisors. So it wasn't surprising that Nixon took Burns's advice and not Friedman's, for Nixon was a Burns patron and wanted Burns as his Federal Reserve chairman to replace William McChesney Martin. (Nixon made him Counselor to the President in 1968 and Federal Reserve Chief in 1970.)

Long-opposed to the fixed exchange rate system, Friedman had first-hand experience with its flaws a year before he wrote the confidential memo to Nixon. At that time, individuals who wanted to speculate in foreign currencies were generally barred from the forward market, although there were no laws prohibiting private speculation. The Federal Reserve Board and the foreign banks it dealt with exerted informal pressure to prevent private speculation because of its potentially disruptive effect on the exchange rates.

One autumn day in 1967, Friedman telephoned a Chicago bank seeking to sell short $300,000 in British pounds sterling with the idea that Great Britain was about to devalue its currency. To his dismay, the bank refused to accept his order even though he was prepared to pledge $30,000 in cash as a security deposit for the transaction. Friedman then contacted two major New York banks with the same proposal. Again, he was refused.

"The reason they gave was that they disapproved essentially of speculation against the pound," Friedman said. "But the real reason was that they thought the Federal Reserve wouldn't like it or the Bank of England wouldn't like it." For Friedman, it was bitter disappointment compounded by the fact that three weeks later—just as he had predicted—Britain devalued the pound by 14.3 percent to $2.40. Had he been allowed to sell short, Friedman would have more than doubled his money. That experience would subsequently link Friedman with the Merc and Leo Melamed three years later, when the Chicago Mercantile Exchange was on the cusp of innovation with the International Monetary Market, the first financial futures market.

A year after Friedman's futile attempt to trade currencies, Merc trader Richard Boerke had better luck with the banks than did Friedman. Boerke also had designs on shorting the British pound and convinced fellow traders William Goldstandt and Bill Henner to go in with him. "I called the American National Bank," Henner said, "and we sold the British pound short." Unfortunately, the pound rallied and the trio lost money on the trade. Most individuals at the time, however, still couldn't trade currencies because the banks had a monopoly over them. Only large corporations were allowed to protect themselves through trading a so-called forward contract, which was merely a cash market transaction between two parties agreeing to buy and sell a security at some time in the future. Individuals could go short cocoa, coffee, soybeans, grains, cattle, eggs, and even copper, but not the British pound. Unlike a futures contract, the forward contract is not standardized and usually not transferable. Banks, in the late 1960s, demanded commercial motivation for currency speculation. Why was an individual less important than a corporation? If General Motors had a right to protect itself, why, then, didn't the average citizen?

In the meantime, the Merc was riding a long-awaited wave of success. Diversification was producing record trading volume. That's not to say the industry was content solely with futures trading in agricultural products. In 1968, for example, the National Produce Exchange (NPE) actually had a plan to trade futures on the Dow Jones Industrial Average. But the Securities and Exchange Commission vetoed the plan because the NPE wasn't a registered securities exchange. Little noise was made over the rejection.

As far as the CME was concerned, the language of statistics spoke loudly and clearly. In 1968 the CME accounted for about 20 percent of all commodity futures trading in the United States, up from only 3 percent four years earlier. The 1968 volume of contracts had climbed 33 percent above the record-breaking 1967 figure of 1,388,010 contracts. The most popular contract was, of course, pork bellies, which had been around since 1961; they had become one of the most actively traded type of contract on any exchange in the nation. The activity was reflected in the membership price.

On 25 July 1968 the price of a CME seat hit a new high of $38,000—the highest price for a seat on any commodity exchange in the country at the time, and more than tenfold above the price in 1964, when a membership cost a mere $3,000.

Just as industrial firms looked to diversification to spur earnings growth, the CME managed to broaden its base for futures trading in agricultural products. Besides pork bellies, there were Idaho potatoes (launched in 1967), a revised egg contract to coincide with industry demand, a live cattle contract modernized and increased in size from 25,000 to 40,000 pounds, hogs, hams, turkeys, and plans to start a boneless beef contract in early 1969. Shell eggs—once the darling of the Exchange—had pretty well run their course by now. Limited to fresh eggs, the new egg contract closely reflected the fact that a realistic value of fresh eggs provided a better price for forecasting means. In 1945, an estimated 50 percent of all storage eggs found their way into the retail market. By 1968, there were approximately a half-million cases of eggs produced in one day, and in the market the next. Modern production had become a year-round business. Producers, processors, and users had a better guide for price insurance through hedging.

The CME's confidence and upbeat aura were reflected in Marty Cohen's breezy and often impish advertisements. The Merc's strategy was simple enough: to attract a hearty crop of speculators. "Let's face it," one CME pamphlet began. "Most people don't know what commodity futures are and they're a bit apprehensive about getting into a mysterious field involving big profits ... and losses." Almost any "strong-hearted person" with the money, intelligence, the stamina, and the time to study "these fascinating markets" can be rewarded with an "exhilarating experience" sweetened by "tremendous profits," proclaimed yet another CME brochure. But the CME never lost sight of reality. For in the same promotion it cautioned, "there are more losers than winners in commodity speculating."

The campaign to attract newcomers was under the scrutiny of Alex C. Caldwell, administrator of the Commodity Exchange Authority (CEA) in the USDA. "Speculators are essential to the futures markets," declared Caldwell, "But anybody who gets into it simply must know what he's doing."

There was little doubt that trying to popularize commodity trading was a delicate challenge for the shrewdest of admen. "Trading futures is only for the very rich . . . guys who have $500 or $1,000 to throw around," needled one Merc advertisement. Another advertised: "See your broker for stocks, mutual funds, convertible debentures, tax-free municipals, and strictly fresh eggs."

The Merc's hottest commodity—pork bellies—presented a special promotional problem. That message was clear from the cartoon strip on the wall of E.B. Harris' office. The strip showed a middle-aged couple having dinner. "I'm thinking of buying some pork belly futures, Shirley," exclaims the husband eagerly. "What do you think?"

"I think," snaps Shirley with a glare, "that that's not a nice thing to discuss at the dinner table."

Semantics was the least of the CME's worries. Credibility was at stake. In January 1969 new regulations designed to protect commodity futures customers were announced by the Department of Agriculture. Issued under the Commodity Exchange Act, the regulations set minimum financial standards for futures commissions merchants. Now they had to have adequate capital resources. The CEA required that a customer initiate and maintain a discretionary account with a $5000 minimum equity. If the equity fell more than $100 below the minimum, the firm would be required to liquidate the entire account. Six months later, the CME and CBOT would be the only two exchanges with such rules in place.

Indeed, the CME and other exchanges found themselves vulnerable on a number of cases from the onion growers to the potato growers to irate shoppers demanding to know why the cost of bacon and steak were so high. Collectively they pointed the accusatory finger at the speculators in the trading pits. It was, however, the DeAngelis soybean oil scandal that threatened to sink the boat. At its height, the critics in Washington were blasting the CEA as weak and not up to the task. At one point, Congress tried pushing a measure that would have established then-Secretary Orville Freeman as absolute czar of all commodity markets. It would, in effect, have given him powers equal to those exerted by the Federal Reserve Board, the Treasury, and the Securities and Exchange Commission over the stock markets.

In mid-January, Melamed, a general partner in Dellsher Investment Company, was elected chairman, replacing Robert J. O'Brien, president of John V. McCarthy & Co., Inc. The new team also included Glenn Anderson, first vice chairman; Gerald Hirsch, second vice chairman; Michael Weinberg, Jr., secretary; and William Muno, treasurer. The group was solid and dependable. Anderson, president of Andco Inc., had served as chairman of the pork bellies, live cattle, and hog committees. Hirsch, then a newly named vice president of Saul Stone & Co., had been first elected to the board in 1964 at the age of 30, making him the youngest governor in CME history and one of the youngest serving on any exchange in the country. Weinberg, who held an MBA from the University of Chicago, had been chairman of both the rules committee and public relations committee. It was the 50th anniversary of the Exchange. And it promised to be a special one from the start. Just two weeks (on 31 January) after the new officers were elected, a CME seat sold at a record $43,500, up from the previous record of $42,500 set on 29 January. "We were hoping that the price of a membership would reach $50,000 sometime during 1969 as a fitting tribute to our 50th anniversary year," Harris said. It reached $90,000.

In congratulating the CME on its anniversary, President Richard Nixon wrote, "By fostering sound practices in futures trading and by encouraging active trade in an increasing number of commodities, you continue to contribute meaningfully to the growth and well-being of American private enterprise and the national economy."

The CME had budgeted $325,000 for advertising and descriptive literature that was to fall into the hands of 100,000 potential speculators and hedgers. Among the booklets, for example, was one hailing the benefits of hedging for both the banker and the commodity producer called "Price and Loan Protection Through Hedging." Such efforts apparently paid off, for in the first ten months of the year, the CME more than doubled its trading volume over that for all of 1968.

It was a good story and the newly hired Ronald Frost set out to tell it. "Our volume has grown to such an extent," Harris announced, "that our public relations obligations require us to have a full-time specialist internally, as well as an outside firm."

The Merc's advertising program at the time was handled by Haggerty & Sullivan, a small Chicago agency that ran 95 percent of the CME ads in *The Wall Street Journal*. "No one really knew what futures trading was then," Frost reflected. "We were still scrambling and a distant second (behind the CBOT) in trading volume. But business was coming our way and we wanted to be the best." Years later, on the wall of Frost's office hung a sign that summed up the lament of the public relations man: "When I'm RIGHT no one remembers. When I'm WRONG no one forgets."

In 1969, when the Merc chose Marty Cohen as its ad man, the purpose was, as Frost remembered, "to become better known. We became the talk of the industry. We were probably spending more than the industry as a whole." One ad in *Playboy* magazine that stated "Cattle Futures are not for Widows or Orphans" drew an unexpected response from aspiring speculators. For the first time, Frost noted, the CME began to identify locations of commodity traders. The responses came from Illinois, Iowa, and California. As a result, "we began meeting brokers in Los Angeles and began producing more brochures than just contract specs," said Frost. "To the major brokerage firms futures markets were stepchildren at best." In addition, a series of radio promotions were launched following a University of Wisconsin survey that revealed that after truckers, farmers were the next biggest group of radio listeners. "We figured farm radio was the most effective means to reach farmers on hedging," said Frost.

At the time, most of the stories in the press, according to Frost, were usually related to exchange volume. "We need more exposure," he told Harris. "What if I could get you on the Johnny Carson Show or Joey Bishop Show?" Harris shook his head in disbelief as if Frost had offered to send him on a trip to the moon. Several days later, Frost told Harris that the Merc was going to give Joey Bishop (his nightly show had more than 20 million viewers) a champion steer. The next week, Frost, Bob O'Brien, and a blanket emblazoned with "Chicago Mercantile Exchange" were off to Los Angeles in search of a champion steer.

At the Los Angeles stockyards, they got into what Frost described as "a bidding war" over a huge champion Angus steer. "Sold to the man with the white hat!" bellowed the auctioneer, pointing to O'Brien, whose $8,000 bid won. Frost promptly hired a herdsman to handle the steer. After some promotional visits to various Los Angeles banks and brokerage houses with steer in hand, it was off to the Joey Bishop show. Bishop graciously accepted the steer dressed in its Merc blanket before millions of viewers. It was the first time the CME had gone from coast to coast.

An even bigger milestone was reached in March when pork bellies moved ahead of corn as the most actively traded contract in the nation. Bellies had replaced such popularly traded commodities as corn, wheat, soybeans, oats, and rye—the pets of the Chicago Board of Trade. "This is akin to a relatively unknown American Stock Exchange issues' topping American Telephone & Telegraph in volume," *The New York Times* observed. Though pork bellies were initially shaky, they eventually gave the Merc the stability it needed. In January 1969 some 109,000 pork belly contracts changed hands during the month compared with 103,000 corn contracts.

Suddenly, records and myths were shattered. The *Journal of Commerce* on 26 March 1969 noted that the frozen concentrate orange juice futures contract on the New York Cotton Exchange, "along with that of the spectacularly successful pork bellies contract on the Chicago Mercantile Exchange, have blasted the once held opinion that processed food products do not lend themselves to futures trading."

The proof was in the volume. In 1969, the 50-year-old Merc surpassed the 122-year-old Chicago Board of Trade in dollar volume for the first time. More than $39 billion worth of commodities futures contracts changed hands, easily doubling the Merc's 1968 volume and surpassing the CBOT's 1969 total of just under $37 billion. (The CBOT, however, remained the leader in number of actual contracts traded: 4.9 million, compared with 3.6 million at the Merc.)

Commodity trading had experienced its greatest activity in United States history. Trading in government-regulated futures markets rose to a record $81.5 billion in 1969, up 36 percent from the previous year. The increase in national volume was led by the Merc, at least in part, because of a large amount of money freed by investors who liquidated positions in the securities markets.

The increased trading volume naturally reflected higher membership prices as well. A seat on the Merc jumped to a record $90,000 in mid-December, while the value of CBOT seat sold for $44,000, the highest price since 1929, when the record $62,500 was paid. By contrast, a seat on the New York Stock Exchange sold for $270,000 on 9 December, off 48 percent from the record $515,000 paid in December 1968.

The eyes of the financial world were beginning to focus on the Chicago Mercantile Exchange. Stories about the Merc appeared in virtually every major newspaper in every major city across America. "We had become a conglomerate before that word went out of vogue," Harris said, "and now we were being described by a new and more popular word—multimarket."

The Merc had added lumber and boneless beef to its growing list of contracts. Other exchanges, too, were moving to diversify. In an attempt to become less dependent on government loan programs to farmers, the CBOT developed new, non-grain futures contracts. It had added iced broilers, plywood, and silver to its list and was about to establish a marketplace in securities options.[3] New contracts didn't just happen. They took time and effort to develop.

The CME, for instance, began studying lumber in 1961 and concentrated on it intensively in 1968 through three independent studies, a computer model, and advice from people in the lumber industry. For softwood lumber, a research team made 3,000 correlations covering prices in a seven-year period from 1962 to 1968. The finding: two-by-four lumber prices correlated well with other sizes in a given species, and that two-by-fours of different species—but similar grades and dryness—also correlated. Close correlations were found with unseasoned two-by-fours, and weaker, but still practical, correlations were found in matching standard grade prices with utility grade. The result: It made possible effective hedges on purchases and sales.

As it handled its swelling business, the Merc was also preparing for the future. "In the past decade we've suffered because our image was one of a small exchange," Melamed told a reporter. "The things we've done administratively this year were necessary in order to expand further and to prove to the public that our integrity is unimpeachable."

The staff in the Merc's research and administrative departments was bolstered, as was the department of audits and investigations under 34-year-old vice president William M. Phelan. A faster means of recording trades in operations among the 74 clearing members was in the works; the Exchange was about to trade in its IBM 1400 series for the speedier and spiffier IBM 360 model. For the renovated trading floor—expanded by 40 percent—a new Translux Jet display of prices on the New York Stock Exchange, Chicago Board of Trade, and Chicago and New York Mercantile Exchanges was installed. The public relations department moved to larger quarters on the third floor. The trading floor was already too small for the activity and there was talk of a yet-to-be-constructed Mercantile exchange building within or adjacent to the Loop in the next two years. The Merc had sprung up like an adolescent with a can-do attitude and a desire to discover the world.

There was no doubt that the once-sluggish Merc now had momentum, perhaps more so than any other exchange in the nation. It was on its way to becoming a multinational corporation. The changes that swept the Merc came from a better feeling among the Exchange members about themselves and the leadership. Its leaders wanted to be more than visionaries. They wanted to see around corners.

18

New Book, New Look

No matter how it was analyzed, the intellectual premise behind a new Chicago Mercantile Exchange was diversification coupled with a strong set of newly fashioned bylaws. Melamed and his associates were helping to put it together. Their plan for reshaping the Exchange internally was simple enough: to create a level playing field for its members through rules that made sense and brought order. The days of steamrolling were over.

In the past, members who had adapted the Exchange to suit their needs were now being forced to adapt themselves to the Exchange's demands. It meant, to begin with, rewriting the rulebook. That, in turn, meant a checks and balances system. For instance, the business conduct committee—the watchdog over market manipulation—would no longer have any Board members on it other than the chairman of the committee. Many Board members reacted predictably: "There was a lot of screaming," according to Melamed. On the other hand, the Board maintained control over the Exchange finances. That meant giving the rules teeth that could give the Board, or segments of it, the power to go to a clearinghouse member to demand additional capitalization.

Like a hand-embroidered tapestry, the rules were tediously stitched together over an 18-month period by a constitutional convention–style committee comprising 23 members who represented every aspect of the Exchange. There were those with expertise in the meat complex, others in eggs, still others in marketing, and so on. For the greater part of a year, the committee met two and sometimes three times a week at the Bismarck Hotel in a rented room, where ideas were freely traded like contracts in a crowded pit. The idea was to get away from the Exchange environment, to loosen ties and let hair down, and to haggle over points concerning each and every rule. Each rule was updated or amended, some were discarded, and a host of new ones added. The process was time-consuming; fortunately, no deadline had been set. As needs arose, however, some of the new rules became effective immediately.

To help pick through the legal details, the board of governors turned to Jerrold E. Salzman, a young Harvard-educated lawyer from Lee Freeman's firm.

In a strategic sense, Salzman represented a new wave of thinking that swept the exchange—sort of a bridge connecting the past to the present. He was a modern-day lawyer who could quickly study the markets and who knew how to apply the rules. No longer would the new Exchange officials have to depend on institutional memory. The business world had grown far too complex.

Out of his own legal background, Melamed fashioned a more dynamic role for exchange counsel. He explained,

> Perhaps it was my legal training. Or because we sensed we were entering a litigation-oriented era. Or perhaps it was to strengthen my hand in enforcement policies. Whatever the reason, the attitude of the past which we inherited—lawyers were used as a last resort—was discarded. In its place, we promoted the concept that our attorneys must be kept abreast of every significant move by the Exchange and must be in constant communication with us regarding our problems and programs.

The old leaders of the CME personified Tolstoy's view of history: smug and powerful generals who had less freedom than their foot soldiers, becoming prisoners of the events and forces they sought to manipulate. The Merc had suffered from a hardening of its arteries, offering one contract after another without much apparent thought as to whether it made economic sense. Financial sleight of hand twisted old formulas into new shapes. The problem was that no one had really been in charge.

In his first state-of-the-CME message, Melamed set the tone of his administration, explaining that the Board no longer headed the same institution as it did a decade before. "We are now directors of a business which will soon rank among the nation's biggest," he stated. "Our potential is virtually unlimited."

The trump card Melamed held was his implicit understanding of traders. It enabled him to artfully commingle a trader's instinct with a businessman's pragmatism. "Be a lover, not a fighter" was his philosophy toward the markets as well as toward the Exchange, which had found romance in pork bellies. He had reminded himself and his fellow traders not to fight the market because the market was always right. Cut losses and let profits run. Every trader knew that. Discipline was the key. A large trader wasn't successful because he traded big numbers. It took skill as well as the the ability to be right more often than wrong. Moreover, it took the considerable risk of time and money to build competence and confidence. And in the quest for success, if a trader played for peanuts, he would win peanuts.

Those same principles could also apply to running an exchange. Yet an overemphasis on stability, rules, and procedures could drain the entrepreneurial fuel that had driven the Merc from the beginning. That would surely decrease willingness to take business risks and challenge competitors, making the Merc's organizational climate as stale as a day-old doughnut. There were 500 members of the Exchange, all of them entrepreneurs in their own right, all more or less fending for themselves as traders, all with their own space in a trading pit defined by the width of their shoes and length of their soles. Each was an individual. "Getting them to think collectively as an institution was a task in itself," said Harris.

It was going to take more than a change at the top to restore the Merc's luster. Simply throwing money at the Exchange wouldn't guarantee success either. Instead, it would take a change of heart.

Probably one of the most significant factors to change the spirit of the institution was the fact that all the members of the Board were putting in a full day's work for the Exchange. In the words of Bill Muno, "Being a Board member was no longer merely a matter of prestige. It now meant a great deal of time and effort in the form of scores of meetings and special conferences. Just as important, it meant being concerned on a daily basis and responsive to new ideas and expanding goals."

The members also profited by the Merc's good fortunes as the Board passed on benefits. With a healthy treasury, the Exchange voluntarily reduced its income by the authorization of full use of Treasury bills as margin. This action allowed brokerage firms and their customers to earn interest on margin money. At the same time, clearing fees were cut by 50 percent, increasing the profits of both member firms and individual members. Another change was the tightening of the rules pertaining to discretionary accounts. A speculator was required to put up a minimum of $3,000 to open an account and to maintain a balance of at least $2,000. The more stringent rule, said Harris, was designed to protect "widows and orphans" and those financially unqualified to speculate in commodities. To bolster the rules, stiffer penalties were adopted; the maximum fine for a minor offense was hiked from $500 to $2,500, and for a major offense from $1,000 to $10,000, with a possible expulsion from membership.

The value of memberships more than kept pace with the activity. The golden anniversary pamphlet disclosed that 102 of the Exchange's 500 seats had changed hands over the year as membership prices rose to $85,000 from a 1968 high of $38,000. Thus, it came as no surprise that in June 1970, the Merc announced plans to stretch its legs in larger quarters. It had outgrown not only its space, but the era. Through a referendum, the members voted overwhelmingly in favor of the move. Of 350 votes cast, 320 members voted to seek new quarters—a symbol of their renewed faith and belief in the Merc's future.

The hunt was on for new quarters. Over the next several months a special CME committee considered new sites in the downtown area—145 of them. The $1 million remodeling program completed in 1969 was already inadequate. In October 1969, Melamed, in a letter to CME members, said that despite a recent 40 percent expansion, "our present trading floor is busting at the seams." The board believed that the Franklin street building facilities—dedicated by Will

Rogers in 1928—would suffice for perhaps two or three more years. Perkins & Will was retained as advisor, architect, and designer of the new trading floor. As a stopgap measure, the third-floor area was under renovation to accommodate the CME's public relations department, new warehouse, delivery points department, and a new theater and lecture hall for public presentations.

Some of the old guard traders, led by Sol Rich, advised against a move. Even Chicago magnate Henry Crown thought it unwise, though he did have a vested interest. Crown, who had once owned the Empire State building, was the Merc's landlord. He had bought the building at 110 North Franklin in the late 1930s, after missing out on an opportunity to buy the Merchandise Mart. When Crown got wind that the Merc was on the prowl for new space, he invited Melamed to lunch.

"I was scared to death; didn't know what it was about," Melamed said. He found out soon enough. Crown simply tried to talk him out of the move. Melamed left the lunch the same way he had entered—scared. "I spent that night thinking," Melamed said. "By morning, I was convinced I was still right." Three years later, the Merc was in its new building, 444 West Jackson Boulevard.

By 1975, the Merc again needed space. The only way to expand the building, said architects, was to cantilever the building out over the Clinton Avenue sidewalk. To get the city's permission to do that, Melamed paid a visit to Mayor Richard J. Daley at City Hall. "What's it gonna to do for the city?" Daley asked. "Well, Mr. Mayor," Melamed replied, "if I'm right and the IMM grows the way I think it's going to grow, it will move the center of gravity of finance in the country a couple of feet west of New York." "I like that," the Mayor said, "You've got the right to build that building." And the Merc expanded.

During this time, the Board had the foresight to switch from a manual clearing procedure to a computerized operation in 1967 which gave the Exchange the ability to handle increased volume swiftly and accurately without the paper logjams that had plagued Wall Street back offices. Much of the surge in the Merc's activity stemmed from the addition of new contracts and revisions in others designed to better meet the needs of their respective industries. But it took promotion, pre-selling, advertising, and public relations to make research and planning mean anything.

An equally important task, however, was to rebuild the public's faith in the Exchange. During the summer of 1969, everyone knew that the cost of living had begun rising—a penny here and a penny there. At the time, meat accounted for about a third of the family food budget, which totaled $32 per week for a family of four. But supply and demand had caught up with meat prices that were rising faster than the cost of living. Beef prices rose dramatically for an obvious reason: Cattle numbers could not keep up with the population growth and its beefed-up appetite; in 1960 Americans ate 99 pounds of beef per capita and 111 pounds in 1969. Moreover, the growth of fast-food hamburger chains, led by McDonald's™ and Burger King™, had expanded the market tremendously. "You might say cow prices were jumping over the moon," Harris said of those days. "But it wasn't the fault of the Exchange, although there were always people in the wings trying to pin it on us." Pork prices rose even more dramatically than those of beef, because farmers had cut back production in deference to the demand for beef.

One finger-pointer was Julian Kramer, president of Tanleff Beef Company in New Jersey, who charged the Merc with contributing to high beef prices through "wild speculation in cattle futures." Ironically, at the time, the futures market for live cattle was below the cash price. Cattle began trading in 1964 and hit a record of $34.50 per hundredweight on 2 June 1969. On that same day, top-grade cattle in Chicago was $37.50 on the cash market. (Since 1964, the prices had ranged from 22.5 cents per pound to 34 cents on a spread of $12 per hundredweight. After World War II, cattle prices had fluctuated as much as $18 per hundredweight.)

Kramer had aired his complaints in a full-page advertisement in the *Newark Evening News*. The ad urged readers to write their congressional representatives and senators demanding to know why prices were higher. New Jersey Senator Clifford Case had received about a thousand letters from readers of the ad inquiring about the meat prices. In spite of all the noise created by Kramer, he later appeared to hedge his claims in an interview with *Supermarket News*, a trade publication. "I'm not saying that my charge [in the advertisement] is 100 percent accurate," he conceded, "but if it's only 75 percent true, the public is taking an awful beating." Then he added, "The major factor is the whole inflation climate."

In January 1970, the Merc initiated a financial innovation that was unique for futures markets and was bound to improve the image of the exchange. By that time, the Merc had become a profitable entity and Uncle Sam came to collect some back taxes. The Board called on its tax counselor, attorney Ira Marcus, and he devised the Chicago Mercantile Exchange Financial Trust, a trust fund to protect investors from the failure of any CME clearinghouse member.

In creating this trust fund and contributing to it year after year (by 1991, the fund held $35 million), the CME not only provided security to the people dealing with Merc firms, thereby greatly improving its financial standing; it also insulated a great deal of CME income from taxation. Similar action had been earlier established by the New York, American, and Midwest Stock Exchanges, but the Merc was the first commodity exchange to institute such a fund.

Coincidentally, the CME action in 1970 came on the heels of an incident in late 1969 that forced the CME, CBOT, and Minneapolis Grain Exchange, along with several commodity companies, to indemnify customers of Minneapolis-based Q Commodities Company, which had gone out of business. The indemnification of more than $400,000 came after audits disclosed the company had a heavy loss of credit balances of segregated customer accounts.

It was only the beginning of a string of incidents that stirred public resentment against the industry. In March, a Scranton, Pennsylvania commodities dealer's empire collapsed, leaving more than 250 investors and creditors with losses. Named in the class action suit were the CME and CBOT. Shortly after, another class action suit against an East Coast egg distributor prompted a federal district court judge to state in a strongly worded opinion, "Defendants should be enjoined from the making of further false, misleading, or knowingly inaccurate reports . . . because if further releases are issued, plaintiffs, the public, and the Chicago Mercantile Exchange, will suffer damages which cannot be repaired."

A month later, a $9 million class action suit was filed in Federal district court against the Merc by a group of futures speculators who claimed the Exchange had manipulated the March 1970 shell eggs futures contract. Though they weren't the Merc's most actively traded commodity, the egg contracts had become a source of allegations against various traders and commercial interests for manipulating prices in violation of the Sherman Antitrust Act. The wave of suits kept the Merc's audits and investigation department on its toes. And in October 1970, the Exchange came down hard. The Board meted out heavy penalties to four individual members and three member firms for rule violations in trading July 1970 pork belly futures. Among the violations cited were trading in excess of speculative limits, acts detrimental to the interest or welfare of the Exchange, the furnishing of funds to other clearing members without approval of the Exchange, and improper recording of customer orders.

It was a watershed case for the Merc, not because of what was involved, but who was involved. "The board was taking on the Merc establishment," Harris recounted. "That meant going up against the old guard and proving the Exchange could clean its own house." Because of the gravity of the case, the Merc for the first time allowed defendants to be represented by non-Merc members, or outside counsel.

When Melamed became chairman in 1969, the Merc was still a roughhouse of trading cliques known not so fondly among outsiders as the Whorehouse of the Loop. "The Merc's reputation was green eye shades and sleeve garters," said Laurence Rosenberg, who had left the CBOT in 1967 to trade pork bellies at the Merc. "When I bought my Merc membership in 1965 for $7000, I got a lot of ribbing from the guys at the Board of Trade." In 1961, Rosenberg paid $6,000 for a CBOT membership—double the Merc's price—and traded corn and soybeans. "I found it difficult to crack the committee system politically," Rosenberg continued. "That wasn't so at the Merc, which had come from minus to zero and was ready to progress in the Sixties. There was a feeling we were going to turn around."

Within a matter of months, Rosenberg was asked by Melamed to become a member of the clearinghouse committee. By 1969 Rosenberg was on the board, and he served as Merc chairman from 1977 through 1979. (As of 1991, Rosenberg had served on the Merc board of governors for 22 years, the second longest duration, behind former chairman John T. Geldermann, who has been on the board for 24 years.)

At times, the Merc seemed less a big exchange than a federation of trading fiefdoms that had given the place a casino image. In a desperate hunger to change that image—and to shed labels with harsh overtones—the new leadership refused to look at the past as a blur and was unapologetic that the Merc was at war with itself. The Exchange needed regulatory focus, and if it couldn't police itself, someone else would. The onion fiasco had proven that. It was a message that Merc leaders would relentlessly reiterate to the membership over the next two decades. The alleged violators in the pork belly case included David G. Henner and Robert J. Murphy, both associate brokers of L.D. Schreiber & Co., an old-line clearing firm; John F. Staren, a principal owner of Staren & Co., another clearinghouse; and Ann Cuneo, who had inherited her membership from her deceased husband. Others who appeared before the Board during the inquiry included Sidney Maduff and L.D. Schreiber, two of the most prominent and successful Merc traders at the time, and associate member Beness Enterprises Inc.

The board was on a tightrope. It wanted neither a kangaroo court nor a moot court, and it didn't want to turn into a bunch of hanging judges. If punishment had to be meted, of course, it had to be in line with the violation. But then again, examples had to be made to discourage others from trying the same thing. There were reputations and livelihoods as well as the Merc's image at stake. That, however, was only part of the conundrum. If the Merc were to move forward, it had to draw upon that single characteristic that had driven its founders from the underclass to prosperity—not self-esteem, but self-discipline. It was the key to being a successful trader. Why shouldn't it hold for an institution made up of traders? Now, in a sense, the Merc itself was on trial.

On a crisp fall afternoon in October 1970, the hearings opened before the board of governors in the office of the Merc clearinghouse. Staff members present included William Phelan, vice president of Audit and Investigations; Karl Heimke; and outside counsel Lee Freeman Sr.. A bill of particulars prepared by the business conduct committee was officially presented; the charges, in part, stated, "In May 1970, or shortly prior thereto, Henner, Cuneo, Murphy, and Maduff agreed that if circumstances allowed, they would act together to squeeze or corner either the 1970 July or August pork belly contract and manipulate the price thereof."

In May 1970, Henner had taken delivery on 200 pork belly contracts and Cuneo on 211 contracts. These contracts, Schreiber told the board, "represented a very important part of the bellies that were immediately available." Schreiber had financed the outright purchase of at least 61 of Cuneo's pork belly contracts, amounting to some $813,000. All along, Exchange officials tried to monitor positions taken by the bigger traders.

In late 1969, Harris called Schreiber, who was wintering in Miami to tell him that there was a "tight fit in the market" and he wanted to see it loosened up by deliveries. Then Harris outlined what he perceived to be the scheme:

> "Here's what these people are shooting at," Harris said. "They're going to take delivery of these bellies, 400 cars in May, and they're going one of two ways. In either July or August they were going to withhold these bellies from sale, then go short either one of those contracts and deliver the 400 contracts and break the market to their own profit. Or, the other alternative was that they would sell those cars at any price obtainable during July and in one of those months, after they got rid of the 400 cars, they would step in and buy freely and tighten up a squeeze because of the absence of product.

In the first instance, they would capitalize on the short side of the market; in the second instance they would capitalize on the long side.

Even those in the market, it seemed, had trouble following the testimony. Take, for instance, board member Dan Jesser, a veteran trader himself. Somehow the arcane machinations were a bit too muddy for his vision. Seeking clarification, Jesser lapsed into a kind of theatrical aside that sounded like a stream-of-consciousness monologue when he was called on to comment:

> I don't quite understand this. If you have loaned the money to finance the outright ownership of cash bellies, and obviously the person to whom you have loaned this money does not have the money to pay for those bellies until such time as he sells them, I don't think he can sell them without lifting the hedge because the increment may acquire to the paper, if the hedges are not lifted. In other words, the sale is made according to the price on the market, I presume, according to futures purchases, and hedges must now be lifted at that very moment in order to establish a basis for the sale. Is that normal?

There was drama in and out of the board room during the hearing as tensions ran high. Recalled Michael Weinberg, Jr., then on the board: "An early break in the case came when a witness for Commodity News Service annoyed with a lack of response by the defendants said he would 'blow the whistle on them' if they continued to be unresponsive." The next day Weinberg handed out dime store whistles to each board member, as a symbol—and reminder—that Merc members were blowing the whistle on each other. "Not everyone appreciated my sense of humor," said Weinberg.

Throughout June and July 1970, Phelan observed Henner's trading on the floor of his own account and of Cuneo's. Phelan also discussed the trading of the July 1970 pork belly future with a number of other people on the Exchange floor. He learned that Henner had a controlling effect on the trading of the future. "The market was being affected by a couple of people," Phelan testified, "that when they waved their hand one way, the market would go one way. If they waved their hand the other way, the market would go the other way. It seemed like the fact that they had possession of this product, plus the way they were treating the market, scalping every day, that they had quite a hold on this market." The techniques employed by Henner and Cuneo were subtle and sophisticated in the early stages. The manipulators knew that from the moment they had the cash market cornered, they were in a position to manipulate the futures market in small swings.

Harris and Phelan were aware of the potential for manipulation in May 1970 when they learned that Henner and Cuneo had cornered the cash market. Henner had failed to establish bona fide hedge accounts and instead engaged in speculative trading that whipsawed the market to their advantage through day trades and changing positions. Henner and Cuneo were accused of reaping windfall profits from their manipulative efforts in excess of $240,000 each.

To the detractors who gave exchanges poor marks for self-regulation, the Merc showed a tough side. Besides a $10,000 fine, one broker was suspended from the CME for three years, another for two. One clearing firm was suspended for two months, and the principal owner of a second firm was suspended for two years and his firm's clearing privileges were revoked. In addition, the member rates of an associate firm were revoked. A fourth individual whose membership remained intact was fined $30,000, the biggest fine ever slapped on a Merc member up to that time.

When the smoke had cleared, the Merc showed that it could clean its own house. "This should be an indication to people that the Exchange isn't going to tolerate any nonsense in our markets," Melamed said afterward. "This action should help boost our image." Besides the largest fines, the penalties were the severest ever meted out by the board. It was an important case for the Merc. From then on, Merc officials believed, it would be easier to break up squeezes and corners.

The incident sparked the old debate over gambling versus speculation in the name of futures trading. To start with, the open outcry system was "a type of free-form auction that combined elements of primal scream, aerobic dancing, and the Battle of Hastings," a description given by Eugene Finerman, a Merc public affairs writer, in one of the Merc's more jocular and popular brochures. There was nothing divine in that. But if an exchange was not a church, neither was it a casino; in truth, it was a bit of both. It was a place where buyers and sellers, set apart from the physical impact of the world's harsh realities, struggled against the odds in a purely economic sanctuary. They met solely to trade futures contracts.

Professors Charles V. Harlow and Richard J. Teweles made the following written observation:

> Gambling involves the creation of a risk for the sole purpose of someone taking it. The horse race, poker game, and roulette wheel create risks which would not be present without them. Gamblers are willing to accept these risks in return for the opportunity to win some money. No particular social good is accomplished unless

one believes that gambling provides a needed outlet for the gamblers, whose needs might be satisfied by something worse if they could not gamble.

Speculation, on the contrary, deals in risks that are necessarily present in the process of marketing goods in a free capitalistic system. . . . If the speculator was unwilling to take them, someone else would have to do so.

In July 1976, administrative law judge George H. Painter summarized the pork belly trial:

Futures markets perform a valid economic service to society, especially in the areas of price insurance and price stability, and nothing in this decision is intended to disparage that worthwhile function. There are striking similarities, however, between futures trading and pari-mutuel wagering. New money is not generated in the futures market. For every dollar lost on a losing contract, one dollar, minus commissions, is won on a winning contract. There is one winning contract for every losing contract. Winners buy low and sell high, or sell high and buy low. Losers do the opposite. The possibility of delivery on the exchange is the single element distinguishing futures trading from wagering. And to repeat, delivery is the exception, not the rule, on most futures markets, including the Chicago Mercantile Exchange.

Such incidents involving price tampering, corners, or squeezes reflected on the shakiness of the federal regulators as well. The federal watchdog over the futures exchanges in 1970 was still the CEA. Its critics, however, characterized it as more a puppy than a watchdog for its lack of regulatory bite. It was administered by 20-year CEA veteran Alex Caldwell, who supervised a staff of 170 in Washington and in four field offices (Chicago, New York, Kansas City, and Minneapolis), all with an eye on some 21 commodities that were being traded at the time. Caldwell was a complicated man with a "friendly" line of patter and an ironic scowl that creased his face. He saw the CEA's approach as preventive. "We try to prevent manipulation before it occurs rather than go after the manipulator after the thing is all over, because by then the damage has been done," he pointed out. But, argued the regulators, to catch up with mischief in a trading pit required placing a police officer in every one. No federal agency had enough resources and labor to do that.

Clearly the burden had to be shared between the exchanges and the CEA. The relationship between futures trading and the cash egg market was a case in point. Caldwell conceded that it was possible to manipulate both the cash egg and futures egg markets. Thus, the spot market in eggs on both the New York Mercantile Exchange and the CME, he concluded, had "outlived their usefulness." Both exchanges through their own initiative had discontinued spot trading in eggs. Had the cessation of spot trading resulted from pressure by the CEA? It was a question to which Caldwell replied "We had conversations with officials of both exchanges and we made clear to them our feeling that potentially they could be used for price manipulation and they were not used for merchandising eggs. We did not think they were serving a useful purpose. But the action was taken by the exchanges themselves."

From the early days of the commodity exchanges, shady speculators devised more and faster ways to make a buck than there were types of contracts to trade. Squeezes, corners, price manipulation, curb trading after hours, bucketing (whereby orders are matched elsewhere than in the pit), not to mention the old-fashioned noncompetitive trades known in the industry as a "wash sale," "cross trade," "accommodation trade," or "fictitious sale"—"methods and techniques of manipulation limited only by the ingenuity of man," was the way a U.S. Court of Appeals put it in a 1963 case involving the giant Minneapolis grain merchant, Cargill, Inc. Markets also moved on rumors ("Sell the fact, buy the rumor," quipped many a trader). And there was even "regulatory manipulation," a term used by Philip McBride Johnson, the former chairman of the Commodity Futures Trading Commission which replaced the CEA in 1975. Johnson referred to those types of actions imposed on futures markets in the "face of a real or perceived danger" that the market may overheat. In November 1976, for example, the CFTC forced the New York Mercantile Exchange to confine trading in the November Maine potato futures contract to the liquidation of open positions and to raise the margins on the contract to 100 percent of the value of the commodity. In March 1979 the Chicago Board of Trade was unsuccessfully ordered to stop trading in its March wheat contract. In 1980 the CFTC for two days closed the grain futures markets in Chicago, Kansas City, and Minneapolis, following President Carter's grain embargo on the Soviet Union.

There were those in the business who actually believed that stopping corners and squeezes would kill the markets, because they provided the fuel to run the market machine. "That was the sex of trading for a lot of people," Harris said "It was the oil that made the markets work, even though people complained about it."

19

Who Were We?

If the Chicago Mercantile Exchange had developed anything in its first half century, it was a nose for opportunity. That, coupled with the new management team's zest for tomorrow's tasks, drove the once-staid butter-and-egg exchange hard into the future.

The Merc hit record volume just as the gross national product broke the lofty trillion-dollar mark. But the decade of prosperity came to an end. The 1960s indeed were golden years. Inflation was now beginning to chip away at the economy, and a recession loomed. It didn't help that stocks were collapsing along a broad front (the Dow sank to 631 in May 1970), and the Penn Central, formed in a merger several years earlier, was bankrupt. The offshore mutual fund business of Bernie Cornfeld had crumbled, and Robert Vesco fled to Costa Rica, accused of siphoning hundreds of millions from Cornfeld's fund operations. With inflation rising, the dollar sinking, and trade deficits appearing, Richard Nixon was in search of new economic policies that would bring economic order.

Amid such chaos, the Merc announced its dramatic plans to expand. With pork bellies sizzling as the most actively traded of all commodity futures—and the demand for bacon remaining fairly inelastic—the mood at the Merc was upbeat. The go-ahead attitude prevailed on a sunny April morning in 1970 in the office of Mayor Richard J. Daley. Flanking the mayor were Harris, Melamed, Jesser, chairman of the CME real estate committee, and Freeman, the Merc's outside counsel, in a press conference detailing plans for the most modern futures exchange in the world.

Later that day, immediately after the close of trading, a more elaborate presentation was made to the Merc members on the exchange floor. Using a combination of three slide projectors, the Merc officials, along with representatives of the exchange's real estate consultant, Perkins and Will Partnership, and the new building's architect, Skidmore, Owings and Merrill, laid out the details for a building complex that would take nearly two years to complete.

The new headquarters and trading floor complex—housed in a six-story rect-angular building adjacent to the south side of a thirty-five story office building—was to be located in Gateway Center, immediately west of the Chicago River between Jackson Boulevard and Adams Street. It would have 43,655 square feet of floor space with more than half of it for the trading floor. The cost: $6 million.

There was no doubt that the Merc was preparing for more business.[1] The floor would have eight to twelve trading pits, compared with the present five. There would be ten to fourteen board-traded commodities, compared with eight. The new administrative offices alone would account for another 11,697 square feet. The gallery level covered 8,029 square feet. As recently as 1964, the Merc had accounted for only 3 percent of the total U.S. trading volume in futures contracts. Five years later, it was 40 percent. In the dollar value of the contracts traded (nearly $40 billion), the Merc now led all futures exchanges.

It was apparent that growth was not a temporary matter. The Merc had even prepared a new ad for newspapers and magazines across the country that showed the architectural rendering of the new Merc. The headline was simply, "Build-ing," symbolic of what the Merc had been doing for years: creating liquid markets for commodities among a wide range of users in accordance to their needs. Perhaps more important than the newly proposed building, however, was the distribution of the CME's new rulebook. It had been in the works for nearly two years, toiled over by a dozen committees, scores of members, and legal counsel. A copy of the book was given to each member on 1 June 1970.

The new rule book reflected meticulous care and a great deal of study of each area of the Exchange. Practically every previous rule had been refashioned or modified to some degree. Some rules had only been reformatted for clar-ity. Others were either partially or totally revised in concept. Still others were completely new, replacing unused or antiquated ones. Naturally, the updated rulebook was an immediate best-seller among the members.

In June the CME had also voted to increase its minimum commission rates. A special committee headed by Barry Lind had studied the commission rate structure and recommended the general increase (an average of 13 percent) be-cause of increasing transaction costs. The last general adjustment in commission fees came in 1950, when commissions were lowered. The new rates were keyed to a letter Harris had received from the Association of Commodity Exchange Firms that noted, "Unless the level of minimum commission rates which can be charged to a customer is brought more in line with the current cost of handling the business, and done so promptly, a number of firms which have been promi-nent in commodity business in recent years may be forced to abandon it." The letter also pointed out that under the existing commissions, single buy or sell transactions were simply not profitable.

That summer, the Merc paused just long enough to honor one of its veterans, an elfin, white-haired fellow known around the Exchange as Sam. Sam Newman was retiring after 39 years as a telegrapher. He had started on the floor of the exchange in 1931, working for Western Union, and then joined the Merc in 1954. Sam had spent nearly 40 years on the floor, and at age 69, Florida beckoned. During the Depression, he recalled at his retirement ceremony at the Bismarck Hotel, "Some days not one car was traded." He even remembered the day Ken Mackay, then CME executive vice-president, had started as a board marker. In accepting a special plaque, his speech was characteristically to the point. "I see a more progressive spirit at the Exchange," he said. "They'll [the members] be okay." It was the end of an era and the flickering of an institutional memory.

By design, the Merc would no longer live in the past. Melamed called the Merc's new posture "the coming of age" as it geared itself to more business. Martin Cohen continued to churn out a series of spellbinding ads that portrayed the Exchange as an aggressive institution chasing public business on the heels of a stock market downturn. The new ads flashed such headlines as the following:

- Were you born under the sign of the pork belly?
- Was Charlie McCarthy cut out to trade commodities?
- Sell now. Raise later.
- Teddy Roosevelt would have made a great commodity trader.
- Price Insurance. Our policy.
- Was Toulouse Lautrec too short to trade commodities?
- One man's Polaroid is another man's pork belly.
- Where does Wall Street go for eggs?

Image became a priority, and Melamed used his chairman's message as a reprimand of sorts and as an outcry for unity in a speech given to Merc members in January 1971.

> Image is perhaps our most difficult problem. To a large degree, image is affected by the attitude and impression conveyed by our members and governors. One of the principal reasons for our problem in this regard is the intermittent publicity about a so-called attempt or "squeeze" of one of our markets. Where there is reason to believe that such might be the case, it becomes the primary duty of the Audits and Investigations Department and the Business Conduct Committee . . . but more often than not, our image suffers severely because . . . unnecessary loose talk, hearsay and unwarranted gossip . . . invariably finds its way into the public ear and our reputation invariably suffers, whether or not there is a grain of truth in the gossip at hand.

Like a big brother chastising his sibling, Melamed continued on a hard line: "It is my strong opinion that with the coming of age of the 'Merc' it is also high time our members come of age." "How do we make our members grow up?" Melamed asked rhetorically. "Well," he emphasized, "we already have a rule on this subject and I propose we begin strong enforcement of it. But the primary responsibility lies with our governors. You, as members of the Board, must constantly be on the alert to prevent and stop public unwarranted member orations and set for them the pattern and style that if they have something to say—fine—we want to hear it, but in the proper place and manner. I cannot sufficiently stress this point."

Nor could Melamed overstress the importance of policing. The four sources of self-regulation—the Department of Audits and Investigations, the Business Conduct Committee, the Clearing House Committee, and the Floor Practices Committee—were expected to take a no-nonsense approach even, as Melamed put it, "if it should be unpopular." From that point forward, corners became a footnote in the history of the Chicago Mercantile Exchange. Although markets would eventually grow too big to corner, there would always be brokers and traders trying to sting customers through rigged trades of one kind or another. But even better regulation and enforcement could hardly wipe out the dubious reputations of futures, which dated back to the nineteenth century, when the CBOT was known as a symbol of "wicked" capitalism. The surge in food and commodity prices in the mid-1970s, much of which was blamed—rightly or wrongly—on futures speculation, continued to tarnish the images of the exchanges in Chicago and elsewhere. Partly in response to the consumer uproar, Congress created the CFTC to replace the ineffectual CEA and gave the new agency more power and money. "It was a classic case of an industry trying to live by 1890 robber-baron standards in an age of public accountability," John Rainbolt, one of the first CFTC commissioners, told the *Wall Street Journal* in 1977.

Implicit in a strong enforcement policy, the Merc officials reasoned in 1969, was an unimpeachable board of governors. That meant that board members and their respective clearinghouses were expected to behave in a manner beyond reproach. To this end, the Department of Audits and Investigations was reorganized into a decentralized operation with various staff members assigned to specific committees. The head of the department was to function as the primary administrator and troubleshooter. The day-to-day job of each staff member was clearly defined so there would be no confusion.

On the educational front, the Merc became even more aggressive. After all, it was the responsibility of the exchanges to drive the industry, or so Harris believed. To do that required intensive education on a broad front. Advertising and public relations could take the process just so far. Those areas dealt with form; Harris would say that education showed substance. With Ron Frost serving as the point man and traveling as far as Seattle and Vancouver, the Merc, in conjunction with a number of universities, put together a string of hedger seminars. In addition, there were banker seminars, expanded fellowship-in-futures programs, telelecture programs, establishment of college courses on futures trading (including a YMCA study course in commodities), correspondence courses in futures, development of a common examination program for all commodity exchanges, an annual CME conference on meat and livestock, a host of new materials for use by brokerage firms, universities, and CME users, and a number of booklets designed for noncommodity areas as a service to agribusiness. The list also included a series called *Trading in Tomorrows,* which subsequently was turned into a semidocumentary on the exchange and futures markets, as well as a book entitled *Futures Trading in Livestock—Origins and Concepts.*[2] Responsibility for research and education fell largely on the shoulders of Mark Powers, a young Ph.D. in agricultural economics who had joined the exchange in January 1969 as a vice president. Much of his work was to be involved with researching new commodities. In the first year on the job, he had reviewed some 30 prospects.

Powers, a thoughtful and articulate bespectacled 31-year-old University of Wisconsin economist, had written his doctoral dissertation on pork belly futures. One of 11 children who had grown up on a Wisconsin dairy farm, Powers had a deep understanding of agricultural commodities but was ambivalent about commodity exchanges. "There I was in a room with no windows," he recalled. "I was a farm boy in the big city. I had a deep skepticism about the social good of exchanges."

It wasn't long before he became a believer and a student of the futures industry. In that windowless room, Powers began to think about the value of exchanges like a physicist contemplating the Big Bang. In a sense, the Exchange was his cosmos, and, for him, delving into it was more than an intellectual exercise. Exchanges, he concluded, make a great deal of sense if one considers them as being in two businesses: communications and credit.

An exchange was a meeting place, a forum for disseminating information. The clearinghouse was the credit aspect. As long as there were enough market participants, the system functioned well. In short, the success of a market was highly dependent on its ability to attract and hold hedgers. Powers had implied in his study of the pork belly market that the changes in the pork belly contract specifications made the contract more appealing to hedgers and that hedgers subsequently drew speculators into the market.

This was the area where the exchanges needed the most help, Powers maintained. "They were backward on their approach to the business they wanted to list," he said; "the contracts weren't written correctly." The industry, as he determined it, was in rather "bad shape and pushed against the wall." It wasn't long before he became a master at analyzing and writing contracts to more closely reflect the activity in the cash markets.

The trading of futures contracts, reasoned Powers, is a financial service. And like any other financial service, it had to be packaged, advertised, promoted, financed, and distributed. It took a first-class marketing job. "Improper marketing of even the best written and most economically necessary contract will spell doom for a contract," Powers said.

Exchanges had not traditionally viewed themselves as being in the business of selling financial services. They were in that business, nevertheless. The result of this attitude was obvious to Powers. "They have taken a very passive attitude toward marketing activities," Powers noted. "The fact that exchanges are not-for-profit membership organizations, whose members can be and are assessed to meet operating expenses, has contributed to this attitude." How, then, did it manifest itself? "Most notably," Powers continued, "in the almost benign neglect that has been afforded almost all new contracts on exchanges after the initial hoopla of the opening ceremonies is completed." The relatively low cost involved in listing a new contract provided little incentive for an exchange to do a better and more complete job of developing and marketing its contracts. Thus, if the contract failed, little had been lost.

Recognition was also a factor to the success of a contract. Consider live cattle, for example. One of the reasons for its immediate success was the fact that the public speculators knew what a steer looks like. "Trading in live beef futures conjured up romantic images of old West cattle drives and cowboys," said Powers. "People who bought cattle futures felt just like the cattle barons."

Pork bellies, on the other hand, were not easily identifiable or understood by people at the start of trading. One radio announcer called them "pork tummies." As it turned out, however, the name pork bellies was so unusual that it worked to the advantage of the exchange. By the time Powers came to the Merc, it was all academic. Both cattle and bellies were booming. Now there were new contracts to consider on an item that every man, woman, and child was familiar with—money.

Harris had recruited Powers. Changes in the world currency system were in the wind and Melamed wanted the Merc ready to take advantage of them.

There were few places to turn to in order for Powers to do his homework on the subject. One source that came immediately to his mind was University of Chicago free-market economist Milton Friedman, who had been lecturing to his students that the system of fixed exchange rates—then on the threshold of being discarded, he believed—was something that should have been done away with years earlier. Friedman had been snubbed by the banking establishment when he tried to speculate in currencies. Subsequently, that experience would gain the Merc a much-needed friend in Friedman when it came time to launch the International Monetary Market.

When Melamed came across the story of how Friedman had wanted to short the pound and couldn't, "I was convinced the idea of a futures market for currencies was a good one," Melamed said. "But who the hell was Leo Melamed? But Milton Friedman was somebody!"[3]

Now the Merc could tap into Friedman's insights. Powers sent Friedman a letter on 30 March 1970. As a graduate student, Powers had first heard the laissez-faire economist in a heated debate in Madison, Wisconsin with University of Wisconsin professor Leon Kaiserling, a devout Keynesian. "Kaiserling got so mad in the middle of the debate," recalled Powers, "he stormed off the stage. So Friedman stayed and started talking about foreign exchange forwards."

Friedman had been predicting the breakdown of Bretton Woods since 1950, while individuals such as Federal Reserve chairman Arthur Burns, a close advisor to Nixon, favored fixed exchange rates. Fixed exchange rates were orderly. Floating rates introduced uncertainty into the world, and that could make the problem of trading more difficult. And that, in turn, could open a market for futures.

Less than two weeks later (on April 10) Friedman replied to Powers's letter with three points:

> (a) There is certainly an important economic function served by an efficient market in futures in foreign currency. I am under the impression that such a market does exist today. I do not know enough about the detailed arrangements to know whether that market would be improved by your Exchange establishing trading in futures. If so, it would be extremely desirable.
>
> (b) I doubt that we are entering a period of flexible exchange rates in the major currencies. I do believe that we are entering a period in which there will be more frequent changes in the exchange rates of major currencies but, as in the past, I believe that these will be changes from one temporarily fixed parity to another rather than truly flexible rates. The difference will be that the changes will be smaller and more frequent than in the past.
>
> Again, I do not know enough about the detailed market arrangements to know whether an organized exchange in currency futures would have a function to perform in addition to the trading by banks.
>
> (c) I do not have enough expertise to answer this question.
>
> Sincerely,
> Milton Friedman

The message from Friedman was clear to Powers: No one really knew whether the idea would work. In true Merc fashion, there was enough information for the Merc officials to push the idea of a currency market. Once again, the Merc was off and running on a new contract.

Trading French francs wasn't exactly what the founding fathers had in mind when they launched the Merc in 1919. Of course, times were different then, and every cent was measured by the gold standard. A rose by any other name might have smelled as sweet; but for a buck to be a buck to be a buck, it had to be backed up by something you could sink a tooth into (or fill it with). But with inflation rising, the dollar sinking, and trade deficits appearing, Nixon launched his New Economic Policy in 1971.

The new policy was a mixed blessing for the Chicago Mercantile Exchange. The bad news came on 15 August, when the administration froze wages and prices for 90 days and imposed a 10 percent import surcharge. At the same time, however, Nixon closed the gold window, thereby suspending the convertibility of dollars into gold.

The next morning Powers entered Harris's office to find him on the phone with CEA head Alex Caldwell.

"What does this mean?" asked Harris.

"I don't know any more about it than you do," Caldwell replied.

Immediately after the conversation with Caldwell, Harris turned to Powers and said, "Mark, from now on you'd better get going full steam on coming up with a currency contract."

The reaction to the freeze was mixed. Liberal economists saw it as a way to break the momentum of an inflation that was showing signs of turning worse. The free marketers saw it as an intrusion. "I applaud President Nixon's proposed reduction in both taxes and Federal spending," Milton Friedman commented at the time. "I applaud also his action in ending the fiction that the dollar is convertible into gold. But I regret exceedingly that he decided to impose a 90-day freeze on prices and wages . . . "

Friedman said the freeze was like freezing the rudder of a boat and making it impossible to steer, in order to correct a tendency for the boat to drift one degree off course. History had shown that trying to control wages and prices often failed. It had been tried time and time again. The emperors of Rome and China issued edicts. So did the monarchs of medieval Europe and England, relying on an ethical code backed by severe penalties. Except for brief wartime periods, when measures were reinforced by patriotic fervor, controls were met with scant success. There would be stability for a while, then a flood, a poor harvest, or a siege, and prices would soar. In the long run, the ancients weren't very successful at holding down prices—nor, for that matter, were the modern theoreticians, even with their huge bureaucracies and communications networks to mobilize public support behind them.

Three days after the freeze—on 18 August—the Merc advised its members that the order affected the sale of cash pork bellies, skinned hams, and lumber. It didn't, however, preclude trading in the futures markets of these commodities. Specifically, the presidential order did not apply to the cash or futures prices of fresh eggs, live cattle, live hogs, fresh Idaho russet potatoes, or grain sorghum.[4]

While Powers was busy researching a currency contract, tremors from a series of monetary crises were jarring the world's economies. International currency speculators had mounted a massive attack against the already bruised dollar by shifting huge sums into stronger currencies, notably the West German mark and the Japanese yen. To keep the values of their own currencies from rising beyond the fixed price "ceiling" set by the 1944 Bretton Woods agreement, West Germany and Japan were forced to sell unlimited amounts of marks and yen for dollars, amassing between them nearly 24 billion U.S. dollars.

The Bretton Woods Agreement (named after its birthplace in New Hampshire), forged by a group of ten signatories, had been signed by Harry Truman on 31 July 1945. Simply, it governed the world trade and payments system and established a narrow band of fluctuation of European currencies in relation to the

U.S. dollar. At the same time, it set up both the International Monetary Fund—designed to promote exchange rate stability, mutilateral trade, and currency convertibility—and the International Bank for Reconstruction and Development to promote investment. In 1960, the United States and seven other nations sold gold in the London market while the United States maintained the official price of gold at $35 per troy ounce. By March 1968, active gold pool members had established a two-tier gold arrangement.

As banker for the world, the United States was learning a painful lesson: the vicious monetary cycle built into the Bretton Woods agreement. The United States had found itself caught in an economic vortex. The more currency it spent, lent, or gave away, the more the global economy became lubricated. But the more currency floating around the world, the less confidence other nations had in it, and the sooner an international financial crisis was likely to occur. Unable to take the pressure any longer, West Germany and Japan cut their currencies' moorings to the dollar and allowed the mark and yen to float—to fluctuate in value in response to economic influences. In floating their currencies, these countries were in violation of the rules of the International Monetary Fund, the supranational agency that watched over the Bretton Woods agreement. Suddenly it was monetary anarchy, and every country, including the United States, for itself. The entire system was collapsing. The United States could no longer honor its pledge to exchange gold for foreign-held dollars.

Nixon's announcement stunned the international financial world. The reason for his drastic action: In the first six months of 1971, the United States had reached an all-time record deficit of $11.6 billion in its balance of payments. That amount was more than all the gold left in Fort Knox.

Under the fixed exchange rate system of Bretton Woods, importers knew what they would pay for goods in their domestic currency, and exporters knew how much they would receive in their local currency. If the importer could sell at a profit to the consumer, and the exporter's costs were below the export price, then everyone gained from trade. Once Bretton Woods broke down, the rules changed.

On 13 December 1971 finance ministers of the leading industrial nations met in Washington's Smithsonian Institution to scrap the Bretton Woods agreement and hammer out a new one. It was give-and-take all around. The United States agreed to devalue the dollar by raising the official price of gold from $35 an ounce to $38. That meant, in effect, that an American would pay more for a Volkswagen; West Germany would pay less for a roll of Kodak film. More U.S. goods, it was hoped, would be sold overseas, and fewer foreign articles would be bought by Americans, thereby improving the U.S. trade balance. For their part, the other major industrial nations agreed to adjust their currencies upward, making them worth more in relation to the battered dollar. In short, the financial tune-up was designed to relieve pressure on the dollar in its reserve currency role.

Equally important decisions were made. The 10 finance ministers decided to permit the exchange rates of the world's major currencies to fluctuate against the dollar by 2.25 percent above or below the official exchange rate—a total of 4.5 percent, instead of the 2 percent total fluctuation previously allowed under the Bretton Woods system. Both sides of an import-export transaction now faced exchange rate risk. Each party sought to transact in his own currency to prevent being whipsawed by the market. For example, take the American importer who ordered British automobiles worth $5 million. Based on a British pound worth $2.60, the autos would cost £1,923,077. Assume that the payment was due in nine months, but during that period the pound in relation to the dollar increased by 2.25 percent to $2.6585. Now the importer was faced with paying $112,500 more for the autos than he had anticipated. However, if, at the time he bought the autos, he had purchased futures contracts in British pounds equaling $5 million, he would have locked in a price and saved $112,500. It was all academic, however, without a freer-floating exchange rate.

Foreign exchange forward contracts had been available for years, but they involved the extension of credit and thus had turned into an interbank market. For that very reason, both individuals and firms were unable to take advantage of the forward market.

Almost unnoticed among all the other historic monetary moves, was the agreement to allow greater fluctuation in the exchange rates. For the Merc, the stage was now set for an idea whose time had come sooner than anticipated. In January 1970 Friedman had predicted the collapse of the Bretton Woods system by 1975. Suddenly, the timetable changed and the Merc had to climb into the foreign exchange trenches.

As early as March 1970, Melamed told the CME Board he was exploring the idea of foreign exchange futures. At first there was some skepticism, but he maneuvered past it. Nevertheless, he urged Powers to pursue the concept in light of the fact that the International Commercial Exchange (ICE) in New York was also pondering the notion of foreign exchange futures.

On 23 April 1970 the ICE actually listed nine currencies and began to trade futures contracts on them. Predictably, these first currency futures were unsuccessful.[5] The ICE lacked a sufficient marketing scheme. But more significantly, there was a lack of exchange rate volatility. The rates were still fixed under Bretton Woods, and from all official indications out of Washington, the situation appeared unlikely to change. "No change in the structure of exchange parities is necessary or anticipated," Treasury Secretary John Connally said on 4 May 1971. Four days after Connally's comment, West Germany and the Netherlands let their currencies float. The mosaic of international finance was beginning to show signs of cracking.

Once Nixon closed the gold window, the Merc moved swiftly to lay the groundwork for what would become the International Monetary Market. "An era had ended," Melamed said. "We believed that a new era was dawning—not only with respect to currency exchange rates—but in the very psychology and manner of operation of American citizens. We were to begin the process of realizing that the U.S. was no longer alone in the financial world."

The central banks were coming to grips with this new reality. It had become impossible for a government to hold its currency at the agreed rates when all the economic and financial forces dictated a higher or lower value. The gesture was futile for one or a number of central banks to continue to support a given currency at the established rate when all the world's so-called speculators responded to the reality by selling or buying against the fictitious rate. The continued pressure toward the real value of a currency had caused some nations to go nearly bankrupt in an attempt to support an arbitrary agreement.

In the midst of the monetary changes taking place, one thing became clear: The American public would soon realize that the United States was no longer alone in determining the value of its currency. The value of the dollar would grow more dependent on the relative value of the Deutsche mark or the yen. America's financial status would become dependent on such international factors as balance of trade and balance of payments. Outside world forces could even cause the almighty dollar to be devalued. Indeed, Americans were about to be rudely awakened.

There was still a hurdle to overcome as far as public awareness. Once balance of payments became a front-page item rather than one exclusively limited to the finance section, the Merc reckoned, then many citizens would begin to look for a way to be involved in this "new" internationalism. It seemed reasonable, then, to assume that many people would seek investment and speculative opportunities in vehicles of an international monetary nature. Merc officials saw it as a developing trend that would grow for decades to come.

Thus the philosophy of the International Monetary Market (IMM) was born: to organize a futures exchange for the express purpose of listing and dealing in monetary instruments. "As it was not our nature to beat around the bush," said Melamed, "our first instrument was the real thing itself—money."

The Merc had moved quickly during the autumn of 1971, just one month after the closing of the gold window. In September, Harris telephoned Milton Friedman at his retreat in Vermont, persuading Friedman to meet him and Melamed in New York City to discuss the idea of an International Monetary Market. The three of them spent two days trading ideas at the Waldorf Astoria. It was several months before the Smithsonian Agreement, and most observers assumed that fixed exchange rates were doomed. In *Essays in Positive Economics,* published in 1953, Friedman had argued the case for floating exchange rates. In Friedman they also found a strong advocate of a public market in exchange rates. "It was intolerable that people should not be able to buy and sell short foreign currencies if they wanted to," Friedman said.

But Melamed wondered whether the timing was right. Would the new monetary order include flexibility? If so, would there be a need for a futures market in currency? These were questions posed to Friedman during the New York meeting. "I thought it was a splendid idea and a very imaginative one," said Friedman of that meeting with Melamed and Harris. "I also thought it was a courageous idea because you were betting on something that was going to have to happen, not on something that had already happened."

Friedman told Melamed and Harris that "there wasn't a chance in a million" that the world was going to have an honest gold standard. "What we have is a standard," he said, "a pegged price for gold. It was like the pegged price for wheat. It wasn't that gold was determining money, it was that money was determining gold."

In effect, the Merc was asking Friedman to put his reputation on the line. A new financial exchange needed credibility, someone with stature and impeccable credentials who could give it a stamp of approval. "Friedman's unqualified affirmative response to our queries gave us the courage to proceed," Melamed later recalled. In September 1971, for $5,000, Friedman was commissioned by the Merc to write a paper on the feasibility of foreign currency futures. Powers, meanwhile, began preparing a justification paper.

Released on 21 December 1971, Friedman's 11-page paper was titled *The Need For Futures Markets In Currencies*. It was clear, concise, and to the point, written in a manner that could be easily understood by a layman:

> Changes in the international financial structure will create a great expansion in the demand for foreign cover. It is highly desirable that this demand be met by as broad, as deep, as resilient a futures market in foreign currencies as possible in order to facilitate foreign trade and investment . . . . Such a wider market is almost certain to develop in response to the demand. The major open question is where. The U.S. is a natural place and it is very much in the interests of the U.S. that it should develop here.

As long as currencies would float in an expanded band, there would be a major need for a broader, widely based, active, and resilient futures market. Transitional floats, Friedman said, had now become respectable. The only true futures market in foreign exchange at the time took place among the world's major banks, which tended to be highly selective. Friedman had learned that lesson back in 1967 when he tried to short the British pound. But times were changing and so were attitudes.

Moreover, Friedman argued, foreign trade would not be hampered by foreign exchange risk if, and only if, there were futures markets in which currencies could be hedged. At the time there was such an off-exchange futures market among the banks in London, Zurich, and New York, but it lacked the necessary breadth, depth, and resilience.

Friedman turned part of his paper into a primer by explaining the previously inexplicable relationship between hedgers and speculators. "A really satisfactory futures market cannot depend solely on hedging transactions by persons involved in foreign trade and investment," he wrote. He reasoned that foreign payments might be in balance so that, over a long period, forward sales of currencies for hedging purposes just balance forward purchases. But within short periods, there was nothing to ensure such a balance for each foreign country separately. "The market needs speculators," Friedman emphasized, "who are willing to take open positions as well as hedges. Fortunately, the same features that make a futures market so essential for foreign trade assure that it will also attract speculators."

Friedman was not alone in his opinion. A number of notable economists concurred and indeed encouraged the Merc officials. "But I must admit," Melamed later said, "that without Professor Friedman's credentials on our team, we might never have started."

The first government official to receive the Friedman paper formally was George P. Shultz, who became U.S. Secretary of the Treasury shortly after the IMM was launched.[6] He had also been a colleague of Friedman's at the University of Chicago. Melamed felt like "the immigrant kid from Poland" on the morning in 1972 when he and Harris waited in the anteroom outside of Shultz's office for a scheduled meeting. "The Merc in those days was very small," he said, "a secondary futures market and a distant second to the Chicago Board of Trade, though we were dealing successfully in cattle, pork bellies, and hogs."

Shultz's free-market views were in sync with Friedman's. Melamed talked about heading into the unchartered waters of floating exchange rates, and that would surely dictate the need for a new market for hedgers and speculators. After listening to Melamed carefully, Shultz responded,"It's not a bad idea, if you can make it work."

Their next appointment that afternoon was with Fed chief Arthur Burns. Burns, who had Friedman's paper lying on his desk, welcomed Melamed and Harris warmly. Though he liked the idea, Burns predicted an uphill battle for the fledgling IMM.

Melamed remembered leaving Washington that day "on cloud nine, assured that the U.S. government wouldn't oppose the idea." On that return flight to Chicago, he realized the essence of Friedman's paper—worth its weight in gold, Melamed boasted—was a marriage of two unique elements: his theory and "our" traders' intuition.

It would take at least three years before the Merc realized that the IMM had arrived. Along the way, there were some encouraging signs, such as Melamed's 1973 meeting with senior executives from Merrill Lynch in New York. The IMM was trading seven currencies, and volume was a sluggish two to three thousand trades a day. But Melamed forgot about that when he entered Merrill Lynch's lobby and was confronted with a sight his eyes couldn't believe: There blazing across an entire wall for all the world to see was a tote board flashing the change of prices of international currencies being traded in Chicago. It was a clear sign that perhaps the IMM had the heart—and drive—to become the little exchange that could.

While the banks outside of Chicago were standoffish, wirehouses E.F. Hutton and Shearson, along with Merrill Lynch, were early supporters of the IMM, which Melamed referred to as "a dream on a hope." They knew, as the Merc leaders did, that currency was the fundamental commodity that made the world go 'round.

Of course, without the Smithsonian Agreement, the idea of an international monetary market would have remained on paper. On Friday, 18 December 1971, Nixon announced the agreement to expand the Bretton Woods bands. Although the new system was too rigid to last, it provided the market with a 4.5 percent range, enough to justify a futures market in foreign currency.

Two days after Nixon's announcement, the Chicago Mercantile Exchange hurriedly organized a press conference. Melamed, Harris, and Powers told the world of the CME's plans to trade futures in foreign exchange and financial futures. The news from the press conference received widespread coverage, appearing in nearly every major newspaper and on a number of radio stations, as well as in newspapers in Europe and Asia. The Merc viewed the response as favorable. To the popular press, the idea was more of a financial curiosity far removed from its daily readers. But to the aloof banking community in the United States and abroad, the idea of individuals speculating in currencies was threatening; such individuals were generally barred from the forward market, although there were no laws prohibiting private speculation. In 1971 the Federal Reserve Board and major domestic and foreign banks continued to exert informal pressure to prevent private speculation because of its politically disruptive effect on exchange rates.

Now that they had told the world of their plan, the Merc prepared itself for one of the toughest fights it had ever faced: to convince the world the plan would work.

20

Making Allies

The wheels were in motion. Melamed, in his third term as chairman, had committed the Merc and there was no turning back. There were many details to be covered and a strategy to refine. Clearly the Merc was off in a new direction. It was a time when most organizations were caught up in the headiness of the holiday season, that period between Christmas and New Year's, when the entire world seemed to be at ease—but not the Merc.

Two days after Christmas in 1971, the Merc's Foreign Currency Committee met at 2:35 P.M. to lay out a plan. Besides Melamed, Harris, and Powers, also gathered in the boardroom were John T. Geldermann, Laurence M. Rosenberg, Ron Frost, Richard Boerke, William Goldstandt, Bill Henner, Lee Freeman, Jr., and Lee Freeman, Sr. The group represented nearly every aspect of the Exchange, from public relations to the pit.

Powers reported on the trip to New York he had taken the week before. There he had met with officials from several banks, including the First National City Bank (predecessor of Citicorp) and the Federal Reserve Bank of New York. The purpose of such meetings was clear-cut: to explain the Merc's strategy to the current and potential players in the world's financial markets.

At the same time, the Merc sought to determine whether it was subject to any regulatory agency—the Treasury, the Fed, or the SEC? No one knew precisely. The Federal Reserve Board had already assured the Exchange, through correspondence with Powers, that it had no regulations on commodity futures trading in foreign currencies. But, cautioned the Fed, if the market was successful, it would be paying closer attention. The Securities and Exchange Commission had no jurisdiction over money trading, and neither did the Commodity Exchange Authority, since money is not an agricultural commodity. Plans were also being made to meet with officials of the Treasury Department. Both the Treasury and Fed acquiesced to the formation of this newly proposed market. How could they intercede? Nothing had yet been traded, and thus it was impossible to determine whether there would be a harmful effect on the dollar.

The Merc was like a country engaged in building strategic alliances; but it wasn't like the old days, when Harris would don a ten-gallon hat and string tie to thump the stockyards and ranches from Peoria to the Panhandle, rousing interest among ranchers in the cattle contract. Now it was strictly pinstripes and boardrooms as Merc officials indeed were practicing financial diplomacy, shuttling to rounds of meetings in Washington, New York, and Chicago.

On 13 January the Merc officials were to meet with the New York brokerage houses. A week later they would be back in Chicago to gather support from the Merc clearing members based in the Windy City. A February symposium of American economists was planned. Thought also was given to obtaining banks as clearing members. Freeman, however, cautioned that having banks as clearing members could cause legal problems for the Exchange. Harris and Powers thought that priority should be given to bringing in multinational firms as clearing members rather than banks. These were questions to be debated.

There was a tremendous amount of ground to cover, and virtually every inch required spadework. It was new turf for the Merc and an entire industry that still had its heart and soul in agricultural commodities. There would be skeptics to deal with and hundreds of questions to be answered. There were also legal considerations and tax consequences.

The main question facing the Foreign Currency Committee was the kind of structural organization to be developed within the Chicago Mercantile Exchange for handling foreign currency trading. Members of the committee unanimously agreed that the CME board should develop a separate not-for-profit exchange in which current CME members would receive a membership at a nominal price. The governing bodies of the original CME and of the new exchange would overlap.

No one, of course, knew whether the new market would work. The early indications were hardly encouraging. In the back of everyone's mind was the failed attempt of the currency futures begun in 1970 by the small International Commercial Exchange, which languished on the 1971 volume of 14,623 contracts worth some $376 million. The poor showing of the ICE's currency market was caused by a lack of local market makers, small size of contracts, and perhaps most important, the premature start.

There was also the entrenched competition and firm opposition from many of the big U.S. banks, which had provided their clients with forward exchanges to hedge for business reasons against changes in foreign currency value. The banks took a conservative position, pointing out that new futures markets, such as those in pork bellies and cattle, had been organized to make hedging possible for producers and their industrial consumers. Such facilities for hedging currencies, the banks argued, already existed.

Hence, said one New York banker, a currency futures market wouldn't "serve any real function other than to cater to people slightly more sophisticated than those who go to the track." Such digs were common from the banking establishment, which seemed incensed over the prospect of a bunch of Chicago pork belly traders challenging the world monetary order.

The Merc saw the situation differently. Under the old monetary system, only a few hundred American companies did enough international business to be affected by currency fluctuations. Now the risk had increased with floating rates. And there were thousands of firms—importers, exporters, multinationals—that had never used the foreign exchange markets.

Shortly after the currency committee meeting, the Merc officials met with Chicago bankers. Harris had tapped into the old boy network to introduce Melamed to Chicago's power bankers. One such meeting took place on a blustery December day in the august boardroom of the First National Bank. On one side of the conference table sat Melamed, Harris, and Powers. On the other side was First National Bank chairman Gaylord Freeman, heir apparent A. Robert Abboud, and executive vice presidents Richard Thomas and Robert K. Wilmouth (Wilmouth would later become president of the Chicago Board of Trade and then head the National Futures Association).

Melamed carefully laid out the plan for the International Monetary Market, with the prospect of a healthy capital flow into the bank's coffers as a result. Looking into Freeman's eyes, a tight-jawed Melamed said, "I want First National on the first IMM board of directors." There was an icy silence. Melamed continued.

The old script was dead, Melamed assured the bankers. The fixed-rate system would never be reinstated. The alarm bell rang when Bretton Woods was scrapped. With confidence and clarity Melamed pleaded like an attorney who knew he was going to win an airtight case. The new monetary order required a broad foreign exchange market—one that would grow geometrically—for a public and business community that was then "highly ignorant" of the use of foreign exchange markets as a protective tool. The prospect required a market of wider scope than the interbank market, and particularly one of much easier access; this was the obvious solution to the CME, but those on the other side of the table weren't as convinced.

Abboud challenged, "How do you know speculators will trade these currencies?"

The Merc's trading pits were loaded with locals who were already providing plenty of liquidity for the cattle and pork belly markets. In fact, therein lied the economic justification for including the International Monetary Market on the Merc's menu: to provide hedge services to businesspeople who sought to protect themselves against the risks that arose from changes in the exchange rates—and opportunities for speculators to participate in the pricing process. Both parties were vital to the lifeblood of any futures market.

In reply to Abboud's question, the ever-tactful Harris said, "We could put anything up on the board and they'd trade it."

Indeed, there was some truth in Harris' sardonic response. At one time or another, the Merc pushed shrimp, apples, onions, potatoes, butter, eggs, cheese, scrap metal, cow hides, turkeys; once it even considered pecans.[1] With a sort of lunatic optimism that declared, as Harris once put it, "We didn't know it couldn't be done," the Merc was comfortable in the vanguard of the futures industry.

Now it was Freeman's turn to respond. The insouciant chairman leaned back in his chair, thought for a moment, placed his hands on the table, and said, "I like this idea. We're gonna get behind it." Abboud was a bit more direct. "We want some of the business," he added.

The Merc had made an important ally in the First National Bank, as well as in the other two major Chicago banks, Continental Illinois National Bank and Harris Trust & Savings Bank. The banks were friendly, but not solely out of sympathy for an underdog. It was a matter of business. The Continental became the IMM's delivery agent; First National did a brisk clearing business, with more than a dozen clearing members; and Harris Bank handled the Merc's clearinghouse account.

At Continental and First National, the Merc was banking on credibility. At the time, both banks were leading Chicago to the position of an international banking center. The Merc's list of credible backers was growing: Friedman, First National, Continental.

The Chicago banks had lived with the Merc's agricultural markets for many years. Many of the traders, brokers, and clearinghouse members were good customers of the banks, and the banks understood the need for hedging and futures. Continental, for instance, helped the Merc create a mechanism for the delivery of the various foreign currencies. If someone, for example, bought Deutsche marks on the IMM and held the contract until expiration, he would have to get the actual Deutsche marks delivered to a bank account in Germany. The Merc couldn't handle that procedure. Continental, then Chicago's largest bank, with branch offices and correspondents in nearly every major city in the world, was an ideal delivery agent. Powers wrote the specifications for the currency contract while working closely with Continental's John McPartland, who was busy designing the delivery mechanism. (Several years later the Merc hired McPartland as a vice-president of its clearinghouse.)

Drawing talent from these banks, Melamed sought to create a board of directors for the IMM that would be the Merc's showpiece of credibility to the world. "I needed names, big names," Melamed said. Robert Abboud, then vice-chairman of First Chicago, joined the first board of directors, along with Beryl Sprinkel, a Milton Friedman protégé and the Harris Bank's chief economist, who subsequently became chairman of the Council of Economic Advisors in the Reagan administration. The others on that first historic board included Melamed, chairman; John Geldermann, first vice-chairman; Carl E. Anderson, second vice-chairman; Robert J.

O'Brien, secretary; Laurence Rosenberg, treasurer; and members Lloyd Arnold, Richard Boerke, William Goldstandt, Henry Jarecki, Daniel Jesser, Marlowe King, Barry Lind, Donald Minucciani, William Muno, Frederick Schantz, and Michael Weinberg.

Unfortunately, outside of Chicago, all the prestige the Merc could muster didn't mean much at first. "We went around the world using the First and Continental as references," said Powers. But that was hardly important to the nine U.S.-based foreign exchange brokers, including those at the First and Continental. "Continental's chief foreign exchange trader called me names and said he would do everything to stop us," recalled Powers, a monetarist and strict free-market economist.

Powers found himself faced with the challenge of writing the specifications on a currency contract that would influence international finance for years to come. Less than a year earlier in his assessment of the fixed-rate system, Powers concluded, "It would be difficult to start futures in the major currencies because banks are against it. They fear regulation of the market if an exchange starts trading and allows speculators in. Currently no government agency regulates the banks' trading." As for corporations, they were getting their foreign exchange service from their banks for free. Why, then, would they want to put up margin and pay a commission to an exchange?

Another concern was the contract size. Powers reasoned that contracts too large would only attract the wealthiest of speculators. "The big criticism I had heard of the New York currency contracts was that they were too small," recalled Powers. "They should have been in units of at least $250,000 to be useful for any hedger."

Powers wrapped up his memo with the following observation:

> If exchange rates become truly flexible I'd be surprised to see the banks continue to carry on their exchange operations as they do now. I suspect it would be too risky for their conservative nature and they would as soon give it up as to take the risk. Don't expect, however, that flexible exchange rates will appear right away. They may be five years off. Further, I think if we want to develop a currency future for trading, we should devise the thing primarily for the speculator. I know that flies in the face of theory and the image we're trying to build, but I think our chances of attracting much hedging to the market are pretty slim under current conditions.

The case for more flexible exchange rates, as Merc officials viewed it, was as simple and powerful as the case for the free market economy in general. Exchange rates were nothing but prices, which, if determined in the market with all other prices, ensured a more efficient allocation of resources than would occur under a planned and carefully controlled system.

The Merc wasn't entirely alone in its vision. The media, too, began to sense a new monetary system around the corner. The very day that the group of ten met in Washington (18 December 1971), a *BusinessWeek* story noted that although the world "probably will still be using gold a decade from now," one of the major changes was that "the network of exchange controls that nations have put in place to insulate their currencies from the crisis must be taken down before they strangle the monetary system."

Writing in the December 1971 issue of *Fortune,* economist Lawrence Mayer noted that "after the costly experience of the past, countries may be willing to change outmoded parities sooner. It's not beyond the realm of possibility that the IMF will legalize transitional floats." Another international finance expert, Gunter Reinman, editor of *International Reports,* believed that any revision of the world monetary system would not follow a blueprint. "There will be floating rates, official and free market rates of exchange and changes of parity, sometimes at relatively short intervals," Reinman predicted.

Such comments were sweet music to the ears of the Merc and its supporters, who by now saw the impending situation as obvious: The monetary risk of doing business internationally was going to become greater. As Milton Friedman had put it, "Foreign trade will not be hampered by these risks, if and only if, there is a futures market in which they can be hedged."

The market at the time, which primarily existed in London, Zurich, and New York, was an active spot market in foreign currencies. The forward contract market, however, was far less active. The market itself was composed almost entirely of banks and a handful of brokers. With limited swings in exchange rates, the little hedging in forward contracts was easily facilitated. With the wider bands, a businessperson faced the possibility of as much as a 4.5 percent change in the value of his or her transactions. On a $1 million transaction, that was equivalent to $45,000, a fair amount by most standards. The new bands would undoubtedly lead to a substantial increase in the demand for hedging services.

The forward contract market among the banks was neither broad nor deep enough to handle the increased volume, the Merc argued, mainly because participation in the market was limited. Building its rationale around the potential hedger, the Merc provided a liquid market that was quick, low-cost, and efficient. Speculators were just as important as hedgers.

Earlier, Nobel Laureate Paul Samuelson pointed out in his well-known basic text, "Aside from their possible influence towards stabilizing prices, speculators have another important function. By being willing to take risks on their own shoulders they enable others to avoid risk. They do this through a process called hedging." Wharton School of Finance professor Herbert Grubel in his book *The International Monetary System* had argued that the broader and deeper a foreign exchange market was, the greater the likelihood it would render stability to the market.

Thus the Merc would complement and even improve the efficiency of currency markets among the banks. A liquid futures market would provide banks with more flexibility in their foreign currency dealings. It would also provide an alternative market for them to consider in attempting to service their customers' needs. Of course, it would mean competition.

The highly emotional nature of the foreign currency market had to be considered as well. At times, a chance remark by a finance minister or a rumor of a currency realignment was enough to trigger major price swings. The bank forward markets, under certain conditions, actually had a destabilizing effect on the spot market. The forward exchange rates reflected expectations of traders who reacted quickly to changes in sentiment.

Because central banks of IMF member countries were obligated to work harder to maintain spot rates, the forward rates often fluctuated more widely and frequently outside of the official spot rate limits. Banks that dealt in forward currencies therefore usually maintained low open positions as they tried to even out their forward positions—whether those positions were long or short— with offsetting spot transactions. In their attempts to maintain low risk exposure, they had transferred the sentiment and expectations of the forward market to the spot market, making it more volatile. That, in turn, forced the central banks to work harder to maintain spot prices. A futures market where banks could hedge their forward contracts could lower pressure on the spot markets.

At the same time, an alternative market had the potential to help stabilize exchange rates. Conventional wisdom, however, argued that a market in which speculators could participate in the price discovery process for foreign currency would tend to destabilize rather than stabilize. Many feared that speculation simply reinforced the hopes and fears of the usual participants in the market, so when the exchange rates became unsettled by political or economic uncertainties, the speculators swooped in to form a perverse force that threatened established parities.

Speculators, by pouncing on a currency, made it weaker and forced its depreciation, only to reward the speculator for his actions. "The arguments are not well founded," Grubel had emphatically stated. He went on to point out that in international currency, natural forces, if allowed to operate, would set a limit on the ability to do this. He argued, "Only if a government through inflationary policies, keeps interest rates low and domestic goods prices high, and thus prevents these real forces from developing, can there be a cumulative depreciation of the currency. Under these circumstances the blame for the domestic inflation and exchange rate depreciation should be put in the government's inflationary policies, not on the speculators."

It was a convincing argument for those who cared to listen. Whenever historic experiments with the use of freely flexible exchange rates were attempted, the speculators were close behind. But those experiments were really not a fair test, Grubel countered, "since they were always introduced after major economic crises and after conventional pegging operations proved totally inadequate to deal with the problems."

There was a more practical view to consider. The usefulness of a futures market to the general economy was much greater than that of hedging, which merely transferred risk from dealers to speculators. It provided information. Well-informed dealers could give definite opinions in determining the market price. Besides, the true test of the value of any commodity is the price people were willing to pay for it by actually putting their money on the line.

If the price of a currency changed and then remained at the new level, it was probably a good indication of the true value of the currency. To the extent that speculators profit from such activity, the Merc argued, they were being rewarded not for raiding the market, but for accurately anticipating the correct value of the currency.

Despite the growing support by the world's leading economists and finance experts for a currency futures market, the critics—mainly the banks—were still carping. They saw the Merc as a bunch of sandlot ballplayers trying to break into the big leagues.

At 53 years old, the Merc was hardly a kid. If anything, it was a seasoned veteran as skillful as anyone playing the game it knew best—futures. Its $6 million stadium—the new trading complex—was on schedule, and it even managed to break new ground by learning more about its players. For the first time, it produced a profile of a commodity trader.

In mid-1970 Powers surveyed more than half of the CME clearing members who provided details on over 4,000 traders. The typical trader was a man, about 45 years old, with a college background, an income over $10,000, and a rather modest trading appetite (he traded only a few contracts at any one time).

The Merc had always suspected that futures lured novice investors, and the survey confirmed that speculation did attract new investors. Seventy-three percent of the respondents had traded for less than five years. Nine percent had commodity accounts for 14 years or more. At least 69 percent also had securities accounts in addition to their commodity accounts. Of trades that were concluded, 85 percent held positions for less than 30 days, which led Ronald Frost to conclude that traders had no predetermined plan. One factor the study was unable to measure: the psychology of the people in the market.

"One caveat about speculating in foreign exchange," Melamed sarcastically said shortly after the profile was completed, "it's not a market for the faint-hearted, and one definitely should not enter it with grocery money. Pay your bills, prepay your life insurance, set aside money for your kids' college education, build up a contingency fund for alimony and then, if you have anything left over, you have the necessary risk capital for speculating in foreign exchange."

Merrill Lynch, at the time, was interested in only currency speculators with seasoned knowledge of the risks and $50,000 in liquid net worth. "We are not going to make our customers sacrificial lambs just to make a market go," said Robert Hagan, a Merrill Lynch vice-president in charge of commodities research. Bache, on the other hand, had set no net worth minimum.

Now it became clear to the Merc membership that battle lines were being drawn and the exchange was digging in for a tough (and perhaps long) fight. This time, though, it had made sure it had plenty of ammunition.

21

Pounding the Pavement

Just one month after the Merc announced its decision to enter the currency futures field, the members were asked to vote on the plan. Although most of them were unsure as to what the International Monetary Market would mean to the future of their exchange, they had faith in the Merc leadership. They showed it on 17 January 1972 when the CME members voted 321 to 19 to approve the organization of the IMM.

Under the terms of the proposal, Merc members automatically became eligible for membership in the IMM for a $100 fee. Additional memberships would then be made available at $10,000 each to "a new public and industry not previously connected or involved with our markets," according to the proposal. Ten days later, the IMM was chartered by the state of Illinois. Shortly thereafter, the IMM disclosed the currencies to be traded: British pounds, Canadian dollars, Deutsche marks, Swiss and French francs, Japanese yen, Italian lira, and Mexican pesos.[1]

Had the IMM not been launched as a separate exchange, the idea may have died on the Merc trading floor. At this point, the Merc was still known as the "Meat Exchange," the house that pork bellies built. As far as the members were concerned, the $100,000 price of a Merc seat was ample proof that there was money to be made trading hogs, pork bellies and cattle.

Of the 500 members, 300 were on the Exchange floor, where many had started trading butter and eggs. Now they were finally making money. The notion of turning bacon and eggs into an international omelette didn't sit very well among a bunch of hungry traders who had gone through some lean years. By the same token, gold bugs like Henry Jarecki, who was to be a charter member of the IMM board, wanted nothing to do with pork bellies. The untested IMM was a new market, dealing strictly in finance, fertile ground to breed a new kind of trader. "Here we could attract young traders with less money and build a trading population limited to foreign exchange," Melamed told Harris shortly before the IMM memberships were offered.

197

Although there was no limit on the number of seats that were offered at $10,000, they were for sale only one year. At the end of the year, the Merc had garnered 150 new members to bolster its strategy. Few, if any, of the new population of younger people left the new trading pits. No novice really wanted to compete head-on with a veteran pork belly or cattle trader. Thus a new generation of trader was being groomed for a new and untested market. The Merc had plenty of unexplored territory and its own legion of pioneers who could help fashion a "financial futures" image unencumbered by the history and impressions of age-old agricultural futures. These new members, limited to the contracts provided by the IMM, were captives of the currency pits, unable to participate in the more active meat complex and forced to generate business in their own arena. "It was a crucial element in our growth," said Melamed.

Melamed was elected the IMM chairman, and Harris, president, in addition to maintaining his role as Merc president. (Both would be the only people to hold those two particular offices until the IMM was merged as a division of the CME in 1976.) Michael Weinberg, Jr., then 47, replaced Melamed as CME chairman, a position Weinberg held for two consecutive years. A soft-spoken former newspaperman whose business acumen was shaped at the University of Chicago Graduate School of Business, Weinberg was a Merc's blue blood. His grandfather, Max, was a charter member of the Chicago Butter & Egg Board and its successor, the Chicago Mercantile Exchange, and his father, Michael Weinberg, Sr., who retired in 1983, had been the youngest president of the Butter & Egg Board, and had served as Merc chairman from 1955 to 1957.

The first son of a former chairman to be elected to the Merc's top post, the younger Weinberg joined the Exchange in 1954. He had been a director since 1967 and a tireless Merc loyalist, having served as secretary, treasurer, second vice-chairman and the head of a half-dozen different committees before he assumed the chairmanship.

Other key board officers included John T. Geldermann, first vice-chairman of the CME and IMM; Carl Anderson, second vice-chairman of the IMM; Daniel Jesser, second vice-chairman of the CME; and Barry J. Lind, CME treasurer. Robert O'Brien became IMM secretary, and Laurence M. Rosenberg, treasurer. It was a veteran leadership pool, out of which would come two more CME chairman in the years ahead.

The shift in leadership allowed Melamed to concentrate on marketing the IMM. At the same time, he maintained his role as secretary of the CME. The Merc spent the entire month of January getting the word out that, ready or not, the IMM was coming. On the 14th, Melamed and Harris met with Illinois Senator Charles Percy in Chicago to discuss the new exchange.

Percy was an ideal ally. Not only was he a strong supporter of the Chicago exchanges, but he was also chairman of the powerful Senate Foreign Relations Committee. Moreover, Percy was an advocate of free markets, having been schooled at the University of Chicago before becoming the wunderkind of Bell and Howell Corporation. The meeting resulted in a letter from Percy to Arthur Burns sent in early March:

> The Chicago Mercantile Exchange has announced its intention to offer futures trading in foreign currencies. This, in my judgment, could be of major significance to the foreign economic policy of the United States.
>
> The economic functions of this market are compatible with the desire of the U.S. to increase its exports. If the U.S. is to reduce last year's $2.5 billion trade deficit, we must provide all the incentive we possibly can for our firms engaged in exporting. The market contemplated by the Chicago Mercantile Exchange will, in my judgment, serve a useful economic purpose for exporters who desire to hedge their foreign currency exposures. It will also supplement, and perhaps improve, efficiency of the forward market that currently exists among the major international banks by providing them a greater deal of flexibility in their foreign exchange operations and an alternative market to consider in serving their customer's needs.
> ... The Chicago Mercantile Exchange officials are anxious that members of the Federal Reserve Board, and other officials of the government be kept fully informed of their efforts and activities in this endeavor. Hence, I think it would be beneficial if we could arrange a meeting between yourself and officials of the Exchange to discuss the progress they are making. I respectfully request such a meeting at your earliest convenience. . . .

Although the CME counsel assured the IMM it needed no governmental sanction to proceed, the Merc board believed it imperative that the appropriate U.S. officials be fully aware of the Merc's intentions. There indeed were compelling reasons to touch base with the U.S. government as well as with foreign governments.

Melamed explained the reasons for his support of communication with the government: "First to give the IMM concept the proper level of support and prominence; second, to gain, if possible, a positive reaction which we might be able to use in promoting the idea; and third, if the opposite were true, to control any negative fallout." Courtesy calls had already been paid to George P. Shultz, who became Secretary of the Treasury shortly after the IMM was launched. Shultz had been the first government official to formally receive the Friedman paper; although, as Melamed recalled, Shultz gave the IMM "long odds, he recognized its inherent values." Shultz had been Milton Friedman's professorial colleague at the University of Chicago, and his own free-market views were in sync with Friedman's. In similar fashion, Melamed, Harris, and Powers called on Arthur Burns, Federal Reserve Board chairman, and Herbert Stein, chairman of the Council of Economic Advisors. In each instance, the response was similar to that of Shultz's: cordial, but skeptical.

Ten days after the Percy letter, Melamed and Powers met again with officials of the Treasury Department in Washington before making the CME's biggest splash on 24 February with the IMM monetary conference at Chicago's Palmer House. The crowd totaled more than 700 representatives of the largest U.S. and overseas banks, industries, brokerage houses, academia, speculative interests, and exchange members.

The impressive lineup of speakers included Nobel prizewinner Paul Samuelson of the Massachusetts Institute of Technology, finance professor Paul Cootner from Stanford University, Talat M. Othman, vice-president of the international banking division at Harris Trust and Savings Bank, and Michael P. Seibel, assistant vice-president in international loan and money market administration at Bank of America.

The next month, on the morning of 15 March, Melamed and Harris met with Governor James Mitchell and his staff at the Federal Reserve in Washington. A few hours later and a few blocks away, Melamed was discussing the economic need for foreign exchange futures with Stanley Katz of the Commerce Department.

On the very same day, the Merc's 500 members were offered IMM memberships at the low price of $100 each. At first, the board was going to dole out the IMM memberships free; but Ira Marcus, the exchange's outside tax expert, convinced the governors otherwise. A seat needed value, however nominal, Marcus explained, in order to establish a tax basis for the membership. The following day, the IMM seats were offered to the public at $10,000 each. (A year later, 150 seats were eligible for resale on the open market, with the first sale at $8700; a membership never dipped below $10,000 thereafter.)

In April, the currency contract specifications were translated into German, French, Spanish, and Japanese and printed in separate brochures. In addition, a detailed 40-page booklet entitled *Understanding Futures in Foreign Exchange* was developed along with a study course. On 21 April, the agreement among the finance ministers of the European Economic Community to narrow their intracurrency band of fluctuation by 2.25 percent was implemented. Thus, the EEC "snake" in the "Smithsonian tunnel" was born, with the French franc at the top and the Italian lira at the bottom. Nevertheless, the skeptics wouldn't let up. The next day, 22 April, a *BusinessWeek* article entitled "The New Currency Market: Strictly for Crapshooters," preached that "if you fancy yourself an international money speculator but lack the resources. . . . your day has come." By now the Merc's skin had grown thick enough to withstand such barbs. "Not what you'd describe as a friendly endorsement," Melamed would later say. "The world not only misread our purpose, but our potential as well."

On 16 May 1972 the old trading floor at 110 North Franklin took on the cachet of a United Nations festival. There were seven young women for seven currencies; each wore a native costume as they led a group of dignitaries that included William S. Dale, executive director for the U.S. to the International Monetary Fund, to the IMM area. There, Dale cut a ribbon made of the IMM's seven currencies. "It is no accident that the IMM is opening only five months after the Smithsonian agreement of last December," Dale said, "The wider bands provided by that agreement indicate the usefulness of a market like the IMM in assessing risks and appraising the future."

At precisely 9 A.M., chairman Michael Weinberg rang a gold bell to open the first currency. Thereafter, he rang the bell at two-minute intervals and each time one of the costumed women carried the flag of each currency's nation to the designated trading area. That morning the ghosts of the Merc's past met face-to-face with the spirits of the future. Ironically, trading in this modern futures contract was still recorded on a blackboard. There was both excitement and confusion that day. Veteran trader Marlowe King ran up to Mark Powers, asking, "Should I buy or sell?"

Even before Weinberg rang the last bell, a clerk scribbled the first trade across the blackboard as Charles Mattey purchased British pounds. Mattey, a vice-president and director of Bache & Company, bought contracts for two million British pounds, worth $5,220,000, for the account of the First National Bank of Memphis; he represented a Memphis cotton merchant involved in an international transaction. The seller was Henry Jarecki's New York–based Mocatta Metals Corp., hedging business in the London bullion market. (On 1 January 1975—the first day U.S. citizens could own gold in more than 40 years—Jarecki sold the first ounce of gold.)

The philosophic and gregarious Jarecki was not your ordinary trader by any means. He was even further in style from the bankers of the day. As a teenager, Jarecki with his family escaped war-ravaged Europe in 1941, settling in the U.S. After graduating from the University of Michigan, he headed for Heidelberg in 1950 to attend medical school in the footsteps of his father. He returned to the U.S. in 1957 and started a psychiatric clinic in New Haven, Connecticut. At the same time, he began dealing in silver coins on the side. "Psychiatry seemed to me like arbitrage: You invest 30 hours with a patient, you get 30 years of productive life," he once told a reporter.

By the time the IMM got started, Jarecki was well established as a world class metals mogul in the gold and silver markets. "Melamed believed that because I represented a long-standing bullion-dealing company, I must have had relations with British banking, which I did," said Jarecki.

Jarecki was the consummate arbitrageur, but unfortunately not a risk taker. At first, Jarecki was reluctant to buy an IMM seat, but Melamed prevailed with an offer that Jarecki couldn't turn down. He virtually offered Jarecki a "put" on his IMM seat for one year, with the understanding that Melamed would make up the difference if the value of the seat declined. Jarecki never had to collect.

The first day's total of currency contracts traded was 333. By year's end, a respectable 144,928 contracts had changed hands as volume rose to more than three times that of the following year. Clearly, the IMM was an idea whose time had come.[2]

On the day the IMM opened *The Wall Street Journal* ran a page-one story with an unflattering twist, headlined "New Game in Town." It was in that article that the bitterness of the banking establishment was expressed. "I'm amazed that a bunch of crapshooters in pork bellies have the temerity to think that they can beat some of the world's most sophisticated traders at their own game," said one New York bank's foreign exchange dealer. No one denied that currency strategies could be tricky for even the sophisticated traders.

A few years earlier, First National Bank of New York had incurred an $8 million pre-tax loss in its foreign exchange operations because a trader in its Brussels branch misgauged the market for the British pound. In the same *Journal* article, economist Paul Samuelson questioned whether the IMM could really offer users significant advantages over the network of banks and money dealers. He also speculated that even if the IMM became successful, it could incur the wrath of both the U.S. and foreign governments by fanning currency speculation and thereby disrupting exchange rates.

The devaluation of the dollar the year before had caught the attention of more Americans than ever before on the foreign exchange market—especially those who traveled abroad. Particularly jarring were the stories of the inability of U.S. tourists in Europe to exchange their dollars for foreign currencies the week after Nixon's 15 August speech when he closed the gold window. "Since last year's monetary crisis, Americans have finally awakened to the fact that the dollar is no longer king of the heap but subject to the same vicissitudes as any other currency," observed A. Robert Abboud, executive vice-president of the First National Bank of Chicago and an IMM director. "The IMM certainly stands to benefit from Americans' growing concern over the strength of the dollar."

Despite the fact that Abboud was on the IMM board, the First National's foreign exchange trader wasn't interested in the IMM. Merc officials knew the banks would have to cooperate at some point if the IMM were to work as designed. Without the banks' participation, the IMM ran the risk that its transactions might not have any connection with reality. No one would know whether the IMM price for, say, Swiss francs was the real price, or whether it was merely the Merc price.

To encourage the banks, the Merc went an extra step: It created a class B membership of official arbitrageurs who would keep the liquidity flowing between the IMM and the banks and who were exempted from capital requirements. It was yet another component critical to the success of financial futures.

The class B arbitrage device was a means by which the IMM could be connected to the real world, since banks did not ordinarily cater to individual speculators. Once again Harris tapped into the good-old-boy network, this time introducing Melamed to Continental Bank's chairman, Tilden Cummings—an unassuming gentleman called "Tilly" by his friends, he was one of the world's most powerful bankers at the time.

In trying to set up the program with Continental, the IMM had run into a snag with the bank's legal department. After Melamed convincingly explained the strategy to Cummings, the chairman picked up the phone and instructed his legal department to clear the way. A special clearing account was set up for class B arbitrageurs with the sole purpose of dealing in foreign exchange. Continental had the lien on the position, and the Exchange set no margin requirements.

Among the first class B arbitrageurs, who paid $50,000 for the privilege of arbitraging foreign exchange, were Maurice Levy, Gerald Hirsch, and Philip Glass. These traders were usually bank customers, buying, for example, yen from the bank in the cash market and selling yen futures on the IMM, or vice versa. The bank would have the opportunity of reviewing the arbitrageur's position daily to assure itself that the positions were true hedges.

The banks had been guaranteed that these arbitrageurs would lay off their positions every night. In effect, the system bridged the banks to the Merc trading floor. At the same time, the banks would have the backing of the commodity firms at the Merc who were its customers. Class B arbitrage, however, was destined to become obsolete as soon as the major banks realized that dealing directly with the IMM was safe and profitable. Though it was a good deal for the banks, they remained at arm's length from the IMM for quite some time.

Predictably, the European bankers were no more enthusiastic than the American bankers. Typical of the polite rebuke among foreign bankers was a letter to Harris from Edmund de Rothschild, of the great European banking family. Rothschild earlier had declined an invitation to attend the February IMM conference in Chicago. His sentiment toward the fledgling IMM was obvious from his letter; the following is an excerpt:

> I am writing to thank you for your letter of the 28th January, in which you have outlined an interesting development on the Chicago Mercantile Exchange. The extension of a futures market in certain foreign currencies could no doubt be of interest to small individual investors but, as you are aware, there is a very highly sophisticated international market for foreign exchange operations in which the major banks of the world participate. Banks are, therefore, able to offer their customers all the requisite services for futures trading in the major currencies and they are also able to arbitrage their own requirements with each other. . . .

It was precisely this attitude that sent a Merc contingent across the Atlantic to win the hearts and minds of European financiers in the summer of 1972. Using New York–based consultant Curtis J. Hoxter Inc. to set up the Merc's itinerary, the band of Merc officials took off on a two-week trip (from 17 June to 30 June) that took them to London, Milan, Zurich, Geneva, and Frankfurt in an effort to put the IMM on the European corporate and monetary map. The Merc commando team included Melamed, Harris, Powers, Lind, Rosenberg, Geldermann, Frost, O'Brien, and Jesser.

The division of labor was carefully mapped out. Chairman Melamed outlined the IMM's philosophical concept. President Harris provided the background of the CME, and vice-president Powers presented the technical operational data. Lind and Rosenberg fielded questions from a trader's perspective. Frost handled the local press, dispensing brochures not only in English, but in French, German, Italian, and Spanish as well. The group quickly discovered that skepticism toward the IMM was universal. At many of the meetings, to the Merc team's dismay, they outnumbered the audience.

The low level of attendance, Hoxter concluded, was caused in part by the monetary machinations that were taking place in Europe at the time. There had been a crisis in the pound sterling, forcing many people to stay at their trading desks. The domineering role of the banks in the European scheme of things also had to be considered. Major European corporations were particularly circumspect about engaging in activities contrary to the wishes of the banking community. In addition, British companies were prohibited by the Bank of England from trading currency futures.

The Merc contingent spent the first two days in London. On 17 June at 12:15 P.M., they met with the Bank of England's governor and senior economist. "Would you like to see our boardroom?" asked the governor. "It was like being in a church; everyone spoke in hushed tones," recalled Powers. The message, however, was loud and clear: The Bank of England had no intention of participating in the IMM.

At the end of the meeting, the bankers politely asked the Merc officials if there were anything else they could do. "Yes, you could float the pound," replied Melamed with a chortle that was met with icy silence by the British bankers. And the Merc crew was off that night for Milan.

The next morning it was all over *The Herald Tribune* and the Italian papers. The Bank of England had floated the pound from $1.60 to $1.40. (Due to pre-established price limits, it took 20 days before the futures caught up with the cash market.) Over breakfast at a sidewalk café that morning, Powers began doodling on a napkin as he scribbled out a plan for expandable price limits in the currencies in an effort to give traders a chance to set up a line of credit should the markets become too volatile. The rule change had only to be posted on the exchange floor, and if there were no major objections, it would automatically go into effect.

With the pound sterling crisis unfolding, most of the Merc contingent headed back to Chicago to oversee the activity on the IMM. Harris, Powers, Geldermann, and O'Brien carried the IMM torch to the other money centers of Europe.

There were four meetings in London, three in Milan, three in Zurich, one in Geneva, and two plus a seminar in Frankfurt. An analysis of the trip by the Hoxter organization pointed out the pluses and minuses of the effort:

Throughout the sessions it was evident that the IMM does still have a deep-seated credibility problem on the Continent which is mainly caused by the prejudice and jealousy of foreign exchange dealers and bankers. To some extent if a confrontation was possible this was overcome. But there is no doubt about it, to a large extent this prejudice derives from the reactions and non-reactions of U.S. banks and particularly brokerage houses in Europe as was vividly demonstrated by the response of the head of the Merrill Lynch operations in Zurich to a telephone call to the effect 'I cannot afford to come to this meeting since I have to deal on a permanent basis with the local Swiss banks.' It should be added that in many instances the Chicago banks did not shine by their attendance, particularly the Continental, which only put in one appearance in Geneva. The First National Bank of Chicago was also noticeable by its absence in any of the London sessions. . . .

On the positive side, the European trip served as a solid introduction to the Merc and the IMM. "The quality of our message was not to talk down to people, but to challenge them to think," said Powers. News organizations such as Reuters and the London *Economist* exchanged views with the IMM contingent. Among the financial institutions that the Merc team met were Commerzbank of West Germany, Italy's Banca Commercial Italiano and Bank of Italy, Swiss National Bank, Deutsche Bank, Dresdner Bank, Bank Venteble, First National City Bank, Chase Manhattan Bank, and the Bank of England. The corporate connections, a virtual who's who of European commerce, included West Germany's foremost multinational chemical concern, Hoechst, IBM Italy, Alitalia Airlines, Nestle, Brown Bovery, Dow, and Firestone. If the IMM were going to become accepted on both sides of the Atlantic, it would have to do so by explaining itself in a detailed way, the CME officials realized.

They also came to another realization a few years later. Ironically, if the banks had participated in the IMM from the start, the Exchange may never have gotten off the ground. "You can prove mathematically," Jarecki said in 1988, "that a guy just standing in a pit and trading when the futures market is not the primary market can be picked off by the guys in the primary market." Instead, the 40 or so class B arbitrageurs were able to make a market inside the banks' forward market in those currencies traded on the IMM. Consequently, the IMM didn't have to focus solely on secondary currencies such as the Mexican peso in order to avoid competing with banks.

Even before the IMM had a chance to settle in, the futures markets already had begun to take on a new dimension from the summer of 1972 into 1973. As the Merc was preparing to trade a new type of future in currencies, the long-dormant grain markets were boiling over with activity. The reason: The Russians were buying massive quantities of American wheat. The critics called it the "great grain robbery" that summer, when the Soviet Union secretly bought a quarter of the U.S. grain at bargain prices. The purchases depleted grain reserves, sending prices to their highest levels since 1917 and eventually wreaking havoc on American food costs. Moreover, it had boosted the futures markets to a new speculative plateau and focused the exchanges in the eye of the public. As it turned out, the USSR's disastrous 1972 grain crop unleashed the greatest bull market in the history of grain trading. Now commodities were denationalized; food had become a global market.

In the pre–World War II days, world grain trade amounted to some 30 million tons a year. By 1975 it had risen to more than 150 million tons. For nearly 40 years before the early 1970s, the government, through subsidies, encouraged the American farmer to produce surpluses in order to keep farming economically viable. During the later 1940s, some of the surpluses helped in the recovery of war-torn Europe and Japan. Despite the bountiful bins, however, the lid remained tight on domestic prices. All through the 1950s and 1960s, the United States simply did not know what to do with its surplus grain; it was stored at a cost of billions of dollars per year. In the 1960s, some of the grain was used to win friends and influence people abroad. American farm products were sold mainly to Great Britain and to the Netherlands or were given away to India, Pakistan, Egypt, and other developing nations.

All the while, the world food situation had its peaks and valleys. There were the mid-1960 droughts in India and Pakistan that caused a food crisis, followed by the Green Revolution—the development of more durable short-stemmed varieties of wheat and rice fertilized with heavy doses of nitrogen—that led to self-sufficiency for such countries as India. In 1970, a corn blight destroyed a sizeable portion of the U.S. corn crop. But there was always enough—so much so that during the early 1970s the grain-exporting countries cut back grain production to reduce surplus stocks.

Almost overnight, the situation drastically changed through a combination of circumstances. The Soviet Union experienced severe drought in 1972, forcing it to enter the world grain market. It did so again in 1973 in order to fend off a decline in livestock production. Ultimately the USSR purchased 20 million metric tons of wheat and 10 million tons of corn, soybeans, oats, and other coarse grains, boosting its total grain imports to three times the previous season's.

On top of that, American wheat was sold to China for the first time in 20 years. Demand was equally stiff from other countries as well. Drought had hit Africa that year and Korea had a failing rice crop. Japan and western Europe were big buyers, as was Canada, normally a grain exporter. Adding to the pressures were nagging weather problems: As one-fifth of the world suffered from drought, America's farm belt was under a prolonged wet and cold spell during the 1972 harvest, which upset forecasts of record yields.

At the same time in South America, there was a shift in the Humboldt Current, a cold Antarctic current flowing north along the coasts of Chile and Peru. The result was the virtual disappearance of the normally plentiful supply of Peruvian anchovies, a major source of world fish meal products. This loss of a key protein source for animal feed sent buyers scrambling for a substitute—soybean meal—and prices soared.

As supplies of feed grains tightened and prices rose, cattle, hog, and poultry farmers cut back production. The easing of controls on retail food prices by the Nixon administration did the rest. Between 1972 and 1973, the price of sirloin steak jumped from $1.35 a pound to $1.75, and pork chops from $1.25 to $1.56. All told, in 1973 Americans paid some $2 billion more for food than they had in the previous year. By 1975 the food bill had grown to a startling $50 billion. Secretary of Agriculture Earl Butz commented on the Soviet grain sales: "This is by all odds the greatest grain transaction in the history of the world. And it certainly is the greatest for us."

The great bull market of 1972 to 1973 was well under way. As grain reached its highest price in 125 years in Chicago, "beeflation" also set in. A live cattle contract on the Merc between 2 January and 1 August surged to $7,480 on just a $400 investment. Supply and demand economics had kicked into high gear. The Soviets and Chinese, on a shopping spree for U.S. food, added one billion new mouths for American agriculture to feed, wiping out the surpluses and giving farmers their best net income in history. It was happening at a time when living standards the world over were rising and populations expanding, at a time when every American man, woman, and child was on the average eating 116 pounds of beef per year—up from only 56 pounds 20 years earlier. It was a small wonder, then, that for the first time since 1964 pork bellies accounted for less than half of all trading, thanks to record volume in the CME's live cattle and live hog contracts. Hogs, bellies, iced broilers, and shell eggs reached record prices. In the first nine months of 1972 alone, the value of contracts traded was some $47 billion, compared with the previous full-year record of $40 billion. (Value figures did not include the activity on the IMM, which was worth $10.6 billion after five months of trading.)

As the price of bellies, hogs, and cattle rose, so did the prices of bacon, hamburger, and pork chops, along with scores of other items on supermarket shelves. That, in turn, sent the tempers of grocery shoppers soaring. In protest, some picketed the Merc and Board of Trade. Clearly public interest in commodities had grown as never before, spurred by the profit potential of the futures markets and the rapid rise in food costs.

Bowing to public sentiment, Congress demanded answers. Testifying before the House Select Small Business Subcommittee on 25 September 1973, Frederick G. Uhlmann, then chairman of the Board of Trade, explained the bloated food prices this way: "The problem is the result of record worldwide demand at a time of shrinking surpluses at home. The buying spree that ensued can only be described as panic. Virtually every country of the world suddenly wanted to trade dollars, which were becoming less valuable, for food that was becoming more valuable, and the prospects of hunger only increased the eagerness of the buyers."

On 14 October, Michael Weinberg, Jr. testified on behalf of the Merc before the same subcommittee with good-humored logic. "If an evil group of speculators pushed commodity prices to new highs," he told Representative Neal Smith, Democrat of Iowa and chairman of the committee, "then an equally good group of speculators theoretically pushed prices down the 35 percent that the livestock and other markets have dropped in recent weeks." As commodity prices soared, so did commodity fever among the speculation-hungry public. The prospect of cashing in on fast changing commodity prices had gripped nearly everyone from the Des Moines dentist to the New York psychoanalyst, from the Miami construction worker to the Los Angeles barber. Many of them had forsaken the stock market when the go-go years ran out of steam. Now they saw other opportunities.

Meanwhile, the Chicago Board of Trade was busy establishing an entirely new market. Called the Chicago Board Options Exchange (CBOE), the new exchange traded call and put options on stocks. The CBOE—the brainchild of former *Wall Street Journal* reporter Joseph Sullivan—opened on 26 April 1973, a year after the IMM, in the old smoking room next to the Board of Trade trading floor. Among the CBOE's early movers and shakers, along with Sullivan, were a pair of silver-haired brothers, Edmund J. O'Connor and William F. O'Connor, who had made millions trading soybeans at the CBOT and saw unlimited possibilities in equity options. Edmund became the CBOE's first chairman, and the brothers went on to build one of the biggest and most prominent options clearing and trading firms in the world. In 1990 William O'Connor became chairman of the Chicago Board of Trade.

Though Chicago was no longer the hog butcher of the world or the stacker of wheat, it was still the stormy, husky, brawling commodity trader of the world. Chicago's city fathers recognized that fact, leading Mayor Richard J. Daley to proclaim the week of 12 through 16 November 1973 to be Commodities Week.

No one knew it then, but Chicago was also on its way to becoming the financial futures capital of the world.

22

Still the Evangelists

"Free Markets for Free Men" was the opening day theme as Melamed rang a model of the Liberty Bell to begin trading in the new $6 million CME building at 8:30 Monday morning on 27 November 1973.

The reflective steel and dark green glass exterior resembled the first six floors of the landmark John Hancock Building. And the 170-foot-long trading floor—unencumbered by interior columns or walls so traders didn't have to crane their necks to see the electronic boards at either end of the floor—was bathed in mercury vapor lights recessed in bronze-colored sound-absorbing baffles 34 feet above. The layout had allowed the number of work stations to be increased by 40 percent, and there was a box seat view for up to 100 visitors in a glass-enclosed gallery.

As usual, it was noisy. Not even the black synthetic rubber flooring could soften the tumultuous outcries exploding from the trading pits where the open-mouthed traders faced off, their jaws jutting forward, their eyes narrowed to the gaze of people at the limit of their endurance, their faces mottled with exertion. People were making and losing money in this free-market cradle, but you couldn't tell the winners from the losers by their sweat or screams. One thing was apparent: The exchange had already outgrown its new space.

Plans for the new quarters were completed in 1969, after Exchange volume had grown to more than 40 percent of all U.S. commodity trading from 4 percent in 1964—and well before the International Monetary Market was founded. In 1964 contracts traded totaled 250,000 and memberships sold for $3,000. By 1969, volume had increased to more than 3.7 million trades, and a membership was worth $90,000. Earlier, in November 1972, volume had surpassed the record high total set in 1969. Trading in the IMM was the unknown quantity. During its first six months, the IMM had recorded more than 82,000 trades.

While most Americans had taken a long weekend for the Thanksgiving holiday, the staff members of the Chicago Mercantile Exchange were singing a variation of Lydia Maria Child's Thanksgiving Day verse that went something like this: "Over the river and down the street, to our new Exchange we'll go."

Taking advantage of that weekend, the CME packed up 45 years of records and memories as it moved from 110 North Franklin Street to its new headquarters beside the Chicago River at 444 West Jackson Boulevard. Like the new kid on the block, the Exchange stood amid such famous architectural denizens as the Sears Tower, rising directly across the river. A few blocks to the north was the Kennedy family's flagship—the Merchandise Mart, the world's largest commercial structure. Just to the west was the sprawling University of Illinois campus and the downtown transportation hub joined by the Union and North Western railroad stations, where some 150,000 daily commuters filtered into the city. Only one day of trading was missed in the move.

No sooner had the Exchange settled into its new surroundings when word began circulating that the Merc was about to settle another matter: the end of minimum rates for negotiated commission fees. Both the Merc and CBOT had approved the new rate structure as part of a settlement of eight antitrust suits that had challenged the exchanges' rules and process of setting rates. The negotiated rates were to be introduced in a transition period of four and a half years. The futures exchanges were following the pattern adopted earlier by the stock exchanges. In return for the elimination of the minimum rates, the Merc and CBOT were released from any liability for alleged damages resulting from their establishment of commission rates in the past or during the transition period.

A year later, the Merc and CBOT would find themselves embroiled in yet another battle over money matters set off by city reflexes. This time the Chicago City Council wanted to impose a tax on all commodity and stock transfers that would add $36 million to its coffers. It hit the Merc and other Chicago exchanges like a Lake Michigan squall. Ironically, the proposed tax was announced on 14 November, the opening day of Commodities Week in Chicago proclaimed by Mayor Daley and the city council. "It was a strange show of appreciation for what the exchanges had brought to the city of Chicago," Harris mused in recalling the shock of the proposal. "With one hand the city fathers were patting us on the back. While the other hand was reaching for our wallets."

The Merc moved swiftly to fight the tax. Led by the Merc, the CBOT and the Midwest Stock Exchange, Chicago's exchange community mobilized to battle the city council. Weinberg wrote a seven-page letter to the press, Mayor Daley, and the city council finance committee five days after the tax was proposed; an excerpt follows.

> The Chicago exchanges and their members strongly believe in supporting their city. They are proud that Chicago has been gaining recognition as a new world financial center, and has long been the world agricultural capital. They know that its commodity markets have been the envy of everyone, involving 80 percent of all U.S. commodity futures business. And they feel sorrow that the function of their markets, and their services to agriculture and to Chicago, are so greatly misunderstood, with success being met with penalty, rather than support. . . .

The morning of 19 November when the Merc letter was released, Harris and Weinberg met with Mayor Daley and his staff, requesting reconsideration of the tax proposal. A few hours later, Melamed and Weinberg were facing off with the finance committee. "It's a confiscatory tax," railed Melamed before committee members. "Our paramount objection is that commodity futures transactions don't represent an actual exchange of goods," he continued, emphasizing that "the same contract may be traded 25 times a day and, therefore, would be taxed over and over."

The Merc had traveled a tortuous road to success, potholed with the usual rejections. Along the way it had learned to fend for itself, to build alliances, and to play hardball if it had to. In the old days it warbled like a lightweight Caruso whenever it voiced its opposition to attacks from outsiders. Now there was an invigorating directness synchronized smartly with the 1970s American work ethic: Get it done, whatever the cost.

Earlier in 1973 the Exchange had set up a new government relations committee, co-chaired by Melamed and Weinberg, in addition to a new pricing committee. The government relations committee, coordinated by Merc staffer Jordan Fox, played a growing role in dealing with both the executive and legislative branches of local and national government.

The Merc had responded to a debate that was brewing over efforts to give margin-setting powers to the federal government as well as to give more control to the CEA over the operations of commodity exchanges. In a CME membership letter dated 18 April 1973 and entitled "The Government, The Mercantile, and You," Weinberg summed up the Exchange's posture:

> We will oppose efforts to hamper free markets with all the legitimate tools at our disposal. . . . Until now, we have operated on the theory that discretion is the better part of valor. We do have eyes and ears in Washington, and we do have friends whom we have used, in order to modify, remove, and oppose restrictive measures. It would have been pointless to cry "foul" when no one attacked us, and our membership of 500 is much less impressive than the many-hundred-thousand-member allies of farm groups, with whom we have counseled and worked. . . .

Three years later, the Merc could afford to have its say—if not its way. It had amassed a fund of $137,000 for political contributions, most of which was aimed for dozens of sympathetic politicians running for congressional elections. It was perfectly legal. In fact, it had been encouraged by Congress through changes in the federal election laws in 1974. Nearly 500 corporations, trade groups, and labor organizations had flocked to establish so-called political action committees (PACs).

The Chicago Board of Trade's Auction Markets Political Action Committee, formed in September 1976, was initially envisioned as the political fund for members of Chicago's five markets: the CBOT, the Merc, the Chicago Board Options Exchange, the Midwest Stock Exchange, and the MidAmerica Commodity Exchange. But exchange egos and personalities caused the collective PAC idea to fall apart.

Six months later, the Merc set up its own fund, the Commodity Futures Political Fund (CFPF), with Melamed as chairman. In an aggressive three-month drive, the Merc PAC raised $125,000, giving it the shape of a political heavyweight. In the past, Merc members had been on their own in giving support to political candidates. But, as Melamed put it, "that had very little effect in terms of telling our story."

"We were apolitical," he recalled. "We were like babes in the woods when we went to Washington. They thought the Chicago Board of Trade was a chamber of commerce and, if they had heard of the Merc at all, they assumed it was a bank." In the coming years that would all change, partly because of the Merc's active PAC and the Washington lobbying office it would establish not far from the White House. The Merc and the other Chicago exchanges managed to fend off the proposed transfer tax and make peace with the city council.

It was an easy truce, given what the exchanges brought to the city in the way of economic vitality in 1973. Outside of the 1,500 futures and options traders at the time, the exchanges were among the city's major employers. Combined, they accounted for 10 percent of the 110,000 service sector employees in finance, insurance, and real estate working in Chicago; the payroll: $150 million.

The exchanges and member firms rented in excess of one million square feet of space in the city of Chicago, and alone paid more than $2 million annually in real estate taxes. In addition, the Merc and CBOT clearinghouses handled an average of $507 million each night in margin funds deposited among Chicago's major banks. Because the margin represented only minimum maintenance, the full total of member firm and customer funds on deposit in Chicago banks was in excess of $1.5 billion. The economic ripple included investment capital, service business, computer time requirements, banking services, related labor, employment, attorneys, accountants, and so on.

Chicago exchanges, the pioneers and innovators of futures and options markets, were turning the Windy City into the risk capital of the world. The exchanges themselves had become tourist attractions, hosting thousands of visitors in their galleries each year. The trading floors had become open classrooms for foreigners seeking to emulate the Chicago exchanges in their own countries. In response, the exchanges offered an array of educational courses, scholarships, work programs, grants for academic research, and donations for all sorts of civic projects, such as the $50,000 given to the Lincoln Park Zoo in 1969 to develop a poultry building as part of the zoo's farm complex. By the mid-1970s risk management was becoming one of Chicago's major industries as well as one of its major exports.

It was a dreary political time when everything was overshadowed by Watergate, but in the summer of 1973 public attention once again turned to commodities. Senator Henry Jackson's Permanent Investigating Subcommittee opened hearings on the Soviet wheat sale. The government had subsidized the exports—thereby giving away resources, making the United States poorer, and stimulating inflation, according to an editorial in *The Wall Street Journal*. The USSR had indeed been able to buy wheat at $1.60 a bushel before anyone had recognized the effect of its purchases on U.S. prices. (Three years later, in 1975, the American harvest would be so great that even grain exports and stocks would be higher at the end of the year than at the start.)

During the Jackson hearings, questions concerning the regulatory power of the Commodity Exchange Authority were raised. The weakness of the CEA had first been challenged in 1966 following a major commodities scandal—the Anthony (Tino) DeAngelis salad oil swindle, a $150 million hoax. The general accounting office (GAO) and the Agriculture Department itself found evidence that the CEA had known in advance of some of DeAngelis's illegal activities but failed to act. The GAO issued a list of recommendations for tightening the federal policing of commodities markets, but the CEA largely ignored the GAO's advice.

By 1973 the Agriculture Department's inspector general accused the CEA of exercising only "minimum surveillance" over commodity trading without ensuring that corners, squeezes, and other types of price manipulation by dishonest traders were being prevented. CEA administrator Alex Caldwell, who had been on the job for 13 years, was sharply criticized by Inspector General Nathaniel Kossack as relying "primarily on self-regulation by the commodity exchanges."

Caldwell was a calm and precise man whose tidy office directly contrasted with the bedlam and paper-strewn trading floors of the futures exchanges. He had little ambition to expand the CEA's activities, once telling a newspaper reporter, he was "no empire builder." He was a friend of the exchanges more than an adversary, a champion of free markets who believed strongly in self-regulation. Consequently, the CEA had been a reluctant enforcer.

During the trading turmoil of 1973, the CEA suspended the trading licenses of only five floor traders and two firms for a mere fifteen days to six months and issued fewer than a dozen cease and desist orders. Now Caldwell and the CEA were under heat from such critics as Representative Neal Smith and Senator Richard Clark, both Democrats from Iowa. The congressmen wanted tighter control over the markets.

"The system simply must be harnessed," insisted Minneapolis Democrat Hubert Humphrey to the chagrin of his friends on the Minneapolis Grain Exchange. "It's like a train getting longer and longer and still being pulled by the same tired locomotive." Part of that tired locomotive included the CEA. What was needed, the politicians insisted, was actual reform. It came shortly after the round of congressional hearings in the summer and fall of 1973. Caught somewhere between smugness and despair, the commodity exchanges had been too defensive. In fending off the congressional investigators, they conceded that perhaps an overall agency to regulate commodities was needed. "Once you've said that," Weinberg later mused, "you can't be totally aggressive on the offensive."

With Watergate unfolding like a political passion play, the halls of Capitol Hill were suddenly filled with reform-minded congressmen. Not even a well-fortified lobby could turn back the bills that were introduced to strengthen futures trading regulations in January 1974. One such bill, which came out of the House Agriculture Committee, was the Commodity Futures Trading Commission Act. It set up the framework for the Commodity Futures Trading Commission (CFTC) in April 1975, replacing the CEA.

The CFTC promised to be to commodities what the SEC had been to stocks. Moreover, the CFTC's authority was extended to nonagricultural commodities, which meant that the IMM and currencies would be under the jurisdiction of a federal agency. At the same time, the definition of a commodity was expanded to the broadest terms: anything "that is or becomes the subject of futures trading, intangible as well as tangible."

Some were nervous about the prospect of a new and perhaps more stringent agency. "Some individuals believed we could duck this and maybe it would pass," said Melamed of that period when hearings on the new agency had just begun. "Then there was the more enlightened view that it was coming because we were successful and it was going to happen," he added. If it was indeed going to happen, the Merc and other futures exchanges were faced with two alternatives: either to ignore it or to help direct it.

The Merc was in the second camp. The growth and acceptability of futures in general had made exchanges like the CBOT and the Merc more visible than ever. "We actually participated in the process," explained Melamed. "We helped change words, mold sentences. There was a give and take." In fact, Melamed was on the list of five candidates to head the new agency; this list was to be submitted to Gerald Ford. At the time, Melamed had been on a vacation in Hawaii when he received a call from White House aide Beverly Splane, who was responsible for finding candidates to fill the posts of chairman and commissioners for the first CFTC. She told Melamed he was one of the candidates for CFTC chairman.

Melamed asked Splane if she would hold decision until he could meet with her in person. She agreed. The two met in Washington shortly thereafter. "I tried hard to convince him," recalled Splane. "But he refused because he wanted to build the exchange." Of the opportunity, Melamed said, "You can't say 'no' to a president. If I had been appointed to head the CFTC, all my plans for the IMM would have been over." (William Bagley became the first CFTC chairman.)

Part of the plan for the IMM included preparations for trading a gold contract on 2 January 1975. Five months earlier, on 14 August, Ford repealed the 40-year ban on private ownership of gold in the United States. The repeal was to become effective after 31 December 1974. Preparations for an IMM gold contract had been under way for more than a year. "We have exhaustively researched the market and utilized the expert knowledge of gold bullion assayers, refiners and brokers," Melamed told IMM members in a quarterly review.

The IMM had additional ammunition in its marketing arsenal: the expertise of Henry Jarecki, an IMM board member, chairman of Mocatta Metals Corp., and a director of Mocatta Goldsmidt Ltd., one of the world's largest bullion dealers. As one of five members of the London gold market, Mocatta participated in the daily London gold fixings. The specifications for the contract were relatively simple (minimum price fluctuations were in multiples of 10 cents per troy ounce), and the expanded price-limit formula that enabled currency futures prices to catch up with the spot market quickly following large price movements had been adapted to the gold contract.

Great Britain was the first country in modern times to officially tie its paper currency to gold when, in 1816, it fixed the value of an ounce of gold in terms of the pound. Other European countries followed suit, and eventually, so did the United States; the dollar was first fixed in terms of gold in 1900. Actually, a two-tier gold market had already been established in 1968.

It simply meant that there existed a private or free market price for gold and an "official" rate at which the price of gold was pegged for making international payments among nations' central banks. Milton Friedman called it a "pseudo-gold" standard, applying the term particularly to the period from 1934 to 1971. Supply and demand determined the world's private stocks of gold, free of any intervention by governments. By 1974 it was obvious that gold would come to play an increasingly minor role in the international monetary system, replaced by special drawing rights (SDRs) as an instrument for making international payments. Gold itself was held more as an unofficial reserve asset.[1]

London's bullion dealers in particular were paying close attention to the Merc's proposed gold contract, which had the same specifications as the London contracts. Thus, by design, it made direct arbitrage with the London gold market easier. Even the U.S. Treasury liked the idea of a gold futures market. Speculation in gold futures was expected to help reduce gold to the status of other commodities and to demonetize the precious metal. Other exchanges in New York and on the West Coast were also preparing gold contracts.

The IMM had already expanded by trading a copper contract on 1 July. The first trade was a sale of ten January contracts, each calling for 12,500 pounds of electrolytic copper. Harold S. Brady, one the nation's major copper traders, had sold to an undisclosed buyer, with Philip D. Lind of the Lind-Waldock Corp. executing the trade.

The politics of the Exchange continued in orderly fashion with the election of John T. Geldermann as chairman in 1974. He succeeded Weinberg, who had held the post for two years. Geldermann, a tall man with a droll wit, had started his career in the pits of the CBOT shortly after his return from World War II.

The eldest of four brothers, in 1948 he founded Geldermann & Company, Inc. with his father, Godfrey, who had been a member of the CBOT since 1921. In 1964, the firm expanded its clearing operations to the Merc, where Geldermann began trading pork bellies. He had spent 19 years at the CBOT mainly as a corn trader. "When you came from the Board of Trade in those days," Geldermann said, "you carried some of the aura with you. At the Merc there was always that feeling of playing catch up." That was one reason why chairman Nate Werthheimer asked him over lunch one day to run for the Merc board of governors in 1967. He has been on the board ever since. Geldermann would never return to the CBOT, and he went on to become Merc chairman from 1974 to 1975 and then again from 1989 to 1990.

During the late 1960s Geldermann was a member of a CEA panel to study automation in the futures industry. "At that time," he recalled, "it was the general determination of that panel that, technically and practically, the exchange trading functions could not be automated for 15 years."

Along with Geldermann there was Carl Anderson, assistant vice-president of Merrill Lynch, Pierce, Fenner & Smith, Inc., as first vice-chairman of the CME; Laurence M. Rosenberg, president of Grow Investments, second vice-chairman; Donald Minucciani of Weinberg Bros. & Co., treasurer; and Melamed, still chairman of the IMM and secretary of the CME.

Melamed, Harris, Frost, Powers, and company were now dividing half their time to the Exchange daily operations and the other half to pushing the IMM. They had been busy criss-crossing the country to plant the idea of the IMM like seeds in harsh soil. They met in New York with bankers, in St. Louis with brokers, and in San Francisco with financial industry representatives. "The first four years were very slow," said Melamed. "There were moments when we felt the pressure of it all. We were still the evangelists."

23

The Public Takes Notice

"I am here to listen and to get acquainted. I am looking for intelligent discussion," Senator Hubert Humphrey told Melamed and Weinberg during his visit to the Exchange in late 1973. As a member of the Senate Agriculture, Nutrition, and Forestry Committee, Humphrey came to the CME to discuss his bill to strengthen and improve commodity futures trading and its regulation.

New worldwide influence spurred the demand for commodities, coupled with unpredictable factors that converged to throttle supply. The result: skyrocketing prices, consequent heavy futures trading, and a consumer outcry for scapegoats. At least that was the public's view. The media—a relentless critic of the futures exchanges in the first place—shared equal skepticism. Many stories in the popular press seemed to fuel the fury. *Forbes* magazine ran a 1 August 1973 cover story entitled "Commodities—Is the Public Playing Russian Roulette?" The cover photograph showed a man with a pistol pointed to his temple.

Humphrey and his colleagues[1] came to the Merc for a first-hand look. They mingled among the traders on the floor and got a birds-eye view from the gallery as well. Given the fact that the Commodity Exchange Act of 1936 had not been revised since 1968, the CME officials agreed with the congressmen that an overhaul was important.

Over the next few months Merc officials Melamed, Weinberg, Geldermann, and Harris testified before various committees with the same message: More controls were needed both to upgrade the professionalism of some marketplaces and to increase the services and protection afforded the public. "We would draw the line, however, at any effort to diminish the self-regulatory responsibilities of the nation's 18 individual exchanges in favor of a 'Big Brother' federal agency," Weinberg told Humphrey the morning of his visit to the Exchange.

Earlier, in testimony before Representative Neal Smith's House Subcommittee on Special Small Business Problems, Weinberg had outlined a nine-point legislative program that would expand the size and scope of the CEA and at the same time require increased self-regulation by the exchanges themselves.

Everyone, it seemed, had a bill up his political sleeve. In the House there were Poage's and Smith's bills. In the Senate three bills were prepared by Senators Humphrey, George McGovern, and Gary Hart. All meant the end of the CEA. Four bills called for a new commission similar to the SEC that would be tied to the Department of Agriculture. The new agency would regulate all commodities traded on futures exchanges that were not covered by the SEC. Violations would also mean stiffer penalties, providing civil fines up to $100,000 to replace the $500 to $10,000 fines. The Hart bill provided for civil actions brought by individuals for damages and up to $1 million for criminal violations.

When it came to dual trading, there was considerable disparity. The Poage bill would empower the Commission to set terms under which a floor broker could trade for his own account and at the same time execute customers' orders; in cases not specified by the Commission, no floor broker could execute a customer's order and transact his or her own or discretionary order on the same day except to correct an error. The Smith and Hart bills prohibited dual trading at any time. The McGovern bill provided such a ban during a single day. And the Humphrey bill left the rule intact.

Margins were also up for political grabs. The Poage bill prohibited anyone except the exchanges from setting margins. The Hart bill required exchanges to set margins with Commission approval. The Smith bill gave the Commission approval over margins. The McGovern bill allowed the Commission to change margins only after written request to an exchange and hearings. The Humphrey bill would not change the then-current CEA rule.

Other areas the bills considered were manipulation (the McGovern bill wanted to leave the act unchanged, but the other four included various procedures, along with court action in two bills to enjoin a practice or a position); registration (anyone associated with a futures commission merchant [FCM] would be required to pass examinations and be registered with the commission); and customer insurance (the Poage and Hart bills both called for creation of an insurance fund to protect customer accounts in case of a firm's bankruptcy).

Hogs, cattle, and soybeans gained as much status during the period from 1972 to 1974 as politicians lost. The gaggle of proposed bills clearly showed that commodities were tasty political food for the hungriest of politicians. Why not? Every constituent eats. Besides, commodities was a story the media were anxious to report. It had drama—the intrigue of international wheat deals with the cold war enemy, explosive price increases, angry consumers, skeptical farmers, profiteering. The bills also showed something else: an ignorance on the part of some congressmen as to how futures exchanges worked.

The Exchange officials were thus spending more and more time in Washington explaining the fundamentals. In his testimony in May 1974, Melamed told members of the Committee on Agriculture, Nutrition, and Forestry that the CME opposed neither a new commodity commission nor many of the provisions in proposed legislation. "Indeed, many of the provisions," he pointed out to the congressmen, "were the result of suggestions that we ourselves initiated."

Melamed had written his own testimony, part of which later inspired adman Martin Cohen to create a series of award-winning CME advertisements that to this day are considered classics. "Mr. Chairman," Melamed continued, "there are no commodity exchanges in Moscow; there is no Peking Duck Exchange in China; there is no Havana Cigar Board of Trade. The farmers of those countries have no need for a vehicle which offers projection or price protection. There the governments themselves establish the prices which they will pay for the farmers' products."

Indeed, it was unfortunate, bemoaned Melamed, that legislation relating to the futures markets was prompted in large measure by the upward food price spiral. He explained,"To act as a messenger is, in fact, one of the primary functions of futures markets. Futures markets, by their definition, must act to provide us with a glimpse of what is coming. If these markets had failed to predict the high prices to come, they would not have functioned correctly. As a matter of fact, they did not fail, and moreover they responded to the emergency far better than might have been anticipated."

In some ways appearing before Congress was beneficial, though trying. From time to time, it offered a forum for the exchanges to air their differences, a kind of escape valve. "It was healthy confrontation," said Harris. "Congressmen saw the faces behind the names and it gave us a chance to update them on our thoughts and markets." On some points, however, the Merc stood its ground, refusing to give an inch. Margins was one such point. The Merc's stand on outside tampering of margins was simply stated by Melamed in the mid-1970s and unaltered in the 1980s, when the markets were explosively volatile. "We are vehemently and unequivocally opposed to any legislation which would transfer this authority from the exchanges themselves," he emphatically told Senator Humphrey and his fellow subcommittee members.

In the first place, *margin* is a misnomer with respect to commodities. There is a fundamental difference, both from a conceptual and an operational standpoint, between margin on securities and those on commodity futures contracts. Unfortunately, that fact was not always understood. Securities margin is a direct measure of the creation of bank credit, but futures market margin acts as a surety or security deposit. The futures margin therefore was not measured by the value of the product or contract, but was determined by the volatility of the market and the possible change in daily price movement.

In 1967 the Agriculture Department commissioned the Nathan Report, which concluded that margin on commodity futures markets could not be utilized for any other purpose without impairing the actual operation of the market itself. Furthermore, the margin was a security deposit and could not relate to payment on credit toward the purchase of the product. No agency, the report added, was better equipped or situated to regulate this area than the exchanges themselves.

Controlling margins by federal edict, Merc officials argued, would push the exchanges toward the threshold of price control. It is an ongoing argument whenever the markets heat up, and the issue came to a head in the stock market crash of 1987, when stocks plummeted. But this was all before the crash, and, in the dog days of August 1974, no one had dreamed of such things as stock index futures, portfolio insurance, and program trading, which raised the markets to a sophisticated level of hedging.

The currency futures market was limping along, despite the fact there was plenty of evidence that corporate America needed to hedge its foreign exposure. Only two years earlier, the very year the IMM opened, Americans were watching the 1972 Olympics from Munich through the ABC network, which was losing $2 million because someone apparently overlooked a simple fact: The network was collecting receipts and paying its bills in two different currencies, dollars and Deutsche marks.

ABC wasn't the only multinational corporation that hadn't mastered the ABCs of currency hedging. Among and outside of the nation's top 500 firms, there were those who had never used the foreign exchange markets. Earlier, for instance, Chesebrough-Pond's had attained record sales and earnings despite increased losses on foreign exchange, equivalent to nearly 5 percent of its net income. Farm machinery maker John Deere & Company, in its 1971 annual report, included a 10-year summary of consolidated income showing write-offs for foreign exchange losses for every year since 1962, ranging from nearly $6 million in 1967 to $546,000 in 1971. F.W. Woolworth in 1967 wrote off nearly $3 million, or the equivalent of about 6 percent of its income, while Proctor & Gamble found it necessary in 1971 to increase its reserves for foreign operations because of currency volatility. In 1974, Gulf Oil lost $25 million on one of its foreign loans.

There were, of course, plenty of success stories, too. Outboard Marine Corporation attributed earnings gains to foreign exchange trading as did Hewlett Packard, as well as some of the major banks such as Chase Manhattan and Morgan Guaranty. Obviously the new monetary world demanded a broad foreign exchange market. It also demanded a great deal of educating of the public.

In the first two and a half years of the IMM's existence, the Merc published more statistics and information on the use of foreign exchange than had been produced in the entire decade before. In addition to an array of study courses, there were a variety of lectures, symposiums, conferences, courses for universities, taped cassettes, and a 30-minute movie as well as the constant flow of published reports.

Despite the effort, there was still reluctance among corporate executives to use the futures markets in general, much less the currency markets. "Because some companies don't understand how the markets work, they are afraid they will hedge themselves into a loss," observed Raymond J. Doll, senior vice-president of the Federal Reserve Bank of Kansas City in Missouri.

Yet at the time, a growing number of bankers were urging their customers to use the futures markets. The Chicago banks, closer to these markets, seemed more inclined to do so. Said Harris Bank vice-president Wallace Weisenborn at the time, "We tell our clients that if they want to speculate by not hedging, they can do it with their own money, not ours." Down LaSalle Street at Continental Illinois National Bank & Trust Company, John Goodrich, Jr., a vice-president, echoed similar sentiments. "We can give a bigger percentage advanced against hedged inventories than we can against unhedged ones," he said.

But the Merc wasn't about to sit and wait for the business community to catch up with the IMM. The financial world was changing too rapidly to lag behind in finding new and innovative tools that could be used to cope with uncertainty.

That August, Melamed met with Jack F. Bennett, the undersecretary for monetary affairs at the Treasury Department. The subject was gold. Melamed gave a compelling reason for the Treasury to modify its regulations to allow the opening of futures contracts in gold in light of the fact that if gold prices were to substantially rise between 14 August 1974, and 1 January 1975, the U.S. government would receive severe criticism both from the American public and from Congress.

"It would be as if the Europeans and other non–U.S. citizens were given a sure bet at the expense of the American public," Melamed wrote Bennett in a follow-up letter. "They can buy gold now and later sell it at much higher prices to Americans." It wasn't an idle theory. At the time, many foreign speculators were doing just that. A futures market in gold would effectively alleviate the problem, insisted the Merc.

Four months later, on 31 December 1974, the Merc gold contract sprang to life on the IMM. Illinois Governor Dan Walker clanged the golden bell to signal the start of trading in a pit next to a $2 million display of gold bullion.[2] Action bristled from the outset with 798 contracts changing hands in the first hour. The day marked the first time in 41 years that U.S. citizens were allowed to own gold. (The contract called for 100 ounces of .995 fine gold to be delivered in seven contract months.) It was a time when New York City was sagging under a mountain of maturing debt, rattling the municipal bond market. It was also the era of negotiated commissions among stock brokers, many of whose firms were battered by recession, the paperwork crunch, and the 1973 to 1974 market collapse that melted institutional trading profits like ice in boiling water.

Activity in the gold contract, however, didn't begin to pick up until 1978, when the country was in the grip of inflation, higher interest rates, and a see-sawing stock market that sank the Dow Jones Industrial Average to a low of 750. Not even the bicentennial and the tall ships that glided through New York harbor could distract people from the harsh economic realities of the times. The auto industry felt the brunt of competition and began to lay off workers as foreign cars grabbed nearly 30 percent of the U.S. market; takeover mania in the corporate jungle went on a wild binge that continued into the 1980s.

With the new Commodities Futures Trading Commission came William T. Bagley, the first CFTC chairman, who had an evocative and individualistic style. Though he had spent 14 years in the California state legislature, he had no previous experience in the complex futures industry. The new position was not exactly a comfortable one, and industry reaction was mixed. "Nothing is free any more, but we were the closest thing to it in terms of how our markets were developed and how they operated, and I hate to see it change," bemoaned Frederick Uhlmann, vice-president for commodities at Drexel-Burnham.

Bagley, a man with an engaging smile who favored wide ties and suspenders, took the helm of the new agency at a time when government regulation was passing out of vogue. In fact, the five-man commission was named by Ford just as he was attempting to reduce the efforts of government regulation. Congress had imposed the new bureaucracy on an industry reluctant to accept federal regulation. Nevertheless, Bagley viewed the CFTC as "a classic example of Congressional initiative . . . spawned by Congress in response to what seemed to be a public demand." Bagley was quick to point out that the CFTC was different as a regulatory agency because it wasn't created as a result of an industry scandal, a specially appointed task force, or industry demand. As for the opponents to a CFTC, Bagley would simply smile and say, "It is not so much resistance as a head in the sand attitude."

In a resolved and diplomatic tone, Melamed said, "We could have been left alone and still done a good job in self-regulation. However, I will admit that I am not unpleased by the fact that the CFTC is now in existence and will have larger regulatory authority and teeth to carry it out."

Within a year, the Merc felt the bite of the CFTC's teeth. In a crackdown against the illegal use of futures trading to avoid taxes, the CFTC charged the Siegel Trading Company and 10 individuals, including Joseph Siegel, the firm's president, and Alvin C. Winograd, its vice-president, with committing fraud through fictitious prearranged trading of currency futures on the IMM. Joseph Siegel's older brother, Sam, had been known for his exploits of trying to corner the Merc's ill-fated onion market. Now Joseph was wheeling and dealing with Mexican pesos through a scheme that began in October 1974 when he persuaded Harold Brady, a highly successful Chicago copper trader, to open an account for the purpose of sheltering income from taxes.

In the 1970s sheltering income could be done legally through spread trading, which involved the simultaneous purchase and sale of futures positions in the same commodity, but in different delivery months. Whichever way the commodity price moved, one side of the spread would show a gain and the other a loss. The spreader could then defer the income, thereby turning short-term gains into long-term ones. The Internal Revenue Service had accepted the strategy as long as it involved risk to the trader—the contracts actually had to be owned, and the potential to make or lose money on the trade itself had to exist.

Using the discretionary power granted by Brady, Siegel and others had rigged artificial trades that created no economic risk. Normally, such prearranged trades required two traders willing to offset each other's position. But Siegel used Brady's account to form one side of the rigged trade. The respondents, trading in their own accounts, then took the opposite side for income tax advantages. Siegel had falsely reported to Brady and the IMM that the trades had been competitive. In all there had been 28 false trades in Mexican pesos and Swiss francs between December 1974 and January 1975. Brady had paid out commissions of $91,225 in a scheme that created more than $2 million in phony tax losses through rigged trades.

In July 1977, an administrative law judge levied a $100,000 fine against Siegel Trading and suspended it from certain kinds of commodity trading for six months. In 1978, the U.S. Attorney's office went after Siegel and Winograd, convicting the pair of conspiracy, fraud, and violation of the Commodity Exchange Act. Siegel was fined $500,000 and given probation; Winograd received a nominal fine and probation.

The young CFTC was busy. In June 1977 a federal grand jury in Chicago, assisted by the CFTC, indicted five CBOT soybean traders on a variety of offenses that included tax evasion and defrauding customers through rigged trades. At the time, one CFTC official estimated that more than $500 million in taxes had been evaded in recent years through illegal commodity trades and that the IRS had lacked the resources or knowledge to ferret them out.

Though the Merc itself was not a target of the CFTC probes, the peso case was hardly the kind of the publicity the struggling IMM needed. But it encouraged the Merc to enhance its surveillance and auditing capabilities. In 1979, for example, the Merc levied one the biggest fines up to that time against clearing member Refco, Inc. for repeatedly violating recordkeeping and order entry procedures and margin requirements and for exceeding position limits. Although Thomas Dittmer, Refco's president, never admitted to wrongdoing, he was suspended from the Merc for six months, and Refco was fined $250,000.

As soon as the CFTC had gotten on its feet, a flash of controversy tied to the Merc arose in the late fall of 1975. It dealt with the Exchange's hiring of Beverly Splane, a 31-year-old former White House personnel aide who had been acting executive director of the CFTC in charge of screening applicants for the commission. Some congressmen likened the move to a Pentagon general going to work for a major defense contractor. But Splane had taken all the necessary steps to ensure propriety.

Immediately after receiving the first call from the CME, she contacted Bagley to inform him she wished to start negotiations for the job if it were legal and proper to do so. Together the two then notified the CFTC commissioners and Bagley obtained an opinion from the commission's general counsel that there was no conflict of interest or law violation.

With that approval, she negotiated her move to the Merc, which had four complaints pending against it before the CFTC. It made the issue all the more sensitive since the complaints were technically under the purview of Splane, who had broad control over compliance, enforcement, and investigations, although no actual role in the handling of the cases. Splane had been cautioned that she would be violating criminal law if she sought to represent the CME on any matter that had been pending before the agency during her time as acting executive director. The prohibition was absolute for a year, and in matters where she was directly involved, the barrier was extended indefinitely.

At 3 P.M. on Friday, 7 November, Splane resigned her post to join the CME as executive vice-president. In doing so, she became the highest-ranking woman executive at a major exchange. In Splane the Merc had not only a valuable resource with Washington connections and insight into a new federal agency, but a superb administrator. The statement by Bagley said simply that she had held the job of acting director since April and added,"The excellent organizational ability of Beverly Splane was of immeasurable assistance in establishing an entirely new commission . . . . Without her help, the commission would not have been able to make the relatively smooth transition from an agricultural-related agency of the Department of Agriculture to an independent commission with authority over all futures trading—agricultural, non-agricultural, and international."

Splane was typical of the new kind of staff talent the Merc began to develop in the 1970s and 1980s to handle a more bureaucratic organization and to deal with emerging markets. With an M.B.A. from the University of Chicago, Splane had been a management consultant and professional recruiter before serving as director of career development at the Harvard Business School from 1973 until her appointment to the White House in August 1974.

When she got to the Merc, she said, much of the staff was composed of clerks who had worked their way up from the trading floor. "There was no one who could deal with Wall Street and federal regulators. I brought in new people and worked the old people down and sideways," she explained.

A decade later Splane would be instrumental in helping the Merc forge its historic link with the Singapore Monetary Exchange as the forerunner of 24-hour global trading. Splane and the Merc walked the legal tightrope in 1974 with relative ease. As for the CFTC, it maintained its status even in the eyes of a skeptical press. "The CFTC—under the chairmanship of William T. Bagley—replaced the toothless and limited Commodity Exchange Authority of the Agriculture Dept. and is equal in muscle to the Securities & Exchange Commission," remarked *BusinessWeek* 16 months later.

By the time the CFTC faced reauthorization in 1978, however, the regulatory darling of the futures industry was fighting for its life. "We have beaten back every jackal that came out of the jurisdictional jungle," declared an embattled Bagley who had waged the fight in the halls of Congress, where he had appeared about 15 times over a 10-week period to argue that the CFTC should be allowed to continue. Under the 1974 law that created the agency, Congress had to decide to keep it going or not.

The understaffed, underfinanced CFTC had been criticized as ill-managed, uncooperative, with other agencies, and unknowledgeable about the complexities of the futures markets. Moreover, some critics accused the agency of being obsessed with the relatively minor task of policing fraud in the sale of commodity options, which eventually became legalized. The CFTC had successfully argued against suggestions that its authority over futures trading in financial instruments be given to the Treasury and its authority over registered securities be given to the SEC.

The Carter administration threw into the hopper an eleventh-hour proposal that the CFTC be replaced by an agency headed by one person responsible to the president. But it received little congressional support. In any case, commissioners and critics agreed that the CFTC spent too much of its time on congressional debate at the expense of some of its other business. The reauthorization process, complained former CFTC vice-chairman John Rainbolt, "has turned the commission and staff into lobbyists to a certain extent."

The process did the same thing to the Merc and to other exchanges. One lingering cause of concern was a Capitol Hill campaign to allow states jurisdiction over the futures business, particularly the power to prosecute fraud. This worried the exchanges, which saw the prospect of 50 different interpretations of the same law. The London options scandal was the prime reason why state securities commissioners asked Congress to give them greater clout with commodities sales. The proposed law never left subcommittee.

Although the CFTC won its reauthorization, Bagley lost his credibility and was expected to resign before his term expired in 1980. "I don't want to color myself gone," he cautioned shortly after the reauthorization hearings. A year later, he was replaced by Carter's appointee James Stone, whose expertise was in insurance regulation rather than in commodities. By 1982 the situation had hardly changed. Philip McBride Johnson, partner in the law firm of Kirkland and Ellis and the chief outside counsel for the CBOT, succeeded Stone; in his book on commodity regulation, he wrote that the commission didn't gain the "full respect and confidence of the Congress and other agencies with which it must work and compete."

Educating the lawmakers in the arcane world of futures was never an easy task for the exchanges. On one hand, the traders, with their leather lungs and sharp elbows, were always a paradox to themselves and a perplexity to the public. On the other, the exchanges viewed Congress as a surly beast, one particularly dangerous when unhappy. Initially the Merc opened its Washington office in 1977 to educate Washington officials. Bill Bagley actually gave the Merc the idea. In a speech to the Merc members in the winter of 1976 at the Bismarck Hotel, Bagley said he was appalled at the lack of understanding of the futures markets in Washington. "That speech was the genesis of our Washington office," said Laurence Rosenberg, who opened the office during his tenure as Merc chairman.

For all the Merc's liquidity, it refused to rest on its laurels. Diversification was still in the minds of Merc officials, but so were cultivation and refinement of the new markets such as the Treasury Bill contract. Just as 1974 was a period of intense preparation for the gold bullion contract, the Merc was busy gearing up for a new contract to be traded in January 1976: a 90-day U.S. Treasury bill futures contract.

Why the optimism? First, there was a trend toward the use of short-term monetary instruments. Second, the T-bill was the principal instrument from which short-term interest rates emanated, which made it a good hedging device against rate volatility in other instruments such as commercial paper, bankers' acceptances, agency paper, and certificates of deposit. Third, T-bills offered a primary market of more than $3 billion and a secondary market with daily trading volume of up to $5 billion; It was indeed a highly liquid market.

On 6 January 1976 Milton Friedman, now a Nobel Laureate in economics, rang the bell to begin trading the 90-day T-bill. Over the next six years, Treasury bill futures would become the most actively traded contract at the Merc.

The planning of the Treasury bill futures contract proved to be tougher than a Rubik's Cube. The problem was easily understood: T-bills were quoted on interest rates, but the futures contract had to be based on the price of the bill. When interest rates rose, the price of the bill would go down, and vice versa. Traders thus had to think inversely. To solve the problem, Melamed turned to Melvin Unterman, a former banker, who, along with Philip Glass, William Goldstandt, and Atlee Kohl, was a member of the T-Bill specifications committee.

Unterman came up with the so-called IMM index, which represents the actual annualized T-bill interest yield subtracted from 100. Thus, to find annual interest yield represented by a particular futures quote, one must subtract the quote from 100. If traders expected the annualized interest rate to go from 5.83 percent to 6.56 percent, they reduced their bid from 94.17 to 93.44. In contrast to interest rates, the index moved down as the contract lost value, and vice versa. This is the way the Treasury Department sold T-bills on a discount basis. Rather than getting a $10,000 piece of paper that pays $162.50 interest in three months, the purchaser pays $9,837.50 for a piece of paper that turns into $10,000.

As he had done with currencies, Mark Powers almost out of instinct wrote the specifications for the T-bill contracts. Although those specs have changed somewhat over time, they still apply in basically the same form in which Powers wrote them. The fertile-minded Powers, Melamed once wrote, represented the handful of "brave soldiers" compared "with the armies who viewed the idea of financial futures with disdain."

Shortly after T-bills were introduced, Merc officials were back in the trenches. Just as currency futures had been sold to the banks, T-bill futures now had to be sold to the investment bankers, who again waited to see whether this new contract, pegged to soaring inflation and interest rates, would work. A target firm was Salomon Brothers, where Melamed met with senior partner

William Salomon. Melamed recalled,"He listened to me and said, 'This is not for Salomon to start. But if you prove it will work, I'll join, and I promise you Salomon will be your number one trader.' And when we showed it would work, it gave the bond dealers a huge security blanket; and he was as good as his word: Salomon did come in and did become number one."

The instant success of the T-bill contract inflamed the competitive fires in Chicago as the Merc and the CBOT began frantically to search for new contracts in the interest rate sector. The problem was to choose an instrument. While the Merc had zeroed in on the short-term market with T-bills, the CBOT launched a mortgage-backed futures contract, or so-called Ginnie Mae (Government National Mortgage Association, or GNMA), in 1975. The brainchild of Richard Sandor, a former finance professor at the University of California at Berkeley, the contract looked like a sure winner, given the fact that Americans borrowed more than $1 trillion to buy homes. At least one-third of that debt was securitized, whereby mortgages were bundled and traded as securities. In the early 1970s these securities were a bonanza for Wall Street firms. The total principal amount of mortgage securities sold to fixed-income investors was $8 billion in 1977; a decade later it was $120 billion.[3] This was one area the Merc had no interest in pursuing. When the CBOT opened its mortgage-backed contract in 1975, Roger Gray, a Stanford finance professor, predicted a rough road for the contract because of potential delivery problems.

With a lock on the short-term interest rate futures market, the Merc thought the world was going toward the shorter end of the interest rate spectrum. Consequently, the IMM chose to go after the middle-range market with a 4-year Treasury note contract. The success in the T-bill market and failure in the Ginnie Mae market encouraged the Merc to think short-term. It turned out to be a critical error, given the enormity in volume of the CBOT's Treasury bond contract.

Although the Merc's star flickered on the "wrong decision," Melamed looking back views it as a twist of fate that benefited the exchange over time. He explained,"Thank God they [the CBOT] made the right decision. If we had made the right decision, we would have been the only ones in financial futures because there was nothing left. In the subsequent years, we wouldn't have won the battles [against the regulators, Congress, and so forth] without being in lockstep with the CBOT in financial futures. In effect, our loss made it successful for this market in Chicago because we now had both exchanges playing a dominant role in promoting and protecting the financial futures markets."

One exchange didn't make an industry—many exchanges did. As the Chicago exchanges—the Merc, the CBOT, the CBOE, and the Midwest Stock Exchange (MSE)—began to physically expand their facilities with massive additions and new buildings in the 1980s, that fact became apparent. As they grew, they attracted more people and more money. In 1986, nearly 33,000 persons were employed by Chicago's exchanges and the member firms (including the CBOE and MSE), spending some $870 million on rent, taxes, data processing, telecommunications, and professional services, according to a November 1987 study by the Commercial Club of Chicago. The Commercial Club had been convinced to do the study in order to show the economic impact of the Merc and of Chicago's other exchanges. Even though the report projected an annual growth rate of 10 percent to 15 percent for the industry, it boasted,"Cities around the world are trying to emulate the success of Chicago and its exchanges."

Yet even today a stigma still hangs over the futures markets like a polluted haze. In West Germany, for example, options trading was forbidden by law because it was considered gambling. That law was repealed only in 1989. Options and futures, the critics say, have nothing to do with capital formation—an argument the Merc is constantly battling.

The ferocity of the battle varied with the mood of the times. For instance, on the heels of the stock market crash of 1987, a strong undercurrent of fear and anger ran through the two exchanges as securities officials and some Washington lawmakers blamed the stock index futures contract for causing the 508-point plunge in the Dow Jones Industrial Average and driving small investors to seek other havens.

Recriminations over who was responsible for the 19 October crash turned skirmish lines into a good old-fashioned turf war: On one side was Chicago, a world financial center shaped, as *Time* stereotypically put it, by "young, brash, speculative and unabashedly noisy" futures and options traders. On the other side was New York—the heart of the world's securities and banking industries—whose stock traders and brokers, by contrast, were "tradition-bound, analytic, fraternal and relatively demure." Both entities reflect the dark side of what appeared to be a healthy rivalry. Each city appeared to be vying for the title of Clout City as they jockey to influence the nation's lawmakers.

The free-marketeers, however, saw the struggle as not so much between the Midwest and East as between today's high-tech global financial market spinning on volatility and a past in which Wall Street operated as a private club and competition was limited. John A. Wing, president of Chicago Corporation, in defense of stock indexes, summed up the tone of LaSalle Street eight months after the crash when he told the *National Journal,* "The stock market is sacred; it's got God-like qualities. And so the securities industry is able to cloak itself in the American economy. That's somehow more appealing than risk transfer and free markets."

The "battle" with lawmakers began in Illinois as far back as 1876, when the state legislature called futures contracts gambling contracts in a law that slapped a $1,000 fine on the would-be perpetrator and a sentence of up to a year in the Cook County jail. Seven CBOT traders were arrested under the law, which was repealed a year later. Illinois politicians such as Senators Alan Dixon and Paul Simon and Representative Dan Rostenkowski vigorously championed not merely one institution, but the Merc, the CBOT and the CBOE.

The Merc and the CBOT have tried to reinforce their positions in Washington politics over the years. Edgy and eager to head off trading regulations, and in reaction to the shift in authority from the CFTC to the SEC, both exchanges developed sizeable political action committee (PAC) contributions, amounting to more than a half million dollars in the period from 1985 to 1986.

The flow of PAC funds, of course, depends on the political activity in any given year. Each PAC also distributed $20,000 to 1988 presidential candidates, with one or both giving $5,000 donations to Republicans George Bush and Robert Dole and Democrats Richard Gephardt, Albert Gore, and Paul Simon. Honoraria and expense-paid trips have also been part of the strategy. In 1987, for example, 24 of 43 members of the House and Senate Agriculture Committee—the authority over the CFTC—received $1,000 or more in honoraria, mainly for speeches before the Merc and CBOT. That year both exchanges also anted up another $24,000 for 10 of the 19 members of the Senate Agriculture, Nutrition, and Forestry Committee for a round of hand shaking, speeches, and tours of the exchanges.

The result can be a public relations bonanza in photographs of the lawmakers flanked by exchange officials striding amid the trading pits. The exchanges have never hidden their on-again, off-again relationship with politicians. The walls in the offices of exchange officials are festooned with photographs of Washington's best and brightest, not to mention the thick photo albums lying on coffee tables like family archives.

The wooing process doesn't end when the lawmaker lands back in Washington. Every May, the Merc carries its political romancing to Capitol Hill with its annual Washington reception. Every U.S. senator and congressman who has visited the Exchange, as well as congressional aides, cabinet members, and regulators from the CFTC and SEC are invited to the annual cocktail party—from 6 P.M. to 8 P.M.—held in the House Agriculture Hearing Room, filled with food, fine wines, azaleas, and Washington gossip, all overflowing onto a long veranda directly across from the Capitol.

The reception has grown from a handful of congressmen since the first one in 1977, when the Merc opened its Washington office. In 1990 about 15 senators and 76 congressmen attended, in addition to Secretary of Agriculture Clayton Yeutter and 135 other VIPs and staffers, according to Carol Sexton, the reception's coordinator, the Merc's vice-president of public affairs, and sister to former Chicago Mayor Jane Byrne. During the 1988 and 1992 presidential conventions, the Merc hosted parties for both Democrats and Republicans.

The futures industry constantly complains that Congress doesn't understand its business, much less stock index futures. Consequently, in seeking allies and sympathetic friends, the industry has become a political animal, ironically without a political constituency. There are only half a million futures traders and

25 million stock traders. But the Merc, over the years, has developed a working relationship with some of the nation's leading pension fund managers as well as institutional investors.

The Chicago exchanges at this time were on an innovative run, driving against each other in heated competition. A year earlier, the CBOT launched the futures markets in interest rates, when it created a contract in mortgage certificates of the Ginnie Mae. That enabled participants in the mortgage market to hedge against fluctuations in long-term rates. The CBOE volume was already more than a third of the NYSE volume, although the CBOE traded only in calls—options to buy a stock at a fixed price at some future date—and only in 80 issues. But it was about to begin trading in puts (options to sell stocks in the future), too.

Another frontier looked as if it were going to open soon. The CFTC had hinted that it would let the exchanges trade in options on commodity futures, which made sense. The exchanges were already trading the underlying commodities, and established markets in commodity options could lower the entry fee and limit some of the inherent risks in commodity futures.

By now, the four-year-old IMM was trading some $13.7 billion in eight foreign currencies and an additional $6.8 billion in gold. Such volume helped the Merc capture one-fifth of the nation's commodity trading business, second only to the CBOT. The 11 smaller U.S. exchanges in places like New York, Minneapolis, Kansas City, New Orleans, and San Francisco saw the share of their futures trading volume grow from 17 percent in 1970 to 30 percent in 1976.

"In the last decade we have bitten off so much we had better take time and chew it," Melamed told a *BusinessWeek* reporter two months after the T-bill contract began trading in 1976. "Even in cattle—which is one of the most successful contracts of a decade—we've only tapped 3% to 5% of potential industry usage. We have not yet begun to touch the potential of the currencies. And the Treasury bill market potential is bigger than all our other markets put together—it boggles the mind."

Part III

The Age of
Financial Instruments
(1976 to 1992)

24

Spreading Its Wings

In the mid-1970s the Malthusian predictions of overpopulation caught the fancy of gloomy forecasters, who predicted that early in the next century there would be only one square yard of land for each man, woman and child on earth. The Merc managed to attain an even tighter compression of the humanity on its trading floor shortly after its new building was occupied in late 1972—about one square foot per trader in the more active pits.

The overcrowding was the price paid for success of such contracts as live cattle, live hogs, pork bellies, eggs, lumber, and feeder cattle, as well as currencies, gold, and Treasury bills on the IMM. The Merc since the early 1950s had moved from underdog to top dog by establishing markets that older members—and then bankers—said were taboo. First it was unstorable items, then currencies, gold, T-bills. It was, in the words of Warren Moulds, a former newspaper man hired by Frost to beef up the public relations department, "An embarrassment of riches."

The seat prices spoke eloquently of the health of the CME's markets. Memberships reached a 57-year high of $150,000 in 1976, surpassing the former record by more than $20,000 and equaling the record for any commodity exchange. (At the time a seat on the CBOT was $125,000 and $89,000 on the New York Stock Exchange.) The IMM seats, too, reached record highs at $40,000. For those who had held on, the IMM seat turned out to be the bargain of the decade. Just four years earlier, 500 Merc members bought IMM seats for $100 apiece, and an important infusion of young blood came into the exchange when 150 IMM seats were sold to outsiders for $10,000.

Of course, not every trader hit it big. Some, in fact, struck out. There was a turnover of around 40 memberships—a good number of which belonged to traders who hadn't been able to make it—every year.

"The markets have no mercy," Melamed reflected from the floor of the Exchange. "They don't care about the pedigree of your lineage, only your sense of survival. That produces a hard and smart individual." Every trader knew that it cost money to learn how to cope with markets and that indeed the market was an equalizer in terms of bankroll and number of contracts traded when it came to who made money and how much. "It isn't who's big that matters," said Larry Rosenberg. "It's who's right."

Alex Kittner apparently had been right more often than wrong in his 48 years as a trader in the Merc's egg pit. The 80-year-old Kittner was turning in his trading badge and the frigid Chicago winters for a place in the Florida sun. He had paid $500 for his seat on 10 August 1926 and sold it for $75,000 in 1975. A native of Austria, the unpretentious, almost shy Kittner, who indulged in gin rummy when trading was slow, sold eggs door-to-door in his early years. (He became so proficient at gin, the Merc established a permanent gin-rummy trophy in his name that was awarded at the Exchange's annual outing and field day.) Kittner was truly the last of the butter-and-egg men, staying clear of the glamorous newer contracts, such as those for pork bellies, cattle, hogs, and currencies. Yet, he hung on to his IMM membership, not as a means to get back into the pits should he someday get the trading itch—It was far more basic than that. He could return to the floor to visit friends anytime in a place, he said, "where I spent more than half of my life."

The year Kittner bought his CME membership, Kenneth Mackay joined the Merc as an office clerk. Later he served as board marker, then manager of the clearinghouse in 1954, and in 1961 he became executive vice-president. During World War II he was in charge of the cheese subsidy program for the Dairy Products Marketing Association, a group of cheese cooperatives that purchased butter and cheese for the lend-lease program, the armed services, and the cheese subsidy program. Now he too, after 48 years, was retiring from a post he had held since 1961. Mackay, who was replaced by Beverly Splane, had the longest institutional memory of any Merc employee, and he agreed to continue as a consultant to the Exchange. After eight years, William Phelan, vice-president in charge of audits and investigations, also was resigning to go into private law practice. The search was on for his successor.

Another key resignation, accepted "with regret," as John Geldermann noted in the chairman message, was that of Mark Powers as vice-president in research and education and senior vice-president of the IMM. The troika of Melamed, Harris, and Powers had been the impetus behind the early days of the IMM. While Melamed was the driving force in implementing currency and interest rate futures and Harris the goodwill ambassador, Powers turned theory into practicality by creating tradeable contracts. Now Powers was to join the CFTC as chief economist. A decade had passed since his path first crossed Milton Friedman's as a graduate student at the University of Wisconsin, where Friedman had come to lecture. Now Friedman was a Nobel Laureate and Powers was on his way to Washington.

In the back of the board's mind was the fact that in less than two years Harris would retire, too. That meant a search for a new president, the first in 25 years. The plan was to go outside for a successor and, if possible, to bring the person in at least a year before Harris retired. "The transition would be more effective that way," explained Harris. But there were other matters far more pressing to consider, matters that threatened to create civil war on the trading floor of the Exchange between Merc members and IMM members.

With the Merc's success predictably came problems in organization. They fell into three major and related areas: membership, the potential of disunion among members, and space. In true fashion, the Merc set up a special committee in 1975 to find effective solutions. This was a critical time for the Merc.

"Agriculture was never going to be the future. Finance was going to be the future," Harris reasoned. "So if the Merc had any future it was on the back of the IMM. But that was something I couldn't prove at that time. The only way to resolve all that was to find a Solomon-like merger whereby everyone got what he wanted or a little bit of what he wanted."

The Merc officials had only to observe what happened at the Chicago Board of Trade in its relationship with the Chicago Board Options Exchange (CBOE), its 1973 spinoff. There was outright animosity between the sister exchanges that had created an invisible wall of independence, competition and, worst of all, divided loyalty. The CBOE was treated more like a stepchild, with its different markets and different players from those of the CBOT. Two separate cultures emerged and the antagonism grew, especially during those periods when equities were booming and commodities were at a lull, or vice versa. The schism exists to this day, although the animosity is more subtle. And each exchange remains a separate entity, housed in its own building.

It was clear in 1975 that the base of 500 traders was too narrow to operate from. "This fault in our structure is in fact more pronounced than the figure of 500 would indicate," stated the hard-hitting Merc report on the merger and reorganization of the CME and IMM. The limitation of members, the board determined, had hurt the liquidity in the Merc's trading pits, virtually limiting the Exchange to three primary markets: cattle, hogs, and pork bellies. Thus, the report concluded, there were insufficient members to markedly increase volume of business in the Merc's other successful markets, such as lumber and eggs, and to concentrate on potentially large markets, namely, boneless beef, butter, hams, milo, potatoes, and turkeys. "We certainly lack a sufficient number of members who could successfully promote any new futures market yet unlisted," the report noted.

Two conclusions emerged from the report. The first was obvious: The Merc needed more members to keep its markets viable and continue to grow. The second conclusion, although equally obvious, needed more explanation to the membership. Even if the Merc had sold 100 new seats, the new members would focus on the three primary markets with few, if any, members left to participate in the other markets. New members themselves, it was concluded, would not solve the CME member dilemma. The primary markets were not the ones that needed additional traders. A simple split of the membership was not the answer either. There would be too many objections with regard to seat price, broker competition, and such.

The IMM had faced a similar situation four years earlier when it was launched. By selling separate memberships, traders gave their full attention to a new field of business. It was the new flow of traders that helped give the gold contract a promising start. The CME thus needed more than new members, but these had to be a special kind of new member, one whose activities would concentrate on the markets that were in need of new and continuous liquidity.

Although the second problem facing the Merc was not as imminent, it was equally as serious. The single most important element that had moved the Merc into the forefront of the U.S. financial scene was, in a word, unity.

"It was a unique force of unity of purpose by our members which enabled the CME to innovate, to explore, to brazenly promote our ideas, and in the end, to succeed," the report expressed. Already there existed a current of disunity, the board determined, that, if left unchecked "will create a climate of bickering and squabbling between members." That, in turn, "will without fail be the cause of stagnation, if not downfall of our institution. We must prevent this at all cost."

The cause of disunity came from the fact that a number of those who had held dual seats had sold off either their IMM or CME membership. Their loyalty became divided; they were members of only one exchange and not the other. The division had created problems with respect to equitable use of floor space and facilities between the two exchanges. Worse, however, was the friction building between members. The boards of the CME and IMM agreed that the exchanges together could do more business than they could apart. The lack of adequate space added to the tension on the trading floor. While the new CME building was programmed for a 30 to 40 percent increase in business, much of the planned expansion area had been used up by the IMM. At the same time, the IMM needed more space as well, especially once the gold, silver coin, and T-bill contracts came on line.

The Merc board knew it would be a battle to get support for a merger plan. "It was a major controversy," said Melamed. "I lobbied that as hard as I've ever lobbied anything in my life." Some members of the IMM opposed the union. Merc officials fanned out on a crusade, meeting members one-on-one, pitching the "united we stand, divided we fall" speech as if they were stumping a World War II bond rally. The CME was getting its markets back, but the IMM was asking, "Why are we giving them our markets?"

The IMM members had to be convinced that they needed a unified community that included the CME's infrastructure, real estate, clout, and money. "Your future is dependent on you being together with them," Melamed told the IMM members. It was a very difficult sell both ways, but in the end, the call for unity prevailed.

The proposal roared through on a referendum. There were virtually no dissenters on the afternoon of 6 October, 1975, when the boards of the CME and IMM approved the reorganization plan proposed by the special committee. Under a single integrated plan, a comprehensive solution had been found. On 3 November, the CME members voted 343 to 23 in favor of the plan and the IMM members approved it 396 to 57. The IMM was merged into the CME as a division.

A second division was created, tentatively called the Non-Livestock Market Division (NLM), whose members could only trade eggs, lumber, milo, butter, and frozen turkeys. (Shortly thereafter, the NLM was renamed the Associate Mercantile Market Division, or AMM.)

The CME was the surviving entity. Its members could trade on all the Exchange's markets, including those of its two divisions. The board was authorized to sell up to 300 NLM memberships at $30,000 each. The initial offering opened on 20 November and was fully subscribed by 9 February 1976. The merger gave the IMM a sound financial base for its future promotion and growth. The CME members, in turn, gained access to the potential of the IMM, which had some of the world's most active markets. Under the reorganization, the CME board was expanded from 12 to 21, and it took nearly a year to combine the CME and IMM rules into one set of bylaws. Shortly after the election of the new board members, Melamed was elected chairman of the reorganized—and unified—Chicago Mercantile Exchange.

Some wounds remained from the bickering among IMM and CME critics of the merger, but none that Melamed thought couldn't be healed within a year. Next, the board turned to the problem of physical expansion, an issue that strongly resonated with members. The merger had set up the posture and finances for a realistic solution. Financially, the Merc was in its strongest position in years with the IMM assets having been merged into the CME assets and an additional $3 million gained from the sale of 150 NLM memberships. The noted architectural firm Skidmore, Owings & Merrill was hired to develop expansion plans. By mid-April a plan was presented to the CME board that extended the total trading area by 9,000 square feet, or nearly 60 percent more than its present size. The CME building was to be extended 90 feet to the west with a 9-foot overhang along Canal Street. The overhang, which required permission from the city of Chicago, prompted the Merc to observe in its annual report, "[this will] mark one of the few instances in our city's history of such approval. It is a measure of the value the City places on the Exchange and its industry."

One important trend in the 1970s that carried into the 1980s was the involvement of Merc members on the committees. In 1975, for instance, more than 50 committees involved about one-half of the total membership. Some met two or three times a year, others as many as 30. Among the busiest was the Business

Conduct Committee, meeting 27 times. It considered such allegations as holding excessive positions in a market, executing prearranged trades, exceeding daily trading limits, trading for one's own account ahead of customer's order, or refusing to appear before the committee. These were the sort of problems that had haunted the Exchange in the past and would do so in the future.

But in the 1970s the CME reaped the kind of headlines that were good for business. On 8 January 1976, the day T-bill contracts began trading, *The Chicago Daily News* featured the Merc in its lead editorial under the headline "Chicago's Promising 'Futures.'" "The International Monetary Market has enhanced Chicago's reputation as the nation's leader in commodities trading," the editorial began. "The aggressive imagination and technological expertise displayed by the IMM and its members continues a tradition that has made Chicago an international marketplace."

Part of the credit for expansion was given to the CFTC's relatively swift pace in approving new contracts. The commission had taken less than four months to review and approve the IMM's plan for T-bill trading. The year before, it only took five months to clear the way for the CBOT's market in government-backed home mortgages. The speed with which the CFTC acted was in marked contrast to the four years that the SEC took to approve the CBOE.

Unlike other regulatory agencies at the time, such as the Interstate Commerce Commission and the Civil Aeronautics Board, which were notorious for procrastination, the CFTC seemed to be more concerned with laying ground rules to prevent abuses than attempting to dictate the operations of the exchanges. Milton Friedman believed the CFTC's early track record stemmed from the fact that it hadn't yet had time to become tangled in bureaucratic red tape.

It was therefore not surprising when in 1976 the CFTC was about to give the go-ahead to commodity options trading, long tucked in the scandal-ridden corner of the securities industry. In May a CFTC advisory committee recommended that such trading be permitted, along with off-exchange commodities options trading that afforded the same customer market protections as on-exchange trading. The Commodity Exchange (COMEX) in New York had already applied to the CFTC to trade options on its silver and copper futures. The Merc and CBOT were also considering options.

Although options had less profit potential than futures (because an options buyer lost her options premium to the options seller), they increased the speculative capital flow into futures markets because many professional options sellers bought the futures contracts against which the option was sold. The inflow, in turn, facilitated hedging, the ultimate justification for futures markets.

The prospect of options trading worried some industry and government observers, given what had happened in 1932 on the CBOT during the so-called Great Wheat Collapse. Options trading had accounted for more than 10 percent of the Exchange's wheat futures volume as a group of speculators sought to corner the wheat market by massively buying wheat calls and futures.[1] The corner, however, failed. But in a panic, the speculators unloaded their positions, selling off the calls and futures and forcing wheat prices to plunge 30 percent. Corn, oat, and rye prices were dragged down. The resulting furor, in part, led to the 1934 ban on domestic commodity options trading.

Commodity options trading had practically died out until the early 1970s. A number of options houses based mainly in California began selling options on world commodities (silver, gold, and copper), which were left virtually un-regulated by the 1936 Commodity Exchange Act.[2] This time, naked options were sold; that is, there were never any futures contracts or physical stocks of commodities to back the options. Instead, they relied on new investor money to pay off winners. Once again, the options business became contaminated. Boiler-room operators and off-exchange swindlers selling naked options bilked investors out of an estimated $100 million.

By 1976, under the watchful eye of the SEC, options on equities had won legitimacy, owing to the brisk trading on the Chicago Board Options Exchange, the American Stock Exchange, the Philadelphia Stock Exchange, the Midwest Stock Exchange, and the Pacific Stock Exchange. Now the regulators were inclined to reconsider the merits of the derivative product. It helped too that in 1978 the CFTC's budget was increased by $1.6 million, which permitted the hiring of 50 new staffers to police a three-year options pilot trading program on several exchanges.

But it wouldn't be until January 1983 when the Merc offered its first option on a futures contract on the Standard & Poor's 500 Index.[3] In August 1983 the CBOT had begun trading options on T-bond futures; the New York Coffee, Sugar and Cocoa Exchange traded sugar-futures options; and the New York Commodity Exchange traded gold-futures options. Options were a more basic and fundamental instrument than futures contracts in that an investor or hedger could create synthetic futures with options, but not with futures contracts.

During the 1970s the Merc was learning to adjust to economic conditions. For example, when the currency contracts looked weak, the size of the contract was reduced twice over a period of three years. The speculators simply couldn't handle contracts that were too big.

The turning point for the IMM came in September 1975, when Mexico devalued the peso. At the time, the IMM was the only market in the world trading the Mexican peso. The IMM withstood the trading shock of $96 million changing hands, a large sum for those days. Looking back, Melamed called it "the watershed of credibility" for the Exchange. "We didn't have to borrow any money, we had done it right, and we were still open," he said. "There was no bank market. What was the forward market for the peso? They all looked to the IMM. And that's where it began."

With the transition of the CME-IMM merger completed, Melamed chose not to run for chairman of the Merc in 1977. Instead, he accepted the newly created position of CME special counsel and continued as a member of the powerful executive committee. In the new role, he was to act on behalf of the CME in matters relating to local, state, and federal government and continue his leadership for strategic long-range plans.

He was replaced by Laurence M. Rosenberg, the vice-president of broker Anspacher & Associates. The mustachioed Rosenberg, then 38, had been a member of the Merc since 1965 and on the board since 1970, serving as vice-chairman in 1967. Over the years he chaired several committees, including the Business Conduct Committee. A graduate of Lake Forest College and a veteran of the U.S. Army counterintelligence corps, Rosenberg was popular among his fellow Merc traders. There was a bit of daring in Rosenberg; he was a skier, 20-mile-a-week jogger, and pilot, who likened the risk of flying with that of trading. "There are bold pilots and old pilots," he'd say, "but no old bold pilots." Rosenberg started as a runner at the CBOT in 1960, and the following year he bought a membership and began trading corn. Two years later he formed a partnership in a trading firm with Hank Shatkin, a former taxicab driver and one of the CBOT's great success stories. Leslie Rosenthal later joined the firm; his nickname, the "Romanian Prince," reflected his European roots. Rosenthal eventually became chairman of the CBOT in 1981. At one point (from 1974 to 1978) he served on the boards of both the Merc and the CBOT at the same time. Rosenberg had worked closely with Melamed over the years, and he had a no-nonsense style and a direct management philosophy. "The only time things go wrong," he said "is when somebody tries to tamper with it."

One of the new board members was Barry J. Lind, who was recruited by Melamed after previously serving on the board. Another board member was Jack Sandner, a young attorney with strawberry hair and an engaging smile, who would become chairman in 1980. Others included James Paul, Robert Ascher, Donald Minucciani, Joel Greenberg, Jerry Wetterling, and Joseph Miller, as well as old-timers William Katz and Carl Anderson. In addition, there were eight carryover members and three public members.

Jack Sandner possessed a hard-nosed work ethic, a self-igniting chuckle, and a fount of amusing anecdotes; he represented the kind of single-minded leadership the Merc needed during the 1980s. As a Notre Dame–educated attorney, he shared more than a professional background with Melamed. Their personal histories were different—Melamed was the Jewish immigrant from eastern Europe, and Sandner an Irish-Italian Catholic born and bred in America—yet they were both shaped by dramatic upheavals early in their lives. Melamed had escaped the Nazis; Sandner, the mean streets of Chicago's south side. Both were survivors.

Sandner's journey to the Merc's top elected post in January 1980 came largely by chance. A steely, intense individual and small in stature, Sandner was a scrappy kid with quick fists. As a youth, he was too small to be a bully but gutsy enough not to back away from one. His Irish father was a merchandise manager for a major downtown women's retailer, and his Italian mother, as he described her, was a "Back of the Yards girl who worked two and three jobs."

Back of the Yards got its name from the stockyards where Chicago had earned its reputation as hog butcher of the world. The area was typically ethnic Chicago, a politically powerful Irish bastion bordered on the east by blacks and on the west by Slavs, where the late Mayor Richard Daley had been born and raised in a section called Bridgeport.

Problems at home caused by his father's heavy drinking had their impact on young Jack. By the time he was 16, he was a high school dropout prowling the streets for action. He was a pump jockey at a gas station with a career goal that didn't extend beyond his neighborhood.

At this time, Sandner began venting his hostilities through organized boxing, first in the Golden Gloves. His boxing career took a serious turn when the former world middleweight champion Tony Zale became his mentor. A strong natural counterpuncher and swift on his feet, with a jab-quick ability to size up his opponents weakness, Sandner racked up 58 wins against two losses. He had a champ's killer instinct, his admirers told him. They also urged him to try for a boxing scholarship to college—advice he took. He returned to high school and hit the books as well as the punching bag. Sandner graduated high school as valedictorian, won his scholarship, and went to Southern Illinois University, where he majored in psychology, wrestled on the varsity team (college boxing had been banned in 1961 following the death of a boxer in the NCAA finals), was active in student government, and graduated with honors.

Set on attending Notre Dame law school, he was turned down because he had applied too late. The class was already closed. But that didn't stop Sandner, a man who didn't like to retreat and was used to meeting people (and opponents) face-to-face. Sandner went directly to the dean of Notre Dame's law school, where he finessed the situation with a lot of verbal footwork, talking about the ups and downs of his life, about his comeback, and about how much Notre Dame meant to him. Throughout the two-hour conversation, Sandner was quick, logical, and persuasive. In the end, he won the dean over and was accepted by the law school. Sandner's ability to verbalize ideas with convincing ease made him a star in law school—he went on to win a scholarship, the moot court competition, and graduated with honors in 1968—and later proved equally useful at the exchange.

Sandner began practicing law in Chicago. As fate would have it, one of his clients in a personal injury case turned out to be E.B. Harris's wife, who had been involved in an automobile accident. The meeting with Harris and his wife in 1971 changed the direction of Sandner's career. Harris, always on the lookout for fresh trading talent, gave the young attorney a tip: Buy a Merc membership for "only" $80,000 and do some trading on your lunch hours. The markets, Harris predicted with good old boy charm, were about to explode. (Indeed, they were.)

Ironically, Sandner's fists almost kept him out of the Merc. During the Christmas holidays in 1970 he attended a party hosted by Dellsher Investment, Melamed's firm. He did not know Melamed at the time and was the guest of a mutual friend of theirs. Shortly after his arrival, a couple of tipsy traders began harassing him. Why, they insisted on knowing, was an "outsider" at the party? The pair backed him toward an elevator bank and began pushing. After walking away three times to avoid a confrontation, Sandner finally let go, slapping one in the face and punching the other unconscious. Sandner excused himself and left the party. The incident was forgotten until Sandner applied for a Merc membership six months later. The traders he had whipped tried to block his membership. But friends intervened and he got his Merc seat.

Sandner had taken Harris's advice. He borrowed the money from a bank and began spending lunch hours in the pits, trading first live cattle, then eggs and pork bellies. After a year he became a full-time trader and a part-time lawyer, just like Maury Kravitz and Leo Melamed and so many other member-lawyers had become. In 1976 Sandner joined the commodities firm of Rufenacht, Bromagen & Hertz, one of the nation's biggest livestock operations, and rose to president. A year later he proved himself a fairly polished arbitrator when he deftly reorganized members' space and telephone allotments on the exchange floor without shattering anyone's ego. Such efforts paid off not long after, when a group of fellow traders asked Sandner to run for a Merc directorship. He agreed, and was elected by a rare write-in vote. The next year his fellow directors elected him vice-chairman, and in January 1980 he became Exchange chairman. At 38, he was a millionaire and one of the youngest chairmen in Merc history, with the solid backing of Melamed. As new Merc chairman, Sandner reflected the spirit and image of the Merc itself—a hustling, scrappy, frenetic, young and wealthy upstart. These were some of the same qualities that had propelled Melamed to the forefront of Merc leadership.

The Melamed-Sandner alliance was a powerful force in moving the Merc through the 1980s. Both were tireless when it came to Merc business, and despite their hefty egos, they never clashed openly. "We may have had differences, but never aired them publicly," Sandner said. "We worked things out." They played off one another as sounding boards, often discussing problems and issues facing the Merc well into the early morning hours. From the start, Melamed recognized Sandner's skill as a top-notch negotiator with the knack of making complex issues palatable.

In 1978 the Merc's new board meshed well with its new president, Clayton K. Yeutter, a 47-year-old affable, outgoing man who knew his way around a farm, around Washington, and around the world. Initially, Yeutter had reservations because of the Merc's past image. Melamed, who had chaired the search committee, nevertheless convinced Yeutter that the Merc job would be good for his ambitious career. Always a free market advocate, Yeutter brought to the Exchange a governmental halo and an international perspective. Yeutter was set to take the top staff job in May, when Harris retired at age 65. A former assistant secretary of agriculture and U.S. deputy special trade representative for President Ford, Yeutter, noted *The Chicago Daily News*, boasted "one of those rare Renaissance résumés."

Indeed he did. He had both a Ph.D. in agricultural economics and a doctorate in law. While working in both government and law he had been running a farm in Eustis, Nebraska, where he grew wheat and corn and raised cattle. The son of an immigrant farmer who came to the heartland from southern Germany at the turn of the century, Yeutter was reared on a Nebraska farm. Even as a youth Yeutter was an overachiever. A tall man with a hefty presence, he excelled in academics, athletics, and 4-H activities. At the University of Nebraska he graduated first in his class as an undergraduate and first in his class at law school. Moreover, he was well-versed in state, national, and international political affairs.

In the spring of 1977, his business address was in Washington. When the Ford administration was turned out of office, Yeutter had returned home to Lincoln to become a senior partner in the respected law firm of Nelson, Harding, Yeutter, and Tate, where he specialized in government relations. It was a role that proved to be a key factor in the Merc post. "He knew his way around Washington," said Rosenberg. "We realized the day of the rainmaker was history. But we needed a man who knew where the doors were in Washington and who wasn't afraid to knock on them."

The very same month Yeutter's appointment was announced, the Merc opened its Washington office. And on 17 November, during his first press conference as president, he made it clear that the Merc was going to become active in the Capitol because, as he put it, "that's where the action is." Yeutter, who was instrumental as an assistant agriculture secretary in drafting the legislation that created the CFTC, said he would establish an "amiable, straight-forward and discerning" relationship with the agency. At the same time, he laid down the law for the regulators: "We won't kow-tow to the CFTC. If we have a problem we'll tell them so, either formally or informally. However, we don't want an atmosphere of constant confrontation with the CFTC."

The polished Yeutter, with a quick smile and forceful presence, was the perfect emissary at a time when the Merc wanted to gain new influence in Washington. Like Beverly Splane, he had worked the private and public sectors and knew the hazards of bureaucratic red tape.

"Nobody likes to be regulated and I guess I headed more regulatory bodies than anyone else in the world when I was at the Agriculture Department," he told reporters. "I'm well aware of the dissatisfaction with regulators that occurs in a regulated industry." There was no doubt in anyone's mind after the press conference that Clayton Yeutter was indeed ready to knock on some doors.

25

Tangibles and Intangibles

While the Chicago Mercantile Exchange was trying to build a dynasty as the world's premier financial futures market, another dynasty on the other side of the world was crumbling. The Ayatollah Khomeini in 1979 overthrew the U.S.-backed Shah of Iran, creating turmoil in one of the largest oil-producing nations. It wasn't long before the oil shocks from the Shah's downfall reached American motorists, who were waiting in long gas lines just like they had in 1973. The Organization of Petroleum Exporting Countries (OPEC) lost little time in doubling crude prices to over $30 a barrel. The predictable result: double-digit inflation.

The sudden turn in economic events favored the futures markets. As stock and bond markets reeled under the strain of runaway inflation, soaring interest rates, and economic uncertainty, the futures markets were booming. Investors scrambled for commodities and collectibles as well as gold and silver. Amid rising interest rates bond prices collapsed (from 83 to 62 on the Salomon Brothers index), wiping out some $500 billion in market value.

In response, the newly appointed Federal Reserve Board chairman Paul Volcker—a tall, cigar-smoking inflation fighter—promised to tighten the nation's money supply. "Swarms of U.S. and foreign investors, both institutional and individual, are rushing into futures because of the small margin required and because of the variety of contracts being traded," *BusinessWeek* noted in June 1979. During the first four months of the year, trading volume on the 12 U.S. futures exchanges totaled 23 million contracts, a 28 percent increase from a year earlier and nearly equal to the volume of all the contracts traded in 1974. A year later, when frenzied metals-buying sent the price of gold to a startling $850 an ounce and silver to $50 an ounce, volume on the Merc alone reached 22.3 million contracts, of which the IMM accounted for 45 percent.

Following the 90-day T-bill contract launched in 1976 (on 6 January), the Merc introduced the one-year T-bill in 1978 (on 11 September) and the four-year Treasury note contract a year later (on 10 July). The success of these contracts had proved that those who dealt in interest rates were just as willing to allow speculators to bear the risk of changing interest rates as grain elevator operators were to allow speculators to bear the risk of changing grain prices.

As the Merc added new trading contracts, it also attempted to keep the old ones stoked, from eggs to currencies. For instance, it streamlined the delivery for its currency futures, departing from a more complicated system. Delivery in five European countries and in Japan would now be handled by the foreign branches of Continental Illinois Bank. All the paperwork involved was centered in Continental's Chicago headquarters and then handled by a single bank in each delivery country through Continental's worldwide wire network.

Even the venerable egg contract was reinvigorated. A decade earlier the Merc had run an advertisement with a picture of an egg and the caption "Our Founder." Now the Founder—the mainstay of the Merc, reaching peak volume in the early 1970s—was updated. The basic change called for delivery of a certificate rather than the eggs.

"This is the most exciting thing to happen in my ten years at the Exchange," said Milton Stern, who at the time headed the Merc's delivery department. Traders, it was believed, would be less hesitant to trade paper, while those accepting delivery would find it more convenient to switch delivery locations. The Merc had listed other egg contracts in the past, such as a nest-run contract in 1974, but volume remained low and no contract had traded since 1975. A frozen egg contract was listed in 1949. It got off to a slow start, accelerated to a high of 134,617 contracts in 1961, then tailed off to nothing in 1974 when nationwide production and per capita consumption declined.

Frozen eggs lost their market, too, as users such as bakers, candy makers, and mayonnaise processors switched to liquid eggs, which had the advantage of no storage charges and no lost time in thawing them.[1] But eggs remained more a vestige of the past. The future was in financial instruments.

In the race with inflation, speculative cash was flocking to the options markets. But that flow was rivaled by the torrent of money that had shifted from stocks and bonds to futures. Trading volume in financial instruments had more than doubled on the exchanges between 1978 and 1979. It was enough to encourage such traditional investing centers as the New York Stock Exchange and the American Stock Exchange to attempt to siphon off some of the business. The Amex Commodities Exchange began trading futures on Ginnie Mae bonds in 1978, and in March 1979, the NYSE announced plans to start its own futures market, to be called the New York Futures Exchange. In the spring of 1978, the New York Mercantile Exchange (NYMEX) said it was considering reviving a dormant contract in foreign currency futures. Contracts covering nine different foreign currencies were listed on the exchange in September 1974, but by July 1976 the market was inactive. The Merc's IMM had a two-year head start on the NYMEX in currencies, which showed the strategic importance of initiating markets in the futures business.

Nevertheless, the NYMEX was willing to try again as it assessed the interest of the New York banks, the primary market makers in foreign currencies. "It is relatively easier to reactivate a dormant contract than start a new one," explained NYMEX president Richard Levine. Of the nine currencies listed for trading, the exchange focused on reviving contracts covering the German mark, the Swiss franc, the British pound, the Canadian dollar, and the Japanese yen—all currencies traded on the Merc.

The NYMEX strategy to revive currencies grew out of a last-ditch effort to keep the exchange alive. Two years earlier, its most important contract, Maine potatoes, suffered a default in the May contract. The result devastated the exchange, pushing it to the brink of extinction as seat prices plunged from a high of $47,000 to a mere $5,000.

Shortly after Levine's announcement, the financial press drew the battle lines between the two exchanges. The situation prompted Levine and Melamed to exchange letters that summer reminiscent of two diplomats tiptoeing around a sticky incident involving the boundaries of their respective countries. Levine wrote Melamed the following letter on 1 August 1978:

> I thought a personal note might be appropriate in the face of the "newspaper war" between Chicago and New York. I am sure you realize that, at least for our Exchange, this "war" exists in the press alone. We shall certainly not contribute by comment or attitude to any possible cause of deterioration to a long and warm relationship between our two exchanges.
>
> The press has correctly reported our interest in reviving (starting!) currency futures trading in New York. And, yes, we believe currency futures should be traded here as well. Quotes, however, taken out of context or distorted by recollection may easily have seemed more confrontational then was intended. Frankly, we've been as chagrined recently as we've been pleased with the publicity.
>
> As eager as we may have been to enjoy the volume that currency trading has produced, we have been even more pleased that interest in a New York market for currencies has, essentially, been brought to us! As you know, the New York banks and securities firms have been chauvinistic about a local market. Some of your own members, too, seem to feel that another market would complement rather than undermine the IMM's. We agree. The potential for currency trading has been barely scratched. In all likelihood, our own markets—should they be successful—will stimulate trading rather than draw interest from Chicago. The arbitrage opportunities, of course, need no explanation.... If anything, our prospective currency markets should prove once again that imitation is the sincerest form of flattery.

Melamed, then CME special counsel, responded to Levine's letter on 11 August:

> ... You are indeed correct that I realize the alleged "war" is more newspaper rhetoric than reality. You are also correct that I do not believe you or the New York Mercantile would contribute by "comment or attitude" to any deliberate deterioration in the relationship of our two exchanges.

With respect to the New York Merc's revived interest in currency futures, my response is also predictable. As you know, I am today and have always been a staunch advocate of competition. Your entry into a contract which is already successfully traded at the IMM does not, in my mind, violate any holy principles. Indeed, it is your privilege to do so. As you are aware, currency futures are a much more complex and intricate market mechanism than any other and, therefore, present many more difficult and different problems. The road to a successful currency market is therefore full of unforeseen pitfalls and complexities; but these difficulties are certainly not insurmountable.

Thus, I wish you success and welcome you to the competition between us that this will no doubt generate.

At the time, the Merc was already locked into battle with a New York market—the Commodity Exchange of New York (COMEX)—in trading gold contracts. For a while, the Merc was on top, but in the wake of the 1980 gold market retreat, when gold plunged from a high of $850 an ounce in January to $500 in March, the Merc subsequently lost its grip on the market. Three years later, the COMEX had the gold market pretty much to itself. The plan to trade currencies on the NYMEX was shelved. Instead, the NYMEX began trading a fuel oil contract; it was on its way to turning itself into a major energy exchange.

In the heat of the markets in the late 1970s what bothered critics most was a realization that the bubble of speculative capital in futures was growing primarily because of the fundamental problems that were shaking the world economy. There were serious questions to ponder. Did the futures markets feed inflation? Did the futures markets siphon risk capital away from the stock and bond markets, impairing the ability of American industry to raise cash with which to operate? Who should regulate financial instruments and proposed stock indexes, the CFTC or SEC? Was there economic justification for such contracts in the first place? These were questions not easily answered.

"Even when gold goes up and I happened to have picked the right contract at the right moment," Melamed told a reporter in the summer of 1979, "I ask myself what it really means. Gold is not really a valuable asset. And if I am buying it, I am admitting that the system is failing."

As for those worried over skewed capital flows, the futures pool was about $6 billion, compared to many billions of dollars in the debt and equity markets. Moreover, the number of market participants hovered around half a million people in the futures markets and more than 20 million in the stock market. In the meantime, the CFTC was still under fire, hampered by vacancies at the top, a lack of familiarity with futures on the part of staff, and a paltry budget. "Unlike the SEC, the CFTC has never had a clear vision of its mission," said Beverly Splane who had helped set up the CME's Washington office. The new CFTC chairman replacing Bagley was James M. Stone, former Massachusetts insurance commissioner and an economist with a reputation as a tough regulator.

For all its weaknesses, the CFTC still made sense to the futures industry. It was true, as the SEC pointed out, that there had been significant changes in the nature of futures contracts. Treasury bills and Ginnie Maes were financial instruments traded as futures. No one denied that fact. However, the actual securities underlying these futures contracts were not regulated by the SEC. Nor did the agency have expertise in futures markets. Even if it had the expertise, there was reason to have trading regulated by a single agency. It avoided fragmentation and duplication of authority and interagency rivalries. Jurisdiction by the SEC, argued opponents, would add a second layer of regulation to each of the exchanges in the futures industry and the costs of regulation were soaring. The jurisdictional question would continue to haunt the futures industry whenever the markets overheated or the exchanges were embroiled in controversy.

It was during this period that Melamed and others were busy putting together a plan for an organization that could monitor the off-exchange brokerage community.[2] He talked about a proposed self-regulatory body, called the National Futures Association, on 22 February 1978 in Washington during congressional testimony on CFTC reauthorization before members of the Agriculture Subcommittee on Conservation and Credit.

The way the Merc saw it, there were three areas where the CFTC seemed inadequate: It had burdened the markets with "misguided and erroneous" regulation; it underutilized the expertise available within the industry, approaching problems with an inherent suspicion of the exchanges' motivation; and it mistakenly assumed the futures markets were the same as the securities markets, leading to a blind attempt to apply SEC regulations and procedures. The Merc's contempt surfaced when Sandner took the chairmanship in 1980. The fellow who had convinced the Merc to bend the rules in order to allow him to put a "Free Markets for Free Men" patch on his firm's trading jackets found an adversary in the new CFTC chairman James Stone. Sandner, the former boxer, came out swinging. "Realizing the won-loss record of strong regulatory agencies versus weak institutions," Sandner said, "we became determined to create a strong, powerful, and visible exchange, one that could act affirmatively."

For example, when Stone and the CFTC demanded that the Merc delist its January Treasury bill cycle the day after it was listed, the exchange refused. The Merc vigorously argued its case during the congressional hearings that followed. The result: The CFTC's temporary restraining order was vacated. When the CFTC suspended trading on the Chicago Board of Trade after President Carter's 1980 grain embargo, the Merc jumped in on behalf of free markets. Sandner met with Stone in Washington. The dialog was icy and Stone's message blunt: It was none of the Merc's business since none of its contracts were suspended. Sandner followed up with a letter to Stone, reminding him that "an attack on free-enterprise no matter where it takes place is an attack on us." The Merc managed to counter in other areas as well. It fended off the CFTC's effort to require pit brokers to time-stamp their trades by the minute. And it helped defeat

Senator William Proxmire's proposed bill that called for credit curbs and margin regulation. It even managed to ward off an attack by Congressman Benjamin Rosenthal over alledged manipulation of the cattle market. The Merc indeed had a busy year trying to hang on to self-regulation.

Sandner began his chairmanship on a regulatory note that turned sour for Bunker and Herbert Hunt, the sons of the late Texas oil tycoon H.L. Hunt. The Hunts, long enamored with commodities, were billionaires and had the appetites to match. First they traded in oil, then sugar, and, in 1976, soybeans. The brothers along with other members of the family, accumulated some 21 million bushels of soybeans, far surpassing the CBOT's allowable 3-million-bushel speculative limit. The CFTC forced the Hunts to reduce their holdings to the allowable limit for an individual or company. All along, the Hunts were buying silver, too. But instead of offsetting their futures contracts and taking profits and losses, they took delivery of silver bullion, amassing huge amounts in warehouses. In the process they even tried to gain control of the nation's largest silver mine. At the same time, they were speculating in cattle futures on the Merc. In early 1980 the prices of gold and silver began to plunge, along with those of most commodities. The per ounce price of silver fell from $48.70 on 17 January 1980 to $10.80 by 27 March, and the Hunts were left holding the bullion. They had huge positions in the silver futures contracts as well, so they were faced with the choice of liquidating their positions or coming up with tremendous margin calls to hang on. Everything turned against them, including their position in both live and feeder cattle futures. They had bought the market, instead of selling it, and as prices dropped they continued to buy more cattle contracts, hoping the market would turn around and rally. The cattle market had moved limit—the maximum price a contract is allowed to move in a single trading day—down against them. The Hunts had bought their cattle contracts through Bache & Co., of which they were part owners. On 27 March 1980 Sandner met with Hunt representatives, who were seeking an extension of credit rather than having Bache liquidate their positions. The Hunts were in trouble. Bache was feeling enormous pressure, and so were the banks that had lent the Hunts millions to finance their speculative binge. "My sympathies are with you and what's happening," Sandner told the Hunt contingent. "But this is a no debt system. We have never extended credit to anyone on a margin call. I'm not going to be the first Merc chairman to change that." The Hunts sold out of their cattle positions and took the losses.

Self-regulation was the lynchpin of the futures industry, and for most of its 150-odd years it was entirely self-regulated. Out of threat of increased federal control, the National Futures Association (NFA) was proposed by Melamed in late 1979. The NFA would come under CFTC jurisdiction and relieve some of the vexing burdens of the agency. The NFA, with its own legal and investigative staff, would be responsible for such areas as minimum financial requirements, protection of customers, examination and registration of commodity salesmen, and arbitration and reparation procedures.

It would be, however, more than two years before the CFTC gave the nod to the NFA. Although approval was granted on 30 September 1981, the NFA did not operate until 2 August 1982. NFA chairman Melamed tapped an industry stalwart as the NFA's first president: Robert K. Wilmouth, former president of the Chicago Board of Trade, who also had been executive vice-president of the First National Bank of Chicago. In Wilmouth the NFA had an outspoken, nuts-and-bolts executive who knew the players in both the futures and banking worlds. This blend of experience had made him sensitive to customer confidence and service.

"Starting the NFA was adventuresome," recalled Wilmouth of that sweltering August morning in 1982, when the NFA opened its doors in downtown Chicago with a meager staff of 12 and a "tiny" budget supported by the exchanges. "I wasn't sure we'd get the full support of the industry. We didn't recognize the enormity of the job. But once we were set up, support rallied quickly." Initially, the NFA office was set up with borrowed equipment and a quick-fix loan of several hundred thousand dollars from the Continental Bank. The staff since has grown from a dozen to 330 people, including 30 in a New York office, and a budget of $26 million.[3]

For their part, investors didn't seem as concerned with the merits of the CFTC or the SEC as they were with the markets themselves. Large institutions— pension funds, banks, and securities dealers among them—that had never traded futures before were now hedging their portfolios with financial instruments.

Consider that autumn weekend in October 1979, when the Federal Reserve Board decided to get tough on inflation by leaving the marketplace free to send interest rates soaring. The timing could not have been worse for International Business Machines Corporation, which had just floated a $1 billion debt issue and was caught in the downdraft of plunging bond prices. As bond prices fell dramatically, Salomon Brothers, a lead underwriter of the IBM offering, was able to recoup much of its loss because it had previously sold short interest rate futures.

Financial futures were becoming legitimate—and important—strategic finance tools. Money managers now saw the Treasury security market as three separate but equally important components: the cash or actual securities, futures, and options. It was impossible to ignore any part. The nation's central bank, the Federal Reserve, had also become a believer. In the mid-1970s it worried that interest rate futures would turn into a speculative merry-go-round to distort interest rates and bond prices while diverting long-term capital from industry. Now the Fed officials were conceding that the futures were having the positive effect of providing better liquidity to the Treasury securities market. In 1979 the futures markets helped absorb $43 billion of Treasury debt, which ballooned fivefold to some $200 billion by 1983.

The rash of new and proposed futures contracts in financial instruments was part of the financial revolution that started in 1972 with the IMM. Heading

into the decade of the 1980s, the Merc—and the other futures exchanges—
were poised for the introduction of even more useful and intriguing contracts,
contracts that had no deliverable supply. They would be settled in cash. The
futures bandwagon was rolling, and far up in front of the caravan was the
Chicago Mercantile Exchange, the place that once traded only butter and eggs.

"I still can't believe how far we've come in the past 25 years," Harris reflected
a few days before his official retirement as CME president. "The financial world
has changed and the Merc with it."

He paused, took a long draw on a cigarette, releasing a plume of smoke, and
then added, "I suppose you can say the Merc helped change the world, too."

26

Good to the Last Drop

Even before Clayton Yeutter had settled into the Merc presidency, the Exchange had opened its window in Washington with an office on Pennsylvania Avenue a short distance from the White House. Heading the office was C. Dayle Henington, a former administrative assistant to Representative W.R. Poage.

It was clear that Congress needed to understand the Exchange and that the Exchange needed to understand Congress. There were basic changes in an industry evolving at breakneck speed. While stock prices and volume had ebbed and flowed under the bearish impact of government economic policy during the late 1970s, futures volume had been expanding at a staggering pace.

Like Yeutter, Henington knew his way around Capitol Hill and agricultural matters, having served Poage when he was chairman of the House Committee on Agriculture. He had joined Poage after a 20-year career in the U.S. Air Force. In heading the first Washington office to be opened by any futures exchange, Henington's goal, as he explained at the time, was "mainly to make the economic functions of futures markets better understood by legislators."

The learning curve was fairly steep in late 1979 and in 1980, given what was happening in the tumultuous metals markets. There was too much silver in too few hands. Some of those hands, of course, belonged to the Hunts. Margins were boosted (from 5 percent to 60 percent on the Commodity Exchange, or COMEX) and limits on the number of contracts a speculator could hold were set. The result was a sell-off that sent prices plunging limit down, or the lowest level to which prices were allowed to move in a single trading session. Gold had also taken a precipitous drop because of an announcement of an unexpectedly large U.S. Treasury auction of the metal. That, in turn, depressed silver prices even more. The situation for the futures markets became even more tenuous a year later when Jimmy Carter retaliated against the Soviet Union's invasion of Afghanistan by ordering an embargo on the sale of $2.6 billion in corn, wheat, and soybeans. The embargo's long-term effect on grain prices eventually meant somewhat lower food prices for the American public. It also benefited U.S.

farmers who bought their grain for livestock. Experts figured that the grain embargo cut farm income that year by 10 percent. The loss rippled through the farm economy, affecting rural bankers, store owners, feed companies, and fertilizer manufacturers.

On the heels of the embargo, trading was halted for two days at the Chicago Board of Trade in order to prevent a panicky overreaction. Within the week the market stabilized. The cattle and pork belly pits at the Merc also adjusted to the embargo's impact. Prices settled to meet market demand, and once again the world of futures caught up with the geopolitics of the day.

1979 ranked as one of the most stable periods for the world's currencies since 1971, when floating rates took hold. The central banks, including the U.S. Federal Reserve Board, had turned interventionist in the foreign exchange markets. This stability provided fresh determination to back up their intervention with domestic monetary policies aimed at correcting underlying causes of exchange rate instability. The Fed had played a pivotal role in its willingness to raise interest rates, despite the onset of a recession. The economy was slowly sliding downhill as corporate profits began to stumble. Skyrocketing housing costs and rising interest rates coupled with a federal budget whose expenditures far outpaced receipts chilled the economy even more. Incomes from noncorporate business, including farming, began to decline and manufacturers uncertain about business prospects were keeping a tight rein on inventories.

There was more than a whiff of inflation in the air. The markets caught the scent and began to teeter. From late 1979 to early April 1980, the Dow dropped more than 100 points to below the 800 level. During this period, even more money found its way into the futures markets, especially in inflation-hedged vehicles such as gold. With the increasing attention of Congress on futures trading, it was not only prudent, but imperative in the minds of Merc officials, that the futures industry work closer with the lawmakers. The establishment of the Washington office was a well-timed and strategic move by the Exchange to establish an ongoing dialogue with the lawmakers.

Marketing the Merc's contracts abroad became another priority. There were no European futures exchanges, so the concept of hedging with futures was indeed foreign. The London banks continued to use the interbank markets for currency trading, and there were an active London gold market and an options market in metals.

The potential for exchange-traded products in Great Britain and the European continent was sizeable. The European traders, brokers, and bankers were just becoming aware that financial futures trading in Chicago was having an effect on their cash money markets. That's why in early 1979 the Merc began thinking about establishing a beachhead for its assault on Europe. A London office seemed the logical choice.

Locally, there were still some old quandaries to work on. One of the most difficult issues confronting Exchange members was the way decisions were made.

At the Merc, most policies were usually approved by the board. The more controversial ones, however, were subject to referendum and had to be approved by a majority of the strongly opinionated floor traders, a process more akin to political campaigning than to corporate management. But that was the point of Exchange life: It was an egalitarian system. The traders were the shareholders of the Exchange and each had a vote that counted. There were no corporate rituals to overcome, no convoluted relationships between bosses and workers, professionals and staff, insiders and outsiders. There was no pulling rank like Henry Ford II did when he'd remind Ford executives whose name was on the building. Unlike the Byzantine politics and motives of corporate executives, the culture of the Merc was one of shared values in a highly fluid economic environment.

The governing board was made up of members such as Melamed, Rosenberg, Geldermann, Weinberg, and Lind, and later Jack Sandner and Brian Monieson. They had been pit traders, activists in exchange politics, and, perhaps more important, entrepreneurs as either the heads of their own clearing firms or CEOs of others. In essence, they knew about futures and how to run businesses. Their entrepreneurial instincts allowed them a certain flexibility and speed to move when opportunity appeared. Yet they weren't Henry Ford–type entrepreneurs, the autocratic prototypical business leaders of the early 1900s, nor did they fit the Alfred Sloan model with its modern style of management that evolved during the 1920s and 1930s. For that matter, they were not Harvard-trained MBAs with computer-driven rationales who were possessed, as author John Brooks observed, "by an impersonal scientific spirit that went beyond Sloan's rationalism." Perhaps the board, critics would say, was too inbred and the power structure built to serve Melamed's goals for the Exchange.

As the Merc grew, so had Melamed's stature and single-mindedness to build a world-class exchange. In the process he had built a power base like that of any other corporate chieftain, keyed to enhancing value and return on equity. As long as the Merc's trading volume and seat prices grew, the members would support the leadership.

Melamed used his position to influence the thoughts and actions of those around him when it came to nettlesome issues. He began with a light hand that became heavier as time went on. He had long learned that compromise took the sting out of solutions, and while he could be relentless in pushing an idea he believed in, always in the back of his mind was the guiding tenet of his convictions: The Exchange ranked higher than any single member.

"I didn't have the influence with the floor traders to put the IMM together," E.B. Harris said. "Leo did. He could change his mind quickly. He was a bull-dog." By nature as well as by profession, Melamed was a risk taker. But the Merc was far from the typical organization. Like any organization the Merc had a logic of its own, also dictated by the nature of risk, yet it didn't suffer from the inertia of tradition. How could it in its volatile world?

Even as a youth escaping the Nazis, Melamed, it seemed, was constantly struggling to attain some sense of order. It was the trials of adversity that gave Melamed his "twice-born" personality, a phrase coined by turn-of-the-century psychologist William James and later used by Harvard's renowned social psychologist Abraham Zaleznik to describe a key characteristic of leadership. Leaders, according to Zaleznik, grow through mastering painful conflicts—death of a parent, sickness, rejection by a role model—in their lives during their developmental years. Melamed's escape from the Nazis, Sandner's youthful struggle to reenter the mainstream of life, and John Geldermann's return from World War II wounded and somber were the kinds of traumas that helped shape individuals for leadership roles. And although the methods to bring about change among leaders in all walks of life varied, the object was the same, Zaleznik believed: "to profoundly alter human, economic, and political relationships."

During more than two decades, Melamed's vision had profoundly altered the Merc's economic and political relationships. "I'm an integral part of the institution," he told a reporter in 1987 in an appraisal of his position. "It walks with me . . . I don't know if I can be divided from the institution." The comment was indicative of how Melamed viewed his imprint on the Merc, an imprint that several years later would be vigorously challenged by members who accused him of a me-versus-them attitude.

Regardless of what leadership mantel he wore—Merc chairman, special counsel, chairman of the executive committee—over the years, there is little doubt that Melamed was the guiding hand behind the succession of chairmen that followed when he stepped down from the official role in 1976, after three years. "My genuine intent was to share the limelight by offering the way for someone else to be a chairman and then divide the responsibility between the two of us," candidly explained Melamed.

That didn't mean a rubber stamp by the board. Melamed's favorite strategy was to lobby board members individually—and often—before a meeting that required policy decisions. He would concentrate on key members: the chairman, vice-chairman, former chairman, and other officers. "It was always with the idea that if I was right then I could convince them to vote that way," said Melamed, who had carefully gathered a coterie of supporters over the years.

Melamed had become mentor to a trio of protégés—Laurence Rosenberg, Brian Monieson, and Jack Sandner—who were attracted to his personality, wit, and style. First there was Rosenberg, who succeeded Melamed as chairman in 1977. Though today Rosenberg balks at being called a Melamed protégé, he was also at one time vice-chairman of Dellsher Investment Company, Melamed's clearing firm. Over the years, Rosenberg served as Merc chairman from 1977 to 1979 and first vice-chairman, first in 1976, and then from 1983 through 1987. Sandner, president of Rufenacht, Bromagen & Hertz, Inc., which shared the nineteenth floor of the Merc building with Melamed's firm, followed Rosenberg as chairman in 1980 through 1982 and then took the rein again in 1986, 1987, and

1988 after serving as second vice-chairman in 1978 and 1979. After Sandner's first tenure came Brian Monieson, Melamed's co-champion bridge-playing partner, who was first vice-chairman from 1980 to 1982 and chairman from 1983 to 1985. It was with Melamed's backing that John Geldermann became chairman in 1974 to 1975 and again in 1989 and 1990. The leadership thread remained taut. When, for example, Sandner had stepped down as chairman in 1988—after having served the maximum number of consecutive terms—the Merc governors created for him the $150,000-a-year position of senior policy advisor. When he became chairman again in 1991, Rosenberg was elected to the senior policy post Sandner vacated.

Before Melamed became chairman of the executive committee in 1985, Rosenberg, Sandner, and Monieson all had chaired that key committee as Board Chairman at one time or another, beginning in 1979. Each chairman had particular strengths that Melamed had hand-picked: The affable Rosenberg was strong in the areas of advertising and public relations; the brainy Monieson knew technology and systems; and Sandner, a tough-minded pragmatist, eloquent speaker, and strong negotiator, could simplify the most complicated issues in concise and clear language. They all shared Melamed's vision—and his power.

Melamed had thought about the notion of power shortly after the board passed a rule limiting the CME chairmanship to three consecutive one-year terms. "Power is very enticing and very dangerous," he said. "I realized this when I was re-elected chairman for a third term. I could have gone on forever. It wasn't right. How are you going to test yourself against the truth? I wanted to hear people argue with me. If I couldn't be dissuaded then I felt strongly about my opinion. To outsiders I may have come off as powerful and opinionated, but the board knew I was flexible." Melamed was a person who could adopt other people's ideas because, as John Troelstrup, former CFTC attorney and head of the Merc's regulatory compliance department for several years, put it, "He's a doer. If the idea was a good one, it got done."

The Merc had changed over the years and so had the balance of power from the early days, when Melamed led the Young Turks in revolt. "We were selling boy genius stuff," said Melamed of the 1960s and the early IMM years. "Harris represented the old era. He was the door opener, the guy selling the soap. The Exchange needed someone who was fresher, younger, and probably crazier."

To keep his own balance, Melamed, whose voice constantly juggled humor and seriousness, learned to laugh at himself from time to time. For instance, a party celebrating the merger of the Merc and IMM was given. It was a black-tie roast with Melamed on the spit. He was introduced by Beverly Splane, as "Leo, a legend in his own mind."

Melamed's strength as a manager lay in his ability to perceive issues and developments. The onset of regulation was easy to see. Building up the Merc's financial integrity by making sure no clearing firm defaulted was another priority, as were establishing a strong administration, diversifying the product line, and developing a solid support staff to accommodate growth. "These were all moves of anticipation, not reaction," said former chairman Bill Katz. "Leo's a superb tactician."

Even the Merc committees had definitive structure. Barry Lind and Melamed had collaborated to overhaul the committee system into some 20 committees covering virtually every segment of the Exchange, including a pit oversight committee to review all trading practices. To ensure that ideas and people wouldn't grow stale, one-third of the members of each committee were to be rotated to a different committee on an annual basis. The rotation system also answered those critics who had attacked the committee system as a way of doling out rewards among Exchange members for their support on issues or of individual board members.

Melamed knew how to recognize and tap into the Merc's cultural network to accomplish goals. To do so, he became the consummate networker, exposed to a constant flow of information and ideas. There were official channels of information, but Melamed also developed his own private network by talking to industry sources, academics, government officials, politicians, traders, and other Exchange executives. Growing stodgy was the last thing the Merc's board of governors would put up with.

In 1979, for example, when the Merc had a big surplus income off a record volume year of 19.9 million contracts, rumors spread across the floor that dividends would be dispersed to members. (Unfortunately, such a windfall was not allowed by Illinois law under the Merc charter.) But always direct, without qualification, Melamed told Yeutter, the executive committee, and members of the financial instruments marketing committee, "I hear that we have a big surplus. . . . I propose that we re-evaluate our programs and our budget. I believe we need to redouble all our efforts. I believe that we must hasten the start of our present marketing programs. I do not mean to sound panicky. . . . I have seen more successful institutions than the CME and IMM go down the drain because of a combination of complacency and misdirection." That same year, the Merc added a four-year Treasury note contract to its other interest rate contracts (90-day T-bills and one-year T-bills). Even the Chicago Board of Trade hoped to garner some of Melamed's energy and stamina. In January 1979, the CBOT offered him a directorship on the CBOT board. It was, as Melamed wrote CBOT chairman Ralph Peters, "one of the highest plaudits anyone could bestow upon me."

But Melamed was already on overload. As the Merc's special counsel, he attended every CME board meeting and a host of ad hoc committee meetings. He was also chairman of both the CME Financial Instruments Steering Committee and a member of the CME's Executive Committee, as well as the Real Estate Committee and several other committees. In addition, he was chairman of the National Futures Association and a director of the Futures Industry Association. Among it all, he traded for a living.

Given his load, not to mention a possible conflict of interest, Melamed had no choice but to decline the CBOT's offer. In doing so, the statesman in him took the opportunity to ease tensions between the exchanges and to lay the groundwork for an alliance. In industry matters, Melamed believed, a united front between the two biggest futures exchanges was imperative. "I must tell you," his response to Peters continued, "that your offer has had and will have some meaningful and lasting effects on CBOT and CME relationships. I need not tell you that we in Chicago are faced with formidable competitors from New York, not to speak of continuing altercations with Washington. Thus, it is incumbent on our two institutions to coordinate our efforts in these regards and to work closely and in harmony whenever possible . . . because our joint cause is beneficial to Chicago futures markets. I promise you that I will make myself available to you and the CBOT should any occasion arise where I could give counsel or undertake specific assignments on behalf of our mutual goals. Please convey these thoughts to the members of your Executive Committee."

Melamed's impact, however, and indeed the Merc's image on the other side of the Atlantic, were somewhat out of sync with its domestic stature. The Exchange had hired Streets Financial, a London-based public relations firm, to gain much-needed media exposure to the European financial communities. But at best the Merc had received token press from foreign publications. "American futures exchanges were still somewhat of an enigma in those days," said former Merc public relations vice-president Ronald Frost. "We were looked at as a curiosity. The Europeans wondered whether financial futures were a temporary phenomenon or a permanent one."

The Chicago Mercantile Exchange was the second biggest futures exchange in the world, viewed as a liquid market for pork bellies, cattle, currencies, and T-bills. But the International Monetary Market's image abroad was, in the words of Jack Sandner, a member of the Financial Instruments Steering Committee at the time, "at best second rate." The Merc had still not learned to effectively hype itself internationally, especially in marketing its gold futures contract. This became evident to Melamed on a trip to London in October 1979, which left him with a definite impression. He had gone to London to attend the sixtieth anniversary celebration of the London Gold Market. The COMEX — the Merc's biggest competitor in the gold futures contract — was well represented by a contingent of its officials. New York's gold market was perceived as the most liquid and efficient.

Merc officials realized that the IMM had failed to adequately publicize its gold market and to bring European gold business to Chicago, despite the fact that Merc gold traders such as broker Maury Kravitz were among the heaviest hitters around. At one point, Kravitz — with the biggest order deck in gold among the brokers — filled orders for contracts of more gold in a year than the 53 million ounces annually mined throughout the world.

The London visit was an eye-opener for Melamed, as he shared his observations with colleagues upon returning to Chicago. "I came away with the belief that we must retain someone in London for our office there who is conversant with and known in the field of gold or else we will surely lose any possibility of bringing European gold business to Chicago," he told members of the Merc's financial instruments steering committee. "As a matter of fact, time is of the essence to do this, irrespective of many other things we must do to regain a gold presence with the world gold community. If not, we stand a good chance in the next year or so to lose this market to New York entirely."

It wasn't going to be easy to win gold. The COMEX was an exchange devoting all its energy, resources, and time to one contract. The local traders had only a single pit to concentrate on and there was plenty of liquidity in their gold contracts. One alternative strategy was to create a reason for a second gold market in the United States. That would have required a different delivery system, logically in London, because that's where the cash market was located. There was no reason why two markets in the same commodity should exist in the same U.S. time zone because there would not be enough traders to provide the necessary liquidity for each of the markets.

The sense of urgency spurred the process of opening a CME London office as major wirehouses such as Merrill Lynch, Bache, and Thompson McKinnon were getting into the futures business with overseas offices. Beverly Splane hired Kimberly Albright, an American expatriate who had been working for Citibank's London operation, to help find space and to serve as an administrative assistant to the head of the CME London operation. Spencer Stuart, an executive recruiting firm, went about the task of finding someone to manage the office. It had to be someone British who was familiar with the financial markets. "The Merc meant little to the international financial community," said Rosenberg, then chairman. "But the IMM was gaining some respect."

"I didn't know an awful lot about the Chicago Mercantile Exchange at the time," recalled Keith Woodbridge, one of the candidates Spencer Stuart found. "Only one or two British banks were using the Merc. It was pretty patchy." Woodbridge, a genteel man with a firm handshake and quick smile, had worked for Citibank for 26 years. Though he didn't know a lot about trading futures contracts, he knew about trading and open outcry. During the 1960s he had been in charge of the bank's foreign exchange dealing room in Paris, where he'd daily buy and sell currencies at the Bourse around a pit. "The only problem was that all the currencies were traded in the same pit," said Woodbridge. (At the time, all stocks on the Paris Bourse were traded by open outcry.)

When Woodbridge was approached by Spencer Stuart, he was treasury manager in Citibank's London office. In Chicago to be interviewed by the members of the Merc board, he looked out across the floor of the Exchange from the visitors' gallery one day. "I had the feeling that all those people were doing the same thing I had been doing, but in a different way. It was another dimension of the same market."

Woodbridge didn't know what to expect in his interview with Melamed. He was surprised by Melamed's first question.

"Can you write?" Melamed asked.

"Yes I can," Woodbridge replied.

It was the kind of question, Woodbridge later thought, to which the answer would have been more revealing than the answers to queries about his knowledge of the futures markets. Woodbridge got the job. And the Merc became the first American exchange to establish a London office.

In January 1980 the Merc hosted a black-tie dinner in London's Guild Hall. Beneath huge golden chandeliers sat the Merc's entire board of governors, along with bankers, brokers, exchange officials, and others from London's financial community. Sandner toasted Queen Elizabeth and Rosenberg welcomed the guests.

The Merc's London office would call on central banks and the local branches of the Exchange's member firms. Albright had found a prime location in London's financial district at 27 Throgmorton Street, nestled among a warren of streets near the Bank of England, Mansion House (where the Lord Mayor of London lived), and the statue of Lord Wellington. The Merc office was also around the corner from the venerable London Stock Exchange and near the Royal Exchange building that would house what would become the first financial futures market outside of North America, the London International Financial Futures Exchange (LIFFE), which opened in 1982.

LIFFE's first chairman, John Barkshire, one of London's financial whiz kids, was to spend five months during 1979 in New York and Chicago studying futures markets. "Melamed and Sandner encouraged the formation of LIFFE," said Woodbridge. "The Merc gave LIFFE a lot of help in 1981 and 1982." The Merc's London office was running three multi-day seminars per month to teach traders and brokers who were getting ready for the rigors of futures trading.

From the start, it wasn't an easy sell. The Merc's London office offered a one-day futures course for beginners. Woodbridge called on old friends and talked to bankers and the press about the futures business. The reactions, as Woodbridge puts it, "were all polite." Most were negative. Some money men were skeptical. Others complained that the contracts were too small. Still others thought it impractical because the Merc was six hours behind London time. "We went into a marketing, education, and sales dimension," said Woodbridge. The second week after the office opened, the Merc held a press conference for some 50 London journalists. The questions were basic, the answers specific.

Back in the United States, inflation was playing havoc with investors holding fixed income securities. Without the hedge of interest rate futures, they were being battered. The financial storm began on Saturday 6 October, the so-called Saturday night special, when Fed chairman Paul Volcker announced an increase in the discount rate—the rate charged on borrowings by member banks—of a full point to 12 percent, and an increase in the reserves member banks held. The development touched off turmoil in the money markets. Interest rates soared higher and billions of dollars in securities values were wiped out. By the year's end interest rates rose to 15 percent. In his determination to end high inflation, Volcker squeezed harder, sending the prime rate to 21.5 percent in early 1981.

Stock market investors following the doomsday advice of market letter advisor Joseph Granville to "sell everything" poured billions into money market funds, whose assets jumped from $77 billion to $190 billion. Like a summer tornado, the recession tore through the economy. Housing starts, auto sales, and corporate profits tumbled. The Dow skidded from 1024 in April to 820 in September. And by the end of 1980, outsiders invaded Wall Street taking over Shearson, Bache, Salomon Brothers, and Dean Witter Reynolds. It was the beginning of the economy of the 1980s, distorted and inflated by leveraged buyouts, massive junk-bond issues, vast fusions of credit, and the sale of a Van Gogh painting for an astonishing $53.9 million.[1]

At the same time, debt was becoming one of the world's growth markets, for amid the volatile interest rates, financial futures were getting their biggest boost. There were several reasons for this. There was liquidity in these markets. The deliverable supply of bonds (about $20 billion) in 1979 was already twice as big as the soybean market. And by 1988 the bond market had grown more than 10-fold to $210 billion.

Not surprising, then, was the proliferation of new products and new exchanges that were either started or proposed between 1980 and 1982; these included the New York Futures Exchange, the New Orleans Commodity Exchange, the International Futures Exchange, Ltd., the World Energy Exchange, the London International Financial Futures Exchange, and the European Options Exchange.

By this time, banks and government securities dealers who had been skeptical of T-bond and T-bill futures were using these markets, which transferred risk, discovered prices, and disseminated them around the world in as fast and efficient a method as possible. In fact, in 1981 Treasury bond futures for the first time outperformed, in terms of volume, all other futures contracts on any other exchange.

At the Merc, gold, foreign currency, and T-bill futures had overtaken the agricultural products. The T-bill contract, only five years old, represented a daily turnover of $20 billion, a market three times the size of the underlying cash market in Treasury bills. Moreover, trading volume in the Merc's Treasury bill contracts had set records for 25 consecutive months.

Besides the banks, the corporations were also becoming end-users. Firms such as General Telephone & Electronics, Allied Chemical, Esmark, Republic Steel, Union Carbide, Sears, DuPont, and General Electric were among the corporations using financial futures as part of their overall business strategies. Investment bankers, too, realized the advantage of the markets. This became apparent during the period when the Fed had tightened the monetary screws.

Interest rates had moved against Salomon Brothers, one of the underwriters of a $1 billion debt issue offered by IBM. Salomon, however, hedged its portion of the offering to avoid millions of dollars in losses.

Such success stories attracted more underwriters to use interest rate futures in the domestic markets as well as in the Euromarkets and beyond. The financial futures markets were becoming international in scope. The Bank of England had given the green light for the new London International Financial Futures Exchange to trade foreign currencies, sterling instruments, and Eurodollar certificates of deposit when it opened in 1982. Already the Sydney Futures Exchange in Australia was trading currency futures. And in Canada, interest rate futures in Canadian T-bills and T-bonds were traded, as well as gold futures on the Winnipeg Exchange.[2] Hong Kong, too, had a gold futures market.

Clearly the currency markets had passed the critical stage, although start-up, as vice-chairman Jack Sandner put it, had been "excruciatingly slow." In 1975 currency futures totaled less than 200,000 contracts, or about 10 percent of total volume. Five years later, currencies accounted for 45 percent of the IMM volume. During 1980, trading in the British pound alone hit one million contracts, a total that exceeded all the currency volume on the IMM in the previous year. The mushrooming volume in currency futures made clear the need for an alternative market, even though the interbank market still had a viable, well-tried forward market in foreign exchange. It was proof to the critics that futures markets could indeed operate side-by-side with cash and forward markets.

Given the growth of the markets, the Merc was taking its ideas to other parts of the world. In addition to the London office, seminars were planned in 1981 in a dozen European cities as well as Singapore, Hong Kong, and Tokyo. "We took the concept of financial futures trading to Europe and Asia because we were convinced that they were becoming international markets," Yeutter said. As the Merc's goodwill ambassador, Yeutter had become chairman of the Chicago Association of Commerce and Industry and began attending international conferences such as the Swiss Commodities Futures and Options Association's (SCFOA) annual meeting at Burgenstock, Switzerland. The Merc, in fact, was the first U.S. exchange to support SCFOA, and Yeutter was a founding director. At SCFOA's tenth annual meeting in September 1989, Yeutter returned to greet old friends and to give the keynote luncheon speech as the U.S. Secretary of Agriculture.

The public had fiscal confidence in the CME and IMM clearinghouse based upon its historic record and system of financial monitoring by the Exchange. Not a single dollar of public funds had been lost as a result of financial failure of any Merc clearing firm, a record that held up going into the decade of the 1990s. One of the primary reasons for this financial safety was the fact that the markets operated in a no-debt manner and that all positions were marked to the market daily so that each clearing member paid in cash for its customer's position every day. The no-debt policy was unique in the credit-conscious world.

But the Merc went beyond the general no-debt system of futures. Merc officials had long before concluded that, for the CME to become a global force, it had to devise a secure financial structure. The idea was to actually codify the principle that had generally been believed to exist; that is, if any Merc clearing firm would fail, the other clearing firms would make up the loss. It was a principle that in fact had never been tested or adopted legally.

To do so, Melamed enlisted two colleagues upon whom he always relied in financial matters. The first was Barry Lind, who had previously helped to establish the financially sound CME Clearing House; and second, Ira Marcus, the outside tax counselor who had been instrumental in creating the CME Financial Trust, which guaranteed customer protection. The result was Rule 802, or the so-called "good to the last drop" rule, adopted in 1977. It stated that the financial failure by any CME clearing member was a liability to all other clearing members—to the full extent of their assets. Rule 802 put the CME's financial integrity and strength in a unique position in relation to all other futures exchanges and gave the Merc the financial strength it sought in its quest for global futures market dominance.

The clearinghouse at the CBOT was different from the Merc's in that it was an entity separate from the exchange. That meant that if the CBOT clearinghouse went under through default, it wouldn't take the exchange with it. Support of the CBOT clearinghouse came from the clearing members who had purchased shares of stock in the corporation. The Merc, on the other hand, adopted a "we're all in the same boat" approach. Its clearinghouse was an integral part of the exchange organization. A clearing member had a guarantee worth billions of dollars—the strength of combined assets of all the Merc clearing members. In that respect, Lind's committee devised a "fairness doctrine" based upon the annual amount of volume, trades, and capital of a clearing member. In short, everyone would participate in the failure of any individual clearinghouse. The Merc, according to Melamed, became the first exchange to ever put the fairness doctrine in writing. "If we had attempted to do it in today's [1990s] environment," Melamed said, "it never would have happened—never. It had to be done when the exchange had its muscle, at a time when the futures industry was still unorganized."

Specifically, if a default arises from a clearing member's house account, the Merc will transfer all customer positions and funds to another nondefaulting clearing member. The Merc will then apply to the defaulting clearing member's debt the member's security deposit (between $200,000 and $2 million per firm, based on a formula that is recomputed at least quarterly as of 1991), its house margins on deposit, and its Merc memberships. (To qualify as a clearing member a firm must own six seats, two in each division.) Customer margin accounts cannot be used to satisfy defaults in a house account. Instead, the Merc applies its own surplus funds (some $48 million of the end of August 1991) and the pool of its members' security deposits ($47 million at the end of August 1991), and makes assessment calls to meet a default in a house account. Similar steps are taken should a clearing member's customer account default. The Merc will attempt to transfer positions and funds of the customers not in default. In order to meet the default, however, the Merc would apply any of the defaulting clearing member's customer margin on deposit as well as any security deposit, assets, and memberships. In addition, the Merc would apply the clearing member's house margin on deposit.

To alleviate the risk of nondefaulting customers of a clearing member, the Merc has a $44.2 million trust fund (as of June 1991) that can be used on a discretionary basis to assist customers of a Merc clearing member that becomes insolvent. If a default exceeds the clearing firm's deposits and memberships, the Merc will fund the loss to the Clearing House out of its own surplus. If that amount is insufficient, the Merc will next apply the security deposits of its clearing members.

Of course, there was a final source of funds to draw from. The "common bond" or "good to the last drop" rule provided for the balance of the loss to be allocated among the remaining clearing members. The assessment powers provided to the Clearing House (under Exchange rules) are unlimited but must be made in accordance with a formula that calls for the first half of the assessment made on the basis of adjusted net capital. That part of the assessment is capped at $2 million per firm. The second half of the formula has no limit and is based on each firm's share of trading volume for the past six months as well as each firm's share of the open interest (the number of futures or options contracts that at a given time are outstanding). By 1989 Merc clearing members had some $11 billion in shareholders' equity, plus $5.2 billion in subordinated debt. What would happen in the event of a massive default that required assessments? The Merc is prepared to borrow from banks, using collateral provided by its good to the last drop rule. If a settlement bank[3] informed the Merc clearinghouse that it refused payment on behalf of a particular clearing member forcing a default, the Merc's emergency financial procedures are triggered.

The process of clearing is one of the most misunderstood points about futures markets. A transaction in the forward markets was executed privately between buyer and seller. The two parties were accountable to each other for the life of the contract. That meant they could create their own terms for the contract. In the futures markets, however, the clearinghouse created a relationship far different from that of a typical forward transaction. With the clearinghouse, a customer was not concerned about the financial performance of the party on the opposite side of the trade. At the end of the day, the clearinghouse of the exchange took the opposite position: It became the seller for every buyer, the buyer for every seller.

In contrast to the securities industry (which formed the Security Investment Protection Corp. in the early 1970s after the collapse of several major firms), the futures industry didn't provide customer account insurance. It relied, instead, on rules that required strict segregation of customer funds at the clearing member level and guarantees at the clearinghouse level. As early as 1976, the CFTC had considered whether to compel the futures industry to adopt some type of account insurance. It tabled the issue, but revived it again in 1985 in the wake of a default by Volume Investors Corporation, a clearing member of the New York Commodity Exchange (COMEX), which, unlike the Merc, had no trust fund at the time. Volume Investors defaulted in March 1985, when customer margin deficits exceeded the firm's capital. The nondefaulting customer and clearing funds were applied to the deficit to make up the shortfall. However, these customers were unable to recoup their funds until subsequent receivership proceedings in 1986. In a 1985 report, the CFTC observed that the rapid growth of institutional trading and increased volatility of the futures markets heightened the potential for a default of far-reaching consequence. But in November 1986, the National Futures Association's Customer Account Protection Study chaired by Sandner concluded that there were "currently substantial and wide ranging customer account protections in place" and recommended maintenance of the systems already in place.

The Merc's system of financial integrity would be put to the acid test a year later, when the foundations of both the securities and financial futures industries would be shaken to their cores by the biggest market break in American history.

27

Shaping the Mosaic

Going into the 1980s the Chicago Mercantile Exchange had established itself as a world-class player and innovator in the emerging financial futures markets.

"If you were forced to name one person whose influence has been the greatest in the futures industry over the 15-year period," observed *Futures* in a 1987 retrospective, "you would be hard-pressed not to select Leo Melamed, although, to be sure, other influential people contributed greatly to the industry's growth during that time."

The article continued, "Melamed was instrumental in establishing the IMM, the breakthrough into the financial area that has set the tone of futures markets ever since. His involvement in the rise of the CME, the growth of the Futures Industry Association (FIA) into a significant industry voice, the development of the National Futures Association (NFA) and many other industry activities make it difficult for anyone else to top his accomplishments during the 15 years."

It was obvious to those who had worked with him over the years that Melamed didn't settle for little dreams. He went for the big ones. "The Merc became my ideal," he said. "The institution and I became one and during that time my wife was a widow and my children, orphans. I lived inside the four walls of a board room. I didn't have time to smell the flowers."

The Merc had grown bigger and faster than even Melamed had anticipated. When the Exchange moved into its new complex at 444 West Jackson in 1972—with the then-largest trading floor in the world—the Board had allowed for 20 years of growth. Within five years it had outgrown the facilities and expanded them by 30 percent to accommodate the increased trading volume. It was all that Walter Kowalski, the Merc's venerable statistician for nearly 40 years, could do to keep up as his computers churned out an array of record-shattering statistics on a daily basis. By 1980, membership expanded from 500 to more than 1300. And annual trading volume rose from 3.5 million contracts to 23 million. In dollar value, that represented an increase from $139 million to $23 billion traded on a daily basis. The number of contracts had grown from just five agricultural products to 20 and included forest products, gold, currencies, Treasury bills, and certificates of deposit. Already planned in 1981 were new futures contracts on the Eurodollar, Standard & Poor's Stock Index, and even options on various futures.

Given the growth curve and the plans for new contracts, it wasn't surprising that on the drawing board was a new exchange to reflect the future. The new building on 30 South Wacker Drive along the Chicago River and a block from the old exchange was to have two 40-story towers. Adjacent to the south tower the Merc would occupy a 40,000 square foot trading floor with the capability to construct a second trading floor above the first of approximately 30,000 square feet. Part of the south tower would eventually house the administrative offices. On 11 August 1981 ground for the new exchange was broken. The Merc was scheduled to move into its new home over the Thanksgiving weekend in 1983.

To raise the money for the new building, Melamed put together a kind of financial SWAT team that included tax counselor Ira Marcus, Barry Lind and Jack Sandner, who had taken over the chairmanship from Larry Rosenberg after completion of his third term. The key plan: to sell more memberships. That meant developing new products as well.

In the months ahead, the Merc began planning a host of new products that included a contract on a stock index. Merc officials were sure that index futures were the next wave of the futures markets, so convinced of that prospect, the board decided to fashion an entire division around this new index product and options on all existing and new futures, which still awaited CFTC approval. Through long and tiring negotiations with Standard & Poor's Corporation, a subsidiary of McGraw-Hill Inc., the Merc had designed a futures contract based on the Standard & Poor's 500 stock market index to be traded on and marketed exclusively by the Exchange.

The primary question was whether or not a stock market index was public or private domain.[1] While counsel advised that an index was in the public domain, Merc officials believed it was in the private domain and therefore Standard & Poor's deserved compensation. Consequently, Melamed, Sandner, and Salzman met with S&P officials in New York, where a deal was worked out at "a ridiculously low price," according to Melamed, to obtain exclusive rights to trading the S&P 500 as a futures contract. The initial contract was based on a "cap" payment tied into the trading volume during the first two years of trading. With the explosive volume that came with the bull stock market beginning in 1982, the contract was quickly outdated. In 1984, a more equitable contract was renegotiated that gave Standard & Poor's a bigger royalty payment and the Merc exclusive rights for the new stock index derivatives that the S&P might produce.

With new products like the S&P, there was an equally compelling reason for yet another division. The new division—to be called the IOM, for Index and Options Market—would be a way of also infusing new members into the Exchange who didn't have enough money to buy either a CME seat or an IMM seat. The IOM membership was based on a two-tier price: An existing member was permitted to buy one IOM seat for $30,000. The public would have to pay double, or $60,000. Predictably, and in light of what had happened to the value of IMM memberships, no one needed arm-twisting to buy an IOM seat. The sale netted the Exchange $30 million.[2] Best of all, the income was tax free, since memberships in the new division represented a sale of a capital asset. The Merc had 30 million tax-free, debt-free dollars to invest in its future. Now all it needed was the right contract.

Philip McBride Johnson, a partner at Kirkland & Ellis in Chicago, had been the chief counsel for the Chicago Board of Trade. It was Johnson who, on behalf of the futures industry in 1974, had added language to the legislation that gave the CFTC "exclusive rights over futures," effectively barring the SEC from regulatory oversight of futures. There was every reason to believe that index contracts would clear the regulatory log jam that had held them up. The appointment of Johnson as CFTC chairman in 1981—replacing James Stone— set the stage for industry expansion. Johnson was the first CFTC chairman familiar with the futures industry from the inside.

Johnson's first contact with the futures business came in 1965, when the Merc hired Kirkland & Ellis to fight an antitrust suit for allegedly manipulating onion futures trading. Kirkland & Ellis had represented the CBOT since the 1930s, and Johnson was one of the few attorneys with expertise in the futures industry. He had been called on to help draft the framework for the Chicago Board Options Exchange in the early days and worked on the CBOT's GNMA contract, the first interest rate futures contract. Johnson also had become the outside counsel of the fledgling National Futures Association. At the time Johnson took over, John Shad was selected as the SEC's new chairperson. The two began meeting in July 1981 to hammer out the framework that would determine jurisdictional lines between the CFTC and the SEC. The conflicts between the two agencies ended on 7 December 1981 with the unveiling of a joint plan called the Shad-Johnson Accord that gave the CFTC control over financial futures and options on financial futures, and the SEC control over options on the securities underlying the financial futures.

The disagreement over regulatory jurisdiction dated back to the creation of the CFTC as the overseer of futures trading in 1974. Just three years later stock index futures were proposed by the Kansas City Board of Trade, raising the jurisdictional clash between the CFTC and SEC because the underlying instruments involved corporate stocks. The Merc and four other exchanges subsequently applied to trade stock index futures, but approval was hampered by the agencies' jurisdictional dispute. Although the SEC had traditionally regulated equity securities and the CFTC commodities, the new financial instruments had characteristics of both, which led to fuzzy jurisdictional boundaries. After months of negotiations, the roadblocks had been removed for such novel trading instruments as stock index futures, options on debt securities, and options on foreign currencies, which were all cash settled. These new-breed futures contracts incorporated an innovative departure from traditional commodity contracts by using a cash delivery system—no actual stock shares changed hands, only money. (Here, for example, is how the Merc's S&P 500 futures work: This index consists of a "point score" based on the price of 500 individual company stocks. The contract based on the index rises and falls in value depending on whether the 500 individual stocks go up, pushing up the index point score. Instead of making an investor buy shares of all 500 stocks for ultimate delivery, this futures contract uses a mathematical formula to calculate an equivalent cash value—say, $500 times each index point—at final settlement. If the index drops, the futures contract likewise drops in value.)

The agreement reached between the two agencies, related in a 1 February 1982 joint statement, divided the contested trading universe. The CFTC would regulate all futures contracts; "broadly based" stock or bond index futures; options on futures contracts, including financial futures; and options on foreign currencies trading on commodity markets. The SEC would regulate all options directly on securities, such as corporate stocks and bonds, Treasury bills, and bonds; and options on bank certificates of deposit or corporate stock indexes; and options on foreign currencies trading on stock exchanges.

When stock index futures began trading in early 1982, they were welcomed by investors rather than seen as a threat by the investment community as a whole. Federal regulators and stock exchange officials wondered what effect this type of futures would have on capital market formation and volatility. There was also concern over whether narrowly based index futures could be manipulated. The accord addressed this concern by allowing approval of futures contracts only on broadly based stock indexes—those representing enough different stocks to prevent manipulation of any individual stock price through the futures market. The oversight and policing of the stock markets themselves by the SEC remained uncompromised.

By 1974 futures trading had expanded well beyond the agricultural products. Yet items such as gold, silver, foreign currencies, propane, iced broilers (processed chickens packed in ice), plywood, and Ginnie Maes that the CBOT was setting up to trade had not been included in the list of commodities defined under the Commodity Exchange Act, nor had coffee, cocoa, and sugar, commodities that had been produced overseas although they traded on U.S. exchanges. In the past, as Philip Johnson pointed out, Congress had excluded the foreign products because it was thought impractical. "There may have been less need to regulate for the sake of protecting domestic commerce," Johnson wrote in his book *Commodities Regulation,* published in 1982, not long after he became CFTC chairman. That attitude, however, changed with the passage of the Commodity Futures Trading Commission Act in 1974, which radically amended the Commodity Exchange Act. The Act was revised to include contracts in foreign-grown products as well as any other item that would be used in futures trading by adding the phrase "and all other goods and articles, except onions as provided in Public Law 85-839 (the ban on onion trading), and all services, rights, and interests in which contracts for future delivery are presently or in the future dealt in." The definition of commodity had been expanded, as Johnson summed it up, so as "to encompass virtually anything that is or becomes the subject of futures trading, intangible as well as tangible." Thus, any object—including a security—that could be traded in a contract for future delivery on an organized exchange fell into the CFTC regulatory camp. (However, although the Act defined a commodity, it gave no definition of a futures contract.)

In the two years preceding Johnson's arrival at the CFTC, only five contracts had been approved. The long list of products collecting dust on the CFTC shelf included a commodity options pilot program, a Eurodollar futures contract, and stock index futures, the first of which had been proposed to the Commission in 1977. The stock index future was a political hot potato. The SEC wanted to regulate futures on securities. The CFTC held its ground. The infighting and indecision between the agencies had placed the Merc and other exchanges in limbo as far as new product development. Besides the jurisdictional question, another looming issue begged resolution: cash settlement.

The industry had been wrestling with an alternative means to make cash and futures prices converge at expiration. In pursuing cash settlement as the mechanism, the Merc argued that futures markets were never meant to be physical delivery markets. Delivery in most cases provided a way to ensure that futures prices and cash prices converged. Historically, less than 2 percent of all the contracts traded resulted in delivery.[3] Moreover, exchange economists questioned why, if there were good cash prices, one should have delivery at all. On the other side of the world, the Sydney Futures Exchange (SFE) was paying close attention to the debate over cash settlement. The Sydney exchange wanted to trade a U.S. dollar contract and because of various controls on currency, cash settlement seemed to be a good way. The first cash-settled futures contract was launched at the SFE in 1980.

In the United States, it was the Chicago Mercantile Exchange that first pioneered cash settlement by winning the CFTC's approval to offer a contract on three-month Eurodollar time deposits. Cash settlement on this particular instrument made a great deal of sense, given the environment of the Eurodollar time deposit, a nonnegotiable deposit with a well-developed cash market involving a large number of banks. Without cash settlement the delivery mechanism would involve short-sellers setting up bank accounts on the part of longs. It made physical delivery cumbersome. Cash settlement on the other hand, in the words of Merc economist Rick Kilcollin, was "a much neater mechanism."

Before the CFTC approved cash settlement, a strong lobbying effort had been undertaken by Melamed, who employed his favorite technique: the one-on-one meeting. Melamed had managed to meet with each CFTC commissioner to plead the cause for cash settlement. One of his chief supporters was CFTC commissioner Gary Seevers, who later was to become a governor on the Merc Board after he left the CFTC and became a partner at Goldman Sachs. Federal regulation had to be introduced to preempt state gambling laws that would have prohibited the practice of cash settlement. With approval of cash settlement in the Eurodollar contract, the Merc was leading the futures industry to a new plateau. Indeed cash settlement was the biggest innovation since the introduction of currencies in 1972 because it opened the way for the cash-settled stock indexes, the futures product that would dominate the 1980s.

The Merc introduced the Eurodollar contract on 19 December 1981 in a departure from its usual opening day festivities. "The Chicago Mercantile Exchange put on a $60,000 show Wednesday to open its new Eurodollar futures contract," the *Chicago Tribune* reported. The "show" centered around a transatlantic press conference and broadcast to London with Sandner, Yeutter, and Melamed wearing earphones as they fielded questions from reporters in Chicago and London. The Exchange had arranged for a live broadcast in London via satellite.

The unusual steps to promote the contract (covering $1 million in 90-day Eurodollar time deposits, or dollar-denominated deposits outside the United States) were taken because the Merc officials expected half the business to come from outside the United States. "This is an intercontinental contract," Melamed told the press, noting with a grin that the opening was indeed a departure from typical debuts, which involved "coffee, donuts and the mayor, and the mayor comes free."

Opening day trading was brisk. With 2,765 contracts changing hands, it was the second highest opening day activity for a futures contract, behind the Merc's certificate of deposit contract, which had opened on 29 July with volume of 4,246 contracts. There was competition in these contracts. Waiting for CFTC approval were applications for similar contracts from the Chicago Board of Trade and the New York Futures Exchange; both these exchanges were already trading a CD contract. But more than 75 percent of the business in CD futures was flowing to the Merc.

As for the new Eurodollar contract, traders were moving into the pit with coaxing from board members. While Merc officials long believed that the market determined the life or death of a contract, they also believed that each new contract needed the initial support of members. After all, the Exchange was a not-for-profit organization whose members operated for a profit, and it paid its bills by collecting fees on every transaction. Increased volume also provided the capital for more services to improve and expand the markets. But even more importantly, a successful exchange meant a higher net worth for its members. With seats trading competitively, the price of a membership reflected market perception of the income stream to members. That's why membership expansion had to be carefully planned. Exchanges that issued more seats than the amount of business would support found themselves with bargain-basement membership prices and a lack of traders to create liquidity.

That was part of the problem for the slow start of the New York Futures Exchange, a subsidiary of the New York Stock Exchange formed in 1978 to trade futures and futures options contracts. NYFE had launched currencies and bond futures trading when it first opened its doors. But trading languished and seat prices with it. "Within two years," said Lewis Horowitz, NYFE's president and chairman, "we realized the markets were not there. Trading was relatively dormant until 1982." Today most of NYFE's trading activity is in the New York Stock Exchange composite stock index futures.

Unfortunately there is no set formula for a successful exchange, but Merc officials understood what the blend of new products and expanded membership could mean. The opening of the IMM in May 1972 boosted Merc volume that year from 4,673,462 contracts to 6,059,766 contracts in 1973. It was the same for the IOM; volume in 1981, the year before the IOM was launched, totaled 24,527,020 contracts. A year and three new contracts later (CD, Eurodollar, and stock index), volume had leaped to 33,574,286 contracts. The basis for rapid expansion globally took more definitive shape in 1980, when futures markets in Europe and the Pacific Basin began to emerge. Some brokerage firms that were CME members were reporting that as much as 30 percent of their futures business was coming from overseas. At the same time, overseas firms were not only purchasing memberships on the Merc, but they were also purchasing member firms of the Exchange. In 1980, for example, UK-based Mercantile Holdings Ltd. acquired CME member Woodstock, and Guinness Peat bought a 20 percent stake in Geldermann & Co. A year earlier, the New York–based firms of Salomon Brothers, Goldman Sachs, and Discount Corporation became Merc members. There was little doubt that the need for financial markets was being expressed.

Under Johnson, the CFTC helped restore momentum to the futures industry. "Our philosophy has changed 180 degrees," said Johnson. "We now believe the marketplace ought to decide whether a product will sink or swim, not whether it is economically justifiable." Approval of cash settlement, said Johnson, was the most important decision made while he was CFTC chairman. It was indeed, because waiting in the wings were stock indexes. The Kansas City Board of Trade (KCBT) was first in line with its value line stock index. But 24 hours before the CFTC was to approve the contract, Johnson was visited by the chairman of the KCBT with a problem. The Federal Reserve Board, the KCBT was advised, would not allow margins as low as 3 percent to 5 percent. Johnson called Fed chief Paul Volcker to discuss the matter. Johnson posed the question directly: What could be done to accommodate the Fed's concerns without dredging up the fight between the Fed and CFTC over who had margin authority? Volcker told him he had problems with the low margins. Johnson asked if 10 percent was acceptable. Volcker said yes and the KCBT agreed. After years of bickering over margin control, the problem had been solved, as Johnson later put it, "in a five-minute horse trade."

After four years of planning and waiting, the new era was ushered in with the first index futures contract, traded on 24 February 1982 in Kansas City.[4] Two months later—ironically, three weeks shy of the tenth anniversary of the IMM—on 21 April the Merc opened its S&P 500 index. No other contract in the history of the futures markets ever matched the start of trading in the S&P 500 stock index. During the remainder of April, 27,544 contracts traded. Seven of the nine months through December 1982 were record volume months. By November, more than half a million S&P contracts were changing hands.[5] The S&P index consisted of 400 industrials, 40 public utilities, 20 transportation, and 40 financial issues. Most of the stocks were traded on the New York Stock Exchange, but some were traded on the American Stock Exchange and over-the-counter. The Merc's agreement with the S&P to use its index provided for exclusive use for 18 months.[6] After that, S&P could authorize other exchanges to use its index. But by that time, the Merc reckoned, it would have the market.

That assumption proved correct. Better times for the stock market were just ahead, but it didn't seem so in early 1982. The economy was shaky from the worst economic setback since the Great Depression as unemployment rose above 10 percent, imperiling dozens of companies with bloated borrowing and energy costs. Banks took their lumps, too. The failure of Penn Square Bank in Oklahoma set off a shock wave of write-offs among such big-city lenders as Continental Illinois and Chase Manhattan.

The Volcker recession began to ease during the summer, when the Fed discount rate was cut three times between 20 July and 13 August. That's all it took to ignite the stock market. On 12 August the Dow bottomed out and over the next five days climbed almost 100 points. The bull market of the 1980s was underway. And so were stock index futures. The long-awaited start of the commodity options program at last arrived in early October 1982. On 28 January 1983, the Merc took yet another first step by offering an S&P 500 options contract. Now there were options on the stock indexes themselves.

The index race heated up even more on 11 March 1983, when the Chicago Board Options Exchange began trading its CBOE 100 index options. Merc officials believed that the SEC had approved the product quickly in order to help its constituent exchanges compete with the futures exchanges and their stock indexes—a product the SEC had previously opposed. Following a whirlwind romance with the Merc and S&P, the CBOE turned its index into the S&P 100 index or the so-called OEX.[7]

The world of index futures and options enabled investors to play the stock market without owning a share. It was used by brokerage firms and large institutions to hedge their stock market risk. Just 17 months after the fledgling instruments were introduced, they accounted for 9 percent of the total activity of the futures markets. No futures contract had ever taken off with such speed and impact.

"Most commodities have moments of calm—but not the S&P," Melamed told a reporter in August 1983. "You literally have to close out your position if you want to get a cup of coffee or smoke a cigarette."

At the Merc, traders were arriving at 7 A.M.—two hours before the S&P contract opened—jockeying for choice positions in a trading pit jammed with more than 200 traders. Among the 17 agricultural and financial futures contracts listed on the Merc at the time, stock index futures were too immense for those interested in America's financial markets to ignore. On one particular day in August 1983, the underlying value of stock index futures traded in Chicago, New York, and Kansas City totaled $6.4 billion. The market value of shares on the NYSE that same day was $3.5 billion.

Institutional investors, who accounted for at least two-thirds of the trading in stocks, were beginning to use the new instrument to limit the risk of owning stock. Acceptance of the index contracts had been nothing short of remarkable. In the first year, for instance, the S&P contract was used by Harvard Management Company, which managed Harvard University's huge endowment fund. "Suddenly the speed picked up," said NYFE's Horowitz. "Once the concept of adding return through hedging caught on, indexes were off and running. Chicago used the academics to pull the engines. If Harvard does it, 'Why shouldn't we?' said the pension funds."

It wasn't surprising that almost 3 million S&P contracts were traded on the Merc during the period from April through December 1982. The following year, annual volume increased to over 8 million contracts. In 1984 the S&P 500 futures contracts became the first Merc product to reach an average monthly volume of more than 1 million contracts.

Helping to produce that kind of volume were such firms as the Los Angeles-based money manager Leland O'Brien Rubenstein (LOR), which began using the S&P futures on 30 March 1984 for two of its pension fund accounts. The new accounts launched LOR on a new career path: selling insurance, or the so-called hedging tactic known as *portfolio insurance*. Institutional investors found that they were able to get hundreds of millions of dollars into the market quickly without having to make specific stock decisions and disrupting the market. And transaction costs were less than 10 percent of what it would have cost to buy the actual stock. "It was like wearing suspenders and a belt," said Horowitz of portfolio insurance.

Another name for portfolio insurance is *dynamic hedging*. Based on a formula, a short stock index futures position is increased or decreased to create a synthetic put on the portfolio. Thus, any loss in value in the underlying stock market would have been made up by gains in the derivative market. The new instruments were, in effect, an equity-commodity hybrid that afforded the first practical way of reducing systemic risk—a stock portfolio's vulnerability to economic news and global events as opposed to news that affects a particular stock. They also provided an edge in asset allocation.

"The dizzying array of strategies available to institutions makes a Rubik's cube look like child's play," observed *BusinessWeek* of index futures in the summer of 1983. By then index fever had spread from Chicago to Hong Kong. The SEC and CFTC had already approved 25 stock index futures, options on stock index futures, and options on actual indexes. The U.S. exchanges were already busily breeding a second generation of indexes. Some were keyed to industry groupings such as technology, utility, and financial stocks. Others were based on key economic indicators such as housing starts, auto sales, and the consumer price index, called by Milton Friedman "the ultimate inflation hedge." There was even talk on the Merc financial instruments committee about a possible contract based on the S&P over-the-counter index of 250 industrial stocks.[8] The deluge of index products in June 1983 prompted the Securities Industry Association to ask for a moratorium. But the Merc and other futures and securities exchanges ignored the request.

The scramble to get market share took some marketing muscle. In one effort, the Merc mounted a massive advertising campaign to promote the S&P 500 among the nation's brokers and investors. The ad effort was designed by Michael Weiser, who had previously worked for the CBOE before establishing his own agency. The response to its campaign in one month produced several thousand telephone inquiries.

In the ebb and flow of the history of the futures markets there were tides that swept in the most profound changes. The Merc sensed such a tide washing over the industry in 1972, when it launched currency contracts. Now, a decade later, another tide had washed over the financial futures markets. But no one knew just how big—and controversial—it would be.

There was mystique and controversy surrounding these new markets. They were evolutionary and at the same time revolutionary. The days when big institutions concentrated solely on the stock market were quickly ending. Now the experts were comparing what was happening in index futures to the impact of interest rate futures, which quietly transformed the debt markets. There was one major difference: Indexes were catching on faster. Yet at the time, only about 10 percent of the institutions were using index futures. Sixty percent was evenly spread among floor traders, stock market specialists, and brokers who hedged their stock inventories and speculated in their own accounts. The general public accounted for the remaining 30 percent. (Index options, CBOE officials had estimated, among individuals accounted for 30 percent of the options activity, with the rest coming from floor traders and member firms.) Nevertheless, the large pension funds now had the ability to effectively hedge market risk, placing them in a better position to hold larger equity positions.

"We look to (stock index) futures as our first line of defense or offense with a major market move," Richard Szczepanik, a partner of Harvard Management Co. (which controlled the university's $2.4 billion endowment fund), told *Business Week* in the summer of 1983.

But institutional business was still slow in coming. To be perfectly hedged, an institution's portfolio had to duplicate the broad index. The index products thus opened a floodgate of arbitrage specialists, each trying to construct a unique computer pricing model and portfolio of stocks that would track the indexes. The strategies were aimed at cashing in on the discrepancies between the actual indexes and futures prices. But it wasn't that easy a play because of the volatility in the basis—the difference between the cash and futures prices. In the Merc's application for CFTC approval of the S&P index contract, it had argued that the futures contract wouldn't influence the daily prices in the stock market. Consequently, arbitrage would be impossible because of the difficulty of buying or selling 500 stocks at once.

Another drawback for institutional business was the morass of legal and regulatory paperwork that had to be waded through before trading could begin. Internal controls to monitor activity had to be set up to satisfy directors and regulators. The Labor Department issued a "no comment" letter, signaling that it wouldn't prevent pension funds from using index futures. Mutual funds had to seek approval on a state-by-state basis and then ask permission from their shareholders. Bank trust departments and insurance companies also needed regulatory and client approval. But the change in tax structure favored the institutional business.

The tax treatment of speculative futures positions (as opposed to hedging) had three major phases—1980, 1982, and 1986—in tax reform legislation during the 1980s. Before the Economic Recovery Act of 1981, futures positions were treated like capital assets. Gains and losses were realized upon the liquidation of the position; those held for more than six months were taxed as long-term gains. Thus came the tax straddle strategy as a means of allowing wealthy persons to defer payments of unrelated capital gains. Merc economist Todd Petzel explains, "Relatively risk-free offsetting spread positions would typically be established. As the underlying market moved, one so-called "leg" of the spread would have a gain, another a loss. The losing leg would be realized by rolling it into another spread. In that way a loss in the current year would be generated and the offsetting gain preserved until the next tax year. With a bit of planning, it could be translated into a long-term gain qualifying for lower tax rates."

The juggling of profit and loss figures to reduce tax liability soon caught the attention of other wealthy individuals who realized that they, too, could apply the same complex maneuver to offset high-income gains with paper losses. The straddle didn't catch the attention of the Internal Revenue Service until the late 1970s when it was discovered that doctors, entertainers, and other wealthy Americans were using the tax straddle on the advice of their accountants. At the time, Merrill Lynch, as *Common Cause* noted, was pushing the tax straddle through a company memo that was read during congressional hearings. The firm avoided using a form letter to tell its customers about the straddle because that "might bring the attention of the Internal Revenue Service to this area . . .

[which] might then take steps to end the tax benefits obtained through the use of tax straddles." A congressional Joint Tax Committee study presented several examples that included a securities broker who had sheltered his $11 million income using a straddle and ended up paying no taxes at all.

This practice, however, was unsuccessfully challenged in the courts by the IRS in 1980 and then effectively eliminated by the revised treatment of futures in the Economic Recovery Act of 1981. In effect, the tally of gains and losses had to be accounted for in the current year. That destroyed the possibility of rolling gains from year to year and ended the concept of tax straddling. "There were genuine hardships created by this change," noted Petzel. As partial compensation, however, futures gains and losses were deemed to be 60 percent long-term and 40 percent short-term regardless of the length of period held. With the maximum marginal rate for individuals at 50 percent, this produced a tax of 32 percent for futures (0.40 at a short-term rate of 50 percent and 0.60 percent at the long-term rate of 20 percent). Initially, traders argued that closing the loophole would discourage speculators from continuing to take long-term risks. According to Clayton Yeutter, the futures industry had asked Representative Marty Russo (D-IL) to protect the traders from the tax straddle legislation. He obliged, *Common Cause* magazine reported, by offering a bill that would have cracked down on the tax straddle for everyone, except the futures traders, who numbered about 2,500 and who stood to gain at least $400 million a year under the Russo proposal. Another supporter was Representative Tony Coelho (D-CA), chairman of the Democratic Congressional Campaign Committee in 1981.

In July 1981, Russo's proposal passed the House Ways and Means Committee, whose chairman was Dan Rostenkowski (D-IL), a friend of the Chicago futures exchanges. Leslie Rosenthal, then chairman of the CBOT, said, "Marty Russo has saved the commodity industry." The Senate, however, took a tougher stand. Led by senators Daniel Patrick Moynihan (D-NY) and Robert Dole (R-KS), both the Senate Finance Committee and the full Senate voted to close the loophole for everyone. The revised tax law wasn't a total loss for the traders; the maximum tax rate on trading profits was reduced from 70 percent to 32 percent and allowed traders to qualify for long-term capital gains rates even on investments held for less than six months. The law also gave traders five years to pay taxes they had deferred using tax straddles.

Options on futures were not part of the IRS tax equation until 1982. Treating them as stock options, critics feared, would lead to another form of tax straddle. So, under the IRS Code § 1256 they were afforded the same treatment as futures contracts. These exchange-traded futures included contracts on foreign currency futures or forwards, equity options on futures, or contracts on broadbased indexes like those traded at the CBOE. The Tax Reform Act of 1986 specifically eliminated the distinction between rates on long-term and short-term capital gains for both investors of futures and stocks.

Taxes and regulations, noted University of Chicago economist Merton Miller, were the greatest impetus behind financial innovations. Changing tax structure both motivated and defined a change. Each innovation that did its job successfully, Miller believed, earned an immediate reward for its adopters in the form of tax money saved. The Eurobond market, for example, had grown in the 1960s out of U.S. regulations that placed a ceiling on the rate of interest that commercial banks could offer on time deposits. Eventually a 30 percent withholding tax on the interest payment of these bonds sold in the United States to overseas investors drove the market from New York to London, where it still thrives today, even though the withholding provision has since been repealed. The swaps markets evolved during the early 1980s, when firms sought ways to avoid British government restrictions on dollar financing by British firms and on sterling financing by non-British companies.

By now it was clear to most investors and observers the bull market was more than a premature blip on the technicians' charts. This became apparent when the Dow Industrial average's 17-year struggle to break 1,000 came to an end in October 1982 as the recession lifted. After four years of poor earnings and big spending to reposition itself, IBM was making a blue chip comeback. A rising market, of course, meant less institutional business in index futures. Futures and options were the tools used in bear markets. "It's going to take a bear market to really educate the major institutions about the usefulness of these products," said Richard Sandor, a senior vice-president at Drexel Burnham Lambert at the time. Nevertheless, by some estimates, there were at least 50 major pools of institutional money on the sidelines ready to invest in stock index futures. These were watershed years for the Chicago markets. The S&P futures contract, along with cash settlement, helped to define the Chicago-style futures markets, which began to claim advantage over the New York–style stock markets. For the speculator there was a high degree of leverage; moreover, the up-tick rule did not apply to go short a futures contract or to buy put options. And the transaction costs were reasonable.

Of course, there was no assurance that the new contracts would work. No matter how much the Exchange studied the potential of a contract, it was the members who bore the risk if it failed. The Merc had invested $3 million to develop the S&P contract, nearly 10 percent of the CFTC budget. While the S&P index futures had taken off beyond expectations, long-term success was in doubt. After all, the gold contract had a fast start, too. The IMM and the COMEX in New York each had launched a gold futures contract on 31 December 1974, the first day American citizens were allowed to own gold since the 1930s. During the first year the IMM won the volume battle, edging out the COMEX by 407,000 contracts to 393,500. Over the next four years, the two exchanges ran even in the gold contracts. Then, in 1978, the COMEX sprang ahead, tripling volume and surpassing the Merc by nearly 1 million contracts. Two years later, as gold bounced between $500 and $800 an ounce, the trading volume in gold on the IMM dropped by 1 million contracts. By the end of 1980, the IMM's gold volume had fallen to about one quarter of COMEX's annual volume of 8 million contracts. The decline continued until the CME ceased gold trading in 1985.

What happened? Too many out-trades and poor order fills were some of the reasons traders gave for the gold pit's demise. Others attributed the deterioration to spreaders skipping to New York because of better settlement procedures. At one point, the Merc sued the CFTC in an effort to get its price settlement procedure changed to a committee decision similar to the COMEX's rather than price averaging. (Some traders, the Merc argued, bid out of line on spreads for margin purposes. Eventually the Merc won the right to committee-determined settlements, but too late for its gold market.)

There were more obvious reasons for the loss. One had to do with the COMEX's location. Most overseas customers who dealt in gold knew New York better. Moreover, the COMEX had established itself in metals with silver and copper futures. The COMEX also had the advantage of attracting tax straddle business. The New York market had a post-market trade rule that allowed spreading—which provided the market greater liquidity—after the close of the market. This attracted an enormous amount of straddle business. The Merc lost out on that business because spreading could only be done during the course of the trading day at the Merc. Consequently, the Merc petitioned the CFTC to allow a similar session so that it could adequately compete with the COMEX. The Merc's request was ignored.

Looking back on the gold race, Merc officials knew there would be a healthy arbitrage between the two markets. But in the long run there wasn't a need for two gold markets because they were too similar. The odds were long that the Merc's gold market had a chance from the start. Could the same fate, wondered observers, befall the S&P 500? The chances were highly unlikely since the S&P 500 index was exclusively licensed and accounted for 75 percent of the stock index market. It wasn't the case for gold. The burgeoning S&P pit of some 500 traders was proof of the enormous activity that had helped push 1982 exchange trading volume up 40 percent over that of the previous year's.

In the early stages, however, the traders needed a little encouragement.[9] A few months after the S&P contract began trading in 1982, Melamed and Sandner were on a trip to London in an effort to market the new product along with the Merc's other contracts. No sooner had they arrived in London when they noticed with trepidation that volume in the NYFE's index contract was rising, while S&P volume at the Merc was slipping. Given what had happened to the Merc's gold contract and the fact that the cash market in stocks was in the NYFE's own backyard, there was deep concern that the new S&P contract could come unglued. The two cut their trip short. "On that flight back," said Melamed, "I thought of a gimmick." Melamed reasoned that if every member on the floor gave the new market 15 minutes it would undoubtedly boost the market's liquidity. The plan was simple: a "15 minutes please" campaign. Hundreds of buttons were made up emblazoned with "15 minutes please" while Melamed and Sandner stood at the door of the trading floor for a week handing them out to every member. The hunch proved right. It helped that a bull stock market was underway, although the go-go euphoria had not quite taken hold. But the efforts to prod the membership added to the momentum of the S&P contract. Within a week after the campaign, volume turned around and the Merc has never looked back.

The rapid rate of growth begged for administrative expansion as well. The Merc staff had increased from 155 employees in 1972 to 450 a decade later. More contracts, more people, more bureaucracy. Now the Merc faced the challenge of any fast-track institution: how to avoid bureaucratic burnout without diluting the Exchange's sense of mission and vitality. Melamed and Sandner were putting in 15-hour days and needed relief from the day-to-day operations as Yeutter raced around the country with a heavy speech-making load. He had given 67 presentations of one kind or another around the world in a year. On one day he was the lead-in for President Reagan at the National Corn Growers Association convention in Des Moines; then he left for a presentation to the New York Society of Security Analysts and, shortly thereafter went to the annual meeting of the National Livestock Producers Association. From there he moved on to Washington, where the Merc hosted a dinner in honor of retiring CFTC commissioner David Gartner, who, as Yeutter put it, "shared our basic economic and regulatory philosophy."

Yeutter described his role within the Exchange and the industry "as somewhat different from anyone else's" because of his Washington experience. "I was there for six-and-a-half years and a lot of the people in power in Washington either in the Executive branch or in Congress are longtime friends, many close personal friends," he told an interviewer. "I simply cannot devote the time to day-to-day management that other exchange presidents can," he continued. "So what we have here at this exchange is more of a Mr. Outside, Mr. Inside relationship. Mr. Inside functions on day-to-day management responsibilities . . . I can't afford to spend the time on that here." Yeutter was never reticent about discussing the Merc's lobbying efforts. "I don't want to be immodest about it, so please handle it properly in the story," he said in a 1985 interview with *Common Cause* magazine, "but I've been around Washington for a long time and I really believe I can evaluate Washington performances as well as anybody in the country. And I would say that as of right now, we probably do our job as well as anybody in Washington."

The year Yeutter made that statement, the Merc's Commodity Futures Political Fund was the highest contributor among corporate PACs without stock, giving $324,000 to cultivate such congressional allies as Representative Dan Rostenkowski (D-IL), chairman of the powerful House Ways and Means Committee; Senator Robert Dole (R-KS), former chairman of the Senate Finance

Committee in the 1980s and majority leader of the Senate in the Bush Administration; and former Speaker of the House Jim Wright (D, TX). These men were among the power brokers sympathetic to the futures industry over the years. In 1988 the Merc, the CBOT, and the Futures Industry Association gave $1.2 million to a host of candidates, more than 70 percent of them incumbents. The Merc had raised $668,528 and the CBOT—through its Auction Markets Political Action Committee—$548,594. The FIA's Futures Industry Political Action Committee chipped in $10,050.

The exchanges tended to downplay the importance of their PACs, the Merc's headed by Melamed and the CBOT's by its president, Tom Donovan. In fact, the policy of the Merc's public relations department was not to comment on the Merc's political action committee. Nevertheless, PAC efforts of the futures industry have been well documented by the press, prompting *Common Cause* to observe several years ago, "The story of the commodity industry's Washington lobbying operation, fueled by the industry's well-timed, well-placed and increasingly generous campaign contributions provides a textbook example of what's wrong with the legislative system."

There were few who would argue that the Merc's political clout was being felt in the Capitol. Yeutter had strongly disagreed with any suggestion that the futures industry was buying its way in Congress. "We don't make quid pro quos on campaign financing for any member of Congress on any issue ever ... We don't buy votes and don't intend to buy votes," he told a reporter. But it never hurt to have a few friends in high places. During the period from 1981 to 1982, at the time the futures industry was coping with the closing of tax loopholes, it was faced with another congressional battle. The House and Senate agriculture committees wanted to levy a user fee on each commodity trade, with the proceeds going toward the cost of running the CFTC. A similar fee had been levied on stock transactions since 1934, with the funds helping to pay SEC expenses. Officials of the Merc and other exchanges argued that such a fee would be punitive and unfair. A decade later the futures industry was still warding off user fees, despite the government's efforts. The user fee—a 13-cent tax on each futures trade in the United States—was part of President Bush's 1991 budget and was also mentioned in the CFTC's reauthorization bill that was before both houses of Congress in 1991. (The fee was increased to 15¢ in the 1992 budget.) The House bill calls for only a feasibility study of the assessment, whereas the Senate's bill calls for an actual schedule of service fees that would range from a total of $3.8 million in 1992 up to $21.7 million in 1996. Together the Merc and CBOT execute nearly half of all futures and options bought and sold around the globe. Exchange officials argue such a transaction tax could push the futures markets overseas the way of, for example, the electronics and shoe industries. "The futures business does not have an affinity to the U.S.," said Sandner, shortly after he became Merc chairman in 1991. "Business today will move, with a push of the button, to that market where the cost of doing business is lowest."

How much clout did the Merc have with the CFTC? Some individuals, such as former CFTC chairman James Stone, thought that it was a great deal. "This industry can be righteously indignant if someone is appointed that didn't either come from the industry or come with specific industry approval," charged Stone, the former commissioner of insurance for Massachusetts, who was appointed CFTC chairman at age 32 by President Carter in May 1979 over the objections of futures industry officials. Stone resigned the CFTC chairmanship on 20 January 1981, nearly two years before his appointed term was to expire on 15 April 1983. But he stayed on as CFTC commissioner until 31 January 1983. In 1985, when Yeutter was asked whether he had recommended all of the CFTC commissioners, he replied, "Recommended would be too strong a word in some cases. But I really don't want to answer for publication because if I do, then everyone at the CFTC is going to want to figure out which I recommended and which I did something less than that . . . I certainly had conversations with the White House personnel office on all those appointments."

Even if money doesn't buy votes, it buys access. There's hardly an office wall of a Merc or CBOT official that doesn't display him or her with an auto-graphed photo with a U.S. president or congressman. Some exchange executives collect the photos of the influential and famous the way children covet base-ball cards. Although exchange officials don't trade the photos, they hoard them in albums. Even today, it is the lure of PAC money that has made congres-sional representatives frequent flyers to the Windy City, a sobriquet in refer-ence to Chicago's brand of blustery politicians back in the 1890s. In 1989 and 1990, according to a report by Ralph Nader's Washington-based Public Citi-zen, 282 members of Congress visited Chicago, more than any other city in America, including New York, Los Angeles, and Miami. It was enough to call Chicago, as the *Sun-Times* put it, "the capital for clout-seeking in the nation." The chief reason, the *Sun-Times* observed, was the "vigorous" lobbying activi-ties of both the Merc and the CBOT. Over the two years, the two exchanges had sponsored 118 trips. The National Cable Television Association in Wash-ington, D.C. came in second with 75. It paid to be cordial to politicians. In September 1988, for example, when President Reagan was on the campaign trail raising funds among GOP backers, the White House used the Merc trading floor for a reception. (Prior to the affair there was a photo session with the president, exchange officials, corporate executives, and their spouses.) Educat-ing the lawmakers in the world of futures had never been an easy task for the exchanges.

In late 1982 three Merc executives—Melamed, Sandner, and Yeutter—had absorbed most of Beverly Splane's administrative responsibilities, while she took on the role of managing director of a six-month joint feasibility study between the Merc and the Singapore Financial Futures Working Party. The study would determine the synergism of a Far East venture at a time when markets—driven by greed and self-interest—were becoming more valuable than territory, and information more powerful than military hardware. The financial markets were on the cusp of becoming a global village linked to a trading technology of microseconds. While the Merc was trying to operate efficiently under drastic space constraints, the search for a chief operating officer was underway, a Mr. Inside, as it were. In late March 1982 an executive recruiter on behalf of the Merc contacted William J. Brodsky, then the 38-year-old executive vice-president of operations at the American Stock Exchange. At the time, he knew something about the Board of Trade and the Chicago Board Options Exchange, but nothing about the Merc. Brodsky met with Melamed and Sandner in Washington and with Sandner, Melamed, and Yeutter in Chicago before meeting the CME executive committee. The discussions centered around three points. One dealt with the Merc's vision of international expansion, the second with options, and the third with stock index futures.

Like Melamed, Sandner, and Yeutter, Brodsky was an attorney who happened to be an authority on options. He knew the mechanics of the options markets, having helped the Amex establish itself in equity options, as well as the regulatory side. Moreover, Brodsky was considered a strong administrator. He had spent his entire career on Wall Street, as had his father, Irwin Brodsky, a veteran of 61 years in the securities business that included 32 years with J.W. Seligman & Co. and 15 years as managing partner of Model, Roland & Co.

At 17, Bill Brodsky had landed his first job on Wall Street, working a summer on the floor of the New York Stock Exchange for DeCoppet & Doremus, a firm that dealt in odd lots. As an undergraduate at Syracuse University, he was business manager of the basketball team and at Syracuse law school, he was president of the class. After graduation, Brodsky joined Model, Roland & Company, where his father was managing partner. In 1974 he was hired by the Amex and eventually assumed the responsibility for stock options, market operations, trading analysis, and planning. Because of his expertise, Brodsky was also a board member of the Options Clearing Corporation, the clearing body for all listed stock options. Raised and bred in the New York City area, Brodsky and his wife, Joan, a Latin teacher, were strictly New Yorkers. They had never entertained thoughts of moving west of the Hudson.

During negotiations with the Merc, the Exchange had launched a massive promotional campaign to promote the S&P stock index contract with full-page ads in the Wall Street Journal and video tapes featuring Louis Rukeyser. "You had to be blind not to notice the Merc during that period," said Brodsky. Nevertheless, he still wasn't convinced the Merc was the right place for him. A fourth point, however, that came up in talks with the Merc may have had more of an impact on Brodsky's thinking than anything. He explained, "I recall discussing the new building concept. The IOM seats had just been sold, which raised $30 million. It was a tremendous figure. Just the concept that an institution of this size could sell 1,300 seats and raise that much money and build a new building was highly impressive. By contrast the Amex, which was always an aggressive exchange, and the New York Stock Exchange, were unable to build new buildings, which they later regretted. And when the Amex got into the options business and offered 200 memberships, it was only able to sell 97. Here was the Merc selling 1,300. Can you imagine the impression it had on me of the institutional capability of the Merc?"

Brodsky was even more impressed, given the fact that at the time the Amex had a larger staff with an annual operating budget of $50 million, compared with the Merc budget of under $30 million. After much soul-searching, Brodsky decided by early August to take the offer of executive vice-president and chief operating officer. The announcement on 24 August indicated that every department of the Exchange was to report to him except for the Washington operation, which Yeutter would oversee. "It's a sign of the time that William Brodsky doesn't know beans about pork bellies," the *Chicago Tribune* remarked in an October feature story on the new Merc official.

A man who possessed a firm handshake and a ready smile and who didn't mince words, Brodsky came to the Merc at a time when the competition between Wall Street and LaSalle Street was heating up over financial contracts. Both the Merc and the CBOT were Goliaths being chewed up around the edges by increasingly strong Davids. "I didn't know the futures business that well," he recalled. "But certainly from a New York securities perspective, there were things greeted with a certain amount of skepticism—such as split price openings. The entire agricultural side of the business was totally alien to me."

As an Amex administrator, one of Brodsky's strengths was his ability to deal with all elements of the membership. "He's one of those people who can draw the proper balance between different points of view," said Options Clearing Corporation chairman Wayne Luthringhausen shortly after Brodsky joined the Merc. During the first several weeks, Brodsky met staff members and visited a different pit every day to meet the floor traders. The days of knowing everyone on a first-name basis were long gone with the expanded memberships and a vigorous turnover on top of that. It didn't mean, however, that centralized power had to exist in a vacuum. Close contact with an amorphous membership would always be a problem for a dynamic organization.

The administrative problems at the Merc were more vexing than that. Morale among staff members had deteriorated in recent months, and when Brodsky looked at the Merc's organizational chart, he said to himself, "This can't be." There had been 11 people reporting to Beverly Splane. No manager, Brodsky believed, could function effectively with that many subordinates to deal with on a daily basis. It didn't make any organizational sense. One key position—vice-president of operations—had been vacant for nearly six months. And in the first week of Brodsky's tenure, the head of data processing quit out of frustration. "I begged him to stay on for a reasonable period until we could fill the spot and because we needed someone to run the computers." The computer operation was treated as just another small department, run, in Brodsky's words, like the mailroom. Clearly, the Exchange from an operations standpoint had fallen behind the pace of its growth. The Merc staff organization, as Brodsky saw it, was loose and poorly structured.

By December Brodsky began to reorganize and streamline the administrative staff, which had grown by one-third to 457 between 1980 and 1982. He moved quickly and decisively. First, he brought in the consulting arm of Arthur Anderson to review the clearing operations. Next, he hired Don Serpico from Zenith Corporation to run data processing. Then came Anthony Ward to oversee the operations group. Ward—recommended by Joe Sullivan, the founder and first president of the CBOE—was from Booz Allen Hamilton, the consulting firm which had set up the CBOE's floor operations.

The Merc restructuring took nearly a year to complete and involved the marketing, operations, research, administrative, and regulatory divisions. Besides Ward, four other executives were placed in newly created posts as senior vice-presidents: Rick Kilcollin, chief economist, was in charge of research; Barbara Richards became head of marketing; Gerald Beyer was in charge of legal and regulatory affairs; and Glenn Windstrup directed administration and planning. All Merc departments reported to one of the five senior vice-presidents, who, in turn, reported directly to Brodsky.

Brodsky was emphatically against what he called the "narrow operational capacity" of exchanges. He explained: "Exchanges had to have operational overcapacity rather than undercapacity, because the entire industry depended on an exchange's ability to run its operation, churn out reports and to provide a constant flow of services and information. There really can't be a good excuse for not doing that well all the time."

The old structure of committees running the Exchange daily had long given way to a professional staff. Committees were still important, however—particularly the executive committee. During the World War II years the heavy flow of regulatory measures from Washington forced the Merc Board to refer emergency matters to a small committee with the power to act. Called the executive committee (in accordance with Rule 217.5), it was comprised of the officers of the Board and several other Board members. Melamed had been involved in some capacity the executive committee since he first became chairman in 1969. In 1977, after stepping down as Merc chairman, he took the title of special counsel and several years later became chairman of the executive committee. When Melamed gave up the Board chairmanship, he continued as special counsel to the Board and continued to serve on the executive committee. It was in 1985 that Melamed realized he needed an exchange title for the outside world. This became apparent on a trip to Japan when he realized that his title of special counsel had been translated as "staff attorney." Upon his return the Board appointed a committee to review an appropriate title. The committee recognized that all along Melamed had been de facto chairman of the executive committee. This was now codified in his title.

In recent years it brought up the question among some journalists and Exchange critics of whether the power was too concentrated, resting in the hands of Melamed and a tight-knit group that included Jack Sandner, Laurence Rosenberg, and Brian Monieson, all Merc chairmen at one time or another and tireless workers on behalf of the Exchange. True, it was more cumbersome to deal with problems as the membership grew. But the Board attempted to be accessible for open dialogue on any issue.

"People who didn't believe the possibility of open dialogue," insisted Sandner, "are those who didn't understand the process and didn't take time to learn it." The Board's hard-nosed approach to problems and the fact that the business conduct committee had teeth were subsequently illustrated when, in 1985, Monieson, his partner, Myron Rosenthal, and their firm, GNP Commodities, Inc., were found guilty of and were fined for exceeding speculative limits in pork bellies. Rosenthal was fined $70,000 and Monieson, $10,000. Monieson's fine would earn him, as *The Wall Street Journal* put it, "a dubious distinction" as the only Merc chairman to be found guilty of trading violations while running the exchange.

"The exchange had become international in scope and to maintain our credibility we had become tougher on violators no matter who they were," said Larry Rosenberg, chairman of the Business Conduct Committee in 1976 and from 1980 through 1989. When Rosenberg became chairman of the committee, it was in the days before what he called "the megafines." In the 1970s each offense carried a fine of up to $50,000. By 1989, the per offense fine was $200,000. "The fines got bigger because the S&P dollars got bigger," said Rosenberg.

Brodsky had arrived during a transition period. The Merc members, though willing and anxious to play a role in Exchange matters, neither had the time nor the expertise in the technical aspects of running an exchange. Moreover, the scores of younger members inhabiting the pits seemed to suffer from institutional and generational amnesia when it came to supporting the Exchange through committee work. "The typical member doesn't involve himself in the committee structure," conceded Sandner in an 1987 interview. "The majority of members leave as soon as the bell rings." Yet the Merc was still dominated by its floor members, who were much like equity owners of a business. In contrast, other exchanges were beholden to their member firms, which brought them their business. It was a balancing act at the Merc, as Brodsky saw it, between the old members, new members, member firms, and professional staff.

The complexion of the Board had changed over the years, too. The Merc had 18 directors, or so-called governors, who were Exchange members: three public directors and industry representatives appointed from Merc clearing firms. The Merc was the first futures exchange to have outside directors on its board. Three representing the producer, the consumer, and the general public were appointed in 1942, when membership had dwindled to 225 seats owing to the war. By 1945, however, the effort, as chairman Maurice Mandeville remarked in a letter to the membership, "proved to be only partially successful." The Board, continued Mandeville, "was forced to go far afield for appointive Governors with the result that they attended our meetings so infrequently they were unable to keep currently informed of our problems." For the following year, the Board decided not to appoint outside directors.

Typical of an outside director in 1983 was Nancy Clark, who knew little about the futures markets but a great deal about Washington. For five years she was a Washington lobbyist for Bendix Corporation and for a year Boise Cascade. Clark was also on the board of Sears, Roebuck & Company. "Washington is compromise," she told a *Chicago Sun-Times* reporter shortly after she joined the Merc board. "That's why businessmen get so frustrated." Her basic experience taught her that no individual lobbyist ever got a bill passed without involving a "tremendous" coalition. Understanding how to deal with the federal regulators became a way of exchange life. At times it had been adversarial and combative, but by the early 1980s—following CFTC reauthorization—there was a fluid dialogue between Congress and the futures industry.

In January of 1983 the chairmanship changed hands from Sandner to Brian Monieson, who had been first vice-chairman during the three years Sandner served as chairman. A champion bridge partner of Melamed's, Monieson held an MBA degree from the University of Chicago and ran GNP Commodities Inc. , a clearing and research concern. In the 1960s he had been a pioneer in computers, having worked at Honeywell Corporation before turning to consultancy in 1965 with his own firm called Indecon. The first program was an econometric model for harness racing. The model's bets were featured in the *Chicago Herald American* where, according to Monieson, every two-dollar bet on his system returned to an individual some $400 in the course of a year. The major consideration for successful betting: A horse's performance against better competition was more important than its speed or time. Soft-spoken and precise, the bespectacled Monieson—more reminiscent of a professor than a futures trader—went on to develop a trading model for pork bellies on behalf of Commodity Corporation of Princeton, New Jersey. He began trading for himself at the Merc in 1971. By 1983 Monieson's trading skills and mathematical savvy had earned him respect among a number of his peers. Indeed, over the years Melamed had used Monieson as an "intellectual sounding board" in financial matters. "I was always the numbers person," said Monieson, who referred to Melamed, Sandner, and himself as "the inner group" during his tenure as chairman. Not only would they strategize during the week, but the three would meet to discuss Merc business nearly every Sunday evening from 10 P.M. to midnight at a fast-food restaurant on Highway 41 not far from where they lived in Chicago's north suburbs.

The financial pits were now in a manic bustle and the Merc felt the pressure of keeping pace while looking to the future. The markets were racing ahead at a time when institutional investors began to see the possibilities of financial futures. Some 200 U.S. banks, including 19 of the top 30, were now using financial futures in asset and liability management and government bond trading. Morgan Guaranty Trust Company, through a subsidiary called Morgan Futures, was the first commercial bank to join a futures exchange. The Merc had been instrumental in helping Morgan obtain approval from the Federal Reserve. Others such as Citibank, Bank of America, Bankers Trust Company, and First National Bank of Chicago also were taking steps to become full-fledged futures brokers and Exchange members through holding company subsidiaries. As futures brokers they could deal directly in the market for their own accounts and for their correspondent banks and corporate clients. The pension funds, too, saw the advantages of futures in financial risk management. Several large ones, including those of Exxon Corporation, General Motors, Kodak Corporation, and Westinghouse Electric Corporation, began using stock index futures as market-timing and trading vehicles.

With cash settlement in 1981, of course, the shape of trading changed. Once the CFTC approved the mechanism of cash settlement, said Melamed, "we all went scurrying about for the stock market of our dreams." Analysis indicated that eventually the portfolio manager, who measured performance on the basis of the S&P 500, would be the one to drive the business toward the Merc. Fortunately, at this time the economy was off and running. The gross national product was on its way to recovery, though not fast enough to save a record 31,334 companies from bankruptcy. Unemployment was dropping steadily, but farm debt was soaring. It cost farmers six dollars to grow a bushel of wheat that could be sold for only three dollars at market. As the DJIA regained lost ground of previous months, spirits along the farm belt sagged. That was bad news for the agricultural futures, but good news for the financial futures.

Against the backdrop of record trading volume and the introduction of options on futures, the Merc was anxiously awaiting the completion of its new building on Wacker Drive between Madison and Monroe Streets with 1,000,000 square feet of office space and a 40,000-square-foot clear-span trading floor. There would be room to expand the trading space by another 30,000 square feet. The second phase called for the twin to the first office tower to be built on the Madison end of the block. Both towers would be connected by the trading floor, which sat between them on the east bank of the Chicago River. Tenant enthusiasm for the building was apparent. A year before opening, more than 50 percent of the space in the first tower had been leased. The $350 million project, of which the Merc owned 10 percent, had moved ahead with hardly a hitch. "People squabble more about putting up a three-story building than we have," Yeutter said. The Merc had chosen the Levy Organization as its consultant to coordinate construction of the new building, designed by Fujikawa Johnson & Associates. The developer was a joint venture between Metropolitan Structures and JMB Realty, two of Chicago's major firms. John Geldermann, chairman of the Merc's 12-person building committee from 1976 to 1989, had put in long hours to coordinate the entire plan from breaking ground to moving into the new building when it was completed. He was proud that the entire project was brought in at $200,000 under budget.

"The design," said Larry Levy, head of the Levy Organization, "was not a trendy one; it is a strong architectural statement . . . for an organization that was growing at the rate of 40 percent a year." Part of that "statement" used granite to convey a quality institution. Melamed put it this way: "The Board of Trade has always been an image, it's a landmark. We expected our building to be equal to, if not more of, a landmark."

During the preceding 10 years, the Merc concentrated mainly on creating new products and on ensuring the liquidity to make those products work. Little had been done in automation. But the new trading floor was a preview of what was to come in the next decade. Atop each pit stood the animated arbitrage clerks, their eyes glued to the telephone clerks along the trading floor perimeter, firing off bids and offers in the familiar financial shorthand using hand signals that, in turn, were relayed to the broker in the pit for execution. Dividing the floor into grid-like sections were rows of some twelve hundred work stations—each capable of handling 128 incoming telephone lines—threaded together with some 14,000 miles of telephone wire. Into these stations poured the buys and sells from around the world as runners carried the orders into 19 pits that represented a smorgasbord of futures contracts. Beneath the massive, crowded, and boisterous trading floor—in a concrete bunker—beat the heart of the telecommunications system. It was, said Don Serpico, senior vice-president of the Merc's operations department, "like a small telephone company servicing 8,000 customers in a square city block." Some 85 Merc member firms used one main communications system, which included 8,500 telephone circuits and 2,400 phones. In any given year, that meant 7,000 requests for moves, adds, or changes in phone equipment among these firms. The Merc's telephone system, by design, was more a Jeep than a Ferarri—dependable, not flashy. It remained a low-tech operation, whereby the programming of specific lines to telephones came through physical single hard-line connections rather than through a keyboard and computer. These connections, by design, were distributed throughout the Merc's telecommunications room and decentralized across member firms.

On 28 November 1983, the day the Merc was to begin trading in its new building, its snazzy electronic system nearly gave Geldermann heart failure. Geldermann had arrived at the Merc by 5:00 A.M. The switches were turned on and all the computers were supposed to kick in at 6:30. But they didn't. All the digital clocks were out of sync. Something was drastically wrong. Serpico began checking the hardware, but he could find no apparent malfunction. Then it suddenly hit Geldermann, a tall, low-keyed man who almost never showed panic. Now he was frazzled. "We began to wonder if our brand new exchange would go down the first day," Geldermann said. The traders were milling about the floor and dignitaries were arriving. Within minutes of the opening bell, the computers clicked back on line. As it turned out, there had been a glitch in the software. Nevertheless, for the next six hours, recalled Geldermann, "We held our breaths."

At 7:30 sharp Chicago Mayor Harold Washington rang the gold ceremonial bell, which signalled not only the start of currency futures trading, but also the official opening of trading on the new Chicago Mercantile Exchange Center—the largest column-free futures trading floor in the world. It was, Monieson said, "our dream for the future." Once again, the ongoing romance between Chicago's mayors and the Merc was evident in Mayor Washington's remarks: "I am amazed at what I see here," he said, "and what the Merc has done for this city. We need you, we want you, and we want to help build an atmosphere conducive to your doing business here." The Merc had come a long way, but it had never strayed far from the neighborhood where it was born. Over the years it managed to stay within a few square blocks of where it all started. The Merc began in a building long demolished at the corner of Lake and LaSalle Streets. There board markers kept track of bids and offers on the trading floor from 1899 to 1921, the location that housed the Butter and Egg Board, which was renamed the Chicago Mercantile Exchange in 1919. From there the Merc moved a few blocks away to a building at Wells and Lake Streets, where it set up trading facilities from 1921 to 1928. The wrecker's ball took care of that one, too. Its members thought that it had certainly found a permanent home in the 14-story building at Washington and Franklin Streets. It spent the next 45 years there, from 1927 to 1972. Then over Thanksgiving weekend in 1972 it moved yet again to 444 West Jackson Boulevard and a 14,000-square-foot trading floor built over the air rights of the Union Station Company, abutting the Chicago River. A decade later—again over Thanksgiving weekend—the Merc moved into the 40-story CME Center on Wacker Drive (its current location), boasting a 70,000-square-foot, 10-story high trading complex—with the largest clear-span, column-free trading arena of any futures exchange in the world.

Among the more than 100 guests who were treated to a champagne breakfast that morning in 1983 were Susan Phillips, chairperson of the CFTC, and Illinois Democrat Dan Rostenkowski, chairman of the House Ways and Means Committee. "The Merc is to Chicago," Rostenkowski remarked, "what oil is to Texas and Oklahoma, what milk is to Wisconsin, and what corn is to Iowa." For Merc officials, the CME Center represented a promise to the city of Chicago and a step toward shifting the center of gravity for finance to Chicago. In their minds the new building represented the last piece in the mosaic, making the Chicago Mercantile Exchange a world-class player.

28

Exporting the Evolution

The first trade in the Chicago Mercantile Exchange Center the morning of 28 November 1982 was 10 futures contracts in Swiss francs traded at 0.4608. The buyer was Brian Connor of Collins Commodities, Inc., for his own account; the seller, Andrew J. Brinkman of CSA, Inc., trading for his firm. Two days later, a new single-day trading record was set with 236,149 financial and agricultural contracts changing hands—more than double the total volume for all of 1952.

The new center opened to rave reviews. Joe Simms, the Merc's vice-president of public affairs, summed it up in a memo to Brodsky: "I have never seen a single story so dominate a paper as did our opening. We had a prominent front page picture—even though there was a space shot the same day. In addition, the business section of the *Chicago Tribune* on Monday featured the bell-ringing shot of Mayor Washington, Clayton, Brian, and Leo. When our first page picture moved into the business section on Tuesday, the bell-ringing shot continued to be featured there. Even more satisfying than the picture, though, were the headlines, 'New Merc off to a smooth start,' 'Extensive preparation pays off; few hitches reported. . . . ' "

In January 1983, Ronald Reagan signed the Futures Trading Act of 1982, renewing the CFTC's mandate to regulate futures trading for four more years. That year also marked the start of Wall Street's takeover mania as Drexel Burnham Lambert Group began an insatiable drive to finance leveraged buyouts with junk bonds—debt instruments that pay high rates of interest on distressed companies—that would eventually snowball into a $200 billion market by the end of the decade only to fade with Drexel's bankruptcy in February 1990.

The Merc had clearly established itself an innovator. "With the Merc leading the way in developing new types of futures contracts, the industry has resurged," *The Wall Street Journal* reported in February 1983.[1] Much of the success was attributed to the Merc's S&P contracts, which represented about 60 percent of all stock index trading at the time. Now the Merc was about to take yet another innovative step as its attention focused on the other side of the world.

Beverly Splane, based in Singapore, busily laid the groundwork for the first exchange link of its kind anywhere—a trading connection between the Chicago Mercantile Exchange and the Gold Exchange of Singapore, 14 hours and 9,400 miles away. Plans for the trading partnership were announced in the summer of 1983. Almost immediately, the skeptics aired their concerns. How would the trading cultures mesh? The futures markets in Chicago were a raucous affair with traders screaming and shouting in a free-for-all spasm of capitalism, whereas the Singaporeans, as one observer stated, traded in a "sedate and gentlemanly" manner gathered around a blackboard. Simply, it meant that Singapore traders would have to be schooled in Chicago-style futures trading.

The Chicago-Singapore plan was dubbed "revolutionary" by the media because it called for a mutual offset between the Merc and the Singapore exchange, which became the Singapore International Monetary Exchange, or SIMEX. A trader could establish a position in Chicago and remove it in Singapore, or vice versa. A customer, for example, in the United States could buy a gold contract in Chicago at noon and close out the same contract twelve hours later—midnight Chicago time—on the Singapore exchange as if it were carried out at the Merc. The Merc had spent two years and $1 million to develop the venture, which Melamed described as "the same kind of challenge if one wanted to start a new exchange in Denver." Yeutter saw it as a long-term investment without leading to "major increases in our trading volume any time soon." In short, the Merc's optimism was hedged with caution. The two exchanges were connected by a $16,000 a month (both sides combined) telecommunications link that included sophisticated banking and programmed computer ties.

To placate the federal regulators, namely, the CFTC, the Merc had gotten Singapore to agree to strict American rules aimed at protecting U.S. customers, such as requiring firms to segregate customer funds from their own. The Merc also required that financial obligations for Singapore clearing members be comparable to those for Merc clearing firms. For months several Chicago traders lived in Singapore, helping to train the local traders. Despite the city-state's tiny size of 2.5 million people and its lack of natural resources, financial services in Singapore were a growing and integral part of its economy.

The Western-educated technocrat Ng Kok Song, chairman of the SIMEX and a senior official in the powerful Monetary Authority of Singapore (MAS), viewed the link as an important step in diversifying his nation's economy. Ng Kok Song, who had spent time in Chicago observing the Merc in action, was excited over the prospect of Singapore jumping ahead of its Asian rival, Hong Kong, in moving into the financial futures field. Adjacent to his office at MAS was a cavernous trading room that Kok Song liked to show visitors. Behind the battery of screens were teams of sophisticated currency traders who moved billions of dollars in and out of world major money centers to bolster Singapore's surplus treasury.

On 29 August 1984 the CFTC approved amendments to the Merc rules that allowed it to establish the link with SIMEX. One week later, on Friday, 6 September, at 8:05 P.M. (it was 9:05 A.M. on 7 September in Singapore), cymbals clashed as four dancers circled the SIMEX trading floor, performing the oriental lion dance of good luck to herald the historic trading link between the Merc and the SIMEX. Dr. Richard Hu, managing director of the MAS, unveiled a commemorative plaque, and then rang a golden bell—a gift from the Merc—as trading began in Deutsche mark (DM) and Eurodollar (ED) futures contracts identical to those at the CME. (Japanese yen contracts were added in October.) The first trade was for a DM contract, sold by Krishna Jagatheesen of the Republic National Bank of New York to Jeremy Heng of Citibank for 0.3432—and the dream of round-the-clock trading was on its way to becoming a reality. The Merc-SIMEX link, reported *The New York Times* that morning, "is considered a historic step in the direction of 24-hour trading." Actually, after-hours trading existed, but on an informal basis. Interbank trading, for instance, took place in London and Hong Kong when the Merc was closed. The Singapore link, however, formalized such trading and made it cheaper and more efficient. "We're accommodating something that already exists informally: around-the-clock trading," said Brodsky, who had been named president-designate to replace Yeutter. "The idea is not just to create more business, but to create efficiencies that don't already exist." The disparate trading cultures blended into an unique concoction of style and practicality that marked the beginning of global and connected markets. The telephone and microchip had become the tools of the trade. Once again the Merc—led by Melamed and Sandner, who would serve as chairman for six years during the 1980s and then step in again in 1991—was able to sense the movement of futures markets half a beat before the rest of the exchanges, providing a map of where the industry would be heading. (Nearly three years after the 1984 Merc-SIMEX link, the Chicago Board of Trade established its after-hours trading program on four weekday nights. It subsequently extended each evening session to three and one-half hours and allowed trading on Sunday evening to coincide with the opening of business in Tokyo.)

"At the Merc," Melamed once said, "we were never looking for vindication, but we sure were looking for business." If Melamed had to pick a "vindication" date it would have been 1 September 1976. That was the day the Mexican peso was devalued 50 percent. Where was the only place to get a forward price in the peso? At the Chicago Mercantile Exchange. "Our market was right there," Melamed said. "It opened up. It never had to sweat. A hundred million dollars changed hands, and we were safe and secure. And the world took notice that the Chicago IMM stayed in business and continued to trade Mexican pesos. . . . "

That same feeling now prevailed toward this new Asian venture. But the Merc was exporting more than trading savvy and style. Launching the golden age of financial futures in the early 1970s had become more than just the cloning of a pattern set by the Merc. What had occurred worldwide since then, in effect, was what some industry observers called "speciation," or the creation of new species. By 1989 more than 30 futures and options exchanges existed around the world, each with its own constituency and its own types of contracts to differentiate it from its cousins around the globe. World centers of futures trading had joined the ranks of their North American counterparts with exchanges in London, Paris, Switzerland, Montreal, Tokyo, Singapore, Hong Kong, Australia, and New Zealand, among others. Moreover, the number of futures and options products had grown from 70 to 370 between 1980 and 1990.

Expansion efforts bred new competition for the Chicago exchanges. Banks, investment banks, and risk-management boutiques began to design competitive products. No longer did a money manager have to dump a stock portfolio or sell off $500 million in bonds to adjust a position. It could be done by using new products, both on and off the exchanges: stock index futures, options on indexes, Treasury bond futures, Treasury bond options, currency options, currency swaps, currency warrants, interest rate caps and collars, putable bonds, Eurodollar futures, Eurodollar options, long-dated options, range-forwards, and so on. In the course of a day, a corporate treasurer could trade Eurodollars in Chicago, Brent crude futures in London, and Nikkei stock index futures in Singapore. And even if a treasurer never traded a futures contract directly, chances were good that his banker used some type of interest rate contract to offset the risks in a corporate bond underwriting or interest rate swap. In essence, the over-the-counter market was competitive but complementary.

A true intermarket system had evolved in futures and options during the 1980s. The corporations purchased the tailor-made futures and options products from banks and financial institutions, which would then channel large portions of their natural hedge demand to the major exchanges like the Merc. "It is difficult to imagine how the current willingness of banks and financial institutions to offer tailor-made products would exist without the ability to hedge with exchange traded products," observed M. Desmond Fitzgerald of Mitsubishi Finance International Ltd. "It is also difficult to see how the exchanges would provide such good liquidity without the institutional hedge demand." All along, the Merc was positioning itself to enter the twenty-first century, when time zones would no longer be an obstacle. One needed only to glance at the cover subtitles of the Merc's annual reports to know where it was heading: the 1985 and 1987 reports boldly proclaimed, respectively, *A Global Perspective* and *A Universal Exchange: An Integrated Marketplace*.

On a humid morning in Singapore in 1986, Sandner expressed his feelings about global risk taking in a speech to SIMEX traders and officials. Quoting from George Gilder's *Wealth and Society,* Sandner said, "There is a vital link between the speculator's money chase and the well-being and growth of a society. It is from the individual's willingness to take a risk that anything of any consequence results." More and more investors, it seemed, were willing to take that risk in the 1980s. With stock market averages down 10 to 20 percent at one point in 1983, the flexibility and low cost of stock index futures looked attractive. According to a *Barron's* survey, more than one in four active stock market investors queried were thinking about the futures markets. In mid-1983 some 123 of the 300 largest domestic and foreign banks operating in the United States were using futures. Similarly, pension funds loomed as serious users. An annual survey by *Pensions and Investment Age* revealed that 26 public and corporate pension funds used futures in 1983, double the number that did in 1982. Among the new pension players were American Can, Atlantic Richfield, Chrysler, Delta Airlines, Grumman Corporation, IBM, Phillips Petroleum, Sears Roebuck, and Texaco.

The insurance companies, too, were following suit: Within the year, 10 states, including California, Illinois, New York, and Virginia, passed legislation that struck down barriers to using futures. In New York, for example, insurance companies were given the nod to hedge 2 percent of total assets; in California, 5 percent; and in Illinois, futures positions were linked to a company's capitalization. Chicago's Kemper Investors Life Insurance Company had sunk $1 million into a computer futures accounting system designed especially for its bond manager. Yet another survey, taken in 1982 by accounting firm Arthur Andersen & Company, found that only 15 out of 394 corporations, mortgage bankers, thrifts, and other financial institutions said that they used interest-rate futures. Another 65 percent, however, added that they were weighing the idea.

In just a little over a decade, financial futures had caught on with amazing speed. In 1983 among all U.S. exchanges, 140 million contracts had changed hands, compared to 17.3 million in 1972. More than one-third of futures trading in 1983 involved financial instruments, stock indexes, and foreign exchange. At the Chicago Mercantile Exchange, volume had set a new record for the seventh year in a row, reaching 38 million contracts, of which 22 percent were the S&P futures. The S&P 100 stock index futures contract was introduced in July, following a landmark tripartite agreement between the CME, Standard & Poor's Corporation, and the CBOE.

New products in the pipeline included petroleum futures—gasoline and No. 2 heating oil—and options on Deutsche marks. The new products committee was also busy shaping contracts on agricultural options, which hadn't been available since the 1920s. The Merc's strategy was obvious: an emphasis on index contracts and options—both for finance and agriculture—with an occasional excursion into a new product line such as energy contracts. The index contracts clearly offered a plethora of potential product possibilities limited only by imagination and practical resources. Options, on the other hand, offered a natural entrance to markets and users who had never before contemplated futures.

By late summer 1984 the U.S. economy was becalmed, but not until after the nation's financial system was somewhat shaken by several events. Earlier in the year, AT&T had spun off its seven regional operating companies under an antitrust settlement. Shortly thereafter, both Fed chief Paul Volcker and Martin Feldstein, President Reagan's top economic advisor, cast gloomy forecasts for the economy. The result: Stocks fell again, sending the Dow average below 1100. The nation's financial community was given another jolt with the near collapse of Chicago's Continental Illinois Bank after the failure of Penn Square Bank in Oklahoma. Continental, which had purchased more than $1 billion in oil loan participations from Penn Square, was rescued by the Federal Deposit Insurance Corporation. On the plus side, Congress managed to cut the capital gains holding period from one year to six months, while Great Britain cut crude oil prices, resulting in a worldwide oil glut. All along, the federal deficit crept up, topping $200 billion. After the Dow gained 12 percent in 1982 and 20 percent in 1983, it closed down at 3.7 percent at the end of 1984. As for the Merc, things only got better in 1984, when volume surged to yet another record — 44.8 million contracts. For the industry as a whole, volume in futures climbed only 6.7 percent above 1983 levels, but the Merc recorded a 14.8 percent increase. Combined options and futures volume industry-wide had risen 11.7 percent, while the Merc recorded a healthy 17.7 percent, thanks to its first 4 million-contract month in March.

To put the Merc's volume growth in perspective, the historical view was even more impressive: More than 25 percent of all trading activity in Chicago Mercantile Exchange history had taken place in 1983 and 1984. It had taken the Exchange 60 years to trade its first 100 million contracts, but just over four more years to trade the next 100 million. (On 26 October 1984, the Merc traded the 250 millionth contract in its history. The S&P 500 contract had become the second most actively traded contract in the industry, achieving average monthly volume of more than 1 million contracts.)

The only marketing disappointment during the year had been in the energy products — leaded gasoline and heating oil contracts — which could not overcome the lead developed by the New York Mercantile Exchange. Typically it had been difficult, if not impossible, for a second futures exchange to draw volume away from an existing market. The Chicago Board of Trade had also tried to crack the energy futures markets but was forced to drop its gasoline and heating-oil contracts because of poor volume. Not even the Merc's proven ability to move new contracts by inducing its members to fill the trading pits could work in the energy markets. The reason, Merc officials quickly discovered (the energy contracts traded for only three months), was the fact that exchanges offering virtually the same products were not needed in time zones only one hour apart.

It wasn't the first time the Merc lost out to a rival; it lost the gold-trading market to the COMEX in New York and bypassed Treasury bonds, which became the industry's largest-volume contract for the Board of Trade. The Merc leadership, which had been right far more times than wrong, took the setbacks in stride. "Our record in launching new contracts is the best in the business," Melamed boasted, "but that doesn't mean we can't fail now and then. The strength of this institution is that we admit it and go on to the next show."

Expansion had its price. Unfortunately, record volume wasn't enough to offset the costs involved in reconfiguring the trading floor to make room for the new options products. While revenues reached a record $52.3 million, operating expenses jumped 21.7 percent, to $49.1 million over the previous year's. The result was a slim income of $3.2 million from Exchange operations, down from $8.5 million in 1983 and only a 2.6 percent increase in members' equity to $58.1 million. Nevertheless, the Merc was perhaps the most fiscally sound futures exchange in the nation. It had flourished well beyond expectation since 1970, when it accounted for a relatively small percentage of the industry's trading volume. In 1984 its share was a healthy 30 percent and growing. And despite numerous membership expansions, the value of a full Merc seat during the 14 years had soared from $35,000 to $159,000.

Although Melamed urged Merc members to "not panic during selective periods of relatively low economic activity," the future wasn't altogether cloudless. In the fall of 1983, a note of caution crept into his outlook despite the immense success of financial futures. "Success on this scale will also bring us commensurate problems and dangers," Melamed said. "The federal bureaucracy will step up its internal struggle for jurisdictional control. There will be Congressional demands for stronger enforcement policies, stronger regulations and stronger federal agencies. The SEC and CFTC will face off over issues of our turfdom and, without predicting a winner, their composition and division of authority may dramatically change—especially as the lines between futures and securities markets continue to blur as they are bound to. Alas, there will also be scandals and failures and surely there will be new legislation." To be sure, the threats were not confined to the public sector alone. Futures trading had triggered the wrath of critics ranging from consumer advocates to the Colorado and Iowa cattlemen, who, miffed by the volatility in prices, wanted to end trading in live cattle futures. There would always be those who harbored a deep-seated antipathy to the marketplace and its workings and who "would strangle the messenger," remarked Robert Bleiberg, then editorial director and publisher of *Barron's*. Consequently, Ron Frost, who stormed the prairies with his team of Merc marketers, carried on a number of seminars in major cattle feeding areas across the country.

Part of the challenge in 1984—the CFTC's tenth anniversary—was to clarify the tax situation and to refine the concept of cash settlement. Congress had cooperated on the tax front by allowing options contracts the 32 percent tax treatment, just as it had done for futures contracts in 1981. Legislation had also eliminated an IRS cloud that had been hanging over the futures industry for three years on tax treatment of certain spread transactions. As for cash settlement—no deliveries—it already existed in such contracts as the S&P 500 and Eurodollars; now the Merc wanted to extend the concept to other futures and options contracts. The most controversial point was cash settlement on the feeder cattle contract, submitted to the CFTC for the first time in 1985. All the while, the Merc worked with members of Congress, 62 of whom visited the Exchange in 1984, an election year. In the five years from 1980 through 1984, well over 200 congressmen had come to the Merc to meet its officials, ask questions, and tour the trading floor. Visitors from Washington included Tip O'Neill, Vice-President Walter Mondale, Gary Hart, Robert Dole, and Dan Rostenkowski. The Merc's political beliefs were aided by its political action committee, a $300,000 fund, under the chairmanship of Melamed. "Without the PAC the industry would be in sorry shape," Sandner remarked. "You can't buy votes, but over a period of time, the donations do open a congressman's door."

As Clayton Yeutter prepared to leave the Exchange early in 1985, Brodsky, as incoming president, was ready to take over. Brodsky had done a lot to depoliticize the staff by reorganizing not only the departments, but also the procedures in which employees were promoted. In June 1984 Glenn Windstrup, who had started at the Merc as an 18-year-old board marker and whose job it had been to make sure the new building went up on time and on budget, left the Merc after nearly 18 years of employment. He was replaced by David O'Gorman, a former executive with the CBOE, the NYFE, and the brokerage firm Rouse Woodstock. The biggest organizational bombshell, however, was yet to drop. On 7 November 1984, Melamed sent a letter to the Merc membership announcing a painful decision: to substantially reduce his role at the Exchange. Melamed was torn. He needed more time, he said, to devote to his family, his business, and a science fiction novel he had started writing. He had been on a nonstop marathon since his arrival as a runner at the Merc in 1953 while still a law student. Melamed would remain as special counsel, an unsalaried post he held since departing as Merc chairman in 1977.

"As special counsel, I plan to continue serving the best interests of our Exchange on a federal level," he explained. "But I will no longer allow myself to be as comprehensively involved in the day-to-day CME management as in these many past years." That meant he intended no longer to attend board or executive committee meetings, nor, as he put it, to maintain a role in the ongoing Merc decision process. At the time, he was also coordinator of the floor planning and services committee and chairman of the influential financial instruments steering committee, which approved and marketed new contracts. Monieson described Melamed's new role as a change "from an operational manager to basically a strategic planner."

Melamed had often spoken of decreasing his role but was dissuaded by associates from carrying out his avowed intent. Now, he felt, the time was right. There was the new building, and an array of new products. He had also helped

lead the industry's battle to gain the right to trade options on agricultural products, and he had participated in the Merc's transition to a new leadership as
Yeutter prepared to leave early in 1985 to be succeeded by Brodsky. Moreover,
Melamed assured the Exchange members that the cavalcade of products would
not slow down. "The plans already in place for our next wave of option contracts
will materially strengthen our options presence and again broaden our over-all
base," he said in the 7 November letter.

Melamed would be sorely missed. "He is the guts of the Exchange," brooded
trader Ronald Wild, upon reading Melamed's letter. No one ever doubted
Melamed's influence. He had become the industry's most persuasive lobbyist
and was considered a force behind the skyrocketing financial futures industry,
a market that transformed a tiny exchange once known mostly for insider trading cabals into a worldwide power. In 1972 the Merc's foray into financial
futures with the International Monetary Market was "a scary thing because nobody understood the concept of trading currency futures," recalled former Merc
vice-chairman Barry Lind. "You had to be a blind believer."

Melamed had sold the idea to traders one by one; he even wrote promotional material for the new contracts. Then he appointed "team captains" to
monitor the pits and to remind members of their pledges to trade the new contract. "He was able to get membership backing for projects they didn't even
understand," marveled former Merc president Everette B. Harris. And in 1984,
when a group of powerful floor brokers offered discount commissions in a grab
for market share, it was Melamed as chief troubleshooter who placed a midnight telephone call to their leader with the reminder, "By hurting the entire
Exchange, you hurt yourself." The group backed off, averting civil war among
the brokers.

"I love the power, the decision-making," Melamed conceded two months
before he issued the November letter. "That's hard to let go of." In an exchange
full of thousands of risk-takers, no one was giving odds that Melamed, though
cutting back, was going to remain on the sidelines for long. In fact, five months
after Melamed's announcement that he was cutting back on his day-to-day activities, he issued another letter to the Merc membership. This one was shorter
and it sparkled with literary flair:

> The other day I was asked by an out of town acquaintance how I was enjoying
> my new free time. Alas, I had to tell him the truth: To paraphrase Mark Twain,
> News of my early retirement is grossly exaggerated.
>
> So, notwithstanding the chorus of "I told you so's" that this letter is bound
> to provoke, I thought it advisable to set the record straight. The truth, as most
> informed observers know, is that I was not allowed to withdraw from CME affairs
> as much as I had originally planned.
>
> Indeed, at the behest of Chairman Monieson, Dr. Yeutter, William Brodsky
> and all the other senior members of our Board, I agreed for the time being to
> continue with my previous responsibilities on the Board as well as direction of

the Financial Instruments Steering Committee. Their arguments, that it was not a propitious moment to carry out my announced intent, ultimately won.

Oh well, as Robert Burns told us, "The best laid schemes o'mice an'men gang aft a-glee." I just thought you ought to know.

Very truly yours,
Leo Melamed

Melamed was back in the full Merc picture by mid-April. There was too much to be done. The competition was heating up as never before as the complexity of the marketplace became more pervasive. On 1 June 1985 Brodsky succeeded Yeutter, who left the Merc following his appointment by President Reagan as U.S. Trade Representative, a sensitive and highly visible ambassadorial and cabinet level post that includes responsibility for conducting trade negotiations on behalf of the U.S. government. "This position gave him and consequently the Merc instant credibility in the international market," Monieson said at the time. For nearly a decade the Merc's trading volume grew; more than 56 million contracts were traded in 1985 to capture 31.6 percent market share.[2] During the period in which Yeutter had served as Merc president, from July 1978 to June 1985, Exchange volume had grown from 15 million contracts and revenues of $12 million to 55 million contracts and revenues of $55 million.

By 1984 the CBOT's share of the worldwide futures business stood at 46.7 percent, compared with the Merc's 28.2 percent share. For the Merc, the activity was reflected in the value of membership prices: A full Merc membership had risen from $155,00 in October 1984 to $175,000; an IMM membership from $115,000 to $158,000; and an IOM membership from $38,000 to $60,000. A Board of Trade membership, however, had slipped from $250,000 in October 1984 to $185,000 in October 1985. Over the same period an options membership on the Philadelphia Stock Exchange dropped from $82,000 to $32,000. A seat on the New York Futures Exchange had fallen to a low of $1,500 with the annual dues of $3,000 double the value of a membership. The competition in financial futures had obviously heated up. Now the New York Stock Exchange had the NYFE; the American Stock Exchange, the ACE; and both the Chicago Board Options Exchange and The Philadelphia Stock Exchange traded currency options.

With the addition of options on Eurodollars, the Merc became the only exchange to trade options in four major product areas—agriculture, currencies, interest rates, and stock indexes. Groundwork also had been laid for the 1986 introduction of four more new contracts: futures on ECUs (European currency units) and T-bills and options on Japanese yen and Canadian dollars. Despite the rosy prospects for growth, the Merc took a conservative approach, paring its 1985 budget by 10 percent and virtually freezing staff hiring. The Board was also losing one of its stalwarts, Carl Anderson, who had been a Merc governor for 11 terms—22 years. During that time he had been an officer, a member of the executive committee, and a major proponent of the agricultural complex.

For investors in the stock market, 1985 was a year of confusion. Early in the year, the dollar had ceased its long climb against other currencies. With Japanese long-term bond rates at 7 percent and the Tokyo stock market trading at around 30 times earnings, American investors turned their attention to international mutual funds and foreign markets with such schemes as asset allocation. The action on Wall Street continued to be fueled by the free market fury of leveraged buyouts and takeovers like General Electric's acquisition of RCA. The realities of supply and demand had also grabbed the world's cartels. Attempts to fix prices of tin, cocoa, rubber, sugar, and coffee had failed. The invisible hand even forced OPEC to shed its price-fixing oil strategy like an outdated wardrobe.

Meanwhile, the foreign exchange markets were sending a clear message: The United States was a threadbare trillionaire living beyond its means—who could no longer afford to do so. The key, of course, was the negative balance of trade situation. Only a positive balance would mean greater demand for a country's currency. If a country other than the United States had racked up such deficits, the rest of the world would have forced a correction by simply refusing to accept any more of its currency. For most other countries, that would have meant dipping into the International Monetary Fund for a quick-fix loan. But fortunately for the United States, the world cannot ignore its dollars because many economies are too dependent on American purchases. Even more important, the dollar is the world's reserve currency and principal means of international exchange. Thus, to exact reform from the United States, the world's other industrialized nations had but one choice: to push the dollar down.

On 22 September 1985 the so-called Group of Five (the finance ministers from the United States, United Kingdom, Germany, France, and Japan) deliberately set in motion the decline of the dollar. Actually, market forces had already sent the dollar into a funk to end its four-year-long bull market. By early September the dollar had fallen 23 percent against the Deutsche mark, 33 percent against the British pound, and 10 percent against the Japanese yen. The Group of Five's action was taken during the final stages of consolidation, Melamed later observed in a commentary supporting flexible exchange rates that was published in *The Wall Street Journal*.

Indeed, with the prospect of lower interest rates, the dollar had responded to the added pressure. "Had the ministers not acted," Melamed wrote, "I dare say free-market forces would have achieved a similar result soon enough." Melamed had railed against the rekindled notion among some U.S. congressmen to go back to fixed exchange rates.[3] By February 1987, the dollar's fall said that the industrialized nations had reached a point of diminishing returns. So Japan, West Germany, and the others bought dollars to cushion the sliding American currency. Some $150 billion swirled daily though the currency markets during that time as the fragile dollar backslid against the yen and mark at even a hint that the United States budget deficit would grow larger.

Nowhere was the reaction to the fate of the dollar more evident than on the floor of the Merc. For some currency traders such as Gordon McClendon, who grew up on Chicago's South Side and joined the Merc in 1986, the tension started long before he'd entered the pit where he traded the yen contracts.[4] On one particular day at 1:00 A.M. Chicago time (4:00 P.M. Tokyo time), a telephone call from Tokyo roused McClendon from a fitful sleep. To his tired ears, the caller seemed to be muttering numbers in rapid-fire succession, but McClendon caught the essence of what was said: "The yen looks lower . . . it's moving lower." The stream of words was devoid of vigor and power, yet like a bucket of ice water they suddenly roused McClendon to his senses. Now he was wide-eyed and anxious.

"Sell ten," he instructed the caller. "Sell ten." From that point he was on the phone every 15 minutes for another quote. Between calls, he was mesmerized by his computer terminal, which flashed the yen's decline as he lapsed into a Star Wars monologue: "The market is 126.5 . . . it's 40 lower . . . the trade figures must be bullish. . . . " By 5:30 A.M.—two hours before trading started—he was already at the Merc, gazing at more computers and chatting with colleagues as he prepared a trading strategy. There were other factors that affected exchange rates as well; interest and inflation rates, monetary reserves, seasonal flows of funds, civil unrest, and wars were among them. But on this day, it was the U.S. trade figures—released at 8:30 A.M. Washington time—flashed across a television monitor, computer terminal, or wire-service ticker that ignited the trading crowd (and money managers elsewhere) into an explosion of noise and action.

That's how it was by the mid-1980s. There was only one market—the world. Everyone from New York to New Zealand was using computer and telephone clout to usher in investment opportunities. It was no longer enough for a foreign exchange trader to eyeball his or her own market; everyone had to watch stock, bond, and options markets and trade in these instruments in German marks, Swiss francs, and Japanese yen and the broad range of long- and short-term interest rate products. Moreover, making one's way through the labyrinthine menu of systems to find commodity prices or stock quotations or interest rates could be done from a computer at home or upstairs in an office away from the tumult of a trading floor. Useful information had to be easily accessible in the drum fire volatile markets. Better, cheaper, and faster were the links to the bottom line.

The Merc claimed five of the industry's ten most actively traded contracts. Ten of its futures each accounted for more than 1 million contracts traded—more than any other futures exchange. In its first full year the SIMEX traded more than a half million contracts, mostly in the Eurodollars, and work had begun on a futures contract based on the Nikkei Stock Average, the most widely used stock average in Japan, to be introduced in the third quarter 1986. The Merc scored its ninth consecutive annual volume record in 1985: Some 56,548,476 contracts traded—a 26 percent increase—compared with the 1984 total of 44,870,922. During the year, the single-day volume high was recorded on 11 December with

354,069 contracts traded—104,000 contracts more than were traded for all of 1964. New contracts listed in 1985 that helped push volume to record levels were options on live hogs and options on three-month Eurodollar futures. Another new contract listed that year was SPOC, the acronym for S&P over-the-counter industrial stock price index futures.

Each year the Merc drew more than 100,000 people to its visitor's gallery and trading floor to observe free enterprise like a drama unfolding in a theater in the round. They came on buses as part of a city tour that included the heart of Chicago's financial district. Many simply walked off the street spontaneously to satisfy curiosity. But there was nothing spontaneous about the Chinese delegation that paid a visit on 26 July 1985. Led by Li Xiannian, president of the People's Republic of China, and his wife, Madame Lin Jiamei, the delegation numbered 60. President Li was accompanied by an additional 20 members in an official American delegation that included Selwa Roosevelt, U.S. Chief of Protocol, and Arthur W. Hummel, Jr., American ambassador to the People's Republic of China.

The groundwork for the visit had begun five years earlier when the Merc hosted representatives from the Bank of China. In September 1984 the Bank invited members of the Merc's SIMEX steering committee to participate in the opening of SIMEX and then to visit Beijing. Having the president of Communist China look in on the bastion of free enterprise in the Windy City had all the cachet of a first-rate diplomatic coup. And while the trading of the Merc felt the effects of many major world events over the years, there were few instances in which trading activities stopped. Li's presence in the visitor's gallery on that Friday morning touched off wild applause and cheering among the traders.

Why not? History was being made on the floor of the Chicago Mercantile Exchange. Li Xiannian was not only the first head of state ever to visit the CME, but also the first Chinese president to visit the United States. The 80-year-old Li, who had fought in Mao Zedong's guerrilla army in the 1940s, became president in June 1983, the first Chinese head of state since the end of the Cultural Revolution in 1969. As he gazed down upon the color and excitement of the floor below, he wondered whether or not all the tumult was staged for the occasion.

"Your Excellency," said Brian Monieson, "I assure you the floor action is not staged. In fact, it is probably a little less hectic than normal since Fridays are usually quieter than other days."

At this time, the agricultural markets were struggling against tough odds brought on by the curse of glut. Farmers, stricken by the plagues of shrinking demand, debts, falling land values, and overproduction, searched for schemes to boost crop prices and head off creditors. The salutary effects of letting the market run its course had raised the specter of bankruptcy for farmers from the Oregon plateau to the piedmont of the Carolinas. The harsh economic realities brought little hope to the corn fields of middle America—and to the trading floors of the exchanges, where many locals in the grain and meat pits began to pull up stakes and migrate to the action of the financial instruments, which were dominating the futures markets (at the CBOT agriculture futures had plummeted from 64 percent of total volume in 1980 to a mere 25 percent in 1985) as never before.

Financial futures, including interest rate, equity and currency contracts had rocketed from 18 percent in 1980 to 59 percent in 1985, according to a survey by the Futures Industry Association. Precious metals and petroleum futures made up most of the remainder of the market. By 1986, both the equity and financial futures markets were still pushing skyward. But a tragic start to the new year occurred in January, when the space shuttle Challenger exploded before the eyes of millions of viewers shortly after takeoff. An explosion of another kind rocked Wall Street in the following months as the SEC began a series of insider trading actions against a group of hard-driving, high-earning investment bankers. All the while, the dramatic rise in the stock market strained the logic of the most astute analysts. How high could the market go? In January the Dow industrial average roared to 1600. In February it passed 1700; in March, 1800. At mid-year the average stood at 1900. Most analysts were convinced that the Great Bull Market of the 1980s would continue its charge into the next decade with, of course, a correction or two along the way. There, in 1986 looming on the financial horizon, was the tantalizing prospect of the Dow Jones industrial average reaching 2000.

In mid-January 1986 the Merc began trading the European currency unit (ECU). The ECU—developed in 1980 by what were then the ten Common Market nations—is a ten-currency composite or "basket" of currencies pegged to the prevailing exchange rates and the amount of each currency in circulation. Although it is a monetary standard for the European Community based on the relative strength of each country's economy in the EC, there have never been ECU bills. Instead ECU credit cards and bonds are issued. The ECU, in fact, had grown as a popular medium of exchange for trade and finance transactions throughout the world and by 1984 it had become the third most frequently used vehicle for new Eurobond issues. Dominique Rambure, a director of Credit Lyonnais and chairman of the ECU clearing committee in Paris, rang the opening bell on 15 January, opening trading on the Merc's first new contract for 1986.[5]

The ECU was yet another example of how the world's financial markets had grown more sophisticated and how banks, corporations, and money managers were trying new tools to hedge currency rate fluctuation. As companies with far-flung international operations used tools like the ECU as a standard for intercompany transactions, ECU-denominated bonds played a growing part in international capital markets with the World Bank and other international bodies using them.

A week before the ECU contracts began trading, the Merc had chosen Tokyo as the site for its second overseas office with plans to staff it before the year's end. Six years earlier, the Merc had become the first offshore exchange to open an office in London. Brodsky's first official trip as president of the Merc was to the Far East, where he visited exchanges in Hong Kong and Tokyo; he also paid a visit to the SIMEX. Brodsky's report was to the point: Asia was the emerging market for the Merc's products. Brodsky thus recommended a marketing office in Tokyo. The Tokyo venture indicated not only the Merc's interest in Asia, but also Asia's interest in the Merc. The offset trading link with the SIMEX reinforced the notion that tremendous growth potential existed in that part of the world.

The Merc, as the Board saw it, was following the global evolution of the financial markets. "The thousands of Japanese and other Asians who have visited our Exchange in the past year or so reveal just how great the desire for information is," said Brodsky, who in 1985 had already met with officials of Japan's powerful Ministry of Finance,[6] the arm of the Japanese government that oversees the securities and financial futures industries. By early November 1986, the Merc had appointed Takeo Arakawa as managing director of the Tokyo office. He was an ideal choice. A spunky man speaking fluent English, Arakawa knew his way around the Ministry of Finance, where he had worked from 1946 to 1964 before joining Nippon Kohkan Company, a major Japanese steel maker. Four years of Arakawa's tenure at Nippon were spent at the company's New York City office.

Several Japanese securities firms were already represented at the CME, and several domestic CME members had set up shop in Tokyo. Japan's first experiment with financial futures came in October 1985, when the Tokyo Stock Exchange listed yen bond futures. Eventually, it was the highly influential and somewhat Byzantine Ministry of Finance that took control of financial futures. Founded in 1870, the Ministry of Finance is older than even the Japanese cabinet and has influence that bureaucrats in Washington, London, or Bonn can only fantasize about. Although its regulatory power over the financial system is detailed, its administrative guidelines can be somewhat vague.

Liberalization would increase on 22 May 1987—not coincidentally, the very day the Merc opened its Tokyo office—when Japanese financial firms were allowed to deal in their own accounts in overseas futures markets. The Japanese had used the floor of the CME as a classroom. Such financial powerhouses as Mitsui Bank and Nikko Securities quietly bought seats in an effort to learn all they could about the markets and to train the staffers that they needed to trade in Japan. Strategic planning among Japanese firms—keyed to what the Merc had started nearly 15 years earlier, when it launched the IMM—prompted the Nomura Research Institute to forecast Japan's role in the world markets during the coming decade: "In the U.S., financial futures and options have become an integral part of the financial market to such an extent . . . that many feel that securities investment without financial futures and options is inconceivable. There is a real possibility that such a situation will develop also in Japan within the next ten years."

Development of the international marketplace was among the critical issues now facing the Merc. The domestic markets were far from mature, but the international markets remained virtually untapped. In January, 1986, Sandner—who had served as Merc chairman from 1980 to 1982—was elected to a fourth one-year term as chairman.[7] He replaced Monieson as head of the 29-member board that included three public and three industry governors. Sandner's election brought with it the benefit of continuity that had long given the Merc a leadership dimension few other exchanges could match. Not only would the new chairman help guide the Merc in international waters, but he would also carry the banner of vigorous opposition to two major regulatory issues. Earlier in the month, the CFTC had ordered the Merc and CBOT to establish audit trails capable of tracing trading activity to the nearest minute. The second CFTC proposal called for a stringent increase in the minimum capitalization standards for trading firms.

Both exchanges, allied over the issues, came out swinging. Over the next two months, verbal skirmishes between the Merc and CFTC took place as Brodsky, Sandner, and Melamed voiced concern during Senate hearings that dealt with CFTC reauthorization. "Unless the issues which our industry is bringing before you at these hearings are favorably addressed," opened Melamed, "we will become subject to a repressive yoke of federal regulations which make little sense and are the result of inexperience or motivations beyond our comprehension."

As for the CFTC's one-minute time stamping rule,[8] Melamed called it "the foremost example of regulatory meddling in areas which the Commission inadequately comprehends." But the CFTC, which charged the Chicago exchanges with dragging their heels on the audit trail issue, was quick to point out that there were already several exchanges—the Kansas City Board of Trade, the Philadelphia Board of Trade, the Minneapolis Grain Exchange, and the New York Mercantile Exchange—using one-minute systems. A few years earlier the Merc had voluntarily instituted a system of computerized surveillance over brokers and traders. An updated version of the plan, which Melamed called "consistent with the requirements of the open outcry auction system," had been rejected by the CFTC.

In April, the Merc submitted a counterproposal for increased capital requirements to the CFTC. Barry Lind, a "number cruncher" that Melamed had relied on so often over the years, was chairman of the committee responsible for responding to the CFTC. Lind had viewed the CFTC proposal, issued 5 August 1985, as grappling with only one element of risk. He instead proposed a three-step procedure based on margin as a measure of risk that resulted in a 48 percent increase in the capital requirements of the firms in the CME study.[9]

By now the Merc was well entrenched in the business of options. During the first week in March, options on Japanese yen futures began trading. It was the fourth option on a currency future as the Merc boosted its efforts, following the CFTC's decision in the previous year to expand its financial options pilot program.[10] A month later, on 10 April, Richard Thomas, president of First Chicago Corporation, signaled the start of trading in options on T-bill futures.

The celebration of the opening of the new CME trading floor at 30 S. Wacker on November 28, 1983. From far left to right are Chicago Mayor Harold Washington, Illinois Representative and Chairman of the House Ways and Means Committee Daniel Rostenkowski, CME President Clayton Yeutter, and CME Chairman Brian Monieson.

Traders and staff gather for the official opening day commemorative photograph. The new trading floor at 30 S. Wacker Drive opened for business on November 28, 1983.

Illinois Governor Jim Thompson opens the Live Cattle options contract on October 30, 1984. With him are, from left to right, CME President Clayton Yeutter, CME Special Counsel Leo Melamed, CME Chairman Brian Monieson, Cattle Committee Chairman Jack Sandner, and CME Public Governor and past President of the National Cattlemen's Association W. J. (Dub) Waldrip.

Nobel Laureate George Stigler rings the opening bell for the Eurodollar options contract on March 20, 1985. Helping him with the countdown are CME Chairman Brian Monieson, CME Executive Committee Chairman and Special Counsel Leo Melamed, and CME President Designate Bill Brodsky.

People's Republic of China President Li Xiannian acknowledges his reception on the CME trading floor during his July 26, 1985, visit.

Taking part in the opening ceremonies for the Nikkei 225 contract at SIMEX on September 3, 1986 are, from left to right: Akinobu Kojima, President & CEO, QUICK Corp; Ang Swee Tian, General Manager, SIMEX; Ko Morita, President & CEO, NKS; Ng Kok Song, Chairman, Monetary Authority of Singapore; CME Executive Committee Chairman and Special Counsel Leo Melamed; and CME Chairman Jack Sandner.

December 15, 1986, marks the day the CME and NYSE agree on changes for the expiration of the S&P 500 contract to deal with the so-called "Triple Witching" phenomenon. From left to right are NYSE Chairman John Phelan, CME Executive Committee Chairman and Special Counsel Leo Melamed, NYSE President Robert Birnbaum, CME Chairman Jack Sandner, and CME President Bill Brodsky.

U.S. Trade Representative Clayton Yeutter is "welcomed back" at a reception in honor of his return visit to the CME on February 20, 1987. From left to right are former CME Chairman Brian Monieson, CME Executive Committee Chairman and Special Counsel Leo Melamed, Clayton Yeutter, former CME Chairman Larry Rosenberg, CME Chairman Jack Sandner, and CME President Bill Brodsky.

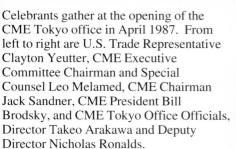

Celebrants gather at the opening of the CME Tokyo office in April 1987. From left to right are U.S. Trade Representative Clayton Yeutter, CME Executive Committee Chairman and Special Counsel Leo Melamed, CME Chairman Jack Sandner, CME President Bill Brodsky, and CME Tokyo Office Officials, Director Takeo Arakawa and Deputy Director Nicholas Ronalds.

The October 19, 1987, stock market crash creates a variety of reactions from traders on the CME floor. Pictured is CME trader Ben Rubin.

Traders and staff regroup at the end of the trading day after the October 19, 1987, stock market crash. (COPYRIGHTED 10/20/87, CHICAGO TRIBUNE COMPANY ALL RIGHTS RESERVED, USED WITH PERMISSION.)

CME Chairman Jack Sandner explains the workings of the trading floor to Australian Prime Minister Robert J. L. Hawke on June 20, 1988.

A view of the CME trading floor "after hours" as it is used as the site of the October 21, 1988, Illinois Olympian Salute.

From left to right, Richard Grasso, President, New York Stock Exchange; Kenneth R. Leibler, President, American Stock Exchange; Joseph Hardiman, President, National Association of Securities Dealers; and CME President Bill Brodsky testify in Washington, D.C., before the House Subcommittee on Telecommunications and Finance on September 28, 1989, regarding the stock market crash of October 1987. (COPYRIGHTED, MARTY LAVOR, ALL RIGHTS RESERVED, USED WITH PERMISSION.)

Russian visitors to the Chicago Mercantile Exchange participate in a mock trading session on August 23, 1990. (COPYRIGHTED 8/23/90, CHICAGO TRIBUNE COMPANY, ALL RIGHTS RESERVED, USED WITH PERMISSION.)

CME Chairman John Geldermann demonstrates the GLOBEX ® trading system screen to visiting former Japanese Prime Minister Nakasone during his visit on September 12, 1990. Former CME Chairman and Senior Policy Advisor Jack Sandner, Executive Vice President and COO Rick Kilcollin, and Vice President of GLOBEX Marketing Jack Walsh watch the presentation.

CME and CBOT leaders pose beneath a bust of Lenin during a jointly sponsored trip to Moscow in November 1990. From left to right are CME President Bill Brodsky, CBOT President Thomas Donovan, CME Executive Committee Chairman and Special Counsel Leo Melamed, CBOT Chairman William O'Connor, and CME Chairman John Geldermann.

CME Chairman Jack Sandner delivers testimony to the Senate Agriculture Committee on February 20, 1991, as it considers Commodity Futures Trading Commission reauthorization. Looking on is CBOT Chairman William O'Connor. (PHOTO COURTESY OF THE CHICAGO BOARD OF TRADE.)

President of Mexico Carlos Salinas de Gortari (*center*) demonstrates free trade with CME President Bill Brodsky (*left*) and CME Chairman Jack Sandner (*right*) while on the CME floor on April 11, 1991.

Chairman of the Joint Chiefs of Staff General Colin Powell addresses CME members and employees on the trading floor during his May 12, 1991, "Welcome Home" visit to Chicago. Accompanying him are, from left to right, CME President Bill Brodsky, CME Governor Norma Newberger, CME Chairman Emeritus Leo Melamed, and CME Chairman Jack Sandner.

Exchange leaders and traders celebrate thirty years of trading Frozen Pork Belly futures on September 17, 1991. From left to right are CME President Bill Brodsky; Chairman Emeritus Leo Melamed; Glenn Andersen, former Chairman of the CME's New Commodities Committee; Chairman Jack Sandner; former Chairman and currently retired member Bill Katz; and Joseph Fox and Gary Mainiero, both members.

Ireland's President Mary Robinson tours the CME trading floor with CME
Chairman Jack Sandner during her first official visit to
the United States in October 1991.

The CME trading floor is the signing site for a friendship pact between the cities of Chicago
and Mexico City on October 10, 1991. From left to right, seated are The Honorable Richard
M. Daley, Mayor, City of Chicago, and The Honorable Manuel Camacho Solis, Mayor,
Mexico City. From left to right, standing are Mrs. Alejandro Carrillo; CME Chairman Jack
Sandner; The Honorable Alejandro Carrillo Castro, Consul General of Mexico; and CME
President Bill Brodsky.

Chairman Jack Sandner presents a CME trading jacket to President George Bush during his historic visit to the Exchange on December 6, 1991. Looking on are CME Chairman Emeritus Leo Melamed and CME President Bill Brodsky.

On December 9, 1991, President Bill Brodsky, Chairman Emeritus Leo Melamed, and Chairman Jack Sandner sample an anniversary cake in celebration of the CME's ten years of trading in Eurodollar Futures contracts.

On February 13, 1992, the CME launches the S&P MidCap 400 Index contract. From left to right are CME Chairman Jack Sandner, CME President Bill Brodsky, and Patrick Ryan, Chairman of the Aon Corporation.

Former Soviet President Mikhail Gorbachev receives a close up view of the CME's idea of "free markets for free men" during his unprecedented visit to the Exchange on May 7, 1992. He is accompanied on the trading floor by CME Chairman Jack Sandner.

CME Chairman Jack Sandner presents Mr. Gorbachev with a customized trading jacket to commemorate his visit to the Exchange.

A glimpse into the future of futures trading shows testing of a prototype hand-held A.U.D.I.T. trading terminal on the floor of the CME.

CME, CBOT, and Reuters officials begin celebration festivities for the GLOBEX ® trading system launch on June 25, 1992. From left to right are CBOT Chairman William O'Connor, GLOBEX Chairman Leo Melamed, GLOBEX Managing Director Gary Ginter, CME Chairman Jack Sandner, CME President Bill Brodsky, Reuters Chief Operating Officer of GLOBEX Murray Finebaum, Reuters Managing Director of Transaction Products Rosalyn Wilton, and CBOT President Thomas Donovan.

From left to right, CME Chairman Jack Sandner, GLOBEX ® Chairman Leo Melamed, and CME President Bill Brodsky pose for a June 26, 1992, nationwide advertisement in recognition of the Exchange's 2,724 Members and 92 Clearing Firms. The copy read:

EXPANDING THE ENGINES OF LIQUIDITY.

Record-level open interest in excess of 3 1/2 million contracts. Daily volume up 25% over a record-breaking 1991. Options trading over double the 1991 rate. Membership prices highest of any U.S. exchange. And rising. This is the kind of unprecedented growth and experience that have become synonymous with the Chicago Mercantile Exchange.

And unprecedented growth leads to unprecedented expansion. To accommodate regular trading hours growth, construction is beginning on a second trading floor. When completed, the CME will be the world's largest trading facility. And to accommodate worldwide demand for CME currency and interest rate futures and options contracts, trading hours are being expanded to nearly 24 hours a day via GLOBEX, the world's first global electronic trading system.

More liquidity. More volume. More trading space. More hours. More and more reasons the world is coming to the Chicago Mercantile Exchange to manage risk.

CME Chairman Jack Sandner, CME President Bill Brodsky, Nobel Prize–winning economist and CME Public Governor Merton Miller, and Stephen Friedman, Co-Chairman of Goldman Sachs & Company, preside over the bell ringing for the opening of the newest CME contract, the Goldman Sachs Commodity Index on July 28, 1992.

For the month of April, the Merc had posted a record trading volume of more than 6 million contracts. Stock index futures led the way with an unprecedented record of 1,847,177 contracts, up 71 percent from the volume in April 1985. The S&P activity reflected the breathtaking stock market expansion. Already the bull market had lasted for 44 months, well past the 30-month average life of postwar bull markets. The momentum encouraged some prognosticators to predict the Dow's march to a peak of 3600 by 1988. Others were forecasting 2700 by late 1988.

Everything, it seemed, was on a record-paced course. On 21 May currency options traded at the Merc ended the day totaling more than 79,000 contracts—the greatest number of currency options traded in a single day on any exchange. Options on the yen futures had led the pack with a volume of 64,673, more than a five-fold increase over the previous Merc single-day record of 11,766 set on 9 May. Such volume, in turn, drove seat prices to new highs. On 22 May the price of Index and Options Market (IOM) membership reached a record $98,000, up 30 percent since January and double the cost of a year earlier.[11]

Early in June, Brodsky turned his attention to the marketing division, headed by senior vice-president Barbara A. Richards. Four areas, each under a vice-president, were set up to reflect the Merc's business operations as a whole: commodity marketing, agricultural futures and options; international financial marketing—financial products including the Merc's London office, Tokyo office, and the SIMEX link; domestic financial marketing, the U.S. and Canadian programs; and market development, special projects for domestic and international marketing.

The reorganization coincided with the new post that had been created for Michael Apatoff, a former congressional aide, who took charge as the Merc's chief operating officer on 1 June. He reported directly to Brodsky. Though Apatoff knew little about the futures markets, he had solid government contacts from his work as a special aide to Majority Whip Thomas S. Foley, a Washington Democrat. Apatoff's early initiative came a few weeks later, when he helped create a separate division for the Merc's clearing organization, which matched buy and sell orders along with monitoring the risk exposure of clearing firms.[12]

Late in June, the Merc was preparing to trade the fourth futures contract, the British pound, in the mutual offset system (MOS) link with the SIMEX. The other existing MOS currency contracts included the Deutsche mark, Eurodollar, and Japanese yen. It had been nearly two years since the SIMEX venture began (on 7 September 1984), allowing investors to trade a futures position at the Merc or SIMEX and offset, or liquidate, the resulting position at the same or the other exchange.

Since the SIMEX opened its first trading pit à la Merc, it had managed to attract non-Chinese locals. One of them was Steven Schoenfeld, a 27-year-old former Fulbright scholar, who became the first American to trade Japanese stock index futures on the SIMEX. Like a wandering mariner lured by a foreign land and a new market, Schoenfeld in May 1986 bid farewell to his family and friends in New York City and headed for Singapore, where a year earlier he had done graduate work. First, however, he stopped in Chicago to take the Merc's floor orientation program to learn more about trading. "I figured that if I could learn the ropes in Chicago, then the smaller Singapore market would be less intimidating," he reasoned.

While his mind told him one thing, his gut said something else on 1 August, that first day he entered the SIMEX trading pit. "I could feel my stomach churning and not just because of the chili peppers in my lunchtime bowl of noodles," he recalled. Schoenfeld continued, "I felt pressure to perform even though I was a novice. Many other locals looked up to me—and not because of my relative height. The CME was SIMEX's role model, and being American, they expected more from me than other new traders. At the same time, I hoped to discover whether the Chicago-style risk-taking could be successfully transplanted in Asia."

As he planted his feet in the yen pit, the chattering in Chinese and "Singlish" bombarded him. "Waaah, a new Ang Moh trader," shouted an inscrutable face.[13] And Schoenfeld said to himself, "Oh boy, what am I doing here, 12,000 miles from home with a 25 million yen exposure?" Eventually Schoenfeld found out that, indeed, risk taking is universal, as did John Morse a year later, when he left Chicago and the Merc, where he was a local in the S&P pit, to become an American in Paris trading bond futures in the Marché à Terme des Instruments Financiers (MATIF). Opened in February 1986, the MATIF adopted Chicago-style pit trading and by 1987 it cleared more than 11 million long bond contracts.

What the Merc had started in 1972 with the IMM and currencies had grown into a global network of financial futures and options markets with scores of trading floors competing for markets. By 1987 more than 310 million futures contracts traded worldwide, representing some 350 different financial and agricultural products. Not only were the exchanges feeling the competitive heat from one another, but the banks were designing over-the-counter products for the management of risk.

Perhaps even more threatening to the open outcry style was the Exchange of Futures for Physical (EFP) transaction, by which, say, a basket of stocks underlying an index futures contract is used to close out the contract at the expiration of the contract period. Or in the case of oil, paper barrels are converted to real oil at the expiration of the contract. Thus, the EFP—generally executed after exchange hours—bypassed the standard cash settlement mechanism—and the trading pit of an exchange. The rapidly growing EFP market was without a doubt taking its toll. During the period from June through August 1986, EFPs accounted for 2.1 percent of the Merc's overall futures volume, and nearly 98 percent of those EFPs occurred in four major currency contracts.[14] There were several hundred billion dollars a day swooshing through this market, which was growing at an annual rate of 116 percent. Such growth, Merc economist Rick Kilcollin told a meeting of the CME's strategic planning committee on 28 October 1986, "demonstrates strong market demand for services not currently provided by the exchange floor."

Merc customers had been using EFPs for block trades (involving large volume and large amounts of money between two institutions) that were impossible to execute on the trading floor because of liquidity, size, and price constraints. In short, EFPs were used to get a large order executed at one price without being split up. Depending on the market, the use of EFPs varied. With currencies, for example, EFPs were used to compensate for the differences in time zones; with agricultural products, users desired delivery at locations other than exchange-designated delivery points. Or they wanted a product altered from exchange specifications.

Daytime EFP trades, in addition to those of the overnight market, took place because they reduced the risk in spread transactions between spot and futures positions. As a rule, however, EFPs were initiated after Merc trading hours; most of the EFP transactions took place 45 minutes after the Merc closed, just as the Singapore and Hong Kong markets first opened and immediately before European market opening. EFPs were also used by customers to obtain one-price fills of orders. Simply, the large institutional traders would probably go elsewhere if the Merc restricted these trades. The four major firms that at the time had been doing sizeable EFP business were E.F. Hutton, Refco, Shearson/American Express, and Drexel Burnham Lambert. These firms basically handled EFP transactions in one of three ways: as large block trades on the floor of the exchange, by trading at night in the interbank market with European banks, and with limit or stop orders throughout the night.

EFPs had become a major after-hours market, with night trades accounting for 80 percent of all currency EFP volume. Yet despite the positive influence on the Merc's foreign exchange business, EFPs were a cumbersome solution to the needs of market users. Now there were serious questions to consider: How should the Merc respond to the growth of the currency EFP trading? How should the Merc accommodate demand for block trading—at least 20 percent of all EFP volume were block trades—in currencies and other contracts? Should the Merc open earlier? Did it make sense to establish a Merc facility for night trading? Were elaborate computers the solution?

These were questions not easily answered. For the strategic planning committee, there was no question regarding what was needed: a way to accommodate the demand for 24-hour markets. Finding the strategy to meet that demand was another matter. It would take imagination, planning on a global scale, and some political maneuvering as well. It would also take a great deal of soul-searching; part of the solution would surely tamper with sacred ground that Merc leadership had vociferously defended over the years, begging the toughest question of all. What would be the fate of open outcry?

29

Seeds of Volatility

How far had the Chicago Mercantile Exchange come since currencies began trading in 1972, when the International Monetary Market traded 144,000 contracts? That volume was now being surpassed during an average four hours of trading. On the eve of the IMM's first anniversary, Melamed wrote a letter to the membership which, in part, stated, "The new era will afford us the opportunity to expand our potential into other areas within the monetary frame of reference.... We must be willing and ready to explore all possibilities."

Those pioneering currencies reflected close economic ties with Europe. The markets of the late 1980s showed a growing economic interdependence on the nations of the Pacific Rim. In addition to its trading rights on the Japanese yen, the Merc had an exclusive license to trade futures on the Nikkei 225 and Nikkei 500 stock averages, which represent the Japanese stock market. (On 3 September 1986 the Nikkei 225 futures contract already began trading on the SIMEX.)[1] The Australian dollar was set to be traded the following year.

Government debt, world trade and international investment had dramatically increased the flow of capital and its inherent risks. The term *risk management* became a part of nearly every multinational's lexicon as domestic and foreign companies alike sought to hedge the vagaries of currencies and interest rates the world over. Now continents half the world away were inseparably bound by the microcircuit that turned the marketplace into a perpetual insomniac that dared not sleep.

The Merc's venture into the twilight of 24-hour trading began in 1981. As time zones longed for economic synchronization to compete internationally, an exchange had to have an instrument traded while its market slept. The fact that the universe of futures was expanding and not contracting gave focus to the other side of the world. The obvious route, Merc officials thought, was Hong

310

Kong, where currencies flowed freely in one of the world's great staging posts for trade, industry, and communications.

Melamed, Sandner, and Rosenberg traveled to Hong Kong, where beyond the neon glitz and Manhattanized skyline they were dismayed at what they found. "The community was divided," said Melamed. "The British didn't talk to the Chinese. The Chinese wanted their own exchange. And the government didn't talk to anybody. Who were we going to talk to if we were going to create this major step in the evolution of our markets?" There was also an undertow of anxiety tugging at the legs of the financial community over the prospect of Hong Kong's new landlord, the People's Republic of China, set to regain control after Great Britain's lease on the crown colony expires 30 June 1997.

At this time the Monetary Authority of Singapore (MAS) was reexamining the role of the Gold Exchange of Singapore (GES) in an effort to upgrade the island's status as a global financial center and to rekindle its smoldering gold market singed by insider manipulation. To this end, there was a push by some Singaporeans to tie in with an American futures exchange before rival Hong Kong did so. Among those who were pushing the hardest was Lim Ho Kee, the former deputy chairman of GES, and Ng Kok Song, a key MAS official. They were men after Melamed's own heart—positive, aggressive, single-minded— who would argue why things should work as opposed to why they shouldn't. Equally important, they understood futures markets.

In May 1982 the MAS invited the Merc to visit Singapore. Melamed, Sandner, and Monieson flew to Singapore for a get-acquainted meeting that merely touched on the possibility of a joint financial futures market between the two exchanges. The result of that trip left the Merc officials with a hopeful afterglow that Singapore—not Hong Kong—was the better prospect. They were impressed with Lim Ho Kee's knowledge of financial futures. "That was crucial," Melamed later explained. "We didn't have to start from the very beginning and so our threshold of understanding was a higher one." But it was in the following month, when Lim Ho Kee and Ng Kok Song came to the Merc, that things started to gel. The two had come to gather information about auditing methods and regulatory systems and to see the dynamics of a marketplace in bloom. From the Merc gallery they saw the expansive floor carpeted with traders bidding, buying, and selling in open outcry fashion; a free-form auction, some would say, gone mad, with all the elements, as the Exchange humorously put it in one of its guides called *The Merc at Work*, of primal scream, aerobic dancing, and the Battle of Hastings. Every trader was an auctioneer in a system that allowed only the best bid and offer to surface, while defying conventional wisdom: In the trading pits it was far better to be heard than to be seen. The law of the pit was simple enough. You couldn't bid below someone's higher bid, and you couldn't offer above someone's lower offer. Any trader willing to pay the highest price announced that, and all the lower bids were silenced.

There was enough energy emanating from the floor, it seemed, to stoke the market around the clock. Yet the notion of night trading sessions and 24-hour trading were on distant horizons. Even mutual offset with a Far East partner, it seemed, was a decade away, rather than a mere two years. Ho Kee convinced the Merc of two things: Mutual offset was the only way to succeed from the start and Singapore was likely the place where the Merc could make the deal it wanted. Such notions simmered at the Merc for a year.

In May 1983 Lim Ho Kee was back in Chicago with a contingent of some 18 GES officials that included Ng Kok Song and Elizabeth Sam, both of whom would become SIMEX chairmen in subsequent years. The Singaporeans had come to negotiate with the Chicagoans—Melamed, Sandner, Monieson, Rosenberg, Yeutter, and Brodsky—in what turned out to be a marathon session of three nonstop days at the Merc.

There were numerous points to consider. And at times the banter was salted with skepticism over whether these two exchanges half a world apart could get together. True, they were separated by an enormous ocean, 13 hours, and a cultural gap, but they were inexorably bound by a common thread—the one that the Singaporeans called "*ziben zhuyi*," the Americans, "capitalism." Those discussions, wound through a maze of concerns, were characterized, in part, in *SIMEX and the Globalization of Financial Futures*, by coauthors Robert K.G. Chia and Doreen Soh:

> The negotiations and meetings proved to be protracted and fretful sessions for both the Chicago and Singapore parties as they were in untested waters. Problems revolved round such touchy issues as sovereignty, trade-offs, and the lack of precedence. The huge numbers of negotiators representing different interests compounded the situation. Answers to questions such as the degree of independence to be enjoyed by each exchange, the financial safeguards demanded by the CME, financial obligations in the form of margins and guarantees that Simex had to put up in relation to the mutual offset system, operational and technical aspects of the clearing mechanism, membership, seats, trading regulations, legal entity, interpretations, had to be resolved to the satisfaction of both sides in a relatively short period of time.

When the discussions began, Melamed would later concede, "I did not necessarily believe it would end the way it ended—that we could get to the final signing of the mutual offset system."

The Singapore delegates had convinced the Merc officials that the Monetary Authority of Singapore was ready to pass rules compatible with CFTC regulatory policy. "We would never have been able to achieve that in Hong Kong," said Sandner. During the three days, there had been a confluence of thought and feeling on that viewpoint. It wasn't the lure of prospective new business to American shores that persuaded the Merc it was on the right course with Singapore. It was the hidden persuader, the *modus operandi*, as he referred to the mutual offset system, in which ultimately financial transactions would be global. "And if it was the case in time," Melamed reasoned, "whether it be ten years from then, why not be the pioneer to do it?"

In August 1983 a letter of intent between the two exchanges was signed. There were, of course, more intense discussions to follow—and some 15 drafts— before an agreement on the CME-SIMEX linkup was reached in June 1984. As previously noted, the MOS link was activated on 7 September 1984. And once again, the Merc had become the wellspring of innovation. In doing so, it had forged a strategic alliance that was both offensive and defensive in anticipation of the global battle for new markets and to protect its existing markets.

The mutual offset system took time to get off the ground. But even after it did, it never satisfied the Merc officials. While it was able to succeed in one contract—Eurodollars—it was unable to succeed in the currencies or other contracts. In short, mutual offset was a hit or miss proposition, leaving the Merc vulnerable, Melamed believed, to an exchange "that recreates itself without mutual links and just tries to wrest your business away during its time zone." The Japanese were bound to do that, the Merc reckoned. Unfortunately, mutual offset didn't provide an ironclad guarantee that enabled the Merc or SIMEX to hold on to their respective markets. Moreover, mutual offset dealt with one time zone. Continued Melamed, "You needed something that served the 24-hour clock. If it was going to work, we would have to set up a similar link in a European time zone. Then we asked: What were we going to do when Japan came on board? Japan was so strong that it might overwhelm the Singapore market."

It was clear to Melamed, Sandner, Geldermann, Lind, and other members of the Merc's Strategic Planning Committee[2] that the Exchange had ignored automation and technology in the face of crucial questions: How to deal with the flood of hybrid off-exchange products and EFPs? And how to prevent market share from shrinking? There were internal operational snags to consider as well. The S&P contract, for instance, had the largest concentration of small orders, yet the sector lacked enough information and quotation facilities. In July 1986 Geldermann noted that technologically the Merc was at least a year behind. He made the point in a report he prepared and distributed to the Strategic Planning Committee entitled *A Method to Improve and Automate Commodity Exchange Trading Floor Entry and Reporting Operations*. To bolster its efforts in these areas, the Merc hired Kenneth Cone in September as director of strategic planning. A Stanford University Ph.D. economist who taught at the University of Chicago Business School, Cone had been an associate management consultant at Booz Allen Hamilton. For Cone and the Strategic Planning Committee, the single most important item to focus on in the months ahead was to be a concept that came to be known as P-M-T—post (pre) market trade.

The Merc was finding it increasingly difficult to stay ahead with new exchanges and new products cropping up in the United States and overseas. "Success is a magnet," Sandner told the Merc membership at the 1986 semiannual meeting. "Not only is there an army of regulators and legislators, there is New

York, Chicago, Philadelphia, London, Paris, Australia, Hong Kong, Tokyo, all breathing down our necks . . . we have something they want. A successful, thriving, unique marketplace . . . ."

By then, the Merc had 60 different committees, 2 executive vice-presidents, 6 senior vice-presidents, 17 vice-presidents, a professional staff of 304 people, 546 other employees, 53 CME clearing members, and 36 IMM clearing members (class A and class B). Between 30 and 35 percent of Merc volume was coming from overseas. On an average day 275,000 contracts traded, enough to keep the computers busy until 4:15 A.M. to get through the day's processing cycle. Two hours of that time was recovered each evening after the Merc traded in its old IBM mainframe for a spiffier model that increased the processing from 1.8 million instructions per second to 6 million per second. And a new laser printer spit out 14,000 lines per minute, replacing the old 2,000-line per minute printer.

The world in 1986 was far different from the one that Melamed wrote about in 1977 in an article for the *Hofstra University Law Review* on the mechanics of a commodity futures exchange. In it, he had concluded that an automated transaction process could supplant neither the trading floor nor the open outcry system. If the Merc intended to maintain a leadership role as an innovator in the futures markets, it had no choice but to think globally on a 24-hour basis. And that meant automation.

Meanwhile, there were other pressing matters to cope with in the course of a normal trading day—also having to do with man and machine. Terms like "quants" and "triple witching" began to seep into the mutterings of Wall Street and LaSalle Street traders. On 8 January 1986 the stock market plunged nearly 40 points. Within a few days critics had accused an alleged culprit for the accelerated downturn: program trading. This fairly new phenomenon linked to computer-driven trading systems was increasingly being used by major banks and brokerages. Program trades permitted institutions thousands of trades in hundreds of stocks simultaneously. The massive buying and selling was executed in minutes. Brokers called the number crunchers who did the quantifying "quants" or "techies," among other monikers. During that hectic Wednesday, program trading involved a flurry of arbitrage transactions that involved selling stocks and buying the S&P 500 stock index futures contracts.

As the market headed down in the morning, a window of opportunity opened widely. The price of the futures contracts on the S&P 500 index dropped below the cash price of the index, a proxy for the value of a basket of stocks. The program trades began to kick in, essentially selling stocks and buying into the futures market. The cycle worked in three stages: The first step, dictated by the program trade, bought futures contracts on the S&P 500 stock index; step two sold stocks representing those in the index, thus helping the market to its 40-point decline; then the arbitrageurs reversed the earlier trades when the futures contracts expired and the price of stocks and the index converged, thus making a profit out of the disparities in the two markets. With critics viewing the demons of volatility as program trading and index arbitrage, it wasn't long before their fingers were pointing in the direction of futures.

There was nothing really sinister about program trading. In its purest form it was simply the use of a computer to make a trade—Model T stuff, one observer called it, compared with other computerized systems that delved into the heady world of artificial intelligence to make investment decisions. Initially program trading techniques were considered a healthy development because they improved portfolio management by allowing index funds to add or subtract from their stock portfolios. But that was long before the days of huge price swings, before the crash of 1987, when the market plummeted some 508 points on 19 October, and then two years later on 13 October, when it dropped 190 points.

The controversy over program trading would rage into the next decade. Most of the debate focused on extraordinary volatility that frayed the nerves of the steeliest investors. Did program trading induce market volatility? Stock market volatility was indeed greater in the 1970s and 1980s than in the 1950s and 1960s, but the economic environment was also far less stable than it had been in the past 20 years. Matters were hardly helped by the fact that trading had become more concentrated in the hands of fewer institutions. By 1986 U.S. investment managers represented some 33 million mutual fund shareholders and more than 60 million pension plan participants and beneficiaries. These funds totaled nearly $2 trillion in assets, compared with only $400 billion a decade earlier. There was a growing awareness that traditional market mechanisms, particularly in stocks, were simply not structured to accommodate the massive and sudden money flows these managers commanded. It was a small wonder that "volatility" became the watchword of the day.

"The futures markets arose to cope with this increased underlying volatility," Princeton University economist Burton G. Malkiel argued in a *New York Times* opinion piece more than four years after that 40-point decline in January 1986. "Thus blaming futures and program trading for the volatility is as illogical as blaming the thermometer for measuring uncomfortable temperatures."

Fueling the controversy over drastic short-term market swings in 1986 was the so-called Triple Witching Hour. That was the term given to the hour before the market closed when stock index futures, index options, and options on individual stocks all expired the same time of day, setting off wild trading spasms—and extraordinary volatility—in futures, options, and underlying securities. The triple congruence occurred on the third Fridays of March, June, September, and December.

On 10 September 1986, in the wake of big price swings during each quarter's triple witching hour, the SEC stepped in with implicit instructions: Traders placing orders for execution at the market's close on triple witching days had to do so at least a half hour before the market's close. The 30-minute window was intended to allow stock exchange specialists to take care of order imbalances. The adjustment worked. During the subsequent triple witching hour on 19 September, the order flow was relatively evenly matched and there was only a small move in the Dow average.

The Merc and NYSE, too, did their part to de-hex triple witching. In June 1987 both exchanges altered settlement procedures, whereby the Merc would cease trading in expiring S&P 500 futures and options contracts at the close of business on the day preceding triple expiration. Expiring contracts were settled by using a special opening quotation for each S&P stock. The quotation comprised the next day's opening prices as listed on the New York Stock Exchange and American Stock Exchange, as well as the first price for all the over-the-counter stocks in the index. Finally, the Merc displayed on the trading floor the special opening quotation of the S&P, along with the NYSE-produced order imbalances in relation to the opening. After reviewing the expirations in June and September, exchange officials agreed that the triple witching effect had vanished. In September *Barron's* called that month's expiration day "quiet and uneventful . . . the quietest day of the week."

The joint Merc-NYSE effort to squelch triple witching in Melamed's mind represented more than fire fighting. "It was a big breakthrough," he said, "in our relationship with the New York securities community, which had always assumed we wouldn't do anything about triple witching—as did many in our community."

Before the year was over, in early November, the two exchanges again had shown their respective communities that the futures and securities markets were intertwined, for better or for worse. During the previous weeks discussions had been quietly held between the senior officials of both exchanges; Melamed, Sandner, and Brodsky represented the Merc, and the NYSE sent chairman John Phelan, Jr., president Robert Birnbaum, and vice-chairman Donald Stone. The result, Sandner and Phelan jointly told the press, was a newly formed task force headed by Brodsky and Birnbaum to explore a range of mutual areas that included the possibility of a trading link between the two markets. There was talk about the use of electronic systems in trading portfolios, or "baskets," of common stock; improvement of communications between traders at both exchanges; the reduction of transaction fees for members of both exchanges; and the resolution of issues involving program trading, among a long list of items. The task force was short-lived, however, overshadowed by events that would dissipate goodwill and good intentions, changing the character of the relationship between both exchanges from that of a healthy rivalry into a war of the wills.

In early January 1987 investors around the world were caught up in the drama of Dow watching. When, they wondered, would the Dow Jones Industrial Average reach the 2000 mark? The answer came on Thursday, 8 January: As the closing bell rang on the New York Stock Exchange, where floor traders filled the air with confetti and cheers, the Dow settled at 2002.25. "An exhilarating achievement," *Time* magazine called it, heralding one of the longest and strongest bull markets in U.S. history. Since the advance began in 1982—on a 52-month run—stock prices had more than doubled. Nowhere was the market's momentum reflected more than in the Merc's trading pits, where 40 percent of the volume came from the products the Merc had developed in the past five years. Trading volume during 1986 marked a tenth record year with more than 68 million contracts, 16 percent of which was option volume. The 25 percent a year growth rate pushed the value of a Merc membership up $56,500 for the year. An IMM seat jumped $54,500 and an IOM membership $62,000, a gain of 107 percent.

A good portion of the volume came from the S&P pit, where enormous amounts of money were at stake daily. The S&P futures contract traded an equivalent of between $11 billion and $13 billion in stocks on an average daily basis from mid-February to mid-March 1987, according to figures compiled by Kidder, Peabody & Co., the Wall Street firm active in program trading. During that same period, the average daily value of shares traded on the NYSE was between $6 billion and $8 billion.

Triple witching wasn't the only unsettled matter bedeviling the S&P pit. "Traders were falling out of the pit due to the congestion and quotations were running as far as 50 points behind actual real-time prices," reported *Futures* magazine. The volume and volatility, admitted Sandner, "stretched the pit to its absolute capacity." In August 1986, Melamed and Sandner organized a committee to study the S&P situation and to find out, as Sandner put it, "if we're in the horse-and-buggy age." Like a man stricken with gout from the overindulgence of the good life, the Merc was feeling the pain of success. And the S&P pit was only a symptom of the Merc's ailment. It was evident to Merc officials that the system of futures, open outcry, order execution, competition, and dual trading was being tested as never before.

Getting S&P orders filled on volatile days had become "a nightmare," complained Jack Lehman, senior executive vice-president of Shearson Lehman Brothers Inc. Brokers and traders began hurling manifold accusations at one another—on the floor and in the press—that included poor order executions, slow reporting of trades, mismatched trades (called out-trades), prearranged trading, and the "shaving of points" from customer orders. The linchpin was dual trading, which allowed a broker filling customer orders to also trade for himself. The pressure increased on 23 January, when the DJIA dropped 115 points in an hour and the stock index futures gyrated wildly. The March S&P 500 contract swung 16.6 index points—a single day record.[3] The value of the move per contract was $8,300. The hectic day was enough to push Shearson Lehman to advise its clients to switch to stock index options on the Chicago Board Options Exchange, where small orders were executed by computer. The consequences of the Merc's high volume were congestion and volatility.

As the arbitration cases between traders began to mount, so did the pressure to do something dramatic in light of the fact that it was the Merc's showcase contract in the middle of a hailstorm. Tempers turned sour and snappish. "Traders bitch about a lot of things," Melamed told a *Chicago Tribune* reporter. "When they lose money, they feel a lot better if they can say it's someone else's fault." Among those who went on record to defend the S&P contract was John Conheeney, chairman of Merrill Lynch Futures Inc. "In any busy market," he said, "you have problems getting orders out of the pit . . . by and large those problems have been managed well."

By now an S&P study committee, headed by IOM governor Howard Dubnow and Harry "The Hat" Lowrance, chairman of the floor pit committee, was looking at trading practices. Another committee, chaired by board member Robert Hammer, was to study broker groups which had slashed commission rates as low as one dollar, half the rate of 1982, in order to attract business. The probe also included an analysis by the Tellefsen Consulting Group—at a cost of $250,000—of the S&P order execution process. The Board promised results within 30 days.

For the locals, whose trading lives were measured in nanoseconds, a month may have seemed a lifetime. On 25 February a petition, signed by some 300 floor traders, to ban dual trading was submitted to the Merc's board of governors. It stated, "We the undersigned, petition the President of the Chicago Mercantile Exchange, William Brodsky, to hold the referendum prohibiting a member from filling customer orders and trading for [his or her] own account in the S&P 500 futures and options, on any given day."

The petition was a disappointment to Melamed, Sandner, and other board members who had to ask the petitioners to hold back until the various committees—which subsequently held 50 meetings and heard concerns from more than 100 market users—had presented their recommendations. The plea was ignored. Once the petition was submitted, the Board had two weeks to respond. After that, the petition would have to be brought to a referendum. The dual trading issue had been debated in good faith for more than a century. Opponents saw it as a potential conflict of interest. Proponents argued that the ban would adversely affect liquidity and eliminate many high quality brokers.

Outsiders wondered whether the Merc was at civil war. Initially there was concern among some Merc officials that the antipathy between the petitioners and Board might divide sympathies and even weaken the spirit that had held the Exchange together like cement. The Merc was a common enterprise and though each trader and broker was an independent agent, they were all dependent on each other. Their fortunes, as measured by the value of a membership, rose and fell together. They shared the same outcome of change together. Melamed had ensured that when he fought off the old guard 20 years earlier to create the process of referendum—the mechanism for exchange members to be heard—that was now before the Board. Melamed was the first CME chairman to allow petitions from the floor. But now, when the Merc needed to show the world a united front, his stance had tempered. "The Board," he told a reporter, "does not like to run the Exchange by petitions from the floor."

There was danger in communicating through rumor and the business pages of newspapers. It was apparent to Melamed and Sandner what was needed: face-to-face interaction. After closing hours on 12 February a meeting was called with some 500 traders to air the catalog of concerns plaguing the exchange. "We won't tolerate a tearing down of the Merc's image," Melamed told the group, reminding them that the Exchange would not take any action until the study committee's report was issued. He promised the proposals would be a comprehensive package that would go beyond dual trading. The committee had already proposed a change to prohibit brokers from occupying the pit's top step—a prized location because of its vantage point—if more than a quarter of their total trades were for their own accounts. The proposal, however, had been put on hold, pending the full committee report.

The day before this meeting, the Merc board had voted to ask the CFTC for permission to strap a 12-point limit in the daily price move of the S&P 500 contract as a year-long pilot program. The board's action had reversed the Merc's prior position against price-move limits in all its financial futures contracts, including the S&P 500 index. The move, Melamed maintained, was to keep buy and sell orders flowing in a volatile market. Price limits were unpopular with many traders, who believed they dampened volatility, and institutions were wary of limits since the stock market had none. Thus, in futures one could get trapped in a limit situation while the cash market continued to trade. The proposed limit was a compromise of sorts. If the price limit were reached on two consecutive days, it would be dropped on the third day to permit prices to adjust to market conditions. On the fourth day the limit would then be reinstated.

Two weeks later, on 23 February, a letter signed by Melamed and Sandner was sent to the S&P 500 traders stating that the pit had a "negative image" and vowing the Merc "will take all necessary action to correct the problems and deal harshly with all violators." By the end of the week, it had done just that. Early Friday morning, on 27 February, notices of a series of penalties were posted near the entrance to the trading floor, drawing clusters of traders. The disciplinary action included the expulsion of two members, who were also fined $100,000 and $50,000. The two had violated rules that prohibited trading against customers' orders and prearranged trades. In addition, smaller fines of $500, $375 and $100, respectively, were levied against three other members for pushing, elbowing, and spitting in the S&P pit.

By March Melamed was on the warpath. "Our image has to be reconstructed immediately," he told a *Chicago Tribune* reporter. "If heads have got to roll, then let them." Using the Tellefsen report and committee findings, a package of reform proposals was unveiled for the Merc's busiest market that included an internal review and overhaul of the Exchange's surveillance procedures. In a gesture that seemed to put his reputation and intellectual integrity on the line, the Merc's chief strategist snapped, "If I don't see something I'm proud of in 60 to 90 days, I'll walk."

Melamed and Sandner were determined to face anybody on the reform issues—subject to CFTC approval if the impending referendum to end dual trading failed—which were outlined in a letter sent to 3,000 Merc members on 12 March. Two days earlier the request to end dual trading had been rejected by the Board in favor of a more far–reaching approach because, as Melamed and Sandner explained in the letter, the petition "suggests a single sweeping solution to complex and multi-faceted problems."

Among the board's recommendations, hammered out in two days of special meetings, were as follows:

1. The top step of the S&P pit—where 95 percent of customer orders were executed—was banned to dual trading (a "high-priced piece of real estate," Sandner called the top step).

2. Brokers throughout the S&P pit had to manually record to the minute their personal trades in order to complement the new CRT (computerized trade reconstruction) system, which was to go on-line 1 July 1987.

3. Broker groups—to be defined and registered with the Exchange—were limited to trading customer orders and personal accounts. Broker members could not make more than 15 percent of their personal trades with other members of the same association or more than 25 percent of their customer orders. Fines for violations ranged from $1,000 to $50,000 and/or suspension and expulsion.

4. No more than one member of a broker association could serve on a CME disciplinary or pit committee or arbitration panel.

The recommendation placing limits on trading within a broker group Melamed described as "the toughest one for the brokers to swallow," but the most important. If approved by the CFTC, the Merc would become the first exchange ever to restrict broker group trading. There was even tentative talk about automating the execution of orders, for which Melamed said that the "jury's out" on that prospect. On 7 April, a week before the referendum was to take place, the Merc announced the appointment of Paul B. O'Kelly as vice–president of compliance. It was a strong choice. A 13-year veteran of the SEC, O'Kelly, 38, was the assistant regional administrator in the Chicago office when the Merc hired him to begin in May. The Merc also beefed up its compliance department by 50 percent, adding eight investigators to its 16-person staff. Three of the investigators were to be the first permanent ones assigned exclusively to the trading floor, a step called "outstanding" by John Troelstrup, the Merc's former vice–president of law and compliance. To assist the regulatory support, the Merc also increased the number of computer programmers from five to eight.

Then came referendum day. On 13 April Merc members went to the polls. The vote surprised some, but not Melamed and the Board, who had used friendly persuasion in the form of telephone calls to solicit members' support. The petition to ban dual trading was overwhelmingly rejected by a weighted vote of 3,393 to 1,214. The results, tabulated by Arthur Andersen & Company, represented a 74 percent vote against the petition. Even members of the Index and Option Market (IOM), where the dual trading petition originated, had defeated it by a two-to-one margin. (The weighed vote allowed CME members six votes, IMM members two votes, and IOM members one vote.) The unweighted totals showed 1,272 members against the petition and 525 in favor. By division, the unweighted numbers showed that CME members voted 348 to 103 against the petition; IMM members 381 to 174; and IOM members 543 to 248.

Defeat of the referendum cleared the way for the Board to submit its proposed changes in the floor practice rules to the CFTC in late April. Approval came on 15 May. The victory was a reaffirmation of leadership and indeed the political structure of the Exchange. The outcome of the referendum signified "a strong vote of confidence in the CME board of governors," Melamed said. "Our members understood that the board's proposals, based on committee recommendations, were more responsible and responsive to the issues involved."

The new rules governing the S&P pit took effect Monday, 22 June. The traders were faced with not only some psychological adjustments, but also a physical one: the S&P 500 pit was to be enlarged by 250 square feet, the market reporting "perch" expanded, and a railing installed between the top step and the rest of the pit. The structural changes—completed during the three-day Fourth of July weekend—were made to help ensure compliance with the new rules.

Also in June a special committee, headed by Merc vice-chairman Laurence Rosenberg, scrapped the old sanctions for new and stiffer ones. A major offender faced expulsion or suspension and a maximum fine of $250,000, up from the old maximum of $50,000. Fines for "minor" offenses were increased from $5,000 to $25,000. Throughout the months ahead, bad news bulletins citing disciplinary action repeatedly created gaper's blocks of traders craning to see who the latest culprit was. Those who were caught found it costly. By mid-September one veteran trader, Alan L. Freeman, was found guilty of prearranged trading in 1986. Freeman neither admitted nor denied violating Exchange rules. Nevertheless, he was fined $250,000 and his membership privileges suspended for a year. For the year 1986, the Merc levied fines of $190,000 against 27 traders compared with $1.68 million (including Freeman's fine) against 38 members in 1987. Publicizing such disciplinary actions in the press was sometimes viewed as more of a penalty than the fine itself. The Merc's 1987 total open interest—the number of contracts outstanding—exceeded that of any other futures exchange. That meant plenty of activity and liquidity. The enormous success of the S&P futures—and, indeed, all the Merc's markets—brought to mind what old Elmer Falker had ominously told his trading pals some 30 years earlier. "Don't let our futures markets get too successful," he warned, waving a big cigar in the air in the days when smoking was still permitted in the pits and the spittoon was nearby. "Why not?" a young runner innocently asked. "Because," Falker replied emphatically, "futures markets tell the truth and nobody wants to know the truth. If the truth is too bad and too loud, they'll close us down."

For Merc officials and traders the noise would grow louder in and out of the S&P pit as the 1987 stock market opened with a bang. And eventually, everywhere the Merc turned, it would seem as though someone was coming after it, spurred by the bogeyman of Wall Street—volatility. As long as stock prices were rising, the Wall Street interests who blamed stock market volatility on the Chicago markets remained at ease. All was quiet on the Merc's eastern front when the new year began.

Despite the Dow's record breakthrough in January 1987, there lingered traces of uncertainty as to where the market was heading. Now that it had passed the 2000 barrier, would it be propelled to greater heights? Or would it fizzle? After a five-year bull market, wasn't a correction overdue? In all the fervor over market mania, most people had forgotten what happened to the Dow when it passed the 1000 historic benchmark: It took a decade before it cracked 1100. But there was even more fodder for fretting.

What was to keep the market moving higher in the face of a lackluster economy? And there were concerns over several other issues: some dire predictions about inflation as well as recession; the Federal Reserve Board's tightening monetary policy; federal legislation that would disallow interest deductions for any significant takeover borrowing; the specter of protectionist trade legislation; and the disparity between the return on stocks versus the return on fixed income investments. Fundamentals aside, there were also international tensions of the day: an unsettling Persian Gulf situation with increasing Iranian hostilities; a falling dollar; falling prices on foreign stock markets; and a policy disagreement between the U.S. Treasury and the German Bundesbank, spelling an end to the Louvre Agreement targeting exchange rates, thus ending the hotly debated notion that foreign exchange values could be preordained by government edict. The crash, believed some observers, was in the wings.

The investment sages couldn't agree as to how much life was left in the bull market. While some saw rainbows, others saw clouds. In January 1987, for example, one of Wall Street's most popular gurus, Robert Prechter, applied his analysis known as Elliott Wave Theory to predict that the Dow would peak at 3600 by 1988. By September another hot shot analyst, Marty Zweig, who managed $1.3 billion in pension funds, had turned bearish. His "Zweig Forecast" newsletter predicted the Dow would soon plunge 1000 points to 1755.

On 19 October came the crash that was heard around the world. It was far more than just stocks falling from Himalayan highs to hellish lows. It was the bubble of painless prosperity bursting: tax cuts without a price, a chronic trade gap, and a budget deficit clearly reflecting a country living beyond its means that could no longer afford to do so. The makings of a Black Monday had always been there. Only the psychology lagged.

30

The Crash

The gust of ill wind that blew over the markets the week before 19 October turned into a tempest.

On Wednesday, 14 October, the Dow stood at over 2500. By noon on Tuesday, a week later, the Dow was just above 1700, a decline of one-third. On the day of the Crash, however, the S&P futures contract implied a Dow level near 1400. From 14 to 16 October the Dow fell 250 points in a flurry of selling triggered by chronically declining trade figures, which had pushed the dollar lower in currency markets as long-term interest rates edged higher. Another factor that added to the drab picture: the filing of anti-takeover tax legislation, which caused risk arbitrageurs to sell stocks of takeover candidates pushing the market even lower. That, in turn, created a huge overhang of selling pressure—enough, subsequently concluded the Brady Commission report, "to crush the equity markets in the following week." The overhang was concentrated among mutual fund managers and the portfolio insurers, who administered between $60 billion and $90 billion in assets, selling in anticipation of further declines. During the three-day period the portfolio insurers unloading S&P futures sold the equivalent in stocks of some $530 million on Wednesday, $965 million on Thursday, and $2.1 billion on Friday. The market climate had grown steadily darker and its texture coarser with the prospect of more selling on Monday into a market already down 10 percent. The computer models of the portfolio insurers had called for the selling of at least $12 billion in equities, but less than $4 billion had been sold. Mutual funds—whose redemptions on Friday alone exceeded stock sales by $750 million—had also received substantial requests over the weekend. These mutual fund customers were entitled to repayment based on the prices at the close on Friday.

On top of that there were the index arbitrageurs—who attempted to profit from intraday price disparities between the futures market and stock market—and the smaller number of aggressive trading institutions, who could smell the blood of a selling onslaught and were anxious to close in with the prospect of rebuying stocks at lower prices. This latter group understood the strategies of the portfolio

323

insurers and mutual funds and anticipated the selling by these institutions into a declining market. On Friday, seven of these aggressive trading firms sold more than $100 million each, and four of the seven purchased more than $100 million. That day, traders as a group had sold $1.4 billion of stocks and bought $1.1 billion. Clearly, by the end of the week, the market and its players teetered on the edge of an abyss with no bottom in sight. The Dow average had fallen 108 points to 2246, ending the worst week, according to the 17 October issue of *Barron's,* since 18 May 1940, when a 15 percent drop resulted from the crumbling resistance of the French armies by the German Blitzkreig.

After a five-year run that saw the Dow peak at 2722 in August, stock prices, it seemed, could no longer ignore the air of unreality that swept over the market like a plume of stale cigar smoke. Based on interest rates, corporate earnings, and other fundamentals, the market was ahead "700 points on sheer greed," lamented one analyst. Stock prices, complained other pros, were out of line with expected corporate earnings and dividend yields to fall below the interest return on bonds, giving fixed-income securities an investment edge. One thing was certain: The United States was fidgeting on a bed of economic travails that included sliding interest rates, a weak dollar, and a double whammy to boot: ballooning trade and budget deficits. In late September the August figures of the U.S. trade deficit were released to mixed reviews. On one hand, the $15.7 billion deficit was a slight reduction from the previous quarter's. On the other, investors hoping for a greater reduction were discouraged. They viewed the deficit as a clear sign that U.S. finances were out of control and that no one in the Reagan Administration knew how to fix them. The consequence: stock dumping. Others singled out a more tangible villain in the form of Treasury Secretary James Baker. Over the weekend of 18 October, The Sunday *New York Times* wrote a story about Treasury Secretary James Baker's excoriating the West German central bank, which permitted four increases in German interest rates in three months. Higher interest in other major countries lured international capital away from U.S. shores to cover the federal deficit. The *Times* article quoted an unnamed "senior administration official" as announcing "an abrupt shift in policy," which implied that the United States could retaliate against the Germans by driving the dollar down. Baker seemed to bristle when reminded of the *New York Times* story that some believe pushed the market over the brink. In his defense, he told *Time* magazine a week after the crash, "What triggered it was not my remarks but a front-page story in one of our major newspapers. It quoted an unnamed government official, not me, and drew inaccurate conclusions from my remarks in a way that could not but contribute to market nervousness." On a television interview on Sunday, 18 October, however, Baker had said, "We will not sit back in this country and watch surplus countries jack up their interest rates and squeeze growth worldwide on the expectation that the United States somehow will follow by raising its interest rates."

In any case, the specter of chaos in the currency markets gave investors a queasy feeling that the so-called Louvre accord—the 1987 agreement among the United States, Japan, West Germany, France, Great Brittain, Canada, and Italy to keep the value of their currencies within a narrow trading range—was about to come unglued. Market players took Baker's statements as a hint that the dollar would be allowed to fall against the Deutsche mark as the American response to climbing West German interest rates.

Reacting to such press accounts, Japanese and European investors began selling the dollar in early Monday trading. Black Monday had begun, well before dawn rose over the U.S. securities, options, and futures markets. Their counterparts across the Atlantic and Pacific Oceans were in a state of high anxiety, brought on by too many unanswered economic questions. Volatile emotions turned into a selling crush, aided by computers that enabled the exchanges to execute trades swiftly and in huge volumes that would have been inconceivable a decade earlier. Volume that perhaps would have been stretched over a week was now crammed into a day with one-sided sell orders driving prices down violently. As sell orders piled up on brokers' desks, computer screens began flashing rows of the bad news numbers: reported price breaks in Tokyo, Hong Kong, Sydney, London, Paris, and Zurich well before trading began in Chicago and New York. Concerns over a "correction" after five years of a bull market were no longer vague. The day of reckoning had arrived. Prices were in free-fall. The market crumbled like a kind of financial Tower of Babel, spewing forth a jumble of languages all saying the same thing in the next day's headlines around the globe: "Crash." "Le Crash" in Paris, "Crolla Wall Street e transcina le Borse" in Madrid, "Schwarzer Montag an der Borse" in Berlin, "CRASH" in London.

The markets on the nineteenth had moved fast, fast, fast as prices went down, down, down. That morning in Tokyo, where price limits on individual stocks were a long-established concept, the Nikkei Index, Japan's equivalent to the Dow, fell 2.5 percent. At 10 A.M. panic moved across the floor of the Hong Kong Stock Exchange as the Hang Seng index of 30 stocks dropped 133 points in the first 40 minutes of trading. The FT-SE market index in London—which was six hours ahead of Chicago—had slipped 10 percent by midday. The sell-off in the London market was exacerbated by U.S. mutual fund managers who tried to beat the anticipated selling on the NYSE by unloading U.S. stocks in London. One mutual fund, for example, dumped $95 million of its U.S. equity portfolio in London prior to New York's opening. Based upon the trading activity in the London market by 5 A.M. in Chicago, the Dow would be down at least 200 points, estimated traders. The large U.S. brokerage firms with overseas branches knew that further selling by foreign investors was on the way to both the cash and the futures markets in the United States. By 7 A.M. Melamed was already on his way to the Merc when NYSE chairman John J. Phelan, Jr. reached him on the car phone. "It looks like a very bad market," said Phelan, alerting

Melamed to the fact that an inordinate number of sell orders were building up in the Designated Order Turnaround (DOT) system set to hit the market. (DOT handled up to 2000-share orders.) Melamed then called Brodsky in his office to let him know of the warning from Phelan.

The call from Phelan was all the more significant because it had come over an hour before the NYSE opening. Normally the exchange did not see that kind of order flow that early. "We knew we were in for a bad day," said Brodsky, whose fourth-floor office became a sort of command center where Melamed, Sandner, and Brodsky could man the telephones, monitor the markets flickering across the television screens, and walk just a few steps to the VIP lounge to observe the massive trading floor below.

At 8:05 A.M. New York time, yet another news flash on the wires jolted already uneasy investors. The United States had responded to Friday's attack by the Iranians on a U.S.-flagged Kuwaiti tanker by bombing an oil platform that Iran had converted to a military command center for its operations in the Persian Gulf. Of the Gulf incident, the Brady Commission was later to conclude, "[Despite] a flight by investors to dollar securities in the wake of Gulf tensions, fears of the demise of the Louvre currency accord proved stronger, causing the dollar to weaken substantially as foreign currency trading began in New York." These events caused domestic investors to fear that foreign institutions, especially Japanese ones, would dump the large equity portfolios that they had accumulated earlier in the year. (Economist David Hale points out that the precedents for the October Crash were not the crashes of 1929 and 1962 so commonly referred to in the press, but the crashes of the late nineteenth century, which resulted from the dollar's links to the British pound sterling.)

Prior to the openings on 19 October, the sell orders were piled high in both stock and futures markets. Each market responded with its own—but quite different—opening procedure. The NYSE rules encourage specialists to delay opening when the overnight accumulation of orders for a particular stock is too far out of balance to allow establishing an opening price near the previous close. The delayed opening is thus intended to give the specialist a few minutes to search for balancing orders on the other side. At the NYSE that morning, the huge order imbalances had overwhelmed the specialists. An hour after the opening bell more than one-third of the Dow stocks, including IBM, Sears, and Exxon, hadn't started trading. Throughout the day there were a total of 187 opening delays, seven trading halts, and three stocks that did not resume trading after halts. (Exxon, the last of the Dow stocks to open that day, opened at 10:23 A.M. Chicago time, down about 9 percent from Friday's close.) On 20 October, there were 92 opening delays, 175 trading halts, and 10 stocks that did not resume trading. Unopened stocks inhibited trading in the derivative instruments, namely, the S&P futures on the Merc and options on the Chicago Board Options Exchange as well as other exchanges' stock index futures and options contracts. Transaction delays through the NYSE's DOT and the eventual decision to prohibit index arbitrage through the system also disconnected the market segments.

The pathology of disconnected markets, as the Brady report would point out, fed on itself. The surfeit of sellers and scarcity of buyers, in both futures and stock markets were at times on 19 and 20 October nearly in free-fall. Sellers were putting downward pressure on both stock and futures markets. What had looked like a tightly woven carpet was turning into a rag rug made of scraps and fraying fast. As large discounts developed between futures and stocks, those investors who could switched from selling futures to selling stocks. Those unable to switch continued to sell futures, driving prices down further. The discounts in the S&Ps sent a grim message—creating a so-called billboard effect—to hopeful stock buyers: Declines were imminent. The futures discount made stocks appear expensive and inhibited buying support for the market.

On 19 October, both the stock and index futures markets suffered their worst single-day declines in history. The Dow's Black Monday plunge of 22.6 percent was the largest one-day drop ever, almost doubling the record 12.8 percent fall on 26 October 1929. By the time the Dow closed the day at 1738.74, more than $500 billion in paper value—a sum equal to the entire gross national product of France—had vanished. Throughout the day specialists on the New York Stock Exchange were drowning in sell orders as the trading volume reached 608 million shares, nearly double the 16 October record. The record 108-point plunge in the Dow on the sixteenth was surpassed in the first hour of trading on the nineteenth. The retreat in stocks was along a broad front. The top 15 selling stocks on 19 October accounted for 20 percent of the total sales, or $4 billion. The top 15 buyers accounted for 10 percent of the volume, or $2 billion. Index arbitrage involved some $1.7 billion worth of stock. On the American Stock Exchange volume surged to 35.4 million shares as the Amex composite index dropped 41 points, or 12.7 percent, to 282.5. The over-the-counter market suffered similar trauma; the NASDAQ composite index plunged 46 points to close at 360.2, for a loss of 11.35 percent on volume of 222.9 million shares.

Things were just as bad in Chicago, the hub of the derivatives. The Merc's S&P futures contract fell 80.75 points, a 28.6 percent decline. The CBOT's index future, the Major Market Index (MMI), composed of 20 stocks, 17 of which were in the Dow Jones industrial average, sank 24.38 percent. And the most popular index option for retail investors, the CBOE's S&P 100 index (OEX) contract, lost 21 percent of the value of the underlying index.

Throughout the chaotic day, portfolio-related futures selling accounted for at least 16.7 percent of the contracts traded in "spooz," the nickname traders gave the Standard & Poor's 500 futures contract, based on its ticker symbol—SPZ. In the first half-hour of trading New York time—from 9:30 to 10:00—portfolio insurance strategies accounted for only 5.6 percent of spooz volume. It grew 32 percent from 10:30 to 11:00 and 25 percent from 12:00 to 1:00. In total, portfolio insurers sold $4 billion worth of stock index contracts, or about 40 percent of the public volume. And the top 10 sellers accounted for 50 percent of the volume. The result: massive one-sided volume. During the day one major pension fund alone sold 27.3 million shares on the NYSE. The same fund also sold 7,000 spooz contracts—equivalent to 17.6 million shares with a dollar value of $706 million—on 16 and 19 October. This institution spread its stock sales throughout the day divided into thirteen 2-million-share programs.

Those trades, based on the deep discount of the futures from the cash, were believed to be executed by Wells Fargo investment advisors on behalf of one of Wells Fargo's major clients, the giant General Motors $33 billion pension fund. Wells Fargo unloaded 13 so-called baskets of stocks on the NYSE—each order amounting to $100 million, for a total of $1.3 billion. In executing its trades Wells Fargo had made a tough decision: It ignored the NYSE numbers. (The reason the numbers should have been ignored is that when a stock doesn't open, the index is computed based on the last sale—even if it is from the day before and even if the stock is trading dramatically lower somewhere else, such as London.) The pioneer of portfolio insurance—the Los Angeles–based Leland O'Brien Rubenstein Associates—had taken the opposite tack and suffered. Because the steep discount made it impossible to hedge well against further stock market drops, Leland O'Brien on the afternoon of the nineteenth made a fateful decision: It under-hedged in anticipation of futures prices snapping back. The firm ended up selling some 2000 S&P futures contracts, equivalent to about $250 million. But that total only represented less than half of what Leland O'Brien needed to sell to get its hedge levels up to the desired proportions. And on the following day, when stocks began to rebound, the firm's accounts were only 65 percent hedged, and it was unable to participate in the turnaround. In short, trusting the numbers out of New York on 19 October dictated one strategy; believing that the futures prices in Chicago were closer to the actual value of the underlying stock suggested another. Had market conditions permitted, Wells Fargo would have sold an additional 27 million shares, or their futures equivalent, in the final hours of the nineteenth. The program was instead halted shortly after 2:00. Of that eventful day, Gordon Binns, who ran the General Motors pension fund—the nation's largest corporate fund at the time—will only say, "We had some protective strategies in place, which we tried to follow in October with some degree of success. That, plus the fact we were diversified among a number of asset classes, protected our fund from serious erosion. I'd also like to discourage anybody from thinking we were following a strategy that involved turning over what we were doing to a computer and letting the computer decide what to do. Human beings make all our decisions."

Binns perhaps was the archetypical institutional investor that evolved in the 1980s: sensitive and responsive to a wide array of investment tools. Responsible for the pensions of some 800,000 GM participants and beneficiaries, Binns reigned over an in-house staff of 10 and 60 outside investment managers who laid down a road map of strategies that included the use of stocks, bonds, options, and futures. As a spokesperson for the pension industry, he testified before various congressional committees before and after the crash and was claimed as a friend by both the futures and securities industries. After the crash Binns was the only pension fund manager who served as a director of the Futures Industry Association, as well as being a member of the Pension Manager Advisory Committee to the NYSE (set up after the crash) and the Equity Advisory Committee on the Merc. Most of the pension funds, like General Motors, came through the crash intact, thanks to a five-year bull market that left many of them overfunded. Diversification was the key to withstanding the shocks. The average pension fund, according to the Employee Benefit Research Institute in Washington, D.C., had only about 40 percent of its portfolio in equities. So for the average pension portfolio the 25 percent plunge in stocks from August 1987 to October 1987—along with a rise in bond prices—resulted in only a 12.6 percent drop in value.

The market's jittery and fragile nature became more apparent during mid-morning on the nineteenth, when SEC chairman David Ruder told reporters during a press conference that the SEC might consider a short trading halt of perhaps 30 minutes to an hour to let the market "sort itself out." After his comments hit the newswires, the market slid another hundred points or so. Referring to Ruder's comments at the time, Princeton University economist Sanford Grossman called them "the most frightening idea I've heard in a while. Shutting the market down for a half-hour is a sure way to cause a panic."

Despite the massive delays in stock openings, the NYSE managed to keep from shutting down altogether on 19 and 20 October, if for no other reason than a psychological one. "For all practical purposes, the exchange was closed," concedes Robert Birnbaum, who was president of the NYSE at the time of the crash. "I think the world would have been anxious and apprehensive if the New York Stock Exchange had physically closed its doors."

What would have happened if the New York Stock Exchange had closed? No one knows. Not John Phelan. Not President Reagan. Not even David Ruder. "I don't think anybody knows," said Birnbaum. "If they do, no one knows if they're right." In the past, however, panic had closed the doors of the NYSE, once for 12 days during 1873, and for a period of four months and 11 days in 1914, in anticipation of panic brought on by the Great War. The war came, but not the panic. Storefront stock operators sprang up in Chicago, Boston, and Philadelphia to fill the Big Board's void. But the financial press of the day refused to cover the action of these storefront auction rooms, which in some ways were a throwback to the earliest exchanges in American history. Once the exchange resumed trading in all its listed stocks on 1 April 1915 it was business as usual. But not even during the Crash of 1929—the Big One—had trading ceased. "The times were different when the exchange closed in the past," said Birnbaum. That's certainly true. Although the circumstances surrounding the eras were different, the emotions that drove investors to react in panic were the same. This, however, was 1987 and the market systems of stocks, options, and futures were inextricably linked through strategy and automation. Mind and machine were at work here, along with a human trait that couldn't be programmed into a memory chip: fear.

"First and foremost," the Brady report concluded, "these apparently separate markets are in an economic sense one market. They are linked by instruments, participants, trading strategies, and clearing flow." Oddly enough, they were linked by the abstract as well: illusion.

The market that came unglued had been held together by the illusion of liquidity, which had led institutional investors, portfolio insurers, and the like to adopt strategies that required a liquid market far in excess of what could be supplied. At least that's what the Brady Commission thought. The liquidity during periods of normal volume provided by specialists, market makers, and traders on both sides of the market was "something of an illusion," the report emphatically stated. With everyone showing up on the same side of the market at once, the authors of the Brady report metaphorically observed, "As with people in a theater when someone yells 'Fire!' these sellers all ran for the exit in October, but it was large enough to accommodate only a few."[1]

Late Friday afternoon, on 16 October, the Merc executive committee had voted to increase margins on both speculative maintenance and hedge accounts to $7,500 from $5,000, effective on Monday. By 9 A.M. on the nineteenth, large sell order imbalances were reported on the NYSE; a net of $500 million, or 14 million shares, was waiting to be sold through DOT, which electronically routes orders from NYSE member firms to the specialist in a particular stock on the exchange floor. Between 9:30 A.M. New York time—when the S&P 500 futures began trading on the Merc—and 10 A.M., another $475 million was loaded into the DOT pipeline. By then, the Dow was already off by 104 points. In the next half hour volume reached 154 million shares.

The traders in the S&P pit that Monday were more depressive than manic. No one knew what to do. There was a great deal of anticipation prior to the Monday opening bell. Alan Ross, the head of floor operations for Merc clearing member Rufenacht, Bromagen & Hertz, Inc., remembered that day, when the opening price in the S&Ps fell 7 percent at the opening—an enormous gap by past standards—from the prior settlement price. "The atmosphere was surreal," Ross said. "There were blank stares. No one could believe it was happening. Some people began to leave the pit." An estimated 40 to 60 of the 500 participants in the S&P pit had left during the course of the day. Some 20 percent of those who walked away were locals, the market makers of the pits who buy and sell for their own accounts to provide liquidity in at least 40 percent of the trades.

As in all futures index contracts, the selling began promptly at the 8:30 Central time opening bell. The institutional traders led the way. They started unloading December S&Ps, a hundred contracts at a crack. At least 13 firms sold 771

S&P contracts between 8:30 and 9:00 central time, before most of the component stocks had opened. Eventually, an eerie silence came over the pit. "There was a big hole in the middle of it," said Ross. At the opening there was the usual crush of traders jammed into the S&P pit. An hour later there was half that amount. What had happened to the screaming, jostling, beseeching, imploring, cursing? The traders in the pit that day were a microcosm of the rest of the world: They were like soldiers on the frontline of war who know nothing of the battle at large—or its causes—but only the few yards around them. Beyond that perimeter they were powerless. Everyone that day was powerless. The market had become a victim of its own intensity as traders seemed to strive for answers that eluded them, and everyone else.

Those who were trying to get out of the market were long and wrong. They listened for bids that never came. They offered down. And the market plunged. There was a huge drop. Then another, two minutes later. Around 10:00 Central time a big foreign investor stepped in to buy, pushing the December contract a tad higher than the underlying cash index. The rally took place in the blink of an eye. Minutes later the S&Ps began their precipitous drop. The lack of bids eventually pushed the futures 24 points below cash value, but cash value didn't reflect real value for stocks not trading; the S&P index on the nineteenth lost 20.39 percent, and the December S&P futures lost 28.61 percent.

At 1:50 P.M. Brodsky called SEC chairman David Ruder to update him on the Merc's situation. The markets were thin, Brodsky said, and the clearing-house was in good shape. The Merc was adequately coping with the situation, he assured Ruder, adding that members of the Merc's staff were in touch with Richard Ketchum, director of the SEC's division of market regulation. Five minutes before Brodsky's call, Ruder had been on the phone with John Phelan. For the first time in the history of the financial markets, the lines of communication between the futures industry and the securities industry were connecting—in a crisis situation. Throughout this period, Brodsky was in constant contact with NYSE president Robert Birnbaum, his former boss at the Amex.

All that day the market was irrational, as S&P futures volume reached a record 162,000 contracts, the equivalent of nearly $20 billion in stocks comprising the S&P 500 index. (The "cash index" represents the weighted prices of the 500 index stocks.) Without a doubt, futures provided liquidity to so-called synthetic stock sellers, thus absorbing selling pressure on the stock market. Merc floor traders accounted for about 31 percent, or 50,000 contracts traded in a market overshadowed by sheer fear. Some traders stood in the pit shielding their badges with their hands so as to avoid any trading mistakes. Others refused to venture back into the pit. Their biggest anxiety: out-trades. An out-trade is a trade that doesn't clear because key informational elements—11 criteria that include the price, quantity, month, and so forth—do not match between buyer and seller. (The Merc's clearing method is known as a four-way match system because the four parties involved in the transaction—the buying and selling clearing members and the buying and selling brokers—all must agree that they were the participants to the trade.) The number of S&P futures out-trades on the nineteenth was 8,464, or 14.4 percent of the total contracts cleared, but down from the 11,421 out-trades on the sixteenth and the record 15,862 out-trades on 23 January 1987.

"From an operational perspective," the CFTC would later conclude in its report on the crash, "the order routing, trade execution, and clearing procedures employed by member firms and the CME performed well during this period. . . . With few exceptions, clearing firms were able to process orders . . . the CME was able to process and clear trades in a reasonably expeditious manner."

To accomplish that task over the high-volume days of 16, 19, and 20 October, the Merc used special trade-checking sessions. Volume in the S&P futures pit on Friday, 16 October totaled 135,344 contracts; on Monday, a record 162,022 contracts; and on Tuesday, 126,562 contracts. The volume was considerably above the daily average of 92,258 contracts in September 1987 and 81,150 contracts during October. The out-trades on each of the three days were above the out-trade rate of 11 percent for the prior six-month period ending September 30. The Merc, however, stepped up its efforts to accelerate settlement of the trading disputes with special checking sessions. The first was held on Saturday, 17 October. The second occurred in the late evening of Monday, 19 October, lasting until 3:00 A.M. on 20 October. Staffers of member firms and out-trade representatives had worked around the clock to reconcile the trades. The all-out push had paid off with dramatic results: The S&P futures out-trade percentage by transaction for 16 October declined from 16.6 percent (11,421 transactions) to seven percent (4,908 transactions), below the six-month average. Out-trades on the nineteenth were reduced from 14.4 percent (8,464 transactions) to 8 percent (4,767 transactions), and on the twentieth to 13 percent (4,969), slightly above the Exchange's average. These percentages were at a level low enough to resolve before the opening of trading the next day.

There were still, however, those touch-and-go moments in the settlement process of a wheezing market. A heart-stopper came on the morning of 20 October. The nineteenth was a long day, but the night was even longer. In spite of the crash, Merc officials went ahead with previously scheduled plans. Earlier in the evening, Melamed, Sandner, Brodsky, Rick Kilcollin, and Kenneth Cone had dinner with Reuters officials Andre Villenueve, president of Reuters North America, and John Hull, Reuters executive vice-president. They were in the process of negotiating plans that had been announced in September 1987 to globalize futures trading on a 24-hour basis through a Merc-Reuters computer hookup. It was the most ambitious plan yet toward an around-the-clock automated trading system.

Following the working dinner, the Merc executives returned to the exchange to join Brian Monieson, Barry Lind, Jerry Beyer, and John Davidson, head of the clearinghouse, in addition to members of the Clearing House staff. The group ended up spending the night in the Merc's clearinghouse sweating out the unmatched trades. Much of the time the Merc officials huddled in the Clearing House's conference room on the sixth floor, monitoring the trades as they cleared. Unlike the securities industry, which took five working days to settle accounts, the futures industry operated on a pay-as-you-go basis in which accounts were squared up each night or before trading opened the next morning. This daily process, known as "market to market," was keyed to a zero-sum arrangement, meaning that for every winner in the futures market there was a loser. In short, the sum of profits had to equal the total of losses, and that tally was based on the day's price change. There were those in the securities industry unfamiliar with the pay-as-you-go system, as the Merc found out the hard way on the morning of the twentieth when it was faced with a number-crunching headache that put its financial integrity on a tightrope.

As the 7 A.M. deadline for confirmation of settlements—based on trading during the nineteenth—drew near, a sticky problem arose. A major Wall Street investment banking firm owed the Merc $207,169,087.50 in trade settlements plus margin calls of $136,318,789.50, for a grand total of $343,487,877. It was a significant sum, given that the total settlement from trading on 19 October 1987 amounted to $2.53 billion, versus $120 million on a normal day. The Merc had collected $1,620,300,000 of that total through intraday calls during the nineteenth. The balance of $1,100,125,356.50 was due by 7 A.M. Tuesday. (The figures do not add up because of noncash payments and netting effects.) In addition, there were margin calls of $1,007,169,501.53. Therefore, the funds owed by the firm represented 19 percent of the outstanding settlement funds and 14 percent of the margin payments. That was but one side of the equation. On the other side, the Merc owed $670 million to Goldman Sachs and $917 million to Kidder Peabody.

Normally, the bank—in this case Continental Bank—would transfer the money without a hitch in paperwork shuffling, based on a telephone call from the Merc Clearing House. It was normal procedure. But not this time—not a day after the crash, and not with such huge sums at stake.

The 7 A.M. deadline passed and the investment firm's account had yet to be settled. John Davidson was on the phone, trying to convince the Continental Bank to arrange the transfer. Continental was having its own problems that day with First Options, its wholly owned subsidiary that was the nation's largest clearing firm in terms of the number of options market makers. On Tuesday, First Options had severe liquidity problems brought on by large losses among certain market makers, restrictions imposed by the comptroller of the currency on Continental's ability to infuse additional capital into First Options, and extensive market makers' withdrawals of equity from their accounts. For the month of October alone, First Options would lose $79.5 million before its crisis was resolved through an infusion of $312 million from Continental Bank and its holding company. Meanwhile, Don Serpico, vice-president of operations, told Lind of Continental's refusal to budge, given the sums involved. Lind quickly relayed the message to Sandner, urging him to contact the investment firm's top management.

Sandner made the call. According to Merc clearinghouse records from 19 and 20 October, there are no notes or other memoranda relevant to Sandner's conversation to a specific senior official at thefirm. The clearinghouse telephone conversations were not tape-recorded then as they are today. Both Sandner and John Davidson believe it was the firm's chairman with whom Sandner spoke on that Tuesday morning. The conversation took place in the old clearinghouse conference room, and, while Sandner was on one phone, Brodsky was on another with Continental officials Wilma Smelcer and Ken Chalmers, trying to get the payment confirmed and giving them "comfort" with the source of the funds.

The firm's chairman had been called out of a meeting to take Sandner's call. "This is the chairman of the Chicago Mercantile Exchange," opened Sandner, raising his voice to convey a sense of urgency. The chairman, believed Sandner, felt neither the gravity nor the urgency of the situation because of the five-day settlement period in the securities business. Then Sandner unloaded.

"You don't understand," said Sandner. "Let me tell you the facts. This is a no-debt system. Payment and collection of the previous day's trading must be settled by 7 A.M. of the next morning or before trading begins. Yours is the only firm that hasn't made its payment. If the money isn't forthcoming, the headlines in tomorrow's newspapers will say that your firm defaulted."

"I understand," the voice on the other end of the line assured Sandner.

Within 45 minutes the settlement was resolved. The clearinghouse itself bears some responsibility for the snag, according to Davidson. When the settlement reports first went to the banks—just after 4 A.M. on the morning of 20 October—they indicated that the investment firm owed more than $427 million, a figure nearly twice the amount that was actually due. The clearinghouse staff had not credited the firm with three intraday margin calls that it paid during 19 October. "Continental's decision making may have been slowed by the need to consider a figure almost twice as large as what was really due," Davidson explained. The error was caught at 6:30 A.M., and the bankers were alerted over the phone. By 7:10 corrected reports had been faxed to each settlement bank.

In any case, there were lessons to be learned by the brush with financial gridlock. "It afforded us an opportunity to completely revise, update, and automate processing in the financial area and to strengthen our resources and available collateral," Davidson said. "With respect to the financial services industry in general, it highlighted the benefits of the pay-as-you-go market-to-market system to the senior decision makers in the industry."

Throughout those hectic hours a situation involving margins occurred that became a first for the Merc: Cross-margining took place between futures and equity options. No one reported the fact, nor did the Merc bring it to anyone's attention. But it happened and it is worth reviewing at this point because in October 1989 the Merc established a program with the Options Clearing Corporation to allow a cross-margining system to help eliminate drains in cash flow. In the futures market both buyer and seller deposit margin money with their respective clearing member. The initial margin or original margin thus serves as a performance bond. If the account loses money, additional margin or variation margin is required to ensure the position's financial integrity. All the options exchanges, including the CBOE, clear through the Options Clearing Corporation (OCC). In contrast, the Merc maintains its own clearinghouse exclusively for its clearing member firms. Whereas the Federal Reserve sets initial margins for stocks and options, the commodity exchanges set margins in the contracts traded on their floors. Precisely what happened on 19 October to one particular firm that cleared through both the Merc's Clearing House and the OCC shows the kinds of machinations the clearing system underwent during the crash. It also shows that the notion of cross margining was more than wishful thinking.

Going into trading on 19 October, the firm had long positions in the S&P 500 futures, which were offset by a portfolio of broad-based CBOE securities index options (OEX) cleared at OCC. As the S&P 500 futures contracts declined in price, at 10 A.M. the clearinghouse made the first of its intraday calls for settlement, asking the firm for $5 million. (Twelve other clearing members were called at the same time for a total of $290 million.) The request was promptly met by Harris Trust and Savings Bank, the firm's bank. In the early afternoon the firm received a second intraday call of $5 million (This time 20 other firms were called to come with a total of $660,500,000). Again, the call was met by Harris. Late in afternoon the clearinghouse issued yet a third call, this time for $6 million. (In total, 15 firms were called for a total of $669,500,000.) Rather than meet the third margin call, James Colville of Harris Bank called the Merc's John Davidson to explain that the firm had cross-market positions between the Merc and the CBOE and that settlement on the long position was being financed by the Harris Bank. Harris had collateral from the firm, including long puts— options that give its holders the right to sell the underlying stock—which were in pledge accounts at the OCC. Throughout the day the puts had appreciated, but there was no mechanism for the OCC to inform the bank of the increased value of these puts on an intraday basis. Consequently, Harris could not determine with any certainty the value of its collateral and would not extend additional unsecured credit to the firm.

After the close of the market, OCC chairman Wayne Luthringshausen called Brodsky (Brodsky had worked with Luthringshausen since 1975, when Brodsky served as Amex's director on the OCC board for a period of seven years). Luthringhausen confirmed that there indeed were long put positions on the firm's books at OCC that had appreciated "substantially" in value. It meant that, if the firm's position were considered in total, its options positions could be viewed as cross-margining the futures positions. Thus, with an established offset mechanism, the firm would not have to come up with margin on the third intraday call.

Under the circumstances Brodsky was willing to proceed, but he suggested two additional steps: First, the firm's principals were requested to come to the Merc to confirm their positions and their intent to meet the margin variation call the next morning. Second, the Merc's Clearing House staff had to be on the phone with the OCC staff during the night to confirm—prior to the 7 A.M. settlement time the next morning—that the positions and their values were in the appropriate account for the benefit of Harris Bank.

By 8:30 P.M., the firm's officials arrived at the Merc, where they met with Jerry Beyer, John Davidson, and others in the Clearing House. There the firm's contingent satisfied the Merc executives with respect to its positions and its commitment to make payment on the morning of the twentieth, meeting the first condition that Brodsky had outlined. Consequently, the firm was informed that its third intraday margin call had been cancelled. "This can accurately be said to have been the first use, albeit ad hoc, of cross margining," Brodsky said.

Throughout the next two weeks of trading, the Merc's Clearing House, the OCC, and Harris Bank were in constant contact with each other over the firm's positions. On days when the market was rallying, OCC would take comfort from the gains in the futures positions, which offset losses in the options positions, just as the Merc had taken such comfort on 19 October. Nearly two years later, on 6 October 1989, cross-margining for proprietary accounts—the brokerage's own rather than that of its customer's—between the Merc and OCC went into operation. The firm just discussed became a participant in March 1990. (Phase two cross margining for CBOE and CME floor traders went into effect on 26 November 1991.)

Thus, the day of the crash—19 October 1987—was an institutional panic, dispassionately fueled by computers with little participation by the public. Were computers really to blame? Some insisted that they were. Others with equal conviction said that they weren't. Suddenly, the computer was like an unconventional artist bursting into the limelight, only to be misunderstood and acclaimed at the same time. If computers did help accelerate the Black Monday slide, they were most certainly not responsible for initiating it. What existed in the financial world was a clear case of what author Richard Wurman calls "information anxiety," the gap between what people understand and what they think they should understand. The data was available because the computers had tucked it away. But coming to terms with it and understanding the whims of panic was like trying to figure out when the San Andreas fault is going to unleash the big one. Everyone knew that computers didn't move stocks; people did. Yet even before the experts began their autopsy on who or what killed stocks, most of the press was playing Taps for program trading and portfolio insurance. Conventional wisdom had computers making quick decisions without regard for a company's prospects or the health of the overall economy. Some saw black humor in the black box that brought on Black Monday: What was the difference between the crash of 1929 and 1987? In the crash of 1987, it was the computers that jumped out of the windows, joked some brokers who were still able to laugh. No one could blame computer trading in the 1929 crash because there were no computers. Then, the perceived villain was margin buying; now it was computerized trading. Some saw it as a market correction; others, simply as a panic, like a classic bank run. Most, however, were bewildered and numb as the debate over causes of the crash sought to seek simple answers to complex situations. Perhaps at no time in American history had a financial panic so quickly undergone analysis with such unflinching scrutiny.

The post-crash scenario became a remake of *Rashomon*—everyone had a different version of the events. Reports poured in from regulators, independent commissions, and exchanges, including the Merc's blue-ribbon effort from a committee that was chaired by University of Chicago economist Merton Miller, who three years later would win a Nobel prize for his research in finance theory; Yale School of Management economist and dean Burton Malkiel, a former member of President Gerald Ford's Council of Economic Advisors and author of *A Random Walk Down Wall Street;* Stanford University finance and law professor Myron Scholes, co-developer of the Black-Scholes options pricing model widely used by traders, investors, and portfolio managers; and attorney John D. Hawke, Jr., former general counsel for the board of governors of the Federal Reserve System, who specialized in regulation of financial institutions at Arnold and Porter, a Washington law firm.

The NYSE-sponsored report, made public in December 1987, was not a study of the crash. Commissioned long before the crash to study the effects of computerized trading on market volatility, it took a hard swipe at the economic function of futures markets. The crash had ignited the feud between Wall Street old-timers who had aged on stocks and fundamental investing and the younger, computer-bred "rocket scientists"—so called because they are trained in mathematics and computer science—who used stock index futures and options in the design of sophisticated trading strategies that included portfolio insurance. Since the crash this coterie of youthful math and finance whizzes, also known as "quants" for their quantitative, number-crunching analytical style, were on the defensive, along with Chicago's futures exchanges. The New York Stock Exchange report had widened even more the generation gap—between the prostock and antistock index traders—that already existed within the big investment banking firms such as Morgan Stanley and Salomon Brothers. Directed by Nicholas Katzenbach, former attorney general under President Lyndon Johnson, the report purposely avoided analysis of trading data. Rather, as one observer noted, issues were examined "impressionistically." The report emanated more whining than wisdom by painting the stock market as the haven for long-term-minded investors, whereas futures and options were the lure for short-term speculators. Program trading was the artery that carried the speculative blood to the cash market. Merc economist Todd Petzel interpreted the Katzenbach findings this way: "If futures cannot be banned outright because they may serve some hedging function, any activity like program trading that would link the markets should be made prohibitively expensive." (Again, the Katzenbach report was in the works even before the crash and was intended as a survey of program trading. That's why the rather slim volume—compared with the other reports—was the first one to be released to the public.)

The Katzenbach report appealed to those uneasy over the rocket scientists' new financial inventions and instruments. It was the same kind of ammunition fired by the traditionalists in the 1960s at the wunderkinder of that era, who also had altered concepts to create the new-fangled investment model known as the mutual fund. Predictably, the Merc leadership dismissed the NYSE report as spurious and self-serving, a ploy to draw attention away from the argument that the meltdown should have been traced to problems on the NYSE floor, where the trading systems and the specialists could not cope with the selloff because no one had the necessary capital. The specialist gridlock precluded a great deal of program trading because the NYSE had stopped trading in a number individual stocks. About a month after the crash, *The Wall Street Journal* ran an article that reconstructed the events of 19 and 20 October and detailed the specialists' problems on those days. The lengthy story found "little to suggest program trading or portfolio insurance caused the crisis." The truth of the matter is that there were fewer program trades than usual on 19 October. All along, however, NYSE chairman John Phelan believed that program trading increased volatility in the markets and that the volatility would eventually discourage people from investing in stocks. "When the data behind the events were examined closely," Petzel said, "the Katzenbach Report conclusions could not be supported."

That certainly was not the case with the major government studies made over the six months following the crash. They included "The Report of the Presidential Task Force on Market Mechanisms" (the Brady Commission Report, January 1988); "The Final Report on Stock Index Futures and Cash Market Activity During October 1987 to the U.S. Commodity Futures Trading Commission" (the CFTC report, January 1988); "The October 1987 Market Break: A Report by the Division of Market Regulation—U.S. Securities and Exchange Commission" (the SEC report, February 1988); "Financial Markets: Preliminary Observations on the October 1987 Crash" (General Accounting Office, January 1988). Though these titles may have sounded a bit somber—and even foreboding—great care had been taken in checking the trading data during preparation of the reports. The SEC report, for example, had a 10-minute breakdown of the index-related selling on the NYSE on 19 and 20 October, as well as the chronologies of portfolio insurance selling on the Merc. After reviewing the reports even Petzel conceded, "There were no stones left unturned."

A recurring theme in these crash commentaries was that program trading, portfolio insurance, and arbitrage trading sent selling pressure from the futures exchanges in Chicago to the NYSE. Buyers, asserted both the Brady and SEC reports, were overwhelmed by portfolio insurance or by the fact that portfolio insurers were significant sellers, causing a selling overhang that dampened the chances of a price recovery. But the CFTC report in late 1987 (and its two follow-up reports in 1988) found that volume from both index arbitrage and portfolio insurance was dwarfed by other institutional sales. For instance, during the first half of trading on the nineteenth, one mutual fund alone traded some 17.5 million shares, or 34 percent of the total volume. Consequently, none of the studies recommended direct curbs on program trading, portfolio insurance, or index arbitrage. On the contrary, they all concluded that the derivative index markets provided valuable hedging and market timing benefits to institutions. That, however, didn't stop some of the large Wall Street brokerage firms from voluntarily stopping index arbitrage for their own accounts.

Birnbaum's boss at the NYSE, John Phelan, seemed ambivalent when it came to the futures markets, despite the fact that the New York Futures Exchange was the futures arm of the NYSE and that Phelan was the NYFE's first chairman. The NYSE had even bought the American Commodities Exchange from the American Stock Exchange to beef up its efforts. But in the process of the crash, the market had redefined itself with a new term: an interlinked market. Stocks and futures were inseparable. Suddenly, futures were in the limelight. But Phelan still didn't care about futures. He was a securities man who grew up on the floor of the NYSE as a specialist, having learned the business from his father. Getting the NYSE into the futures business was a defensive move, Birnbaum maintains. "Someone once asked what would happen if they'd ever start trading IBM futures," he said. "And that question prodded the NYSE to get involved with futures."

The markets now appeared in a harsh floodlight, personified by an intruding—and intriguing—technology that seemed to be taking over. On one level there was a philosophical clash over the economic function of stock and futures markets. The stock market played an economic role—raising capital for American companies—whereas the value of the futures market was limited. That argument, however, ignored the risk-transferring function of the futures market and the hard fact that during the crash the futures market was a safety valve that absorbed selling pressure. The derivative products thus enabled investors to reduce their exposure to the stock market during uncertain periods, and they provided an alternative to removing capital from the market entirely, which is what happens when investors sell their cash stocks. Futures, then, are risk management tools that in essence are an adjunct to the capital formation process. That is a fact, claim proponents of derivative instruments, often overlooked or misunderstood by critics. Index futures, in another role, serve as indicators for future price levels in fast-moving and volatile markets. This price discovery mechanism is an indication of the value of the cash market where individual stocks can be bought or sold when calm is restored.

On yet another level—under the heading of efficiency—there were things such as speed of trades and transactional costs to consider. Portfolios that included pension, insurance, and mutual funds were wielded by huge institutional investors. At the time of the crash, these institutions held an estimated $950 billion in stocks supported by batteries of computers programmed to signal where managers could sell whenever numerical trip wires were hit. Hundreds of millions of dollars cascaded in and out of the markets, affecting the value of hundreds of stocks simultaneously. Even though these institutions controlled only 33 percent of the equity on U.S. exchanges, their activity accounted for nearly eight out of every ten stock trades each day. "Pachyderms," one observer called the institutions that now traded on the New York Stock Exchange, where 1,523 stocks worth some $2.1 trillion are listed. A decade earlier a 30-million-share day would stretch the limits of the NYSE, causing hours of delay to complete transactions. But bigger, faster computers humming in the bowels of the exchange changed all that. Banks of IBM and Tandem computers ran the NYSE's DOT system, which recorded trades and relayed confirmation back to brokers. The NYSE's computers and those of the American Stock Exchange are owned and operated through a joint affiliate known as the Securities Industry Automation Corp., which harbors a complex of six miles of fiber-optic and coaxial cables with a number-crunching capability said to rival that of NASA's mission control. Today every exchange has its own spiffy acronym for the equivalent of the Big Board's SuperDot order processing operation; at the American Exchange it's PER (post-execution reporting); at the Chicago Board Options Exchange, RAES (Retail Automatic Execution System, which allows public customers to purchase or sell up to 10 contracts through automatic execution); at the Merc it's TOPS (Trade Order Processing System); and at the Chicago Board of Trade, EOS (Electronic Order System). Neither the Merc's nor the CBOT's systems were yet in operation during the crash.

The electronics of the 1980s offered institutional investors a scale and sophistication they could not resist. In the early 1980s selling or buying more than 30 stocks at one time was the trading art of the day. By the mid-1980s trading in subsets of the 500 different stocks was routine. And so was program trading. Basically, there are four kinds of program trades. The first type, and the most widely used, involves the simultaneous placement of buy or sell orders for a portfolio of at least 15 different stocks valued at more than $1 million. The second type, known as portfolio insurance or dynamic hedging, uses the futures market whenever the cash market index falls to a predetermined level, usually by 3 percent. Rather than sell stocks as their prices are falling, portfolio insurers sell stock-index futures. If the decline persists, the futures are repurchased at a lower level that yields a big profit, which offsets some of the loss sustained on the stocks. Losses in the cash market (stocks) are thus made up by gains in the derivative market (futures). So traders who buy the futures hedge their positions by making computer-aided sales of the underlying stocks, which puts more downward pressure on a plummeting market. That's why critics during the crash pointed to program trading as the culprit. The third program-trading strategy is tactical asset allocation, which employs stocks, bonds, futures, options, and cash equivalents. Through a predetermined formula and programmed computers, one asset is exchanged for another in order to get the highest yield from an investment portfolio. The fourth strategy is index arbitrage. Traditional arbitrage is as old as the markets themselves. Simply, it worked this way: If a widget market in Chicago is higher-priced than the widget market in New York, an arbitrageur will sell New York widgets and buy Chicago widgets, or vice versa. The same approach takes advantage of momentary differences between the price of a futures contract and of the stocks themselves. When that spread becomes sufficiently wide, a trader can lock in a profit at no risk by, for instance, buying the futures and selling the underlying stocks. It was index arbitrage that was blamed for the market's sudden burst in volatility, though the point was never conclusively proven. Indeed, some experts believe that the opposite is true: Index arbitrage reduces volatility by helping the market reverse course when it goes too far in one direction. On the day of the crash, however, most of the arbitrageurs were on the sidelines because the computers that tracked stock prices had fallen too far behind.[2]

There were few who truly believed that derivatives alone had caused the crash. After all, exchanges in Japan, England, France, West Germany, Australia, and Hong Kong had been hammered with equal or larger declines, yet none of them had a sufficiently developed futures market to allow arbitrage or portfolio insurance trades of significance. "To assign all of the blame on program trading is perhaps convenient, but far wide of the mark," observed First Boston analyst Scott Hamilton four days after the crash. Indeed, the term *program trading* was somewhat misleading. It was derived not from the fact that trades were executed by computer programs but that they involved the systematic sale of portfolios of stocks as if they were one stock. The first program trades, executed in the 1970s, didn't involve computers. It wasn't until 1982 that program trading came into its own with the advent of stock-index futures, which, in essence, enabled investors to speculate how the entire market was going. The strategy opened a variety of opportunities.

If anything, the crash proved that the world was one big global financial village, as each foreign market responded differently. It was in the Asian cradle of capitalism—Hong Kong, long a model of free markets—where the system vaporized. Nowhere did the ticker shock of Black Monday rattle an exchange more than in the Crown Colony. When the Hang Seng Index dropped 11 percent within the first few hours of that day, Hong Kong Stock Exchange chairman Ronald Li simply took the easy way out: He closed the exchange. Four days later, when the exchange reopened, the value of shares had dropped by a third, to some $50 billion, wiping out any gains that had been made over the year. Even before the Hong Kong Exchange reopened, local money men were characterizing it as a poorly run casino. Confidence in the Hang Seng was badly shaken among locals and international investors, forcing British officials to ante up $512 million in loans to support the stock-futures market while Beijing forked over $42 million to shore up imperiled stock prices.[2]

Even before the crash, market volatility had been pushed onto center stage. The system showed serious signs of overload in September 1986—the year in which Big Board volume soared to a daily average of about 140 million shares—when the market suffered a severe plunge as a then-unprecedented 240.5 million shares changed hands on 11 September 1986. The Dow had dropped 120 points during 11 and 12 September. Not long after that day—nearly a year before the crash—John Phelan, chairman of the New York Stock Exchange, gave a speech in which he warned that a combination of the various program trading strategies could bring about a market "meltdown." Price volatility struck again on 23 January 1987, when the Dow took a 115-point fall. And long before the ink was dry on the Securities and Exchange Commission's thorough and voluminous report on the October market crash 10 months later, SEC chairman David Ruder had begun to share publicly some of his thoughts on the impact of derivative products. The former dean of Chicago's Northwestern Law School had chosen familiar turf from which to make his first public address as the newly appointed SEC chairman. On 6 October 1987 he told members of the Bond Club of Chicago, "I have no magic answers to volatility concerns. What is clear is that index futures and options are valuable products and that measures to address potentially destructive market volatility must be developed." He also talked of a "meltdown" scenario and ways of reducing the "likelihood of a market 'cascade'" without significantly reducing the benefits derived from index products."

An SEC analysis of 11 and 12 September attributed the sharp market sell-off strictly to fundamental economic conditions at the time rather than to "artificial forces" resulting from index-related trading strategies. Nevertheless, index trading was seen by Ruder as a catalyst that rapidly "changed investor perceptions to individual stock prices and may have condensed the time period in which the decline occurred." Ruder, however, was quick to remind the Chicago audience, "In reality computers make ongoing calculations and alert traders to potential opportunities. They generally do not automatically initiate or execute trades." (It was a point frequently misunderstood by much of the media in the early days of the crash.) As far as the use of derivative index products, no one from the SEC, including Ruder, would deny the advantage they offered institutional money managers: the opportunity to adjust quickly at low transaction costs the debt and equity holdings in their portfolios.

At 11 A.M. on 20 October, the S&P pit closed in anticipation of the NYSE's closing. Closing the Merc was, as Brodsky put it, "a scary and ultimately unprecedented decision." The decision was made by Melamed, Sandner, and Brodsky (with approval of the Merc executive committee), based on a conversation with Phelan over the speaker phone in Brodsky's office that morning.

"Phelan said he was considering closing the NYSE," recalled Brodsky. "It was viable at the time and we read into what he was saying." The closing of the S&P pit was met with cheers, even from the die-hard traders who lived by the Merc's unofficial motto, "Free markets for free men." Under normal circumstances, Brodsky said, "they would have run us up the flag pole" had the exchange officials interfered with trading. But the conditions were far from normal. If the NYSE closed, the Merc would have been exposed in the futures markets under circumstances where intermarket trades couldn't be offset with trades in the stock market. The Merc didn't want to have a futures market that predicted price movements on the stock exchange unless traders were able to know the prices on the stock exchange. Wisely, the Merc closed for an hour, thus inhibiting the so-called "billboard effect," whereby stock traders based their purchases on the predicted futures prices. The fact that the futures prices were showing dramatic declines—50 to 60 points compared with prices on the NYSE—was terrifying for stock traders. For the few brave souls the right strategy at the time was to buy futures because of the dramatic discounts from actual stock prices. (In fact, some major U.S. pension funds did precisely that with great success.) Buying stock index futures at a deep discount is similar to buying premium merchandise in, say, a department store at a 50 percent discount from the normal price—with the knowledge that the price will return to normal and that the merchandise can be returned at full retail price.

As for index arbitrage, it couldn't be properly executed because there were too many stocks closed or effectively closed. Even though the NYSE had the "up-tick" rule—the short sale of a stock permitted only when the stock's most recent price change is an up tick, or upward price movement—there were institutional investors who could execute their strategies without selling short. (The up-tick rule was imposed by the SEC in 1938 under SEC chairman William O. Douglas, who would go on to become the renowned Justice of the United States Supreme Court. It was aimed at reducing volatility and manipulation.)

The closing had been the Merc's toughest moment of the week. Contrary to its philosophy, it had closed the market for the stock index futures for some 49 minutes—something akin to a bomb scare. Shortly before the closing, Phelan had told the Merc that there were no buyers and that the NYSE couldn't open as many as 90 major stocks. In effect, as the Merc saw it, it was the only U.S. equity market in full operation at that point. "We decided to suspend trading rather than leaving our exchange as an island to be dumped on by the rest of the world," Sandner told a press conference at the time. "Phelan said the New York Stock Exchange was on the verge of closing, and then he went into a meeting." If word had gotten out, Merc officials reasoned, its market could have dropped another 10 or 20 points on the S&P 500 stock index, equivalent to 80 to 160 Dow points. Faced with that prospect, the Merc took a breath. The billboard effect disappeared in that time, and the stock market turned around, spurred in good part by a rash of companies buying back their own stock at bargain prices with SEC blessings. Trading in stock-related futures and options also was halted at various times during the morning of the twentieth on the CBOE, NYFE, KCBOT, and Amex.

The Merc's board of governors had also taken other emergency action on Tuesday to help keep brokers who filled customer orders in the S&P pit. Monday's volatility had reduced the number of traders willing to act as brokers on the top step of the pit. A shortage of brokers threatened the pit's liquidity, making it difficult for some brokerage houses to get orders filled. In a notice to Merc members, the exchange amended its rules to temporarily allow clearing members to verbally release and requalify brokers to fill orders. Merc rules had specified that those releases and qualifications were to be submitted in writing to the exchange. Going into Tuesday 20 October there were serious questions. Could the markets sustain another selling onslaught? Would the Federal Reserve step in with funds to sooth frayed nerves of Wall Street bankers? And what about the clearing systems of the futures exchanges that worked on a "market to market" basis of adjusting accounts to reflect gains and losses at the end of the trading day? That morning the Federal Reserve Board made a crucial announcement: Before the opening of the equity markets, it would pump needed liquidity into the pipeline by making repurchase agreements. The Fed planned to buy securities from government dealers for immediate delivery with an agreement to sell the securities back at the same price within 15 days. This allowed the Fed to inject reserves into the banking system on a temporary basis to meet a temporary need. The reserves would be withdrawn as soon as that need passed. The Fed had learned from its past sins of omission that a financial system under severe shock needed assurance to avoid panic. A sudden lack of money had a domino effect; nervous banks would not lend money to securities dealers and brokers to meet margin calls. Unable to borrow money, they would have to sell holdings, thus driving prices even lower. And finally, if brokers and specialists could not do business, neither could the exchanges, as was the case in 1929.

Throughout the years the Merc had to hose down fires over everything from the onion scandals in the 1950s to the broker squabbles over commission rates on the trading floor in the 1980s. The press had always covered the incidents, but not in such detail and with such zeal. In its second-day coverage of the crash, the headline of a *Wall Street Journal* story out of Chicago stated, "Chicago's 'Shadow Markets' Led Free Fall In a Plunge That Began Right at Opening." The story opened with the line, "The panic began here."

"We were surprised at the press reaction and media onslaught," said Andrew Yemma, the Merc's vice-president of public relations. "We weren't accustomed to such intense national attention." The former financial editor of the *Chicago Sun-Times,* Yemma had only been at the Merc for six months before the lightning struck. In fact, none of his staff of four, including a secretary, had been there more than six months. Suddenly, every newspaper, magazine, and TV station was knocking at the Merc's door asking for interviews, explanations, backgrounders. "Papers that never covered us as well as TV networks were showing up demanding interviews and comments with little preparation and understanding of the futures markets," Yemma said.

Like a frustrated teenager screaming at parents that "you don't understand," the Merc sought to explain itself. Within two weeks after the crash, it held press conferences in Chicago, Washington, New York, Paris, and London, issuing a fact book to explain index futures, program trading, portfolio insurance, margins, and index arbitrage, among other subjects. "We needed outside help. We needed to be proactive," said Yemma. The Merc turned to Hill and Knowlton, the high-powered public relations specialists geared to crisis management. A media analysis and random survey were taken by the H&K, which revealed that most people weren't familiar with futures and options or program trading. As it turned out, the H&K people didn't know much about the Merc either. H&K flew several of its vice-presidents from New York and Washington to Chicago, where one of them spent an hour interviewing Melamed and Sandner about the Merc. During the course of that interview in the Merc's executive conference room, the two became skeptical about the queries, which indicated a lack of understanding of futures markets. "What are you prepared to give up?" asked an H&K executive. "Are you willing to be regulated by the SEC?" After that question, recalled Yemma, the Merc officials had lost faith in the outside public relations effort.

In a series of editorial meetings, Merc officials meet with *Wall Street Journal* editorial chief Robert Bartley and writer George Malone. Then on to *Newsweek* and *Fortune* magazines. At *Fortune,* managing editor Marshall Loeb hosted a round table discussion of the crash with 20 of his editors, firing questions at Melamed, Sandner, Brodsky and Yemma. "Marshall said it was the biggest turnout of his staff in years," Yemma said. "They didn't understand the futures business. They viewed us as a bunch of speculators, allowing bets on the stock market."

At times there was almost a circus atmosphere on the media's part. One day after the crash Jonathan Brandmeier, a Chicago FM radio disc jockey, got out on the catwalk above the trading floor set on doing a colorful commentary. He was immediately hustled away. Hundreds of interview requests poured into the exchange from every corner of the United States and from overseas publications as well. Even Ted Koppel, in one of his "Nightline" town meetings, tried to explain the crash to Americans with the help of the Muppets. Sandner, representing the Merc and the futures markets, was one of 15 guests from all sectors of the financial world who appeared on the Nightline special. Koppel and the Muppets did little to enlighten the public.

Merc officials, however, had better luck enlightening the powers of the securities industry. They lost little time explaining their perspective on the crash. On 24 October, the Saturday following Black Monday, Brodsky called SEC chairman David Ruder, who was spending the weekend at his home in the northern Chicago suburb where Brodsky also lived. A meeting was set for 3:30 that afternoon. The Merc contingent that showed up at Ruder's home included Melamed; Brodsky, Rick Kilcollin, the Merc's senior vice-president of research; and Donald Jacobs, Dean of Northwestern University's Kellog School of Management, who was an outside Merc governor and Ruder's friend and former colleague. Jacobs served as the intermediary between the Ruder and the Merc officials who reviewed the week's activity, carefully explaining why the Merc had temporarily ceased trading on Tuesday and how the market was able to keep its nose above water after it had nearly drowned on Monday. On the nineteenth, Brodsky explained, arbitrage on the NYSE had accounted for only 10 percent of the NYSE total, down from the 16 percent to 20 percent it usually accounted for. The result was a large discount between the futures and cash market. Melamed confirmed that, on Tuesday, Phelan had told him that the NYSE was on the brink of closing and that the Merc had responded by closing because it didn't want to be the only market. If the futures market had not existed, Melamed said, there would have been greater pressure on stocks. Jacobs emphasized that during the week as the automated trading systems—the NYSE's DOT in particular—became unavailable, the futures market had become the only indicator of price. In response to Ruder's question as to who futures buyers were on Monday and Tuesday, Kilcollin, who had spread sheets with him, responded as if he were rattling off a bill of particulars: On Monday, institutions were net sellers—selling some 28,000 S&P futures contracts and buying 24,000 contracts, including 8,000 institutions, 10 index arbitragers, 2,000 market makers, and 4,000 unknown. Throughout the week, the floor community was intact and there were no cash or capital problems, the Merc officials assured Ruder. All through the hour and a half meeting Ruder listened patiently, asked questions, and took copious notes on a legal pad. Throughout the crash and its aftermath, Ruder and the SEC were at the center of a communications web that reached every corner of the financial community.

Determined to keep the lines of communication open, Merc officials again met with Ruder four days later, on the evening of 28 October in Washington, where they had come to testify before a congressional committee on the crash. The dinner meeting at the Melrose Restaurant in the Hyatt Park Hotel was attended by Melamed, Sandner, Brodsky, and Charles (Chip) Seeger, senior vice-president and government counsel, who worked out of the Merc's Washington office. Ruder was accompanied by Richard Ketchum, Director of the SEC's division of market regulation; he would oversee the SEC's report on the crash, which the agency euphemistically called the "market break." The dinner was more social than business, a sort of get-acquainted round. To the futures industry, Ruder, a legal scholar straight out of the university and only two months on the SEC post, was an unknown entity who needed educating in the futures markets. The futures industry, however, believed that it already had at least one sympathetic ear in the agency, that of Joseph Grundfest, an attorney and economist, who had been an SEC commissioner since 1985.

Even before the week of 19 October was over, tension built between the futures and securities industries in a war of words—and ideas set off by recriminations over which side was responsible for the crash and just how markets should be regulated in its wake. Soon the media had painted it as a turf war, pitting the SEC against the CFTC, as well as the securities powers in New York against the futures powers in Chicago. In between were the Washington politicians as referees, promising to introduce bills to change the way markets worked. "The markets today are a hybrid between an equities and commodities market that nobody knows about," asserted NYSE chairman John Phelan. "The assertion that our market was the villain and caused the fall of the stock is blatantly false," opined Melamed. "We are going to look at the problems created for [market] regulation by having two separate regulators," promised Ruder. "We have to ask ourselves if we can afford a technology that slips out of human control," mused Representative Edward Markey (D-MA), head of the Securities Subcommittee of the House Energy and Commerce Committee.

Based on all the comments, confusion, and market aftershocks, the media drew its own conclusions. "New York and Chicago fight a turf battle that is depressing markets and stalling reform," proclaimed *Time* magazine a month after the crash in a three-page article headlined, "The War of Two Cities." Before the *Time* article appeared, however, officials from the Chicago exchanges and NYSE already had begun a dialog unbeknownst to the media. Melamed, Sandner, and Brodsky, along with CBOT president Thomas Donovan and chairman Karsten (Cash) Mahlmann, met with Phelan in New York. The purpose of the meeting was to present a united front between New York and Chicago that would tell the world that the leaders of the securities and futures markets were working in tandem toward solutions. All along, the Merc wanted to present an industry solution in an effort to ward off intrusive new congressional regulations. That meant that the exchanges had to speak with one voice. The outcome of the meeting was to be presented in a press release like a communique dispatched following a political summit between superpowers. But the meeting backfired. Donovan and Mahlmann saw Phelan as being too high-handed and were not as eager to cooperate with the NYSE as the Merc had been. The meeting ended in a standoff and feelings of deep animosity between the CBOT and Merc officials that lasted for months. And, of course, a news release was never prepared. Yet the Merc vowed that it would continue to work with the NYSE on its own.

On the morning of 4 December at 9:30 A.M., Ruder, who had given a speech in Chicago the day before, visited the Merc, where Sandner accompanied him around the exchange and explained how the prices were determined at the opening of the market. In mid-March 1988, Ruder, appearing before the Senate Agriculture Committee, warned that talks between the regulators and exchanges had yet to produce any agreement on new measures, including coordinated trading halts, price limits, and other circuit breakers. Ruder's comments echoed the sentiment that had arisen among members of the futures and securities industries that the hodgepodge reaction of the stock, options, and futures exchanges to the market pummeling lacked coordination.

The Brady Task Force had recommended a unified clearing system for options and futures, but the SEC thought the problems of such a system would outweigh the benefits. Ruder had repeatedly proposed raising margins on stock index futures and giving the SEC regulatory authority over them. The CFTC had agreed that higher margins were necessary, but only to levels that guaranteed financial protection. The CFTC didn't want circuit breakers unless there were price limits across all markets, and there was no way that it would ever consider giving up authority over the index futures market. One thing Ruder and then acting CFTC chairman Kalo Heineman did agreed on was to bring the exchange powers face to face. On 10 February 1988 an informal meeting was held in Ruder's SEC office in Washington, attended by Phelan, Melamed, and Heineman. For two hours they discussed the problems that existed between the derivative market and stock market. The problems, Ruder and Heineman agreed, had to be solved by the markets, not by the regulators. "New York had treated Chicago as a stepchild and here was this stepchild growing to be huge," Ruder said. Ruder was trying to assume the role of the ideal party host who tries to keep the conversation among the guests flowing, embarrasses no one, and sends the guests home in a pleasant mood. Indeed, Phelan and Melamed left the meeting upbeat, agreeing to maintain a dialog over ways to cope with another market decline in the future.

Four months later, on 6 June, Ruder paid an unofficial—and unexpected—visit to the Merc. Although he had called in advance, it was still somewhat surprising to the Merc officials that the very person who was pressing for SEC jurisdiction over the derivative products would walk into the enemy camp. "We didn't know what to make of the visit," Brodsky said. "We looked at it as an effort to gather information first-hand and to extend an olive branch." Ruder met with Melamed, Sandner, and Brodsky to informally discuss the interaction between the stock market and stock index futures. It was a Merc first: the first time a chairman of the SEC had come to the exchange to talk things over. Ruder had visited the floor of the Merc in the fall of 1987, but in the mode of a dignitary paying a courtesy call. By now the Federal Reserve had made it clear that it wasn't interested in overseeing the nation's futures exchanges in any way. "Ruder told us he believed the SEC had jurisdiction over the derivative markets, but that reaching that goal wasn't high in his priorities," Brodsky recalled.

Ruder showed concern that the market was still in danger. "There's less danger than you'd think," Sandner replied. "Current market prices for stocks are lower than the underlying fundamental values. Systems were being enhanced and progress is being made in the area of cross margining. Traders are aware that bank credit might become tighter in a down market and that has made them more cautious." Melamed shifted the conversation to another area of concern: the index participation. Index participations are contracts based on the value of a basket of stocks, indexes, or securities. Investors never own the underlying stocks, but take profits or losses in cash based on the overall performance of the index. Both the Merc and CBOT argued against characterizing the index participations as stocks, because to do so would restrict innovation in the futures markets. The SEC disagreed, believing that these hybrid financial instruments were a form of securities and that it thus had jurisdiction over them rather than the CFTC. The SEC went ahead and allowed the Philadelphia Stock Exchange, the American Stock Exchange, and the Chicago Board Options Exchange to begin trading these various forms of the instruments. One such form, for example, which the Philadelphia Stock Exchange was trying to market, was called cash index participation shares, or CIPs. In mid-March 1988 the SEC had approved Philadelphia's trading of CIPs based on two stock indexes: the S&P 500 CIP and the blue-chip CIP (an index of 25 stocks that correlates with the Dow Jones industrial average). The idea was to bring small investors into the market, and the Philadelphia exchange moved to aggressively market the product. Its efforts, however, were short lived. On the heels of SEC approval, the Merc and CBOT challenged jurisdiction of the U.S. Court of Appeals for the Seventh Circuit in Chicago. The futures officials argued that CIPs were actually futures contracts and did not constitute stocks or baskets as the Philadelphia officials contended. Therefore, the Chicago exchanges concluded, it was the CFTC that held full, lawful authority over CIP jurisdiction—not the SEC. Cash index participations traded briefly before the court challenge stopped them in August 1989. The CIPs, which were ruled a futures product by the Court of Appeals, had been offered and margined as a security to individual investors. Had they been traded as futures, the number of qualified brokers and customers would have been greatly diminished. The SEC let the matter drop without challenging the verdict in a higher court.

Meanwhile, the Merc continued to work with the NYSE. On 14 June 1988 Melamed, Sandner, and Brodsky met Phelan, NYSE president Richard Grasso, and NYSE vice-president Donald Stone in New York, where, over dinner at the posh Four Seasons, they discussed some of the Brady Commission's key recommendations and made suggestions as to what could be done to implement some of them. At a critical point during the October crash, the markets for stocks and futures had disconnected, exacerbating an already bad situation. In an effort to stave off future disconnection, the Merc persuaded the NYSE to abandon a 50-point collar that had barred high-volume program traders from using its SuperDOT computer system at any time in which the Dow declined 50 or more points. Beyond that, in an unprecedented show of cooperation, the Merc and NYSE voluntarily had agreed to institute coordinated circuit breakers and "shock absorbers," which would allow the markets and their participants to catch their collective breath in times of tumult.

The Merc wasn't the only one in a defensive posture. There were the rocket scientists, or quants, those mathematicians and academicians trained in computer science who put together formulas for options pricing and risk management strategies using futures contracts. Across the nation, from Columbia University to the University of Chicago to Stanford University, the futures industry had strong academic support. On the day of the crash, Fisher Black, at Goldman, Sachs & Company, said that program trading deserved no blame for the decline. "People have changed their minds about the future of the economy," Black added. It was Black, a former University of Chicago professor, along with his colleague Myron Scholes, who tied the theory of risk analysis to a pricing structure in the 1970s. The result: the Black-Scholes formula for determining the value of an option. Options—from which synthetic futures could be created—thus became the darling of the academic finance community. "The academics became defensive because they believed in financial futures," said economist David Hale, vice-president of Kemper Financial Services.

And so did the Wall Street establishment. Birnbaum, the former SEC attorney and president of both the Amex and NYSE, explained on a rainy morning at the Four Seasons Hotel in Chicago in the winter of 1991: "In the past 15 years the biggest developments to impact Wall Street were junk bonds and the derivative products. In terms of the marketplace, financial futures products are well entrenched in the mainstream. They are here to stay."

Considering his Wall Street pedigree, Birnbaum sounded like a turncoat. He had spent a 40-year career in the securities business as an SEC attorney (he had worked on the SEC's landmark 1963 special market study) and as president of both the Amex and the NYSE from 1985 to 1988. Shortly after the crash, he had even delivered a series of speeches calling for the SEC's jurisdiction over the stock index futures markets, a gesture that put him square in the enemy camp, by the futures industry's reckoning. But Brodsky, too, had grown up in the securities business before he became a part of the futures industry. He knew first-hand, he'd say, how the SEC had been an impediment to innovation and growth of securities options. Brodsky, in fact, had convinced Birnbaum to join the Merc's board of governors, which he did in 1990 after retiring from NYSE.

The trading volume of stock index futures had grown spectacularly since their introduction in 1982. In the week preceding the October crash, trading in the S&P 500 index futures contract averaged 106,400 contracts, equivalent to $16 billion worth of equity securities and representing more than two times the average daily dollar volume of trading on the NYSE during September 1987. Options on stock indexes, whose contracts were about one-fifth the size of index futures contracts, grew equally fast in 1987 and by October accounted for more than 43 percent of total options contract volume. Clearly, the dramatic growth of the derivative products reflected institutional use of the markets and of market basket trading, coupled with the change in investment strategies.

The question, then, wasn't whether the market was efficient, but whether it had any connection to reality. Did it indeed reflect the financial and political chaos in the rest of the world; the highly leveraged takeover binge, whose by-product was a surge in insider trading: the investment community's short-term quarterly focus on earnings; and the United States living it up on borrowed money? Was the reflection coherent and real? Markets remain volatile for one reason and one reason only: too many unanswered questions, and too many unanticipated events.

Before the crash there was a general feeling in the United States and abroad that, given the lessons of history learned from the 1929 crash, coupled with the money, brains, and technology circulating in the world of finance, disaster could be avoided. How could another crash happen? It seemed that a crash wasn't all that different from a tornado—if the conditions are right, there's no stopping it, even if you see it coming. Both are spontaneous outbursts and both spread devastation and ruin. Apparently the precise mixture of emotions and events created the right conditions in 1987. In any event the crash of 1987 sent a clear message: The global financial system—locked in a maze of immense institutions and intricate trading strategies—and its players were fallible.

31

The Sting

Fifteen months had passed since the crash of 1987, and the dust from the fallout was still settling when yet another storm lashed the Merc, plunging it into perhaps the most controversial time in its history.

Many people believed that a deep recession would hit after the crash, but sheer momentum pumped up by the debt of the 1980s had kept the economy growing for a year or so—"Much like Wile E. Coyote running off a cliff and standing for a few seconds on thin air," was the way *Time* magazine characterized it. The oil shocks of the 1970s had led to double-digit inflation and eroded incomes in a process that economists dubbed "stagflation." Between 1973 and 1989 the median income of American families had risen from $24,345 to $25,830—an annual gain of just three-tenths of one percent a year. By contrast, incomes between 1959 and 1973 had grown at a rate of 2.7 percent a year.

By 1989 the economy was already inert and beginning to pay the price of the colossal credit binge brought on by leveraged buyouts and reckless consumer and business borrowing. Neither had the federal government shown restraint. Since 1980 the federal deficit tripled to more than $3 trillion; interest on that sum alone ate up $286 billion a year, accounting for the third largest expense in the budget. Consumers also relied on credit during the decade, increasing their debt from $1.4 trillion to $3.7 trillion; there were similar figures for U.S. industry. As corporate America downsized, workers lost manufacturing jobs, especially in the automotive, steel, and computer industries. By the early 1990s, the jobs in areas such as retailing and banking that had been created in the service sector during the 1980s would shed workers by the tens of thousands as American companies began to undergo long-term structural changes.

1988 was the first time in 13 years that the Merc had not set a new volume record. Trading volume on all exchanges, including the NYSE, slowed down after the crash. Trading in the S&P 500 futures contract, second only to Eurodollar futures in 1987, fell by 40.5 percent in 1988, leading to an overall decline in total Merc volume of 7.5 percent. The result was a drop in clearing fees, the

Merc's primary source of income. But the loss in clearing fees was partially offset by increased demand for the Merc's quotation vendor fees, which had been raised in 1988. The year had ended with an increase of 4.6 percent in members' equity and a profit of $3,490,000. The Merc was also able to add $5 million to the Chicago Mercantile Exchange Trust, an important component of its financial safeguard system.

Despite the lower volume during the post-crash period, memberships continued to rise, owing in part to the growing globalization of the U.S. futures markets. With Japanese institutional investors holding some $65 billion in U.S. government securities, it wasn't surprising that they sought access to the U.S. futures markets as a means to hedge against sudden market swings. In particular, 33 Japanese financial firms bought Merc memberships in 1988 to help push prices to record highs: On 5 August 1988 a CME seat sold for a record $525,000, and during the previous week an IMM seat sold for a record $417,000.

The Merc began to spend money in the late 1980s, preening itself like a proud bird. To accommodate its growing staff, in 1988 the Merc leased floors two through ten in the north tower of the CME Center. The year before, $2.5 million was spent to remodel the fourth-floor executive offices that included a new boardroom to reflect the Merc's growing global status. David O'Gorman, senior vice-president of administration and finance, described the new boardroom as "international in nature and simple in design." Designed by Powell-Kleinschmid, whose principal, Robert Kleinschmid, was a devotee of renowned architect Ludwig Mies van der Rohe's skin-and-bones style, the room was 60 feet long and 30 feet wide. It truly had an international flavor; the walls were paneled with Brazilian teak, and the ceiling was composed of raised fabric mesh panels imported from Switzerland. Dominating the center of the room was a massive mahogany conference table, 30 feet by 12, that comfortably seated more than 30 people. At the east end of the room was a long buffet and a projection screen. On one side of the room, suspended from the ceiling, were television monitors that tracked the markets. On the other side were clocks ticking time from Chicago, New York, London, Tokyo, and Singapore. It had its own air conditioning and heating system separate from the rest of the building. The boardroom, across from the escalators that carried Merc members to the trading floor, was situated to give it visibility.

In 1989, the Merc completed work on the mezzanine level as part of the final construction phase of the North Tower. On the mezzanine was located CME Club—the restaurant for members only—along with the learning center, library, meeting halls, and auditorium. A half million dollars alone was spent on the corridor with its terrazo floor, a glass baffle ceiling, and walls of marble, granite, and stainless steel that gave it a touch of art deco. The Merc's logo of a globe embedded in the floor at the entrance of the CME Club cost $12,000. "The cost of the corridor brought out a lot of screaming from some members," said John Geldermann, who was Merc chairman at the time. "But we were determined to make a statement on behalf of the Merc—strong, long-lasting, and durable like the exchange itself."

The roster of visiting dignitaries during 1988 included 13 U.S. Senators and 77 members of the House of Representatives. In June three members of the Japanese Diet toured the exchange. Also that month Australian Prime Minister Robert Hawke made his way across the trading floor, nearly bringing trading to a halt in some pits, as well-wishers sought to shake hands with the flamboyant man from down under. There had not been such commotion over a celebrity, recalled traders, since 1972, when actors Paul Newman and Robert Redford took a break from the filming of *The Sting* in Chicago to visit the floor. And in October Ronald Reagan, making his final trip to Chicago as president, used the Merc as the location to do some fund raising and politicking for George Bush's 1988 presidential campaign.

For the coming year, Merc officials were set to push GLOBEX, a 24-hour international electronic trading system, as a strategic priority. "The crash of 1987 did us at least one favor," Brodsky said in the 1988 annual report. "It proved conclusively that 24-hour trading is no pipe dream; it's a reality."

But 1989—the year the CFTC was up for congressional reauthorization— began on quite another reality that was unforeseen. On the cold Wednesday evening of 18 January 1989, federal agents, subpoenas in hand, rapped at the doors of a number of traders' homes across the Chicago area in a tactic calcu- lated to scare the wits—or information—out of them. The surprise visits were the culmination of a two-year undercover investigation in which several FBI agents carrying hidden tape recorders had penetrated the trading pits at both the Merc and CBOT as part of the biggest investigation to ever hit the Chicago markets. The sting operation was designed to catch traders who were allegedly defrauding customers, and the canopy of subpoenas covered some 40 traders at both exchanges. The nighttime swoop by the federal agents gave a new meaning to free markets for free men as the threat of RICO—the Racketeer Influenced and Corrupt Organizations Act—was intended to pry pleas from the stunned traders, or to get them to testify against others or lose their Rolexes, cars, or even houses on the spot under the pretrial asset seizure provisions of RICO. (Passed in 1980, the RICO Act was intended for use as a tool in the war against organized crime and drugs to confiscate the ill-gotten gains of drug dealers.) No one caved in that night; the operation was characterized by *The Wall Street Journal* as "Sentence first, trial later." The agents had shown up as late as mid- night; some were accompanied by one of the moles, playing incriminating tapes and talking about the penalties for commodity law and wire- and mail-fraud vi- olations. Technically, the traders did not have to be represented by counsel that night because they were not in custody. The government had based its midnight raid tactic on pure fear and confusion.

Later a *Wall Street Journal* editorial would criticize the strategy: "Whatever the alleged crimes, these tactics violated the Justice Department's own guidelines prohibiting RICO threats 'solely or even primarily to create a bargaining tool.' Coerced pleas under these circumstances raise credibility problems."

The Merc's usually tough face acquired a look of bewilderment. That night, Melamed, Brodsky, Sandner, and newly elected Merc chairman John Geldermann, along with top CBOT officials Karsten (Cash) Mahlman (chairman) and Thomas Donovan (president) were steeped in the pomp and three-ring revelry of President Bush's inaugural festivities in Washington. During the evening the futures executives mingled with a host of politicians that included Illinois Governor James Thompson and Samuel Skinner, then Secretary of Transportation; he became Bush's chief of staff in December 1991. It wasn't until they returned to the Park Hyatt Hotel, recalled Sandner, that they found out about the late-night visits to the traders. "It was shocking," he said.

The next morning, 19 January, the *Chicago Tribune* broke the story with a banner headline: "U.S. probes futures exchanges." The subhead stated, "FBI key to fraud investigation." The *Tribune* story had caught virtually everyone by surprise. "Everyone was out of touch," said Jerry Salzman, the Merc outside counsel. "The *Tribune* made it sound like millions had been stolen, as if our own compliance department was unaware, that our surveillance system was defective, and that the exchange was complicitous. We didn't know what the full magnitude of the investigation entailed."

Details in the *Tribune* story were sketchy, but what was available was astounding. The FBI had planted undercover agents known as moles on the trading floors of the Merc and CBOT. These moles recorded conversations in the trading pits and in various bars and restaurants. They even hobnobbed and schmoozed with the targeted traders and their families at their homes. They threw lavish parties in their high-rise apartments and became members of the East Bank Club, a gym popular with commodities traders. The objective of such affections was to gather information, to become one of the guys in an effort to solicit stories about illegal trades. It was an incredible tale of subterfuge and espionage through an elaborate sting devised by the feds that lasted two years. It was, in fact, the most ambitious financial sting in FBI history, according to Anton Valukas, the U.S. attorney for the northern district of Illinois, who had led the investigation.

The FBI sting had turned up allegations of widespread cheating of customers, market manipulation, fraud, and tax evasion involving hundreds of traders and millions of dollars. It also turned up the heat on the exchanges, which sat like wooden ducks as the media opened fire. "The exchanges will be forced to change their arcane, century-old trading system, and scores of go-go traders could find themselves gone-gone to jail," sneered *BusinessWeek* by the first week in February. The finger wagging didn't stop there. The media blitz was on. By Andy Yemma's count, the story played 14 straight days on page one of the *Tribune*.

The local and national headlines seemed relentless to the Merc and CBOT officials in what appeared to be the biggest Chicago story since the fire of

1871. Asked the *Chicago Sun-Times*, "Will probe outcry peril open outcry? Commodity scandal: 'Pits full of pitfalls. How four moles exposed market abuses." Another *Sun-Times* story the same day (Sunday, 22 January 1989): "How Traders Got Trapped. The 'moles' who shook Chicago." Pronounced the *New York Times*, "FBI Said To Study Chicago Cheating In Futures Trades." Stated *The Wall Street Journal*, "FBI Sting Operation In Chicago Staggers 2 Futures Exchanges. Government Probe of Trading May Implicate Up to 150, And It Aims for the Top." And with a ring of the Roaring Twenties that left Chicago with its rat-a-tat-tat image, *Time* magazine called the FBI sting the "Crackdown on the Chicago Boys" that rounded up "evidence of widespread fraud in the city's freewheeling commodities markets." Even the political cartoonists grabbed a piece of the story. The *Tribune*'s Richard Locher rendered an alley scene in which an FBI agent with drawn gun closes in on two thieves. One of the crooks asks the FBI man, "Why aren't you out trading commodities like the rest of them?"

The result was predictable. A wave of paranoia swept the trading floors of the exchanges, and, at times, the mood turned dark. Suddenly traders were rubber-necking for unfamiliar faces in the pits, and others who had stood side by side for years in the same pit ceased to speak to one another. There were rumors of wires; tape recorders, it seemed, were everywhere. The FBI had the goods on the heavyweights, one story claimed. There were rumors reported in the *New York Times* on 21 January that Merc officers had been subpoenaed. Skeletons rattled as stories of the legendary figures who used to corner markets crept into the sidebars of the current stories. Wagging tongues dredged up old (and unsubstantiated) stories based on rumor that the mob allegedly had used the Merc's trading pits to launder money. Once again, as in the stock market crash, the exchanges were suspect, showered by a fusillade of accusations. The Merc eventually issued a statement that such allegations were "unfounded and unwarranted." Matters became so tense that on 24 January the Merc sent out a letter to members urging them "not to be driven to irrational or self-destructive behavior by the adverse publicity."

The calamitous situation caused Melamed and Sandner to cancel plans so they could stay close to the members on the Merc floor. The pair were scheduled to visit Australia on 27 January to give speeches at the dedication of a new trading building for the Sydney Futures Exchange. Instead, Brodsky attended the dedication and spoke in their place.

Whatever else it did, the news initially hurt volume: Trading volume was down about 25 percent in the week following the news of the investigation. The sudden drop in volume was reflected in the price of exchange memberships. In the three business days following news of the investigation, 32 seats were sold at the Merc and CBOT. The value of a full membership at the Merc on 4 January was $520,000; on 21 January it had dropped to $480,000. But the setback was temporary. By the end of January, futures volume was bouncing back. At the Merc, total trading volume from January through mid-March rose

35 percent over that of the same period in 1988. In the first week in April a Merc seat—the best indicator of an exchange's health—sold for a record $550,000, up 15 percent from the drop in the price after the FBI sting, and 6 percent higher than it had been prior to the news of the sting. At the time, the Merc seats were the most expensive in the industry.

The *Chicago Tribune* had been the exclusive beneficiary of a Justice Department leak out of Washington and Chicago and had as many as 10 reporters working the story, which attracted other journalists from across the country as well as a host from Tokyo to Paris. On Friday, 13 January, Valukas had flown to Washington and briefed Attorney General Richard Thornburgh on the investigation. During that meeting, it was decided to end the undercover operation and to seek indictments. On Monday, 16 January, word of the investigation had reached the *Chicago Sun-Times*. By then, however, the *Chicago Tribune* had a jump start. When *Tribune* reporters got an inkling that Valukas was about to start handing out indictments, they met with him, offering to wait to break the story until the indictments were dispensed—in exchange for an exclusive story. Valukas turned the offer down. And instead of waiting another four days—until 22 January—as planned, Valukas moved immediately in anticipation that the *Tribune* would break the story before the subpoenas were handed out. Ironically, he was trying to head off a leak out of his own agency, the Justice Department. The G-men paid their visits on the evening of 18 January and into the early morning hours of the nineteenth. The *Tribune* broke the story in its morning edition on 19 January. The *Sun-Times* caught up a day later, on 20 January. By then hordes of reporters had swooped down on the exchanges.

"What began as a government leak swiftly became a torrent of intrusively gathered news stories that were frequently misleading and sometimes inaccurate," observed David L. Protess, a professor at Northwestern University's Medill School of Journalism, who had his students do a content analysis of newspapers' first 10 days of coverage.

John Geldermann, who was elected Merc chairman on 18 January, became, as Protess put it, "one of the first victims of the journalistic excess." On the evening of 19 January, Cable News Network reported that three brokerage firms, including Melamed's Dellsher and one "owned by" Geldermann, had been subpoenaed. As it turned out, no subpoenas had been issued to any of the firms and Geldermann had only a minor interest in the firm that CNN said he owned. (The firm under the Geldermann name had been sold to ConAgra in 1984 and Geldermann maintained a small interest until 1989.) CNN retracted the story the following evening.

Seven months later, in a *Columbia Journalism Review* article on the media's coverage of the sting, Protess wrote, "All the stories had one common characteristic: none of the allegations was attributed to anybody with a name . . . almost two-thirds of all information contained in the stories was attributed to anonymous sources."

The pursuit of the story by the media became a story in itself. Once the *Tribune* broke the initial story, each news organization tried to advance the story with its own scoops, tips, and leaks. The avalanche of media questions bombarding the exchanges and traders caught Merc officials off guard. *The Wall Street Journal*'s Chicago bureau even sent its own confidential survey on trading practices to nearly 2,000 traders. The survey, mailed in late February to both Merc and CBOT traders, asked a dozen questions pertaining to criminal and unethical behavior at the exchanges. The responses, the *Journal* noted in an accompanying letter, would be the basis for one or more feature stories in coming issues. The *Journal* considered the method a standard reporting technique, but it also noted that the questionnaire was designed without control numbers or identifiers in order to preserve confidentiality. A sampling of the questions: "Will the FBI probe ultimately improve investor confidence?" "Do you think the exchange should be doing more to publicly defend its practices or do you think it should be prepared to make major reforms to restore investor confidence?"

The response rate was only 15 percent, yet on April 18 the *Journal* ran a story headlined "Violations Are Common At Chicago Merc, Poll says." One expert pollster, quoted by Protess, called the survey "pretty severely biased" because of the low response rate and the questionnaire's format. The Merc's spokesperson, Andrew Yemma, dismissed the survey as "typical of the high-pressure methods used by the *Journal* at this point." Eventually Protess himself came under attack when the *Chicago Tribune* accused him of a conflict in his coverage of the media through a bias toward self-regulating organizations since his wife, Joan, was an attorney for the National Futures Association. At one point a *Tribune* editor even tried to persuade the editors of the *Columbia Journalism Review* not to run the Protess article. Such were the media machinations as the story of the FBI sting grabbed the hearts and minds of aggressive editors and reporters.

On 24 January the government widened its net as FBI agents handed out subpoenas to secure the trading records of virtually all futures clearing firms, which handle the floor traders' paperwork and the collection and disbursement of funds. According to the *Chicago Sun-Times,* 200 new subpoenas were served targeting as many as "10 billion documents." (Some 500 subpoenas were issued in total.) Trading records had been subpoenaed dating back to 1 January 1983. The next morning the *Sun-Times* called the sweep an "extensive new demand"; the investigation was now focusing on companies rather than on just individual traders and brokers. The *Tribune* called it "a sweeping escalation," and *The Wall Street Journal* said the investigation had "widened substantially."

Such conclusions, observed Protess, appeared to be "a quantum leap in logic." He explained: "A futures firm's relationship with a trader is like a bank's relationship with a customer. The firm has no supervisory authority and is no more responsible for what a trader does than a bank is for what a customer does."

The Merc's Yemma was faced with the same problem that the exchange had faced during the crash. "Most of the reporters assigned to the story," Yemma said, "had almost no idea of how the exchanges worked."

The subpoenas had just been issued when the *Tribune* had a team of reporters on the streets and on the phones to randomly interview traders whose names were culled from newspaper articles, directories, and other sources. "Together, the *Tribune*'s telephone calls and stories produced an atmosphere of panic and paranoia that may have been calculated by Justice Department leakers to frighten traders into cooperating in the investigation, a tactic used in previous sting operations," stated a March 1989 editorial in *Chicago Lawyer*.

The FBI investigation of the CBOT was code-named Operation Sourmash. One of the undercover agents who called himself Richard Carlson claimed that he specialized in soybean contracts and was a native New Yorker; another, who called himself Michael McLoughlin, a Treasury bond trader, said that he was from Florida. The pair had been described by fellow traders as friendly, pleasant, and constantly asking questions. The sting operation at the CBOT was allegedly launched partly in response to a complaint from the Decatur, Illinois-based Archer Daniels Midland, a $6.8 billion grain and soybean producer whose outspoken chairman is Dwayne Andreas. ADM, in fact, helped the FBI infiltrate the CBOT pits and the private lives of the traders. Both Carlson and McLoughlin started out by working for ADM as low-level employees before eventually buying memberships with government money.

ADM, a major soybean trader, had blown the whistle out of frustration with brokers who gave priority to their own accounts over their customers', a violation of exchange rules and federal law. The CFTC requires that traders and brokers must try to get the best possible price for their customers when executing trades. The potential conflict of interest from dual trading had become a major target of the FBI probe, and the investigators began to look at a practice called "bucketing a trade." This practice involved taking the opposite side of a customer's trade privately instead of executing it in the open market. The broker sliced an extra profit margin by buying a contract from a confederate known as a "bagman" at a bit more than going price in the pit, or selling one for a bit less. For example, say the price of soybeans opens at $6 to $6.10 a bushel on a contract of 5,000 bushels. Under the law, the floor broker should try to buy the contract for his customer at $6.10 or less. Instead, the broker turns to his pal in the pit and buys it at $6.11—a price that guarantees the confederate a profit, some of which he kicks back to the broker. The FBI probe also pried into other alleged violations such as "wash" trades, which are actual or false trades that result in no change in a customer's position; and "curb" trades, which are executed outside of the pits or after the market closes.

From its experience with the market crash, the Merc had learned a lesson: that nothing focuses attention like pain, especially one that grows worse. To assuage the potential critics, the Merc therefore used Rolodex diplomacy in mounting its damage control campaign after the FBI investigation. Valukas, said Salzman, assured the exchanges that they themselves were not the target of the investigation. "It was a rational decision, the consequence of which was that the exchange would fully cooperate in the federal investigation," Salzman said.

Full cooperation left Merc officials walking a tightrope between acquiescing to the authorities and standing up to them in defense of the membership. "The membership thought the leadership had abandoned them," Melamed later said. "In the process many members were angered we didn't come out with a clear-cut defense."

Despite the Merc's strong political base in Washington, there was a fear of legislative retaliation, with the CFTC up for reauthorization and the prospect of SEC jurisdiction looming in the background. Now the Merc's ability to regulate itself was called into question. "Many argued we lagged in automation," Geldermann said. The last thing that Merc officials wanted to end up in was a no-man's-land of empty rhetoric, battling legislators, regulators, and the press, which were becoming mouthpieces for reform. The Merc's job, the board agreed, was to hold nothing back for at least two reasons: to bolster investor confidence and to tighten surveillance procedures.

The FBI allegations had challenged two of the exchanges' sacred cows: self-regulation and open outcry. Although the CFTC was the futures industry regulator, the exchanges actually were the initial level of regulation. Now the federal investigators were claiming that traders had routinely ignored trading rules and committed fraud, and that violations of the Commodity Exchange Act had gone undetected. The integrity of the open outcry system, which purported to deliver the best and most efficient price to market participants, also was under attack.

Was there a defect in the Merc's compliance system? It was a question that Merc officials asked themselves as they stood behind the Merc's surveillance record of the previous 12 months. The Merc's surveillance department routinely scrutinized trading records and had caught violators. During 1988 it had opened 145 trade practice investigations, prosecuted 179 members, and obtained convictions of 103. These convictions had resulted in fines amounting to $1,747,250; suspensions totaling 4,798 days; and four expulsions.

Under the CFTC rules, the Merc was required to do its own investigation even though the federal probe was still in progress, according to Salzman. Fearing that the Merc's investigation could interfere with its own, "The U.S. Attorney wanted the CFTC to send us a non-action letter to stop our investigation," said Salzman. Valukas later allowed the Merc to continue its internal investigation, after being assured that it would not interfere with federal efforts. The CFTC, which had been aware of the FBI sting from the start, did not attempt to stop the Merc with its own probe. Moreover, on 25 January, a week after the

FBI sting was made public, the Merc's board of governors set up the Special Committee to Review Trading Practices. The committee was to complete its findings within 60 to 90 days. Merc chairman John Geldermann headed the panel, and Melamed and Susan Phillips, former chairperson of the CFTC, served the Merc committee as vice-chairpersons. Phillips, chairperson of the CFTC until 24 July 1987, became a member of the Merc board in January 1988. Because Phillips had known of the investigation, some Merc members thought that she should not have been allowed to join the Merc board. From the start, the CFTC knew of the probe, according to Valukas. Phillips, however, claimed that the Enforcement Division's investigation could have been undertaken with the CFTC's knowledge, but not necessarily with that of the chairman's or commissioners'. The other members of the panel included Thomas F. Eagleton, a Merc public governor and former Democratic Senator from Missouri; Donald Butler, also a public governor and former president of the National Cattlemen's Association; Louis I. Margolis, a Merc industry governor and managing director of Salomon Brothers, Inc.; and John A. Wing, president and chief executive of the Chicago Corporation, a highly regarded member of Chicago's financial community, and a former *SEC* attorney. Past Merc chairman Jack Sandner, who was now senior policy advisor to the board, and William Brodsky also were on the committee. The review of the compliance system was handled much the same way an accounting firm does an audit. Trading practices would be scrutinized and enforcement procedures examined, promised Melamed, "from top to bottom and there [will] be no sacred cows." In addition, the committee would interview customers, futures commission merchants (FCMs), floor traders and brokers, and others who could provide relevant information.

On 1 February the Special Committee had its first organizational meeting, and its first comprehensive working session was on 9 February. Weekly meetings were scheduled through mid-March in both Chicago and New York. In an attempt to soothe a rattled membership, and to lash back at the media blitz, the board of governors sent a letter to members on 13 February, stating, in part,

> ...It is imperative at this juncture to make it absolutely clear that the Chicago Mercantile Exchange, as an institution, is not the focus of the federal investigation. This should have been clear from the outset. However, the relentless media coverage has created an environment of confusion and misinformation.... As a consequence, the damage already inflicted on the futures industry may outweigh the good that may yet be achieved by the ultimate exposure of wrongdoing by some Exchange members.... Indeed, before a single indictment has been issued—before anyone has been brought to trial, let alone been found guilty—this media frenzy has unjustly cast doubt on all futures business, the Commodity Futures Trading Commission (CFTC), as well as the self-regulatory process. It has resulted in a delay of CFTC reauthorization and instigated at least one Congressional probe....

On the nineteenth, all the Merc's trading records from 1 January 1983 to 18 January 1987 were frozen by subpoena. Immediately, the Merc's compliance staff, headed by vice-president Paul O'Kelly, met with Merc outside counsel Glynna Freeman, a former assistant U.S. attorney and colleague of Salzman. Freeman was briefed on how the records were kept. She in turn explained to the staff the significance of the subpoena and how extensive it was. "We supplied enormous amounts of trade data on individual traders," recalled O'Kelly. "Wave after wave of requests for information came in from the Justice Department. There were a couple of requests each week over the next eight months."

A procedure had been set up: First, the government investigators would contact Glynna Freeman with a request for specific information on a particular trader. She then called O'Kelly, who would contact the Merc's management information services department, which produced the computerized printouts that eventually totaled 50 to 100 boxes of documents. They would be given to Freeman, and she would turn them over to the authorities. Meanwhile, O'Kelly, Salzman, Beyer, and Davidson met intermittently with officials at the U.S. attorney's office to discuss the Merc's investigative and compliance procedures in trading activity. These meetings, as O'Kelly put it, were aimed "to give the authorities comfort with respect to how the markets operated."

The Merc was in a clearly defensive posture, and there was no way, said Salzman, to mount a rebuttal. "We spent the next three years fighting to keep our heads above water," Salzman said. The Merc estimated that it spent anywhere from 5,000 to 10,000 labor-hours and between 1987 and 1990 in dealing with congressional hearings and federal officials in connection with the investigation. Part of the defense included producing some 50 boxes of computer printouts for the U.S. attorney. In its defense, explained Yemma, the Merc decided to handle the public relations itself and "to be proactive" from the beginning. To this end, Melamed became the primary voice for the exchange in dealing with the media. Initially, interviews were doled out carefully and strategically to the *Chicago Tribune, New York Times, Wall Street Journal, Chicago Sun-Times,* and the local CBS affiliate, WBBM-TV.

The code name of the FBI's investigation at the Merc was called Operation Hedgeclipper. Special agents Randy Jackson and Peter Vogel were assigned to work undercover in the Merc's trading pits. The pair had started out working the S&P 500 pit in June 1987, where they reportedly lost money during the October crash. They had established their false identities six months earlier, in April 1987, assuming memberships in the East Bank Club and moving into luxury apartments at Presidential Towers, a few blocks west of the exchange. The two claimed to be cousins trading on the floor for Vogel's rich Uruguayan uncle, Friedrich Krupp, and had set up shop as the Dolphin Trading Company on the twelfth floor of the Merc building.

Unlike the procedure used at the CBOT, where ADM helped train federal undercover agents, the Merc operation was almost entirely clandestine. Vogel and Jackson cleared their trades through a division of LIT America, which had no knowledge that the two were undercover agents. Jackson, whose real name is Randall Jannett, moved to the Swiss franc pit. Vogel, whose real name is Dietrich Volk, moved to the yen pit. Until the two agents paid visits to traders' homes on Wednesday night, 18 January, they had maintained their secret identities. Jackson claimed that he had attended St. Mary's College in California. Volk—like his persona Vogel—said that he had graduated from the University of Kansas in 1976. On his application with the National Futures Association, Vogel had listed fictitious employment with Peach State Capital. "He was real cleancut—wing tips, clipped hair, tie always knotted tightly," Merc trader Tom Hicks told *Time* magazine. "He didn't dress like the rest of us. They called him the 'accountant.'"

All the while, they wore their hidden tape recorders and took copious notes in the form of a daily diary. Every night, the moles from both the CBOT and the Merc would go to a safe house, where they would unload the day's events to other agents—a daily debriefing. "It was nerve-wracking for the agents [the FBI moles]," said Valukas. "They were under tremendous pressure because they became friends with the traders, spent time with their families, and got to know their children."

The use of undercover agents in the investigation was similar to the FBI's approach in so-called Operation Greylord, the probe of the Cook County justice system. As of January 1989—five years after Operation Greylord—the U.S. attorney had convicted 84 persons (15 judges and dozens of lawyers, police officers, and court officials) of federal crimes from fixing tickets in traffic court to bribing judges in drug cases. And there were more convictions to come. It took a massive effort to infiltrate the notoriously corrupt Cook County Court system using undercover agents and moles wired with hidden recording devices. The FBI sting of the U.S. futures traders came at a time when there were heavily publicized indictments and convictions of Wall Street's inside traders, who were manipulating the stocks of target companies involved in mergers. Prosecutors first snared Dennis Levine, a Drexel Burnham Lambert Group investment banker, who had pleased guilty in 1986 to four counts of profiting from insider trading. The authorities then got Levine to implicate Ivan Boesky, a Wall Street speculator who was fined $100 million for insider trading and sentenced to jail for three years. Boesky in turn helped prosecutors pursue Michael Milken, Drexel's billionaire junk bond king of the eighties, who was once described as the most powerful financier since J. P. Morgan. He, too, ended up in jail. And 152-year-old Drexel was bankrupt and in disgrace in the biggest failure in Wall Street's history.

Now the futures traders were under attack. The intention of the federal prosecutors during the nighttime visits was to seek cooperation from various traders at both the Merc and the CBOT. In some cases cooperation required exchange members to wear electronic wires in the hope of incriminating their colleagues.

In other cases, the feds cajoled or threatened. Valukas had moved swiftly, issuing scores of subpoenas to traders and demanding trading documents and disciplinary files dating back to 1983 from the two exchanges.

Valukas's reign as a $75,000-a-year U.S. attorney had been a successful one, but it seemed inevitable that he would return to the futures market. There had, as the *Washington Post* noted, "probably never before been a U.S. attorney who understood the Chicago markets so thoroughly." As defense lawyer for Jenner & Block in Chicago from 1976 to 1985, the 45-year-old Valukas, whose father was a Cook County circuit court judge, defended more than a few futures traders accused of trading violations at the Merc and CBOT. When he succeeded Dan Webb in 1985, he inherited the Greylord investigation, in full swing, along with Operation Hedgeclipper and Operation Sourmash, which were in the seminal stage. In 1988 he had become the first federal prosecutor to successfully use RICO to gain an indictment in a securities case involving a Chicago attorney in an insider trading scheme.

The Greylord experience had made Valukas a true believer in the effectiveness of undercover work. But it was as a defense attorney that Valukas had learned just how effective the government's nocturnal tactics could be. It happened in 1984 when two FBI agents paid a surprise evening visit to the home of Walter Brinkman, president of the Chicago Board of Trade Clearing Corporation and Valukas's client. After an 18-month investigation by the FBI, IRS, and office of U.S. Attorney Dan Web—whom Valukas would replace a year later— Brinkman and James Johnson, executive vice-president of the CBOT Clearing Corporation, were charged with illegally eliciting corporate campaign contributions in 1981 and 1982. Brinkman had instructed his vice-presidents to ask more than 20 employees to use their personal checks to make campaign contributions to members of Congress with the understanding that the employees would be reimbursed from the corporation's own funds. Under federal law it is illegal for corporations to make campaign contributions to federal candidates using corporate funds. As part of the investigation, a pair of FBI agents showed up unannounced at Brinkman's home one night. By the time Valukas arrived, it was too late. Though Brinkman was under no legal obligation to talk to the agents without the presence of his attorney, he had spent a considerable amount of time telling them about his role in the illegal scheme. In the fall of 1984, Brinkman, Johnson, and the CBOT Clearing Corporation pleaded guilty. The Clearing Corporation received a maximum fine of $100,000. Brinkman was given eight years of probation and fined $35,000, and Johnson received four years of probation and a $1,000 fine.

As a prosecutor, Valukas had an unflinching stance against white-collar criminals. The press was comparing him to his counterpart in New York, U.S. Attorney Rudolph Giuliani, the terror of Wall Street's inside traders. "Don't expect Valukas to show his compassionate side in the ongoing federal probe into trading practices at the exchanges," observed *BusinessWeek*. "He has invested hundreds of thousands of taxpayers' dollars—and great personal prestige—in the investigation. He can ill afford to come up empty-handed."

On 25 January, some 20 traders were called to testify before a federal grand jury. The industry became even more jittery at this point. Melamed's firm, Dellsher Investment, severed its clearing relationship with millionaire yen broker David Horberg, co-chairman of the yen pit committee, after he was subpoenaed in connection with the FBI investigation. Horberg, who was never indicted, was back trading by mid-March, however, when First Commercial Financial Group agreed to clear his trades.

By the end of January, the story had finally moved off the front pages of the Chicago papers. Not surprisingly, the press had been the target of much criticism from exchange officials in the month following the news.

Although the investigation came as a shock to the Merc, the shenanigans among some traders were hardly news. "There were no new kinds of schemes we didn't know about," O'Kelly said. "We knew there were traders on the floor we weren't catching." But the Merc's compliance department had been far from idle in snaring wrongdoers in the months prior to January 1989. In fact, during the period from 1 January through 18 January 1989, the Merc had taken action against five traders, fining them a total of $928,000, expelling two from ever trading at the Merc again, and suspending two others for a total of 160 business days. The fifth trader, who was fined $3,000, received no suspension. (The fine against Barry Haigh for prearranged trading with his wife, Carlen, was a record $625,000. Carlen Haigh was fined $125,000. Both were permanently expelled.) Compared with the other major futures exchanges, the Merc had been the most active in its discipline of traders, according to a report by the U.S. General Accounting Office (GAO) submitted to the Senate Committee on Agriculture, Nutrition, and Forestry in September 1989. The catalyst for the GAO report was the FBI investigation. The GAO had tracked the disciplinary actions of the Merc, CBOT, NYMEX, and COMEX from 1 January 1984 through 30 June 1989. During that period the Merc had penalized 177 floor traders, assessed $4.47 million in fines, suspended traders a total of 13,562 days, and permanently expelled seven members. This compared quite favorably with the CBOT's results: 64 traders penalized, $1.98 million in fines, 10,558 suspension days, and eight permanently barred. The CBOT's trading volume surpassed the Merc's during the five-year period of the GAO study. Yet the Merc from 1985 to 1986 sanctioned three and half times more floor traders and levied five times as much as the CBOT in fines. The GAO asked whether the CBOT's low numbers showed that the surveillance system in place was an effective deterrent or needed revisions because "it is not finding abuses or punishing offenders severely enough."

Overall, the GAO study found that the regulations in place at the futures exchanges to keep traders honest were inadequate. Both the Merc and CBOT vowed to shore up surveillance without heel-dragging. "We've accelerated the pace," CBOT president Tom Donovan said. "We haven't changed direction, but the car was going 55 miles per hour; now the car is going 65." There was going to be change at the Merc, too, despite the fact that during 1987 and 1988 the Merc's internal surveillance system opened 260 trade practice investigations and prosecuted 188 individuals.

However, there was still room for improvement. Paul O'Kelly, former assistant regional administrator for the SEC, joined the Merc as vice-president of the Compliance Department in May 1987. At the time the Merc had assigned four of eight new Compliance Department employees to the trading floor so that each quadrant had a compliance person present on a regular basis. The first thing that caught O'Kelly's attention when he began his review of the floor practices was the way in which traders reported their trades. The record-keeping system was somewhat rudimentary. The records were hastily written in pencil on trading cards that were neither prenumbered nor presequenced. This cavalier system of record keeping resulted in some traders erasing trades or simply tearing up cards so as not to acknowledge trades that went against them slightly altered. It wasn't until June 1990, in accordance with new CFTC rules, that the card system was changed to include preprinted, sequentially numbered cards with the trader's initials on them. All trades had to be recorded in ink.

On 19 April the Merc's 10-member blue-ribbon committee disclosed its findings in a press conference. Beyer presented the reforms, which included limiting dual trading, doubling the Merc's 10-person floor surveillance staff, picking up trading cards every half hour, and appointing an outside representative to major exchange disciplinary panels. In the binders given to the press was a letter from CME outside governor Eagleton that registered his objections to the way the reforms had been presented. Eight days later, about 150 Merc members met in the exchange auditorium to discuss the committee's proposals. Concerns centered on the dual trading issue and the proposal to allow surveillance cameras on the floor.

The committee's recommendations were reviewed and refined by six internal committees. In August 1989 the board of governors approved the changes — aimed to reduce fraud in the marketplace and to retain self-regulation — which involved seven basic points:

1. Strict sanctions against trading violations, including new guidelines for disciplinary sanctions, which required expulsion after a second major rule violation
2. A stepped-up system that used electronic surveillance technology
3. A full trade data recap available to members on a next-day basis to encourage and facilitate self-policing by members
4. Appointment of nonmembers to all major disciplinary committees
5. Required attendance at a CME ethics and educational program for all members

6. Further restrictions on the trading activity within broker associations
7. Further enhancement of the Merc's computerized trade reconstruction (CRT) system to include separate time brackets from market openings and closes.

Melamed had summed up the Merc's position on 3 August, shortly after the new rules and surveillance changes were announced. "If we lose self-regulation, we lose the other side of the coin, which is innovation," he told a reporter. "We cannot afford to lose that. If that means we have to instill the fear of God into any member on this exchange, we will do that. We will not lose our markets." Under the new measures, the Merc was to install video cameras capable of zeroing in on individual members suspected of wrongdoing. In May 1987, the Merc had considered using roving cameras, but rejected the idea as too intrusive. That was before the market crash and sting. Now, explained Brodsky, "We're willing to try anything legal." (Cameras can only be used for a specific purpose and only with prior written approval of the Merc president. In other words, cameras cannot be arbitrarily turned on.)

The board also approved restrictions on trading within broker groups, which pooled their customer business, and imposed a broader definition of what constituted such a group. In April 1989 there were 191 floor brokerage associations and trading groups registered under the Merc's Rule 515. There were some 931 persons registered with broker associations or smaller trading groups. These broker groups were formed in the late 1970s to allow clearing firms to have the same group of brokers execute their trades in all products. For instance, ABS Partners, the largest broker association at the Merc, with 22 broker associates, executed orders for its customs in only the lead option of six pits—the Deutsche mark, Swiss franc, yen, pound, Eurodollar, and S&P 500—out of 30 trading pits. Those brokers who weren't in groups had complained that the groups didn't expose their orders to the entire trading pit, as required by the Merc's open outcry trading rules. The Merc had already restricted the broker groups through rule changes in March 1987 in an effort, as Brodsky explained at the time, "to level the playing field for all parties."

Dual trading had become a lightning rod for reform. At the end of January 1990, one of the most powerful broker groups, ABS Partners, banned its members from trading for themselves. Initially, the Merc membership voted to eliminate dual trading in the S&P index contract, following charges in 1987 of dual trading abuse that included brokers trading ahead of their customers in a practice called "frontrunning." Now, in the wake of the FBI investigation, the Merc would extend the ban to brokers trading in the nearby contract months of nearly all the financial futures contracts. The practice of dual trading was not illegal, but critics said that it raised serious conflict of interest problems for traders who might have put their own interests ahead of their customers' interests. (Ironically, of the traders who were eventually indicted as a result of the FBI investigation, not one was found guilty of a dual trading offense.) Supporters, however, argued that dual trading kept markets liquid when there was little trading in smaller, low-volume contracts. But a CFTC study released in October 1989 found that dual trading did not have the impact on futures markets that its supporters claimed and that dual traders did not trade more intensively in low-volume markets.

Now the high-profile exchanges sought high-tech equipment to match their images. The Merc found itself an ally in its redoubtable rival, the CBOT. The two exchanges, for example, committed $5 million in a cooperative effort to develop a hand-held terminal for the purpose of real-time recording of each trading transaction by members for their own account in the trading pit; this would provide a more concise audit trail.

Throughout 1989, officials of the Chicago exchanges spent endless hours in Washington, explaining why they thought self-regulation was working, while the federal investigation built toward a wave of promised indictments.

On the afternoon of 31 January, federal agents, standing near the exit doors of the Merc trading floor, delivered 20 subpoenas to yen futures brokers. Over the next eight months, FBI agents continued their investigation, issuing some 500 subpoenas, conducting about 500 interviews, and reviewing more than a million documents.

In February defense attorneys for traders who had been subpoenaed were busy trying to discredit the government's case by arguing before the federal court that their clients had been subjected to unlawful electronic surveillance by the FBI. The exchanges were private entities, the attorneys argued, and the FBI agents had gotten into the pits through a ruse; once inside they became roving microphones, like a bug hidden in a room. They therefore required judicial approval to record, the attorneys maintained. The debate was a replay of issues raised in the Greylord trials, when defense attorneys also protested what they believed to be the illegal gathering of information by hidden microphone. In the Greylord case, the courts upheld the use of hidden microphones to gather information.

At the end of July the court had ruled on the issue of the covert recordings. John Grady, chief judge of the U.S. district court in northern Illinois, decided that the tape recordings made by the FBI in the trading pits (and elsewhere) were admissible as evidence. Without evidence gathered by secretly recording traders' conversations, the government would have had a hard go of it. A potential obstacle had been cleared. On 28 July the Justice Department held a meeting to explain RICO charges to defense attorneys. One thing the indictments promised to do was to heat the debate over the prosectors' use of RICO.

Defense attorneys accused prosecutors of abusing RICO because it was a statute aimed at fighting organized crime. "You don't use a cannon to shoot mosquitoes," said attorney Thomas Breen, a former assistant Cook County state's attorney, who was now defending a CBOT soybean trader about to be indicted. But the Justice Department officials were determined to use RICO in cases of financial fraud and, for the first time, against suspected misconduct on the futures exchanges.

On 2 August, a hot, sunny day in Chicago, the first round of indictments were handed down. At 2:00 P.M. in the Everett Dirksen Federal Building, 46 persons—45 of them traders and one a trader's clerk—were indicted on a total of 608 charges for alleged illegal trading practices at the Merc and CBOT. From the CBOT were 19 soybean traders and three bond traders and from the Merc, 21 Japanese yen traders and three Swiss franc traders. No one was arrested that day; they were given 10 days to surrender. Eighteen of those indicted were charged with RICO or RICO conspiracy violations, which carried penalties of up to 20 years in prison and forfeiture of trading seats (worth $350,000 to $500,000 each) and any other assets (including homes, cars, cash) that may have been derived from illegal transactions. "We are seeking forefeiture of exchange seats for all those who have been indicted for racketeering conspiracy charges," said Valukas. "In six instances we also sought to seize the trading profits of certain individuals."

Valukas' office apparently had struck terror with such threats. Fourteen of those charged had pleaded guilty with apparent hopes of dodging RICO while agreeing to cooperate in the continuing investigation. The prosecutors, too, had hopes that the 14 would implicate their colleagues. Eight of the 14 had also signed civil consent decrees that would bar them from ever again holding memberships in the exchanges.

The room on the twenty-fifth floor in which the announcements were made in a press conference took on the aura of a trading pit in a fast-moving market. As members of the U.S. attorney's office handed out stacks of indictments, journalists pushed and shoved to get inside the hot and sweaty room overflowing with people standing and sitting on the floor as television camera crews tried to get a clear angle. The foreign contingent included correspondents from Japan, France, Great Britain, and Canada. Outside the room other reporters, each loaded down with 1,275 pages of indictments, jostled and jockeyed to be the first to the telephones. It was pack journalism fully packed. The next day, the Chicago exchanges would again make first-page headlines across the nation and overseas.

Speaking forcefully, Valukas said, "We are talking about hundreds of customers and thousands of trades. We are not talking about technical violations. It can be described as wide-ranging activity." Yet, as the New York Times reported on 3 August, "Many brokers and traders who were interviewed said that they thought the indictments pinpointed a few corrupt individuals and that the intense scrutiny of any industry would reveal a comparable level of corruption." Of the more than 6,000 brokers and traders at the Merc and CBOT, 46 people had been identified by Valukas as participants in the "systematic theft of customer funds on customer orders."

Nevertheless, accusations seemed all the more serious with the appearance of Valukas's boss, Attorney General Richard Thornburgh, who had come to Chicago from Washington along with FBI director William Sessions and CFTC chairwoman Wendy Gramm to announce the culmination of the two-year investigation—and to serve notice on market manipulators. It was the first time that the futures exchanges were confronted in person by the government's top law enforcement officials and the top futures regulator—all at once. Thornburgh, however, emphasized that the indictments did not implicate either the two exchanges or brokerage houses. "This probe is part of an expanding Department of Justice crackdown on white-collar crime from Wall Street to LaSalle Street to Main Street with all stops in between," Thornburgh told reporters. "The activities uncovered at these exchanges, the largest of their type in the world, cannot be tolerated." Gramm described the indictments as the "first results of the most extensive and aggressive law enforcement effort in the financial area, ever."

Traders were charged with a wide range of offenses that included racketeering, mail fraud, commodities fraud, filing false income tax returns, lying to Federal agents, and conspiring to defraud the Internal Revenue Service. The indictments also accused the brokers of falsifying trading cards and using advance knowledge of customers' orders to trade ahead of them in an illegal practice known as front running, which had plagued the securities markets as well.

The press conference was a public relations nightmare for the Chicago exchanges, leaving unresolved long-term questions. How would customers of the futures markets react? How would Congress react? The regulators? What would be the effect on open outcry? "In the long run, the indictments will probably be advantageous to the exchanges because they will break down any barriers that remain to electronic trading systems," speculated finance professor Daniel Siegel, who at the time taught a futures and options course at Northwestern University's J. L. Kellogg Graduate School of Management. Indeed, the investigation gave GLOBEX a "positive halo," Melamed said at the time. Other institutions were hardly repelled by the controversy. On 2 February the CFTC approved the Merc's plans to implement GLOBEX in the United States. Less than a month later, on 1 March, three-year-old Paris-based Marché à Terme International de France (MATIF, owned by banks, insurance companies, and brokers, each group with a one-third interest) became the first European futures exchange to sign an agreement in principle to join the GLOBEX system. British government officials had earlier approved the installation of GLOBEX terminals in the United Kingdom, and the Merc was negotiating with Japan's Ministry of Finance to allow GLOBEX terminals in Japan for CME member firms. By April GLOBEX had succeeded in attracting the New York Mercantile Exchange and Sydney Futures Exchange as potential partners in the after-hours electronic trading system. And quietly the Merc had also begun negotiations with the CBOT that would unify GLOBEX and Aurora, the CBOT's proposed after-hours trading system.

There was no question about it—the investigation and indictments sent deep tremors through the futures industry. And although it was too early to tell just what the consequences would be, there was indication that the exchanges could stand the strain. After the investigation and sting were disclosed, the value of the exchanges wasn't diminished among their users. At the CBOT, volume had jumped by 2 million contracts during the first two months of 1989. On 23 February open interest in all Merc products topped 2 million contracts for the first time in the Merc's history.

On 3 August, the day after the indictments were announced, the Merc held a press conference in its boardroom, where Melamed, pounding his fist on the table intoned, "We will put the fear of God in anyone who breaks the rules of this exchange." Shortly thereafter, the Merc received a surprising—and public— rebuke from within its own ranks. Former Missouri Senator Thomas Eagleton, a public member of the Merc's board of governors, lashed out at the exchanges and the regulators. "Self-regulation is the Chicago mirage," he said. "It's something of a myth. The savings and loan industry, we should recall, was an exercise in nonregulation. Many times 'non' and 'self' can be used interchangeably." Eagleton didn't stop there. The CFTC, he added, was "a sleeping pygmy." Obviously, such expostulations didn't go over well in certain quarters. "I was a little surprised at his statements," said CFTC chairman Wendy Gramm. "The Senator has not come to the CFTC to explain his concerns." Later Eagleton received a phone call from Melamed, who said that he was "saddened, not inflamed" by Eagleton's comments.

The Board of Trade was confronted with its own gladiator in the person of Dwayne Andreas, the fiesty chairman of ADM, one of the nation's largest grain and soybean processors, which had cooperated in the FBI sting by employing an undercover agent who gathered evidence on the CBOT floor. In July, 100 CBOT members had signed a petition asking the exchange to take disciplinary action against Andreas over his remarks in an interview with Reuters news agency two days after the CBOT's emergency liquidation order of July soybean contracts. In the interview Andreas said, "They expose themselves to this kind of thing by being inadequate. The CBOT has . . . fallen far behind the times. It's become more of a gambling institution than a hedging center, and that's too bad." Andreas's comment was sparked by the liquidation order, which had triggered a chaotic selloff in the soybean pit and a court battle involving the Italian trading firm Ferruzi Finanziara S.p.A., owner of Central Soya, a major U.S. soybean processing company. Central Soya was forced to sell contracts for delivery of some 22 million bushels of soybeans. The contracts, said Ferruzi, were being held for processing and export, and the company suffered substantial losses as a result of the emergency order. Because of 1988's small soybean crop, there weren't enough soybeans for delivery against the futures contracts. (Ferruzi eventually settled the matter by paying the CBOT a fine of approximately $2 million.)

The members' petition had charged Andreas with violating a CBOT rule that prohibits statements or actions detrimental to the welfare of the exchange. CBOT officials, however, refused to take disciplinary action against Andreas. A letter signed by CBOT chairman Karsten Mahlmann and distributed to members on 15 August stated that such action would be inappropriate, partly because Andreas was not personally a member of the exchange. It was the Board of Trade Clearing Corporation, rather than the board itself, that had jurisdiction over clearing members such as ADM.

By November Eagleton was again rankled. This time it was over what he called the Merc's "circling the wagons," in reference to a CFTC enforcement hearing of GNP Commodities Inc. boss Brian Monieson, the former Merc chairman. The CFTC had charged Monieson with failing to act when he was informed that two GNP salesmen, Norman R. Furlett and Ira P. Greenspon, had diverted profitable trades to their personal accounts while steering losing trades to customers. Eagleton was particularly miffed at the character witnesses listed for Monieson: Agriculture Secretary Clayton Yeutter, National Futures Association president Robert Wilmouth, and Melamed. Wilmouth subsequently canceled his appearance before the CFTC hearing to avoid, he said, "even the appearance of impropriety." Moreover, Monieson's attorney in the case was Jerrold Salzman, the Merc's outside counsel, who had received permission from the Merc to handle the case. "The Merc," wrote Eagleton in his resignation from the board after three years in the position, "has intruded into the legitimate enforcement affairs of the CFTC counter to prudent public policy and against the public interest."

Eagleton followed his resignation letter with a blistering attack on the Merc board, published on the op-ed page of the *New York Times* on 14 November. The Merc's initial response to Eagleton's exit came to 34 measured words. But on 21 November the board of governors released a three-page response to the membership. The letter, a defense of the Merc's honor, culminated in a kind of rationale for the tradition of character witnesses. "We submit that this tradition is sacred to the precepts of democracy and pray that it never be cast as evidence of insiderism."

The Monieson matter, however, became another blow to the image of the Chicago exchanges at a time when there were increased concerns in Washington about the futures industry's ability to police itself—and the effectiveness of the CFTC. The publicity certainly didn't help Monieson. The Monieson case went before CFTC Administrative Law Judge George Painter, who had ruled in December 1976 that the Merc had failed to enforce its rules to prevent manipulation of the July 1970 pork belly contract. In May 1990 Painter slapped Monieson with sanctions, called "draconian" and "unprecedented" by his attorneys, that included an order to cease and desist, revocation of Monieson's broker registration, a bar from personal trading, and revocation of GNP's registration as a futures commission merchant (FCM). Painter also imposed fines of $500,000 on Monieson and $500,000 on GNP. In short, Monieson and his firm were being expelled from the futures industry. The sanctions, as of early 1992, however, were not in effect because the ruling was under appeal before the CFTC.

It wasn't, of course, the exchanges' job to teach traders rectitude and personal morality. That was something they should have had long before they entered the pits. But it was the job of the exchanges to self-regulate and discipline in a manner that created a tone that wasn't heavy-handed, but firm along the lines of, say, tough love. The reputation of business had always had its moral ups and downs. In the early 1960s, for instance, 44 executives of 29 major companies (including General Electric and Westinghouse) were convicted of price fixing and bid rigging. There were monumental business swindles such as that perpetrated by small-time commodities operator Anthony De Angelis, who shocked the financial markets and drove 20 companies into bankruptcy by borrowing $150 million against mostly worthless warehouse receipts for vegetable oil. By the late 1980s the era of deregulation and unbridled greed that turned the period into the decade of the deal seemed to create an anything-goes-if-it-works attitude endemic to the financial world. Markets not only in the United States but also around the world proved that there was no corner on fraud and corruption; it was a global market in that regard, manipulated by the hidden hand of the insider. In New York in December 1988—two years after Dennis Levine, Ivan Boesky, and a whole slew of colorful bankers and brokers were nailed for insider trading schemes—Drexel Burnham Lambert paid a record $650 million fine for securities fraud and other felonies. In March 1989, deposed junk bond king Michael Milken, who operated out of Los Angeles, his brother Lowell, and a former Drexel employee were indicted on 98 counts of criminal racketeering, securities fraud, and other crimes. (In November 1990, all charges against Lowell were dropped.)

The pesky insider was found in foreign exchanges as well during 1989. In Japan a stock market scandal, in which the shares of publishing conglomerate Recruit-Cosmo were handed out on favorable terms to various officials in exchange for political favors, hobbled Prime Minister Noboru Takeshita's government as impugned cabinet members resigned almost every week. In London stock authorities were looking into stock manipulation of such companies as Guiness Mahon, Barlow Clowes, Equiticorp, and Natwest, and cases of fraud in the futures market forced the British government to set up the Association of Futures Brokers & Dealers. In Paris scandal hit the MATIF when the watchdog Chambre de compensation des instruments financiers de Paris expelled brokerage JFA Buisson Cie for its involvement in the $46 million loss by Cogema, the state-owned nuclear fuel group. A few weeks earlier, the Banque de l'Entreprise, admitted that it had speculated away $26.5 million—almost all of its equity—on the exchange. In Hong Kong the Securities & Futures Exchange Commission was established to shore up the shaky ethical reputation of the Hong Kong Futures Exchange, whose chairman was jailed. In Brazil after a four-month hiatus, Brazil's stock index futures and options markets were allowed to reopen by the National Monetary Council after new margin and credit rules that restricted price manipulation were adopted. One investor who had defaulted on $30 million in debts triggered a 54 percent decline in stock prices. In India, with exchanges in Bombay, Calcutta, Delhi, Madras, and Ahmadabad all linked by computer, the Security and Exchange Board of India was set up to combat insider trading, short selling, and misleading prospectuses that had plagued Indian efforts to attract foreign money.

All year long the air in the boardrooms of America's futures exchanges was filled with anxiety and disturbance, too. In January the FBI revealed its under-cover sting at the Chicago exchanges, resulting in 46 indictments in August. In May, the regulators swooped upon the New York futures exchanges. On 4 May federal authorities—the CFTC and the Manhattan branch of the U.S. attorney's office, with the aid of the U.S. Postal Inspection Service—issued subpoenas to nine traders for the records of 45 other traders and the records of four exchanges in a criminal and civil investigation of trading practices. The exchanges involved were the New York Mercantile Exchange, the Commodity Exchange, Inc., the Coffee, Sugar, and Cocoa Exchange, and the Cotton Exchange, all operating in separate quandrants on the ninth floor at Four World Trade Center in lower Manhattan. (New York's fifth commodity exchange, the New York Futures Ex-change, was not involved.) The investigation had no connection to the probe of the Chicago exchanges. But it was yet another blow to an industry already reeling from a slew of bad publicity. In a prepared statement, Senator Patrick Leahy (D-VT), sponsor of the CFTC reauthorization bill known as the Futures Trading Practices Act of 1989, viewed the New York investigation as an indi-cation "that concerns about floor trading practices are not limited to Chicago but rather are industry-wide." In July the CBOT issued its emergency order requiring traders to slash their holdings in soybean futures contracts, touching off wild fluctuations in soybean prices and angering traders, farmers, and the congresspeople who represented them. In September the GAO found that the regulations in place to keep futures traders honest were inadequate. It was a year, proclaimed Senator Leahy, in which the futures industry had suffered a kind of "nervous breakdown."

The CFTC had its problems, too. At the beginning of 1989, Representative Glenn English (D-OK) became chairman of the House Agriculture Subcommit-tee on Conservation, Credit, and Rural Development. In that capacity he was essential to the reauthorization of the CFTC. It was, in his view, a sensitive position, and he sought to distance himself from the pressures of the futures in-dustry. After the FBI investigation broke in January, English announced that he would no longer accept any political action committee money from the futures industry. But the CBOT, which had given English $11,500 since 1985, donated money to him anyway. He promptly returned it.

"The American public needs to feel a greater degree of confidence in this nation's futures markets," English said when introducing his bill in July. CFTC chairwoman Wendy Gramm called English's reauthorization "a strong bill." In addition to making the CFTC a permanent agency—and increasing its budget from $35 million to $40 million—it proposed a ban on dual trading and front running, and called for improved audit trail monitoring and a provision for undercover surveillance. Disciplinary committees were another concern. English wanted exchange disciplinary committees to be composed of a majority of persons who were of a different trading status than the respondent. The bill contended that being tried by peers led to leniency. "The goal is to remove the conflict which occurs when a disciplinary panel of a majority of floor members must try another floor member who may meet them in the next pit," according to the bill's provision.

The day the indictments were announced in Chicago, the House Agriculture Committee approved the Commodity Futures Improvements Act of 1989, with minor amendments, by a voice vote. One provision, sponsored by Representative David Nagle (D-IA) and Representative Fred Grandy (D-IA), banned insider trading from the futures markets, making it a felony with a maximum fine of $500,000 and any profits realized from the violation. One amendment that didn't make it was introduced by Louisiana Representative Jerry Huckaby. His proposal would have required a minimum 15 percent margin for stock index futures trading. After several committee members decried this proposal, Huckaby withdrew it, saying, "We can truly see the effectiveness and power of the lobby of the Chicago Mercantile Exchange."

By mid-year the CFTC, convinced that it was back on sound footing in its bid for reauthorization, approved two Merc futures products in June, an option on the British pound, and Eurorate differential futures contracts, otherwise known as Diffs. The Diff contracts, based on the difference in interest rates paid on Eurodollars and other currencies on deposit abroad, are the futures market equivalent of interbank forward spread agreements. A bank or broker may find it advantageous to borrow short-term money at low interest rates, say, in West Germany, and reinvest the money at higher interest rates in another country. But, in doing so, the firm may be exposed to risk. If, on the repayment of the loan or cashing out of the investment, exchange rates change, the bank may lose money. And, of course, the differences in interest rates can shift over the term of a loan or investment. With the differential contracts, interest differentials could be locked in without using interest rate or currency swaps—exchanges between the bank and client of time deposits denominated in different currencies. The idea of the Diff came from Richard Smith, a former Marine Midland money trader and vice-president who pioneered Marine Midland's forward spread agreement market in 1986. Smith, who had been hired by the Merc as marketing consultant, had high expectations for the Diff complex.

The Diff was the Merc's first new contract in two years; it began trading on 6 July with characteristic flourish, with day-glo green and yellow buttons and typical promotional hoopla. The opening bells were ceremoniously rung by Geldermann, Brodsky, and Melamed. First-day volume in the pound, mark, and yen differential forward-rate futures totaled 1,663 contracts, with a nominal contract size of $1 million. The most popular contract by far was between U.S.

and West German interest rates, with 1,128 contracts changing hands on that first day. In July, 15,000 contracts were traded in differential futures. Trading, however, declined to a small scale, and, as of March 1991, the Diff contract became dormant, but not deactivated, from lack of use by the banks and other financial institutions.

On 13 September the House version of the CFTC reauthorization bill had passed unanimously only to hit a snag in the Senate, where it didn't emerge from the Agricultural Committee until 2 November. This was the bill sponsored by Senator Leahy—the committee chairman—and Senator Richard Lugar of Indiana, the ranking Republican. The Leahy-Lugar bill would beef up the funding and enforcement powers of the CFTC. But the legislation, designed to increase the CFTC's budget by 60 percent through 1994, would be financed through a user fee on each futures transaction. The exchanges argued that such a tax would raise the cost of doing business on U.S. futures exchanges to the point of driving the business to foreign shores. However, the real sticking point to CFTC reauthorization in 1989 came in a last-minute surprise offered by Senator Slade Gorton (R-WA) that didn't sit well with either the Merc or the CFTC: an amendment that would cede jurisdiction over stock index futures to the SEC. Consequently, no full Senate vote occurred in 1989.

If the stock market was any indicator, scandal had little impact on investor attitude. Not even the rash of insider trading scams that rocked Wall Street or the more distant memories of the 1987 crash could keep the market from surging to a record on 24 August. The widely watched Dow average had climbed to 2,734.64, erasing the previous record of 2,722.42, set on 25 August 1987.

If it did anything, the sting yanked the exchanges out of their cocoon of smugness. Eyes were opened wide from the outside and inside of the exchanges. The picture was vivid in what appeared to be porous divisions between good and evil. The investigation proved that there were indeed traders in the pits pulling some fast ones for profit. Yet it also proved another thing: There was no gentlemen's cabal linked from the floor to the clearinghouses bypassing the exchange regulatory mechanism. In short, there was no Mr. Big calling the shots. The perpetrators were rogues bound by an honor system that had fist-sized holes in it, forcing the exchanges to become wistful and introspective. The Merc's drive was rooted in an innate sense of survival and a winning attitude gleaned from years of scrambling as the underdog. And though its spirit had been bruised, it was more determined than ever to take charge of itself and its destiny, while the destiny of the indicted traders would be in the hands of a jury.

32

Into the Nineties

If traders learned anything over the decades in the futures business, it was that nine-tenths of a successful transaction was, in a word, execution. The art of execution, however, went beyond the law of the trading jungle. It was true for trading a futures contract and equally so for putting an exchange strategy in place. Now the Merc leaders were faced with selling the membership on the notion of post-market trading. That meant allaying fears of automation and its impact on the coveted open outcry, which was under attack in the wake of the FBI sting.

In mid-October 1989 leaders of both exchanges appeared before the Senate Agriculture Committee in Washington to plead their case against a pending bill intended to end open outcry trading. To suffocate this face-to-face system, they argued, would drive business to overseas markets. Both Illinois senators—Alan Dixon and Paul Simon—in what the *Chicago Sun-Times* characterized as "a rare move" appeared on behalf of the Chicago exchanges to bolster their position. Such legislation, Dixon and Simon believed, would cripple one of Chicago's and the state's most important industries, one that provided 100,000 jobs and some $4 billion in overnight bank deposits. "No one is implying business as usual," Simon said, urging the committee "to work with the exchanges" and "find a balance" so that business would not be driven to foreign competitors using the open outcry auction to produce liquidity such as the London International Financial Futures Exchange (LIFFE) and Marché à Terme International de France (MATIF) in Paris, each among the world's top five futures exchanges in trading volume.

The harshest critic turned out to be Thomas Eagleton, the feisty member of the Merc's board of governors, who set the tone at the start of the six-hour hearing. He took a swipe at self-regulation and dismissed the CFTC as "emasculated" and "timid," responding only when a crisis occurred. Congress, Eagleton insisted, should push for total electronic trading because "open outcry in pits of hundreds of shouters, winkers, gesticulators, and body touchers cannot be adequately verified and monitored." Melamed later replied to the Senate panel that open outcry is "the economic engine" that made it possible to consider after-hours trading by computers.

The thought of automation had always sent shivers down traders' spines, including Melamed's. He had aired his concern back in 1977 when he wrote in the *Hofstra Review* that "the special nature of futures does not lend itself to an 'open book' execution process. Special orders and expert brokers are required to execute transactions. Liquidity is of primary importance to commodity futures. The sources of liquidity in futures depend heavily on the exchange floor, its traders, and brokers. Thus, an automated transaction system would be detrimental to futures markets."

The article had been written when the world was a different place, before satellites, microchips, and fiber optics lifted the geographic security blanket from U.S. financial markets that had been relatively free from international competition. Moreover, exchange power had been altered by institutional investors as commissions in futures markets and in stocks and bonds had been pared and dealing cartels uprooted. Capital was internationally mobile. And domestic exchanges were pitted against markets overseas, prompting *The Economist* to observe, "Much of the battle for market share will now be fought along the highways and byways of automated trading networks."

The Merc had perceived the reality of globalization five years earlier, when it had instituted the mutual offset link with the SIMEX. There were other points to consider: the pit culture driven by open outcry was primarily an American phenomenon. Most of the exchanges around the world neither had this tradition nor had much success with its application. Consequently, foreign exchanges, including The Tokyo International Financial Futures Exchange (TIFFE), from the outset had opted for either a partially or totally automated execution system.

Secondly, the present-day pits were no longer the only source of liquidity. There now exited an army of "upstairs traders" who no longer depended on eye-to-eye pit contact. Instead, their eyes were glued to computer screens and their ears pressed to telephone receivers. In rapid fashion these traders bought and sold throughout the day, similar to pit traders, to provide a continuous flow of orders to the market. These off-floor traders represented a source of liquidity virtually nonexistent a decade earlier. There also were the institutional traders, such as pension funds and mutual funds, to consider. The institutions moved in and out of positions with their huge buy and sell orders—called block trades— capable of disrupting the markets. On 21 September 1989 the Merc unveiled a proposal to allow block trading of the S&P 500 futures contracts to take place on the trading floor, but only after the big orders were first offered to the pit traders and brokers. Block trading had been used by the nation's stock exchanges for years, but it was the first time a major U.S. futures exchange had proposed the procedure, which floor traders predictably resisted. At the time, volume in the

S&P 500 stock index futures contracts averaged 50,000 trades a day, accounting for nearly 85 percent of stock index futures trading around the country. The proposal, called the large order execution rule, or LOX, allowed a customer to buy or sell more than 300 S&P contracts by finding a party to take the opposite side of the trade without first submitting the order to the pit. Only after a taker was found could the order be brought to the trading pit, where an exchange official would announce the size of the order, but not the previously negotiated price. Pit traders would then have the chance to participate in the trade. Any portion not filled by open outcry would then be executed with the original counterparty at the agreed-upon price. It would take two years before the CFTC approved the proposal, which became effective on 4 October 1991.

There were those who argued that "black-box" electronics could never replicate the quick reactions, subtle instincts, and psychological banter of the floor trader in the process of getting the best price for the customer. But couldn't automation cut down on time, cost, the risk of error, and the lure of fraud in the hectic atmosphere of a crowded trading floor or diffuse telephone market? If so, traditional markets could be rendered obsolete in the future.

These issues were part of a debate that promised to grow stale amid the competitive pressure from the world's financial markets. The Merc began to seriously consider the black-box alternative back in 1987 when, on 24 March, the Merc's Strategic Planning Committee directed Ken Cone to contact Reuters Holdings PLC and Telerate, two of the leading market information vendors, to open negotiations aimed at an evening-hours electronic trading system. From the start, Reuters seemed the logical choice. The collapse of Bretton Woods in 1971—which paved the way for the creation of the IMM—had served Reuters well, too. Though better known as a news agency with a worldwide network of more than 1,100 journalists, photographers, and camera people, Reuters made most of its profit by disseminating price information from banks dealing in the $500-billion-a-day foreign exchange market.

In 1987, Reuters fed information from 125,000 video terminals and teleprinters directly into clients' quotation devices. Information to the news media and business subscribers was gathered from 115 exchange and over-the-counter markets and from data contributed directly by 2,900 subscribers in 80 countries and its army of journalists. Reuters was on its way to effectively becoming the global market for currencies, carrying news and price quotations. Over the next six months Melamed, Sandner, Brodsky, Kilcollin, and outside counsel Jerry Salzman shuttled between New York and Chicago in serious discussions with Reuters officials Andre F. H. Villeneuve, North American president, and John S. Hull, executive vice-president for marketing and development. By August the parties reached an agreement in principle to create a global electronic automated transaction system called P-M-T, which stood for Post Market Trade.

The agreement was announced to the world on Wednesday, 2 September. The basic terms covered a twelve-and-a-half-year period, granting the Merc exclusivity for futures and options during evening hours on the use of the Reuter Dealer Trading System (RDTS), developed for the government debt securities and foreign exchange cash markets. Work on the RDTS had begun in 1984, and Reuters was billing it as the most advanced trader workstation. A prototype had been introduced during the last quarter of 1986 to several key players in the cash markets. And once in place, RDTS would provide access to data carried on the Reuter monitor and other Reuter networks. Traders would be able to deal on a screen displaying bids and offers and to execute counterbalancing orders in the cash and futures markets simultaneously—and automatically.

The Reuters-Merc deal had an immediate effect on life at the Exchange. Prior to the announcement on 2 September, sales of Merc seats were halted. When trading in the memberships resumed at 9 A.M. the next day, records were set: A full Merc membership sold for $478,000, up from $430,000, the previous record sale on 10 August; an IMM membership for $385,000, up from $380,000; and an IOM membership for $175,000, up $1,000 from the 10 April record.

Despite the higher seat prices, the Merc members still hadn't bought the idea of post-market trading. In the fall of 1987, Merc officials faced the problem of arousing an exchange full of pit traders whose reaction to automation was practically Pavlovian. The Reuters agreement needed to be approved by the Merc membership, and a referendum was set for 6 October.

Over the next several weeks, materials for the presentation to the membership, to be made on the upper trading floor a week before the referendum, were prepared on a shroud of secrecy: a slide show and a 25-page booklet entitled "The Future of Futures—A Strategic Plan for the Chicago Mercantile Exchange." The pitch was to focus on globalization, automation, and off-exchange expansion of new products. To encourage members to attend, mailgrams were sent to the homes of each. More than one thousand members showed up—a record turnout—and listened raptly.

The timing seemed perfect. The black-box revolution was already at hand. The roar of traders on floors and on phones was beginning to give way to the clatter of fingers on keyboards. All during the summer of 1987, one exchange after another took a stab at automation in one form or another. In July, the London Futures and Options Exchange automated trading in its white sugar futures contract, following the New Zealand Futures Exchange, which conducted automated trading in wool, wheat, and financial futures contracts. In August, brokers at the Paris Stock Exchange, with its roots dating back to Napoleonic times, were trading their last hurrahs around the pit, due to be removed to make way for a computerized system. A few blocks from the Merc, traders at the CBOE were getting a grip on technology with hand-held computers in an experimental program that would eliminate the need to write out trade information on cards. In anticipation of an around-the-clock equity options market appearing in the near future, the CBOE had acquired the fully automated Cincinnati Stock Exchange. There was also the Bermuda-based Intex, the first totally automated exchange, which was not yet a viable competitor to the Merc's markets.

A year earlier, even the London Stock Exchange, which for 185 years traded on the floor, abandoned the practice for an automated over-the-counter market similar to a NASDAQ-type system (National Association of Securities Dealers Automated Quotation system). NASDAQ's volume had grown at an annual average rate of 25 percent from 1980 through 1986, compared with the securities industry's volume of 19 percent a year during the same period.

The New York Futures Exchange (NYFE) had an arrangement with Reuters to utilize an order routing system. It enabled an NYFE order to be placed from London over a Reuters screen, routed for execution to the floor of the NYFE in a matter of seconds, and then reported back to the British customer. At about the same time, the Tokyo Stock Exchange began trading a yen bond futures contract basically over-the-counter by telephone, with plans in 1988 to completely automate the system. Moreover, Reuters had recently spent $125 million to acquire Instinet, an automated securities system, despite the fact that Instinet had yet to make a profit.

Securities exchanges, for the most part, had begun investing in automated trading systems. Until tested—and severely strained—by the Crash, which would come the next month, these systems had worked to everyone's satisfaction. For instance, the NYSE's Designated Order Turnaround system (called DOT and then later renamed SuperDot after it was upgraded to handle bigger orders) took orders from member firm branches, routed them to a specialist, and sent confirmation back to the branch office, usually within a minute. Once an exchange had order routing in place, it could implement automatic execution systems for small orders almost at will. Although in 1987 the NYSE system did not execute orders automatically, except in limited cases such as openings, other exchanges such as the American Stock Exchange, Pacific Stock Exchange, and Philadelphia Stock Exchange could automatically execute customer orders. (By 1990 the NYSE had planned to launch an automated system for a basket of 500 stocks called Exchange Stock Portfolio and was also thinking about an overnight trading system.)

"It must be remembered," *The Futures of Futures* noted, "the auction market is as sacred a concept to the stock exchanges as open outcry is to the futures exchanges." Clearly, as *Institutional Investor* pointed out, trading was a war of information, and markets on screens changed the balance of power between brokers, market makers, and investors, big and small.

In the Merc analysis, the presentation posed the critical question to the open outcry system, and then answered it. Would open outcry continue to exist without automation? If so, for how long? The response: "Given the pressures of automation around us, given the growth of and demands of our markets, given the competitive threats from other exchanges, given the international implications, it is reasonable to fear that open outcry, without any form of automation, has a limited lifespan."

Night trading sessions in a global strategy, as the CBOT had instituted, made little sense to the Merc leadership. They addressed only a few of the hours of the foreign business day; the growth was slow; it was difficult to maintain a liquid market from domestic channels until foreign business began to flow; and it was doubtful that night sessions in the U.S. time zones would dissuade the Japanese financial community from instituting its own its own exchange in its own time zone, during its own regular trading hours. In fact, night sessions could accelerate Japanese plans to establish competing markets in the same instruments.

A night market, concluded Merc officials, therefore had limited potential. At best, they believed, it would lead to a secondary market niche by way of arbitrage and minor business flow. But a 24-hour facility could become the dominant center for business from its own locale, as well as a magnet for all business during its regular trading hours, and could even impede the growth of a night market on a distant shore.

Initially the odds of the referendum's passing were long. But to hedge its strategy, the board had sweetened the deal for the traders. An incentive had been built into the proposal. For the first time, profits from an exchange venture would go directly into the pockets of the members, not the Exchange. "That was the sex," Melamed said of the proposal that promised to distribute 70 percent of the P-M-T profits to Merc members, with each receiving P-M-T shares based on the divisional membership owned. (In addition, the clearing members would earn commissions for worldwide business conducted by their customers on P-M-T and 20 percent of the P-M-T profits.) The remaining 10 percent of the profits would accrue to the P-M-T organization. The Merc itself would charge a clearing fee that would cover such things as clearing and regulation.

On Tuesday, 6 October—13 days before the stock market's slow fuse exploded boom into gloom—Merc members went to the polls just as they had when they voted on the dual trading issue. By early evening the votes had been counted. It was a landslide for Post Market Trading: The membership voted 3,939, or 88 percent in favor, versus 526 against, demonstrating its approval to create a global after-hours automated transaction system for futures and futures options. The nearly nine-to-one ratio, in fact, was the highest achieved in any Merc referendum.

Over the next several years, the Merc and Reuters applied more than imagination to developing a 24-hour computerized order-matching trading system. In 1988 the name Post Market Trading was changed when it was pointed out that in Great Britain the initials "PMT" stood for "premenstrual tension." The board began groping for a new name that would convey the tone similar to what the International Monetary Market had done in 1972. From scores of names considered, it was Sandner who captured the essence of the system by dubbing it GLOBEX, for global exchange. The system was complex, yet the idea of GLOBEX remained simple: to present regional markets to an international realm with subscribers trading on computer screens when the exchange is closed. The cost was an estimated $30 million, but would climb to more than $70 million over the next several years, provided by Reuters, as the technical kinks were worked out and the launch repeatedly postponed.

By 1989, there was cosmic confusion in the evolution of futures and options trading. Nearly everyone agreed the time had come for 24-hour electronic trading. But there was widespread disagreement over what system to use. Not only was there the Merc's GLOBEX to consider, but half a dozen other systems, from the CBOT's Aurora to the London International Financial Futures Exchange's APT (automated pit trading) to the International Commodity Clearing House's ATS. The futures industry had arrived at the epoch of the automated trading system, with each system standing before the world's traders like a giant monolith out of *2001: A Space Odyssey,* beckoning to be touched.

Technology was fast pushing the industry to the brink of restructuring. The computer promised to create a new breed of upstairs trader. It could also be used to conjure up, as CBOT chairman Karsten (Cash) Mahlmann put it, "what has worked for 140 years—the auction-style pit." Even the exchange local, that leather-lunged pit trader who scalped to create liquidity, was in danger of being replaced by a more aggressive institutional trader. While clinging to its night sessions, the CBOT had finally seen the light, conceding that indeed there was validity to electronic trading. Attempting to electronically emulate open outcry, it created the Aurora system, which embraced Apple's computer graphics, Texas Instruments' artificial intelligence technology, and Tandem Computer's hardware. With computer speed, Aurora had been put together in only eight months and was far from perfected when it was unveiled along with GLOBEX at the Futures Industry Association's (FIA) annual meeting in Boca Raton, Florida, in March 1989. All systems at that point, including GLOBEX, were far from complete.

GLOBEX, however, had the most impressive following at the time. Three exchanges in different time zones had shown interest in joining the system: the New York Mercantile Exchange—the world's third largest futures exchange—intended to list its oil contracts. The Sydney Futures Exchange would trade a 90-day bank bill and 10-year Treasury bond. Only the MATIF had actually signed a letter of intent in the spring of 1989 to trade France's long-term government bond.

Initially, the Merc had a far more grandiose scheme for GLOBEX when it had begun to assess the potential of international futures trading three years earlier. The Merc saw fast-growing competition in the Asian and European time zones in a host of products traded on the interbank over-the-counter market. At the same time, it was feeling pressure from institutional traders to reduce the costs of exchange transactions. In the seminal stage, Merc officials had visions of turning GLOBEX into a monopoly, whereby the Merc would try to keep the system for its own use and to list the products of other exchanges, with the exception of petroleum products, which Reuters had reserved. Those were in the early days of the 24-hour dream, when the Merc's unofficial motto "Free Markets for Free Men" was altered by some Merc members to "Free Markets for Three Men," in a reference to the troika of Melamed, Sandner, and Brodsky. "Obviously we no longer have that mindset," said Sandner in the spring of 1989. "The world won't allow that to happen." Melamed agreed with him: "It was a question of reality. If, say, we had listed French bonds we'd have been fighting the natural constituency and domicile. Why fight for 10 years when you can make love?"

Even so, GLOBEX was far from a love-in during 1989. It was still in the courting stage as Merc officials were continent-hopping to woo partner exchanges. The plan was to establish a sort of critical mass of liquidity. The more exchanges, the more contracts, and the more liquid the markets. Every exchange became a viable source for GLOBEX, so long as it didn't trade contracts that competed with the Merc or with fellow GLOBEX members. And the system offered speed, to boot. A Merc trading pit at full throttle with a thousand arms flailing could probably make roughly 20 transactions each second. GLOBEX would make that look like slow motion.

So the original Napoleonic idea of conquering the futures world had to be abandoned. After all, GLOBEX couldn't provide political grease; one exchange couldn't control the world. The Eurobond market left New York for London in the late 1906s because of a 30 percent withholding tax on interest payments sold in the United States to overseas investors. GLOBEX could similarly be manipulated at the whims of various governments. How, then, was the Merc to handle the politics of GLOBEX? "Carefully," suggested Melamed at the FIA's 1989 annual meeting in Boca Raton where GLOBEX was about to be introduced to the industry. "We say to each government it's bound by its own rules. Nothing changes. GLOBEX simply has allowed us to move this along. I don't think we'll have a political problem."

There were other questions to consider: Was there demand among users of the futures markets for 24-hour trading? Would liquidity be granted by the institutional investors? Could the markets remain liquid without the locals screaming out their lungs in the pits? Could Reuters muster the technology to create a viable trading system? These were the kinds of questions asked by some of the industry leaders in 1989. The available statistics answered many of the questions. The CBOT's night session, which traded mainly Treasury bond futures and options, would have been the twelfth largest futures exchange in the world, based on its evening volume alone. As for the Merc, one-third of its contract volume in futures and options on currencies and Eurodollar time deposits came from outside the United States and Canada. And nearly 10 percent of its daily volume in currencies occurred overnight in the exchange for physical trading, which allowed over-the-counter trading solely for currency futures. Both currency and Eurodollar futures and options were to be traded on GLOBEX.

The GLOBEX strategy was designed to attract institutional business. It was hoped that banks would use the currency futures rather than trade over the counter. Revised capital rules among major money center banks required that capital be held against forward currency contracts but not against exchange-traded contracts. The exchanges offer banks reduced counter-party credit risk, as well as a mark to market settlement system at the end of a trading day. In addition, GLOBEX offers lower back-office costs. To encourage large-volume traders to become market makers, GLOBEX offered 75 special memberships to institutions. These memberships entitled institutions to trade for their own accounts but not for their customers' accounts. Special members were required to put up a minimum number of bids and offers on the GLOBEX screen. Could it work? "Until we try it," mused James Lorie, professor of business at the University of Chicago, "we don't know what we'll miss from the face-to-face. I don't believe we'll miss too much."

In the ongoing global exchange wars, the Merc and CBOT had forged different alliances to carry out their strategies. Each tried to control a slice of technology by taking a different path. The CBOT had hoped to build its better mousetrap from scratch, drawing on the technical expertise of the nation's leaders in the computer industry to develop its system. The Merc, on the other hand, teamed with Reuters to draw on its far-flung information network, but also partly in self-defense. If GLOBEX hadn't been created, the Merc reckoned, Reuters likely would have done it on its own. Or perhaps Telerate. Or anyone else. By 1989 the Merc had spent nearly two years formulating GLOBEX with Reuters. When GLOBEX got the go-ahead from the CFTC on 2 February 1989, it gained the jump on the other exchanges. By the end of the month, the Merc's advertising agency, Lois/USA, had put together a 17-minute high-tech presentation on GLOBEX that used nine projectors, three screens, and a video. On the bright sunny morning in March, GLOBEX was introduced at the FIA's annual meeting, attended by nearly fifteen hundred people representing the brokerage community and futures exchanges from throughout the world.

Melamed, as the newly named chairman of GLOBEX, did the honors on behalf of the Merc. It was clear that the Merc's turf was no longer Chicago, but the world, via the GLOBEX flying carpet. "Those who ignore the march of science and technology will soon be history," Melamed said in a raspy voice, poking a finger in the air. "GLOBEX will offer the world a transaction capability as far-reaching as the future itself," he promised. Like it had back in 1972, when it was about to head into the murky waters of currency trading with the IMM, the Merc now asked the futures industry to follow it on yet another odyssey, over oceans, across continents, and through the channels of high technology.

At the same meeting, the CBOT introduced its vision of the future with the Aurora system, which would compete with GLOBEX. A year later, however, during the days the Cold War was rapidly thawing, the Merc and CBOT, after years as spirited rivals, embarked on their own era of *glasnost*. Chicago was still the world's capital of futures and options trading, but the world's markets were closing in. Early in 1990, however, the Merc set the tone of reconciliation when it set forth its "Blueprint for the 1990s," an agenda that built on its past successes and prepared for new opportunities. The "Blueprint's" six objectives called for the Merc to resolve current trading rule issues and establish a transaction process "beyond reproach"; settle all differences that divide the membership; resolve regulatory and margin issues relating to equity index futures and options; employ the GLOBEX strategy as the centerpiece of the Exchange's international strategy; seek new revenue sources for members by establishing the CME Resource and Service Company; and prepare the Exchange to compete in spheres of trade from which it was then excluded.

The Merc leaders knew that, in a global era, cooperation would be the key to survival. From London to Madrid, companies were jockeying for position as they considered new business realities that would take advantage of a new emerging economic machine. Indeed, corporate alliances—like pre–World War II treaties—were beginning to reshape the traditional European and Asian business landscapes. Why should it have been different for global-minded exchanges? No longer could a Chinese Wall separate domestic strategy from foreign strategy. With geographic barriers vanishing, positioning meant making new allies and setting aside old feuds. In mid-September, at the initiation of CBOT chairman William O'Connor, the Merc and CBOT formed a Common Goals Committee (CGC), in what the Merc called "the next logical step" in a relationship the two exchanges had been forging. In Washington, D.C., the Merc and CBOT had long fought side-by-side to further their interests and those of the futures industry, and now they were in the shadows of the FBI sting and the impending trials of their traders. They were also drawing closer on the technological side, when in 1985 they jointly undertook to develop Computerized Trade Reconstruction (CRT) and in 1990 the AUDIT (Automated Data Input Terminal) system of hand-held electronic trading cards. Then, on 24 December 1990, the CBOT officially scrapped its Aurora system and became a full partner in GLOBEX with the Merc and Reuters PLC. Earlier, GLOBEX got another boost when, on 21 May, the Japanese Ministry of Finance indicated its approval of the installation of GLOBEX terminals in Japan. Testing of the system, involving some 250 key stations in Chicago, New York, and London, was to be begin in the second quarter of 1991.

While the Merc was looking forward to GLOBEX, it also cast a glance over its shoulder in celebration of the 25-year anniversary of its live cattle futures contract. When the live cattle contract was launched in 1964, the cattle industry was situated mainly in the corn belt states. Throughout the late 1960s and early 1970s, the cattle moved west into the high plains region. In a way, GLOBEX and live cattle had something in common: They were radical departures in their respective eras. Back in 1964 futures were traded in storable commodities, and no exchange had attempted the somewhat tricky proposition of creating a contract on a living animal. Skeptics had raised myriad doubts about the proper grade, weight, and other contract specifications that needed to be met. "I thought it was possible even though the textbooks of the time said it was impossible," recalled E. B. Harris, who was the Merc's president at the time. "We were never deterred by fear of failure." Harris had been flown to Chicago from Arizona, where he lived in retirement, to attend the anniversary. Also on hand was Glenn Andersen, who had joined the Merc in 1952 and chaired the steering committee that created and shepherded the cattle contract through the early days. "The members were very supportive of the contract because we were very hungry," said Andersen, who had few doubts about the new product for one reason. "You can look at any successful futures market and see one common denominator," Andersen noted. "A successful cash market. With cattle we had that. That's why I knew it would work, because of the large producer side of the market." Indeed, major meat packers such as Armour & Co. were virtually "enamored" with the contract, according to Lennert Palme, another member of the committee, who in 1964 was in Armour's food research group. As part of the festivities, the Merc awarded ten $2,500 scholarships to college students enrolled in colleges of agriculture and who intended to pursue a career in the beef cattle industry.

Against the backdrop of a weakening U.S. economy, another event took place in 1989 that reminded Wall Street and LaSalle Street of the market's hair-trigger volatility. On Friday, 13 October, just two days after Richard Breeden replaced David Ruder as SEC chairman, and four days after the Dow Jones industrial average hit a record peak, the Dow plunged 190.58 points, or 6.91 percent. It was the Dow's second biggest point drop ever, surpassed only by the 508-point loss—a 22.6 percent decline—recorded on Black Monday. Percentage-wise, the Dow's dive was the twelfth worst ever and was eerily reminiscent of the time two years earlier when the Dow had lost 108 points on the Friday before the crash. This time, however, the severe plunge set off the first test of the circuit breakers that were put in place under a signed agreement between the Merc and NYSE after the market collapse in October 1987. The circuit breakers were to provide the market with a cooling-off period, a chance to give the markets time to regain their equilibrium, because futures prices were reported faster. At 2:07 P.M. Chicago time, trading halted for 30 minutes in the Merc's S&P 500 December futures contract after it had fallen the maximum 12 points, equivalent to about a 100-point drop in the Dow industrials, allowed under the post-crash limits. The halt in the S&P pit broke the link between the futures and stock markets, effectively stopping one form of program trading, stock index arbitrage, that closely linked the two markets. At about 2:30 the S&P futures began trading again, as the futures and stock market started to come back in line. But 15 minutes later, the S&P market careened to a daily drop of 30 points—still another limit—and trading stopped for the day. The spark that had lit the market's fuse, analysts later suggested, was the failure of a UAL Corp., buyout group to secure financing for the deal (UAL Corp is the parent of United Airlines). Fifteen minutes after the UAL announcement, the S&P future started to skid. On Monday the sixteenth, even before the analysts could complete their damage assessments of Friday's market, the market rebounded 88.12 points—the fourth largest point-gain ever.

The Federal Reserve had pumped $2 billion into the nation's financial system to head any potential credit squeeze caused by Friday's selloff.

The way exchange officials viewed it, the two days of hectic activity were a litmus test for the post-crash reforms that had been designed to accommodate heavy trading and discourage panic-selling. On Friday the Merc's circuit breakers had kicked in according to plan, and on Monday the NYSE, in anticipation of massive selling orders, opened its computers one hour earlier than usual to help sort out business before trading began. (The level of coordination between the Merc and the NYSE, according to Brodsky, "went especially well," with regular communication on Friday, throughout the weekend, and into the new week.) The crash proved that the futures markets had become an integral part of the financial markets, and as Melamed had put it on the first-year anniversary of the crash, "Even for the people on the New York Stock Exchange, the futures market can't simply be wished away." That point of view had been shared by Federal Reserve Board Chairman Alan Greenspan, a member of the Presidential Working Group on Financial Markets, who earlier in 1988 had told members of the U.S. House of Representatives that the futures markets had grown so large "not because of slick sales campaigns but because they are providing economic value to their users."

In the months following the crash, Greenspan had flatly rejected the notion of transferring regulation of stock index futures from the CFTC to the Fed. But SEC chairman David Ruder took up the case for his agency. Ruder viewed the futures industry as under-regulated compared to the securities industry. Moreover, futures industry officials, he strongly felt, "didn't give a damn" about the securities industry. Consequently, Ruder pressed for jurisdiction of stock index futures and for higher margins in the futures industry as a possible means, he believed, to dampen volatility. Other members of the interagency Presidential Working Group—Greenspan, Treasury Secretary Nicholas Brady, and newly appointed CFTC chief Wendy Gramm—saw no need for such precautionary moves. The result turned into a smoldering standoff between the SEC and CFTC. It also led to an awkward situation for Ruder and what seemed like a power play by the futures industry when in 1988 President Reagan appointed Mary Schapiro to fill a vacancy as an SEC commissioner, overriding Ruder's candidate for the position. Schapiro at the time was an attorney, working for the Futures Industry Association, the trade group that sharply opposed Ruder's regulatory efforts. Before that she had been an assistant to CFTC chairman Susan Phillips. Some saw the Schapiro selection as Ruder's punishment for his stance on the jurisdictional issue. Ruder's successor, Richard Breeden, picked by President Bush to head the agency in 1989, took up the jurisdictional battle this time with the support of the Treasury's Nicholas Brady. But ultimately the Bush administration measure that sought to transfer jurisdiction over stock index futures to the SEC never made it out of committee, owing largely to an aggressive Merc and industry lobbying effort. Key elements of the defeated proposal included one that would have empowered the SEC to review—and approve or disapprove—exchange-established margins for stock index products. Another would have nullified the Commodity Exchange Act's so-called exclusivity rule, which required that financial instruments with the characteristics of a futures contract be traded only on futures exchanges, solely under control of the CFTC. The jurisdictional bill, S.1729, had met with spirited Senate opposition from the start. The Agriculture Committee's Chairman and its ranking minority member, Senators Patrick Leahy (D-VT) and Richard Lugar (R-IN), respectively, each fought it vigorously. And so did Senator Phil Gramm (R-TX), head of his party's Senate campaign committee, and husband of CFTC Chairman Wendy Gramm. The bill's defeat meant that the entire CFTC reauthorization process had to begin anew on both sides of the Capitol in the coming year.

Just as the summer of 1990 was winding down, two matters sprang upon the world, neither of which was a pleasant prospect: Iraq's invasion of Kuwait and the onset of a recession. The invasion would lead to the Gulf War and a sweeping victory calculated in hours—too quickly for troops to sustain battle fatigue. Unfortunately, the economic fight on the home front looked more like a case of chronic fatigue. The recession lingered; weeks turned to months, months to years. It became the longest, if not the deepest, downturn since the Great Depression. The war didn't cause the recession, but it was being blamed for the growing economic woes as the price of oil spurted from $20 to $40 a barrel. The savings and loan crisis was already in full swing and the real estate market was severely depressed when President Bush dispatched half the entire Army, Navy, and Air Force to the Middle East. The usual terms crept into the economists' rhetoric, including "sluggish," "lethargic," and "lackluster," to describe a traumatized economy in which 1.2 million workers lost their jobs in the first 18 months. It would get worse. In January 1991 alone, another 232,000 workers were laid off, including, as *Time* wryly noted, Minnesota's 1990 teacher of the year. By then some 30 states were deep in debt and were ready to tax everything from personal incomes to pretzels. Eastern Airlines, Continental, and Pan Am (which subsequently folded, along with Chicago-based Midway Airlines) had filed for bankruptcy protection under Chapter 11. More layoffs would follow as industry giants such as General Motors, IBM, AT&T, and Citicorp would begin restructuring themselves to play out the 1990s in the name of increased efficiencies and reduced costs. Such survival strategies became a stake of fear driven through the hearts of America's work force, white- and blue-collar alike. Not since the 1930s had the threat of unemployment hung over the nation on such a large scale. The prospect jittered consumer confidence, which was further shaken by the S&L bailout that between 1989 and early 1992 would cost taxpayers a startling $100 billion—with the meter still running—and force federal authorities to admit that the situation was out of control. It was a small wonder that in late 1990 consumer expectations of business, jobs, and income plummeted.

The economy had become the python that swallowed a hog to trap itself in a cage, as companies and consumers slowly began to work off the vast debt they assumed in the 1980s. It would be at least several years of modest growth in productivity—1 percent to 2 percent—the economists agreed, before American industry could rebuild its long-term future and bring prosperity back. What level of prosperity no one was guessing—never, some insisted, back to the prosperity of the 1960s—not with this kind of staggering budget deficit hanging over the nation. However, what was clear in the dog days of 1990 were signs of protracted recession.

Predictably, the markets reacted to the economic blahs as 1990 unfolded, but not at first. In January, for instance, Merc trading volume was 44 percent ahead of December 1989 volume and 28.4 percent of the previous January's volume. By mid-year, though, volume had slipped more than 9 percent behind that of the first six months in 1989. Clearly, product diversification had buffered what could have been a worse drop in activity. The S&P 500 futures contracts were running 12 percent ahead 1989, along with gains posted by pork bellies and live hogs. These gains, however, could not offset the 24 percent drop in trading volume of Eurodollar futures, the leading hedging vehicle for short-term interest rates and the previous year's pacesetter.

Across the Atlantic, Western Europe was busy positioning itself economically for the twenty-first century with the formation of the European Community (EC). In 1992, Napoleon's fantasy of uniting the states of Europe would begin to take shape, when 12 nations became one market of 320 million people with the "hidden hand" reaching across European borders to touch every facet of life from patent law to the pedigree of bovine animals. Goods, services, labor, and capital were to move freely in this boundary-less economic world, which had a single aim: to counter the industrial might of the United States and Japan. The failure to achieve a common market under the original Treaty of Rome in 1957 had cost Europeans a fortune in lost opportunity and brought the word "Eurosclerosis" to our dictionaries. It was fear of being labeled terminally uncompetitive that was pushing Europe toward harmonization through a monumental deregulatory movement. The last golden age of European economics that bloomed in the 1960s had wilted by the early 1970s from overzealous regulation, nationalistic squabbling, trade bickering, recessionary shocks, Bretton Woods, and oil jolts. Now a barrier-free market had endless possibilities.

Despite rumblings about securities reform, however, the EC had yet to focus on financial innovation and risk capital. It was difficult to get Europeans to make risk investments. For instance, in Germany, where options were illegal and considered a form of gambling until the law was changed in 1990, there had never been a hostile takeover. That meant that European stock exchanges needed to be deeper; because stocks were not traded freely, the markets lacked liquidity. In the United Kingdom, for example, some 20 institutions controlled 95 percent of all stock. At the same time, most European companies were undervalued for tax purposes. There was little incentive for anybody to change. But the prospect of a single market altered that. Perhaps some order could be made out of 12 stock markets with 12 sets of rules, EC planners believed. Moreover, Europe's other exchanges were still jittery over the UK's experience with its so-called Big Bang—the deregulation of its securities markets, which was to usher in a new era of trading and capital formation—that turned into a dramatic change on the London Stock Exchange even before the crash of 1987.

The futures markets stood to gain. Savings of one country could be invested in another country. For instance, if the Italian deficit became too great, people would buy Deutsche marks instead of lira, a prospect that Europe's futures and options exchanges wanted to cash in on. The positioning began to take shape in early 1989, when the Committee of European Community Options & Futures Exchanges (ECOFEX) was formed in London. ECOFEX wanted to be a clearinghouse for ideas and actions in dealing with Europe's emerging futures and options markets, and in lobbying the European Community Commission for the harmonization of contracts and regulations. Early ECOFEX members included Amsterdam's European Options Exchange, France's MATIF, the London International Financial Futures Exchange, and the London Traded Options Market. Among them, ECOFEX exchanges accounted for about 95 percent of total futures and options volume in Europe.

While Western Europe was building its economic future, Eastern Europe was dismantling its political past, struggling to realign itself into a pre–World War II map. With the collapse of the Wall between the two Germanys, and the Baltic states search for independence, the Cold War was in the throes of rapid deconstruction. The dissolution of the Communist system would eventually spread to the Russian homeland itself during 1990, shattering the myth that capitalism would forever remain isolated. Now there existed the possibility that perhaps capitalism could become the dominant system of organizing humans' economic activities. Melamed couldn't let the irony escape notice. It was "bizarre," he opined at a 24 July congressional hearing, that "at the precise moment when the bust of Lenin is unceremoniously removed from Moscow's City Hall, there are those who would advocate major structural changes in the regulatory ... framework of U.S. capital markets." The system that was already in place had achieved, he said, an "unparalleled triumph for capitalism." Shortly thereafter, late in the summer of 1990, the Merc was visited by delegations from Czechoslovakia, Hungary, Poland, and the Soviet Union, exploring free market reform that included the development of commodity futures exchanges.

The global-thinking Chicago exchanges, in turn, saw an opportunity to export their free market philosophy. In late October 1990, the Merc's Geldermann, along with CBOT chairman William O'Connor and president Thomas Donovan, traveled to Budapest to speak at a meeting for the establishment of a new commodity futures market. While there, the three Chicago exchange officials signed agreements with the Budapest Commodity Exchange to provide educational and technical assistance and personnel to help them establish a viable market like the flourishing futures market in grain the Hungarians had prior to World War

II. During the question and answer period that followed a presentation by the Chicago group, an elderly man stood up proclaiming in heavily accented English, "Thank God, I have lived to see this day." He had been an original member of the Budapest Commodity Exchange before it was closed down by the Soviets after the failed revolution in 1956. "He came forward to shake our hands," recalled Geldermann. "And he followed us around the rest of the day."

From Budapest, it was on to Moscow. The three joined Melamed and Brodsky in a meeting with leaders of the city of Moscow, the Russian Republic, and the USSR. The new Soviet markets were only cash auctions, or barter markets, covering a variety of items such as building materials, computers, and other consumer products. As in Budapest, similar agreements were also signed with the three Soviet governing entities that included the Moscow Commodity Exchange.

The visit to Moscow was an eye-opener for the Merc officials. Despite all they had read and heard, the situation seemed far gloomier from a first-hand view. There were acute shortages of every imaginable consumer commodity from apples to vodka. Even worse was the lack of an infrastructure. While visiting the Kremlin, Melamed asked to place a telephone call back to the Merc at about the time the market was opening, and he couldn't get it done—not even from the Kremlin itself. But there was a strong desire on the part of the Russians, the Merc officials would later report upon their return to Chicago, to find a solution to the failure of centralized planning. And they were convinced of one more thing: If allowed to develop freely in these countries, futures markets could be established at a faster pace than could be imagined, particularly in areas such as Hungary, where a free market had previously existed. (Brodsky arranged for one of the hosts, an economist with the Ministry of Trade and Procurement [ag department], to spend six months in Chicago at the Merc and the CBOT. While he was in Chicago, the government collapsed!)

From Moscow, Melamed, Brodsky, and Geldermann traveled to London for the Merc's sixth annual symposium. It had attracted the largest group of industry people ever—more than 300 from all over Europe. The major topic of discussion was GLOBEX.

Despite all the gloomy economic news and threat of a war with Iraq, the futures markets during 1990 showed defiance like the exchanges themselves. In the fall the markets had settled down as interest rates, stock prices, and foreign exchange rates began to adapt to the vagaries of the business cycle and market volatility. On 27 December, nearly a week before the Merc's fiscal year ended, *The Wall Street Journal* wrote in an article headed "Futures Become Hot As Economy Slumps, Sparing Chicago The Fate of Wall Street" that "the Windy City's financial fortunes are based on futures and options trading, rather than on stocks and bonds, investment banking, and corporate takeovers. And these days, with the U.S. economy sinking and war clouds building, that is a crucial difference. Indeed, the bad economic news is attracting some investors to the futures markets."

33

So Long Karl, Hello Adam

By the early 1990s capitalism seemed to have crept into every corner of the world. It even managed to climb the Asian steppes to Ulan Bator, the capital of Mongolia, where for four hours every Tuesday in 1992 shares of five formerly state-owned companies changed hands on the Mongolian Stock Exchange. Could the futures markets be far behind? The land of Genghis Khan, squeezed between Russia and China, had come full circle: in 1921 Mongolia had become the first Asian country to embrace communism, and in 1990 it was the first Asian country to let go of communism.

President Bush's "new world order" was in essence a new world reality. Liberated societies, still traumatized by repression, faced the need to become self-reliant. No longer, for instance, could they depend on Soviet aid and an orderly weaning of their economies away from central planning. The World Bank and dozens of countries, including the United States, stepped up with aid packages of one kind or another to ease the pangs of privatization. Yet countries in transition were finding that it took more than the transfer of state-owned companies to become a free market economy. To become a modern economic state, Russia realized it had to transform the ruble into a convertible currency. To do that required the help of the International Monetary Fund, which would provide a currency stabilization fund, a pool of hard currency that, in effect, guaranteed the exchange rate of the ruble at a realistic level. This action gives the ruble buying power inside as well as outside of Russia. Such a fund, whose contributors would be the industrialized Western nations and Japan, served as did the gold reserves that used to back the dollar. Earlier, Poland had made the transition to a convertible currency without having to draw on hard-currency reserves set aside in an account by the West. The world was facing change—and its institutions, it seemed, had to reinvent themselves to keep up as half the world had abandoned Karl Marx for Adam Smith in pursuit of a capitalistic conscience.

But there was another hook in capitalism's rapture: The nagging recession that was forcing more people to turn their backs on the American Dream with its post–World War II promise of prosperity. Ironically, the two pillars that had so dominated the psyche of most Americans since the late 1940s—the belief in ongoing prosperity and the crusade against communism—were crumbling at the same time. Trapped by a Federal deficit, steep taxes, declining income, and higher housing costs, sons and daughters of middle-class families began to talk about fewer opportunities than their parents had. College graduates (a growing number had returned to live with their parents for economic reasons) were faced with the poorest employment prospects in years and many took on menial jobs with hopes that the job market would eventually loosen up. Others polished their academic resumés and headed for overcrowded graduate schools in order to enhance their credentials while waiting out the recession. But there was hardly any relief in sight. U.S. companies, the economists predicted, would be shedding more than one million jobs in 1992 (a Presidential election year) in their frenzied strategies to downsize and improve profits. The recession had also moved the Merc to pare costs as well, cutting its budget by $5 million in 1990 as trading volume slipped below the previous year's for only the second time in 15 years. Another $10 million was shaved in 1991 that involved scaling back nonessential services and reducing staffing by 52 positions through attrition.

Soured by the hard economic realities, it was not surprising that the polls showed waning consumer confidence, despite the Federal Reserve's cut in the discount rate that helped inch fixed-rate mortgages downward. The drop in rates resulted in a wave of asset allocation, a shifting or a diversification of assets. With low yields on CDs and Treasury securities, investors put money into the stock market: a record $34 billion flowed into stock mutual funds in 1991. That kind of money turned the stock market defiant to the point of ignoring the heavy debt on the economy and the signs of a protracted recession. By December 1991 short-term interest rates were the lowest in 27 years, triggering a rally that sent the stock market to record heights. For the year the Dow Jones average rose 535 points—more than a 20 percent gain—to a record peak of 3168.83. The S&P 500 leaped even more than the Dow during the year, rising 26 percent, and NASDAQ, the barometer for small stocks, jumped a record 57 percent.

It was as if the focus on market volatility since the crash had turned from fear into fascination. When all was tallied, the Merc too benefited from the bullish sentiment and the growing need of financial institutions and corporations to manage risk more prudently. Thus the Merc was the only major futures exchange to register a volume increase—3.5 percent—over the previous year's record. A total of 108,128,616 futures and options contracts had traded, setting a Merc record. Futures and options on currencies were the most actively traded ever, reaching 37,823,810 contracts with record volume recorded in British pound and Deutsche mark futures.

Nineteen ninety-one literally started off with a bang as shortly before 7 P.M. on Wednesday, 16 January, the skies over Baghdad (where it was 3 A.M. Thursday) were aglow with streams of antiaircraft fire, "smart bombs" bursting through bunker doors, and columns of acrid smoke lurching toward a new moon. Desert Shield had turned into Desert Storm as a mighty air armada guided by laser beams, infrared images, and television pictures struck Iraq with precision and relentless fury. The rapid-fire stream of deadly technology turned the Gulf War into a hundred-hour rout by the United States and its United Nations allies. Kuwait was liberated and America's oil interests were secured.

During the war the Merc had taken steps to secure its own markets. Building security was tightened and for a short period the visitor's gallery was closed. (After it was reopened briefcases, bags, packages, and so on were subject to inspection upon request by a security guard.) Margin requirements were temporarily increased for several financial contracts and circuit breakers were placed on currency contracts to maintain orderly markets. Modern wars and modern markets were like multilayered frescoes—complex, technical, strategic, volatile. And in each respective theater there were winners and losers.

January 1991 also brought with it the conclusion to the federal government's battle against the CBOT soybean traders, which had waged longer than Desert Storm. For 13 weeks the government had pleaded its case before a jury of ten women and two men who had to pore over thousands of pages of documents, depositions, and verbatim testimony in a three-week-long deliberation before returning a verdict. On Wednesday 9 January the verdict was handed down: the soybean traders were convicted of scheming to defraud customers through illicit trades at the CBOT. Eight of the ten defendants were found guilty of violations of RICO, a crime that carried the potential penalty of the loss of the defendants' assets, which included their homes and exchange memberships, at the time worth $310,000 each. Key to the convictions, federal prosecutors noted, was the testimony by former traders who had cooperated with the government.

Meeting with reporters in the Dirksen Federal Building following the verdict was U.S. Attorney Fred Foreman, who had succeeded Anton Valukas on 27 August 1990. Foreman, accompanied by Assistant U.S. Attorneys Ira Raphaelson and Thomas Durkin, said, "People are going to have greater confidence when they invest in the future in these markets." Raphaelson had a few words for those who had criticized the government's investigation. "All ten were convicted of the fraud theory," he said, "[which] we were told wouldn't hold water . . . . We said we would answer our critics in the courtroom. The jury has done that today." The prosecutors, in effect, were saying that there was no mea culpa strategy that could work for some and fail for others. The trials were turning out to be an examination of the dark areas of exchange trading and the responsibilities of dealing in a quasi-public organization.

CBOT chairman William O'Connor quickly responded to the verdict by defending the exchange's image as lacking probity. "While any indictment or conviction is one too many for us," O'Connor said, "everyone should understand that the number of members indicted was less than two-thirds of 1 percent of our membership." A few hours later the CBOT announced suspension of the ten traders pending, it said, internal disciplinary proceedings.

The verdict had capped the second trial that came out of the FBI sting operation. In July 1990 a jury delivered what the *Chicago Tribune* described as "a far more ambiguous verdict" in the case involving three Swiss franc traders from the Merc. One of the traders was convicted of 20 charges, another of one charge, and a third was acquitted of violations of commodity law. Now in January 1991, there were 12 Japanese yen traders from the Merc whose case was still being tried. "Bean verdict casts gloom on yen mood," the *Sun-Times* headline proclaimed the day after the soybean traders were convicted. However, defense attorneys for the yen traders told the press that their strategy was different from the approach used in the soybean trial. Defense attorneys for the yen trial, which began 5 September 1990, argued that the government investigators had misrepresented legitimate trades (prearranged trading was a charge central to the government's case) that were not in violation of Merc rules. In contrast, the defense attorneys for the soybean traders conceded that their clients had broken CBOT rules, but had not committed crimes.

After 19 days of emotional deliberations, the jury reached a verdict on 13 March. As in the soybean trial, the outcome was equally as stunning. But this time the scale had tilted completely in the opposite direction. There were no convictions. "In a blow to the federal investigation of Chicago's futures exchanges," wrote *Sun-Times* reporter Greg Burns, "a jury Wednesday returned not a single guilty verdict against any of 12 Chicago Mercantile Exchange traders." The jurors had voted not guilty on more than 100 commodity, mail, and wire fraud counts. Two of the yen traders were cleared of all charges against them as the jury had failed to reach verdicts on 80 counts against the other ten. The outcome forced U.S. District Judge William T. Hart to declare a mistrial. This time, instead of tears from the families of the defendants sitting in the courtroom—as had been the case with the soybean traders—there was scattered applause. And just as defense attorneys for the soybean traders had planned to appeal, now it was the government's intention to retry the case involving 10 of the yen traders on unresolved charges.

The five-month yen trial, which opened in early September, produced a paper blizzard of testimony and court transcripts that apparently proved overwhelming for some of the jurors. "You can't expect people to go through 15,000 pages," bemoaned one juror. "It was too much paper for us." As for the jury deliberations that ended in a 10 to 2 split on many counts, another juror described them as "a cross between a National Lampoon movie and the Twilight Zone." The Merc's official statement gave the yen case a more practical spin. "Our members," the Merc responded, "have been in large measure exonerated."

The matter was far from buried and the controversy continued to surface. On 5 June U.S. District Judge Ann C. Williams publicly admonished the Merc for abusing its disciplinary powers against those traders who had cooperated with the government in the fraud investigation. The judge's criticism was leveled during the sentencing hearing of former Merc traders William Walsh and Mark Fuhrman, both of whom received five-year terms of probation and 500 hours of community service. (Fuhrman was also ordered to pay $10,362 in restitution to cheated customers and $1,675 in restitution to Walsh.) Said Judge Williams, "I am outraged that individuals such as you (Walsh) and Mr. Fuhrman who admitted their guilt and admitted to the way of life at the exchange were punished so heavily when there are defendants who were ultimately convicted who continue to trade." The Merc vigorously denied the charge, stating that it "did not, in any form or fashion, penalize any member for cooperating with the federal government." Walsh and Fuhrman, the statement continued, "pleaded guilty to participation in an ongoing scheme that was injurious to customers. The individuals whose punishments by the exchange were apparently regarded as disproportionate by the court were convicted or pleaded guilty to far less serious conduct." The Merc had expelled both traders and fined them a combined $60,000 after each pleaded guilty to one wire fraud and one commodity exchange act violation. The pair had also admitted to other offenses committed in the Swiss franc pit. Two other Swiss franc traders, however, who pleaded guilty after a federal jury had convicted them were neither expelled nor fined by the Merc. One had received a four-month suspension and a three-year prohibition on filing customer orders; the other a five-day suspension and three-year ban on filing orders. (Pending a full hearing, the CBOT had suspended all 22 of its members who were convicted or pleaded guilty in connection with the FBI sting.)

Nine days later on 19 June the CBOT hired constitutional legal scholar Robert H. Bork to write an amicus curiae (friend-of-the-court) brief that asked the court of appeals in Chicago to overturn the RICO convictions of the eight soybean traders. The CBOT made it clear that it was challenging the application of the RICO law against the defendants and not the guilty verdicts the jury had returned six months earlier. The 64-year-old Bork, who in 1987 had been denied confirmation as a U.S. Supreme Court nominee, told the *Chicago Tribune*: "One of the reasons I accepted the job is to go after the RICO statute. It is a very vague statute because it denies due process, it gives prosecutors enormous leverage and, in my view, it is used for all kinds of oppression."

Eight of the CBOT soybean traders were convicted of racketeering and sentenced to prison terms ranging from probation to 37 months. Two of the defendants, Martin J. Dempsey and Charles Bergstrom, were ordered to forfeit $300,000 each, and three others were ordered to forfeit $150,000 each. "The soybean case was a flagship case for the government and the prosecutors tried to make these guys out to be Al Capones. They tried to make little fish look big," brooded defense attorney James Epstein, whose client Martin J. Dempsey— found guilty of 60 charges and not guilty of 5—was the first among the convicted traders to begin serving his 37-month sentence at the minimum security prison in Oxford, Wisconsin. Besides the soybean traders, three Merc traders had to report to prison that summer: Japanese yen traders Ray Pace and Sam Cali faced one year terms, and Swiss franc trader Robert Mosky faced a four-month term to be followed by four months of Salvation Army work release. Of the 48 individuals indicted two years earlier, 36 had been convicted or pleaded guilty, 10 faced a retrial on remaining charges, and two were acquitted.

The FBI sting and ongoing investigation had left the exchanges hauling apprehension, anxiety, and anger like dirty laundry. Yet Merc officials had no qualms about airing their feelings in public. "Externally, the investigation has had a very negative impact on this institution," Jack Sandner conceded in a 21 April interview with the *Chicago Tribune* shortly after he was elected to a record seventh one-year term as chairman. "It has always been the goal of this exchange to treat any impropriety with seriousness, but you can't have an institution trading contracts worth trillions of dollars a year and not have some impropriety, because human beings are human beings and you're going to have some bad apples. Overall, the investigation has been salutary, because we have accelerated and upgraded many surveillance systems which were in the planning stages before the probe became public knowledge."

The following day, on 22 April, the Merc extended an olive branch to the Justice Department during a meeting with U.S. Attorney Fred Foreman. The hour-long meeting in Foreman's office was attended by Sandner, Brodsky, and Merc outside counsel Jerrold Salzman. The purpose was to explain the reforms that the exchange had put into place since the FBI sting surfaced two years earlier. Among those reforms were the limitation of trading activities of broker groups, a reduction in dual trading, the alteration of trading cards to include more detailed information and the frequency with which they were collected and turned in, as well as an increase in surveillance staff and the use of cameras on the trading floor. "Our objective was threefold," Sandner said of the meeting. "To put a human face on the entire matter, to extend a hand in cooperation, and to let them (government prosecutors) know we also have an agenda of honest markets." Then he added, "Some accounts have suggested that we were heckling at the jury verdicts, but there is nothing further from the truth." Foreman let the Merc contingent know that the investigation of the exchanges would continue. In summing up the meeting Foreman later told a reporter: "I thought it was beneficial. Everyone agrees their business is very important to the city of Chicago, to Illinois, and to the country. Everyone is looking for the same thing, and that is to have a good, honest exchange."

The old fear that government would impinge on the free market machine that drove the Merc was still present, but somewhat muted. Although efforts to shift regulatory jurisdiction and margin-setting authority away from the futures industry were stalled, there were those "lying in wait" to renew the attack on stock index futures, University of Chicago finance professor Merton Miller warned in November 1990. A month before publicly airing his view, Miller had won the Nobel prize in economics. In an interview with the *Chicago Sun-Times* the outspoken Miller promised he would use his clout on behalf of the Chicago futures exchanges, for which he had become the leading academic proponent. "I've long been a champion of Chicago against New York and Washington, and that won't change," he told a reporter. "I hope more people will listen."

Change in leadership at both the Merc and CBOT had also taken place heading into the new decade. After months of deliberation with family and friends, Melamed had reached a decision that could not, he said, be altered. On 5 March 1990 at a meeting of the board of governors he announced that decision: to retire at the end of the year. "There comes a moment in everyone's career when he knows in his heart it is time for a change," Melamed stated in a letter he sent to the membership timed to his announcement. "After twenty-three years at the leadership of the Chicago Mercantile Exchange, that time has come for me."

Melamed's decision came at a time when the Merc was Big Business at its biggest, as the factoids that made up its 1990s profile revealed the following: In 1991 the underlying value of all contracts traded at the Merc totaled more than $50 trillion compared with the underlying value of all equities traded at the New York Stock Exchange of some $1.3 trillion. One-third of the Merc's business came from overseas. On an average day, the Exchange clearing division processed about $500 million in performance bonds that backed market positions taken by customers, members, and member firms. Of the more than 90 member firms, 25 were owned by non-U.S. banks and investment firms. In 1980 the Merc handled nearly 20 million contracts a year. By 1990 it traded just under 103 million contracts—a 460 percent increase over the decade and nearly twice the industry rate. The Merc was doing a third of the future industry's business as the most diversified exchange in the world, trading futures and futures options contracts on agricultural commodities, currencies, interest rates, and stock index products. All of this activity took place in a state-of-the-art complex that encompassed two trading floors (the upper floor was slated to be opened by mid-1993 to trade Eurodollars and other interest rate contracts and currencies) totaling 70,000 square feet, 34 trading pits, 1,200 individual communications trading booths, and more than 5,000 people on the main trading floor doing business amid a whirl of flailing hands, emotional jags, and screaming orders during a day that began at 7:20 A.M and ended at 3:15 P.M.

The explosive growth during the frantically busy years had its price, and the *Chicago Tribune* observed that "it became harder and harder to instill the values and traditions of the exchange into the younger traders. For many, riding the bull markets of the 1980s was more important than regulation or ethics." Had the emphasis on growth and innovation overshadowed playing by the rules? It was a question that promised to stir debate for years to come. There would be other matters to consider as well now in the 1990s. The globalization of markets, new products, and trading them around the clock was even turning the media from "gotcha" exposés to exploration of the more substantive issues facing the exchanges.

It was too difficult to reduce Melamed's tenure to a tidy summation and too early to accurately foretell how history would judge him. "Unfortunately, it isn't certain that history will usher Melamed into any business hall of fame," wrote Terry Brown of the *Chicago Tribune's* editorial board shortly after Melamed's announcement. Then Brown concluded, "Like Henry Ford, Melamed gave his industry something to build on. Like Ray Kroc, he recognized the need for a market and then used his considerable persuasive skills to convince people to use it. After that, it mushroomed because it provided economic value to its users. Some may say it's too early to anoint Melamed a financial wizard and visionary, but there's no doubt he has made his mark and Chicago is the better for it." The headline over the article read, "Leo Melamed, father of financial futures."

For sure, this time Melamed meant it. Three days after his announcement he appeared at the 15th annual Futures Industry Association Conference in Boca Raton, Florida, where on 8 March he gave a farewell address to a packed house of futures exchange officials from across the oceans. His resignation, however, would not completely sever his bond with the futures markets. Although he would no longer take an active part in board conferences, he would continue to be active in working on the completion of GLOBEX. It was impossible to separate the man from the myth, and no one could shortchange the growth of the Merc under Melamed's stewardship. The cumulative value of one original Merc membership in 1969—when Melamed first became chairman and volume was a promising 3.8 million contracts—had grown in worth to well over $1 million by 1989 with volume topping 100 million contracts.

In a tribute to his tireless efforts, the board gave Melamed the title of chairman emeritus and renamed the Chicago Mercantile Exchange-endowed chair at the University of Chicago the "Leo Melamed Chair." The Merc extended the tribute to its annual member's gala, hosting a black-tie dinner on 26 January 1991 in the Grand Ballroom of Chicago's Hyatt Regency Hotel, where nearly a decade earlier the Merc had celebrated the IMM's tenth anniversary in the same room. Among the 1,500 guests were CFTC chairman Wendy Gramm, and E. B. Harris, and brief remarks were made by Mayor Richard Daley, Clayton Yeutter, Merton Miller, Milton Friedman, and John Geldermann. Brodsky acted as master of ceremonies and Sandner led the toast to his "friend and mentor." Part of the festivities included a lighthearted video montage of Melamed's life at the Merc that began in 1954. Of all the speakers that night, however, it was perhaps Barry Lind who captured the essence of the Merc's spirit in his introductory comments of the video presentation. "Remember, those old Judy Garland and Mickey Rooney movies" he said, "where one moment they are sitting in a barn in Indiana saying, 'Let's put on a show' and within ten minutes they are opening in Broadway. It made great entertainment but it wasn't really plausible. Well, imagine Leo walking around an ailing Butter and Egg Exchange telling some guys who just found out that pork bellies were bacon that someday we would be members of the greatest agricultural and financial exchange in the world with a cast of thousands. Just as implausible, but then he went out and did it."

The CBOT had also undergone a change in its leadership ranks. In August 1990 CBOT chairman Karsten Mahlmann, already in his fourth consecutive term, resigned amid fallout from the collapse of the Stotler Group, the firm he was associated with for 27 years. During the boom years of the 1980s, Stotler had overexpanded—through acquisition and the addition of hundreds of new brokers—and was caught in a severe cash crunch that was uncovered by federal regulators who questioned the transfer of customer account funds from the firm's brokerage operations to its parent company. As chairman of Stotler, Mahlmann's credibility became severely impaired and he resigned his position from the CBOT. He was only the second CBOT chairman ever to resign and the first since 1855. Stotler's fall came just seven months after the demise of Drexel Burnham Lambert, proving that even the long-established firms, if not properly managed, are at risk. William O'Connor took over the CBOT chairmanship after Mahlmann's resignation and immediately established the Financial Compliance Committee to regulate capital levels of members firms. "I don't want any more Stotlers or Drexels or anything," he said. A few more such failures, he believed, could lead to greater government regulation over trading firm capital requirements—another blow to the supporters of self-regulation. The 60-year-old O'Connor, perhaps more so than Mahlmann, was also a strong advocate of working with the Merc toward such common goals as sharing technology, combining trade clearing facilities, and building the GLOBEX system.

The Merc had always placed a high value on the continuity of its leadership. It proved it when Jack Sandner, then 49, was elected in January 1991 to a record seventh one-year term as Merc chairman. Shortly thereafter Sandner in a newspaper interview said, "I have always looked to Leo as a mentor and a teacher and a brilliant strategist and I would be foolish not to adopt many of the policies and attitudes he represents. I would also be foolish not to call on him regularly to check my thinking with his." To ensure continuity, Melamed engineered a chain link of positions that stretched into the nineties. From 1967 to 1976 there were only four basic board offices: chairman, first vice-chairman, second-vice chairman, secretary, and treasurer. In 1977 the position of special counsel was created for Melamed, who served in that post from 1977 to 1990. In 1985, the post of special counsel to the board was combined with the chairman of the executive committee, the dual post Melamed served in from 1985 to 1990. Another new post was also created and called legislative liaison and filled by Sandner. In 1990 a senior policy advisor was added and legislative liaison was activated. Sandner became the senior policy advisor and Larry Rosenberg legislative liaison. In 1991, when Sandner became chairman, the board elected Rosenberg as senior policy advisor and Steven Wollack, who had lost to Sandner in his bid for chairman, as legislative liaison.

One priority on Sandner's agenda, as he put it, was to bring "the membership back together." Too often, he believed, members had sought to redress grievances through an outpouring of petitions that at times overwhelmed the board in what Sandner termed "a manifestation of communication gridlock." He started at the board level, adjusting the power structure that existed under Melamed. Sandner sought a more representative board so that members wouldn't need referenda to get their points across. Through a rule change, he also opened the close-knit executive committee to broader participation by allowing elected board members who weren't permanently assigned to the committee to serve on a rotating basis. Those who had not been members of the powerful committee, which generally met two days before the full board meeting, felt, as Sandner put it, "disenfranchised." And no longer were executive committee members grouped at the head of the boardroom conference table. Instead, seating was on an alphabetical basis. For the first time, there was an open door policy in which exchange governors were required to keep office hours in a designated office so they would be accessible to members. It was a modest beginning for what Sandner thought had become a smug and insulated leadership. "We haven't had time to pay attention to the membership," Sandner conceded shortly after his election. "They don't feel they're getting a proper forum to express their thoughts. We need to deal with ideas before they become petitions and referendums." Sandner's comments were made a few days before a referendum to cut trading fees—launched by a petition signed by 400 members in favor of the measure—was to be voted on. The referendum was defeated in favor of the board's alternative fee plan, which went into effect in April 1991.

It was the free-flow exchange of ideas that had given the Merc its entrepreneurial spirit over the years. That spirit needed reviving through change. When an organization became mired in its tracks, E. B. Harris would remind his colleagues, it was on the road to mediocrity. "Next came stagnation and then decline," said Harris.

Throughout its history the Merc never stopped long enough to become bogged down. Momentum was the key to its survival. It had grown into a huge international entity, far from its roots as a domestic agricultural exchange. But its governing structure had changed little over the past half century. In 1991 there were a thousand members serving on 90 different committees. "The system has served us well," reflected Sandner in April 1991, "but maybe it is now time to change it." To determine if change was indeed necessary, in August a Governance Committee was set up to study the situation. It was a nine-person committee chaired by Phillip Karafotas.[1] Each member brought a unique perspective: economist Merton Miller, for example, had served on various corporate boards, including the CBOT's, and Karafotas had spent more than a decade on the Merc board and on various committees, including the executive committee. In 1988 an ad hoc committee that included Brodsky, Karafotas, Larry Leonard, and public governor Donald Jacobs, dean of Northwestern University's Kellogg Graduate School of Management, had made recommendations to the board on limited aspects of the Merc's governance structure. Now there was need for a broader review because governing issues, as the Governance Committee saw them, remained "sensitive and pivotal" to the Merc's future.

Indeed they were. Like most organizations, the Merc was a system with a logic of its own and the weight of tradition and inertia. For 25 years a good part of that logic had been provided by Melamed. In the early days the Merc was more like a PT boat than an aircraft carrier, meaning that it was small and nimble enough to quickly maneuver. But as the exchange and the membership expanded the number of permanent committees, oversight committees, advisory committees, subcommittees, and ad hoc committees rose exponentially. There was a committee for everything, even a committee to review committee structures. Each committee had a chairman and some had co-chairmen. And all the committees reported to the board. At each step of the way that the Merc's governance structure did not provide for leadership continuity, the ad hoc system of tinkering and creating new positions as needed provided it. For instance, in 1979 when Melamed was appointed to the newly created position of Special Counsel to the board of governors, it institutionalized his role as chief policy maker and strategist for the Merc. "While we did not state it all the time," observed Karafotas, "all our jiggling around was to meet a core principle of our success: continuity of leadership."

To that end, continued the analysis, "We all know we created artificial positions, such as special counsel or legislative liaison or senior policy advisor, in order to bypass our governance structure and maintain key people in positions of influence. For the past decade there has undeniably been a Leo Melamed-Jack Sandner team, whatever the machination of our system. In spite of our rules, we accomplished continuity of leadership." But all the "jiggling," the analysis concluded, came with a price: misunderstanding, tension, and acrimony among an increasing number of vocal traders. "We suffer this," Karafotas stated, "because our rules are false to our objectives." The rules and objectives needed to be coordinated if the Merc's governance structure was to reflect its governance principles. Yet it was continuity that enabled the exchange to sidestep the bureaucratic mentality that often undermines most big organizations. Big exchange culture was not like big company culture, which discouraged contact between shareholders and directors. At the same time corporate cultures usually combined the roles of CEO and chairman, allowing the CEO to call the shots, set the board's agenda, dole out committee assignments, and fend off board intervention, not to mention the practice of retaining former CEOs as board members and permitting them to choose their successors. None of these corporate practices held for the Merc.

How did the Merc measure up to other exchanges? Among those exchanges surveyed (AMEX, CBOE, CBOT, COMEX, NYMEX, and NYSE) the Merc was the only one that limited the number of consecutive terms (three one-year terms) the chairman could serve. At the CBOT the entire membership voted on a chairman for a two-year term with no limit on the number of successive terms. The chairman of the Merc was elected by the board. What was the consequence of these differences? The CBOT campaign for chairman often became too contentious, exposing "dirty linen" in the public, and electioneering was done in the newspapers. And because the entire floor voted for the chairman, there was always the chance that the election could turn into a popularity contest. To the Merc leaders, the CBOT's process of selecting a chairman seemed cumbersome and unpleasant. Thus, the Merc concluded, although the CBOT had no limit on the number of years a chairman could serve, the election process itself resulted in frequent turnover in the chairman post. By contrast, the Merc's chairman elections were never obscured by internecine quarrels. Discussions were normally quiet, kept internally rather than aired in the press, there were no efforts to cater to short-term interests with campaign promises, and floor popularity did not prevail over board judgment. The situation prompted Karafotas to conclude, "while our election process has advantages, our artificial term limits run counter to our goal of continuity. This has led directly to our ad hoc, awkward approach." Soon after, a committee on corporate governance was appointed and in January 1992 the chairmanship was expanded to a two-year term, with Sandner elected to an unprecedented eighth term at a salary of $250,000 a year. (Now a chairman can serve up to three consecutive two-year terms.) Morever, the positions of senior policy advisor and legislative liaison were eliminated, which gave the vice chairman more responsibility, and ended the ad hoc continuity bridge.[2]

Byte by byte the markets were taking logical shape toward the twenty-first century. There was nothing to hold back the surge in distance trading as automated systems in various forms could be found all over the globe. In Australia, for example, the Sydney Futures Exchange became the first foreign exchange to announce its intention of joining GLOBEX. (MATIF was the first foreign exchange to actually sign an agreement to join GLOBEX.) In Barcelona, the International Commodity Clearing House (ICCH) offered its automated trading system to the Spanish futures exchange. In Frankfurt, the Deutsche Terminborse exchange wanted to unify six German stock exchanges with an automated system. In Dublin, the IFOX financial futures exchange also planned to use the ICCH system. In Hamilton, Bermuda Intex no longer traded its registered contracts and instead marketed its system with Telerate. In Great Britain, the London International Financial Futures Exchange (LIFFE), spent nearly two years developing Automated Pit Trading, which emulated open outcry instead of the order-matching system of GLOBEX. The London Stock Exchange was among the first to use an automated trading system called Seaq modeled after the NASDAQ system. In Luxembourg, another proposed exchange had been offered the ICCH system. Monep, the Paris-traded options exchange, also looked into ICCH's automated system. In New Zealand, the completely automated New Zealand Futures Exchange used an ICCH-developed Automated Trading System from its beginning in 1985. In Stockholm, the Swedish Options & Futures Exchange planned to market its automated system to the Rotterdam energy futures market. In Switzerland, the Swiss Options & Financial Futures Exchange adopted a system to trade options electronically in an effort to centralize trading in the various centers throughout the country. Called by *The Wall Street Journal* the "fraud-resistant futures market," Soffex offered options on a dozen Swiss equities and the Swiss Market Index.

Indeed it was competitive pressure across the oceans that drew the Merc and CBOT to the same corner. Now it became a matter of protecting not just each one's respective trading turf, but the entire territory. By 1991 the CBOT had spent 143 years and the Merc 94 years to turn Chicago into the world's trading capital of futures and options. At stake was an entire industry that provided revenues, jobs, and incomes to tens of thousands of people. Thus it stood to reason that the Merc and CBOT emerged as the point exchanges in the development of global futures markets. Understandably, the exchanges wanted to continue their dominant position in the years to come and going it alone was not the answer. Why should each exchange spend $5 million to develop a computerized trading card when for $2.5 million each, the same goal can be accomplished? Why should a clearing firm that is a member of both the Merc and CBOT have to employ separate staffs and install separate systems so they can handle trades at each exchange? Why couldn't more than $1 million a year be saved by merging the separate Tokyo offices that each exchange maintained? "There's so much money lying on the table that can be saved," said Merton Miller, who was on the Merc's board of governors and the only nonmember of the exchange on the committee formed to consider common goals between the two exchanges. There was even talk about the possibility of the joint use of Merc's second trading floor.

Would, then, an outright marriage of the exchanges be contemplated? Perhaps someday. But as Miller put it in November 1990, "Not in the near future. Maybe after years of other successes are on the books, there will be more." It would take far more than joint ventures to consummate a merger. There were many organizational differences to overcome, including the way the exchanges chose their respective chairman. The election process was more than a subtle difference in the rites and rituals of exchange life. Each exchange had its own heroes and its own cultural network of formal and informal rules, and at this stage in their histories the instinct to preserve their respective identities seemed greater than ever. Five months after Miller's comment, Sandner reiterated the Merc's position on the prospects of a Merc-CBOT merger in a *Chicago Tribune* interview with William B. Crawford, Jr.: "Way down the road, perhaps," Sandner said. "But I absolutely do not see one exchange in the near future. We can merge certain operations without diluting the competitive edge of our institutions. We will merge our marketing, our clearing systems, the development of certain technologies. But we will fight the Board of Trade tooth and nail when developing a new futures contract, such as a cross-rate contract we expect to launch this summer. We are not going to allow anything that would denigrate the motivation to compete for products and market share, because that is what made the Merc and the Board of Trade leaders."

GLOBEX was a major step toward a possible union, and one that could ensure leadership of the Chicago futures exchanges for a long time to come. The CBOT had scrapped its rival electronic trading system to join forces with the Merc and Reuters in the GLOBEX venture in 1990. But the system described by Sandner as "creating the wheel for the first time" was dogged by technical difficulties and repeatedly missed tentative launch dates. In a perfect world, GLOBEX might have been started in phases. But the plan called for everyone to be up at the same time and that presented major start-up problems. The addition of the CBOT to GLOBEX had increased demands on the system exponentially. "You've added several hundred different instruments and each one must be traded simultaneously. If you want to cut response time in half, it may take four times as much money," explained Gary Ginter, who in April 1991 was appointed managing director of GLOBEX responsible for getting the system on track. Ginter was a founding partner of CRT Ltd. (Chicago Research & Trading Group), a primary dealer in U.S. Treasury securities, and one of the world's major options traders. After 14 years at CRT, Ginter had retired in December 1990 to spend time at the Mid America Institute for Public Policy, a think tank grounded in the Chicago economic school of free markets—the same philosophy coveted by Chicago's exchanges. Ginter had both visibility and respectability in the futures industry. After the stock market crash, Ginter lobbied in Washington on behalf of the futures industry along with Chicago exchange leaders. Moreover, CRT was a clearing member of both the Merc and CBOT, and Ginter sat on key committees at both exchanges and on advisory panels with the CFTC and the U.S. Office of Technology Assessment. He was acceptable, said Melamed, to both the Merc and CBOT and was no threat to either. In short, it was hoped that Ginter could bridge any political squabbles that might erupt among the three major partners, Reuters, the Merc, and CBOT. As the pressures to get GLOBEX running grew, so did the tension within the 19-member GLOBEX board that included Melamed, Sandner, Brodsky, CBOT president Thomas Donovan, and David Vogel, chairman of the Futures Industry Association. After repeated starts and stops, the inaugural date was reset: 25 June 1992.

The fight to preserve self-regulation and integrity of the markets in the face of criticism had thrown the exchanges into a strong emotional tizzy. But the once cloudy future of the exchanges had taken a sunnier turn despite the fact that there were no clear winners after three government trials. Eighteen months after the showy undercover FBI sting surfaced in 1989 the *Chicago Tribune,* the paper that broke the initial story, concluded: "... the multimillion-dollar federal probe has hardly lived up to its billing, and the mixed jury results may make other traders less eager to cooperate." The Justice Department had accused Chicago's futures traders (and in essence their exchanges even though they were not under investigation) of ignoring fraudulent practices. "While it's true that the federal investigation of trading floor practices has cast a shadow on our industry," Melamed said in his 1990 letter to the membership, "the integrity of the CME is not in question."

That became apparent on 11 December 1991 when President Bush paid a visit to both the Merc and CBOT. (Bush's previous visit to the Merc was in 1979 as a congressman.) The Merc saw the indictments in August 1989 as "short-term damage" to the confidence of the futures markets as prosecutors pressed ahead toward a second round of charges. *Sun-Times* financial writer Greg Burns summed it up when he wrote of Bush's visit: "Nearly three years after the news that FBI agents had infiltrated the Board of Trade and Chicago Mercantile Exchange, Bush spent the morning praising the exchanges and declaring that Chicago-style capitalism is the nation's best hope for the future."

Bush opened his Chicago visit at the CBOT, where he made no public reference to the FBI sting operation that led to 48 indictments in 1989 and convictions of all 19 from the soybean pit. As he threaded his way across the CBOT trading floor he handed out handshakes, autographs, and even high fives to cheering traders before ascending a podium overlooking the soybean pit. At 9:29:57, three seconds early, Bush used a silver hammer to smack the opening bell, and trading began. Shortly thereafter, in a closed-door meeting, CBOT officials demonstrated a prototype AUDIT electronic trading terminal for the president. Then Bush was off for the Merc, where again he waded through a mass of jostling bodies and a dissonant symphony of baritone growls that cut through the din of the trading floor. Flanked by Sandner, Brodsky, and a host of stern-faced secret agents, Bush made his way from cattle to currencies to the S&P pit as traders hoisted each other into the air angling for a glimpse. Bush then attended a round table meeting in the Merc's board room where he discussed economic matters with Midwest business executives. After that, Bush moved to the upper trading floor, filled with more than 500 traders, Chicago business and civic leaders, and press. His appearance was seen as a vote of confidence for the futures exchanges. There was no indication to think otherwise. In Bush's eyes Melamed was the "Babe Ruth" of the exchange and Brodsky the man who came "from Wall Street to Chicago." As for the Merc itself, Bush could only offer accolades:

> The Merc has become a bellwether of the future because it never, ever lost the inventive spirit of its founders. You defied the doomsayers when you pioneered that risk-pool management through the Exchange Trust. You established the first financial futures market, the International Monetary Market. You saw an international marketplace and established offices overseas before most exchanges even thought of setting up domestic branches. And you created the Eurodollar futures

a decade ago—and I know you celebrated its tenth anniversary yesterday, and you should be very, very proud of this world leadership.

In challenging times, you've thrived. And this year, you trimmed expenses to improve efficiency—and your business grew by more than four percent, I'm told. Through the ups and downs of the business cycle, you've operated without requiring a dime's worth of assistance from the American taxpayer. And you've taken care of your own without losing your momentum for a single minute.

This outpouring came from a president whose Justice Department had declared open war on the Merc and CBOT, and whose administration pushed for stiffer regulation of the futures markets. The charge was led by Treasury Secretary Nicholas Brady—former chairman of the Wall Street firm of Dillion, Read and head of the government study that lashed the Chicago markets for intensifying the selling panic—and SEC chairman Richard Breeden, both of whom sought to hike futures margins and shift regulation of stock index futures from the CFTC to the SEC. "Ever since the stock market crash of 1987," *Newsweek* magazine observed in the summer of 1990, "everywhere the Chicago Board of Trade and the Chicago Mercantile Exchange turned, it seemed someone was coming after them. The stock market blamed Chicago for their volatility. The Justice Department accused their traders of winking at widespread fraud. As Chicago looked to defend itself at home, overseas markets jumped into the futures business." That statement pretty well summed up the hectic years following the crash when the more conservative Wall Streeters continued to argue that fluctuations in Chicago markets roiled stock prices only to scare away stock market investors. The futures industry countered with equal intensity behind its contention that there was no solid evidence that margin levels affected volatility. It was a battle that had the media asking, "Who will win the clash of cultures?" Brady, it seemed, had put a great deal into the fight, so much so that Merton Miller sniped, "He's ringing more doorbells than a Chicago alderman." And as the Merc looked to defend itself at home, overseas markets jumped into the futures business, snaring 37 percent of the financial futures markets from nothing a decade earlier and prompting Melamed in July 1990 to proclaim, "This is war and we can lose it."

But by late 1990 the battle on Capitol Hill that had pitted the more conservative Wall Street interests against the futures exchanges appeared to be swinging Chicago's way. The Bush bill to stiffen regulations was pulled from a Senate vote because it lacked support, due in part to the futures industry's political clout and efforts by the exchanges themselves to shore up the regulatory procedures and systems. The Merc, for example, began to require traders to attend ethics classes and installed a video camera above the exchange floor focused on a given pit to spot wrongdoing. And in June 1990 the Merc and CBOT chose Spectrix, Synerdyne Inc. of California and Texas Instruments to develop electronic trading cards to possibly replace the pencil and card that had been a trading staple for more than a century. The cost to develop the hand-held computer terminals was $5 million. (On 25 February 1992 some two dozen Merc Deutsche mark traders and CBOT wheat traders, who had traded earlier on a prototype during mock sessions, began electronically recording contracts they bought and sold for their own accounts.)

At the end of 1991, with the Bush visit, the industry's image appeared to have come full circle from the dark early days of the sting operation. "If there was any stigma from the investigation," reflected Laurence Rosenberg, former Merc chairman and a board member since the 1960s, "the President wouldn't have been here." Following the Merc meeting, Bush had invited Sandner, Melamed, Brodsky and others to join him for lunch at the Billy Goat Tavern, a popular lower Michigan Avenue hangout among Chicago journalists, known for its penurious menu of cheeseburgers and chips. The risk appetite of Chicago's traders appeared to have rubbed off on Bush, who after the meal flipped a coin to decide who would pay the bill. "The president called heads," said Sandner. "It was tails." (The restaurant owner insisted on picking up the tab nevertheless.)

As the Merc evolved over the decades, its leaders sought to deliver a visionary long-term plan instead of settling on a minimalist program to move the exchange a notch ahead. The 1970s were a decade of revolutionary change: the IMM came about in 1972, followed a year later by the CBOT's launch of the CBOE, providing new dimensions to the repertoire of risk management tools. The balance of the decade had been devoted to nurturing these innovations. For the Merc as well as financial futures, the 1980s was the decade of acceptance, expansion, and opportunity. Once the value of financial futures and options were proven, the rush was on by both futures and securities exchanges to create a wide range of new instruments for use by money managers, bankers, corporate treasurers, and investment houses. Consider the following: In August 1980 the NYSE launched the New York Futures Exchange (NYFE), which began trading futures contracts on foreign currencies, U.S. Treasury bonds, and 90-day T-bills. That same year the Commodity Exchange listed two-year Treasury notes. In 1981 the Merc introduced futures contracts on the Domestic CD and the Eurodollar, the first cash-settled contract. The Domestic CD was also introduced by the CBOT and NYFE, while the New York Mercantile Exchange (NYMEX) traded for the first time No. 2 Heating Oil and Leaded Regular Gasoline, based on delivery points in New York and the Gulf of Mexico. In 1982 the Kansas City Board of Trade listed a futures contract of the Value Line Index; NYFE listed the NYSE Composite and Financial Indices; and the Philadelphia Stock Exchange (PHLX) listed an options contract on the British pound. In 1983 the CBOE listed options on the CBOE-100 index, which later became the S&P 100 index; NYFE introduced NYSE Composite Index Options; the CBOT introduced futures contracts on gold, crude oil, heating oil, and two-year T-notes; and PHLX listed options contracts on the Japanese yen, the Swiss franc, the Deutsche mark, and the Canadian dollar.

The new product trend continued to the end of the decade under a hailstorm of fierce competition, as one exchange attempted to wrest one successful instrument away from another. Ultimately, as the Merc summed up the 1980s, "Exchanges learned the overriding maxim: He who is firsteth with the mosteth, winneth!" Fortunately, the Merc had learned that lesson well before the 1980s in its role as inventor. Its currency markets were on a consistent growth track: financial futures and options accounted for nearly 90 percent of all trading volume at the Merc and a 60 percent industrywide market share.

By 1991 the Merc, as Sandner liked to put it, had become "a spectacular school of finance, a shrine to free enterprise." Judging by the visiting dignitaries, his point was well taken. President Bush, President Carlos Salinas de Gortari of Mexico, President Mary Robinson of Ireland, and General Colin Powell, chairman of the U.S. Joint Chiefs of Staff, had all visited the exchange for a firsthand look at what the traders often called "the last bastion of raw capitalism." After touring the floor on 11 April 1991, President Salinas, on his U.S. stump for the proposed North American Free Trade Agreement, observed: "Walking on the floor gives one a sense of the precise meaning of free trade. . . . The look in the eyes of those who work down there struck me very strongly. . . . They know the responsibility, they know they can gain or lose in a matter of seconds, but they also have an opportunity to exercise their freedom, their talent, their capacity."

There were other highlights during a year that converged the past and present: On 7 February the Merc reached back to its roots, launching a renewed broiler chicken futures and options contract. (A broiler contract initially traded from 1979 to 1982 and a chicken contract from 1962 to 1963.) Later that month, the Merc celebrated the Silver Anniversary of its live hog futures, the exchange's third-oldest actively traded contract behind pork bellies and live cattle. In March, an early "common goals" venture with the CBOT found Merc public governor Merton Miller journeying to Taiwan, where he urged authorities to enact legislation permitting its citizens to trade on overseas futures markets. On 27 March automated after-hours trading gained an important boost with approval of a CME-CBOT GLOBEX joint venture, ratified at both exchanges via referendum by a wide margin. On 1 April a new clearing fee structure aimed at reducing transaction fees took effect. Ten days later, Salinas came to the Merc. In May, General Colin Powell toured the trading floor as part of the Merc's welcome home to the U.S. troops who had served in the Gulf War. On 23 May the Merc, in conjunction with the CBOT, held its third annual International Finance symposium in Tokyo, which more than 500 guests attended. Entitled "Global Financial Markets in the 1990s: Perspectives from Both Sides of the Pacific," it was the first common goals symposium sponsored jointly by the Merc and CBOT. On 11 June the Merc installed a backup computer and telecommunications system designed to ensure that trading would continue in the event of a major computer failure. On 12 June options on one-month LIBOR futures began trading; by 8 July open interest reached 5,000 contracts and had topped 11,000 at July's end.

During the month of June the Merc announced the addition of two new governors to its board: former Minnesota Senator Rudy Boschwitz, a strong supporter of free markets, and Laurence Mollner, an executive vice-president of Dean Witter Reynolds Inc. On 19 July Chicago and Toronto forged a "sister cities" relationship in the Canadian Dollar pit, where their respective mayors, Richard Daley and Art Eggleton, inked the pact, marking the thirty-fifth anniversary of Sister Cities International. At a July meeting of the Managed Accounts Report Conference, Sandner unveiled the Average Price System (APS) concept that allows a clearing member firm to confirm an average price to customers for a single order or series of orders executed at different prices. In August a formal APS proposal was submitted to the CFTC along with a plan to lift position limits in Eurodollar and major currency futures and options. On 23 August, in the wake of the aborted coup attempt in Moscow, the Merc welcomed Leningrad (now St. Petersburg) Stock Exchange Chairman Igor Klioutchnikov, an advisor to Russian President Boris Yeltsin. "Everything has a good end," said Klioutchnikov, stressing that economic reform should be hastened. (During the failed putsch, orderly Merc markets were maintained, even as volume on Nikkei and currency futures reached new heights and open interest soared.) In September the Merc and CBOT received a $420,000 grant from the U.S. State Department to begin a three-phase project aimed at developing the Budapest Commodities Exchange into a successful domestic and regional commodities market. In early September more than 50 members of the U.S. House of Representatives toured the Merc as part of the Chicago Congressional Weekend that included lunching with Mayor Daley on the upper trading floor. Shortly thereafter, the prototype tests of AUDIT hand-held terminals were conducted by selected Merc and CBOT traders in mock sessions on the upper trading floor—with actual pit testing slated for 1992. On 18 September, in a reverie of nostalgia, the Merc celebrated the 30th birthday of the pork belly. In a conference room festooned by slabs of bacon— one smoked, one fresh-frozen—dangling from hooks at each end, Merc veterans and current leaders gave speeches, munched on bagels and cream cheese and, of course, bacon. "The contract always had a mystery about it, and that accounts for its staying power," mused the 83-year-old William Katz, who helped pioneer the contract while serving as chairman in 1959 and again from 1961 through 1963. (On 27 February 1989, the Merc held a "Bill Katz Day" in honor of his 60th anniversary as a member of the exchange. He retired in 1990.) From 1964 to 1972 pork bellies had been the Merc's mortar and brick, accounting for a major portion of the Merc's business and keeping the exchange well and alive until the advent of currencies and stock index. "Financial futures," Sandner crowed, "were spawned out of the belly of the hog."

On 1 October, the Merc said farewell to Sasha, the nickname of visiting Soviet scholar Alexander Belozertsev, who had spent six months studying organizational operations at the Merc and CBOT through a 1990 agreement among the two exchanges and Soviet officials to aid in the development of free markets. On 4 October the LOX (Large Order Execution) rule was implemented in the S&P 500 futures pit, making the Merc the first futures exchange to adopt the procedure, which is comparable to the block trading rules on major U.S. stock exchanges. On 14 October Sandner presented Irish President Mary Robinson with a Kelly green trading jacket emblazoned with "Ireland Futures" during a tour of the Merc. On 17 October, the Merc signed an agreement with Standard & Poor's Inc. to trade futures contracts and options on the new S&P MidCap 400 Index. Institutional investors have indexed more than $3 billion in assets to the broad measure of medium-capitalization equities. In late October, Chicago and Mexico City signed a "friendship cities" agreement on the floor of the Merc. On 1 November Eurodollar futures contracts cracked the one million mark, closing at 1,009,193 open positions, which are the number of contracts purchased or sold but not yet closed out by investors. The notational value of the open interest contracts exceeded $1 trillion. On 7 November the Merc and CBOT jointly staged an International Finance Symposium in London as part of their common goals effort. On 21 November, total Merc open interest surpassed a record three million contracts. On 10 December George Bush became the first U.S. president to tour the Merc's floor during an actual trading session, and on 31 December the Merc chalked up an all-time record of 108,128,616 futures and options contracts traded in a single year.

In some ways it was a typical year, and in others it was atypical. In any case it was dynamic. The organization is in constant motion, always with an eye on the future and an appreciation of the past. As the panorama of 1991 clearly shows, other exchanges were now seeking the Merc's expertise because it knew how to build markets—and sustain them. In only two decades the Merc had become the Johnny Appleseed of the futures industry, planting its seeds the world over. It had undergone a remarkable change from its days as a faltering butter-and-egg exchange on the brink of extinction in the 1950s. It had repeatedly overcome conventional wisdom while constantly pushing for change. In the process it had to reinvent itself; that is, to create new products and strategies that put it at the forefront of innovation.

Chicago, too, had changed. The stockyards were long gone, the steel mills silent and rusting. Its mighty banks that once sought to become world-class money centers had pared their ambitions. Only the futures exchanges had forged ahead to extend Chicago's status as the premier world center for financial risk management. The once poor butter-and-egg cousin to the vaunted grain markets of the CBOT, the Merc now saw itself as the world's foremost financial futures exchange. By 1991 its Eurodollar futures contract was arguably the most successful, with the largest open interest of any futures market. Its stock index futures were an overwhelming success as well. And the growth of GLOBEX was on the horizon. In less than two decades, financial futures and its array of futures and options instruments had revolutionized the way institutions worldwide managed risk. With pit bull tenacity the Merc had stayed on a course that often defied the odds.

In doing so, the Merc leaders had learned a powerful lesson over those years: no matter how much talent those in control had, if they lacked the right chemistry, leadership stalled. To move an organization like the Merc ahead required individuals with a group consciousness—similar to a championship basketball team loaded with star players who are willing to do things even when the spotlight is on a fellow teammate. "What difference did it make who got the credit," the 79-year-old E.B. Harris said in 1992, "decisions were always based solely on what was good for the Merc, not an individual's career path. That's what made the exchange endure. That's what gives it its spirit. This is an exchange built by people who understood the meaning of survival. All you have to do is walk into any pit and see for yourself. They're filled with capitalists in the heat of competition. Each is a survivor."

Epilogue

Thursday, 25 June 1992, at 6 P.M. on the trading floor of the Chicago Mercantile Exchange, the Chicago futures exchanges began to reach around the globe, across all borders and time zones. GLOBEX was launched.

After four years and an investment of more than $75 million, the 24-hour commodity trading network, as the *Chicago Tribune* put it, "blazed a chapter in the history of Chicago's futures exchanges, processing hundreds of trades without a glitch." Actually, it was 1,939 trades when the overnight session ended at 6 A.M. Friday. A breakdown of contracts traded during that historic period revealed 951 Deutsche mark contracts and 107 Deutsche mark options; 715 Japanese yen contracts and 120 yen options; and 46 futures and options on the CBOT's 10-year Treasury note contract.

It started easily, but not slowly. Only four contracts were initially listed on the system: three Merc contracts (Japanese yen, Deutsche marks, and yen–Deutsche mark cross rate futures) and the CBOT's 10-year Treasury note contract. And just 200 GLOBEX terminals were plugged into the Reuters-owned Digital Equipment Corp. mainframe computer in Hauppauge, Long Island, New York, which matched, cleared, and verified buy and sell orders—within three seconds. The terminals were operated by member firms of the Merc and CBOT, located in Chicago, New York, London, and Paris. The mainframe, on this Thursday evening, was intentionally programmed to operate well below capacity so as not to overburden the system, yet, by any reckoning, GLOBEX was proof that the trading universe was expanding. In the months ahead, plans called for the addition of hundreds of more terminals along with a dozen or more of the most heavily traded contracts listed on the Merc and CBOT. The MATIF exchange in Paris, also a member of GLOBEX, planned to list its contracts on the system by mid-1993, and other exchanges were expected to join GLOBEX as well.

Earlier in the afternoon at the Merc luncheon Mayor Daley officially proclaimed 25 June 1992 as "GLOBEX Day." The Merc, one could say, was on a roll. Six days earlier the exchange had approved plans to build a second trading facility in an empty room three floors above its current trading floor at a cost of

$26.6 million. For the fourth time in two decades, the Merc needed more space to accommodate the interest rate and currency groups along with such new products as the Standard & Poor's MidCap stock 400 stock index, the Russell 2000 Small Cap stock index, and other foreign stock indexes. Under the 32-foot-high ceiling, the new floor—to be completed in 12 months—would add 16 new trading pits and 770 member firm booths. A visitors' gallery would let the public view the markets. The combined trading floors will total 70,000 square feet, making the Merc the largest exchange facility in the world. It was a sizable commitment for those who fretted that the onset of GLOBEX foretold the end of open outcry. Well before the announcement of expansion plans, the man who pursued *glasnost* (openness) and used *perestroika* (restructuring) to try to renovate socialism—and lost his power base and republic in the process—had paid a visit to the Chicago exchanges. On 7 May, Mikhail Gorbachev had come to the Merc as part of a U.S. tour to drum up funds for his international relations think tank, the International Foundation for Social, Economic and Political Research. He toured the trading floor and met the board of governors, and Sandner presented him with a red trader's jacket emblazoned with "Perestroika Futures" across the back and "Free markets for free men" on the front. Gorbachev had clearly embraced the spirit of free-market capitalism: For his 45-minute visit to the Merc, he picked up $15,000 and another $15,000 from his appearance at the CBOT. (All totaled he received $100,000 from various Chicago businesses.)

Shortly before 6 P.M. on 25 June, a three-piece band played the theme to *2001: A Space Odyssey* (from Richard Strauss's "Thus Spake Zarathstra") as exchange and Reuters officials, along with scores of traders and brokers, milled about the floor, sipping champaign and munching on fancy hors d'oeuvres and chocolate cake. Sandner called the occasion "historic"; CBOT chairman William O'Connor asked the "Good Lord above to please bless GLOBEX"; Melamed urged the audience to raise their glasses to join him in wishing "Happy birthday, GLOBEX." Off to the side were Gary Ginter, managing director of GLOBEX, Murray Finebaum, Reuters CEO of GLOBEX, and a brooding Bill Muno, 40-year Merc veteran and member of the board, who was more tentative. "It's scary. I don't know what it means," said Muno, a broker whose two sons are also brokers in the pork belly pit. "I wonder about their future."

Before he could finish his sentence, the hands of Melamed, Sandner, Brodsky, O'Connor, and Reuters executive Rosalyn Wilton ceremoniously tugged at the trading bell, and GLOBEX clicked into operation. At 23.00.00.07 hours Greenwich Mean Time—6 P.M. and seven-one-hundredths of a second Chicago daylight savings time—the first trades took place, all in the Japanese yen contract. Three yen contracts were sold by Credit Lyonnais Rouse (USA) Limited and seven by E.D.&F. Man International Futures, Inc. The buyer of all ten contracts was Dellsher Investment Company, Melamed's firm. Also at the very same time, but at a slightly higher "match token" (or system identification number), E.D.&F. Man International

Futures, Inc. sold one yen contract to Nikko Securities Company International, Inc., and Dellsher Investment Company sold one contract to Credit Lyonnais Rouse (USA) Limited. Meanwhile Joe Gressel, a Merc local wearing his trading jacket, moved about the floor with a broad smile. It was Gressel who had sold those three yen contracts through Credit Lyonnais Rouse—and covered two of them just seconds after. "I made a quick $600 profit," he crowed. "The fills are reported quickly."

Two seconds later (at 23.02.00.40), the first recorded trades in Deutsche Marks took place: Singer/Wenger Trading Company, Inc. bought one DM contract from TransMarket Group, Inc. At the same time, but with a higher match token, Harris Futures Corporation bought 10 DM contracts from FIMAT Futures USA Inc. (the futures division of Societe Generale).

GLOBEX was working—an electronic global trading system in which prices were set by a computer match with incoming orders to completely bypass traders, brokers, and pits. Would GLOBEX eventually replace the mental metabolism of the pits, where a trader's life becomes pure reflex in a rhythm of open outcry? Would the frenetic finger shorthand that spelled prices give way to the speed of fingers typing orders at a computer terminal? Would silence replace noise as the most efficient means of trading the futures contract? Would GLOBEX someday be modified to trade stocks, further blurring the distinctions between futures and stock exchanges? Those were questions no one could answer that Thursday night in 1992. For now in this trading temple of futures and options there was a communion of past, present, and future, of once-strident rivals CBOT and Merc, of low-tech and high-tech. There were no answers, only anticipation.

There among the vacant pits on the cavernous—and quiet—floor of the Merc they awaited the start of a new era.

Notes

Chapter 4

1. The term *bucket shop* first appeared in the United States in the 1870s, but the word was coined in London fifty years earlier and grew out of the habits of swillers rather than speculators. Beer beggars on London's East Side would go from street to street with a bucket in hand, draining every keg they'd come across. They would then park themselves in small darkened dens, where the air was thick with cigar smoke and bawdy jokes, passing the bucket like a loving cup as each took a pull. The den soon came to be called a bucket shop. Eventually the term was used in both England and the United States as a byword of reproach to small places where grain and stock deals were counterfeited.

Chapter 5

1. Later in the year, when a very heavy production of peaches threatened to glut the market, dealers organized a "Peach Week" to draw out demand for peaches at the best prices available. They agreed to supply the retailer at $1.25 per bushel if he would, in turn, sell the peaches at $1.50 and seek to persuade housekeepers to buy in larger quantities than had been their custom. The profit-thin strategy stimulated sales and moved product. Similar efforts followed by other produce associations and before long Chicago had an "orange day," "apple day" and "olive day." There was never any "egg day," according to the records of the Chicago Produce Exchange.

Chapter 6

1. At the time the poem was written, a young poet-journalist was on the staff of the *Chicago Daily News*. He was Carl Sandburg, who had been hired

in 1917 at the suggestion of Ben Hecht. Sandburg was fascinated by the commerce of Chicago's big shoulders, but there is no clear indication that he may have been the anonymous poet who penned the ode to the Mercantile Exchange, though some suspect he was the author.

Chapter 7

1. Unfortunately, Mrs. Sherman—whose husband, Frank, was a broker, trader and eventually a Merc director during the 1950s—could only observe the traders from the doorways, as her poem's title indicates. In those days, there was no visitors' gallery from which to gaze. It would be four decades before the barrier was broken and the first female trader ventured into the pits. However, the Merc could take comfort in the fact that it was the first futures exchange in the nation to open memberships to women, thereby shattering the male mystique that had dominated the trading floors of exchanges since their inception.

Chapter 9

1. No one then could foretell that 40 years later federal agricultural subsidies would metastasize out of control. By 1986, the government was shelling out some $25 billion in farm programs. The record giveaway had cost nonfarm families up to $700 per year in taxes for support.
2. The key provisions of the Agricultural Act of 1948 extended wartime price supports at 90 percent of parity through 1949 for the basic commodities, including dairy products, hogs, chickens, and eggs, and price supports at 60 percent for potatoes, soybeans for oil, peanuts for oil, flaxseed for oil, peas, and beans.

   In 1949, Agriculture Secretary Charles Brannan proposed a new price support program that abandoned the old 1910 to 1914 price base period in favor of a 10-year moving average beginning with the years 1939 to 1948.
3. It wasn't the first such overture proposing a merger of the two exchanges, nor would it be the last. None, however, were really serious, and they were all informal. Two years later, for instance, a somewhat innocuous story on yet another intriguing, but casual, proposal appeared in the *Chicago Tribune* under the headline "Mercantile, Pit Merger Dropped." The following passage is an excerpt therefrom:

   > Attempts to bring about a merger between the Board of Trade and Chicago Mercantile Exchange have ended, even before discussions started. "A few traders presented a petition to the board of directors of the Board of Trade to initiate merger talks. The petition was found to be faulty technically, sufficient to end the matter without objections," according to Robert C. Liebenow, president of the Board.
   >
   > While the Mercantile may be receptive, it will not officially initiate talks.

4. In accordance with the contract, the salary increased to $22,500 in the second year and to $25,000 in the third. In his four and a half years at the Board of Trade, Harris' salary rose from $10,000 a year to $15,900.

5. Typical of the Chicago business writer's rather apathetic view of the Merc during the 1950s is the lead article in the business and finance pages of *The Chicago American* appearing on 28 October 1958. A profile of E.B. Harris and the Exchange, written by the financial editor no less, begins: "Bulky, extroverted Everette B. Harris, president of the Mercantile Stock Exchange, is geared to the future." Referring to the Merc as a "stock exchange" was hardly a slip of the pen, considering the fact that the writer spent a day roving the Exchange floor and observing the action in the trading pits of a Chicago institution that had been in existence for 40 years.

6. One study of Ira Glick dealt solely with professional traders and was based on a sampling of Chicago Mercantile Exchange members. The other, by William Blair Stewart, was concerned with amateur traders. Glick's, an unpublished Ph.D. dissertation written in 1957 for the Department of Sociology at the University of Chicago, was designed "to characterize some of the major occupational problems confronting futures traders and to depict the systems of social relations accompanying futures trading."

   Glick had determined three career patterns that he believed led to success. One pattern was defined by the scalper, described as young, relatively new in the business, flexible, aggressive, exhibitionistic, and always minimizing losses. The second type was the older, more mature trader, who was "very intelligent" and active in some phase of the egg business. The third type was similar to the second, but seldom appeared on the exchange floor, trading through floor brokers instead. Another conclusion drawn by Glick: chartists were a minority and "are not held in high regard by the majority of the professionals."

7. The Merc had an increasing share of the nation's futures business and an impressive growth trend. From 1 January to 30 September 1953, some 190,721 contracts traded, compared with 155,038 in 1952; 158,049 in 1951; 118,219 in 1950; 96,455 in 1949, and 99,441 in 1948.

Chapter 10

1. Crilly was a popular broker at the time. "He was a two-fisted drinker," recalled Bill Katz, "everybody loved him." A week after Crilly's death, E. B. Harris wrote the following poem, which he later gave to Crilly's widow:

   A Broker's Heart

   > A broker's heart just fell apart,
   > For I was there and I saw it;
   > At the call of the bell, he raced and fell,
   > And in line of duty his hour hit.

There are those who feel and with some appeal,
That a life like his was wasted,
But to him and more it was vital and real,
In devotion to duty death hasted.

In a game rough and grim but meant for him,
He played to the end to die brave,
He died as he lived in the pit—on the rim,
And he took no excuse to his grave.

Until the end everyone was his friend,
And that's rare in our kind of gang,
Fight with a grin was his line to the end,
And together his praises was sang.

So it seemed the least to call the Priest,
And his last real wish was heeded,
But at Easter's end for this kind of man,
I'm sure it was not really needed.

Harris wasn't the only Merc official inspired by the muses. In 1987, for instance, Leo Melamed wrote *The Tenth Planet*, a science fiction novel about an advanced alien civilization that discovers a space probe from earth.

2. Released 29 May 1956, the report entitled *Legal Obstacles to Operation of Future Markets* was highly favorable to futures trading.

3. In 1893, a bill that would have put an end to all futures trading in the United States was nearly passed by the 52nd Congress. The following year, a similar bill did indeed pass the House of Representatives, but barely failed in the Senate. During the next 64 years, no government attacks to do away with futures trading came as close as that of the 53rd Congress.

4. The Futures Trading Act of 1921 was passed to regulate futures trading in grains, but was declared unconstitutional by the U.S. Supreme Court in an opinion written by Chief Justice Taft. The decision, noted Stanford University economist Holbrook Working, might have been different if the Act had relied on the commerce clause of the Constitution instead of the congressional taxing power. The very next year, Congress reenacted essentially the same legislation under the Grain Futures Act, asserting that "such fluctuations in prices are an obstruction to and a burden upon interstate commerce."

The Grain Futures Act was subsequently amended through the Exchange Act of 1936, which created the Commodity Exchange Authority and its control over a number of major commodities. The CEA's regulatory list expanded with the growth in volume of a particular commodity.

5. By comparison—and typical of the historic trading pattern in onions—was the activity in the 1955 crop for November delivery. The contract opened on 2 December 1954 at $1.58 for a 50-pound bag. The price touched a high of $2.35, a low of $1.57, and closed out on the last day of trading in

November at $1.90, a profitable price considering that yellow globe onions were grown and marketed at a total cost of less than one dollar per bag.

Chapter 11

1. In October 1973, irked at a subpoena Cox issued demanding President Nixon to turn over tape recordings of White House conversations, Nixon ordered Richardson to fire Cox in what became known as the Saturday Night Massacre.

Chapter 12

1. Ironically, after analyzing nearly 20 years of onion marketing patterns and prices, the U.S. Department of Agriculture in 1973 issued a post mortem showing futures trading did not alter supply and demand. Proponents of the 1958 trading ban claimed that the onion trading was disruptive to marketing patterns—the same argument used in the fall of 1972 against potato futures.
   The Potato Bill, however, was defeated on the House floor after a hard-fought battle. The USDA's report on futures trading was made with two supply and demand models—for the periods from 1946 to 1947 and from 1958 to 1959, when trading was legal, and from 1959 to 1960 and 1969 to 1970, after it was banned. Instead of finding that onion futures adversely influenced marketing and prices, the USDA study reported that researchers found growers influenced by past prices in determining their onion plantings, while current prices simply reflected current production levels. Large drops resulted in low farm prices, which in turn caused growers to reduce plantings the following year, according to the USDA. Therefore the cycle continued; reduced production yielded strong prices, eliciting acreage increases.
2. In New York state, with a somewhat larger number of traders than Chicago, the aggregate open contracts were smaller, with total long positions of 727 carlots and short positions of 306 carlots. The greater part of the Chicago short positions was classified as hedging—1,300 carlots—and these accounted for two-thirds of the total short hedging contracts in the market.
3. It was short-lived lead because the very next month the Board of Trade regained its momentum in terms of the number of contracts traded, and it has never since lost it. By the late 1970s, however, the CME was ahead of the CBOT in the dollar value of contracts traded. It was difficult to capitalize on this fact from a public relations standpoint because the historical benchmark has always been contract volume.
4. Bialystok is the home of the popular Bialy, a cross between an English muffin and a bagel.
5. As a youngster, Melamed began performing at an early age on radio soap operas whenever a male child was needed to speak in Yiddish. He also

gave Yiddish poetry readings at special occasions and holidays. When the Yiddish Theatre was formed by the late Dina Halperin, wife of Chicago Lyric Opera publicist Danny Newman, Melamed began his Yiddish acting career, which lasted until his mid-thirties.

6. The board of governors at that time, in addition to Sieger and Coleman, included Robert Ascher, Frank Sherman, Milton Rich, Hyman Henner, John V. McCarthy, Glenn Andersen, Harry Fortes, William Rankin, and Nathan Wertheimer, who would be elected chairman in 1966.

Chapter 13

1. The Morgan Guaranty Trust Company's index of basic commodity prices had moved from 158.2 in January 1961 to 161.5 by the end of the year.

Chapter 14

1. Employing a "Texas hedge" for other feeder steers on his farm, Colonel Lacy figured that hedging his cattle had resulted in a saving of 0.0436 cents per pound for some 1,200 cattle.

2. Tracking the first five months of trading in live cattle futures on the CME, University of California economist G. Alvin Carpenter had concluded it was "very difficult to sort out the specific influence of the futures market on fat cattle prices" from all the other influences that went into the complex problem of cattle pricing. Sufficient data wasn't available at that point to draw many valid conclusions.

Chapter 15

1. The "vegetable oil bath " to which Ellmore Patterson referred had Wall Street quaking in 1963 over a $150 million salad oil swindle masterminded by a former butcher named Anthony (Tino) De Angelis. His highly lever-aged machinations forced bankruptcy of Allied Crude Vegetable Oil Refin-ing Corp., then the nation's largest supplier of edible oils for export. The collapse started a financial avalanche that led to the failure of 20 banks and commodities and securities firms. Eventually creditors were to learn that much of the edible oil purportedly stored in Allied's tanks never existed. The De Angelis scam came on the heels of a plummeting stock market in May 1962, followed by the Billie Sol Estes scandal that involved the sale of $24 million in mortgages on nonexistent fertilizer tanks to various financial companies. The swindle by this Texas operator eventually became an embarrassment to Lyndon Johnson.

2. Frustrated by the dollar's uncertainty, Charles DeGaulle mounted an assault on the dollar in 1968 by refusing to accept anything but gold in payment of French debts.

3. Agricultural economist Don Paarling, former special assistant to President Eisenhower, views the use of food and diplomacy with mixed results. For instance, food aid was successfully used by the Nixon Administration in 1974 to promote Arab-Israeli military disengagement in the Middle East.
4. The survey was conducted on a personal basis by Beveridge executives Sue Kroening in New York and Ronald Frost in Chicago. At times more than one person was interviewed from a wirehouse. The firms that participated in the survey were Bache & Co., Inc.; Francis I. DuPont & Co.; A. G. Edwards & Sons, Inc.; Goodbody & Co.; Harris Upham & Co.; Hayden, Stone, Incorporated; H. Hentz & Co., E.F. Hutton & Co., Inc.; Merrill Lynch, Pierce, Fenner & Smith, Inc.; Paine, Webber, Jackson & Curtis Co.; Reynolds & Co.; Shearson Hammill & Co., Inc.; Thomson & Co., Inc.; and Dean Witter & Co., Inc.
5. The new measures required 125 personal signatures of bona fide members to stay Board legislation and to cause a referendum. That meant on a vote, 250 members had to cast ballots with at least 126 in favor of the proposal in order for it to carry. Special forms had actually been prepared and available to the members for such petitions.
6. The expanded number of committees—comprising 125 members, or one-fourth of the CME membership—at the time included Approved Warehouse, Arbitration, Beef, Business Conduct, Butter, Clearing House, Egg, Finance, Floor Facilities, Floor Practices, Frozen Egg, Live Hog, Membership, New Commodities, Pork Products, and Poultry Products.

Chapter 17

1. Prior to 1966, other women held memberships but did not trade on the floor; the early female members included Grace E. Hyslop, Charlotte H. Foley, Lois Berger Knight, Nancy Anne McCarthy, and Laura L. Mullen.
2. In his memo, Friedman presented the following six-measure strategy:

Shortly after the inauguration of a new President in January, preferably on the second or third Friday evening or Saturday thereafter (after the financial markets are closed but in time for the announcement to be absorbed over the weekend), he should proclaim the following measures:

1. All restrictions on foreign investment by U.S. corporations are abolished effective immediately and the bureaucratic apparatus for administering them will be dismantled as rapidly as possible.
2. Similarly, all restrictions on foreign lending by U.S. commercial banks are ended, effective immediately.
3. Congress is being asked to repeal the interest-equalization tax.
4. All other restrictions on payments and trade imposed on balance of payments grounds will be removed as quickly as possible.
5. The U.S. will engage in no further gold transactions. For the time being it will keep its gold stock constant, neither buying nor selling gold either

    from or to central banks of other countries or in the private market. (This is already almost the *de facto* situation since the establishment of the two-tier gold system last February, so this point merely makes the policy explicit and open.)

6. The U.S. will engage in no exchange transactions in order to affect the rate of exchange between the U.S. dollar and other currencies—neither to peg the rates of exchange at fixed levels nor to manipulate them.

    The only exchange transactions engaged in by official U.S. agencies will be to acquire the foreign exchange necessary for foreign governmental expenditures or to dispose of foreign exchange acquired in the course of foreign governmental activity. (This point will require an exemption by I.M.F. from present obligations. However, it is an exemption that has been granted to other countries and that can hardly be refused to the U.S.)

3. In 1969, on the drawing board were plans for formation of a Pacific Coast Commodity Exchange, which was to open in 1971 trading coconut oil as its first contract. Eventually, additional contracts would be traded in commodities such as California wines, raisins, tomato paste, cattle, and some exotics like cultured pearls, tuna, crabmeat, and such Pacific currencies as Japanese, Taiwanese, Filipino, and Australian.

Chapter 19

1. In 1970, the CME's New Commoditities Committee considered 39 various items for futures contracts, of which six where either traded or authorized for trading. (See chapter notes for list.)
2. This volume was not intended as a trading guide. Rather, it was a compilation of three different seminars featuring some of the nation's leading agricultural and futures trading authorities, tracing the CME's development of the first futures contract traded successfully in a live commodity. The book, released near the date (1964) of the sixth anniversary issue of the opening of live cattle futures, sold for a modest price of $7.50. By 1970, cattle contracts traded exceeded one million, second only in volume to pork bellies.
3. In 1911 American mathematician and economist Irving Fisher proved that doubling a nation's money supply would double prices. He believed economic booms and busts were caused either by too much or too little money. His use of statistics, mathematics, and economics started a new approach to economics known as "Econometrics." In the 1950s Milton Friedman substantiated Fisher's theories. Friedman concluded that changes in the amount of money are a major influence on our economy's direction and the pace of production, employment, and spending. Friedman's views, known as "Monetarism," have vastly influenced how we think about money, and the way the Federal Reserve controls our money.

4. During the 90-day freeze, it was a violation for a participant in the market to make or accept delivery of actual pork bellies, hams, or lumber (on a futures contract) at a price higher than the highest price at which substantial quantities were sold in the cash market in the 30-day period prior to 14 August 1971. The August 1971 pork belly contract, the November 1971 skinned ham contract, and September and November 1971 lumber contracts continued to liquidate in an orderly fashion.
5. From April 1970 to the end of 1973, a total of 48,709 contracts were traded on the International Commercial Exchange. Trading in these instruments ceased because of a lack of liquidity.
6. Counselor Lee Freeman, Sr. advised Melamed that it would not be legally necessary to obtain approval from the government in order to list currency futures contracts. Nevertheless, Melamed felt that key government officials should be appraised of the Merc's new venture.

Chapter 20

1. Between 1970 and 1972 the Merc's New Commodities Committee considered the following as possibilities for future contracts: ADRs, (American depository receipts, which are negotiable on securities held in custody overseas. They are traded in place of the foreign securities), agricultural credit, canned hams, carcass beef, coal, coconut oil, construction materials, corn oil, cranberries, crude oil, cucumbers, dehydrated alfalfa, diesel fuel, dried milk, Eurobonds and stocks, fish meal, freight rates, frozen spare ribs, frozen strawberries, gold, grapes, honey, insurance, Kraft liner boards, lard, mushrooms, olive oil, paper pulp, peanut oil, pepper, pork loins, rice, safflower oil, Scotch whiskey, sheep, stock indices, tin plate, tomato juice, tomato paste, wine.

Chapter 21

1. Financial diplomacy touched the International Monetary Market from the start. The French franc was not listed as an IMM currency until an International Monetary Fund representative from France showed up on the Merc floor, requesting that the franc be listed; and it was. Similarly, to avoid hurting the monetary pride of its U.S. neighbors, a polite suggestion by the State Department noted what an insult it would be not to list the Mexican peso in view of the fact the Canadian dollar was listed. Again, the IMM obliged.
2. At the tenth anniversary of the IMM, Milton Friedman asked Melamed whether he ever realized how big the IMM would be. Melamed then showed Friedman the 1972 and 1973 IMM annual reports, which stated that "if we succeed with currencies, the sky's the limit."

Chapter 22

1. In the sixteenth century, Queen Elizabeth's Master of the Mint, Thomas Gresham, observed that when gold and silver circulate as money, the cheaper metal eventually becomes the dominant medium of exchange, while the more expensive metal was hoarded, sold abroad, or melted down. The principle that cheap money drives expensive money out of circulation came to be known as "Gresham's Law."

Chapter 23

1. Among other congressional visitors during the fall of 1973 were Representatives Robert D. Price of Texas, Steven D. Symms of Idaho, and W.R. Poage of Texas, chairman of the House Agriculture Committee.
2. The display of gold bullion was put together by Mocatta Metals Corp., Johnson Matthey & Co., Ltd., and the First National Bank of Chicago. Also participating in the ceremonies were Eliot Janeway, syndicated columnist; Leo Melamed, IMM chairman; E.B. Harris, IMM president; and John T. Geldermann, CME chairman.
3. Four times—in 1975, 1978, 1984, and 1986—the Chicago Board of Trade surrendered to market forces that blew away its mortgage-backed contract. During the late 1970s the CBOT's contract was active until interest rates rose and bankers created innovative mortgages. Because the mortgages failed to track the new mortgage securities, the Ginnie Mae's hedging value suffered. The lack of and effective hedging vehicle in 1986 contributed to losses of some $300 million n conventional mortgage-backed instruments on Wall Street. Mortgage-backed securities again took it on the chin in 1987 when Merrill Lynch liquidated its bloated inventory of principal-only mortgage-backed securities at a $270 million loss. On 16 June 1989 the CBOT tried a fifth time to support a new GNMA mortgage-backed contract with hopes of overcoming the stigma of past failures.

   As the Merc pursued the medium-range product, Sandor the CBOT's chief economist, was pushing his exchange toward the long-range instruments with a 30-year Treasury bond contract. Long-term bond futures became the most actively traded futures contract in the world and remain so, making it one of the most successful contracts on any exchange anywhere. It was the Treasury bond that helped the CBOT maintain its momentum through periods of trading drought in its agriculture products. A decade later Sandor, who claimed to have coined the phrase "Ginnie Mae," told a reporter, "The biggest kick for me was watching an industry develop . . . 80 percent of the volume is driven by something that I had a hand in."

Chapter 24

1. The group was headed by Doc Crawford, an Iowa dentist who had turned speculator. The options to buy or sell were called "privileges" and were bought at the close of one day and expired the next morning. A privilege cost roughly one-quarter cent per bushel for 5,000 bushels and was widely used by commercial interests for overnight protection rather than the most costly futures contract.
2. In 1973 the largest of the option dealers, Goldstein Samuelson Inc. of Beverly Hills, was charged with fraud by the SEC. The company's founder was convicted and sent to prison. A year later, some dozen houses were either in receivership or closed down by various regulatory agencies.
3. The Merc's first agricultural option traded in the live cattle contract on 30 October 1984. Its next agricultural option would be offered in the live hog contract on 1 February 1985, followed by options in pork bellies on 3 October 1986 and feeder cattle on 9 January 1987. Options on the lumber contract began trading on 29 May 1987.

Chapter 25

1. The average American ate an estimated 272 eggs in 1990, off two from 1976. All of the decline was in shell eggs, since the use of processed eggs rose from 33 in 1976 to about 37 in 1977. At the Merc the record for shell eggs was set in 1970, when 678,801 contracts were traded. Turnovers dipped for a couple of years before hitting 619,567 in 1973, declining steadily after that. The 130,042 contracts traded in 1977 came to the lowest volume since 29,275 contracts traded in 1967. The downtrend continued throughout the decade of the 1970s and into the 1980s, when a cholesterol-conscious medical profession dampened the public's appetite for eggs.
2. Besides Melamed, the others whom Wilmouth calls the National Futures Association's "founding fathers" include Warren Lebeck, former CBOT president; Les Rosenthal, former CBOT chairmen; John Conheeney, vice-president at Merrill Lynch; David Johnson; George Lamborn; and Howard Stotler.
3. The NFA's budget is based on an assessment fee on every futures transaction of 20 cents a round turn by anyone who uses the market that isn't a member of an exchange.

Chapter 26

1. Art prices of the 1980s reflected the wider economy and meaning of liquidity. In 1987 Van Gogh's *Irises* sold for $53.9 million. In 1987 Picasso's

self-portrait, *Yo Picasso,* sold for $47.85 million, and in 1989 his *Au Lapin Agile* fetched $40.7 million.

2. The Winnipeg Exchange was trading gold futures before they became legally permissible in the United States.

3. A settlement bank is a bank that processes the cash flows relating to margins. The Merc has arrangements with four such Chicago banks: Continental Illinois National Bank and Trust Company, The First National Bank of Chicago, The Harris Trust and Savings Bank, the Northern Trust Company and Chemical Bank of New York.

Chapter 27

1. At the time, the Chicago Board of Trade was embroiled in a court fight with Dow Jones over rights to trade an index futures contract on the Dow Jones industrial average, the venerable average of 30 blue-chip New York Stock Exchange issues. The struggle put the CBOT on the sidelines of the booming index markets that would dominate futures trading in the 1980s.

   Eventually, the Supreme Court ruled that the Dow Jones industrial average was private domain. The CBOT was then forced to list the American Stock Exchange's Major Market Index (MMI), which was designed to closely correlate the Dow Jones index. In fact, 17 stocks out of the 20 that comprise the MMI index are in the DJIA.

2. The sale brought in 1,287 new memberships. From October 1982 through January 1983, the public purchased 125 seats at $60,000 each. From February 1982 through March 1982, seats purchased by existing members totaled 1,039 at $30,000 each. Another 123 AMM (Associate Mercantile Market) members converted to IOM memberships.

   Between 1981 and 1985 the Exchange instituted the Membership Rights Program (MRP). Under this program, each CME, IMM, and AMM membership was issued a quarter of a membership in each respective division. Four quarters were accumulated and converted to equal a full membership in each division. In 1985, all conversions were completed resulting in the following increase in membership: 125 additional CME memberships, 162 additional IMM memberships, and 150 AMM quarters were converted to the IOM division.

   The results of the various sales and MRP conversion increased overall membership in the Exchange from 500 members in 1929 to 2,724 members in 1989. (Today the CME division has 625 members; the IMM, 812; and the IOM, 1,287.)

3. In March 1988 Rick Kilcollin, executive vice-president and chief economist at the Chicago Mercantile Exchange, put the number of contracts that were actually delivered at 0.5 percent of the CME's volume.

4. Initially, the Kansas City Board of Trade applied to the CFTC for a deliverable value line stock index futures contract. After the CME received approval from the CFTC for cash settlement on the Eurodollar contract, it immediately applied for cash settlement for the S&P futures contract. This submission was followed by the KCBT. The New York Futures Exchange also applied for cash settlement. The CFTC approved the KCBT first, then the NYFE and CME.

5. Following are the monthly volume figures for 1982, starting with opening day on 21 April 1982: April, 27,544; May, 123,097; June, 261,282; July, 236,825; August, 373,646; September, 408,085; October, 490,697; November, 515,625; December, 498,731. The months of April, May, June, August, September, October, and November were record months. When the Merc traded 7,878,247 in 1977, it set an all-time exchange record that year. Six years later, in 1982, the volume had quadrupled to 33,574,286 contracts.

6. The S&P-based futures contract would be valued at 500 times the index. In other words, one contract would be $48,935 if the S&P index were at 97.87. The daily price limit would be 3 points for the contract, reflecting a change of 1 point in the S&P index. Based upon analysis at the time, from 1961 to 1978, 99 percent of the daily changes would have fallen within that three-point contract limit, a key point in attracting hedgers, or those seeking price protection.

7. After just 11 weeks of trading volume, the CBOE 100 topped 1 million contracts. The Merc's S&P 500 index reached 1 million contracts in 17 weeks, and the New York Futures Exchange's NYSE index hit the million mark in 36 weeks.

   "Indeed the CBOE has virtually demolished the other index options market as far as volume is concerned," Johnson said in July 1983, about a year after the CFTC reauthorization bill—which included the Johnson-Shad Accord—was approved by Congress. During the reauthorization process, Johnson testified 32 times. On some days he made three appearances before the Senate subcommittee, which showed skepticism over options. In the end, however, the CFTC made a comeback—and so did options.

8. The Merc proposed such a contract to the CFTC in 1985. The contract, dubbed "SPOC" was designed to be an indicator of actual price movements in the over-the-counter stocks. Because it consisted of 250 OTC stocks, the index avoided focusing only on the largest OTC stocks the way narrower indexes did. The index was price weighted, and prices were based on the average of bids and offers of the component stocks. These two factors, it was believed, made the index more responsive to market volatility than capitalization-weighted indexes or those based on either the last sale or current bid. Because SPOC was comparable in size to the S&P 500 fu-

tures contract, it was hoped that there would be spreading between the two instruments, which would enhance the liquidity of both markets.

9. In May 1982 Louis Rukeyser appeared in several promotional tapes that the Merc used to help promote S&P futures contracts. In 1983, his *Wall Street Week* television show was taped from the trading floor of the Merc. The show, reported *The Wall Street Journal,* "prompted some grousing" at the Chicago Board of Trade, which in the fall of 1982 had negotiated to have Rukeyser's show broadcast from its trading floor.

Chapter 28

1. The Chicago Board of Trade, according to *The Wall Street Journal,* had earlier gone 16 years without introducing any new trading product. Its gold futures contract, started in 1975, flopped initially because of its odd-sized lots. But in 1977 it started trading in a Treasury bond futures contract that today is one of the most actively traded contracts in the world.

2. Between 1980 and 1985, CME volume increased by 154 percent—more than one and one-half times the industry growth rate in 1984. In 1984 the Merc boasted a record 68 days with more than 200,000 contracts traded. The standard was replaced in 1985 with nine 300,000 contract days. The S&P 500 futures—trading more than 15 million contracts in 1985—continued to be the industry's second most actively traded contract, with Eurodollars in fourth place on nearly 9 million contracts. And with nearly 6.5 million contracts traded, Deutsche mark futures was leading currency contract of any futures or options exchange.

3. In his essay, Melamed referred to Senator Bill Bradley (D-NJ) and Congressman Jack Kemp (R-NY). Though each approached the issue from a different philosophic viewpoint, both believed that the high dollar value was evidence of a failure of flexible exchange rates, and they called for a new international Bretton Woods—type conference in order to reestablish rigidity in foreign exchange.

4. Gordon McClendon was the first African American board member, elected by the membership to the Chicago Mercantile Exchange in 1989.

5. The ten currencies in the ECU are the West German mark, French franc, British pound, Italian lira, Dutch guilder, Belgian franc, Danish krone, Greek drachma, Irish punt, and Luxembourgian franc. In the cash market in January 1986, an ECU had a value of about 87 cents. ECU futures allow the user to fix the ECU rate of exchange for some forthcoming ECU transactions and was a particularly attractive surrogate for transactions in European currencies, where liquidity in forward markets was problem.

6. The world's first futures exchange was organized in Japan when shoguns were still calling the shots and the military class was deeply in debt to the merchants. The economic conditions—resulting in passage of petty eco-

nomic laws—led to a mingling of the classes and the establishment in Osaka of the Dojima Rice Exchange in 1730. Rice is no longer traded on any of Japan's 16 futures exchanges because it is government controlled. Despite the head start and the fact that the Tokyo Stock Exchange is the world's second-largest share market, Japan's commodity exchanges remained underdeveloped, but not undernourished. On the wave of volatile financial markets during the 1980s, the Nomura Research Institute pointed out that Japan's financial community saw futures and options as "indispensable." Today, control of Japan's commodity exchanges is divided among three ministries: the Ministry of Finance, the Ministry of Agriculture, Forestry, and Fisheries, and the Ministry of International Trade and Industry.

7. Sandner became the third CME chairman in the Exchange's history to return to the chairmanship. The first was William Katz who was chairman in 1959 and again from 1961 to 1963. Melamed, who had served as CME chairman from 1969 to 1971 and again from 1975 to 1977 was the second. John T. Geldermann who served from 1974 to 1975 and again in 1989 and 1990, became the fourth.

8. A CBOT-sponsored study by University of Chicago professors indicated that the one-minute rule would add as much as $10 to the price of each trade because the markets would become less efficient and less liquid, since traders would be occupied recording the timing of their trades. The CFTC staff had found no proof to back up such claims.

9. First, the margin requirements and historical volatility of positions carried by a firm were computed. Then the higher of the two amounts would be a base from which to deduct credits for excess margin and omnibus accounts. The result would be a risk-based capital requirement that would be compared to the CFTC's current capital requirement. The higher of the two amounts became a firm's actual capital requirement. While the CFTC believed that capital be based on the risk associated with the positions carried by a firm, its original proposal had not measured that risk consistently.

10. The others included options on the Deutsche mark, British pound, and Swiss franc. The Merc's first options contract ever tied to an interest-rate futures were options on Eurodollar futures, which began trading 14 months earlier. During Senate subcommittee hearings in mid-March 1986, Sandner had emphasized the need to broaden the options pilot program to the agriculture products as well in order to help farm financing pegged to a new farm bill.

11. An IOM seat allowed its holder to trade in S&P 500 futures, S&P 100 futures, random-length lumber futures and S&P 250 futures, and in options on the S&P 500, British pound, Swiss franc, Eurodollar, Japanese yen, Treasury bill, live cattle, and live hog futures.

12. In March 1986 during the Futures Industry Association's annual meeting in Boca Raton, Florida, a cooperative program between the Merc and the

Board of Trade Clearing Corporation (BOTCC) was announced by Brodsky and BOTCC president Roger Rutz. The joint venture—aimed at reducing costly overlap—involved five areas: pass-through T-bills to satisfy clearing members' daily margin requirements; pay/collect data to enhance financial surveillance; trade data entry and transmission between the two clearinghouses over dedicated communications lines; shared New York office facilities to lower operating costs; and standardized formats for data input and output to enable crosstraining of personnel and to reduce costs.

13. In Hokkien-dialect Chinese "ang moh quee" literally means "red–skinned devil," in reference to what happens to caucasian flesh in the hot equatorial sun.

14. A special EFP committee headed by Rick Kilcollin reported to the Merc's strategic planning committee on 13 August 1986 that EFP transactions had increased from just 3,000 in 1981 to 600,000 in 1985 with at least that many in the first eight months of 1986.

Chapter 29

1. During a ten-day swing through the Far East from 25 August to 4 September 1986 Melamed and Sandner were the Merc's roving Pacific Rim agents. As guests of the *SIMEX* on 3 September, they participated in the opening day ceremony of trading in the Nikkei 225, which was made possible under a sublicensing agreement with the CME. On 27 August the two met with officials of the Nihon Keizai Shimbun, Incorporated (NKS) in Tokyo, which managed and calculated the Nikkei stock average, the best-known index of the Japanese stock market. The Merc had an exclusive agreement with NKS for North American and Asian (except Japanese) rights to utilize the Nikkei 225 and the Nikkei 500 stock averages for trading in futures. The previous day (26 August) the Merc filed an application with the CFTC for approval to trade the Nikkei 225 futures contract in Chicago as part of the mutual offset system trading link with *SIMEX*.

2. The Strategic Planning Committee was headed by Melamed: its members were among the Merc's best and brightest, and it was like a free-form think tank that pondered all sorts of interesting ventures. For instance, in August 1986 the committee considered the creation of a nonspecialist Chicago-based securities exchange. Besides the Merc, the Chicago Board of Trade, the Chicago Board Options Exchange, and the Pacific Stock Exchange (the Midwest Stock Exchange showed no interest) had agreed to explore the concept with Larry Blum, a CBOE veteran.

Blum had retained the law firm of Schiff, Hardin, & Waite to explore the legality of the concept with SEC, along with commissioning a feasability study by Dwight Koop. Eventually, said Bill Brodsky, who was coordinator of the project, the development of 24-hour trading took precedence over such projects.

3. The previous single-day record fluctuation in the S&P contract exceeded 12 points on 11 September 1986, when the Dow Jones industrial average fell 86 points.

Chapter 30

1. Under debate was a thicket of probes that dealt with market infrastructure, financial systems, and the measurement as well as the consequences of volatility. Among the thorniest of questions were those concerning margins. Critics argued that lower futures margins (10 percent) compared with stock margins (50 percent) had increased volatility. "It took six months to convince neutral observers that there was in fact no disparity between stock and futures margin levels if one considered that futures margin levels are collected prior to trading and losses are marked to market daily," Sandner countered before congressional hearings in carrying forth the Merc's defense in the aftermath of the crash. It would be the first time Merc officials appeared before the Senate Banking Committee, whose chairman, Wisconsin Senator William Proxmire, was a tough critic of the futures exchanges. Sandner's presentation on margins was a turning point in the Banking Committee's understanding of how margins worked. "Jack led them through a dollars and cents explanation and now they understand how the markets work in the real world," recalled Brodsky, who appeared at the hearing with Melamed and Sandner.

2. On 18 October, 1990 Ronald Li was convicted—and sentenced to two consecutive two-year prison terms—for accepting, in 1986 and 1987, preferential offerings of shares in Cathay Pacific Airways Ltd. and Novel Enterprises Ltd. in exchange for approving or facilitating the listings of these companies on the Hong Kong Stock Exchange. This case, however, had nothing to do with the problems of the Hong Kong Futures Exchange following the crash, according to Robert B. Gillmore, executive director of Hong Kong's Security & Futures Commission. "Many mistakenly link the two events because Mr. Li was arrested in January 1988," Gilmore said. "It is my understanding that the investigation which led to his arrest and conviction started long before October 1987."

Chapter 33

1. The board of governors approved establishment of the Governance Committee on 24 August 1991. Others on the committee included Robert J. Birnbaum, Robert Hammer, Merton H. Miller, Norma L. Newberger, John D. Newhouse, James E. Oliff, Robert J. Prosi, and Louis G. Schwartz. The committee's basic goals were (1) to create a governance structure to insure a continuity of leadership and (2) to develop a timely decision-making process. In connection with those goals, the Governance Committee had strongly supported the general recommendations of the so-called Com-

mittee to Review Committee Structure (chaired by Lawrence Rosenberg), which had identified seven problems: (1) board members were unable to devote sufficient time to policy making; (2) their time commitments were overtaxed; (3) the number of committees, especially *ad hoc* committees, and committee positions had increased tremendously; (4) most committees were too large and needed to be limited in size by board action; (5) advisory committees were not properly utilized; (6) subcommittees tended to be duplicative and to exist after their purpose had been fulfilled; and (7) committees could benefit from the appointment of nonmember clearing firm personnel with particular expertise.

2. In its examination of the practices of other exchanges, the Governance Committee observed that no other exchange imposed limits on length of term in order to take advantage of a chairman's experience and contacts. However, the committee concluded, a chairman serving for an indefinite period could thwart development of leadership skills in other board members. The committee also upheld the practice of allowing the Board to elect the chairman from among its elected members, a policy consistent with that of all major U.S. corporations and professional associations. Other recommendations by the Governance Committee—also approved by the Board—included (1) retention for unlimited one-year terms of the vice chairman (the name was changed from "first vice chairman" to simply "vice chairman"), second vice chairman, secretary, and treasurer (a proposal to combine the latter two positions as "secretary/treasurer" was rejected); (2) retention of the two-year term for Board members as well as an unlimited number of consecutive terms; and (3) elimination of the positions of senior policy advisor and legislative liaison ("positions," the committee stated, "created to ensure continuity of leadership through some very turbulent times for the CME as an institution and for the futures industry as a whole").

The Board increased the compensation of the chairman from $200,000 a year to $250,000, defining some of the chairman's major roles as "chief policy maker" and "articulator" of the Board's position; "chief spokesperson" for the Merc and the U.S. futures industry; chairman of the Executive Committee; chief legislative liaison; and "ex officio" chairman of all Exchange committees. Annual compensation for board members was set at $20,000 and for public and industry governors, $20,000 plus $1,000 for each board meeting attended. At the time, the Governance Committee believed that no distinction in compensation should be made between those members who served only on the Board and those who also served on the Executive Committee. Moreover, the consensus among members of the Governance Committee was that the size of the 32-person Board—27 nonpublic members and 5 public and industry members—was too large, causing meetings to be run more formally and less efficiently. Maintaining a board of that size, the Committee noted, was also an expensive proposition. Thus the Committee believed that reducing the board size was necessary, but no steps were taken to do so in 1992.

Selected Bibliography

Adams, Henry. *The Education of Henry Adams*. Boston: Houghton Mifflin, 1930.

After the Crash. Washington, D.C.: American Enterprise Institute for Public Policy Research, 1988.

Allen, Frederick Lewis. *Only Yesterday: An Informal History of the 1920's*. New York: Harper & Row, 1964.

————. *Since Yesterday*. New York: Harper & Row, 1972.

Andreas, Alfred T. *History of Chicago*, vol. 3, 1871–85. Chicago: 1886.

Baer, Julius B., and Woodruff, George P. *Commodity Exchanges*. New York: Harper & Brothers, 1929.

Baer, Julius B., and Saxon, Olin Glenn. *Commodity Exchanges and Futures Trading*. New York: Harper & Brothers, 1949.

Berkow, Ira. *Maxwell Street: Survival in a Bazaar*. New York: Doubleday & Company, 1977.

Blum, John M.; McFeely, William S.; Morgan, Edmund S.; Schlesinger, Arthur M., Jr.; Stampp, Kenneth M.; and Woodward, C. Vann. *The National Experience.*, Parts One & Two. San Diego: Harcourt Brace Jovanovich, 1985.

Burns, Joseph M. *A Treatise on Markets: Spot, Futures, and Options*. Washington, D.C.: American Enterprise Institute for Public Policy Research, 1979.

Cameron, James. *1914*. New York: Rinehart, 1959.

Chamberlin, Everett. *Chicago and its Suburbs*. Chicago: T.A. Hungerford, 1874.

Chia, Robert K. G., and Soh, Doreen. *Simex and the Globalization of Financial Futures*. Singapore: Time Books International, 1953.

Cochran, Thomas C., and Miller, William. *The Age of Enterprise: A Social History of Industrial America*. New York: Harper & Brothers, 1961.

Cowen, Tyler. *Program Trading: A Look Behind the Headlines*. Irvine, Calif.: Citizens for a Sound Economy Foundation, 1988.

Cowing, Cedric B. *Populists, Plungers, and Progressives: A Social History of Stock and Commodity Speculation, 1890-1936*. Princeton: Princeton University Press, 1965.

Das, Satyajit. *Swap Financing*. London: IFR Publishing, 1989.

Dedmon, Emmett. *Fabulous Chicago*. New York: Random House, 1953.

Demaris, Ovid. *Captive City*. New York: Lyle Stuart, 1969.

Diamond, Barbara B., and Kollar, Mark P. *24-Hour Trading: The Global Network of Futures and Options Markets*. New York: John Wiley & Sons, 1989.

Dooley, Martin. *Mr. Dooley in Peace and War*. Boston: Small, Maynard, 1898.

Figlewski, Stephen. "Topics in Stock Index Futures and Options: Insuring Portfolio Insurance." First Boston, November 18, 1987.

Financial Futures and Options—Recent Developments. London: IFR Publishing, 1989.

Friedman, Milton, and Schwartz, Anna Jacobson. *A Monetary History of the United States, 1876-1960*. Princeton: Princeton University Press, 1963.

The Functions of the Legitimate Exchanges. Chicago: Hartzell-Lord, 1910.

Galbraith, John Kenneth. *The Great Crash: 1929*. Boston: Houghton Mifflin, 1961.

Gastineau, Gary L. *The Options Manual*. New York: McGraw-Hill, 1988.

Goldman, Eric F. *Rendezvous with Destiny: A History of Modern American Reform*. New York: Random House, 1956.

Goulden, Joseph C. *The Best Years: 1945–1950*. New York: Atheneum, 1976.

Grossman, Sanford J. "An Analysis of the Implications for Stock and Futures Price Volatility of Program Trading and Dynamic Hedging Strategies." *Working Paper Series*, no. 2357. Cambridge: National Bureau of Economic Research, August 1987.

Gunther, John. *Roosevelt in Retrospect: A Profile in History*. New York: Harper & Brothers, 1950.

Hale, David. "Is the Stock Market Crash of 1987 Comparable to 1929 or 1893 or Will There Be a New Jazz Age Before the Next Depression?" Institute for International Economics, November 1987 (unpublished).

————. "Is the U.S. Stock Market Overvalued or Should U.S. Shares Be Valued on the Basis of Japanese Interest Rates?" August 1987 (unpublished).

Heise, Kenan, and Edgerton, Michael. *Chicago: Center for Enterprise*. Vols 1 & 2. Woodland Hills: Windsor Publications, 1982.

Hicks, John R. *The Crisis in Keynesian Economics*. Oxford: Blackwell, 1974.

Hill, John, Jr. *Gold Bricks of Speculation*. Chicago: Lincoln Book Concern, 1904.

Hofstadter, Richard. *The Age of Reform: from Bryan to FDR*. New York: Knopf, 1955.

Holmes, Oliver Wendell, Jr. *The Common Law*. Boston: Houghton-Mifflin, 1881.

Howe, Irving, and Libo, Kenneth. *How We Lived: A Documentary History of Immigrant Jews in America, 1880–1930*. New York: Plume, 1979.

International Chamber of Commerce. *Obstacles to the Operation of Futures Markets: Report of the Commission on Primary Products and Raw Materials of the ICC*. Paris: The International Chamber of Commerce, July 1956.

Irwin, Harold S. *Evolution of Futures Trading*. Madison: Mimir Publishers, 1954.

Johnson, Gale, ed. *The Politics of Food*. Chicago: The Chicago Council on Foreign Relations, 1980.

Johnson, Philip McBride. *Commodities Regulation*. Vols. 1 & 2. Boston: Little, Brown, 1982.

Keynes, John Maynard. *The General Theory of Employment, Interest and Money*. New York: Harcourt Brace Jovanovich, 1936.

Lefevre, Edwin S. *Reminiscences of a Stock-Operator*. Garden City, N.Y.: Garden City Publishing, 1923.

Leuchtenburg, William E. *The Perils of Prosperity, 1914–32*. Chicago: University of Chicago Press, 1958.

Lowe, David. *The Great Chicago Fire*. New York: Dover, 1979.

Lurie, Jonathan. *The Chicago Board of Trade, 1859–1905: The Dynamics of Self-Regulation*. Urbana: University of Illinois Press, 1979.

Manchester, William. *The Glory and the Dream*, Vols. 1 & 2. Boston: Little, Brown, 1973, 1974.

Mathieson, Geo. S. *Wheat and the Futures Market: A Study of the Winnipeg Grain Exchange*. Winnipeg: Hignell Printing, 1942.

Mayer, Martin. *Markets*. New York: W.W. Norton, 1988.

————. *The Fate of the Dollar*. New York: Signet, 1981.

Melamed, Leo. *The Merits of Flexible Exchange Rates: An Anthology*. Fairfax, Va.: George Mason University Press, 1988.

Morgan, Dan. *Merchants of Grain*. New York: Viking Press, 1979.

Nomura Research Institute. *The World Economy and Financial Markets in 1995: Japan's Role and Challenges*. Kanagawa: Nomura Research Institute, 1986.

Paarlberg, Don. *Farm and Food Policy: Issues of the 1980's*. Lincoln: University of Nebraska Press, 1980.

Peters, Edgar. "Portfolio Insurance or Asset Allocation or Both?" The Boston Company, 1987.

————. "Portfolio Insurance and Asset Allocation Strategies." The Boston Company, 1987.

Petzel, Todd E. *Financial Futures and Options: A Guide to Markets, Applications and Strategies*. New York: Quorum Books, 1989.

Powers, Mark, and Vogel, David. *Inside the Financial and Futures Markets*. New York: John Wiley & Sons, 1984.

Powers, Mark J., ed. *The Journal of Futures Markets*. Vol. 1. New York: John Wiley & Sons, 1981.

Prestbo, John A. *The Dow Jones Commodities Handbook, 1977*. Princeton: Dow Jones Books, 1977.

Rogers, George B., and Voss, Leonard, A., eds. *Readings on Egg Pricing*. Columbia: University of Missouri, 1971.

Rolfe, Sidney E., with Robert G. Hawkins. *Gold and World Power*. New York: Harper & Row, 1966.

Rothbard, Murray N. *America's Great Depression*. Los Angeles: Nash Publishing, 1972.

Rothstein, Nancy H., ed., with Little, James M. *The Handbook of Financial Futures: A Guide for Investors and Professional Financial Managers*. New York: McGraw-Hill, 1984.

Samuelson, Paul A. *Economics: An Introductory Analysis*. New York: McGraw-Hill, 1961.

Schaaf, Barbara C. *Mr. Dooley's Chicago*. New York: Anchor Press/Doubleday, 1977.

Schertz, Lyle. *Another Revolution in U. S. Farming*. Washington, D.C.: US Dept. of Agriculture, 1979.

Schlesinger, Arthur M., Jr. *The Age of Roosevelt: Crisis of the Old Order*. Boston: 1957.

Schwanger, Jack D. *A Complete Guide to the Futures Market*. New York: John Wiley & Sons, 1984.

Shannon, David A., ed. *The Great Depression*. Englewood Cliffs, N.J.: Prentice-Hall, 1960.

Sinclair, Upton. *The Jungle*. New York: Signet Classics, 1964.

Smith, Clifford W., Jr.; Smithson, Charles W.; and Wilford, Sykes D. *Managing Financial Risk*. New York: Harper & Row, 1990.

Sobel, Robert. *Panic on Wall Street: A Classic History of America's Financial Disasters—with a New Exploration of the Crash of 1987*. New York: E. P. Dutton, 1988.

Steffens, Lincoln. *The Autobiography of Lincoln Steffens*. New York: Harcourt, Brace, 1931.

Strange, Susan. *Casino Capitalism*. Oxford: Basil Blackwell, 1986.

Tamarkin, Bob. *The New Gatsbys*. New York: William Morrow, 1985.

Taylor, Charles H. *History of the Board of Trade of the City of Chicago*. Vols. 1, 2, & 3. Chicago: Robert O. Law, Co., 1917.

Teweles, Richard J., and Jones, Frank J. *The Futures Game: Who Wins? Who Loses? Why?* New York: McGraw-Hill, 1987.

Time-Life Books. *This Fabulous Century*. Prelude: 1870–1900; Vol. 6: 1950–1960; Vol. 7: 1960–1970. New York: Time-Life Books, 1971.

Walmsley, Julian. *The New Financial Instruments: An Investor's Guide*. New York: John Wiley & Sons, 1988.

Weil, Gordon L., and Davidson, Ian. *The Gold War: The Story of the World's Monetary Crisis*. New York: Holt, Rinehart and Winston, 1970.

Exchange Publications

Butter and Egg Board. *Journals*. Chicago: 1895–1918.

Chicago Board Options Exchange. *Annual Report(s)*. Chicago: Chicago Board Options Exchange, 1987 and 1988.

————. *Fundamental Facts About the World's Largest Options Marketplace*. Chicago: Chicago Board Options Exchange, 1989.

————. *S&P 100 Index Options: The Index Edge*. Chicago: Chicago Board Options Exchange, 1987.

————. *Understanding Options*. Chicago: Chicago Board Options Exchange, 1987.

————. *Commodity Trading Manual*. Chicago: Board of Trade of the City of Chicago, 1976.

————. *Futures Trading Seminar: History and Development*. Madison: Mimir Publishers, 1960.

————. Futures Trading Seminar: *Environmental Factors*. Madison: Mimir Publishers, 1963.

————. *Futures Trading Seminar: A Commodity Marketing Forum for College Teachers of Economics*. Ed. Erwin A. Gaumnitz. Madison: Mimir Publishers, 1966.

————. *Selected Writings of Holbrook Working*, Compiled by Anne E. Peck. Chicago: Board of Trade of the City of Chicago, 1977.

Chicago Mercantile Exchange. *Annual Report* (5). Chicago: 1919–1991.

————. *Blueprint for the 1990's: The Role of the Exchange*. Chicago: Chicago Mercantile Exchange, 1990.

————. *Board Minutes*. Chicago: 1919–1992.

————. *The Chicago Mercantile Exchange's International Monetary Market: The First Decade, 1972–1982*. Chicago: Chicago Mercantile Exchange 1982.

————. *Constitution, By-Laws and Clearing House Rules*. Chicago: Chicago Mercantile Exchange, October 6, 1919.

————. *Events and Meetings on the Occasion Commemorating the Opening of the CME Tokyo Office*. Tokyo: Chicago Mercantile Exchange, April 22–24, 1987.

————. *Financial Safeguard System*. Chicago: Chicago Mercantile Exchange, 1989.

————. *Findings of the Committee of Inquiry: Examining the Events Surrounding October 19, 1987*. Chicago: Chicago Mercantile Exchange, Spring 1988.

————. *Futures Trading in Livestock: Origins and Concepts*. Madison: Mimir Publishers, 1970.

————. *How to Buy and Sell Butter and Eggs*. Chicago: Chicago Mercantile Exchange, 1929.

————. *Implementation: Brady Task Force Recommendations*. Chicago: Chicago Mercantile Exchange, September 1988.

————. *Information for Task Force on Market Mechanisms*. Chicago: Chicago Mercantile Exchange, 1987.

————. *The Melamed Era: A Legacy of Growth and Innovation*. Chicago: Chicago Mercantile Exchange, 1991.

————. *Membership List(s)*. Chicago: Chicago Mercantile Exchange, 1919–1992.

————. *Merchandising Butter & Eggs*. Chicago: Chicago Mercantile Exchange, 1923.

————. *The 1979 Chicago Mercantile Exchange Information Guide and Calendar*. Chicago: Chicago Mercantile Exchange, 1979.

————. *October 19, 1987: The Facts*. Chicago: Chicago Mercantile Exchange, November 1987.

————. *Program Trading: An On-the-Record Symposium*. Chicago: Chicago Mercantile Exchange, 1986.

————. *Studies on the Effect of Stock Index Futures and Options on Stock Market Volatility*. Chicago: Chicago Mercantile Exchange, 1988.

————. *Yearbook(s)*, 1919–1991. Chicago: Chicago Mercantile Exchange, Market News Department, 1969.

Commodity Futures Trading Commission. *Annual Report(s)*, 1975–1991. Washington, D.C.: Commodity Futures Trading Commission, 1975–1991.

Friedman, Milton. "The Need for Futures Markets in Currencies." Prepared for the Chicago Mercantile Exchange, December 20, 1971.

Melamed, Leo. *Book of Speeches, Published Articles and Testimony*. Chicago: 1988–1989.

———. *Book of Speeches, Published Articles and Testimony*. Chicago: 1990.

New York Stock Exchange. *Fact Book, 1988*. New York: New York Stock Exchange, 1988.

Open Outcry: A Monthly Newsletter for Members and Staff of the Chicago Mercantile Exchange, May 1989.

Selected Newspaper Articles

Adler, Stephen J. "Heated Argument: Are RICO Seizures A Violation of Rights As Critics Contend?" *The Wall Street Journal*, February 15, 1989.

"All Corn, Some Wheat and Oats Set Lows in Wake of U.S. Crop Report." *The Wall Street Journal*, December 19, 1957.

Anders, George. "Mixed Bag: Stocks Leap 186.84 In Best Gain Ever, Yet Worries Abound." *The Wall Street Journal*, October 22, 1987.

———. "Portfolio Insurance Helps Investors but Hurts Market." *The Wall Street Journal*, October 19, 1987.

Atlas, Terry. "Brady Seeks Transfer of CFTC Power." *Chicago Tribune*, June 6, 1990.

Baetz, David. "Midwest Livestock Trends Cited at Commission Hearing." *Feedstuffs*, September 17, 1966.

Bailey, Jeff. "Catching Up: Feeling New Pressure, Chicago Merc Stiffens Disciplinary Stance." *The Wall Street Journal*, August 29, 1989.

Bailey, Jeff, and McMurray, Scott. "Futures Shock: Traders Are Indicted for Running the Pits by Their Own Rules." *The Wall Street Journal*, August 3, 1989.

"Bankers Warned: 'Face Facts of Life on Huge Dishonesty.' " *The Chicago American*, September 26, 1958.

Baquet, Dean, and Burton, Thomas M. "Trader Probe is Stingingly Sophisticated." *Chicago Tribune*, August 6, 1989.

Behof, Kathleen. "The Day After: Brief Halt in Trading at Merc, CBOE." *Chicago Sun-Times*, October 21, 1987.

Bennett, Amanda, and McCarthy, Michael J. "Calm Company: Bell & Howell Takes Stock Crash in Stride, Even Discerns Benefits." *The Wall Street Journal*, October 27, 1987.

Berg, Eric N. "Ex-Chicago Merc Chief is Barred." *The New York Times*, May 26, 1990.

———. "F.B.I. Said to Study Chicago Cheating in Futures Trades." *The New York Times*, January 20, 1989.

———. "Forty-Six Commodities Traders Indicted After a 2-Year F.B.I. Investigation." *The New York Times*, August 3, 1989.

"The Big Spill." *Chicago Sun-Times*, October 25, 1987.

Bilitz, Walter. "Mercantile Volume Increases." *Chicago Tribune*, July 22, 1968.

Brashler, Bill. "Fear Rocks High-Rolling Traders." *Chicago Sun-Times*, April 9, 1989.

Briggs, Michael. " 'Crime in the Suites' Targeted." *Chicago Sun-Times*, February 1, 1989.

Burns, Greg. "Bean Trader: I Broke Rules, but Didn't Cheat Customers." *Chicago Sun-Times*, November 29, 1990.

———. "Bean Verdict Casts Gloom on Yen Mood." *Chicago Sun-Times*, January 11, 1991.

———. "First Soybean Broker Reports to Federal Prison." *Chicago Sun-Times*, August 31, 1991.

———. "Globex Debuts amid Doubts About Exchanges." *Chicago Tribune*, June 26, 1992.

———. "Judge Slaps Merc over Penalties to Traders." *Chicago Sun-Times*, June 11, 1991.

———. "Trader Trial Ends with No Convictions." *Chicago Sun-Times*, March 14, 1991.

———. "Traders' Attorneys Tell Jury No Customers Were Cheated." *Chicago Sun-Times*, December 6, 1990.

———. "Two Plead Guilty in Merc Case." *Chicago Sun-Times*, May 2, 1991.

Burns, Greg, and Chandler, Susan. "FBI Agents Tell of House Calls on Traders." *Chicago Sun-Times*, November 1, 1990.

Burns, Greg, and Chandler, Susan. "Verdicts (or Lack Thereof) a Black Eye: Futures Probe Setback Weakens Belief Customers were Cheated." *Chicago Sun-Times*, July 11, 1990.

Burton, Thomas, and Drew, Christopher. "Broker Details FBI Probe." *Chicago Tribune*, February 5, 1989.

Carlson, Elliot. "Wage-Price Curbs Through the Ages." *The Wall Street Journal*, September 23, 1971.

"Cattle: Futures on the Hoof." *Newsweek*, December 7, 1964.

"CFTC Ready to Restrict Dual Trading, Chief Says." *Chicago Tribune*, October 18, 1989.

Chandler, Susan. "CBOT Hires Bork to Rip RICO Law." *Chicago Sun-Times*, June 20, 1991.

———. "Merc Trader Settles Charges; Agrees to 6-Month Sentence." *Chicago Sun-Times*, March 28, 1991.

Chicago Butter and Egg Board Advertisement. *Chicago Tribune*, October 21, 1914.

"Chicago Exchange Announces Fresh Egg Futures Contract." *Poultry & Eggs Weekly*, January 29, 1966.

"Chicago Mercantile Exchange." *The Drovers Journal*, November 30, 1967.

"Chicago 'Merc' Gears for Further Growth." *Journal of Commerce*, February 24, 1971.

"Chicago Merc Margins Rise for S&P 500 Futures Pacts." *The Wall Street Journal*, October 19, 1987.

"Chicago's Plungers in the World Money Game." *Chicago Sun-Times Magazine*, February 24, 1974.

"CME Officials Tell Group: Eye Futures as Industry Skill." *Journal of Commerce and Commercial*, December 10, 1971.

Cockrell, James A. "Commodity Marts Called Aid for Both Consumer, Farmer." *St. Louis Globe-Democrat*, April 13, 1962.

Cohen, Laurie, and Crawford, William B., Jr. "Life in the Pits— Family, Frenzy, Money." *Chicago Tribune*, January 29, 1989.

————. "New Merc Off to a Smooth Start." *Chicago Tribune*, November 29, 1983.

————. "Only Little Problems Crop Up on Merc's Big Day." *Chicago Tribune*, November 29, 1983.

"The Crash of '87: Stocks Plummet 508 amid Panicky Selling." *The Wall Street Journal*, October 20, 1987.

"The Crash of 1987: The Fallout Widens." *Chicago Tribune*, October 25, 1987.

Crawford, William B., Jr. "CBOT Taps Bork to Fight Racketeer Law." *Chicago Tribune*, June 20, 1991.

————. "Charges Against Traders Painted as Trivia." *Chicago Tribune*, December 10, 1990.

————. "Ex-Trader: Chaos Helped Us Cheat." *Chicago Tribune*, January 4, 1991.

————. "FBI Agent Cites Profit from Illegal Merc Deal." *Chicago Tribune*, November 6, 1990.

————. "FBI Agent's Credibility Attacked in Trader Trial." *Chicago Tribune*, November 27, 1990.

————. "Globex Takes Off." *Chicago Tribune*, June 26, 1992.

————. "Globex Trading Network Ready for Takeoff." *Chicago Tribune*, June 21, 1992.

————. "Judge Blasts Merc Penalties." *Chicago Tribune*, July 11, 1991.

————. "Merc, CBOT Chiefs Differ on Defense Against SEC." *Chicago Tribune*, March 9, 1990.

————. "Path Unclear for Exchange Linkup." *Chicago Tribune*, July 20, 1992.

————. "Prosecutor Sums Up Trader Case." *Chicago Tribune*, January 24, 1991.

————. "2nd Floor to Make Merc World's Largest Trading Facility." *Chicago Tribune*, June 20, 1992.

————. "Taping Traders Say They Tried to Warn Friend." *Chicago Tribune*, January 31, 1990.

————. "Trading Probe to Continue, U.S. Tells Merc Chiefs." *Chicago Tribune*, April 23, 1991.

————. "Yen Trader Made Deal to Be Pal, Lawyer Says." *Chicago Tribune*, November 29, 1990.

"Cudahy Commended for Expansion Plans." *The Milwaukee Journal*, May 27, 1969.

"Customer Protection Rules Trigger Clash." *The Washington Post*, November 13, 1977.

Darby, Edwin. "Butter 'n' Egg Volume Hits $2 Billion a Year." *The Miami Herald*, April 14, 1965.

"Dazed Investors Seek Short-Term Refuge." *The Wall Street Journal*, October 20, 1987.

DeMaria, Lawrence J. "Analysts Try to Put Plunge in Context." *The New York Times*, October 26, 1987.

———. "Market is Steady and Tension Eases in Shorter Session." *The New York Times*, October 24, 1987.

DePalma, Anthony. "The Aftermath for Housing and Offices." *The New York Times*, October 25, 1987.

Dietz, David. "The Impact of Regulation on Commodities Trading." *San Francisco Examiner*, November 17, 1977.

Drell, Adrienne, and Burns, Greg. "46 Traders Indicted." *Chicago Sun-Times*, August 3, 1989.

Drell, Adrienne; Burns, Greg; and Herrmann, Andrew. "Traders on Trial: Minor Misdeeds or Major Greed?" *Chicago Sun-Times*, August 6, 1989.

Drew, Christopher, and Cohen, Laurie. "Futures Probe Looks at Common Trading Practices." *Chicago Tribune*, January 23, 1989.

Drew, Christopher; Cohen, Laurie; and Crawford, William B., Jr. "How FBI Worked Trader Sting." *Chicago Tribune*, January 20, 1989.

Drew, Christopher; Cohen, Laurie; and Crawford, William B., Jr. "U.S. Probes Futures Exchanges." *Chicago Tribune*, January 19, 1989.

Drew, Christopher; Cohen, Laurie; and Gaines, Sallie. "No Long-Term Damage, Merc Exec Says: Next Counts May Come As Early As Next Fall." *Chicago Tribune*, August 4, 1989.

Edwards, Franklin R. "Market Pressure Makes Markets Honest." *The New York Times*, January 29, 1989.

Eichenwald, Kurt. "F.B.I. Intensifying Commodity Inquiry on Chicago Trades." *The New York Times*, January 21, 1989.

———. "Nighttime Futures Trading Begins Cautiously on Globex." *The New York Times*, June 27, 1992.

Farina, Nick. "Merc to Occupy New Site in '72." *Chicago Sun-Times*, May 19, 1970.

"Fined for Onion Market Views, Trader Asserts." *Chicago Daily Tribune*, June 10, 1953.

Flynn, Julia M. "Merc Studies a Permanent Curb on Volatility." *The New York Times*, December 14, 1987.

Fuerbringer, Jonathan. "Salomon Brothers Admits Violations at Treasury Sales." *New York Times*, August 10, 1991.

"Futures Market Success." *Advertiser & Gazette*, January 11, 1966.

Gaines, Sallie. "Curbs on Dual Trading Get CFTC Endorsement." *Chicago Tribune*, January 5, 1990.

———. "Merc Puts System 'Under Microscope.' " *Chicago Tribune*, January 26, 1989.

———. "To Outsiders, Futures Exchanges Decidedly Foreign." *Chicago Tribune*, January 19, 1989.

Gaines, Sallie, and Jouzaitis, Carol. "Trader Takes Both Sides in 'Bucketing .' " *Chicago Tribune*, January 20, 1989.

Gilpin, Kenneth N. "Moves to Curb the Volatility." *The New York Times*, March 6, 1987.

Glaberson William. "The End of Business As Usual." *The New York Times*, October 25, 1987.

Goozner, Merrill. "Study Assails Proposal to Raise Futures Margin," *Chicago Tribune*, November 12, 1987.

Gorman, John. "Commodities Interest Gives Valukas Edge." *Chicago Tribune*, January 23, 1989.

––––––. "Greylord-Like Tactics Were Used in Trading Probe." *Chicago Tribune*, January 29, 1989.

––––––. "Indictment Names 3 Merc Franc Traders." *Chicago Tribune*, November 19, 1989.

Gorman, John, and Cohen, Laurie. "Ten Soybean Traders Convicted." *Chicago Tribune*, January 10, 1991.

Gray, Ralph. "Merc Has Look of Youth at 50." *Chicago's American*, March 1969.

Green, Larry, and Frantz, Douglas. "FBI Probes Fraud in Futures Trading." *Los Angeles Times*, January 20, 1989.

Greenhouse, Steven. "A Testing for Chicago's Merc." *The New York Times*, August 16, 1985.

Griffin, Dick. "Curbs May Hit Action on Board Of Trade." *Chicago Daily News*, August 18, 1971.

Gunset, George. "$750,000 Fine Merc's Biggest." *Chicago Tribune*, January 20, 1989.

Harris, Everette B. "Chicago Financial Image Enhanced by International Monetary Market." *The Journal of Commerce*, April 21, 1976.

––––––. "Futures Trading Is Marketing Aid in a Free Farm Economy." *The Drovers Journal*, May 29, 1969.

––––––. "Mercantile Exchange Scores Second Highest Volume Total." *Journal of Commerce and Commercial*, April 30, 1975.

"The Hen, the Egg and the Unvarnished Truth," *Chicago Examiner* January 1, 1915.

Hunt, Ridgely. "The Belly Brokers." *Chicago Tribune*, December 11, 1966.

Idaszak, Jerome. "Bill Would Snuff Out Open Outcry: Exchange Leaders." *Chicago Sun-Times*, October 18, 1989.

––––––. "CFTC Proposes Sharp Curb on Dual Trading." *Chicago Sun-Times*, January 5, 1990.

––––––. "Futures Furor Erupting Anew in Washington." *Chicago Sun-Times*, March 11, 1990.

––––––. "Sander Lays Out New Merc Agenda." *Chicago Sun-Times*, February 24, 1982.

––––––. "We Were Safety Valve in Crash, Merc Says." *Chicago Sun-Times*, October 30, 1987.

Idaszak, Jerome, and Burns, Greg. "Merc Will Install Hidden Cameras, Strengthen Rules." *Chicago Sun-Times*, August 4, 1989.

Ingersoll, Bruce. "Chicago Merc Says Futures Trading Didn't Cause Crash." *Wall Street Journal*, October 30, 1987.

––––––. "House Panel Clears Measure Boosting CFTC." *The Wall Street Journal*, August 3, 1989.

Jensen, Val. "The Year They Closed the Stock Market." *The New York Times*, November 26, 1990.

Johnson, Donald E.L. "Butter Prices Reach 13-Year High; Mercantile Slates Futures Market." *Chicago Sun-Times*, March 1, 1966.

Jones, Howard. "Second U.S. Probe of Egg Trade Started." *Chicago Tribune*, September 19, 1970.

Jouzaitis, Carol. "LaSalle St. Has a Lot at Stake," *Chicago Tribune*, November 1, 1987.

Jouzaitis, Carol, and Cohen, Laurie. "Merc Considers Broker Curb." *Chicago Tribune*, February 27, 1987.

Jouzaitis, Carol, and Winter, Christine. "Halt in Index Trading Short-Lived." *Chicago Tribune*, October 21, 1987.

"The Long Climb Back." *Chicago Sun-Times*, October 22, 1987.

Longworth, R. C. "Japan Inc.—End of an Era Near?" *Chicago Tribune*, October 11, 1987.

————. "Melamed Goes to Moscow to See Future, but Finds Chaos." *Chicago Tribune*, November 9, 1990.

McMurray, Scott. "Chicago Merc Sets Daily Limit on Price Swings." *The Wall Street Journal*, October 23, 1987.

————. "Compliant Officer: Chicago Merc Adviser Faces Heavy Criticism over Regulatory Cases." *The Wall Street Journal*, May 10, 1989.

"Managing a Crisis." *The Wall Street Journal*, October 21, 1987.

"Manipulation Rumors Spur Federal Study of Pork Bellies Futures at Chicago Market." *The Wall Street Journal*, January 7, 1966.

"Market Advances; Buying Is Spurred by Rallies Abroad." *The New York Times*, October 28, 1987.

"The Market Story." *The New York Times*, October 25, 1987.

"Mart Adds Butter Futures." *Chicago Daily News*, March 3, 1966.

Melamed, Leo, and Geldermann, John T. "Mercantile Exchange Polices Itself." *Chicago Tribune*, February 17, 1989.

"Mercantile Exchange, Officers Are Accused of Manipulating Eggs." *The Wall Street Journal*, May 29, 1970.

"Mercantile Exchange Head Urges Fewer Farm Controls." *Chicago Sun-Times*, December 19, 1957.

"Mercantile Exchange Lifts Cattle Margins." *The Wall Street Journal*, March 31, 1969.

"Mercantile Exchange Penalizes Severely 4 Members, 3 Firms." *The Wall Street Journal*, October 22, 1970.

"Mercantile Exchange Volume Rises 91%." *Chicago Sun-Times*, April 4, 1969.

"Mercantile Looks to the Future." *Chicago Today*, July 22, 1971.

"Mercantile Sales at Milestone." *Chicago Tribune*, January 9, 1967.

"Mercantile Volume Hits 3-Month Peak." *Chicago Tribune*, April 4, 1969.

"The Merc Fights for Self-Regulation.' *Chicago Tribune*, April 26, 1989.

"Merc Likes Bacon, Eggs." *Milwaukee Sentinel*, May 27, 1969.

"Merc Says it's No. 1." *Chicago Today*, August 31, 1970.

"Mind and Money: Turmoil's Deep Impact." *The Wall Street Journal*, October 23, 1987.

Mollenhoff, Clark. "Commodity Panel Fuss on 'Conflict.' " *Des Moines Register*, November 13, 1985.

"More Rulings by Cost of Living Council." *The Wall Street Journal*, September 15, 1971.

Murray, Alan. "On the Spot: Stock Markets Frenzy Puts Fed's Greenspan in a Crucial Position. *The Wall Street Journal*, October 21, 1987.

Murray, Alan, and Seib, Gerald F. "Reagan's Reversal: Stock Market's Crash Makes Budget Accord, Tax Rise More Likely." *The Wall Street Journal*, October 23, 1987.

Mutter, Alan D. "Merc Chief Vows Less Government Encroachment." *Chicago Daily News*, November 22, 1977.

Neikirk, William R. "Financial Caution's Back in Style." *Chicago Tribune*, October 22, 1987.

Neikirk, William R., and Widder, Pat. "Crash of '87: Healthy Economy Disguises the Impact a Year Later." *Chicago Tribune*, October 16, 1988.

O'Connor, Matt. "CBOT Hit on Move to Join Traders' Appeal." *Chicago Tribune*, June 1, 1991.

————. "SEC Suit Alleges Fraud by Stotler, Four Top Officers." *Chicago Tribune*, May 28, 1992.

————. "Trader Escapes Jail Term by Cooperating in Trial." *Chicago Tribune*, June 15, 1991.

"One Year After the Crash." *Chicago Tribune*, October 16, 1988.

"Onion Story Costs Trader Fine, Rebuke." *Chicago Sun-Times*, June 10, 1953.

Petacque, Art. "FBI Probes Boasts of 'Laundering' by Traders." *Chicago Tribune*, January 26, 1989.

————. "How Traders Got Trapped." *Chicago Sun-Times*, January 22, 1989.

Petacque, Art, and Drell, Adrienne. "100 More Traders May Be Indicted." *Chicago Sun-Times*, August 4, 1989.

"Pit Moles: FBI Sting Operation in Chicago Staggers Tow Futures Exchanges." *The Wall Street Journal*, January 20, 1989.

Quint, Michael. "Rates Rise in Wild Trading." *The New York Times*, October 16, 1987.

"Rally Spreads Beyond Dow.' *Chicago Tribune*, October 22, 1987.

"RICO Hits the Pits." *The Wall Street Journal*, August 3, 1989.

Robb, Gregory A. "Futures Traders Win in Regulatory Battle." *The New York Times*, October 24, 1990.

Rossi, Rosalind. "Scam 'Ruined My Life,' Says Convicted Trader." *Chicago Sun-Times*, July 18, 1991.

Rustin, Richard E., and Ricks, Thomas E. "Never Again? Stocks' Plunge Brings Calls for the Overhaul of Financial Markets." *The Wall Street Journal*, October 26, 1987.

Sanger, David E. "Global Markets' Role Widens." *The New York Times*, October 28, 1987.

"The Scandal in Chicago: Of Fraud, Markets and the Future." *The New York Times*, January 22, 1989.

Seely, Herman Gastrell. "Mercantile Exchange Has 'Out' for Brokers." *Chicago Daily News*, October 20, 1953.

"Shadow Market: Stock-Index futures Catch On and Spread, Touching Off Debate." *The Wall Street Journal*, April 5, 1983.

Siewers, Alf. "The Pit and the Pendulum." *Chicago Sun-Times*, February 1, 1989.

Sing, Bill. "For Futures Markets, a Shady Past." *Los Angeles Times*, January 21, 1989.

Sorrells, Eugene. "Futures Volume Soars As Stocks Decline; Some See Inflow of Speculative Money." *The Wall Street Journal*, May 18, 1970.

Stabler, Charles N. "To Weather a Crash, It Helps a Little to Be 80 Years Old." *The Wall Street Journal*, October 28, 1987.

Sterngold, James. "The Events That Changed the World of Wall Street." *The New York Times*, October 26, 1987.

Stewart, James B., and Hertzberg, Daniel. "Terrible Tuesday: How the Stock Market Almost Disintegrated a Day After the Crash." *The Wall Street Journal*, November 20, 1987.

"Stocks Fall, but Avert Plunge; Reagan Says He'll 'Negotiate' with Congress on the Deficit." *The New York Times*, October 23, 1987.

"Stocks Fall; Dow Plunges 13.73 Points." *Chicago Tribune*, August 19, 1971.

"Stocks Fall 156, Loss of 8%, After Big Selloffs Abroad; Joint Talks on Deficit Begin." *The New York Times*, October 27, 1987.

Sullivan, Colleen. "Commodities Futures Panel: Some Hill Aides' Views Measured." *The Washington Post*, October 25, 1977.

"Trade Deficit Slams Wall St." *Chicago Tribune*, October 15, 1987.

"Trade Deficit Wallops Wall St." *Chicago Sun-Times*, October 15, 1987.

U.S. Charges Manipulation of Egg Prices." *Chicago Daily Tribune*, September 10, 1953.

"U.S. Will Probe Bacon Trading." *New York World-Telegram and The Sun*, January 6, 1966.

Uchitelle, Louis. "The Uncertain Legacy of the Crash." *The New York Times*, April 3, 1988.

Vartan, Vartanig G. "New Stock Strategies Abroad." *The New York Times*, November 7, 1987.

Wallace, Anise C. "Big Traders' Caution Remakes the Market." *The New York Times*, October 10, 1988.

Washburn, Gary. "Indictments Name 46 Traders." *Chicago Tribune*, August 3, 1989.

Wentworth, Eric. "Chance Seen for Farm Unit's Perennial Bid to Tighten Control of Commodity Trading." *The Wall Street Journal*, January 31, 1966.

"Wider Trade Probe Vowed." *Chicago Sun-Times*, January 23, 1989.

Yates, Ronald E. "Japanese See Futures in Chicago." *Chicago Tribune*, June 17, 1991.

Selected Periodicals

Abbott, Susan. "How Midsized Brokerage Firms Aim for Industry Niches." *Futures*, November 1985.

————. "CME Rejects Petition." *Futures*, May 1987.

Abelson, Alan. "Happy Anniversary... What Now?" *Barron's*, October 17, 1988.

"After the Crash." *Newsweek*, November 2, 1987.

"America at War." *Newsweek*, January 28, 1991.

Baldwin, William. "Chicago's Booming Commodity Markets." *Commerce*, October 1965.

Bentz, R.P. "Fresh Egg Futures Contracts Are Here!" *Pacific Poultryman*, January 1966.

Brownstein, Ronald. "Financial Futures Trading—A Bright Futures or a Bubble Waiting to Burst?" *Financial Institutions Report*, 1983.

"Chicago Merc. Sets Up Security Fund." *Gulf Coast Lumberman*, January 1970.

Continental Bank. *Journal of Applied Corporate Finance*, Winter 1989.

"Does Centralized Power Lead to Decisions in a Vacuum?" *Futures*, May 1987.

Dumaine, Brian. "How to Manage in a Recession." *Fortune*, November 5, 1990.

"Electronic Trading: The Twilight of the Gods." *Intermarket*, April 1989.

Ferris, William. "Mercantile Exchange Growing Fast." *Commerce Magazine*, 1954.

"Fifteen Years of Trading." *Futures*, February 1987.

Friedman, Milton. "Why the Freeze Is a Mistake." *Newsweek*, August 30, 1971.

"Futures Trading in Live Hogs to Start Feb. 28." *National Hog Farmer*, February 1966.

Graves, Florence, and Norrgard, Lee. "Money to Burn: How Chicago's Commodity Traders Get Their Way on Capitol Hill." *Common Cause Magazine*, January-February 1985.

Greenwald, John. "Boom, Boom, Ka-boom!" *Time*, October 23, 1989.

"Guide to Index Futures and Options." *Futures*, Index Guide 1985.

Hirsch, Phil. "World's Butter and Egg Man." *The Lion*, February 1955.

"Hong Kong: Can It Rise from the Ashes?" *Intermarket*, February, 1989.

"How to Handle the Next Black Monday." *Intermarket*, December 1987.

"The Integrity of Markets: Will Congress Intervene?" *Intermarket*, March 1989.

"Intermarket Interview: Brian Monieson." *Intermarket*, January 1985.

"*Intermarket*'s Financial Risk Manager of the Year (And Sixteen Other Outstanding Achievers)." *Intermarket*, January 1989.

"Is the Party Over? A Jolt for Wall Street's Whiz Kids." *Newsweek*, October 26, 1987.

"January 15: Deadline for War." *Time*, January 21, 1991.

Johnson, Donald E. L. "Bringing Home the Bacon." *Generation*, February 1969.

Kahn, E. J., Jr. "Profiles: Dwayne Orville Andreas." *The New Yorker*, February 16, 1987.

Kriz, Margaret E. "First City of Futures." *National Journal*, June 25, 1988.

Kuhn, Arnold J. "Fortunes in Futures," *Chicago Magazine*, September 1956.

"Launch Live Hog Futures." *National Live Stock Producer*, February 1966.

"Life in the Pits Will Never Be the Same." *Businessweek*, February 6, 1989.

McCarroll, Thomas. "Futures Shock." *Time*, June 29, 1992.

"A Man and His Terminal." *Intermarket*, December 1989.

"Managing International Financial Risk." *Euromoney*, supplement to October 1985.

"Manic Market." *Time*, November 10, 1986.

Market Perspectives: Topics on Options and Financial Futures, October–November 1989.

"Mercantile Exchange Volume Up 65 Per Cent to All-time High." *Commerce Magazine*, March 1, 1957.

Merrick, John J., Jr. "Fact and Fantasy About Stock Index Futures Program Trading." *Business Review*, Federal Reserve Bank of Philadelphia, September–October 1987.

Miller, Richard A. "Integrity on the Floor." *Commodities Law Letter*, January 1989.

———. "Interview of CFTC Chairman Wendy Gramm." *Commodities Law Letter*, February–March 1989.

Nelan, Bruce W. "A Chat with the Gorbachevs." *Time*, May 25, 1992.

"1968: The Year That Shaped a Generation." *Time*, January 11, 1988.

O'Donnell, Thomas. "A Maverick at the Merc." *Forbes*, February 1, 1982.

"Overheard." *Intermarket*, April 1989.

The Packer, April 11, 1953.

———, June 6, 1953.

Paulson, Morton C. "Where Pork Bellies Are King: Commodity Exchange Woos Investors." *The National Observer*, May 12, 1969.

Pesmen, Sandra. "A Gift Wish List for Chicago in '88." *Crain's Chicago Business*, December 21, 1987.

Poultry Processing and Marketing, October 1955.

"Profiles." *Futures, Special Issue*, 1988.

Protess, David L. "Commodities Investigation—The Story Behind the Story." *Chicago Lawyer*, March 1989.

"The Real Story Behind the S & L Mess." *American Heritage*, February/March 1991.

Scott, Chris. "Merc, CBT to Develop Trading Computers." *Crain's Chicago Business*, August 21, 1989.

Securities Week, December 12, 1983.

Sellin, Thorstein, gen. ed. *The Annals of the American Academy of Political and Social Science*. Vol. 155, part 1: *Organized Commodity Markets*. edited by S. S. Huebner. Philadelphia: The American Academy of Political and Social Science, 1931.

Smith, Clifford W., Jr., and Smithson, Charles W. "Then and Now." *Intermarket*, October 1989.

Star, Jack. "The Wave of the Futures." *Chicago*, July 1976.

"There's No Such Thing as a Free Leak." *Chicago Lawyer*, March 1989.

"This Triple Witching Hour Could Last All Day: New Regulations Designed to Minimize Mayhem May Backfire." *Businessweek*, June 22, 1987.

" 'This Will Not Be Another Vietnam': A Deadline for Diplomacy and a Plan for All-Out War." *Newsweek*, December 10, 1990.

"Those Who Can't, Teach (Thomas Eagleton)." *Intermarket*, September 1989.

"The 20th Century on Wall Street." *Financial World*, September 16, 1986.

The University of Chicago Law Review. Vol. 21: "Politics and the Constitution" by William Winslow Crosskey: A Symposium. Chicago: The University of Chicago Press, Autumn 1953.

Wallich, Henry C. "The Dollar Viewed from Abroad." *Newsweek*, August 30, 1971.

Wall Street Letter, December 5, 1983.

————, December 28, 1987.

"The Way It Was: An Oral History." *Institutional Investor*, June 1987.

"What Happened to CME Gold." *Futures*, May 1987.

"Who's in Charge? The Crash on Wall Street Spotlights America's Leadership Crisis." *Time*, November 9, 1987.

"Why Gorbachev Is Failing." *Newsweek*, June 4, 1990.

Zaleznik, Abraham. "Managers and Leaders: Are They Different?" *Harvard Business Review*, May–June 1977.

"The Zooming Futures Market: A Bumper Crop of Questions." *Businessweek*, June 11, 1979.

Government Reports

Commodity Futures Trading Commission, Division of Enforcement. *Hearings*, July 19–20, 1976.

Federal Reserve Bank of Kansas City. *Financial Market Volatility: A Symposium Sponsored by the Federal Reserve Bank of Kansas City*. Jackson Hole: The Federal Reserve Bank of Kansas City, August 17–19, 1988.

The Federal Reserve Bank of New York. *U.S. Monetary Policy in Financial Markets*, by Paul Meek. New York: Federal Reserve Bank of New York, 1982.

The Federal Reserve System. *Financial Futures and Options in the U.S. Economy*. Washington, D.C.: Publication Services, Board of Governors of the Federal Reserve System, 1986.

————. *Purposes & Functions*, 1984.

Federal Reserve System; Commodities Futures Trading Commission; and Securities and Exchange Commission. *A Study of the Effects on the Economy of Trading in Futures and Options*. December 1984.

The Presidential Task Force. *Report on Market Mechanisms*. January 1988.

U.S. Congress, Committee on Agriculture. *Hearings on H.R. 11930 and H.R. 12317 to Amend the Commodity Exchange Act*. 1967.

————. Committee on Agriculture, Subcommittee on Domestic Marketing. *Hearings on H.R. 904 to Prohibit Trading in Irish Potato Futures on Commodity Exchanges*. 1963.

U.S. Congress, House Energy and Commerce Committee, Subcommittee on Telecommunications and Finance. *Hearings on Stock Index Futures and Program Trading*. 1987.

U.S. Congress, Joint Economic Committee, Subcommittee on Agricultural Policy. *Policy for Commercial Agriculture: Its Relation to Economic Growth and Stability*, 1957.

U.S. Securities and Exchange Commission, Division of Market Regulation. *The October 1987 Market Break*. February 1988.

U.S. Senate, Committee on Agriculture and Forestry. *Hearings on a Bill to Amend the Commodities Exchange Act to Strengthen the Regulation of Futures Trading, to Bring All Agricultural and Other Commodities Traded on Exchanges Under Regulation, and for Other Purposes*, 1974.

————. *Hearings on a Bill to Establish an Independent Commodity Exchange Commission*, 1974.

————. *Hearings on a Bill to Regulate the Interstate and Foreign Commerce Trading of Futures Contracts in Order to Prevent Unfair and Deceptive Acts and Practices*, 1974.

U.S. Senate, Committee on Foreign Relations, Subcommittee on Multinational Corporations. *Hearings on International Grain Companies*, 1976.

Index

This index is selective, giving only the most important references to characters, sources, and events; this is especially true of the entries for the Chicago Mercantile Exchange itself. The reader is directed to the Table of Contents as a guide to historical events and their relation to the Exchange, and for the general history of futures trading.

Margins on time contracts,
219–20. *See also*
Federal Reserve Board
early regulation of, 13
proposed legislative
controls of, 218
Markey, Edward, 347
Martin, Robert L., 138–39
Marx, Karl, 6
Maxwell Street Market, 57
Mayer, Lawrence, 193
McCarthy, John V., 63, 112,
113, 118–19, 146
McClendon, Gordon, 302,
430
McCormick, Cyrus, 16
McLoughlin, Michael, 359
McNeil, Charles, 41, 43–44,
48
McPartland, John, 191
Meat packing, 21–22
Melamed, Leo, vii–viii, 3–5,
96, 98, 99, 143, 161,
195, 216, 233–34,
274, 288, 289, 293,
301, 313, 318,
325–26, 346–47, 372,
391, 407, 408, 425
and beginnings of IMM,
183–87, 188–91
as board member of Futures
Industry Association,
257
board position on CBOT
offered to, 257–58
and cash settlements,
270–71
as chairman of CME,
150–53, 158
as chairman of CME
executive committee,
285
as chairman of Commodity
Futures Political Fund,
212
as chairman of GLOBEX,
384–85
as chairman of IMM,
197–200
as chairman of NFA,
249–50
as chairman of reorganized
CME, 236–37
chairmanship of CFTC
offered to, 214

as CME special counsel,
163–64, 239–40,
246–47
and dual trading
referendum, 318–21
and Eurodollar contracts,
271
and European promotional
tour for IMM, 203–4
and expansion of CME to
South Wacker, 266–67
and "15 minutes please
campaign," 279–80
force of personality of, in
development of CME,
254–58
on modernization of image
and self-policing of
CME, 171, 176–77
and move to Jackson
Boulevard, 166
and 1989 FBI sting
operation, 360–61,
367
open outcry system
supported by, 314,
378
opposes CFTC regulations
in 1986, 306
opposes CME expansion to
Hong Kong, 311–12
opposes commodity
fransfer tax, 211
opposes legislative control
of margins, 218–19
and promotion of CME
treasury bill contract,
226–27, 230
retirement of, 399–401
earlier plan to reduce
involvement in CME,
298–300
supports CME referendum
rule, 145–47
The Tenth Planet, 298, 420
as Young Turk, 123–27
The Merc at Work, 311
Merrill Lynch, 195–96
Midlin, Samuel, 74–75
Militant Marketers, 76
Miller, Gilbert, 62, 131
Miller, J. Arthur, 74
Miller, Merton, 278, 337,
398–99, 405, 408,
410

Miller, William, 13
Milnarik, Joseph, 41, 67
Minneapolis Tribune, 135
Mr. Dooley, 16
Mitchell, James, 200
Monetary Authority of
Singapore (MAS),
292–93, 311–12
Monieson, Brian, 4, 298,
300, 303
fined by CME Business
Conduct Committee,
286
as head of GNP
Commodities,
sanctioned by CFTC,
372–73
as Melamed protégé,
255–56
succeeds Sandner as
chairman of CME,
287
Moore, William S., 30,
41–42, 48, 49–51,
71
Moscow Commodity
Exchange, 392
Moulds, Warren, 233
Munn vs. Illinois, 32
Muno, William, 100–101,
150, 158, 165
Murphy, Robert J., 169–70
Mutual offset system (MOS),
307, 312–13

Nathan Report, 219
National Association of
Commodity Exchanges
and Allied Trades Inc.
(NACEAT), 78
National Association of
Securities Dealers
Automated Quotation
(NASDAQ) system,
381, 394
National Futures Association
(NFA), 78, 266
Customer Account
Protection Study, 265
"founding fathers" of,
427
proposed by Melamed,
248–250
National Journal, 228